WITHDRAWN

WITHDRAWN

THE PSYCHOLOGICAL IMPACT
OF SCHOOL EXPERIENCE

THE PSYCHOLOGICAL IMPACT OF SCHOOL EXPERIENCE

A COMPARATIVE STUDY OF NINE-YEAR-OLD CHILDREN IN CONTRASTING SCHOOLS

by **Patricia Minuchin**, **Barbara Biber**, **Edna Shapiro**, *and* **Herbert Zimiles**

IN COLLABORATION WITH

ETHEL HORN   ELAINE GRAHAM SOFER
LISA R. PEATTIE   VIRGINIA STERN

Basic Books, Inc., Publishers   **New York**   **London**

FOREWORD

M. Brewster Smith

DEPARTMENT OF PSYCHOLOGY
THE UNIVERSITY OF CHICAGO

This is a complex, honest, and provocative book, one long awaited by those who have been attracted by earlier partial reports of the "Bank Street Study." As an evaluation of "modern" versus "traditional" educational strategies, it is far from conclusive—both for methodological reasons and because, even where clear differential effects appear, evaluation depends crucially upon the competing value perspectives that can be brought to bear on them. But it greatly enriches our understanding of schools and of school children. It provides a usefully detailed natural history of four differing school-and-classroom cultures. It exemplifies a serious and skilled attempt to assess the impact of schools on children, with successes and failures that will be highly instructive to the increasing corps of investigators engaged in evaluating educational and social programs. It gives new and well differentiated content to old educational issues that had become reduced to sterile stereotypes in the controversies of a former generation about progressive education. And, in its multifaceted exploration of the "modern" strategy with its priority on the cultivation of individuality and self-fulfillment, it provides a welcome counterpoise to the present one-sided emphasis on cognitive development and achievement, and on the school as an agency of socialization.

The Bank Street investigators made some difficult and well-considered choices in framing their research plan. On the antecedent side, they put all their eggs in the basket of a single complex independent variable: "modern" versus "traditional." The distinction is drawn with fine-grained conceptual detail and the qualitative data to match it are reported with

v

similar specificity. It remains inherent in the design, however, that the study cannot throw light on the coherence of the various components of educational modernism or traditionalism, or on their relative importance in producing effects on children. Total packages of variables are being assessed.

On the side of outcomes, however, the plan included a broad spectrum of dependent variables, sampling cognitive, self-regarding, and interpersonal attributes. Usually several independent indices are available for each conceptually distinguished variable.

The benefits from thus elaborating the dependent variables are obvious. One is methodological: where the validity of particular measures must remain in doubt, only multiple assessment of the key outcomes can provide an acceptable basis for inference. There is also a crucial substantive advantage. Enthusiasts for particular strategies of educational intervention frequently succumb to the temptation of basing program evaluation on a narrow band of outcome measures focused exclusively on the intended target effect. Thus a program of "cognitive enrichment" might be evaluated solely in terms of its effects on achievement and ability test scores. Possible side effects for good or ill are neglected. The broad-spectrum strategy of the present research provides, in principle, a more adequate cost accounting of the gains attained in particular target areas. It provides evidence that is more likely to be relevant to informed judgment of the value of the program being examined. Unfortunately, since the state of the art is primitive, it also yields complex and inconsistent data that settle few questions definitively and raise many more. Such uncomfortable complexity is vastly to be preferred, however, to erroneous and misleading simplicity.

This book has been long in gestation. The data were collected in the two modern and two traditional schools a dozen years ago—in 1956–1957 and 1957–1958. The intervening years have seen the major impact of Piaget's ideas on American research in cognitive development. Since the authors' rationale for the modern approach is congenial to the developmentalist perspective, they could have drawn upon more sophisticated and conceptually pertinent measures of cognitive attainment were they embarking upon the study today. Similar considerations apply in the area of moral development, where their work could have benefited from building upon Kohlberg's studies, with which their approach is congruent. Today the authors also might not rely quite so heavily on projective techniques, but the scrupulous and objective scoring procedures they employed represent good practice that is not at all dated.

There are also substantial unplanned benefits from the long gestation, in confronting us with enduring issues and giving us better perspective on educational fad and fashion. The recent years have swung the pendulum of educational *and* research emphasis far in the direction of programming for cognitive growth and achievement. Not only have we felt the belated intellectual influence of Piaget: first, there was the post-Sputnik wave of curricular anxiety and reform; more recently, the urgent concern to remedy the academic handicaps of disadvantaged children, mainly black, in inner city schools. For the middle-class child, the heavy push has been to prepare him for college and start him toward increasingly demanding specialized training. (Some of these children have lately been rejecting the pressures in drug-centered alienation or in activist protest.) For the slum child, the main agenda—on which little progress has been made—has been to get him somehow on the middle-class track of academic achievement. The "whole child," an improperly maligned creature of the era of progressive education, has tended to fall from view.

So, at least it seems to me, there is much in this book that is refreshing and very relevant to the needs of the day. We have much to gain from looking once more at middle-class schools that are pursuing different strategies, with reasonably adequate resources, to do what they regard as a good educational job. What we can learn about the impact of educational climates under these favorable conditions may tell us about things we need to know if we are to improve education in more adverse settings where it has been failing utterly. The interplay between cognitive competence, intrinsic motivation, and adequate selfhood may just be such that only through attending to the "whole child" can we come to grips adequately with the cognitive problems of the disadvantaged that have recently been monopolizing our attention.

If the contrast between "traditional" and "modern" approaches, as these authors conceive the polarity, remains a relevant orientation to present-day educational issues, the salient contrast in the theoretical strategies that underlie educational programming has come to pit strategies phrased in terms of specific social learning against those emphasizing emergent developmental stages: Bandura versus Piaget. Is education best viewed as a process of socialization, in which the child acquires a desired cultural repertory of knowledge and behavior by reinforcement and modeling? Or is it better conceived of as an interactive process in which the unfolding capacities, curiosities, and predispositions of the child determine the kind of constructive use that he makes of his educational environment? Matters of values as well as of fact and theory enter into our preferences here. Contemporary research and theory is elaborating the implications of these contrasting orientations and, hopefully, should lead toward a synthesis that takes account of the specifics of learning *and* of the active child's contribution to the learning process.

It is clear, however, that the sympathies of the Bank Street group lie on the latter side. These sympathies come to them naturally as heirs to a strong tradition that incorporates major themes from Dewey and Freud. Since they are scrupulous and undogmatic scholars, the consistent point of view from which they approach the school and its tasks is an asset, not a liability. "Modern" and "traditional" are evaluative terms for them as well as descriptive ones: no harm!

The authors' concern for the multiform ways in which schools affect children makes this book a solid contribution to the mainstream of research guided by newer conceptions of "mental health." Many of us have been inveighing against the older, medically-rooted conceptions that find their most appropriate application to the severest forms of disoriented disability, and have been calling for a reconceptualized evaluation of human functioning that says more about assets and positive goals. Some of us, myself among them, have followed Robert White's lead and have found, in a conception of intrinsically motivated competence, an attractive way of thinking about the characteristics of good psychological functioning. This direction of inquiry points squarely toward the developing self and the cluster of self-attitudes and self-conceptions that McDougall once labelled the self-regarding sentiment and believed to be the keystone of the psychological structure. Here we get considerable help from the Bank Street authors. Their book serves, too, as a useful corrective to the *manpower* orientation of much recent policy-motivated research and theory, that emphasizes competence to meet the role requirements of society. The humanistic values of the authors make them set higher priority on competence to know the self and to realize the projects that emerge from self-commitment.

They also diverge from the Protestant ethic to value *being* as much as *becoming*, to see childhood as having its own intrinsic ends, not just as a stage of instrumental preparation. They can maintain this position the more easily because of their evident faith that the realization of childhood values as good in their own right also lays the foundation for self-realization in adulthood. So they can admire the comparatively full-blown childishness of children in the most modern school, rather than chiding its "immaturity." Unfortunately, this is a cross-sectional study, not a longitudinal one. Some of the questions that are left hanging, including the large one just implied, might be answered if we knew a little about the subjects of the study as they graduate from college. As it is, we must be grateful for the rich fare that is provided.

EDITOR'S PREFACE

PSYCHOSOCIAL STUDIES IN EDUCATION
From the Research Division, Bank Street College of Education

There are times when ideas converge, generate new directions for thought, and stimulate change in programs for research and action. Sometimes this happens to an individual; sometimes—as is the case in the work to be reported in this series—to a group of co-workers; and occasionally this happens to a larger body-politic, as is true at the time of this writing of the war against poverty. The formulation and funding, in the 1950's, of the studies reported in this series was made possible because of the convergence of three lines of thought in education and mental health.

Progressive thinkers in education had conceptualized a new role for the school and had been trying it out for several decades. This model inaugurated radical changes in practice based on the central tenet that education is a primary force in shaping the whole person—his life of feeling as well as his mind, his power to create as well as to adjust, his inner equilibrium and his outer effectiveness. Inevitably, this model included goals for influencing personality. In addition to developing intellectual power, these schools considered themselves responsible for fostering such aspects of development as self-understanding, relatedness to people, motivated interaction with the environment, and personal qualities such as curiosity, spontaneity, and resilience. It was an image of optimal human functioning derived from psychodynamic theories of personality development, which favored humanist values in the individual's interaction with his world and saw the school, in the perspective of John Dewey, as a vital instrument by which to accomplish these goals for people and for society.

National concern about mental illness had begun to spread its ideological wings at the same time. By the 1950's, the term "health" in the mental health movement was no longer a euphemism in the designation of a whole field of activity. The focus had shifted from exclusive concern with mental illness as a disease to a concern with goals for healthy human functioning. In 1958 Marie Jahoda defined the "Current Concepts of Positive Mental Health" as part of the work of the Joint Commission on Mental Illness and Health, established by the Congressional Mental Health Study Act in 1955. As a result, what for a long time had been a vague, somewhat evangelistic concept of mental health was elevated to a condition of theoretical clarity and applied usefulness. Jahoda's roster of criteria for individual functioning was based on a review of the work of personality theorists and clinicians. It was congruent, to an impressive degree, with the goals that had been formulated by the educators. While this congruence added strength and a measure of validity to each position, little might have emerged to influence research and programming had not a third line of thought become increasingly prominent at the same time.

The third convergent line of thinking originated in the field of public health, where programs of prevention had proved effective in the control of physical disorders. The adoption of the concept of primary prevention in the mental health field stimulated new thinking. Whereas the focus had previously been on psychotherapy for the individual, the target now became the relative psychological health of large sectors of the population. Social institutions such as the family and the school became the program locale, and their psychological condition became the programming focus. The rationale was that changes in the modes of functioning of social institutions would bring about such significant elevation of basic ego strength in the general population that vulnerability to the various forms of stress and deprivation associated with the onset of mental disorders would be significantly reduced. On the one hand, there was no hard evidence that positive mental health was specifically preventive of mental disorders and little expectation that the complex relation between health and illness in the psychological field would lend itself to easy unraveling. On the other hand, there was the view that what was needed were programs based on the best available knowledge—from theory and clinical experience—as to the significant etiological forces operating at a community level and activities to ameliorate long-term noxious influences.

These three forceful lines of thought were running in a common channel: the model of a school that took upon itself the extended goal of optimal individual functioning; a concept of positive mental health that was regarded as deserving of a position in the orbit of preventive psychiatry; and a new public momentum toward investment in change in social institutions as a feasible approach to the nation-wide problems of mental health and illness. The school was obviously an important candidate for such investment. The National Institute of Mental Health was ready to support programs working toward change in education in these directions, and in 1958 the Bank Street College of Education was granted support by NIMH to plan a program of research and action on the basis of its prior experience in preschool and elementary education and school consultation that was congruent with concepts of positive mental health.

The choices of what kind of study and which lines of activity to undertake were not altogether open-ended nor exploratory in the sense that one takes a first try at a vaguely perceived problem. At Bank Street College of Education, prior formulations had been made of the nature of educational impact on developmental processes and of the strategies for effecting change in public schools. These formulations provided the frame of reference for what was envisaged and finally undertaken as a comprehensive program. They can be briefly stated:

First, the quality of experience in school has a differential influence on all phases of development during the years of childhood. Knowledge of the interaction between cognitive and affective realms of functioning makes exclusive attention to intellectual skills an archaic and impractical goal for education. Instead, the competence of the child, which it is the school's responsibility to foster, must be broadly conceived in terms of ego strength, that is, the effective interaction of the individual with the work, the people, and the problems of his environment. This calls on the school to elevate its own competence to support simultaneously the growth of the cognitive functions represented in symbolizing, reasoning, problem solving, and ordering information, and the personality processes related to feelings of self-worth and realization, potential for relating to people, autonomy and creativity, the capacity for emotional investment, and the building of a separate identity.

Second, the potency of school influence can best be understood through detailed study of the internal processes of the classroom. The unique pattern of learning experience and interpersonal relations that characterizes each classroom is a product of complex forces not always open to direct observation nor completely to be subsumed under the academic categories of traditional schooling. The teacher's concept of education and her professional mastery of teaching methods interact with her personality, her motivation, and her own development and orientation as a person. The product is a particular kind of teacher-child relationship which, in turn, becomes the vehicle of a particular kind of teaching-learning process. In addition, the flexibility of the teacher's perceptions of the children as members of a social class, her own values for productive living, and her attitudes toward the probability of the movement of the individual in the society, have a direct influence in the way she uses her professional skills with different populations of children. It is the ferment of these several forces—professional competence, the teacher as a person, and the less visible system of values through which her behavior is screened—that constitutes the dynamic processes of learning and socialization in the classroom.

Furthermore, the teacher and the classroom are at the end of a line of other complex and delimiting educational and social forces that, directly and indirectly, act to establish boundaries for possible change in the fundamental educative process. Each school is a society within itself, with a dominant system of values, a pervasive ideology, and a characteristic network of interrelations between children and teachers, teachers and administrators, school people and parents, school people and other professionals, and between school people and the official and unofficial representatives of the community. Any efforts at altering the nature of classroom processes echo and rebound throughout this network. It follows that programs of change aimed at intra-classroom processes are likely to have lasting value only if there is a clear understanding of all these forces and practical wisdom in taking them into account. A prior need, therefore, is to have a more differentiated knowledge of how the "organized complexity" of a school operates as a sub-society within a larger system.

Finally, the promotion of positive mental health in a school cannot be treated as though it were an additional piece of subject matter, concerned with interpersonal relations, to be added to the curriculum. It involves, rather, the infusion of mental health principles into the educative process at all levels—to the way knowledge is transmitted as much as to the transmission of values implicit in the nature of the teacher-child relationship; to the evaluation of new teaching techniques and devices as much as to the reconception of a learning climate. To be consistent with the concept of primary prevention, consultation services to schools need to follow psychoeducational theory and practice as distinct from the clinically-oriented functions, derived from a mental illness model, that are necessary to detection and treatment of incipient disorders.

The Schools and Mental Health program took two directions: research and action. In the research studies, this opportunity was used to put empirically derived postulates, such as the above, through systematic test and observation, to confirm them as far as they could be confirmed, and to differentiate, revise, and raise new questions where prior assumptions proved equivocal. The first two books in this series, *The Psychological Impact of School Experience* and *Teaching and Learning in City Schools*, report two studies of this kind. The first study, which had begun before the program was launched, explores the basic question: Does a school, perceived in its particularity as a life environment, affect the psychological development of children—their thinking prowess and style, self-knowledge, interpersonal perception, and emerging value systems—in predictable ways? The schools selected and studied contrasted widely in their educational ideology. Their orientation toward child development and the purposes of education ranged from the "modern," meaning the integration of developmental-dynamic thinking into the life of the school, to the "traditional," meaning adherence to goals of academic excellence and formal institutional procedures. The children studied were middle class, at a common stage of development, in fourth-grade classrooms. In general, findings of this study support the premise that the quality of schooling, ideologically defined, has a differential effect on development.

It is pertinent to the essential inquiry concerning the role of the school in relation to the concept of primary prevention that, when the modern ideology was integrated into the total functioning of the school, it did indeed support such elements of healthy personality as clearer knowledge of and greater connectedness with the self, a sense of autonomy in relation to adults as immediate authorities or as prototypes of future roles, and the children's deep involvement in their lives as children. The study also shows that these effects do not operate uniformly for boys and girls, for all personalities, or in all contexts. It therefore points the way to further questions and other studies.

The study to be reported in the second book of the series, *Teaching and Learning in City Schools,* made a different attack on the problem of learning and socialization. Here, the schools selected did not vary in educational ideology, practices, and climate. They were approximately similar in these respects and fairly typical of schools in urban centers in that they were all within the traditional range of the "modern-traditional" continuum as we had conceptualized it. They were characterized by didactic teaching, minimal exploration and initiation by the children, little probing for personal or intellectual meaning, and strong adherence to established curriculum and external symbols of success. Yet, not all classrooms in traditional schools have the same impact on the children. In this study, the child population, rather than the total school milieu, was varied, to include low-income Negro and white classes and middle-income Negro and white classes at second- and fifth-grade levels. The primary interest in this study was to test and examine further the premise that the teacher reflects the dominant values of a society in subtle ways and that teaching and learning in the public schools is compounded by stereotyped attitudes toward low-income and minority group children. In order to understand the complex pattern characteristic of classroom life for each of the child populations—the images of themselves and their futures being shaped for them, the resolution they had to make of the conflicting values to which they were exposed—information was gathered from three perspectives: observations in the classrooms, interviews with the teachers, and brief sessions with the children.

These two studies support and complement each other. The basic coherence, within a school, of educational ideology, value sytem, interpersonal styles, and images projected upon the children, showed itself as a major socializing force in both studies. In the first, the milieu created by a traditional authority was shown to be restrictive with respect to the development of personally expressive styles of response and self-relevant images of what the future might hold for these middle-class children. The second study explored the ways in which a traditional educational ideology was related to materialistic values and discriminatory stereotyped attitudes. The result for lower-income and especially for black lower-income children was a more serious restriction, not only of their intellectual development, but also of avenues for the expression of responsibility and initiative, thus impairing their chances for self-realization through occupational achievement. Instead, these children were being led toward identifying with fixed societal roles that are associated with low ceilings of accomplishment and recognition.

The two studies reflected the methodological approach of the program as a whole. The data were gathered inside schools and classrooms, in the "natural habitat" of children and teachers, after appropriate liaison and practical, cooperative arrangements had been made and formal permission secured. Both studies dealt with a complex influence variable—the school in one, the classroom in the other—and both invested heavily in a detailed analysis of the configuration of school as an environment. Both studies had the benefit of interdisciplinary thinking, as distinct from interdisciplinary team operations. The social anthropologists who took part in these studies worked with educational dimensions as an intrinsic part of their purview of attitudes and value formation in school and classroom; and the psychologists and educators paid major attention to the school's functioning as an institution in their purview of the multiple determinants of educational impact. This approach—to include sociological as well as psychological and educational thinking—was a goal of the program and reflected its alliance with the public health point of view as well as a theoretical kinship with ecological thinking.

The second direction of the program concerned the action phase, which will be reported later in this series. It involved two interrelated field projects in a small suburban school system. One of these was a sociological study of the school system and its interrelations with the surrounding community. The sociologists who undertook this study acted as participant observers. The other field project was a program of psychoeducational consultation in an elementary school within the system in which the change process invoked by the consultation was studied.

The superintendent and a few principals welcomed a change process program oriented toward the application of positive mental health principles to elementary education. The small system, the presence of a number of people in the schools and on the local Board who had kindred goals, and the relative quiescence of this educational scene as a whole, made it feasible to take a different approach from that of the other studies, namely, to work inside a school and a school system where, as educators and sociologists, we could study the processes and problems as participants and participant observers respectively. The members of the two disciplines carved out separate spheres of activity while sustaining continuous communication about the central question of how the basic structural-functional conflicts and problems of a school system, orginating within the system itself or in its relationship to the community, affect school personnel at all levels and, in the end, condition the specific nature of the teaching-learning process in the classroom.

The sociological study will offer a model for analyzing the dynamics of a school system, for understanding the interplay of forces which develop and maintain the system's own internal movements and directions of change—movements to which programs for planned change that enter, invited or uninvited, from elsewhere in the community or the educational world, must somehow be adjusted if they are to become viable. The study examines the relations of the school system to the most important of the external systems with which it is connected: the state, the professional associations, the wider educational world, and the local community. The sometimes conflicting, sometimes convergent values, ideologies, and expectations that come from these external systems are shown to be reconciled in various ways within the school system itself. Demands for expansion and improvement of the system are seen to be developed by the professional staff from the logic of their own professional ideology as well as from the internal needs of the organization and are supported at long range by the professional associations. The study describes how these demands are modified and compromised in the endless conflicts and negotiations with and between the several competing groups constituting the local community—whose financial and political cooperation with each other and with the professional educators are needed to keep the school system going. In order to examine more closely how system properties and processes affect the educational process through their influence upon principals, teachers, and children, the sociologists also made a detailed study of the administrative operation and range of teaching styles in one school in this system.

Ideally, this analysis of the system's functioning should have been available as background to instituting the program of planned change through psychoeducational consultation in another school in the same system. For practical reasons, however, both parts of the field program had to be conducted concurrently.

The consultation project followed a set of principles which had been derived from similar work in the public schools. The designation *psycho-educational* accented the main features of the method. The consultants were educators, experienced in a child development approach to education, and skilled in putting psychological aspects of behavior to the service of the teaching function. The consultants established a role with the participating teachers as non-evaluating co-educators who shared the teachers' knowledge of the children and classrooms. The consultation with the teachers was carried on in group sessions, backed up by regular classroom observations and individual discussions. Open discussion about educational matters of immediate concern to the teachers was the medium through which the consultants worked toward the goals of sensitizing the teachers to more differentiated perceptions of the children, and toward freeing them to attempt newer and more flexible curriculum ideas and practices. They tried to create an atmosphere that allowed for the expression of strong feeling and conflicting opinion without allowing the affect to become the focus of the work. While the relationship included affective interchange, the objective position of the educational consultants was not sacrificed. Thus, the consultants enlisted the gains of a dynamic group process without deflecting the activity into one of group therapy. The focus of this part of the program was not to demonstrate effects but rather to engage in concurrent analysis of the process of change, to study the points of resistance and reinforcement experienced by teachers and consultants as old attitudes and techniques were slowly relinquished for new ones. The analysis traces a gradual shift, on the part of most of the teachers, from a behavior trait typology to a child development perspective and a measure of progress as the teachers moved away from a well-meaning standardized didacticism toward a motivated, involved educational transaction between themselves and the children.

In the decade that has passed between the beginning of this program in psychosocial studies in education and this reporting of its major aspects, the two fields to which it has greatest relevance—education and mental health—have arrived at a condition of magnificent turbulence. There is magnificence in the widespread arousal of conscience, at last, concerning the faults in our social institutions and the tragic human waste for which they are responsible. The turbulence has many components, among them, the undifferentiated rejection of past theory and practice in favor of poorly defined innovation with unrealistic promise of rapid remedy, the presence of social forces that cannot wait for trial and assessment of new plans and programs, and a demand for fantastic flexibility on the part of professionals to alter their role identities radically on the shaky presumption that the new roles will indeed serve the new goals effectively.

In education the major upsurge has been on the front of intellectual mastery, with tremendous investment, corporate and scholarly, in programs focused on cognitive skills, new instructional techniques, and modes of learning that involve a discovery route for the child. Though there has been great gain in this ferment about teaching and learning, the dominant vision falls far short of the expanded concept of the role of the school to foster intellectual competence and simultaneously to support the personality processes that mediate the individual's effectiveness in the world of ideas, work, and people.

The field of mental health has burst its former boundaries and is generally considered to be in a state of "revolution," or, as Charles Hersch recently described it, in a "discontent explosion." Skepticism of established psychotherapeutic theory and method, combined with awareness that the population in greatest need is being served least adequately, has led to a major investment of professional energies and federal funding in the primary prevention approach. There is a new set of criteria for individual mental health and new priorities for social planning. Increasing the individual's intellectual and social effectiveness is expected to yield the strength necessary to cope with conflict and anxiety. Social institutions rather than the clinic are seen as the carriers of mental health in the way their internal functions are processed. A major portion of mental health expertise is to be invested in performing consultant and supporting services to the staffs of these institutions, who are in direct relation to the recipients of educational, remedial, and healing functions.

The basic perspective of the school in relation to mental health that governed the choices to be made in our program had a visionary component at the time it was initiated. However, because of the evolutionary shift in the tenets and strategies of the mental health movement, its perspective has since become dominant in the steps being taken to meet the crisis of poverty and to elevate the basic health of the whole population. It is prominent, for example, in the recommendations to be made by the Joint Commission on Mental Health of Children. Thus, the immediate relevance of these studies is greater now than was anticipated in 1958. It will still be a long time and many studies away before the complex and multiple problems we face are resolved. Our knowledge about how primary institutions influence human development is still in an early stage and as yet there are only preliminary guidelines for modifying their impact. It is hoped, however, that the studies to be reported in this series will be useful in the search for solutions that are based on an ecological perception of the school as an institution and that keep the interplay of individual-psychological and social-institutional forces at the center of the vision in planning for change.

The Schools and Mental Health program at Bank Street College of Education was guided in its planning by a Program Policy Board which consisted of the following people: Barbara Biber, Ph.D., Principal Investigator; Elizabeth Gilkeson and Charlotte B. Winsor, Co-Investigators; Viola Bernard, M.D., Donald Horton, Ph.D., Martin Kohn, Ph.D., and John H. Niemeyer. The program benefited greatly from the experienced guidance of this group.

We wish to thank Dr. Leonard J. Duhl, then with the National Institute of Mental Health, for his active and stimulating support.

Finally, I should like to acknowledge our great debt to Joseph M. Bobbitt. As Associate Director of the National Institute of Mental Health, Dr. Bobbitt vitalized our connection with the agency supporting our work, and his unflagging encouragement, confidence, and generosity were a valuable source of support throughout the program.

New York BARBARA BIBER
April 1969

ACKNOWLEDGMENTS

The study reported here was initiated by Barbara Biber, who was then Director of Research at Bank Street College of Education. The project developed as part of a program of research, the focus of which was the relationship between psychological functioning and learning experience in childhood. Barbara Biber provided the original impetus which led to a grant (M-1075) from the National Institute of Mental Health, and she subsequently served as principal investigator of the study. The support from the National Institute of Mental Health is gratefully acknowledged. A later grant from the U.S. Office of Education (Cooperative Research Project 1401) enabled us to undertake additional data analysis which has contributed to this volume.

The design of the study called for the operation of four separate teams, for the study of the schools, classrooms, parents, and children. Each of these four areas of investigation was led by a senior member of the research staff: that of the schools by Dorothy Dinnerstein; the classroom observations by Ethel Horn; the parent interviews by Elaine Graham Sofer; and the interviewing and testing of the children by Patricia Minuchin and Edna Shapiro. Herbert Zimiles had major responsibility for statistical operations and analysis. Elaine Graham Sofer, in addition to leading the parent study team, took part in the interviewing and testing of the children.

Theoretical formulations of the study in its early stages, as well as decisions concerning implementation and research strategies, were thought through by all the above-named people. The project thus benefited from

xviii

a process in which individual contributions and group thinking were conjoined.

We are grateful to other members of the project staff who carried substantial responsibility in each of the four areas. In the study of the schools, Lisa R. Peattie and Virginia Schonborg took part in the collection of data. Lisa Peattie's additional work in the analysis and organization of this material has been invaluable. Zachary Gussow served as an observer in the study of the classrooms and he, Mary K. Weigand, and Raya Wudowsky helped particularly in the analysis of this complex body of qualitative material. Virginia Stern and Lillian Shapiro interviewed parents and coded the interviews. Our warm appreciation goes to Virginia Stern for her help in the difficult task of condensing and simplifying the system of analysis and for the additional work she did in systematizing the parent material. Daniel Rosenblatt and Carol C. Hicks did much of the interviewing and testing of the children. Carol Hicks also took part in the analysis of children's drawings.

Additional staff members who made able contributions at different times were Ann Kirschner and Peggy C. Marquis on preliminary data analysis; Lucretia P. Davis, Lola Gruenthal, and Doris Wallace in the development of coding schemes and analysis of data on the children; Harvey Asch in statistical analysis; Bernard Blitz and Elizabeth Helfmann as classroom observers; and Herman Fine in interviewing the children. We should also like to thank Henrietta Smith, who, on leave from Vassar College, analyzed the material concerning the children's attitudes toward school.

We have greatly profited from consultation with various colleagues. We wish to express our gratitude to Elizabeth Gilkeson, Claudia Lewis, and Charlotte B. Winsor, whose sound advice as educators on the College staff helped us in our initial research formulations and design; to Lois B. Murphy, who was a valuable consultant on research instruments; to Pearl Meissner, who gave us helpful advice on the conduct of the play sessions; to Harriet Linton Barr, who contributed to the statistical analysis of the parent questionnaire; and to Robert Holt, who read several chapters of the manuscript in an early version and made helpful comments.

We are greatly indebted to the officials of the public school system for allowing our study to be carried out in three of their schools; and to the principals, teachers and staffs of the three public schools and the private school in the study. Since we wish to respect the anonymity of the locale and of those who took part in the study, we cannot identify the schools or name any individuals. Without their authority and help, however, we would not have been able to undertake the study. The schools tolerated the presence of our research staff over a considerable period. Their cooperation was an indispensable part of our work and we are profoundly grateful that it was given so generously.

We wish to thank the parents, both for allowing us to include their children in the study and for agreeing to be interviewed. We are also much indebted to the children who were our subjects—for their cooperation and responsiveness, and for making our work with them so enjoyable.

We also wish to thank the President and Trustees of Bank Street College of Education for their continued support beyond the time of outside funding.

We wish to thank Creative Playthings for contributing materials for the play sessions, and Mr. David Linton for providing two still photographs for the Children's Picture Story Test.

It gives us great pleasure to acknowledge our gratitude to our secretarial staff: William Hooks and Ruth Kolbe for transcribing raw data and typing reports and early drafts of the manuscript; Margaret Newman for statistical calculations and for keeping track of large quantities of data and related material; and Carol Carr and Claire Thomas for typing and proofreading the final manuscript. The skill, efficiency, and unflagging devotion of these individuals have been a great support throughout the project.

Finally, we want to thank Doris Wallace, whose remarkable editorial skills have improved every part of this book; her talent for and interest in clear expression have enabled us to sharpen not only the phrasing but the underlying thinking; whatever felicity this book possesses we owe to her untiring efforts.

Although many people have contributed to this study, the authors alone are responsible for the overall organization and formulation of the findings of the study and for the form in which they are presented and interpreted in this book.

CONTENTS

Section IV.   SYNTHESIS

Section V.   APPENDIXES

I

Background of the Study

CHAPTER

1

THE PROBLEM

The research to be reported in this book centers on a question which is both long-standing and contemporary: how do different kinds of education affect the learning and development of children?

When the study was begun, in the mid-1950's, as a large-scale comparison of children educated in schools with differing educational philosophies and practices, it was already germane to a host of questions in the field of education—some naive and sweeping, but many based on the experience and observation of educators and social scientists with a commitment to query and evaluation. The twentieth-century concept of the child had already undergone profound changes. The long strides in knowledge about personality structure, child development, and the nature of motivation and learning had generated changes in child-rearing values and practices, in the goals and methods of child therapy, and in educational theory and practice, though principally, perhaps, at the frontiers of education. Under the impact of this new knowledge and its implications—and in the social context of a period in which the precepts of humanism, the rights of the disadvantaged, and the development of the individual were being affirmed—some educators had begun to redefine the scope of the school's

3

task in educating the child and to found schools in which a new philosophy and a new set of procedures were predominant. Theorists and teachers, such as Dewey, Kilpatrick, Caroline Pratt, and Lucy Mitchell, were among those who pioneered this movement, sometimes building on each other's work, sometimes developing ideas and methods quite independently, but all with a common orientation. For most of these people, the primary goal of the school was intellectual stimulation and development—a goal they shared with educators of all eras and persuasions—but in their theories and their schools they were also concerned with the child's developing sense of himself and his worth and with his relationships to other people. In this emphasis they differed from more traditional viewpoints in two ways—in their view that all these facets are of primary importance in educating a productive and fulfilled human being and in their belief that all these facets depend on and affect each other. When they talked of educating the "whole child" it was not only because of a visionary and humanistic preference, but because they considered it self-evident that the whole child comes into the classroom, whether invited or not, and is perforce educated in many ways, whether recognized or not.

At the time when this study began, this "modern" movement in education had been evolving over a period of three or four decades, and some of its precepts and practices had spread from the group of independent schools in which it originally developed to some schools in the public school systems. There had been, and still was, a good deal of public feeling and opinion about "progressive" education, accompanied often by a tendency to misunderstand purposes and goals and to lump together a wide variety of approaches. There had also been considerable experimentation and change within the movement itself. By this time experienced school people were raising questions which represented maturity rather than early groping. There had been enough experience and adaptation within the framework of the basic ideas for them to be ready to evaluate the effects in a systematic and differentiated way. Though this modern movement had been accompanied, from the beginning, by observation, evaluation, and revision on the part of the educators involved, there had been little attempt to assess the effects of different kinds of education on children in a systematic way and over a broad range of intellectual and psychological functioning. In this sense, the study was a response to the needs of educators and psychologists and their professional interests and to a general public curiosity about these developments in education.

The world today is, if anything, more concerned with education and its effects on children than it was when the study began. Dramatic events and new social forces in the interim period—the exploration of space, the civil rights struggle, the steady advance of automation, the war on poverty—have brought education to the forefront of the national scene and generated newly urgent ideas and programs concerning excellence, quality education, teaching machines, compensatory education for the disadvantaged, and preschool education. Many psychologists and scholars from other disciplines have, for the first time, turned their attention to the education of children. The centering of interest on education has been a convergent phenomenon, but the formulations of goals and procedures have been highly divergent. Some have seen the quest for excellence in terms of preparing scientists more rapidly and skillfully, others in terms of fostering independent thinkers in any field, capable of effective and creative impact on an unpredictable and changing world; some have seen the education of the disadvantaged in terms of the upgrading of reading skills and the correction of sensory deprivation, others in terms of the building of learning motivation, the training of more skillful teachers, and the application and adaptation of preschool experiences known to be meaningful for more privileged children. Though there have been many important ideas and programs, there has been some of the inevitable chaos that attends a sense of emergency and a need for action.

In this current situation, there is a continuous need to clarify the goals of education, to find the relevant variables of child learning and growth as the school can affect them, to evaluate the extent to which psychological knowledge and action programs are syntonic with each other, and to build new developments on evidence from accumulating research and experience. There has been some tendency, in the surge of new efforts, to regard American education of the past as monolithic, static, and a rigid arm of middle-class conservatism, relieved only by misguided and outdated experimentation. It would be more accurate to view education in this country as evolutionary, composed of many strands, and potentially useful as a reservoir for current planning. A considerable body of relevant data—conceptual thinking, program planning, experience in adaptation—lies within the educational field itself, available for evaluation and development in the context of the current national scene; it would be wasteful not to build upon what is available.

To suggest that the study reported in this book bears directly on all the difficult problems of the current era would be presumptuous. Yet it is in many senses relevant to the questions of this era and to the work of a broadening band of professional people. It attempts to evaluate the effects of different approaches in education on the intellectual and psychological development of children. It endeavors to delineate concepts and variables of importance in understanding the nature of a school and its way of working out methods for achieving its goals. It approaches the question of the intellectual and psychological variables in child development that might be affected by school experience, and the problems of their measurement. It presents a body of content on selected schools and classrooms, on a group of parents, and on the functioning of children in their middle years of childhood and of elementary schooling. All these aspects seem meaningful both to the professional world that generated the study and to the wider professional world currently concerned with education.

Summary of Organization. The book is so organized as to carry the reader first through a description of the research procedures and a discussion of their underlying rationale, second through a presentation of the life settings of the children—their schools, classrooms, and families—third through a report on the children and their psychological functioning, and finally through a recapitulation of the findings and a discussion of implications. The important concepts, techniques, and findings of the study will emerge in detail, obviously, in the context of the relevant sections. This introductory section, however, will arm the reader with a very brief and general understanding of the structure of the study and of the major variables—both the influence factors and the effects—on which it has focused.

The Study

The research was designed as an intensive, field-located study using existing situations for the comparative assessment of educational effects. Research centered on 105 children, boys and girls between nine and ten years old, attending fourth grade in four metropolitan schools. The schools were specifically selected because they varied along a "modern-traditional" continuum in educational philosophy. The children came from upper-middle-class families; their parents were generally college-educated, financially successful, and engaged in high-status occupations. To serve the multiple purposes of the research, data were collected concerning the schools as social institutions, the fourth-grade classrooms, the mothers of the children, and the children themselves; the latter were observed in their classrooms and interviewed and tested in a series of six individual sessions. The data collection period extended over two years and involved a staff of approximately 15 people—psychologists, educators, and anthropologists.

As the crux of the assessment, children from modern and traditional schools were compared with each other on a series of measures tapping intellectual and psychological functioning.

The Independent Variable: Modern-Traditional

The contrasting philosophies of education and child rearing which we have called "modern" and "traditional" constitute the independent variable of the research and thus bear general definition here, as well as more detailed discussion and illustration in the chapters on the schools and homes. It might be noted that the basic components of these concepts are common to schools and homes, though educators and parents express their orientations through different specifics, in keeping with their different functions and relationships to children.

The traditional orientation has been conceived as centering on the socialization of the child, through known and standardized methods, toward generally approved forms of behavior and established levels of achievement. By this orientation, adults carry their authority role as one with fixed and unquestionable prerogatives for decisions of right and wrong and for the induction of the young into the established adult world. Child behavior is evaluated in terms of its external impact and its conformity to general standards, and individual differences are seen largely in terms of distance from or correspondence with these preconceived standards and levels of expectation.

The school, in this traditional framework, defines its task in the realm of intellectual growth. It conceives of an established body of knowledge as constituting the intellectual content of the culture and defines intellectual growth in terms of mastery of this subject matter. It assumes a relatively direct training to be the pathway to such mastery. It evaluates pupil progress in comparative and competitive terms, and it tends to foster competition among the children for the approval and recognition of achievement, regarding other aspects of peer interaction as distractions from concentration and learning. It sees the teacher as the fixed authority in whom resides both the content of learning and the judgment of progress.

The modern orientation, as has been noted, draws its philosophy from relatively contemporary understanding of the complex and dynamic forces involved in human behavior, learning, and growth. It expects a more complicated, uneven, and personally determined growth process and it sets a different balance between the general requirements of socialization and the needs and tendencies of the individual child. It incorporates the general view that the child will make his own life, that he will grow into a world different from the one he was born into, and that he must be capable both of adapting to it in a personally meaningful way and of making his impact upon it.

In keeping with this orientation, adults attempt to carry their authority role in a relatively flexible way; they relate more intimately with children, tolerate more challenge, and though they do not conceive of themselves as abdicating their role or functioning as peers, they are more consciously geared to ceding authority gradually as it becomes appropriate, manageable, and constructive for growth. This philosophy evaluates child behavior in terms of its motivation and meaning, as well as its social impact, and sees the individual child primarily in terms of his own pattern of interests, needs, capacities, and rate of growth.

The goals of a school, in this modern framework, are relatively broad. They involve the intellectual growth of the child, the education of his capacity to live and work with others, and the fostering of his development as a confident learner, as a person of unique skills and interests, and as a mature human being. The modern school stresses intellectual exploration and a probing toward integrative principles and depth of knowledge as much as it stresses the mastery of subject matter. It tends to explore new methods, to base its curriculum on understanding of the dynamics of child development, and to offer a variety of pathways and media for the achievement of mastery. It evaluates pupil progress primarily against a profile of the individual's strengths and weaknesses and only secondarily against group norms. It regards the peer group as a vital force for growth and learning, to be nurtured as such, and sees the teacher-child relationship as pivotal in the learning process and as best enacted in a way that is informed, flexible, and relatively close to the children.

The ways in which these orientations are expressed differ in particular settings. Nevertheless, it is an underlying assumption of this research and the thinking that lies behind it that these are meaningful and coherent constellations, distinct from each other, and that institutions and individuals are describable along a continuum conceived in these terms. The schools of this study have been chosen and the families of the children evaluated in the light of this assumption, though the modern-traditional orientation is not considered to encompass the whole of the functioning of a school or the relationship of parent to child, and additional factors have been considered as well.

Perhaps it is important to raise the question of whether the choice of terminology is unfortunate; such relativistic terms as "modern" and "traditional" threaten to trap the researcher in the passage of time, especially in an actively developing field. The phrase "modern education" is apt to conjure up, for many, a specific and literal set of referents, such as teaching machines and programmed instruction, quite different from what is being defined and assessed here. The original terminology has been retained, however, not only for expedience—since partial results of this study have previously been reported—but because the terms appear to have generic meanings that continue to apply. The modern orientation, for instance, is that which attempts to integrate current knowledge from many fields— dynamic psychology and child development, as well as learning processes and cognitive functioning—in order to educate and rear children. While by definition it has selectively encompassed changing methods and content, the modern movement has been, and continues to be, essentially that.

The Dependent Variables: Dimensions of Child Study

The dependent variables of the study are those concerning the functioning of the children. We have been guided in selecting dimensions for study by the central purpose of the research—that is, to assess the impact of school experience—and have thus chosen spheres of functioning that might conceivably be affected by the educational environment. We have taken the position, however, that school influence probably goes far beyond the sphere of intellectual achievement and that, as a total environmental experience, it may affect aspects of developing self-image and the system of expectations concerning people, as well as the style and level of cognitive mastery. The scope of what we have attempted to measure, therefore, has been fairly comprehensive. Though the data on the children have been inevitably limited by practical problems and difficulties of measurement, they represent an attempt to tap aspects of functioning in cognitive, interpersonal, and self-related spheres.

It might be appropriate to note that these data have been used in several ways. In most instances, the material obtained from the children has been analyzed not only to assess school group differences but to describe characteristics of the total group and differences in the reaction of boys and girls. This has been done for two reasons. Perhaps because the concept of "latency" has implied a moratorium in basic processes, children in the middle years have been less extensively studied than preschool children or adolescents. The rather rich data of the study seemed potentially important for their contribution to knowledge about this developmental stage; accordingly, the material has been analyzed and offered to the reader on this basis. Second, this analysis was essential for understanding the central findings of the study, since it was against the known background of group trends and sex differences that the impact of modern and traditional schools could best be evaluated.

In the structure of the study, a roster of predictions connects the independent and dependent variables; this roster is described in Chapter 6, which precedes the child study data. The roster comprises a series of hypotheses concerning differences between children from modern and traditional environments and covers a range of functioning, as noted above. The statements are based partly on the explicit goals and expectations of the contrasting philosophies and partly on inferences concerning effects that are not intended but may be concomitant. The analysis of data has not followed a strict prediction-testing format, but it has been guided by predictive themes and the findings have been weighed against stated expectations. In this sense, the profile of findings in this study includes some that have emerged as predicted, some that have been either contrary to expectations or considerably more complex than expected, and some that are emergent, bringing new ideas to prominent status.

C H A P T E R

2

METHODS

School environments are often described and in many ways, but almost never systematically and comprehensively or with an eye toward determining their psychological impact on children. Moreover, since most procedures for the psychological study of children have been shaped by the needs of clinical diagnosis and laboratory experiments, the psychological assessment of the effects of complex, enduring environments upon the pattern of functioning in children is seldom undertaken. The very purpose of the study, therefore—to examine the school as an environment and its psychological effects upon children—not only had our interest but presented a challenge as to method.

Research Strategy

The relative merits of an intensive, cumulative study of a small number of individuals as opposed to a less thorough study of a great many individuals are determined by the nature of the problem and the temperament and viewpoint of the scientist. In order to cope properly with phenomena whose complexity had eluded systematic differentiation in the past, it was decided that our emphasis would be on an intensive, differentiated study of both the schools (the independent variable) and the reactions of the children (the dependent variables). Our purpose was to gain such a thorough understanding of a small set of school environments that the personality and cognitive characteristics revealed by a comprehensive assessment of groups of children attending these schools could be traced to their experiences in the schools. We did not believe that such a goal could be achieved through brief exposure to the schools and a rapid assessment of the children, no matter how systematic the measurement and efficient the sampling. Measurement technology has not advanced to the point where the complex phenomena examined in this study could be understood without sustained, intensive scrutiny through multiple procedures. Our first emphasis, therefore, was on gaining mastery of the phenomena—to whatever level of complexity was necessary; at the same time, it was a guiding principle that the data be amenable to quantification.

In order to examine psychological variation among children whose school experience had been very different, it was necessary (1) to identify and define the dimension or dimensions of school experience whose effects were to be examined, that is, which would constitute the prior condition (the independent variable), (2) to specify the psychological characteristics which were expected to be affected by variation in this dimension or dimensions of school experience (the dependent variables), and (3) to adopt a research design that would support the validity of inferences made about the effects of variation in school experience while recognizing the existence of other spheres of influence and their interrelated and overlapping effects.

The Independent Variable

It has already been stated in Chapter 1 that the modern-traditional dimension was chosen as the independent variable in this study. The modern-traditional character of a school was judged to be one of the most salient determinants of its influence potential because it acts as an organizing principle that coordinates and integrates many strands of school policy. More specific and refined antecedents, such as class size or curriculum features, could have been studied; but while these are certainly important determinants of school experience, they are not usually independent of each other but are themselves governed by an inclusive set of values and goals. The overall modern-traditional orientation was seen as shaping the final enactment of a school's specific features and as providing the ideological context, thus offering the most useful way of characterizing the integrated forces of influence of the total school experience. The influence of this variable was assessed by the study of children attending schools occupying different points on the modern-traditional continuum.

The analysis of the school environment called for the examination of all characteristics salient to the modern-traditional dimension and for a systematic ordering of their relative contribution. Such a comprehensive synthesis of an institutional environment necessitated prolonged exposure to the schools. It was decided, therefore, that in order to achieve the thorough understanding necessary for the analysis, four schools only would be included in the study and, further, that the schools to be chosen be essentially equivalent in most other, non-modern-traditional respects. Once this was established, two conflicting objectives affecting the actual choice of the schools emerged. On the one hand, it seemed important to study schools which occupied extreme points on the modern-traditional continuum. Some of the most interesting properties of a dimension are associated with its extremities, especially when the middle range is defined as the point where conflicting trends are resolved, thus obscuring the essential character of the dimension. On the other hand, if the findings were to have generality, they would have to be derived from schools representative of the majority and these would not be the extremes.

A compromise, partly circumstantial, eventuated. In order to ensure the representativeness of the schools to be studied, it was decided to work within a large metropolitan public school system, whose schools were typical of many serving large urban communities.[1] Enough variation in school ideology was permitted by this metropolitan system to lead us to expect that we would find four schools within it to occupy appropriate points on the modern-traditional continuum. We discovered, however, that we could not find a school which stood clearly at the modern end of the continuum. This, no doubt, was due partly to the relatively slow filtering process which characterizes the assimilation of new ideas in a large city school system and partly to the difficulties that any publicly operated system—with its central control of crucial educational policy—would have in adapting certain aspects of the modern method. It became necessary, therefore, to include a private school in the sample to ensure representation of a clear modern viewpoint. This circumstance meant the partial sacrifice of the potential generality of the findings since, by virtue of its distinctive educational program, the private school was not typical of most schools. In addition, the children attending this school came from middle-class and many from upper-middle-class backgrounds. In order to equate all the schools in the study with respect to the background variable—an important part of the research design—the public school children in the study had also to be selected from middle- and upper-middle-class families and from schools predominantly serving such populations.

Of the four schools finally selected, three were public schools and the fourth an independently operated private school. By design, the four schools shared certain characteristics: they served relatively homogeneous and stable populations; all had a relatively stable administration and point of view; all had reputations as good schools; all were characterized by a reasonably benign attitude toward children; and all perceived the task of teaching children as a serious professional responsibility. Inevitably, there were also differences among the schools, apart from their modern-traditional quality—in their size, their neighborhoods, and other characteristics. These differences, enumerated in Chapter 3, were not systematically related to the schools' positions on the modern-traditional continuum. With regard to the continuum, the private school was rated as clearly modern, and of the three public schools one was rated as modern and the other two as traditional, one somewhat more so than the other.

The inclusion of the modern private school was, in the final analysis, an advantage. Some of the most decisive differences among the four groups of children pertained to the modern school group, and the fact that it occupied an extreme position at the modern end of the continuum served to enrich the study. In the same way that child development specialists study the radical child-rearing practices of the kibbutz to gain insight into processes and innovations which are relevant under less extreme circumstances, so the study of this clearly modern private school has important implications, both for educational theory and for programming in less unique school systems.

The Dependent Variables

A distinctive feature of this study is its concern to go beyond the measurement of academic achievement in assessing the influence of school. Its aim was, first, to delineate the psychologically meaningful behavior patterns that may be affected by school experiences and internalized by the child and, second, to observe how these were influenced by varying school environments. The underlying assumption was that school does not merely help the child to acquire facts and habit patterns, but that it leads to a partial transformation of the psychological fabric of the child.

The study of school effects in the children, like the study of the schools, called for an intensive approach. Because the variables to be studied lacked established methods of measurement, it was usually necessary to obtain multiple ratings of the same attribute from diverse sources of data, with the intent of converging upon the most accurate characterization of each child. In order to obtain these data, each child had to be seen several times; moreover, sizable samples of each child's behavior were needed—and were obtained by means of standardized tests, interview and projective methods—so that meaningful inferences regarding psychological functioning might be made. The measures obtained from the children were grouped into three broad areas: thinking and mastery, interpersonal attitudes, and self-concept.

It was decided that fourth-grade children should constitute the sample, first because children of this age, with several years of school behind them, would be old enough for the cumulative effect of their differential modes of schooling to be manifest. A second consideration was that children of this age would not yet be involved with the special problems of adolescence, since we wished to avoid the extreme variation and unpredictability characteristic of that stage of development. Third, as stated in Chapter 1, the middle years have received relatively little study and there was need for more systematic exploration of psychological trends during this developmental period.

Other Spheres of Influence

It is apparent that any attempt to delineate the ways in which variations in schooling affect children's psychological functioning must take into account the other social and psychological forces which combine to shape the child's response to a given environment. In this study, the role of social-cultural variables has been minimized by restricting the sample to a metropolitan, middle- and upper-middle-class group. A more complicated problem is posed when one tries to deal with the nature of family life—the significant ways in which variations in the child's experiences at home interact with the effects of variations in school experience.

The evaluation of the home environment, and its relative contribution to the children's behavior under study, presented particular methodological and conceptual difficulty. Although it is a rare psychologist who questions the centrality of the relationship between parent and child, the charting of this relationship with its lines of influence is difficult to achieve. Yet the demonstration of school impact partly depends on an estimation of the relationship between family background and child behavior.

The fact that the children from each school had essentially the same socio-economic-cultural background controlled one obvious source of influence; however, it did not make the families identical. In order to help clarify how the influence of the child's family background might interact with that of the school, data regarding the child-rearing patterns of each mother were gathered by means of a questionnaire and an interview.

In the three public school groups, it was anticipated that variation in family life among children from all three schools would be no greater than variation among children from one. This expectation was later confirmed. However, it would have been unreasonable to expect the child-rearing patterns of the parents who had chosen to send their children to the modern private school to vary to the same extent as those of the three public school groups. The very fact of their choice marked them as homogeneous in some respects, although there was some variation among them. But so long as there was overlap—as there was—between the modern school group and the public school groups in their patterns of family life, it was possible to begin to estimate the relative influence of home and school. The correlation between ratings of family child-rearing practice and measures of the child's psychological functioning was established. By examining school group differences within a context of information about the home, it was possible to identify spheres of school influence, as well as the conditions under which home factors appeared more important or equally so.

It must be reasserted, however, that the design of the study maximized the opportunity to demonstrate school influence, comparing children who were predominantly grouped according to their school experience. The role of family life, therefore, has a relatively modest place in the study when compared with the massive efforts devoted to delineating the school environment. This is a reflection of the primary focus and purpose of the study—to examine the quality of school experience as a source of influence —and does not mean that greater weight has been assigned to the school rather than to the home as a determinant of children's development.

Considerations of Data Collection and Analysis

Precautions were taken to protect the data from bias. Staff members concerned with different areas of the study collected data independently from each other. The material for the study of a child's family life, for example, was gathered by people who had no information about the assessment of his psychological functioning, which, in turn, was conducted independently of the observation of his classroom behavior. The most crucial data were the dependent variable scores, that is, the measures of the child's psychological functioning. It is conceivable that bias could have been introduced during the collection of these data. Interviewers might have made more thorough inquiries with some children, or behaved more—or less—supportively in the manner in which they administered their tests, although they were explicitly reminded to guard against such differential treatment. Five different individuals with varying theoretical predilections collected the dependent variable data. The net effect of their collective biases, however, if indeed these did influence the data collection, was neither systematic nor cumulative.

Ratings of the interviews and projective test protocols were made on masked data, that is to say, any cues which would reveal the identity of the child or the school he attended were removed. Most of the scoring was done by individuals who had not collected the data, to eliminate the possibility that a scorer would recall the identity of a child from the content of his response.

The basic comparison of the mean scores of the four school groups was achieved by applying conventional analysis of variance procedures to examine the significance of main effects associated with the school grouping and sex of the children and with the interaction between school and sex.

Summary

This study is one of the psychological functioning of 105 nine-year-old children, of their experiences and interaction in their classrooms, of the schools they had attended as instruments of psychological influence, and of the contribution of their home backgrounds to the influence process.

Precautions were taken to select schools that were equivalent in most important respects other than their modern-traditional quality. The children in the study were selected from classes considered to be representative of the pervasive educational climate of the school. Home background was taken into account by equating the groups on certain factors and was also handled through assessing the relationship between parent variables and child functioning. Considerable effort was expended to exclude major sources of bias and to use objective measures of assessment and appropriate statistical analysis so that inferences regarding the impact of school experience could be legitimately drawn from the data. The most rigid standards of data analysis were avoided. It would have been wasteful to obscure the very insights the study was attempting to gain through overzealous protection of the null hypothesis. In all, the primary perspective of the study—reflected in its several goals, far-ranging quality of investigation, and varied methodology—is that of a pilot work, breaking ground both conceptually and methodologically in the nature of its attack on a complex problem. It should be read and understood in these terms.

Research Outline

This outline is intended to give the reader a quick view of the research and provides a précis of facts and procedures that may serve as a useful reference as the reader moves through the book.[2]

General Design

The research was conducted in four schools. Data collection covered a period of two years, but focused on fourth-grade children in both years, that is, on successive fourth-grade classes. The staff consisted of 15 people divided into four teams, operating independently, but collecting material simultaneously in the four content areas denoted below. Each member of a data collection team rotated through the four schools, gathering material in each. Material was analyzed by staff members who overlapped but were not identical with the data collection staff.

The Four Areas

THE SCHOOLS

Selection of the four participating schools marked the beginning rather than the end of the systematic study of these institutions as socio-psychological environments. Although the differentiation of the four schools along the modern-traditional continuum was established with reasonable certainty, delineation of the component elements of the continuum needed to be established. Study of the schools provided a microscopic analysis of the independent variable, which was macroscopically conceived for the main purpose of the study. In addition, this study provided data regarding the unique qualities of each school and concerning differences among them that were tangential to the modern-traditional continuum.

1. *Subjects and sources of data.* The four schools were classified as follows:[3]
   Browning (public), the most traditional school
   Adams (public), a traditional school
   Dickens (public), a modern school
   Conrad (private), the most modern school

Adams, Browning, and Conrad participated in the study both years. Dickens was added the second year.[4]

2. *Staff*. Data were gathered by three staff members: a social psychologist, an anthropologist, and an educator.[5]
3. *Techniques*. Observations and interviews.
4. *Procedures*.[6] The staff observed and interviewed in the schools throughout the school year. Procedures were focused on the observation of school events, both formal and informal; interviews with key personnel; and interviews and observations of panel teachers.

   The panel in each school consisted of one teacher at each grade level. Each panel teacher was interviewed and observed in his classroom. Interview and observational data in Browning were limited during the second year because of opposition from the school.
5. *Data analysis*. The schools were ranked on a series of dimensions central to the modern-traditional continuum. Panel teachers were rated on a series of teaching and attitudinal dimensions. School data were also handled through more informal analysis.

   Data were analyzed both by the data collection team and by staff members who had not gathered material.

THE CLASSROOMS

Observations of classroom life served no pivotal function in the design of the study. Cumulative schooling was considered to be the influence factor rather than the immediate classroom situation, and child behavior evaluated outside the classroom was considered more reliable evidence of internalized school effects than reactions shaped by classroom opportunities. Study of classroom processes, however, served two important functions. In comparison with school data, it allowed a systematic verification of the representativeness of the classrooms which had been selected and from which study children were drawn. Further, it offered a detailed view of the processes through which the impact of the school is transmitted to the child.

1. *Subjects and sources of data*. Observations were conducted in a total of six classrooms, as follows:

   Browning—year I
   Adams—years I and II
   Dickens—year II
   Conrad—years I and II
2. *Staff*. Data were gathered by four staff members: two psychologists, an anthropologist, and an educator.[7]
3. *Techniques*. Observations of classroom processes and of individual children in the study. Material was collected in the form of narrative records.

4. *Procedures.* Observations were conducted throughout the school year. Periods of intensive four-day-a-week observations alternated with interim periods of one half-day a week.

Observers rotated among the schools. They followed a schedule covering academic subjects and a sampling of other classroom periods and events. Their records, though narrative in form, followed dimensions of interest specified in an observational guide.

5. *Data analysis.* Records were masked wherever possible. They were coded and rated for cognitive structuring and pupil response in the classroom and for aspects of interpersonal exchange. School differences were determined by statistical analysis.

Data were analyzed by one member of the data collection team and by two psychologists who had not gathered material.

THE FAMILIES

The assessment of home influence focused on those areas which might be expected to affect the child behavior under study: modern-traditional ideology; socio-economic-cultural status; and selected aspects of child-rearing attitudes and practice, some central to the modern-traditional construct and some not. Study of the families served principally as a control and precaution, enabling an assessment of the extent of school influence and of the areas of greatest school impact. It also provided data concerning family influence, however, and the interaction of home and school influence on the child.

1. *Subjects and sources of data.* Subjects were 102 mothers of the children under study (accounting, via two sets of twins and one set of siblings, for 105 children).

2. *Staff.* There were three interviewers: one psychologist and two educators.[8]

3. *Techniques.* Questionnaire, covering attitudes toward child rearing and education and including a section on family background and the child's development.

Interview with mother, covering child-rearing attitudes and practices.

4. *Procedures.* Parents were originally contacted through a general meeting at each school, where the project was explained and permission obtained. The questionnaire was administered at that meeting.

Interviews were conducted at the school and were tape-recorded. They lasted approximately one and a half hours and followed a prepared guide, but were open-ended. Each interviewer talked with an equivalent percentage of mothers from each school group.

5. *Data analysis.* Questionnaire responses were analyzed for socioeconomic information and scored for child-rearing attitudes.

Interviews were coded and rated on dimensions of child-rearing attitude and practice and for aspects of maternal role. Differences among parents of the children in different school groups were tested statistically and the relationship with child study variables was established through correlational procedures.

Interviews were analyzed by the staff members who had collected the data. No attempt was made to mask the protocols. It should be noted, however, that these staff members had no knowledge of the data collected from the children.

THE CHILDREN

The basic and crucial data of this study are those obtained from the assessment of the children. Study of the children provided an estimate of internalized school effects—aspects of psychological functioning which had presumably been activated and shaped by classroom experience and were then assimilated into the psychological structure and organization of the child. Areas of assessment were broad, involving aspects of cognition, interpersonal attitudes, and concepts of the self. Study of the children focused on the differential functioning of children from modern and traditional schools, but provided data relevant to the developmental stage and to sex differences in functioning as well.

1. *Subjects and sources of data.* Subjects were 105 children—57 boys and 48 girls. A breakdown of the subjects by year (I or II), school, and sex is given in Table 2–1.
2. *Staff.* Data were gathered by a total of seven psychologists—five acting as primary and two as auxiliary interviewers.[9]
3. *Techniques.* Individual tests: Intelligence (WISC Performance Scale); Problem Solving (four problems); Projective techniques (Children's Picture Story Test, Drawings, Play Session); Semi-projective and miscellaneous techniques (Sentence Completion, Stick Figure Scale, Similes, Moral Judgments, and so on). (See Chapter 6.)
   Group tests: Kuhlmann-Anderson; Stanford Achievement Test; Group Problem Solving (Russell Sage Social Relations); Sociometrics.
4. *Procedures.* Five individual sessions were conducted with each child the first year. In the second year, a problem-solving session was added. Staff rotated among the schools; each psychologist collected data from an equivalent percentage of children in each school. Individual sessions extended through several months of each school year. Each of the four group tests was administered in a separate session. The sessions were conducted at intervals through the school year.
5. *Data analysis.* Protocols were routinely masked for school, sex, and the identity of the child before analysis. They were scored and rated on

TABLE 2–1

Distribution of Subjects

	Browning		School Total	Adams		School Total	Dickens		School Total	Conrad		School Total	Total
	I	II	I + II	I	II	I + II	I	II	I + II	I	II	I + II	
Boys	6	4	10	9	9	18	12	12		7	10	17	57
Girls	4	4	8	9	7	16	12	12		5	7	12	48
Total			18[1]			34			24			29	105

1. *The percentage of the total class group that could be included in the sample of study children was particularly affected in Browning by requirements of the research design; for example, the children had to be middle or upper middle class and they had to have been in the school at least three years.*

a series of psychological dimensions. School and sex differences were tested by means of analysis of variance, and correlations were obtained between child behavior and parent variables.

Data were analyzed by some members of the data collection team and by others who had not gathered material.

NOTES

1. It is important to note that this study was conducted before the gross regrouping and redistricting prompted by the integration movement and at a time when the issues of decentralization and parent participation in decision-making had not been raised.
2. More detailed presentations appear in Sections II and III and in the relevant appendices.
3. The names of the schools are fictitious. It should be noted that the children's school associated with the sponsoring institution of the study, Bank Street College, was not one of the study schools.
4. While it was obviously important to include a modern public school, time did not permit us to do so until the second year.
5. Dorothy Dinnerstein, Lisa Peattie, and Virginia Schonborg, respectively.
6. It should be noted that selection of the schools was a separate and preliminary procedure conducted before the study proper could begin.
7. Ethel Horn, Bernard Blitz, Zachary Gussow, and Elizabeth Helfmann, respectively.
8. Elaine Graham Sofer, Virginia Stern, and Lillian Shapiro, respectively.
9. Patricia Minuchin, Edna Shapiro, Daniel Rosenblatt, Elaine Graham Sofer, Carol Hicks, and Barbara Biber and Herman Fine.

The Environmental Matrix

SECTION

II

The Environmental Matrix

CHAPTER

3

THE SCHOOLS

The purpose of the study of the schools was to delineate each school as a total milieu and to arrive at an image of the environment for learning it generated. Once the four schools had been selected, on the basis of their modern-traditional views of education, our specific task was to analyze, as systematically as possible, how their separate educational ideologies penetrated and were expressed in the various domains of everyday school functioning. Whereas the general definitions of modern and traditional (see Chapter 1) were adequate for selecting the schools, the detailed analysis was necessary to differentiate these global concepts, perceive them in operational form, and provide the background for interpreting the findings on the children.

While our thesis was that the educational ideology of a school has a differential effect along many psychological dimensions, we were aware that the psychological environment of each school was compounded of more than educational principles and practices and was only partly the deliberate creation of its teachers and administrators. We have therefore taken account of other features, such as the physical and social setting of each school, its distinctive demographic pattern, and the interaction between school and parents.[1]

Settings and Method

Selection of the Schools

An initial list of some 60 public elementary schools in the area was drawn up. This list was reduced to 20 public schools on the basis of census reports, health area statistics, and consultation with members of the school system to estimate the stability and cooperation of the schools and the socio-economic level of the parents. Consultation with knowledgeable educators as to likely cooperation and stability further yielded a possible four independent schools. The principals of these 24 schools were interviewed according to two pretested interview guides, the school neighborhoods were visited, and agreement was obtained from each school to cooperate in the study if selected.

The principal interview, which lasted from one to two hours, covered the following topics: neighborhood changes since the last census; ethnic composition and religious background of the child population; their out-of-school activities; the occupational and social-class status of the parents; their general characteristics and role in the school; the school's admissions procedures or criteria; the number and grouping of the children; the number of teachers—men and women—their background, and their length of service; an overview of curriculum; the nature of the school administration; how supervision of the teachers is carried out; methods of dealing with the topics and problems brought up by the teachers; the principal's view of what a child should get out of school and what the most important qualities are for a teacher; the principal's background and length of service in the school; and an account of the most needed or desired facilities and equipment.

For the study as a whole, the analysis of influence and the assessment of impact employed a common schema. This consisted of three separable though recognizably interdependent domains—*intellectual mastery, interaction among people,* and *individuality*—which have referents both for educational programs and psychological functioning. Data were gathered on the original 24 candidate schools primarily according to the information they would provide in these three areas. Even though the information obtained from these single interviews was relatively limited, it brought out the contrasts in the principals' statements of educational policy and had implications for widely differing psychological impact.

The analysis of the interviews with the principals reduced the 24 schools to a possible eight. The final choice of the four schools in the study was made on the basis of matching socio-economic-cultural level, relatively clear and contrasting educational atmosphere, goals and practice, the presence of a generally benign attitude toward children, and a reasonably convenient geographic location.

The four schools selected consisted of three public and one independent school, as follows:

Conrad. A small independent school which had, for many years, exemplified modern educational values.

Dickens.[2] A large public school, outstanding for its activity in adapting modern concepts and methods within the practical limitations of its operation.

Adams. A large public school which had added a few elements of the modern approach to its fundamentally traditional concepts and practices.

Browning. A small public school which, relatively unaffected by modern trends, valued and sustained traditional methods.

Conrad was judged as the most modern and Browning as the most traditional school. The schools were projected in the following sequence on a continuum from modern to traditional: Conrad, Dickens, Adams, Browning.

The School Settings

CONRAD

Conrad was small, private, and independent. Its building, which was a group of family dwellings reconstructed to make a school, followed no model of school architecture. Nothing about it suggested a public institution. Unstandardized and made-over, with an intimate, homelike quality, it was adapted to what were considered basic essentials by this school staff. There was outdoor play space, rooms set aside for music and dance, clay work, shop work, science, cooking, and classrooms which were set up for different simultaneous activities. A great deal about its appearance was makeshift, old, and inconvenient but, partly because it did not have the problems of bigness to face and partly because it could make its own decisions, the improvisations were functionally adequate. The children's art work, hung almost casually on the walls, its cheerful color, and strong form, created areas of brightness. The children themselves, moving freely about, talking and laughing, contributed to the pervasive quality of sprightly enthusiasm.

The community of which Conrad was a part was a diverse urban neighborhood. It contained a concentration of middle-class professional and semi-professional people (with the arts well represented), as well as many low-income families consisting of Italians and other ethnic groups, all of whom contributed to the community's ethnic, economic, and cultural diversity.

Conrad was the smallest of the schools in the study, with 190 children and 18 teachers—seven of them special teachers. There were 11 classes in this school, one at each level, averaging 18 children in each class.

Since Conrad was not a public school, its pupils could have come from anywhere in the city; however, it actually drew most of its pupils from the surrounding area. The school competed with other private and parochial schools in the neighborhood; less than half the local children attended public schools. Those parents who sent their children to Conrad from relatively distant areas had presumably chosen Conrad after considering other educational possibilities. The school was both expensive and unconventional; it required from its parent body a kind of unique commitment, although within this framework there were disagreements between parents and school, mostly about the curriculum. At the time of the study, the school had little difficulty in finding clientele and was able to maintain its sense of purpose with a few minor adaptations, reluctantly given, in response to the concerns of parents.

DICKENS

The Dickens school was the largest of the four, with 1550 children and 49 teachers who were assisted by special teachers from the central Board of Education. It had 49 classes, with an average of 32 children per class. This large population of children and teachers was housed in a big old school building of another era which showed signs of deterioration and the confusion of repeated makeshift efforts to make it functionally adequate. Its poor physical condition, complicated internal topography, uneven heating and lighting, could have made for a drab, depressing setting. Yet the general atmosphere was cheerful, amiable, and lively, taking its color and quality from the profusion of children's art products in view throughout the building. There was a tone of busy aliveness in the way children and adults moved about in the halls. Abundance of output, more than formal finish, was the dominant impression, and improvisation seemed to be meeting some of the educational needs for which neither space nor equipment were available.

The parents, coming in the main from the middle-income housing development adjacent to the school in a dense urban neighborhood, were eager for the "good" education for which this school was known and expressed their commitment to the school by taking on supplementary tasks, providing certain kinds of equipment, and contributing a certain amount of special teaching help. The relation between the parents as a group and the school staff as a whole was generally accepting and reciprocal but the voice of the parents was limited, both because of the regulations of the school system and because of the self-confidence of the principal as the educator responsible for the school.

ADAMS

The Adams school had a considerable reputation, attracting families to the neighborhood for the sake of the school. It was the second largest of the four schools, with 1120 children and 39 teachers, two of them special teachers. It had 37 classes, six of which were on double session, with an average of just over 30 children per class.

The school's immediate neighborhood showed signs of residential wealth: high-rise apartments with doormen, expensive shops, uniformed nurses wheeling babies to a nearby park. But poverty was not far away; to the east and north were tenements and the stores of the poor, and within the general area of the school a wide income range was represented. The group of people served by the school itself, however, was predominantly upper middle class. At the time of the study, many of the parents were planning to send their children on to private junior high or high schools, and one of their main concerns was whether their children would be accepted by private schools.

The building was new; halls were of gleaming tile and the rooms were painted in pastel colors. In the halls and classrooms were many displays, mounted behind glass with professional competence; children's work was prominent but took second place to professionally prepared exhibits.

Parents and school staff collaborated to maintain the school's privileged, competitive position. The parents gave the school equipment, such as television sets, typewriters, and tape recorders. They provided art exhibits for the halls and musical concerts for assembly. The school stressed its classes for gifted children since through them it could provide "extras" like teaching French and typing which, as the principal frequently said, helped to make Adams "like a private school." The prevailing attitude toward visitors was welcoming and pride was expressed in the school's up-to-date facilities and enriched curriculum. Corridor displays, classroom interiors, assembly programs, all conveyed an outward-oriented attitude.

BROWNING

Browning was the only one of the four schools outside the city's central area. Its location did not provide easy access to the cultural facilities readily available to the other schools. This school was smaller than the other two public schools in the study. Its child population of 560 was half the size of Adams' and its teaching staff of 17 was about a third as big as Dickens', with an average of 33 children per class.

The community surrounding Browning was suburban-like, with families who lived in brick and imitation Elizabethan houses, each with a yard behind, a lawn in front, and plantings of evergreens and rhododendrons. The range of social class and incomes represented here was narrower than that surrounding the other schools in the study. While one part of the district was richer than the other, the whole was middle class.

The school building was in good condition, neat and clean, but extraordinarily bare. Halls were completely undecorated and the bulletin boards in the school office held only such business items as teaching schedules and news items relating to a professional teacher organization. The visitor was impressed by how little was to be seen of children's work in halls or classrooms. The school was spacious but had a barren, institutional quality.

Browning had an active Parent-Teacher Association which provided extra books, audio-visual aids, and the like, as well as such services as lunchroom supervision. Furthermore, a group of parents had demonstrated their interest in the school, shortly before the time of the study, by bringing enough pressure on the Board to replace the principal.

In the circumstances which helped make the schools as they were, one set of circumstances set off three of the schools from the fourth; the three were public schools, part of a bureaucratically organized metropolitan school system, and the fourth was a private school, exceptionally free, even among private schools, of outside controls.

In the public schools, the curriculum was set, generally by the Board of Education; units on clothing and food, for example, were part of the prescribed third-grade program. A teacher, theoretically, was relatively free within this framework to develop each unit as she saw fit, selecting from among suggested alternatives. But she would have had to justify any radical departure from the established curriculum to her principal, who, in turn, would have had to support her to the district superintendent. The principal represented the "system" and acted as an agent of the Board of Education. The areas in which he or she could extend autonomy to teachers were circumscribed; how the principal used the open areas was a matter of educational orientation and what his or her personality projected into the professional role.

When considering the modern-traditional distinction, this administrative framework limited the public schools at both ends of the range. After a brief period of experimentation with quite new ideas, the school system had returned to ideas more, but far from completely, traditional. Modern ideas about child development and the process of learning were prominent in the bulletins on curriculum development—the prescribed basis of teaching in the schools—and were further disseminated through in-service courses and the advisory efforts of specialists in art, music, and so on, sent out from the Board. On the other hand, a public school could not freely experiment with the substance or manner of education so as to move in a direction much more modern than that prescribed. It could deviate either through officially approved experiments or through unofficial modifications which had passed the review of principal and assistant superintendent, but such deviations were limited.

Each school principal could pick his or her teachers, provided there was a vacancy, but the teachers had to be selected from among persons who met the standard qualifications set for the system as a whole. Furthermore, such were the rules protecting tenure that it was extremely hard for a principal to dismiss a teacher who was past his or her probationary period.

The financing of the public schools was determined from above; each school had the number of its teachers set according to a ratio of teachers to student enrollments, and teacher salaries were paid by the Board. A second sum of money, based on student enrollments, came to each school for books and supplies. The financial freedom of the school principal lay in his or her limited ability to juggle funds as between books and other supplies and to select the particular books and supplies deemed best. A large school had a larger budget and more financial leeway, in general, than a small school. In a school with special classes for the intellectually gifted or with experimentally accelerated classes, more than the usual amount of curricular leeway was permitted and even encouraged.

An active, concerned parent body, besides exerting pressure on the school administration, could also donate materials and services. They could give tape recorders and television sets and library books; they could be the added woman-power to make class trips possible; they could provide the material for assembly programs; and they could even (a little irregularly) supply the school with a teacher of French or Spanish. Relative to the total budget, the degree of financial leeway open to the principal, and the material "extras" provided by parents, may seem minimal, but in the general picture which each school presented to visitors and to its pupils, they were important. The curricular "extras" which they provided —the educational television, the typewriting lessons, the French teaching, the concerts in assembly—were from some points of view only frills on a basic core. Still, they were conspicuous and influential.

The private school, Conrad, was free of the restraints of system-wide regulations, uniform curriculum plans, and the hierarchical chain of authority characteristic of a large system. Its administrative structure was a system of agreed-on, largely informal regulations. It had no Board of Trustees to satisfy but was, instead, run by its teachers through an Executive Committee (composed of rotating members) and school-wide staff meetings. Membership on the Executive Committee came to each teacher automatically. There was no such thing as tenure. While new teachers were reviewed annually during a three-year probationary period, every teacher, no matter how established, was subject to periodic review by a committee of colleagues. The principal was the representative of the entire teaching staff.

The weekly staff meetings were of major importance in establishing and revising work goals and standards of teaching behavior. The size and general organization of the school, with one teacher to a grade, precluded the formal establishment of teacher subgroups. Instead there were frequent informal contacts among teachers to discuss particular problems of common interest and *ad hoc* committees on curriculum matters.

In the sense that the institution represented a body of established practice and a system of self-contained values, the autonomy of the teachers was institutionally bound. There were many but not limitless opportunities to extend teacher autonomy but the uses made of these opportunities were related to the views and attitudes of the administrator as a person.

Procedures and Data Collection

The research staff conducting the investigation of the schools consisted of a social psychologist, an educator who was thoroughly familiar with the local public school system and most independent schools in the city, and an anthropologist. The data collection was governed by our view of the school as a semi-autonomous subcommunity—part of a larger social system—on the one hand, and as a separate entity, with microcosmic characteristics, on the other. This made it necessary to become familiar with the public school system and with the social-historical background of which the independent school, Conrad, was a part. Detailed and specific material was needed to enable us to understand how the schools functioned as separate entities.

Officials in the public school system were interviewed on the functioning of the whole system as it affected local schools. Board of Education publications and manuals were scrutinized and a comparison made between the assumptions and educational goals set forth in the Board's curriculum guides and those expressed by the founder of Conrad in a book written about its educational philosophy.

In addition, each school neighborhood was described on the basis of personal reconnaissance and census material, and the chairman of each school's PTA was interviewed. Written material, such as newspapers, assembly scripts, curriculum guides, parent newsletters, and minutes of staff meetings, was collected from each school.

All three investigators observed and interviewed in each school, their visits varying in length from an hour to a full school day. They observed assemblies; life in the halls, lunchrooms, and playgrounds; special events such as science fairs, bazaars, and cake sales; staff meetings; and PTA meetings. All three had both formal and informal conversations with the schools' principals and informal contacts with teachers. Clerks and administrative assistants, specialists in science and art, and other school personnel were contacted informally by all three investigators. Teachers in each school were asked to fill out a questionnaire covering their education, occupational experience, family background, and leisure activities (there was a 100 percent, 67 percent, 35 percent and 82 percent response in Conrad, Dickens, Adams, and Browning, respectively).

In the three public schools, the principal was asked to designate a panel of teachers—one on each grade level (except the fourth grade, where the classroom observation team was already at work)—who might be considered representative of the school.[3] These representative classrooms were visited, both by the educator, who focused mainly on curriculum and classroom practices, and by the psychologist, who focused mainly on the qualities of social interaction, attitudes, and values.

Certain practical problems curtailed the collection of data in all the schools. The planned schedule of interviews and observations had to be adjusted wherever resistance was felt. At the same time that the school and its staff were meeting the requirements of the school study team, they were also accommodating themselves to the massive demands on space, time, and privacy made by the project substudies involving classroom observations and individual sessions with the children in the study. These pressures tended to restrict somewhat the study of the schools, especially the extent of classroom visits and observation and recording of informal activities. However, with regard to such matters as curriculum emphasis, school customs, dominant values of school staffs, styles of adult-adult and adult-child relations, the material collected was generally adequate for our purposes.

It was more serious that the schools were not equally research-tolerant. The teachers at Browning, less accustomed than those at the other schools to outside contacts and visitors in their halls and classrooms, felt the presence of the study team as so unusual and disturbing that it appeared wiser not to attempt to carry out teacher interviews in that school and, in the second year of the study, classroom observations were discontinued on request. Thus the body of data for describing and assessing the practices in Browning is far less complete than the material gathered in the three other schools.[4]

Data Analysis and Related Theoretical Considerations

To be useful, the analysis had to extend our knowledge of the intrinsic processes through which psychological impact was mediated by bringing into focus the concrete ways in which the contrasting theoretical alignments of the schools were expressed.[5] Two questions of central interest were to be answered. First, the analysis would tell us whether the relative positions the schools had been assigned on the modern-traditional continuum were accurate and whether our choice of these schools was valid. Second, the analysis was expected to discriminate among levels of possible differences. We would be able to judge, for example, whether the schools' antithetical views resided in their view of the successfully educated child; or, on the other hand, whether we were dealing with relatively similar *ideals* for children's individual functioning but with clearly contrasting ways of achieving them, that is, a common goal but contrasting means.

In preparing to compare the four schools, moreover, it is well to remember that their potential differences along modern-traditional lines included a relatively small range when compared to conceivable variations in the world's educational practices and do not cover the complete range of known variations on the American educational scene.

Indeed, the four schools were alike in some fundamental respects. While they varied in size, all were large to a small child and all were organized by age-grades. Teachers were mainly women, both young and middle-aged. The content transmitted varied, but around a basic core, which included the "3 R's" and American History. The schools all maintained adults who were in a position of authority over the young, charged with leading them toward goals which the latter may only partially have shared. None exercised extreme forms of rote learning and none allowed children completely free choice of what to learn. Our assumption was that variation within this band of similarity was sufficiently potent to have a differential effect on the psychological development of the children.

The data were organized according to four themes which were identified as salient in the expression and implementation of the school's modern-traditional orientation to education. The four themes were: (1) Education for Competence, (2) Quality and Patterns of Interaction Among People, (3) View of Individuality, and (4) Relation of the School to Its Social and Professional Milieu. Each theme was subdivided into functional categories which define the relevant school practices and values, distinguishing modern from traditional school emphasis. The schools were compared and ranked on each category.

Three sections now follow: first, the comparison and ranking of the schools according to the four themes, accompanied by capsule statements which clarify the relative ranks; second, profile descriptions of the two modern schools and then the two traditional schools according to the four themes; and third, descriptions of those characteristics of each school which are not necessarily associated with the modern-traditional orientation.

Comparison and Ranking of the Schools According to Four Themes

Education for Competence

The four schools reflect the division in current opinion about what the school's responsibility should be for developing competent individuals. One view takes competence to mean academic achievement and mastery; the other view holds that the true meaning of competence also includes attitudes and feelings about work, other people, and the self. Such an extended concept of competence as a legitimate educational goal is usually tied to an image of an optimally functioning individual and an optimal learning environment, in which unseen psychological processes are consciously considered. To take this into account in the analysis, the following five aspects of school functioning were chosen as most relevant to the theme (see Table 3–1): (1) stimulation of intellectual processes, (2) variety of learning modes, (3) sources of motivation: children, (4) sources of motivation: teachers, (5) encouragement of teacher autonomy. The schools were compared on each of these five categories according to the presence and strength of values and practices relevant to each category (see Figure 3–1). The four schools were then given a consensus ranking on each category on the modern-traditional continuum.[6]

CONRAD

Of the four schools, Conrad's implementation of the concept of learning by independent exploration and discovery was the most highly developed. In addition, engaging the child's intuitive, expressive propensities together with his verbal-conceptual-analytic powers was a highly respected value built into the design of the educational program. The school emphasized intrinsic rewards, such as search, discovery, expression, and pleasure, as the most effective motivating forces for learning. By the same token, the

TABLE 3-1
Education for Competence: Relevant Practices and Values

MODERN EMPHASIS	TRADITIONAL EMPHASIS

1. Stimulation of Intellectual Processes

Active exploration and discovery by child	Direct transmission of information and skill from teacher to child
Child's ability to formulate and search for varied solutions to problems	Teaching devices that raise teaching and learning efficiency
Sustaining critical questioning and probing of ideas	Learning tasks with detailed directions for children to follow
Mastery through child's ability to discern relationships among facts and learn to deal with higher-order concepts	Amount and rate of mastering factual information
	Tendency to drift from pursuit of ideas to moral precepts

2. Variety of Learning Modes

Creative expression is integral to intellectual development	Creative arts are supplemental to academic program
Variety of media for expressive activities	Creative activities as skill subjects
Developing techniques to integrate expressive and analytic modes	Reliance on the verbal mode as the proper instrument for learning

3. Sources of Motivation: Children

Stimulation of interest and self-investment in learning activities	Use of established symbols as measure of accomplishment
Use of techniques for making learning individually meaningful and satisfying	Use of an approval-disapproval code of evaluation
Concept of a school climate that matches qualities and impulses of children	Encouragement of comparative-competitive processes

4. Sources of Motivation: Teachers

Enjoyment of spontaneity and curiosity of children	Pride in high achievement scores attained by children
Sense of competence derived from depth and vigor of children's response to learning activities	Ability to control and discipline valued highly as part of sense of competence
Sense of personal worth derived from choice and initiative afforded by administrator	Dependence on administrator's approval as measure of competence
Identification with school's leadership position in the profession	Opportunity for extra-classroom activities

5. Encouragement of Teacher Autonomy

Autonomy extended to teachers as part of general view in which the individual's independence and initiative is highly valued	Autonomy more a by-product of minimal supervision and absence of common value system
Teachers encouraged and supported in innovative, creative approach to curriculum	Teachers expected to follow a directed course in implementing objectives as interpreted by the administration
Teachers made participants in some aspects of decision-making for school as a whole	

FIGURE 3-1
Education for Competence: Ranking of the Four Schools

1. Stimulation of Intellectual Processes	C D	A B	
	Modern	Traditional	
2. Variety of Learning Modes	C D	A B	
	Modern	Traditional	
3. Sources of Motivation: Children	C D	A B	
	Modern	Traditional	
4. Sources of Motivation: Teachers	C D	A B	
	Modern	Traditional	
5. Encouragement of Teacher Autonomy	C D	A B	
	Modern	Traditional	

teachers were unanimously enthusiastic about the personal gratification they felt in stimulating the children's investment in learning and in supporting their general development as individuals.

Respect for the individual's urge to structure and create was an axiom of the educational philosophy at Conrad and applied to teachers as well as children.

DICKENS

The greatest effort at Dickens was to make the child an active, interested participant in learning activities. Within the practical limitations, the range of activities was being vigorously extended, both in the creative arts—especially music—and in social studies. The codes of evaluation established for the public school system as a whole were in effect at this school but efforts were also being made to engage the children's interests, take account of their individual contributions, and reduce reliance on competition as a prime motivating force.

The teachers were enjoying a "discovery" phase for themselves professionally and greatly appreciated the principal's leadership in pointing to new directions. The administrators provided practical support in many ways for those teachers who were inclined to adapt or modify, rather than literally adhere to, the curriculum directives from the Board.

ADAMS

At this school, the teacher was the active, directing figure, interested in what and whether the child was learning, but not oriented to the processes involved. The children worked with a variety of media but creative work itself was ancillary to the program and its products were primarily valued on the basis of performance and achievement. Standard ways of assessing accomplishment, the privileges associated with success, and encouragement of competition were expected to motivate children.

Motivation for teaching was more random at Adams than at other schools and ranged from enjoyment of competence in special subject matter areas to dislike of teaching except for the pleasure it might afford in being a successful disciplinarian; there was greatest common ground in taking pride in the successful performance of the children, especially the bright ones.

The principal's low investment in the educational aspects of supervision gave the teachers considerable freedom; it also exempted them from making the efforts required to reach new horizons in a professional situation.

BROWNING

At Browning, the emphasis was on systematic and accurate fact-finding; mastering the fundamental skills was seen as a prior necessity to any attempts at organizing knowledge conceptually. A narrow range of learning modes included few creative activities. External rewards and conscience were expected to motivate children. Conformity to the principal's expectations and the ability to live up to his goals and standards were inferred to be important components of the teachers' sense of competence.

The teachers at Browning were not encouraged, nor did they show any inclination, to do things their own way; they accepted the principal's interpretation of the Board's directives as part of the authority of his office.

Quality and Patterns of Interaction Among People

This theme was conceived in three ways: as pertaining to the relationship between superior and subordinate, as pertaining to the balance between freedom and control, and as a condition of democratic process. We examined the ways in which authority in the four schools was exercised between two sets of superiors and subordinates (see Table 3–2): (1) authority in the teacher-child relationship and (2) authority in the administrator-teacher relationship. Would both sets of relationships have values in common even though the figures and experiences were different in each case? In examining these relationships we would be making comparisons in terms of the general issue of freedom and control. The third task was to examine the schools' (3) use of peer groups in organization of children's work. In other words, how were contrasting images of a democratic way of life reflected in the different ways employed by schools to engage the children one to another? The schools were compared on each of the three categories (see Table 3–2 for relevant values and practices) and were given a consensus ranking as before (see Figure 3–2).

TABLE 3–2

Quality and Patterns of Interaction Among People:
Relevant Practices and Values

MODERN EMPHASIS	TRADITIONAL EMPHASIS
1. *Authority in the Teacher-Child Relationship*	
Authority mediated through the relationship between teacher and child	Authority vested in the status of the teacher
Rules and regulations adapted functionally to meet needs of varied but simultaneous classroom activities	Rules and regulations fixed to protect high standards of quiet and orderliness necessary to teacher-directed learning
Preference for controls that involve a minimum of restriction and a maximum of reasonableness	Compliance with established authority regarded as positive component of character development
Use of disciplinary measures as corrective expedients intended to remedy disruption	Punishment conceived as retribution for wrong done, presumed valuable for learning distinctions between right and wrong
2. *Authority in Administrator-Teacher Relationship*	
Administrators expect to hold authority by virtue of direct contribution to the educational function of the school	Assumption that authority is based on the powers and responsibilities assigned to the office by a higher authority
Emphasis on individualized working relationship for mediating authority	Role interpreted primarily in terms of efficient management of school enterprise
Supervision carried as joint evaluation, minimizing censor and inspector functions	Decisions made at administrative level and communicated to teachers through the formal structure of the school
Teachers kept informed about reasons for decisions and regulations	Difference in status reflected in style of interpersonal relationship
3. *Use of Peer Groups in Organization of Children's Work*	
Experience in peer group activities encouraged for learning democratic ways of social functioning	Adoption of democratic procedural forms as an experience of democratic functioning
Use of discussion technique to make whole class a peer group forum	Use of political forms of democratic functioning to handle individual and group problems
Engaging the class in problem solving and opinion formation, involving codes of social behavior as well as study content	Whole class organized as a formal unit engaged in individual question-answer exchange with teacher
Shifting composition of subgroups according to task-relevant individual qualifications	Use of small groups, composed according to achievement level, to improve mastery of subject matter
Use of small subgroups that have clearly defined tasks and wide latitude on how to accomplish them	Use of small groups as committees with detailed directions on how to manage their task

FIGURE 3–2

Quality and Patterns of Interaction Among People: Ranking of the Four Schools

1. Authority in the Teacher-Child Relationship	C D A B ←— ⌐——————⌐————————⌐——⌐ —→ Modern Traditional	
2. Authority in Administrator-Teacher Relationship	A C D B ←— ⌐——————⌐————————————⌐ —→ Modern Traditional	
3. Use of Peer Groups in Organization of Children's Work	C D A B ←— ⌐——————⌐————————⌐—————⌐ —→ Modern Traditional	

CONRAD

The teachers at Conrad were confident of their clear preference for an informal authority role with the children, controlling without restricting and allowing for a degree of expected turbulence. The institutional structure, which provided against ukase from above, the common value system, and the direct involvement of the administrator with teachers and children as a person and as an educational leader all kept difference in status to a minimum.

The ways of using peer group formations, whole class or subgroups, at this school were consistent with the conviction of its personnel that the quality of interaction among individuals, more than its formal structure, is the essence of the democratic process and that exploration in this realm is as important as it is in others.

DICKENS

Many teachers shared the principal's goal of establishing a functional and rational basis for the teacher's authority; however, diversity of viewpoint and problems in enacting the role of the teacher were implied. The principal distributed her administrative energies in several directions: she supervised teachers who were trying new ways of teaching, she used the institutional structure to engage teacher opinion, and she upheld her own model of educational excellence in the face of diversity among her staff.

The teachers at Dickens worked with the whole class as an active peer group but only occasionally felt that there was advantage in using subgroups as a means of teaching or forming attitudes.

ADAMS

The Adams teachers took a formal, restraining authority role for granted, entertaining no doubt as to the socializing value of compliance with established codes, but allowing a degree of personalization to enter into their relations with the children. The principal was most committed to keeping the wheels of the school running smoothly. This function involved her in managing pressures from the outside, such as demands from parents, and protecting teachers from practical operational difficulties, but did not require her participation in their teaching activities.

Models for social functioning for the children were drawn directly from adult life, and peer groups were organized according to formal structures established by the teacher.

BROWNING

At Browning, the teachers seemed to maintain an unruffled position of authority associated with a clear, dignified distinction between teacher and pupil such as they would consider fitting between any adult and child. The school also observed the highest degree of formality in administrator-teacher relations.

At Browning, use of the whole class predominated.

View of Individuality

The coherence within each of these schools in the approach to problems of intellectual mastery, in the climate of human relations or in the attitude to creative expression, is no accident, since all these grow out of the school's basic perspective of what is important in the interaction between an individual and his world. If the goal is adaptation to an existing world and the acquisition of competence so as to reap the greatest rewards in that world, a kind of school will take shape that lays greatest emphasis on the process of socialization. Another view, that the world needs constant remaking by individuals who can make an impact, dictates another kind of school, one that considers the nurturing of individuality and concern for the child's identity a major part of its responsibility. To take these viewpoints into account, the following three aspects were chosen as most relevant: (1) self-realization and socialization—that is, how support of the children's self-realization and autonomy on the one hand was balanced with channeling them toward adaptation and acquiescence on the other; (2) perception of children—how the teachers perceived the children; and (3) theory concerning child development and deviation—that is, the connection, implicit or explicit, between the schools' perspectives and child development theory (see Table 3–3).

The schools were compared and ranked on each of these categories on the basis of relevant values and practice (see Figure 3–3).

CONRAD

The opportunity provided for exploration and enjoyment in learning and the minimally restrictive authority system were regarded at Conrad as the

TABLE 3–3

View of Individuality: Relevant Practices and Values

MODERN EMPHASIS	TRADITIONAL EMPHASIS
1. Self-realization and Socialization	
Expression of individual interests, ideas and feelings stimulated by variety of learning modes	Achievement, objectively and comparatively measured, regarded as the major objective of education
Guiding and facilitating individual potential considered essential in teaching	Goal-setting, directing and monitoring accepted as proper functions of teacher
Protection of individual autonomy considered important in socialization	Adaptation to and compliance with pre-established codes considered the most important factor in socialization
2. Perception of Children	
Individualized descriptions in terms of qualities of personality, behavioral style, and intellectual characterization	Children described in terms of brightness, IQ, social background, and behavior
Differentiated descriptions in terms of developmental problems or remedial needs	Characterization of the class in general categories as above
Characterization of the class in terms of qualities of intra-group functioning	Good manners and reasonableness favored by teacher
Vigor and imagination favored by teacher	
3. Theory Concerning Child Development and Deviation	
Learning viewed as continuous growth, involving changes in needs and capacities during successive stages	Early years seen as socializing preparation for intellectual mastery of later years
Concepts of child development used as foundation for curriculum design and teacher role	Children's problems seen in terms of impact of behavior on classroom situation
Children's problems projected against causal factors in child's life situation	Individual differences recognized primarily with respect to achievement in academic subjects and behavioral conformity
Emphasis on school's responsibility for understanding individual differences along multiple dimensions of personality	

conditions most likely to support a full realization of individual propensities and powers.

Both the structure of the educational program and the general school atmosphere contributed toward making the children known to their teachers as individuals, and the educational philosophy influenced the teachers' perceptions in the direction of personal qualities.

The rationale for the educational design at Conrad was based on principles of child development. Some of these principles were idiosyncratic to the school's founder but many were congruent with principles of learning espoused by developmental psychologists.

FIGURE 3–3
View of Individuality: Ranking of the Four Schools

		C	D		A(B)[1]
1. Self-realization and Socialization	← – –	⌐⌐			⌐⌐⌐ – – →
		Modern			Traditional

1. Self-realization and Socialization

C   D   A(B)[1]
←-- ⌐_____⌐_____⌐_⌐ --→
    Modern   Traditional

2. Perception of Children

C   D   A(B)
←-- ⌐_____⌐_____⌐_⌐ --→
    Modern   Traditional

3. Theory Concerning Child Development and Deviation

C   D   A   (B)
←-- ⌐___⌐_____⌐_____⌐ --→
    Modern   Traditional

1. Since the panel teachers at Browning could not be interviewed, the view of individuality at this school has been inferred from observation.

DICKENS

At Dickens, there was particular concern about emotional factors and the environmental influences that may impede the development of individual strength. The teachers' perceptions of the children were mixed. Some were sensitive to the unique characteristics of individuals and groups; others were oriented more to performance and were less aware of other facets of individual functioning. The principal tried to stimulate awareness of developmental and remedial needs.

Interest in applying child development theory was expressed in receptiveness to numerous special projects, among them guidance and remedial programs.

ADAMS

The teachers at Adams felt the school had done well to the extent that the children were high achievers and well adapted. Questions of inner processes and growth were not considered part of the school's responsibility. The teachers tended to have categorized and relatively undifferentiated perceptions of the children, which reflected both the salience of social-class status in this school and the high value given to brightness as measured by academic achievement and IQ.

Teaching was practiced and developed in behavioral terms, uninvolved with child development theory as a way of stimulating interest or as a basis for changing practice.

Relation of the School to Its Social and Professional Milieu

How important is it for a school to maintain itself as an institution sensitive to the realities of its social surroundings and to changes in the professional milieu? Schools differ widely, in general, on this question. For some this goal is peripheral; for others it is of major importance, in fact a measure of a school's viability. Schools that are committed to building functional continuity with the world outside find different ways of working this out—through the children's program of study, through its relation to the community, or in its role as a member institution of a larger profession. A school's commitment to relationships with the world outside, moreover, is crucially influenced by factors such as its relative independence, the investment of the principal in his professional role, and the determination of the parents in defining and demanding what they consider good education.

Three aspects of this topic were considered in examining the differences among the study schools (see Table 3–4): (1) use of the surrounding environment; (2) incorporation of contemporary developments: social-political issues and communication techniques; and (3) adoption of new educational methods.

TABLE 3–4

Relation of the School to Its Social and Professional Milieu:
Relevant Practices and Values

MODERN EMPHASIS	TRADITIONAL EMPHASIS
1. Use of the Surrounding Environment	
Use of surrounding environment integral to curriculum design	Use of surrounding environment for pleasurable excursions in primary grades
Trips for the study of community functioning used as a teaching technique in the primary years	Visits to institutions of general cultural interest in the upper grades
Experience gained on trips integrated with discussion periods, creative arts, and dramatic play	
Environment used to illustrate specific content of studies in the upper grades	
2. Incorporation of Contemporary Developments: Social-Political Issues and Communication Techniques	
Engaging children in study of and participation in contemporary social events and problems	Peripheral attention to current events and problems
Adoption of new communication techniques as part of continuous program revision	Adherence to accustomed modes of communication in teaching
3. Adoption of New Educational Methods	
Experimentation with new methods and procedures	Adherence to established, accustomed methods
Selection and assessment of new methods based on a theoretical rationale	Little or no contact with major sources of professional stimulation and activity
Contact with frontiers of change in the profession	

The schools were ranked on each category as before (see Figure 3–4 for relevant values and practices):

FIGURE 3–4
Relation of the School to Its Social and Professional Milieu:
Ranking of the Four Schools

	C D A B
1. Use of Surrounding Environment	←– – └————└————————└—└– –→
	Modern Traditional
	A
2. Incorporation of Contemporary Developments: Social-Political Issues and Communication Techniques	D C B ←– – └————————————└————└– –→ Modern Traditional
	A
3. Adoption of New Educational Methods	D C B ←– – └————————————└————└– –→ Modern Traditional

CONRAD

In this school, trips were part of a comprehensive method for the study of a functioning environment, linked to other school activities, in all of which the teacher stimulated observation and subsequently encouraged symbolic replication of the experience. Current social and political issues were deliberately not included in the curriculum because it was considered educationally unsound and premature to involve children in the adult problems of contemporary society.

The Conrad staff was satisfied, in the main, that the procedures they had devised in an earlier pioneering period were standing the test of time.

DICKENS

Trips were much used in the primary grades at Dickens to deepen the children's interest and curiosity in the units of study in the social studies program. Social issues were directly discussed; social and political institutions selected for study were ones with which children could have actual contact and a feeling of productive participation.

There was an atmosphere in this school of dynamic change in process; the adoption of new materials and new methods expressed a strong motivation to rethink and rework school practices.

ADAMS

Trips were infrequent here and tended to focus on "display" elements rather than the working activities of neighborhood or community. There was great enthusiasm for bringing new styles and techniques in communication into the school, but interest in current world affairs was minimal.

Adams maintained a certain distinctiveness by the addition of many "extras" in the school program; however, these were fringe activities which did not impinge on the fundamentals of the learning process and did not affect the teaching method or its possible revision.

BROWNING

Use of the surrounding environment at Browning was rare and restricted to the youngest children. The staff relied on accustomed media—books, primarily—for presenting factual material according to syllabus directives. Neither external nor internal forces were operating at Browning to stimulate any appreciable change in its style of schooling.

Profile Descriptions of the Schools According to the Four Themes

---

THE MODERN SCHOOLS

Education for Competence

The heart of the educational philosophy at Conrad was the orientation to learning as a complex process of growth. The staff at Conrad were greatly invested in exposing the child to a variety of learning modes, and they were convinced that full opportunity to learn by exploration and discovery yields both a sounder, deeper mastery of knowledge and builds up a lasting, independent approach to knowledge. The school head stated:

> . . . a school should be a place so set up that a child can carry out . . . discoveries . . . at all levels: in the nursery years when manipulative-constructive activities are self-initiated; in the primary years when the children are re-expressing newly mastered spatial and functional knowledge in two and three-dimensional media; in the elementary years when a "research" method of finding information is established.

Cognitive power was identified with ability to see relationships among facts, to search for origins, causes and conditioning factors, to differentiate and generalize, to formulate problems, and to interpret and form opinions. Facts were the raw material for the intellectual goal of conceptual mastery. This viewpoint had, in earlier years, involved the staff in innovating curriculum design and teaching techniques. In the study of the settling of the country, contrasting ways of life among, for example, the Pilgrims, the Dutch, and the Indians was one central theme; the comparison of what the settlement meant to the Europeans who came and to the Indians who were here was another.

Within the limits of a clearly prescribed framework, Conrad had established a relatively open learning field, low in fixed directives and high in acceptable alternative patterns. The teacher was responsible for selecting and supplying abundant experience, encouraging independent search for understanding by the children, and serving as a resource for guidance and clarification.

Dickens, like Conrad, was predominantly oriented to a view of learning as an active process, but this view was expressed more on an applied than a theoretical level. Through the principal and the group of teachers aligned with her goals, the school was moving vigorously to adopt the techniques, relatively new for them, that bring the child as a learner to the foreground in the learning-teaching configuration. The kindergarten teacher talked about leaving behind the old technique of showing children what to do now that she had learned a lot about letting children do their own work.

The teachers at Dickens were interested in relating what they taught to children's interests and in trying out methods that encouraged questioning and "thinking" in a broad sense. When the kindergarten children were taken to watch a derrick, the teacher engaged them in counting how many loads it took to fill the truck. Another time, a spontaneous discussion about how sand and water mix followed a period of play with those materials. The sixth-grade teacher enjoyed the chance to get off into "deeper aspects of social studies" by teaching the basic concepts of democracy and emphasizing them as part of a system of values.

The rationale for what the Dickens teachers were trying to do could be found in the guidelines from the Board of Education but it was a less broadly conceived philosophy than at Conrad. At Conrad, the practices were in service to an idea, fairly abstract, in which intellectual mastery was subsumed under a broader ideal of total personality development; at Dickens, the practices were closer to being the goals per se, and implications for broader effects were likely to be of the nature of empirical discoveries made by the teachers. Yet, in both schools, education was pointed to the way a child learns when given the opportunity for exploration and self-direction in his position as a pupil.

At both schools, the creative arts were fostered and valued as important modes of expression; techniques had been developed (at Conrad over many years, at Dickens more recently), especially in social studies, for synthesizing the expressive and analytic modes of experiencing and learning. The creative arts were seen as related to intellectual learning in the sense that they deepen sensitivity and contribute new ways of deriving meanings and diversifying perspective. At Conrad, creative-expressive activities were a built-in feature of the school's life—budget, special teachers, use of space, and curriculum design. From an original emphasis on nonverbal media and action and spontaneous expression generally, creative activities had been refined to include standards of technical proficiency. The music teacher, for example, decried an attitude of "just come and sing"; he also expected the children to learn the technical aspects of music.

The social studies program served as the nexus for integrating diverse learning experiences. Each social-historical theme undertaken was approached through reading and discussing the central social, economic, and geographic forces and through exploring and representing the arts and artifacts of the era. A technique of original dramatization had been developed in which the facts and concepts the children had mastered were synthesized with authentic form, color, and movement, the whole communicating a high degree of empathic grasp of the life and feeling of other times and peoples. A play about the Boston Tea Party, which treated the subject with both seriousness and humor, played back and forth between the conservatives and activists who had a part in that moment of history, building up to an impassioned speech about "rousing the people away from tyranny." The plot, music, dance, and props were all created by the children; they danced a gavotte; the emptying of the tea ship was symbolized in rhythmic movement. The closeness of the theme of independence to the children was clear when, intermingled with relatively intricate political innuendoes, one child proclaimed: "England treats us like a child."

At Dickens, the creative arts, especially music, were given an important place in the curriculum but mostly took place in the regular classrooms, with only occasional help from specialists. In addition, some teachers were experimenting with ways of diversifying social studies, by supplementing book work with observation of the community and the way of life of other ethnic groups and, as at Conrad, by writing and presenting plays that synthesized the multiple facets of a social-cultural theme.

The general direction at Dickens was similar to that established at Conrad; but Dickens was in an earlier stage, adapting and trying out new techniques in order to arrive at this goal. Not all the teachers were identified with this movement in the school. Even an energetic principal could support the more experimentally minded teachers (and the panel were among these) only within the limits set by the system. For example, changing goals and practices at Dickens could not bypass the centrally established, relatively fixed ways of assessing achievement. There were no such limitations at Conrad, whose independence enabled the school to keep its position consistent, from goals to practices to assessment.

In both schools there was a strong conviction that the learning tasks could be so interesting and stimulating, so in tune with the impulses of children to explore, discover, and express, that the children would become deeply involved and motivated to learn for the sake of its intrinsic pleasure and fulfillment. In this view, pleasure was in no sense the antinomy of difficulty, nor fulfillment the ready gratification of wish or demand. The intention was not to create ease and avoid struggle. It was, rather, to join the child directly to the actual processes so that his achievement and organization of skills and knowledge should be vivid, personally important, and self-rewarding. "The main idea," the principal at Conrad said, "is to get interest and excitement in learning."

The impact of this educational tenet was similar in both schools, in at least three ways. First, school as a place had qualities to match the children's—it was alive and colorful, receptive to enthusiasm and high spirits, and offered scope for free communication and movement. Second, the adults in both schools placed great importance on establishing a strong bond between the individual child and his class group and school. The principal at Dickens stressed this point: "If he feels that he belongs to the school, feels part of his class—then he will learn," she said. Third, the adoption of new teaching techniques and the revision of old ones were screened by the criterion of "match" with the basic impulses and modes of childhood. This was the basis for emphasizing active exploration, discovery, and personal expression.

The two schools differed in the extent to which reliance on intrinsic motivation had displaced the use of external rewards. At Conrad, there were no report cards or symbols to mark individual success or spur competition. Evaluation was part of the continuous interchange between teacher and child, applied directly to the work at hand. This did not gainsay the presence of the children's own comparisons of each other's competence nor their sensitivity to what the teacher valued most in their work and performance.

At Dickens, on the other hand, report cards were part of the public school system and a source of uneasiness to many teachers and to the administration. A conscious effort was made, at the leadership level, to minimize the comparative-competitive orientation intrinsic to such practices, though this was not unanimously favored as a trend.

In both schools, the image of successful teaching was connected to inner rewards. The teachers enjoyed teaching and felt competent when the children responded with vigor and interest as well as when they showed accomplishment.

The principal at Conrad looked for teachers who had a certain "excitement in learning themselves . . . who could feel the child's excitement in his own terms." The fifth-grade teacher, similarly, talked about the "excitement of watching a kid take an idea and put it together in a really unique and original way." There were no established forms of commendation for good work but an implicit standard-setting operated among the teachers and between teachers and principal, which was activated in instances of inadequate performance.

Teachers who "*want* to teach" was what the principal at Dickens looked for, and for those who were aligned with her views there were the success feelings of an in-group with authority on its side. The rewards were mixed. Many were intrinsic to the teaching process and relationship per se. Some were tied to expressions of approval by the discriminating, articulate principal who was also, as a supervisor, in the position of making official ratings of teachers' performances.

At Conrad, the teachers identified with their school, which they saw as a separate, independent, educational institution with an established philosophy and code for protecting and nurturing individuality. At Dickens, the teachers identified with what they saw as a frontal movement of change within the system and took pride in the shift they had made from traditional to modern modes. The "modern" was more of a fresh personal discovery for them, and their framework was to compare their school with others in the system. At Conrad, reference was to an ideal rather than an existing counterpart.

The basic educational values held by both schools—autonomous learning and intrinsic motivation—were reflected in their administrative styles and practices. Strong motivation to teaching was the first requisite in teacher selection in both schools. In their work with the children, teachers were encouraged to adapt the established curriculum, introduce variations, invent and experiment, so as to keep the interest level high for themselves as well as for the children. They were given opportunities to express their opinions as educators about the conduct of school affairs.

This extension of autonomy to the teacher was different in scope and depth in the two schools. At Dickens, the administration had to strike a balance between the prerogatives of its established educational design and the belief in the value of freeing the individual, teacher or child, to use his own interests and talents. At Conrad, it was relatively easy to achieve balance; the value system was reinforced by its freedom from system-wide obligations.

The principal at Conrad regarded the curriculum as a basic framework not necessarily to be adhered to rigidly. The teacher of the thirteen-year-olds chose to work on American history because she found the children "too ready to be scornful of things American." The fifth-grade teacher did not wish to study Egypt as preliminary to the study of the Middle Ages, as had previously been done. She regarded Egypt as a death-oriented culture and substituted instead a study of the Hebrews and the Old Testament and established connections between that period and the Middle Ages. Such decisions were sanctioned after discussion with the principal or with the staff in a curriculum meeting. Although curriculum changes occurred from time to time, some had remained unchanged for many years. The work jobs traditionally undertaken by certain age groups, such as the complete running of the school supplies store by the fourth-grade children, was a stable feature of the curriculum.

At Dickens, the principal stimulated and invited teacher discussion and opinion on problems of individual children and school affairs but the teachers did not directly participate in the formulation of basic policy. The administrative staff, while recognizing the authority of the curriculum directives from the Board, were inclined to treat them as guidelines rather than prescriptions. The teachers, accordingly, were encouraged to interpret, select, and adapt them, and those teachers who were aligned with the principal's modern-oriented philosophy were consciously pleased with their freedom.

Quality and Patterns of Interaction Among People

The teachers in the modern schools tried to establish a mutually acceptable working relationship between themselves as responsible adults and their pupils as growing children. They tried to find ways of putting the uses of authority to the service of the learning situation by substituting flexible rules and regulations—adaptable to many different kinds of learning situations—for fixed standards of good behavior. It was important to them that the children regard the restraints and regulations to which they were expected to comply as generally reasonable and necessary. Restrictions were moderate; the emphasis on active learning and cooperative group work made talking and moving about acceptable when connected with work.

The teachers in these schools tended toward informality, personalized communication, and expression of feeling as part of their wish to protect a positive relationship with the children. Acceptance of authority, like other essential socialization processes, was looked upon as a gradual process, unlikely to take a smooth, unbroken course toward internalized acceptance of control on a rational, functional basis.

Within this framework, protest and infraction of rules were expected and were always dealt with correctively—even peremptorily—but never punitively. Being sent out of the room was regarded as a relatively severe penalty at both schools, resorted to only after the teacher had attempted to solve the difficulty in other ways. It was also recognized and accepted that this style of authority, in general, would create a somewhat churned-up atmosphere, in which teachers and children were permitted to express relatively strong emotion.

At Conrad, formal authority was at a minimum. Authority was mediated through the relationship of the teacher with the individual members of small classes, often known to her throughout their attendance at the school. The children called teachers by their first names, a symbol of the strong intent to minimize any formalities that might form barriers to close teacher-child interaction.

There were few supernumerary rules for the teacher to monitor; the needs of individual situations governed the limits to be established and the teachers included themselves in the regulations when these were applicable to adults. The whole matter of authority was subordinate to the teachers' intense feeling about getting on with the work, which they considered it natural for the children to share. The fourth-grade teacher did not "approve of any kind of horseplay or tussling around—it takes too long to get reoriented to learning." The fifth-grade teacher tried for an "atmosphere in which it is clearly known that work is the primary purpose of being here." Penalties for infractions were specific but there were no coded punishments such as loss of free time or staying after school. The clear purpose was to get things back into working order again and this was done with a minimum of moralizing.

At Dickens, the panel teachers were similarly oriented but they had, perforce, to observe the more restrictive regulations of the system. They were therefore using externalized methods of control—structured devices, signals, and substitute monitoring by children—while seeking ways to lessen adult-child distance.

Some panel teachers at Dickens were experiencing uncertainty and conflict about how to find a balance between freedom and control that would fit their feelings, situation, and ideals. The fourth-grade teacher thought she had previously been too easy-going and currently maintained discipline by a system of demerits: "I can't stand a fresh kid who talks back." Yet she had a standing invitation from the children to play baseball with them after school. Some, on the other hand, regretted the situational restraints on extending greater freedom. The third-grade teacher who made the children "listen and follow the rules" also worried about the "ones who need more freedom than I can give them."

When pushed to take punitive measures or act in conventionally disciplinary fashion, these teachers felt the need to defend themselves on the basis of circumstance. The principal, as the next authority in line, supported the modern orientation and a child could be sent to her office, not to be scolded or punished, but to get teacher and child out of the deadlock to which events had brought them.

The administrators of the modern schools, like the teachers, were revamping the traditional concept of an authoritative figure.[7] It matched the convictions of these administrators that their authority was respected by the teachers as a result of their contribution to the educative process in the school and their enlightened professional leadership. The Conrad teachers thought their principal had instituted a new era when she had taken over from the founder: "a truly critical look at curriculum," "generally improved organization . . . less spartan, better-mannered style among the children," "a belief that normal academic levels can be reached without stifling creativity," "an enlarged vision of the school's primary orientation—to really look at the child." Appreciation of the Dickens principal was expressed in other terms: "The principal is 80 percent of it" (referring to what sets the character of the school), "she has high standards and we come across," "she doesn't miss a trick . . . but she's not on top of us."

These administrators interpreted their responsibilities to include regular contact with the teachers and children. Thus, as supervisors, they preferred to exercise their influence through individualized work relationships rather than as remote authorities in given positions of superiority. The Conrad head said she enjoyed the chance of substituting for a teacher more than her administrative duties. The Dickens principal enjoyed "the relations with the kids" most. "That part is wonderful . . . relations are so different from when I was a child . . . I looked on teachers and the principal as such august personages!"

By avoiding a censor or inspector stance and cutting through the formalities associated with difference in rank, they consciously attempted a style of supervision that would reduce anxiety and status barriers. New teachers were not visited for the first six weeks at Conrad. At Dickens, new teachers were eased in through a lunchtime conversation and then given the choice of being visited unannounced or by prearrangement. While ready to be a resource as educators, these administrators also encouraged teachers to depend on and learn from each other.

In matters of school management and policy there was room for the teacher's voice to be heard, though at Dickens it was a small voice. Nevertheless, it represented recognition that democratic leadership depends on sustaining genuine communication with those for whom action is taken.

The internal organization at Conrad was close to a pure democracy; the principal, vis-à-vis the teachers, seemed to be "first among equals." Supported by strong group morale, she was a partner in upholding the established lore and values of the school. However, the lines of influence and decision led to her in a way that lent more authority to her leadership than the organizational structure immediately implied. "Don't look at me," the Conrad head said at one staff meeting, when there was a wandering search for an authoritative voice. Yet, it was her word, given in a tone of finality, that closed most of the topics considered, as if she and the others assumed that her stand was crucial for the group. On another occasion, she commented, "Maybe it is harder to battle with me than I want it to be." This principal was part spokesman, part conscience, part enabler for an educational view to which the teachers, as a unified group, were as committed as she.

At Dickens, by comparison, the principal wielded an open, strong, central authority, emphasized as educationally functional and rational. Her stance was the result of several circumstances: she kept close track of the many activities in the school; she maintained her independence of the parents and of her own superiors in the system; finally, she was committed to a given view of education which did not have the unanimous approval of her teaching staff. She was therefore in a position of spearheading an educational view, which she did with energy and determination in putting it over and making it work, enlisting like-minded teachers to give it operational strength and reality. At the same time, the diversity of teaching style she accepted offers some testimony to her investment in stimulation and persuasion as opposed to domination or imposition.

At Conrad, the marked internal cohesiveness of the child peer group was the outcome of two ways of using groups of children in teaching. First, the class as a whole was a working group which, with fullest child participation and teacher guidance, learned by discussion, in a style which encouraged the opening up of issues, the expression of differences, and the pooling of information. For example, the impact of the invention of printing on the people's lives was put to the class as a problem for analysis and a division of labor was planned for gathering needed further information. Second, the frequent use of subgroups, composed according to task-relevant capacities and interests, was another peer group experience which was expected to carry the implicit principle of differentiating worth according to contribution rather than to a generalized superior-inferior status.

It was natural in these classrooms for problems connected with rules of behavior to be brought to open discussion in the same way that matters of work were handled. Thus the formation of social order was content for the children's interaction with each other as members of a group. In their use of the child group in these ways, the teachers were also identifying the element of collective responsibility in a system of values; by depending on the work as the context which transmitted this to the children, they avoided moral abstractions.

These two peer group systems were also part of school life at Dickens, but were less well developed and less consistent from teacher to teacher. While class group discussion was less prominent as an educational technique, it was actively used to explore problems of social interaction. After an inter-class game, the fifth-grade teacher confronted the class with the question: "Why are you such poor losers?" adding, "This is my business and your business—how shall we solve this problem?"

The teachers of the upper grades were invested in making the children participants in the development of a democratic social code. Thus, hearing both sides of an issue and coming to decision by majority vote were principles applied to matters of importance to the children and became part of the peer group experience. Some teachers adopted a political model of democratic organization for the management of intra-class affairs, affording the children a role playing experience and a different form of group interaction.

Some teachers at Dickens found task-oriented activities for small groups valuable, but this pattern was not intrinsic to the curriculum. A number of the teachers did not think they could promote learning through having children work in small groups; in addition, they were reluctant to use— uncritically—new "forms" that they were not ready to integrate into their total educational scheme.

In both schools, codes for group functioning were being formulated together with the children, who were thinking through and talking out elements of fairness and justice in social situations.

View of Individuality

The modern schools' view of learning invited the children to express their interests, ideas, and feelings freely. The value given to independent thinking and to process and pleasure in intellectual endeavor and creative expression illustrate the two schools' philosophy of fostering individuality as a means of self-realization. The acceptance of variation in style of work created a climate in which there was forbearance, at the least, and more often interest in the individual's idiosyncratic response.

At Conrad, the teachers were interested in helping each child identify with the teacher's learning goals for him. In their view, this was at least as important as self-expression. At Dickens, there were more gradations in the teachers' attitudes—from a desire to be less directive to the opposite attitude that the teacher's job is to help children along socially prescribed lines and to establish procedures with which children learn to comply.

When asked to put into words their main objective apart from mastery of knowledge, the Conrad teachers spoke primarily of strengthening the individual by highlighting self-awareness, supporting feelings of adequacy, and stimulating independent thinking. While self-expression and self-drive were important in their image of sound individuality, their interest in socialization was expressed by an emphasis on internalized responsibility for performance and behavior. At Dickens, the thought was more of strengthening the individual through reducing strain in the emotional life. The Dickens teachers were also more concerned about social adaptability—for the younger children the functional aspects of having to cooperate and get along with others, and for the older ones the abstraction and discussion of moral principles and codes.

It is inevitable of course that a differentiated perception of children should be a concomitant of the attitudes and practices inherent in the modern orientation. Relations between adults and children were geared toward maximum personal communication; expanding the activities and varying the teaching methods brought a wider range of a child's characteristics into the open. At Conrad, additional factors, such as the small size of the school and the classes, sharpened the individual's identity. The system of having special teachers for special subjects made each child familiar to several teachers in different contexts.

Characteristically, in the interviews, the descriptions of children by the Conrad teachers were very specific and primarily described qualities of personality, behavioral style, and the idiosyncrasies of the child's responses to school. These teachers spoke from full images of the children as they functioned in school and omitted reference to family background.

Positive feelings were expressed most often about children who were imaginative, determined, robust spirits, tolerant of the unexpected, highly motivated and excited about learning. The teachers' negative feelings centered around what they described as "manipulative" or "scheming" behavior and exhibitionist or "smart-aleck" style.

At Dickens, the descriptions of the children were different. The teachers were more likely to characterize a child in terms of his particular problems or needs and to enjoy most the children whose problems they could lessen, "seeing the quiet ones come out and the aggressive ones quiet down." This fitted in with the principal's interest in stimulating more awareness of developmental problems and individual remedial needs. These teachers' perceptions were most differentiated with respect to children who had difficulties; the intra-family situation was noted as relevant to the children's problems. Some of these teachers, also, were more focused on class achievement than individual personality, leading them to describe brightness in terms of IQ levels and negative feelings about those children whose problems interfered with the pace and smoothness of teaching.

A measure of child development theory had always been a major influence on the development of curriculum at Conrad. These concepts had originated during the general renaissance of "individuality" in the twenties, when the school was founded, and had been influenced by the educational philosophy of John Dewey and the insight of the founder and her associates. They constituted the rationale for much of the educational program. The head explained that the teacher "sets up standards of behavior and achievement for a given class . . . on a knowledge of what to expect in general from a four- or a six-year-old, and on the teacher's sensitivity to each individual's needs."

The incorporation of the developmental approach over many years at Conrad distinguished that school in two ways. First, the Conrad teachers and principal had become emphatically "developmental stage" conscious and repeatedly related their goals and practices to the changing characteristics of successive stages of development. The second-grade teacher based her use of direct techniques of control on the opinion that "children at this stage need to know where you stand." The seventh-grade teacher spoke of the children's "growing competence with tools and ideas and their susceptibility to getting the giggles." These teachers were interested in the progressive sequence of drives, interpersonal relations, and self-perception, as well as in intellectual advances. This was related to their view that learning is part of general developmental processes and the total stream of advancing maturity. Schooling during the preschool years, for example, was considered as contributing to growth and education in continuity with later learning experience rather than as mere preparation for the more regulated life of subsequent school years.

Second, the developmental approach had given rise to new problems and uncertainties at Conrad about such questions as how much expression of aggressive impulses should be tolerated and what the teacher's role was when faced with the child's fantasy life in play activities. When the school decided to enlist professional help in these matters—a step which affected their fundamental beliefs—they turned to a child development expert who involved them in rethinking their own attitudes and practices in terms of psycho-dynamic principles of development. A shift in teacher role was reported: "We used to ignore fantasy because we didn't understand it, but now the attitude is that the teacher should reinforce the reality side while helping the child come to terms with fantasy."

The leadership and a group of teachers at Dickens were in sympathy with the "modern" developmental view advocated by the Board of Education's curriculum guides. At Dickens, contemporary psychological theory entered the school through the special projects provided by the Board, directed primarily to lessening the learning problems of individual children. Remediation was accented more than extending or revising the psychological concepts underlying the educational process. This emphasis filtered through to the teachers who seemed most involved in the children's emotional problems and how to work with them. The first-grade teacher discussed an instance of domination of one child over another as a problem of hidden hostility; the second-grade teacher worked with slow children on projects involving construction but found painting more "therapeutic" for those who were emotionally disturbed.

The concept of learning as a continuous process of growth from the earliest years had not become part of the psychological orientation at Dickens. Early schooling was thought of more as a weaning from one phase of life into another quite different phase. The kindergarten teacher stressed the value of "social adjustment"; the first-grade teacher talked about the first-graders "coming to you as a blank page."

Concern for individuality colored the life of teachers as well as children in the modern schools. This was strongest at Conrad, where it was not only allowed but hoped that in each teacher's use of the given design there would be a quality of uniqueness both as to style and content. This was a strong element in the teacher's allegiance to the school.

Despite the lesser flexibility of operations, a similar view pertained at Dickens, but it was less explicit, not yet to be taken for granted. One of the principal's conscious goals was to make the teachers' work known to each other and she noted with pleasure the occasions when teachers spontaneously praised each other's work.

Relation of the School to Its Social and Professional Milieu

The two modern schools had incorporated the technique of taking trips into the surrounding neighborhood as an integral part of the social studies curriculum for the earlier grades. Though there were certain common assumptions about the value of giving the children direct contact with how things are done in the world around them, the use of trips had different positions in the total educational schema in the two schools.

At Conrad, trips in the primary grades were part of a systematic method of studying how a community, their own, organizes and carries through its functions. Study of the larger city in contrast to the immediate neighborhood was central in the curriculum for the second grade. Their trips were planned to help them clarify concepts of geography, to become aware of the centralization of functions such as traffic control, and to see how concentration of population is met by high-rise buildings and by bridges and roads carrying commuters in and out of the city.

The trips fitted into a sequence of discussion, experience, and re-expression in constructive and dramatic play. With building blocks and school-made carpentry products the children, for example, created a symbolic replica of the city, and in dramatic play they played about stores, offices, hospitals, schools, and playgrounds. This program, known as the "core" program, had been established in the early years of the school as an innovation. It had long since become established as part of the philosophy that the foundation for larger order concepts are best built on concrete, personal experience. Learning how surrounding communities function was considered a tool for later studies of more remote and unfamiliar communities. In the upper grades, trips were used to illustrate and understand concepts of continuity between past and present or the relation between the artifacts of a culture and its work-play morality. In the course of their study of medieval history, for example, the fifth grade visited a private library with a special collection of medieval manuscripts. The sixth grade, studying the Age of Exploration, went to a large city park to work on ideas on mapping.

At Dickens, in the primary grades, many teachers were using the working environment as a similar educational resource, emphasizing the social functions of communication, buying and selling and transportation. The second-grade teacher, working on a unit on transportation, took her class to the railroad station, the docks, and an ocean liner. The third grade visited a fish market and a butcher's shop in connection with a unit on food. These trips provided real-life illustrations for the established sequence of units in the social studies curriculum. They were valued for intensifying motivation and stimulating more probing inquiry but they were not the bricks for a conceptual structure of community functioning.

The schools differed in their points of view and practices about the place that current events, particularly current social-political issues, should have in the program for the older children. Here it was Dickens, not Conrad, which represented what one would expect to be the most modern view, namely, that it is important to involve children—through discussion or participation and in ways appropriate to their youth—in the events and issues on the national and world scene. In one sixth grade at Dickens, the teacher read aloud from a speech by the President in which he mentioned the need for Negro representation in the press. A lively discussion followed in which both children and teacher expressed their opinions. A fifth-grade class took part in UNICEF activities and wrote and performed a play dealing with the role of the United Nations. Both fifth- and sixth-graders wrote and presented plays dealing with space travel from the viewpoint of the scientists' contributions and responsibilities to humanity.

At Conrad, current events were dealt with *ad hoc* according to relevance, and the staff had decided against any active use of contemporary social issues as a regular part of the program. By their rationale, it was undesirable to involve children in the complex social problems of the "adult" world or to confront them with the seemingly inevitable "insolubles" on the contemporary scene with which their experience would permit only vicarious relation. The head deprecated exposing children to the "messes" created by adults. Her goal was to have them "learn to use their minds and imaginations in realms they can cope with" and to avoid experiences likely to lead to a fatalistic attitude that "it is all too complicated and difficult." The school put more educational value on history for understanding how man has faced and solved analogous opportunities and dilemmas in the past.

The schools differed, too, in their receptivity to new kinds of instructional material, Dickens taking the lead over Conrad. At Dickens, an opaque projector and strip films were lent from teacher to teacher. Four television sets had been installed at different locations in the school and were used in connection with science and the new math program. Educational television programs from a local university could be piped in through an intercom system. At Conrad, the staff opposed the use of audio-visual aids on the grounds that they encouraged passivity, thereby diminishing the advantages of first-hand experience and independent discovery.[8]

There was another environmental milieu—the education profession— toward which Conrad and Dickens had basically different orientations. And here, too, it was at Dickens, not Conrad, that the essence of the modern view—experimental venture and receptivity to change—was being expressed most actively. Dickens had an openness to new ideas; it was in a state of becoming. Putting a liberal interpretation on the trend to "modern" ideas implicit in the official curriculum guides, the principal and the group of teachers who identified with her purposes were incorporating new activities, materials, and techniques with self-conscious enthusiasm about their part in changing the old established practices. Their response to the "new" ways in education, furthermore, was not limited to what filtered through in the materials from their own school system. They were receptive to ideas to be found in educational journals, interested in innovations in the teacher-training institutions of their community, and interested in visiting classrooms of teachers in other schools.

What they took on to try out was not random; it had to fit the principle of enlisting more active participation of children in learning and of extending the range of school activities. The readiness to try new ways did not apply to the whole staff; some teachers stood apart from these trends.

The Conrad school presents a more complicated picture with respect to new developments in educational technique. Many of its early premises were still radical to the run-of-the-mill school. Many of its early practices were adopted as "new" thirty years later by schools like Dickens. Through years of experimenting, Conrad had established a program which satisfied its vision of good education and had gradually gained a place in the vanguard of education. Compared to Dickens, only relatively minor changes in basic educational design had been recently made or were being contemplated. Reading was being taught at an earlier age and the principal was considering further examination of "new math." The addition of a psychological consultant to the staff had been the only important recent change. Conrad was not altogether unaware of trends in education but did not see them as relevant to its own, established educational design and the innovations long since incorporated within it.

The staff at Conrad saw themselves as being part of a special stream in the educational profession, unique as schools go, focused more on themselves as a self-evaluating audience than on the profession, the parents, or the outside world. Their identity had a cultural as well as an educational stance. Thus their exclusion of movies or TV experience from consideration in school was part of their resistance to the influence of mass culture and to the vulgarization which it represented to them.

THE TRADITIONAL SCHOOLS

Education for Competence

In the traditional schools, concern for the child's learning was focused on his becoming informed and skilled. Staff energy was devoted primarily toward making more efficient the transmission of a body of knowledge to the child and toward guiding his mastery of fundamental skills in the word and number symbol systems. This focus was given priority in the primary and middle years, since without these foundations children were expected to flounder in their later school years. To accomplish these goals, greatest confidence was placed in practice, drill, memorization, frequent tests, and clear-cut question-answer exchange between teacher and children. Adjustments to differences among children were made according to an expected rate of mastery, not by varying or adapting teaching methods.

Intellectual competence was thus equated with control, mastery and skill of specific operations, factual knowledge, and techniques such as written or oral reporting and test taking. The teacher was the central figure—directing, organizing, and instructing to the level of detail; the children's position was that of carrying out the specific learning tasks she established for them. In teaching social studies, the teacher acted as the middleman between the children and authoritative sources, such as textbooks and encyclopedia, where interpretations could be found and learned as a next order of mastery. The rightness or wrongness of answers as the end product of the activity was of the greatest importance. This was expressed by the way the teachers, after putting a question to the class, passed over wrong or half-relevant replies, until they had elicited a reply that fitted the form and level of correctness as preconceived by them.

At Browning, this approach to intellectual competence was observable in relatively pure form. Factual exactness was expected and praised almost without exception; ambiguity was not tolerated and uncertainties were dealt with by the fiat of established definition rather than by searching for alternative meaning and opinions. In a fifth-grade class, the teacher stressed knowing the exact dates and travel times of the two Mayflower voyages, the exact dates of the Civil War. "What do you mean 'about'?" she said to a child. "Don't guess. Don't speak out if you don't know. Where are the facts?" In a sixth-grade class the teacher offered word definitions of "colonialism" and "imperialism" but did not discuss their meanings in terms of ideas. The principal's concept of children as "lacking the power to reason" and the priority he gave to training for obedience and character provided a rationale that was consistent with the school's educational design. Moves to enrich the curriculum, as advocated by the Board, had a small place in the principal's mind, since they were at variance with his ideas about intellectual development, which assumed a temporal sequence between mastery of fundamental skills and conceptual thinking.

Adams had responded to the push toward enrichment from sources outside the school by increasing the variety of legitimate curriculum activities. It also considered itself to have "modernized" teaching by making enthusiastic use of technological, especially visual, devices, such as film projectors and television programs, and by giving the children more opportunities to share responsibility with adults, in the care and use, for example, of the new kinds of equipment that had become part of the school program. These changes were supplementary to the established methods of educating for intellectual competence, in which the emphasis on achievement was unchanged and good test scores taken as evidence of good learning. In stating their goals, principals and teachers gave priority to bringing the children up to grade level in reading and to keeping the school's general academic achievement level high in comparison to other schools.

To the extent, however, that these supplemental activities exposed the children to greater mobility and interchange, the possibility that some of them might be stimulated to more exploration and self-initiated learning was increased. The teachers at Adams were more aware of the existence of "new" ideas than those at Browning; at the same time, they rejected them as being nothing more than new labels for old ideas.

Both schools emphasized socialization. Adams leaned toward adeptness in social situations and Browning toward conformity to external standards. There was more overt "moral" teaching in these than in the modern schools which interacted, interestingly, with the style of intellectual engagement. When the study content moved away from the clearly factual, there was a fairly rapid shift to moral implications. The process of inference readily took the path of moralistic precept rather than more differentiated or more divergent thinking per se. This represented a sort of reductionistic trend, since the moral was usually a simplified code, whereas the pursuit of the idea would be more likely to have led to more complex considerations.

At Adams, the variety that had been introduced into the curriculum enabled the children to become acquainted with the materials and modes of the creative arts—music and painting among them. These activities were considered supplementary to "real" learning, appreciated by the staff for their colorful embellishment of school life. They were valued for finish, elegance, and their approximation to a hypothesized adult product, thus favoring virtuosity over originality. These activities did not move the teachers to change their assumption that reading and language arts were the most important curriculum areas. This relative indifference to creative process as an aspect of individual growth was evident in the use of prefabricated scenery for a play and in the random mixture of commercial products with child-made materials in a Science Fair.

The use of dramatization at Adams as a medium was consistent with this approach. A sixth grade presented a play in assembly, taken from a book of plays, in which children learn from a dream that they, the "rich" children, should be careful with their toys so they can give them to the "poor" children. The interest was in moralizing, the experience primarily reiterative and imitative. It tested competence in memorization, role-taking, and projection of personal presence, and praise was given for these, yielding commensurate gratification.

There were token attempts, by individual teachers at Adams, to follow the directives of the Curriculum Guides, and to work with a variety of approaches and media in social studies, expressed either by collecting illustrative objects or by using relevant teaching films. Analyzing or integrating content, using creative activities or original dramatization as a way of synthesizing experience and learning, were neither accepted nor rejected; they were not on the horizon. Social studies was treated as a distinct subject matter area, to be mastered through the accustomed strategies of reading, recitation, and preparing of reports.

At Browning, the trend to introduce variety in the school curriculum had not taken hold. There was a marked paucity of activities in any of the arts. The curriculum, the program schedule, the absence of any creative products in the halls and classrooms, testified to the almost complete reliance on the verbal as the proper and effective mode of learning and on verbal interchange as encompassing all the relevant dimensions of school experience. There was some indication of a conscious rejection of expressive experience as proper to the functions of a school. Craft skills in which accuracy and precision are the index of excellence were practiced and displayed in the school.

Dramatization had much the same purpose and meaning here as at Adams, with less investment in the finish of a performance, more obvious teacher assistance, and more formalized schema for presentation.

It can be assumed that many of the children in the traditional schools, perhaps all to some degree, found some personal pleasure in their learning activities—in perfecting skills, in gaining knowledge, in feeling increasingly competent. These schools did not count on the child's intrinsic gratification in learning as a motivating force for his investment in school tasks. Instead, they expected the child to accept the demanding aspects of school life—control, concentration, compliance—as a life task, an essential investment for future gains. They established two stimulants to motivation: first, clearly coded ways of recognizing levels of accomplishment and excellence, and second, competitive evaluation among peers. For the children, successful achievement, as measured by grades, also had secondary rewards: certain school functions were attainable only if a child's grade in conduct and achievement were high enough. This accented competitive strivings among the children and directly influenced specific practices for evaluating children's work and, more indirectly, the general tenor of school life.

Between the two schools, Browning was the clearer example of an atmosphere generated by adults who had an earnest working attitude to teaching and expected an equally earnest and conscientious performance from children. The quiet orderliness of the school, the absence of any emphasis on spontaneity or naturalness in the children's products and dramatic presentations, the emphasis on moral rather than intellectual-expressive meanings, were consistent with this view.

Since the teaching techniques which might match the impulses to learn or adapt to the child's own intellectual or expressive efforts had not been adopted at Adams, there was relatively little opportunity for the child to become self-involved in learning. The system of external rewards was therefore well-suited to the educational climate, in which achievement was the goal. This school did not have quite the sober, serious, all-is-work-and-no-play tone that characterized Browning. There were more opportunities for children to do things they enjoyed, especially in the responsibility they were given to manage the teaching aid equipment. In general, the climate was more relaxed, less demanding of constant control, than at Browning.

In the traditional schools, the value placed on achievement and conformity as goals for the children was reflected in the teachers' assessment of their own competence and constituted the basic motivating force for their work. Professional pride was most frequently vested in getting high achievement measures (taken as evidence of successful learning) and in keeping firm control in the classroom (considered a central component of successful teaching).

At Adams, the principal thought that personality attributes rather than motivation were the primary qualifications for teaching. At this school, there was a wide range of differences in what motivated the teachers professionally, with two predominant themes: willingness to work hard for bright children and conscientious pride in keeping all children up to standard grade-level achievement. For some teachers the opportunity to assume somewhat public roles in extra-classroom activities and to enjoy the accompanying prestige provided motivation. Prestige was important in this school. The school itself had a prestigious reputation in the community, which gave the individual teacher a sense of having an elevated professional position. Within the school there was room to compete for special opportunities, such as assignment to the "good" groups (where there were student teachers), membership on a faculty committee, responsibility for the newspaper, or doing some teaching in an in-service class, all of which contributed to status. The extent to which classrooms in this school were observed to be in the hands of substitutes indicates that the teachers enjoyed activities which took them outside the classroom.

At Browning, approval-disapproval appeared to be the accepted form of exchange from principal to teacher. Praise offered the teachers at a staff meeting, worded in the same symbols used for evaluating children's performance, might have contributed a greater sense of accomplishment to the group as a whole. The first paragraph of notes distributed at a staff meeting read: "Your fine teaching is due in no small part to your excellent preparation. Plan Books today were especially praiseworthy. Everyone gets a star!"

The principals of these two traditional schools differed markedly as people, as educators, and as administrators, though they both had the talents required for keeping a school running smoothly and enjoyed their success in this function. At Adams, the principal approved of teachers who could hold the children by a "personal magnetism" and keep up with the sophisticated urban culture of the parent body. At Browning, the principal valued the competence of his teachers in keeping good control under all circumstances. The teachers echoed the principal's stress on good deportment, manners, self-control, and cleanliness as goals held up to the children. Translated, for adults, as decorum and compliance, they became a paradigm of behavior for everybody in the school.

When the teachers at Adams referred to their school as a relaxed school, they had in mind the kind of freedom they enjoyed in running their classrooms, in the sense that supervision was casual and that there was no pressure to make commitments to new values or change methods in education. They were also free from the responsibility of having a voice in shaping any important school practices. Their position was one of having new practices—recommended from the Board—transmitted to them, not of being asked to analyze or evaluate them. There was no indication that this autonomy for the teachers—by default, in a sense—was being utilized as a condition for independent or creative teaching.

Quality and Patterns of Interaction Among People

It was accepted as part of the teacher's positive contribution to school life in these schools that she establish and maintain a suitable behavioral code and persuade the children to accept and live by it. To be suitable, there had to be rules and regulations that would protect the quiet, orderliness, and decorum of the classroom, since concentration and attention were of paramount importance in the system of predominantly teacher-directed learning. The teachers felt they had to restrict talking and moving about among the children for the sake of keeping the lessons going smoothly. "I like a quiet classroom," the sixth-grade Adams teacher said, in contrast to what "it sounds like at _____," naming an experimental school with which he was acquainted. The first-grade teacher worked for an atmosphere of "quiet calm" by emphasizing "neatness" and allowing absolutely "no borrowing or lending things from each other."

At Adams, the children's acceptance of these rules was considered to have broader significance: it was part of learning in general how to apply oneself to a task and giving up the vagaries of distracting impulses for the sake of it; it had a socializing value as an induction into a clear, unambiguous right-wrong morality. In the teachers' words: "Kids have to be taught a right and a wrong." "No matter how intelligent a child may be, he wouldn't learn a thing unless he had discipline."

The overt methods of persuasion leaned more to punishing infractions than to enlisting the children's participation on ethical or rational grounds. One teacher's view was: "In this world, if you do wrong, you get punished." Another jokingly said: "I wish I could use a hickory stick." In general, the teachers appeared to have little conflict, if any, in these disciplinary functions. For some, disciplinary skill ranked high as a criterion of competence. As one teacher said to another: "I am not an easy disciplinarian and they know it . . . when I say *do*, I mean *do*."

The atmosphere of calm that characterized classrooms in these schools was due in part to acceptance of fixed boundaries in the presence of an authority figure. In one classroom, even when the teacher was out of the room, the children sat straight as ramrods, knowing that the monitor would report those who violated the teacher's parting command to "sit tall." The controlled atmosphere was related in part to the fact that traditional methods of teaching did not arouse as much "stir" as, say, group discussion would and therefore did not call for so much overt control or reminders of the rules of the game. While psychological distance between teacher and children was one of the accepted elements of the teacher's authority, there were some teachers at Adams who made personal appeals to get the attention and affection of the children.

At Browning, a dignified distinction between adult and child dominated the relations between teacher and child, excluding intimacy on any basis. The teachers presented their professional, not their personal, selves to the children. More than at Adams, compliance and obedience to the adult were extolled as virtues in childhood, essential if proper use were to be made of the opportunity to learn. Qualifications for the Honor League included: "Trustworthy—he must obey in school. Courteous—he must be polite to parents, teachers, and classmates." The following appeared in a piece by the principal in the parents' paper: "There is, indeed, a strong case to be made, both logically and psychologically, for the inculcation of habits of implicit obedience. . . . Prompt, unquestioning obedience saves time, profitless talk and subsequent scolding or punishment. . . ."

Both principals of the traditional schools were identified with their administrative roles, especially with the efficient management of their schools. "I love to make things click," the Adams principal said, "to see things run smoothly . . . I probably should have been an engineer." At Browning, the principal was the final authority on all the practical aspects of running the school. He personally arranged all the details for the research project; the school clerk would not allow a chair to be moved from the school office without his permission. These principals had relatively little contact with activities in the classrooms. They accepted the educational authority of the Board and saw their own position as a point of transmission between the Board and the teachers; at Adams, this function was relegated to the assistant principal, with whom the principal said she had "real differences in philosophy," adding "but as long as I am principal my views are going to be the ones to prevail." At Browning, the principal issued printed memos, drawing on Board materials, to the teachers at staff meetings. Thus it was through the service they rendered as efficient administrators, rather than as educational leaders, that they were acting as functional authorities.

At Adams, the principal carried a complicated role in trying to adjust simultaneously to the parents' pressures to have the school approximate private school conditions (with which she sympathized) and to the stipulations of the Board and the limits it set on deviating from established practice and standards. Though the structure permitted teacher participation in curriculum matters, it was only rarely activated either by principal or teachers.

The absence of supervision and the exemption it gave the teachers from being responsible for thinking about the affairs of the school were regarded by most of them as an advantage. A few were discontented with the lack of professional stimulation and guidance and others suspected a system of covert manipulation of privileges that bypassed regular channels. The principal held vaguely formulated ambitions to inspire the teachers and to enlist them in more planning and discussion of school affairs. However, the time needed for administrative matters and what she regarded as the general ennui of the teachers were two obstacles to this ambition. The teachers did not see the principal as salient in guiding the school or influencing their styles of teaching.

At Browning, several factors contributed to the distance between principal and teachers. As a new principal, he was an outsider; as a person, he showed a formal respect for the teachers, which was matched by their attitude of deference toward him. When the principal entered a class-room, the teacher rose and moved toward him, his entrance having prior claim over her engagement with the children.

His authority in practical matters was extensive and unquestioned. The flow of decisions and directives was one way—from principal to staff. The teachers fell in with his emphasis on good behavior and formal manners, either because they agreed with it or considered it their role to respond to his authority. What the principal established as good behavior in his talk to the children in the assembly was reinforced in teachers' remarks and admonitions heard in the hallways: "How many boys will wear ties every day to school?" "Take your hat off in the hall. You know Mr. [Principal] wants the children to remember to take their hats off in the building."

In general, the teachers accepted the authority of the principal's office and did not expect to be part of the decision-making in the school. It was therefore possible for the principal to establish more fixed rules and feel less concerned about leaving room for them to be adapted to circum-stance.

At Browning, the class as a whole was the learning-teaching unit, except for certain skill subjects where the children were grouped according to achievement level. The best readers always occupied the front rows in order to avoid reshuffling for reading periods.

At Adams, the use of committees was valued as a good way of covering subject matter content. The prescribed directives given the children on how to work in committees tended to ritualize the experience and reduced the opportunity for the children to work through, autonomously, the prob-lems inherent in functioning as a group. In one room a poster was exhib-ited for general reading: "A good committee works quietly, is organized and neat, works together, does careful research."

The teachers were interested in transmitting understanding of demo-cratic values and forms. They did not perceive small group work as a means of giving children direct experience in essential democratic proc-esses. The experiences they provided were predominantly vicarious and procedural, for example, studying those commemorated in the Hall of Fame as model leaders who were interested in public service, not self-aggrandizement. By participating in Student Council affairs, children be-came acquainted with election and parliamentary procedures. In part, these activities took the form of play-acting adult forms. Also, within the formal correctness of procedure, when the children acted as a tribunal for other children's transgressions, the subtler aspects of justice were substan-tially lost in the re-enactment by the children of the relatively arbitrary, status-invested authority role carried by the adults in their school. At one meeting of the Student Council, the children had constructively accomplished a change in a ruling about a punchball court by sending a delegation to wait upon the proper authority. But at the same meeting, they entered with great zest into disciplining the children who had chased balls into private property in violation of the rule; the child chairman, using a pompous style, issued frequent sarcastic reproofs about noisiness.

View of Individuality[9]

The curricular design, choice of teaching techniques, and style of interpersonal relationships in the traditional schools expressed in practice the view of the school's responsibility to the individual child. The goal was to bring the child to highest possible levels of achievement according to established norms and to lead him to adapt to the social requirements of accepted standards of behavior. By this concept, control, industry, and compliance were nuclear as values.

With few exceptions, the teachers at Adams thought of themselves as having a directing role in the children's learning and development. In their image of good teaching, the teacher was the most active force, setting the goals, patterning the course of learning, and managing classroom life to ensure the least deviation from pre-established lines of intellectual and social development. This perspective was corroborated in the teachers' statements on what they considered the main objective of school apart from mastery of information and skills. They stressed the passive aspects of adapting to school—in learning to listen and getting along with others. The stress on adaptation as a value appeared, for example, in the public plaudits in the final assembly: the children applauded were those who had been voted the "best citizens." Gains along the lines of developing individuality were mentioned by only a single teacher.

The question of how much each child is known as an individual to the people in his school is largely determined by the basic orientation of the school as expressed in its educational design and administrative practice. In the traditional schools, the reliance on whole class teaching, the relatively few modes and spheres of learning, the identity of the administrators with executive functions which lessened their contacts with the children in their classrooms, the vestment of authority in the status of the teacher as such, were among the factors which led to more formalized and less individualized perceptions of the children.

At Adams, the teachers' interview descriptions of the children were characterized according to a few standard referents—brightness, IQ position, family background, and easy- or hard-to-teach qualities. When problems were referred to, the problem category was the term of communication; how a particular child might stand in relation to his problem remained vague. The kind of children most enjoyed by the teachers were described variously as bright, serene, adaptable, and reasonable. "I would turn myself out for a bright child," the third-grade teacher said.

Family background had an important place in the teachers' identification of the children. The teachers tended to connect children's problems with intra-family discord which, in turn, they associated with unsteadiness in the life patterns of well-to-do families.

Knowledge of child development and its importance were explicit tenets of the guides developed by the Board of Education and in practice involved a developmental view and differentiated concern for each child. The influence of these ideas varied greatly. The traditional schools in the study were among those very little influenced by this mode of thinking about childhood and education. Differences among children in school were recognized primarily in terms of achievement and conformity to behavioral norms. Factors such as reading achievement or IQ level were the basis on which class composition was decided.

Difficult behavior was more often analyzed in terms of the challenge it presented to the teacher's management of the class than with reference to possible causes or origins in the child's immediate life situation or against the background of shifting drives of childhood in successive stages of development. The second-grade teacher at Adams described the problem children as "constantly demanding attention" and the third-grade teacher said she excused obstreperousness in bright children: "If they're bright, they're entitled to it."

It was consistent with this view that what was to be learned in kindergarten and first grade was regarded as preparatory, a period when the young child's primitive condition could be sufficiently altered to admit him to the sphere of "real" school. The first-graders, at Adams, were described as coming "absolutely green" and leaving sufficiently socialized (that is, able to take their clothes on and off, having developed good toilet habits) that they were "human beings."

Relation of the School to Its Social and Professional Milieu

To the teachers in the traditional schools, the immediate neighborhood and the extended environment of the city did not count as a resource for their educational program. The children were taken on trips more in the spirit of a pleasant excursion, requiring no specific preparation and without the expectation that it would reverberate in subsequent classroom work. The places chosen for visits reflected this orientation. The tendency was to take the children where there were pleasant things to see, to the "display" aspects of the environment rather than to the ongoing, daily activities of a neighborhood, since the trips were not part of a study of how a community manages its working affairs.

At Adams, there was more venturing outside the school, especially in the early grades, than at Browning. Several classes went to look at a florist's shop through the window. One teacher arranged a trip to see a statue of a famous writer of children's stories. The older children generally went to museums or libraries. A visit to the post office by several classes was an unusual instance of giving the children a chance to make contact with an essential part of the working environment.

At Browning, there was minimum evidence that the environment was used. The kindergarten children were taken on a walk to see the flowers in the gardens. The discussion that followed concentrated on identifying the flowers by name. In a parents' meeting, the principal briefly mentioned trips as part of the school's enrichment program, but went on to say that the three R's were the main emphasis in the curriculum.

The choice of social studies content for the sixth grades in these two schools—Latin America in one case, the new nations of Africa in the other—reflected the trend in the Board's curriculum guides to give central attention to places and countries where important changes were taking place. The approach to these studies was primarily to advance the children's knowledge of governmental and territorial changes; there was no attempt to penetrate the causes, problems, and controversies intrinsic to these social transformations. A fifth-grade teacher at Browning was observed conducting a lesson on distances and flying times, using a globe to measure the distance between Omsk and Anchorage. The absence of involvement in serious or pressing issues was observed in a fifth-grade assembly production at Adams. The title "A Trip Around the World" suggested a way of dealing with current events material. The play, however, took the form of presenting songs and dances of various nations, ending with a skit which caricatured the current fashion in women's clothes. Other contemporary events and issues, such as would be found in the daily newspaper, did not have an assigned place in the program, although current events was an assigned subject in the curriculum directives.

At Adams, technological innovations in communications had been enthusiastically accepted and were used in every possible way as supplementary teaching aids. The school was abundantly supplied with slide projectors, opaque projectors, tape recorders, and TV sets; the sixth grade kept the city radio broadcast scheduled and piped from the main office into classes that requested them; the public address system was used for song programs as well as announcements and morning talks, labeled "inspirational" by the principal. How these technological aids might affect the role of the teachers or provide new learning experiences for the children or be used for educational planning, in general, did not seem to interest the principal. Her interest appeared to be in abundance of supply: when asked what additional services or materials she would like for her school, her response was "more visual aids."

The forms used in these new modes of communication had an influence on the children, who sometimes mimicked particular program formats. The re-enactment of modes exploited by media such as television produced the effect of making the school world come close to being a replica of that modality in the world outside.

At Browning, there was very little use of these newly devised teaching aids. A fifth-grade teacher encouraged the children to listen to the radio and watch television at home for information relevant to their study of American history. Only in science did the teachers depend on television to supplement their own teaching in school.

The educational innovations associated with the modern orientation—active autonomous learning, study of the environment, experience in the expressive media, relaxation of external controls—were neither interesting nor appropriate to the two traditional schools whose goals lay in different directions. At Adams, however, there was an active seeking for ways to be up to date in its own terms, to fit a self-image of superiority to be maintained, that was not true at Browning. Changes introduced at Adams originated in the wish to keep up with the Board on the one hand and to respond to the parents' image of what schooling should be for children.

In some ways the children were being educated to become appreciative consumers more than active originators. High-quality entertainment was provided for the assemblies, often through parent initiative. At other times, when the children were the performers, the program was likely to consist of a few solos or a "star" performer, inadequately supported by a few other children. This featuring of talented individuals was part of the high value placed on performance.

At Browning, in contrast, show and showmanship had no place. The school appeared to function, with little discontent or ferment, in its own time-honored ways, seemingly insulated from new ideas, new trends, new techniques. In the upper grades, social studies periods followed the question-and-answer pattern; conventional products excelling in precision and accuracy appeared in the arts and crafts exhibit; an assembly play consisted of learned speeches without action or plot.

The principal was disinclined to change things as long as good standing on academic subjects was maintained and was wary of spreading too thin in the effort to follow the path of enrichment. The Bureau of Curriculum's point of view was only slightly represented in this school; it did not seem to have aroused any substantial interest or activity, either because of inertia or because of a deep feeling that the old ways are best and a conviction that the three R's come first. In both the schools, such innovations in actual teaching method as did appear were initiated by individual teachers, not inspired nor substantively supported by the school administrators.

Additional Characteristics of the Schools as Distinct Institutions

In this final section, other characteristics, not necessarily associated with educational orientation, but nevertheless distinct to each school, will be presented. They are the characteristics which involve additional psychological processes through which influence is mediated. They fall into two groups: (1) the teachers and administrators as identification figures, especially the attitudes of the adults to their work and the nature of their professional identity, as these might influence the children's attitudes to their own work roles; and (2) the internal culture of the school, expressed in its cohesiveness, degree of self-containment, morality of success versus search, pleasure-conscience ratio, which taken together could act as an image for the children of how to perceive and what to expect of other life environments.

The separation of these characteristics from those that bear the clear imprint of educational ideology is, to an extent, intellectualistic. Yet, in examining the characteristics which, to a degree, were independent of direct educational matters, we hoped to delineate the ways in which they could be expected to reinforce or counteract the presumed central influence of educational theory and practice.

CONRAD

The teachers and principal in this school were a heterogeneous group of individuals who had arrived, by choice and diverse routes, to a common locus for their work lives. They both enjoyed and created a professional atmosphere in which individuality, nonstandardization, and diversity of life style were respected on a personal level as much as they were valued as part of an educational credo.

Their life patterns represented a wide range of experience. Most of them had lived and studied outside the city in which they were now teaching and they were personally familiar with the subcultural differences of various regions of the country. Educated at liberal arts colleges, they had pursued various professional interests, such as music, archaeology, and Far Eastern art. Before making a clear choice to enter the teaching profession, they had tasted other possibilities. They could integrate their varied interests and experience with their work as teachers because of the school's strong conviction that an extended background contributes greatly to sound teaching.

The teachers, some young, some middle-aged, a few men among them, were very much themselves in their style of teaching. Personalities were reflected in the brisk, crisp style of the teacher who enjoyed intellectual activity and did not indulge in "psychologese," in the tendency of another teacher to interact quite personally with the children and find greatest interest in the creative side of classroom learning, and in the fast-moving, intense involvement of still another teacher who was most keen on expressive productivity.

Thus, teachers who had themselves, in different ways, retained a very personal identity, could be expected implicitly to convey this as a value and, in that sense, reinforce the school's explicit educational strategies to the same end. Similarly, identification with these adults who represented a chosen course within a variety of possible life styles could be expected implicitly, again, to bring home to children the worth of carving one's own path from a variety of alternatives, thus supporting the school's emphasis on autonomous functioning.

There was a striking unity of purpose and organization in this school, a commitment to its basic philosophy. The teachers felt privileged to be able to teach as they believed teaching should be done. The morale was that of a small group of people engaged together in a "good work" and enjoying it.

It can be assumed that the intense involvement of teachers in their work and freely-expressed pleasure would be likely to inspire in children a similar involvement in their own school activities, reinforcing the systematic efforts to deal with learning tasks so that they be intrinsically rewarding.[10] The cohesiveness of this "local culture" also had to do with the fact that the school's traditions had originated in the period which gave rise to the emancipation of women, the rebellion against the standardization of "bourgeois" culture, the veneration for productive work and craftsmanship as contrasted with entrepreneur functions and mass production, and underlying all these, respect for the individual and his autonomy in his life roles. All this was reflected in custom as well as educational design, for example, in the informal dress of the teachers and the work-type clothes worn by the children. Unity and cohesiveness, of course, were easier to sustain in a small school where teachers came together frequently, in the lunchroom, at staff meetings, in committees, and in assemblies.

The teachers did not so much consider this school as better than others; they thought of it as something special and rare. Probably this sense of "specialness" and "differentness" was communicated to the children. Security about the fundamental rightness of its own ways was matched with confidence in its own self-critical, self-evaluating processes.

This degree of self-containment put the school in a defensive position on at least two issues. First, the staff were not entirely at ease with their separation from the public school system. Many had taught children from less privileged populations and were concerned that children in public school were being deprived of good education, as they felt they knew it to be. Yet they could not see themselves working successfully as teachers in the public school system. The second issue concerned the question of how the children would make the necessary adjustments from this special school environment to the standards and expectations in other schools and in the world outside in general. The school relied on the inner strength the children would gain from their educational experience. When, for example, they did make a move to give practice in taking exams in response to parent worries about the children's coping with what lay ahead, the teachers felt that this constituted a violation of principle.

There were strains between the school and the parent body that could be expected to interfere with the school's aim that the educative process be an integrating force in the child's intellectual and emotional development. The school looked with suspicion on some parents' intentness on the training of special skills and talents. Many of the parents were anxious that what they considered to be the school's underweighting of fundamental skill subjects would hinder the children's ability to compete in subsequent school years. For many children this could constitute a conflict or at least considerable divergence in identification with the learning goals held for them by the important figures in their lives.

DICKENS

As a result of the principal's tendency to select as new teachers people of strongly marked character and individual gifts who shared her modern educational ideas, there was, in this large school, among its 49 teachers, a considerable diversity of personal and professional qualities and styles. It was in general a faculty of mixed age, with some concentration of younger teachers, a considerable number of men teachers, and more married than single teachers. Their family backgrounds varied—professional, arts, business, blue collar, were all represented. With few exceptions these teachers had been born and grew up in the city in which they were teaching; relatively few had had any part of their education outside the city.

The teachers who were selected by the principal to be the panel did not fit this general picture; they had many qualities in common with the Conrad teachers. Their interests were varied and, in their formative years, they had explored many possibilities in finding the kind of work that would be suitable and satisfying to them—the theater arts, editorial work, government service. Only one member of this group said she had turned to teaching as the "easier," less demanding career; the others had found teaching a preferred career in which they were willing to invest energetically and which yielded a high level of personal gratification.

Each member of the panel exerted a quite individual presence in the classroom. One was described as commanding, direct, purposefully oriented to intellectual production; another worked energetically to create real learning situations while being very tolerant with the deviant behavior of an overdependent boy; another was described as very intelligent, deeply invested, with few soothing maternal qualities, not from unkindness but because of her preoccupation with keeping things going at a stimulating level. These teachers, and some others like them in the school, could be assumed, just by being the people they were, to be implicitly asserting the values of personal identity, individuality, and exposure to difference. Thus, similarly, though to a lesser degree than at Conrad, the teachers were models of certain fundamental values as well as professionals committed to an educational mode allied to the same values.

It must be remembered, however, that in the school as a whole there was a wide spread of educational convictions and teaching style, which included the views and attitudes represented by vigorous, sophisticated people teaching in the traditional mode. In moving from class to class, particularly in the upper grades, any child may have encountered contrasting teaching modes, classroom atmospheres, and evaluative criteria. While for some children this might have encouraged a degree of adaptive strength, for others it might have had negative effects. The absence of a reliable, consistent learning atmosphere from year to year might have interfered with the development of a sense of mastery and confidence in a steady, knowable, and predictable world. To the extent that this was true, it would detract from the effectiveness of the modern orientation to which the school's leadership was affiliated. This was an inevitable by-product of a situation in which gradual change had, perhaps temporarily, created a school within a school.

The panel teachers (and probably a considerable number of others on the staff) had a lively, positive feeling toward the school, enjoyed its vigorous, stimulating atmosphere, and felt privileged in comparison to their fellow teachers in other public schools. This sense of privilege was partly based on having bright children from educated backgrounds to work with, in a well-run school with good equipment, and the cooperation of parents whose ambitions for the good education of their children were not too divergent from what these teachers wanted to provide. The privilege was felt as an elevation of the job of teaching; the teachers felt gratified with their personal investment in the children as individuals and their participation in liberating trends in education.

The principal was at the nub of the cohesiveness of this group in the faculty. Respected for her administrative skill and her knowledge and values as an educator, she was also the pace setter for whom the teachers expected to work hard in a spirit of "it's worth it." Her role as an authority —inspiring, informing, but also pressuring—was never openly disputed or resented. Some degree of ambivalence might be assumed, however, since, while she embodied the concept of rational functional authority described previously, her forceful personality and strong drive to accomplish her goals were expressed by unpredictable alternation of domineering action and democratic colleague-affiliated behavior.

As at Conrad, the children had before them adult models who worked for purpose and pleasure, who might have been expected to inspire in them similar attitudes to learning. But many of these teachers did not have a great deal of confidence in their own performance. They were trying hard to develop new skills in which they had achieved varying levels of competence. It is an open question how much this kind of teacher uncertainty, acting perhaps as a deterrent to the development of a sense of mastery in the children, might be counteracted by the stimulation to initiative likely to be transmitted to the children by a teacher's open, courageous, experimenting ways. This question applied to the school as a whole. This school was the most receptive to contemporary developments and willing to incorporate educational innovations. To the extent that these were assimilable without loss of coherence, and within the limits of what was manageable by the children and the teachers, the goals of the school's educational orientation were being supported. Whether the advantage of more exposure to variety was outweighed by having teachers who were trying to deal overambitiously with complexity while lacking commensurate experience and techniques remained undetermined.

This school, with its tolerance for diversity of values and methods, its large pupil body and teaching staff, its surge toward new ways, was not, could not be, the unified, self-contained, self-confident "local culture" that Conrad was. Nor did it have the same qualities of uniqueness and separateness. With parents, the school held to a position that was neither appeasing, cajoling, nor rejecting. Realistic plans for involving parents in the school's work tended to shift complaints or protests to participant identification. For the children, their school in clearly recognized ways was very like one of the many schools that the children in the city attended. It was known by a number, the grades were labeled as such, the building was clearly a school building. They were, easily, part of the large community of school children in their city. The hard gains for a new kind of education, which was being sought by their teachers, was not part of a conscious, special school identity for them.

ADAMS

The staff of this school was generally similar to that of the Dickens staff as a whole (though not the Dickens panel group) with respect to the age, sex, marital status, social background, and educational experience of its teachers. The questionnaire data were more partial in this school than in the others.[11] Of the 37 teachers on the faculty, two were men; there were young and middle-aged, single and married women. All had been born in the city in which they were teaching and the majority had had all their education in liberal arts colleges in the same city. In general, these teachers were a more homogeneous group of people than the teachers at Conrad or Dickens, relatively parochial in their interests, having lived within the confines of family and native city. Their choice of teaching seemed to have been made more as a path of least resistance than as an important life decision; they were following a family pattern or had chosen teaching as less demanding than other professions. There was less to give and less to gain from the daily round of teaching children. In their interviews, these teachers seemed less accessible and more self-protective than those at other schools. Even though they spoke fairly freely and expressed pride in their professional experience, personal material was screened out.

Within the strictures of the controlling authority which it was part of their conviction to be, their teaching style in the classrooms varied considerably. Except for the teacher of the youngest children, the exercise of the executive aspects of their role was prominent in all the panel teachers, though it took different forms and had contrasting personal meanings. One of the teachers clearly enjoyed her competence in keeping the class under close surveillance without sacrificing humor and a degree of creativity, and her control had a basically positive quality. Another teacher found ways of establishing herself as a directing presence even when she was physically out of the room. Another exerted an alert watchfulness and was not easily diverted either by a visitor or by a slow child, who would openly be passed by if he could not keep up. One of the teachers made no allowance for spontaneity in any form and controlled the children through the threat of punitive tongue-lashing which she allowed herself even for relatively minor misdemeanors.

Although psychological distance between teachers and children was one of the accepted realities of the teacher's formal authority role, there were some teachers in this school who made personal appeals for the favorable attention and affection of the children. For example, a teacher calling attention to her new eyeglasses said to the class, "Who likes my glasses, raise your hand?" and then, "Who likes me better without glasses?" This kind of invitation to admire surface appearance showed itself as a general characteristic in this school. In the assembly programs, virtuosity, for example, often dazzling, was featured and applauded.

The teachers were important figures in the children's lives, guiding their intellectual competence and inducting them into codes of social behavior.

As such, they exercised considerable potency as models of adult life and exemplars of human values. Their success in establishing a style and façade that matched their social surround exemplified the value of modeling the person on the world around him rather than establishing or asserting individuality. Their emphasis on display, appearance, a "fine show" kind of excellence, expressed an inclination to address themselves to outer rather than inner realms of experience, which was consistent with their ideological position. Those children whose talents brought them to the center of applauded attention may have derived some sense of unique individuality, but there was an implicit disparagement of the children who could not hope to excel in these ways.

The teachers felt privileged to be teaching in this school, most often mentioning the children as an attraction. The latter were bright, alert, and came from sophisticated backgrounds; they came to school well-fed, well-dressed, and well-rested. They were "pleasant to teach." Another attraction of the school was that of being in contact with people of a fairly high social and economic class. Some teachers cited the light supervision, the lack of pressure from the principal, as an advantage; others enjoyed freedom from committee work. The high standards of academic achievement called on the teachers' energies but beyond this there was no inclination to pour one's whole personality into the professional role. The sense of privilege derived from the freedom from pressure, the comfortable setting, from easy-to-teach children, and from the high social status of the parent body rather than from the intrinsic pleasures of being deeply involved in the job of teaching. These values and attitudes of the teachers toward their work lives could have been expected to influence the children toward dutiful rather than committed attitudes to their learning experience; to seek rewards in the secondary rather than the primary sources of gratification. Thus, basic values in the adult community matched educational orientation on questions of motivation and involvement.

The teachers in this school were not divided on educational issues. They held to the long-standing criteria of high academic achievement and good discipline and felt their school to be superior on both counts. Cleavage among the staff, where it existed, followed lines of intra-staff competition, not educational theory or practice.

The strongest unifying force in this school was its sense of audience. It considered itself to be on display, the symbol of how physically attractive and well set up a public school could be. Its most important audience was the parents, in particular a high-status group within the parent body. The school's interpenetration with this outer world was such that it seemed to be partly controlled by it. The principal, not identified with newer trends and lacking any substantial inner direction in educational matters, occupied the difficult position of obeying a double imperative—to please a demanding parent body and to respond conscientiously to what the Board expected of a principal.

Principal and teachers both envied and disapproved of many parents—the broken homes, the too-busy parents, the overindulgence. At the same time, they were eager to impress them. This ambivalent attitude to the parents was probably the most important instance of conflict between personal feelings and convictions on the one hand and the public behavior required on the other. In addition, the "sparking up," the flurry to make things look impressive, did not necessarily fit in with their ideas of the teacher's primary role. The moral views they expressed about treating all children equally were contradicted by their favoring certain children in the classroom; the extra work required for keeping a school in "good show" condition detracted from the advantages of ease and comfort.

As a life environment for the children, there was a morality of success and a marked inconsistency between behavior and feeling. While these qualities could scarcely transmit a sense of a coherent, trustworthy world, there was the possibility that, given the somewhat widened range of learning experience that came in as "enrichment," some children could create a degree of coherence for themselves and achieve their own integration.

BROWNING

The teachers in this school were very different from those in the other schools. They were clearly an earlier generation of schoolteachers. Of the 17 teachers in the school, the youngest was 43 and ten were over 50; all were women, half unmarried. A higher proportion in this school came from families classified as clerical and blue collar. Only two of the 17 had attended a liberal arts college; the others were trained in teacher training institutions. Only one had attended a school outside the city in which they were teaching and more than half had never considered any career other than teaching.

In manner and appearance they recalled a largely bygone image of the schoolteacher—restrained, self-respecting, and plain, quite formal in meeting with strangers. Neither the fashionableness nor the informality of big city life had made an impression. In the classroom, they varied in their ability to live up to their own standards. One teacher could not convey her ideas clearly to the young children she was teaching and grew tense and flustered as a result; another became upset when her insistence that there be no talking or moving about proved ineffective. The other panel teachers, however, were secure, successful by their own standards, quiet and firm in their authority, the children accepting the expectation that there was work to be done and cooperating in the tasks assigned. Beyond this, there were in two of the classrooms two teachers whose genuine interest in what they were teaching communicated to the children.

As people and as teachers, they represented a uniform, uncomplicated way of life—conscientious application to a task, satisfaction with performing well in a restricted sphere, not pretending to be anything other than themselves or engaging in activities that were without value from their perspective. In their view, the activities of the classroom, concentrating almost exclusively on mastery of skills and subject matter, were the boundaries of the life of learning. The almost complete absence of any expansion of the curriculum for the children was matched by the absence of any evidence that the teachers were taking part in professional activities outside the classroom or using the resources of the city for extending their personal horizons.

They required good deportment from the children and bolstered this demand with the teaching of moral lessons, among which compliance to authority and obedience was salient. This was not a hard lesson for them to teach, since they themselves conformed to established order and accepted tasks required of them, whether personally congenial or not. For example, they did better than the teachers at other schools in responding to the questionnaires (which were passed down through the regular lines of school authority) even while they were both anxious and resentful about the presence of the research staff in the school.

They were successful in their work where it mattered most to them: their school ranked high in achievement in the basic skill subjects. In turn, the child who did well in these areas, who conformed to regulations, recognized the teacher as authority, was neat and polite, could also feel successful and enjoy being a source of satisfaction to his teachers. The children who were less competent intellectually or who deviated from the behavioral norms had to accept a disadvantaged position in a stratified society and could not expect to find resources within the school to help them resolve their individual problems. Within these limits, the children were being exposed to conscientious attitudes toward work, to an assumed dichotomy between work—or learning—and the inner self, to adults whose confidence was not disturbed by the conflicts or uncertainties of exploration.

The high degree of self-containment of this school gave it an intellectual isolation, left largely untouched, for example, by the services of specialists from the Board. It was unusually unself-conscious as a public institution with an audience in the outside world, even though its recent history had involved a change of principal, largely in response to parent action. Without apparent embarrassment, it presented an unwelcoming front to visitors generally, symbolized perhaps by the absence of a place to sit, in the office, while waiting for the attention of the clerk (not formidable in her own person) to provide information. The burden of justifying his presence in the school fell upon the visitor.

It was not surprising that the teachers were a close-knit colleague group. They had a built-in homogeneity. An older generation, trained at a time when educational methods in public education were in a state of quiescence, with similar family and social backgrounds, they had long since attained tenure as teachers. Neither their life patterns nor their professional vision propelled them toward search, exposure, or experimentation. They cherished their own group standards and were devoted to maintaining and carrying on a set of practices sanctioned by custom. Though they were inclined to fend off any redefinition of their responsibilities, they were willing to accept minimal compromises with the Board of Education expectations, as these were transmitted to them by their principal. He, as a new appointee, charged with moving the school in the direction of the newer trends, was intent on moving slowly toward any possible change. This he explained as a strategy; however, from the statements of his own convictions and from the formalistic way in which he suggested curriculum change, it was inferred that his own views were substantially in line with those of his teachers.

These teachers were identified with their school. Their allegiance was to a long-established educational philosophy and to the maintenance of a coherent system in these terms.

Impact of the Study

The schools each reacted to the presence of the research project in ways that proved consistent with both their "personalities" as institutions and their educational orientation. The modern schools felt, in general, a professional obligation to cooperate in a study that was investigating issues that they themselves were interested in. At Conrad, the fourth-grade teacher was impressed with the difference in the reactions of the children in the two successive years of the study; she reported a degree of restlessness about the observations and apprehensiveness about the interviews on the part of the children in the second year in contrast to the relaxed attitude and enjoyment of the children in the first year of the study. She herself, in turn, gave the impression, often, of becoming gradually less flexible in the daily adaptation to research demands and increasingly protective of the children in her concern that the project schedule should not interfere in any way with the children's pursuit of their school activities.

At Dickens, the situation in the fourth-grade classroom was without complication. The teacher reported that the children looked forward to the individual sessions and enjoyed them; that the presence of observers had had only a minor effect on her personally and on most of the children. She communicated directly with the research staff about the few individual children who had had special reactions to being observed or to the observers. There was smooth cooperation throughout the study with the teacher, but the complex practical arrangements accumulated tension at the administrative level in the later stages of the project.

The traditional schools accepted the project with minimum enthusiasm but without question when it was clear that it was sponsored by higher authorities in the system. The Adams teachers had no qualms about having the children leave their classrooms for interviews and sent them off with confidence that they would do well in any situation resembling a testing procedure. When they spoke of their own feelings about having observers in the classroom, they reported less strain and self-consciousness than they had expected and a taking-for-granted attitude on the part of the children.

The Browning teacher, by contrast, reported increasing self-consciousness on the part of the children to being observed. Early in the study, this teacher expressed uneasy feelings at being in the presence of observers and discomfort in their presence accumulated so that, in the second year, she joined the principal and other teachers in asking that classroom observations be terminated. At the same time, there was complete willingness to have the children continue to leave their classrooms for individual interviews.

One sees the four schools projected in capsule form in these reactions to the research. Conrad's primary concern was with the children's relative ease or lack of ease and the teachers were intent on protecting the group's learning activities from outside interference. Dickens adapted flexibly to the supplementary activity as long as it could run in the established administrative channels and special needs of individuals could be taken into account. Adams showed a ready acceptance of having children leave their learning activities for "testing" sessions and the teacher's positive attitude toward some adult communication (with the observer) was leaven for her involvement with children. Browning's intolerance of a change in the composition of the "field" of the classroom was accompanied by a willingness to have the children leave their classrooms and make their own adjustment to the situation of the interviews.

Summary Comment

The schools in the study have been described along a series of dimensions which express orientation toward a modern or traditional philosophy of education. Two of the schools were basically modern, two basically traditional. The modern orientation was common to both Conrad and Dickens and, except for some beliefs and practices, Conrad was more clear and consistent in its modern ways, closer to a theoretical model of the modern school, than Dickens. The traditional orientation, while common to both Adams and Browning, differed in kind in the two schools. Browning seemed, on the whole, untouched in its traditionalism; Adams presented a more complicated picture associated with its sensitivity to its social setting. The relative order assigned to the schools on the modern-traditional continuum at the time they were selected for study was corroborated.

Moreover, the analysis has clearly shown that the schools differed not only in their practices but in the nature of their basic goals and ideals in educating children. In each school the modern or traditional orientation toward education was reflected both in the attitudes of its teachers and administrators toward the work of educating children and in the dominant ethos of the school as a small world in relation to a larger one. The interaction among these forces has been presented.

The climate of each of these four schools was an outcome of what a system of ideas had made of given conditions. For example, it was not the case, as might be assumed, that size was a determining factor of how personal or impersonal, how individualized or mass-organized a school would be. In fact, the two small schools—Conrad and Browning—were the respective extremes of the modern and traditional position. While it may be true that the large size of a school places obstacles in the way of individualizing the educative process when this is the goal (as was the case at Dickens), it is equally true that the small size of a school does not in itself create such a goal (as was seen at Browning).

The basic distinction in the educational practices and values of these schools did not obscure the individual character and internal consistency of each. The greatest internal consistency appeared, as might be expected, at the extremes. Conrad's goal, of educating autonomous, committed individuals who would retain the initiative to reshape social processes, was consistently expressed in both the personal and ideational aspects of its functioning. Browning's goal, of carrying out its responsibility of educating skilled people who accepted the established social scheme, was consistently honored in its idea systems and climate of human relations. The two other schools incorporated more conflicting trends. At Dickens, the process of change, spearheaded and supported by administrative authority, resulted in the formation of an enclave of teachers committed to modern views and practices, co-existing with traditional views and practices. The Adams traditionalism was diluted by the common goal of parents and teachers to maintain a front position in the eyes of the community which took the form of embellishing the existing educational program. The professional self-image, modes of work, and personalities of the people shaped and colored the ideas and ideals. In the last analysis, ideas and ideals are forceful shapers of institutions; and eventually become the template to which people must fit.

NOTES

1. This approach is similar to that taken by the authors of *Crestwood Heights* (Seeley, Sim, and Loosley, 1956), whose analysis included the study of the school as a physical plant and as a social system:

    > Environmental forces . . . help to mold the school, and impose the material limits for its operation. On the other hand, the ideological influences within the teaching profession itself are a reflection of the more comprehensive values shaping social living in the total culture. . . . [p. 245]

2. As noted previously, this school was added in the second year of the study.
3. The fact that the principal selected the teachers to be observed raises the question of the representativeness of the teacher sample. It is likely that principals tended to select the more competent, or at least confident, individuals. On the other hand, the choice of teachers for the panel tells us something about the principal's basis for evaluating teachers. The questionnaire given to all the teachers in the school provided a check on representativeness and increased our understanding of the basis of the principal's selection. At the Conrad school, with but one class to a grade, there was no selection of a panel; here *all* classroom teachers (except for two where particular difficulties were encountered) were observed and all specialist teachers and classroom teachers (with these two exceptions) interviewed.
4. Conrad was visited 64 times; Dickens, 40 times; Adams, 43 times; and Browning, 18 times.
5. In connection with the study of developmental stages, Kessen (1962) has called attention in general to the importance of describing the environment:

. . . when there is mention of the "school-age child," we normally mean not merely an elliptical specification of age, but the presence of a typical environment—i.e., school—in which the child behaves. . . . Perhaps . . . there is abroad in child psychology a renewed emphasis on the stimulus; that is, on the specification of environmental events antecedent to behavior which shows "maturational" change. [p. 69]

6. This system of ranking indicates the modern-traditional positions of the four schools *in relation to each other*. It is not a reflection of quantitatively precise differences among them. The dotted lines in Figures 3–1 through 3–4 show that this sample of schools represents only part of the total extent of the modern-traditional continuum.

7. The significance of the administrator-teacher relationship as an index of total school climate has been demonstrated in the work of Halpin (1966). The descriptions of this relation in the modern schools and, later, in the traditional schools are consonant with the dimensions used in his analytic scheme. Tentatively, Conrad would probably rate as an "open" school, Dickens as an "autonomous" school containing an "open" school within it, Adams as an "autonomous" school, and Browning as a "controlled" school. None of the schools in our study fulfilled his criteria of a "closed" school.

8. This view has much in common with the view expressed by Bostwick (1961), who has pointed out that whether materials are abundant or scarce, costly or inexpensive, what matters is that they should have in common

> . . . power to help young persons satisfy their curiosity about the world in which they live, provide them with enough variety to permit their growth in different abilities and capacities and encourage their reaching out for knowledge and understanding. [p. 175]

9. Since the panel teachers could not be interviewed at Browning, their explicit views are not included here.

10. The life style of these Conrad teachers as well as the modern school teachers' motivation toward teaching, previously described, call to mind what Sears and Hilgard (1964) concluded in their study:

> A classroom is a social situation, with a power structure, including peer relationships, and adult-child relationships; hence the most favorable motivational conditions need to take all of these factors into account, recognizing that the teacher is both model and reinforcer and, in ways not fully understood, a releaser of intrinsic motives. [p. 209]

11. This school had the lowest proportion of returns to the questionnaire and some personal data were omitted on the 13 (out of a possible 37) that were returned.

CHAPTER

4

THE CLASSROOMS

The descriptive analysis of the schools delineates the context in which children and teachers functioned; the description of the classroom focuses on a particular set of children interacting with a particular teacher within that frame. The classrooms described in this chapter are the fourth-grade classrooms from which the children in the study were drawn. The observation of classroom life occupied an intermediary position in the study: the classroom represented and was vitally influenced by the school of which it was a part; at the same time, the children in the classroom were the subjects of the study. The children's behavior in the classroom was seen as a composite of their personal desires, predispositions, and capabilities, in response to the opportunities offered by the particular classroom-cum-school.

In any school the teachers create distinctive classroom conditions and the work of Anderson and his colleagues (1945; 1946) indicates that teachers develop a consistent style of teaching and children learn to adapt to its requirements. Within any school, variation in teaching styles is to be expected, but the range of variation is determined by the administrative personnel of the school. Halpin and Croft (1963) have even suggested that a school can be accurately described by its administrative characteristics alone. The assumption underlying the method adopted for the study of classroom life was that the influence of the classroom is continuous with that of the school; that despite the idiosyncratic characteristics of individual teachers, the children would reflect the cumulative impact of their several years of experience in their school. This presupposed that the school (that is, the administration of the school) exerted a constraining influence on the possible range of variation among teachers and that differences among teachers in any one school will be smaller than differences between teachers in different schools.

The purposes of the observation of classroom behavior were as follows:

1. To check the representativeness of the classroom: the congruence of the classroom teacher's modes of functioning with those of other teachers in the school, and the quality of classroom life with the descriptive analysis of the school.
2. To provide evidence of contrasting educational processes by documenting the particularities of the children's experience in school.
3. To provide additional information for better understanding the children's responses in the individual sessions.

The chapter is divided into three sections. In the first, the method of observation is described; in the second, the classrooms and teachers are described and compared, and an assessment is made of the congruence of the teachers in the study with other teachers in the school; in the third, selected aspects of the teachers' and children's activities are submitted to closer scrutiny and statistically compared.

Method

Selection of the Classrooms

In each school a fourth-grade classroom was selected as the source of the children in the study and as the locus of the observation of classroom life. It was crucial that the classroom teacher represent the dominant educational orientation of the school. In the public schools, the principal was asked to recommend the fourth-grade teachers who best represented what he would define as good teachers. These teachers were then interviewed and their classrooms visited as a gross check of their representativeness. On the basis of this information, one fourth-grade teacher was chosen in each of the public schools. At Conrad, there was no choice since there was only one class at each grade level.

The teachers agreed, by free choice, to participate in the study, although obviously the principal's acceptance of the research staff in his school and his recommendation of specific teachers constituted a degree of pressure. However, in recommending teachers for participation, the principal had taken the individual teacher's professional security as well as his view of her competence into account.

Presentation of the Research to the Participating Teachers

The study was described to each teacher as an investigation of the characteristics and capacities of nine-year-old children as ascertained through individual testing and observation of their behavior in the classroom. The teachers were assured that none of the research staff had any connection with school administration and that all data would be treated with maximum confidentiality. The teachers on their side agreed to having only limited contact with the observers and other members of the research staff and no access to the data. It was explained to the teachers that the schedule of observations would mean the presence of a stranger in their classroom on most days for the better part of a school year. Two informal interviews were held with the teachers during the course of the year to give them a chance to air any grievances and to talk about matters of scheduling and the like with members of the research staff.

These teachers, then, gave up the highly valued privacy of their classrooms, put up with a great deal of coming and going of children for individual interviews, and received in return the doubtful satisfaction of "contributing to knowledge." In truth, accepting a long-term observer is difficult and demanding. Few individuals are unself-conscious enough to view such a prospect with equanimity. The fact that these teachers freely agreed to participate in the study when it offered them little in return suggests both professional dedication and a degree of ease in the teaching role.[1]

Observation Schedule

Three observers followed a formal schedule of observations, rotating among the schools. The observations were spread over the school year in three periods of four weeks each, during which time an observer spent two or three hours a day, four days a week, in each classroom. In the intervening periods observations were made for two or three hours only once a week.

The observations were systematically distributed to cover all classroom activities—academic periods, discussions, gym, assemblies, and so on—

and the number of records of each type of activity paralleled the proportion of time allocated to that activity in each school.

More than 800 hours of classroom observation were recorded; the records were distributed among the four schools, the five teachers, and the six classroom groups.

The Records

A narrative-descriptive method was chosen to record the nature and quality of the children's life in school. Although this method seems to have fallen out of fashion in favor of precoded records in studies of the behavior of children and teachers in classroom situations (Gage, 1963), our choice of narrative records was based on two considerations. First, a set of precoded schema would have been too restricting for the range and number of activities we wished to document. Second, the narrative method allowed for the detailed reporting of behavior and interaction without sacrificing context and sequence; we wished to observe the children's activities and behavior in the context of the stream of events in the classroom.

At the same time, observation had to be selective, since no one can observe all the events of a complex social situation. A series of observation guides was therefore devised that indicated pertinent facts and dimensions and detailed the content the observers were to focus on in different classroom activities (see Appendix A for samples). Observational data included behavioral records of the total class group and of the individual children in the study.

While in a narrative-descriptive method there are no guaranteed correctives for possible observer bias, the three observers were deliberately selected to be of different training and experience. We anticipated that their different backgrounds would mitigate against a simplistic bias for or against any particular teacher or classroom and that their observations would yield perceptive records of a complex situation rather than interchangeable sets of tallies.[2] One had been an elementary school teacher and was currently a writer of children's books; one was a graduate student in clinical psychology; the third was an anthropologist.

Additional Sources of Data

The bulk of the data consisted of the narrative records. In addition, the fourth-grade teachers were interviewed at the end of the data collection period. These teachers were also rated by the observers on their teaching performance. The panel teachers (in the other grades) were rated by the school study team on the same series of scales, thus making it possible to compare the fourth-grade teachers with the panel teachers.

General Characteristics of the Classrooms and Teachers and Their Congruence with Their Schools

The Classrooms

While the classroom is conventionally viewed as the teacher's domain, the general tone and mores of the school, as well as the physical characteristics of the room itself, impose limits on what she can do.

There was a general difference between the Conrad classroom and those of the public schools, which followed from the latter's closer adherence to the principle of the self-contained classroom. The children in the public schools spent the greater part of every school day in their classroom. They left for lunch, for occasional gym, assembly, or library periods, and infrequently for special trips. At Conrad, the classroom served more as a home room, the center of school activities, the place for more formal learning tasks, as well as for social exchange; but the children also used the shop, music room, library, and lunchroom, as well as the yard. For all children, however, the main classroom was the focal point of their school experience.

Each classroom is briefly described in terms of its size and general appearance, the equipment furnished by the school, provided by the teacher, and made by the children, and the "displays," that is, the children's work, charts, and maps that conventionally decorate schoolroom walls.

CONRAD

The home room was of average size and, like the school, casually furnished; both had a somewhat shabby, lived-in quality. The home room was less cluttered than those at Dickens and Adams since it did not have to be divided into specific work areas.

The main room of the fourth-grade class had an annex half its size which was the school store, run and operated for the whole school by the fourth-graders. The store merchandise consisted of a variety of school supplies, sold to class groups and to individuals.

There were 19 movable table desks. Children were assigned to specific seats which they kept all year, although they changed seats often to work together. (Seats had a less identifying quality here than in most public schools because supplies were kept in cupboards along the side of the room rather than in the desks.) The teacher's desk, painted gray like the walls, in contrast to the red chairs and desks of the children, was placed at the far end of the room in front of the children. As in all the classrooms, the front wall was a blackboard. The blackboard was used by both teacher and children.

There were no plants or animals in the room.

There was a large bulletin board on one wall. No great feature was made of displays, but what was there seemed to be related to current work or to the children's individual interests (for example, a girl whose great interest was horses had a drawing of horses pinned up). There was no feeling of display for its own sake, and many objects made by the children were not displayed. A mural made for the scenic background of a play may have been hung on the wall until it was ready for use; on the other hand, props for the same play may have been stored in the shop until used. A collection of paid bills brought in by the children in connection with their work as proprietors of the store was hung up. The displays reflected the importance of the store in the children's school life.

DICKENS

The high-ceilinged, large room needed a coat of paint; the plaster was cracking on the walls. The room got dark in the early afternoon and the lights had to be turned on. The acoustics were good and street noises did not interfere (as they did in the Adams classroom). The 31 movable table desks and chairs were arranged in contiguous rows but were moved about often as the need arose.

There was a good-sized free area at the front of the room which was used for a reading circle and other activities and generally reinforced the free use of space in this classroom. There was a painting and craft area with an easel which stood on a piece of linoleum (presumably easy to clean).

Cotton curtains, which the children had helped to make and which they had decorated with crayon drawings, adorned the windows. Later in the year the children made new curtains crayoned with additional scenes of the city, seen on another trip. Because of these touches, the Dickens classroom had an intimate personal quality: it was the children's own room crowded with their things.

Along shelves at the back of the room and on the window sills were plants, three or four fish tanks, and several turtles. Some children were responsible for taking care of these, others checked on their progress, still others took only a casual interest in them. As in all the public school classrooms, authority symbols tended to be at the front of the room: the teacher's desk, the flag. The teacher's desk was placed somewhat off center.

There was no telephone or public address system and the blackboard showed as much evidence of children's use as of the teacher's.

All available wall space was covered with displays. Many children's products were pinned up. One might see, for example, children's crayon drawings of the surrounding neighborhood based on a recent trip. Charts, printed by the teacher, related to current projects. An ever-changing bulletin board contained clippings from newspapers and magazines dealing with current national and international events. The bulletin board items revealed children's handling, were finger-worn and creased; they looked as if they had been objects of a good deal of use and interest.

ADAMS

The two Adams teachers were in the same classroom in successive years, and the general tone of the room over the two years was very similar.

The room was large, light, and functional. The up-to-date equipment included such items as a telephone to the school office, public address system, drinking fountain, and new movable table desks and chairs.[3] The room was painted a pastel color. Shouting and moments of silence were a structural necessity since the acoustics were very poor: sounds in the room bounced off the walls and competed with assorted noises in the street.

The table desks and chairs (38 in Year I, 30 in Year II) were arranged in lengthwise contiguous group areas. This arrangement permitted the children a wider visual field than they had when sitting in formal rows and made it easier for them to talk to each other. The tables, though movable, were never rearranged; the chairs were occasionally moved about and the children changed seats for sectional work.

The teacher's desk was placed catty-cornered facing the children. In addition to the desk and the flag, the loudspeaker was also visible at the front of the room. One feature, unique to the classroom in the first year, was a "bad child's seat." Placed near the door at the front of the room, its occupant was clearly revealed to anyone outside when the door was open.

There was a painting area near the sink. A newspaper was often put under the easel.

The room had an air of immaculate neatness, especially notable in the first year. Also in the first year there was a little-used research table, complete with a lettered sign, RESEARCH, and there was a placard, THINK, on the teacher's desk.

There were no plants, flowers, or animals in the room.

Many displays covered the walls, all carefully arranged by the teacher and mounted on large sheets of colored paper. Displays about current curriculum and charts made by the teacher emphasized rules and procedures to be used in ongoing projects. A large Mercator map of the world, captioned "The World We Live In," dominated one wall. All displays were similarly captioned, looked very neat, and showed no signs of being handled. There were newspaper and magazine clippings brought by teacher and children, mounted under the caption "What's New in the World." There were many examples of children's work.

BROWNING

The size of the room, compared to those at Adams and Dickens, was moderate. Everything was in excellent repair. Walls were a neutral color. The light from the high north window wall was steady and cool. No outside noises penetrated the room and voices within were soft.

Despite a few new features mixed with much that was old, the mixture was thin: the room's appearance was the most old-fashioned of the classrooms in the study. Almost all the floor space was filled by 37 unmovable desks arranged in parallel rows. Passage between rows and sides of the room was sufficient for one person only; there was no free space of any kind available for a special work area. The room was set up for all children to work at the same task at the same time.

The teacher's desk, however, no longer held the center front position; it was set to the side, opening the center front area for the presentation of reports by individual children or groups.

For a short time, the teacher introduced a small easel-table arrangement at the back of the room but this was removed after a few weeks because she said it created a mess and cramped the narrow space even more.

Objects in the classroom consisted of books, textbooks, and an encyclopedia.

Pinned-up displays consisted primarily of samples of the children's good work in spelling, arithmetic, and handwriting. On the side wall was a health chart on which items of cleanliness to be checked were starred daily for each child—shoes shined, nails clean, hair neat, clean handkerchief in pocket, and so on—each child reporting on himself. The bulletin board had an occasional news clipping. Some crayoned pictures made by the children were hung, well above eye level, on the wall.

The Teachers

The fourth-grade teachers shared certain characteristics even while the differences among them resembled the differences among the panel teachers in the four schools described in the previous chapter. They were professionally competent, mature women, well-prepared for teaching, able to keep in equilibrium their relations with children, teachers, and administrative staff. Their satisfaction with the schools in which they were teaching was freely expressed. One of the teachers at Adams said, "If I had to teach for the rest of my life, I'd like it at Adams." Both Conrad and Dickens teachers spoke of their dedication to the goals and ideals of their schools. The Browning and Conrad teachers' satisfaction with their schools was further attested to by the fact that they had taught there for over ten years. All the teachers spoke warmly about the children: "sweet," "refreshing," "good minds," their comments ranging from perceptive remarks about particular children to generalized expression of pride in the children's brightness, sweetness, initiative, or liveliness.

Certain differences between the modern and traditional fourth-grade teachers were noted on the basis of observation and interviews. Those from Conrad and Dickens were somewhat younger and more informal in their dress and general style than were their counterparts at Adams and Browning. The modern school teachers were actively involved with parents who visited the classrooms and were invited to conferences with the teachers—most frequently at Conrad. Group meetings and individual conferences at Conrad were planned flexibly, depending on "how much the parents want to talk." At Dickens, the teacher saw the parents as highly motivated in wanting the "best" for their children. The teachers felt that the parents' expectations were too high at times both for the children and in terms of what the school could do. At the traditional schools there was not much interest in or sense of need for conferences with parents. The teachers were inclined to assess the parents with respect to their child-rearing styles. The Adams teachers saw the parents as cooperative, but sometimes "overzealous," as devoted to their children, but in some cases overindulgent. They decried the lack of continuity in the lives of some children whose parents they felt were too preoccupied with their own adult lives to keep close contact with their children. The Browning teacher was also critical of parents she considered overprotective or of those who "meddle" but, in general, felt the children came from "nice homes."

Congruence with the School

The most important question to be asked about these fourth-grade teachers concerned the congruence between them and their schools. This question was studied systematically by comparing ratings of the classroom performance of the fourth-grade teachers with ratings of the panel teachers who had been chosen to represent their schools.

These ratings were made after the completion of data collection on the basis of cumulative impressions. The teachers were rated on a series of nine-point scales assessing various aspects of their teaching performance (Zimiles, Biber, Rabinowitz, and Hay, 1964). Only those variables which could be applied to both groups of teachers were included. The reliability of the two school observers was not computed, although in general there was good agreement between them. Reliabilities for the three classroom observers on nine of the ten variables were quite satisfactory; they ranged from $r = .78$ to $r = .99$, with a median of $r = .92$ (see Table 4–1). The aberrant variable concerned the assessment of the closeness versus distance of the relationship between teacher and children. The scale required a judgment, at one end, of "very remote and distant" to, at the other, "too close . . . she reacts too keenly. . . ." The observers found this scale difficult to apply, especially to the Adams teachers, each of whom was rated as "somewhat cold and aloof. . . ." and also as "too involved in the emotions and feelings of the children." These teachers were often emotional in class and apparently this was interpreted by one of the raters as overinvolvement in the children.[4]

Two members of the school study team had rated the panel teachers on the same variables. Their ratings were compared with the ratings of the fourth-grade teachers. Although the panel teacher ratings were based on fewer observations, the correlations between the two sets of ratings were generally high (see Table 4–1).

This agreement between the two sets of ratings supports the assumption that the particular fourth-grade teachers with whom this study is primarily concerned were indeed similar to teachers at other grade levels in their schools. This internal congruence of teaching performance might be dismissed as artifactual since these were all teachers whom the principal had selected as representing his conception of good teaching. At the very least, however, the data show that the principal could, in fact, identify a core group of teachers who shared a common orientation to teaching. The fourth-grade teachers were representative of the prevailing philosophy and teaching practices of their respective schools.

The ratings of the fourth-grade classroom teachers also offered an auxiliary means of contrasting the teachers in the different schools. The mean ratings indicate that the ratings of the teachers correspond to the schools' positions on the modern-traditional continuum; and there were reliable between-school differences on most of the variables: the teacher's tendency to foster competitiveness or cooperativeness, her emphasis on needs of the group versus those of the individual children, the coerciveness of control, the extent to which restrictive limits were applied, her approach to learning, her tendency to offer justification of rules and regulations (see Table 4–1). While these ratings were subject to halo effect, they do support the thesis that within each school there was a common mode of teaching and that differences within schools are likely to be less than differences between schools. Most important for the methodology of this study, however, is the corroborative evidence they offered for judging the representativeness of the fourth-grade teachers.

TABLE 4-1

Comparison of Fourth-Grade Classroom Teachers and School Panel Teachers
According to Ratings of Teaching Performance

Dimensions of Teaching Performance[1]	Interrater Reliability Classroom Observers (r)	Schools		Fourth-Grade Classroom Teachers: Mean Rating of Three Classroom Observers	Panel Teachers Summary Ratings		Ratings of Classroom and School Observers (rho)	Analysis of Variance F = Between Teachers
					School Observer #1	School Observer #2		
1. Fostering Cooperative versus Competitive Relations (1 = cooperative, 5 = equal stress, 9 = competitive)	.98	B		6.7	5	—	.95	55.84**
		A	Year I	7.7	7	7		
			Year II	7.7				
		D		1	3	3		
		C		1	1	1		
2. Group versus Individual (1 = emphasis on group, 5 = balance, 9 = emphasis on individual)	.96	B		2.7	3	1	.80	23.63**
		A	Year I	2	2	2–3		
			Year II	2.3				
		D		5	4	5		
		C		6.3	7	5		
3. Approval-Disapproval (1 = much praise, 5 = balance, 9 = disapproval)	.78	B		5.3	4	—	.95	4.60
		A	Year I	7.3	6	7		
			Year II	6.7				
		D		4	4	4		
		C		3.3	3	3		

TABLE 4-1 (continued)

Dimensions of Teaching Performance[1]	Interrater Reliability Classroom Observers (r)	Schools	Fourth-Grade Classroom Teachers: Mean Rating of Three Classroom Observers	Panel Teachers Summary Ratings — School Observer #1	School Observer #2	Ratings of Classroom and School Observers (rho)	Analysis of Variance F = Between Teachers
4. Coerciveness of Control (1 = coercive, 5 = some coercion, 9 = avoids coercion)	.99	B	1.7	3	—	.80	73.85**
		A { Year I	2	3	1		
		Year II	2				
		D	6.7	5	7		
		C	7	8	9		
5. Disciplinary Friction (1 = much overt conflict, 5 = harmonious with some friction, 9 = no friction)	.78	B	4.7	8	—	−.35	4.50
		A { Year I	4	7	—		
		Year II	4				
		D	7	7	—		
		C	7	5	—		
6. Imposition of Limits (1 = severe and frequent, 5 = balance: liberal and realistic, 9 = few and mild)	.98	B	1.3	3	—	.75	53.23**
		A { Year I	1.7	3	1		
		Year II	1.7				
		D	6.3	5	4		
		C	6.3	7	7		
7. Closeness-Distance[2] (1 = T very remote, 5 = balance: comfortable interaction, 9 = T too involved)	.19	B	4.3	4	—	.40	—
		A { Year I	6	3	1		
		Year II					
		D	4	4	5		
		C	5	5	5		

Dimensions of Teaching Performance[1]	Interrater Reliability Classroom Observers (r)	Schools	Fourth-Grade Classroom Teachers: Mean Rating of Three Classroom Observers	Panel Teachers Summary Ratings — School Observer #1	School Observer #2	Ratings of Classroom and School Observers (rho)	Analysis of Variance F = Between Teachers
8. *Rigidity-Flexibility of Program* (1 = rigid, preset, 5 = flexible, 9 = planless)	.78	B ⎱ Year I	1.7	3	—	.90	4.64
		A ⎰	3.3	3	3		
		Year II	1.7				
		D ⎱ Year II	5	5	5		
		C ⎰	4.3	5	5		
9. *Approach to Learning* (1 = fact-centered, 5 = facts + encourage children's inquiry, 9 = encourage inquiry only)	.86	B ⎱ Year I	1.7	3	—	.60	7.09*
		A ⎰	2	3	1		
		Year II	2.3				
		D ⎱ Year II	4	4	5		
		C ⎰	5	5	5		
10. *Justification of Policy* (1 = T explains reasons, 5 = no clear tendency, 9 = very arbitrary)	.92	B ⎱ Year I	5.3	5	—	1.00	11.96**
		A ⎰	6.3	7	—		
		Year II	5				
		D ⎱ Year II	1.3	3	—		
		C ⎰	1	1	—		

1. Note that high scores are not consistently positive or negative.
2. No statistical comparisons were made on this dimension because of low rater reliability.
* $p < .05$
** $p < .01$

Analysis of Differences Among the Classrooms

General Considerations

While the observers had been directed to center their attention on the children (individually or as a group) and to record the teacher's behavior primarily to describe the context of the children's behavior, in many records the teacher became the central figure. More often than anticipated, her behavior was recorded in some detail because of the inescapable salience of the teacher as the center of action and power in the classroom. The highlighting of the teacher occurred in some classrooms more than others and may be related to the modern-traditional quality of the classroom. It is true of course that in general the teacher in a traditional classroom is the dominant figure, from whom the lines of power emanate and on whom attention is focused; the teacher in a modern classroom tends to take a less central role, diffusing the focus of power and interest.

Three analyses of classroom behavior were undertaken, two of *cognitive functioning* and the third of *interpersonal relations*. They are presented separately under the following headings:

The Teacher's Structuring of the Children's Learning
Aspects of the Children's Cognitive Behavior
Aspects of Interpersonal Relations in the Classrooms

For each analysis, a sample of records was selected from pools of records representing the four schools, the three observers, and types of activity periods. All analyses were done on masked records, that is, every reference, name, or comment that could identify the school was deleted. Even so, it was impossible to achieve complete anonymity in all records because some of the activities recorded were typically characteristic of one or another of the schools. Still, the masking procedure did eliminate the identity of the school on many records and focused attention on *what* had transpired and *why* and minimized concern with *who*. It also helped the raters to treat each record as a separate datum.

Essentially, the method was one of coding into predetermined mutually exclusive categories and subsequently rating broad dimensions.

The rating was done by three data analysts working independently. One of the three had served as a classroom observer; the other two were new to the study and not familiar with the schools in the study. It was feared at first that the observer-rater would recognize or remember many of the records. The sheer bulk of the data worked against this, however, and only the most dramatic instances were clearly recalled. In the first analysis (how the teacher organized the children's learning), three raters were used so as to provide a literal double check on the observer-rater. Reliability was quite satisfactory, and the observer-rater continued as rater for subsequent analyses.

It should perhaps be repeated that neither the observers nor the analysts participated in discussion or formulation of the central hypotheses of the study. They had used the observation guides (see Appendix A) and knew from them what dimensions were considered important. They knew also that cognitive functioning and interpersonal relations were being studied elsewhere in the project, but they had no contact with that material.

Method of Analysis for Cognitive Functioning

For the two analyses of cognition, records of academic periods were chosen; they consisted of the periods designated by the school as language arts, social studies, and arithmetic—the major areas of elementary school curriculum. It was in these periods that the teacher most actively directed the children's learning. A sample of 67 academic records was selected, distributed across the four schools, as seen in Table 4–2.

TABLE 4–2
Distribution of Observation Records

Academic Period	B	A	D	C	Total
Language Arts	2	14	5	5	26
Social Studies	2	8	4	8	22
Arithmetic	3	7	4	5	19
Total	7	29	13	18	67

For these analyses, the total record was taken as the unit. Although the periods covered ranged from 15 minutes to over an hour, each record represented a natural unit in that it covered one activity period. Thus the unit of observation became the unit for analysis.

Each record was evaluated according to a series of categories on the basis of which a general rating was made. The judgments and ratings were macroscopic, dealing with broad dimensions of the teacher's mode of approach and the children's response rather than with items of verbal interaction and/or teacher strategy-child response, more characteristic of other recent studies of classroom behavior (see Gage, 1963; Bellack, Kliebard, Hyman, and Smith, 1966).

The Teacher's Structuring of the Children's Learning

We were interested in how the teacher defined what the children would learn and how they would learn it; what kinds of opportunities she offered for questioning, probing; what kinds of responses, skills, and achievements she valued.

DATA AND METHOD OF ANALYSIS

The analysis was based on the teacher's *emphasis on relationship thinking* and *the leeway she allowed for independent cognitive exploration.* Each of these was rated on a five-point scale; the rating was a synthesis of several contributing category judgments. Though the two dimensions overlap conceptually and were highly correlated ($r = .82$), the behavioral cues used in judging and rating were different enough to warrant separate treatment.

Interrater reliability for the two major ratings was quite satisfactory—$r = .90$ and $r = .94$, respectively. For the category judgments, the range was from $r = .74$ to $r = .99$ with the exception of one category, where the low reliability of $r = .51$ was largely due to the low N.

CLASSROOM DIFFERENCES

Comparison of both ratings showed significant differences between the teachers in their emphasis on relationship thinking and the leeway they allowed for independent cognitive exploration.[5] The most striking differences were between the two modern and the two traditional classroom teachers (see Table 4-3). The two traditional school teachers (Browning and Adams) had similarly low ratings on both dimensions; the two modern school teachers (Dickens and Conrad) were notably high on both, though the Conrad teacher's rating was consistently higher. Similarly, comparison of the modern and traditional classrooms on each of the component categories yielded statistically reliable differences (see Table 4-4). As has been noted, these are not independent assessments, but it is of interest that comparison of the two pairs of classrooms shows reliable differences on each dimension.

Relationship thinking was and remains one of the generating concepts of the modern educational movement; it was Lucy Sprague Mitchell's term (1934) for what Jerome Bruner (1964) has more recently called "going beyond the information given." It is defined as the search for relationships among facts and ideas; the connection of facts and concepts to known experiences as a path to understanding and motivation; the expectation that ambiguity may accompany the process of learning and

TABLE 4–3

The Teacher's Structuring of the Children's Learning: Comparative Ratings of Emphasis on Relationship Thinking *and* Leeway for Independent Cognitive Exploration (*Total* N = 67 *records*)

Dimension/ Classrooms	N of Records[1]	Mean Rating[2] (Consensus)	Analysis of Variance
Emphasis on relationship thinking (1–5)			Between classrooms:
Browning	7	1.57	F = 26.51**
Adams	28	1.32	[For B + A versus D + C, t = 8.44**]
Dickens	11	2.91	
Conrad	12	4.00	
Total	58		
Leeway for cognitive exploration (1–5)			Between classrooms:
Browning	7	1.43	F = 31.81**
Adams	29	1.35	[For B + A versus D + C, t = 9.36**]
Dickens	14	3.16	
Conrad	12	4.14	
Total	62		

1. *The variation in N's is due to the fact that not all records could be rated on all dimensions.*
2. *Reliability of ratings made by three judges was computed by analysis of variance; reliabilities for the two scales are .90 and .94, respectively.*
** *p* < .01

reasoning. It is contrasted with a more fact-centered, product-oriented approach to teaching and learning that places greater stress on speed, accuracy, and the definitive mastery of established modes of learning and reasoning.

The component categories concern the teacher's approach to communicating information, and the kind of learning she apparently valued. The raters categorized each record in the following terms:[6]

1. In teaching symbolic skills, such as arithmetic and language, does the teacher *emphasize the underlying principles?* Does she make logical connections to other skills and ideas? Or does she emphasize memorization and repetitive exercises?

2. In her approach to the teaching of concepts, does she *encourage the children to develop concepts,* helping them to put facts together and making implications and connections with other ideas? Or are concepts treated as facts to be learned? Does she stress reporting skills per se?

3. What is her *attitude to problem-solving?* Does she give children an

TABLE 4–4

Differences in the Modern and Traditional School Teachers' Structuring of Children's Learning (Total N = 67 records)

Dimension (Interrater Reliability)[1]	Classroom Frequencies			Comparisons Between B + A Versus D + C
	Traditional B + A	Modern D + C	N[2]	
Quality of Thinking Encouraged				
1. Symbolic Skills (.89)				
Understanding principles	4	9		
versus			37	$\chi^2 = 6.47$**
Memorization or drill	19	5		
2. Conceptualization (.51)				
Emphasis on conceptual development	0	8		
versus			21	$\chi^2 = 8.87$**
Emphasis on concepts as facts	10	3		
3. Problem-Solving Orientation (.89)				
Partly child-determined	3	21		
versus			39	$\chi^2 = 25.03$**
T-determined	15	0		
Cognitive Exploration				
1. Relevance of Subject Matter to Children's Experience (.97)				
Close	4	17		
versus			58	$\chi^2 = 20.83$**
Distant	31	6		
2. Scope of Content Accepted as Relevant (.74)				
Wide	3	7		
versus			16	$p = .025$ [3]
Narrow	5	1		
3. Assistance Given by T (.99)				
Active help	2	15		
versus			37	$\chi^2 = 22.66$**
Ignoring, not helping	19	1		
4. Function of T's Comments (.99)				
Develop	1	15		
versus			35	$\chi^2 = 27.46$**
Interfere with children's ideas	19	0		
5. Pace (.88)				
T's and children's pace Consonant	17	30		
versus			60	$\chi^2 = 14.14$**
Dissonant	13	0		
6. Atmosphere (.99)				
Harmonious or task-oriented	12	27		
versus			61	$\chi^2 = 21.17$**
Discordant or to maintain order	21	1		

1. *Reliability of three judges' categorizations was computed by means of analysis of variance.*
2. *The variation in N's is due to the fact that not all records could be judged on all dimensions.*
3. *The low N made chi square inappropriate and Fisher's test of exact probabilities was used.*
** $p < .01$

opportunity to find the steps to solution? Does she allow them to define their own problems as well as the means to solving them? Or does she mostly set the problem and provide the steps to solution?

The differences in the way the teachers defined the learning situation for the children can be illustrated from the records. The illustrations are presented here in the context of the above three categories of analysis.

One aspect of the way the teachers defined the cognitive realm to be mastered is their emphasis, in the teaching of symbolic skills, such as arithmetic or language, on *memorization* versus the *clarification of principles*. In the following arithmetic lesson, the Dickens teacher helped the children to understand the underlying principles of multiplication.

T begins lesson in multiplication by calling on children for answers to 2×1, 2×2, 2×4, etc., and then for 4×1, 4×2, etc. She writes the tables on the blackboard as follows:

2	4	6	8	10	12	14	16
4	8	12	16	20	24	28	32

Some children immediately perceive a relationship and call out, "I know, I see."
T: Wait, there are two things you should first see about the tables.
BILLY: The answer to the second one is double.
T: Yes, why is it double?
ANNE: Because it's times.
T: Yes, multiplication is a short way of adding, but why?
Lots of hands go up against a background of excited "Ooh's."
SHERRY (very excited): You double the times.
T (realizing they have a beginning grasp): Do you think you can find the 8's table?
JIM: It's like the 4's, because two 2's are four and two 4's are eight.
T: Yes, you double the 4's.
Some children quickly catch on that 4×8 gives the same answer as 8×4 and call this fact out.
SHERRY (hesitates, then says): If multiplication is the same as addition, and we can reverse addition, we can reverse multiplication.

An arithmetic lesson at Browning, on the other hand, illustrates the use of repetitive exercise to reinforce the learning of division:

The T places division problems on the board, e.g., 4/25 cupcakes, 4/18 ribbons, 4/22 ties, etc. Children are instructed to make up a "short story" in reciting the problem and give the correct answer. The children answer, each using the same format, e.g., "There were 22 ties and 4 boys wanted to buy them in a store so that each boy would get 5 ties. There were 20 ties used (T interrupts, tells the child to say "bought," not "used") and 2 ties were left over"—"In the store," adds the T.

During the rest of the period children copy multiplication problems from the board and solve them at their desks. T puts some of the answers on the board to "save time." She tells the class she is deliberately going to make some mistakes and they are to find the error and report it. They are not, however, to say, "Teacher, you made a mistake," but "Teacher, you made a mistake because" and then go on to correct the error.

This was a simple exercise to achieve proficiency in arithmetic calculation and the teacher was trying to make the exercise more interesting by having the various examples dressed up with a story. But when she made the story a formula, which the children *had to* abide by, the story became a ritualized and irrelevant part of the exercise.

One may note that in the arithmetic lesson at Dickens the teacher was introducing the children to concepts, whereas in the Browning record the teacher was drilling on known material. Records from all schools, however, indicated that these excerpts were representative of the teachers' approaches. The two approaches also differed in the level of conceptualization the teacher expected and wanted from the children.

It was in their handling of social studies content that the teachers' *encouragement of conceptualization* and generalization was evaluated. Since social studies consists of facts and concepts, one may ask what the teacher does who does not, in part at least, direct her teaching to the children's learning and understanding of concepts. But when there is little encouragement of generalizations, more emphasis is placed on acquiring discrete facts and ready-made generalizations. In such a setting, concepts are reduced to facts and regarded as such, to be learned as other facts are.

For example, the Browning teacher opened a social studies period by asking the children:

> T: What are we studying?
> SEVERAL CHILDREN: _____ City.
> The teacher then asks a series of questions, e.g.:
> T: Was (colonial leader) liked?
> SEVERAL CHILDREN: No, he was strict and stern.
> T: But was he good?
> SEVERAL CHILDREN: Yes, he kept the colony in order.
> T (telling class to take out paper): What are you going to do with the paper?
> SEVERAL CHILDREN: Take notes.
> T: What must you do to be a good listener?
> SEVERAL CHILDREN: Listen hard.

Another way the teachers' techniques were examined was by looking at the way they posed problems to the children. The teachers in the modern schools mainly used the discussion method. In the following record of a group discussion, the Dickens teacher set a well-defined problem of curriculum content and allowed the children to draw on their own experiences, on factual information, and on their own ability to make inferences. The record, presented in some detail, illustrates the characteristic unevenness of discussions and how the teacher guides them, keeping the children on the topic, and adding and clarifying information. The Browning and Adams teachers did not open up this kind of discussion of curriculum content.

> The children have been reading about maps in the Weekly Reader. The first stage of the lesson is a discussion of some general uses of maps with which the children are familiar. The children's initial responses reflect that they are thinking about this problem both from personal experiences and from what they have read.
>
> T: What kinds of maps do you know about?
> JEFF: Map of the United States.
> T: What are maps used for?
> JEFF: To find out about different states and where they are. For information, find out where places are.
> T: Yes. (She writes *location* on the board under heading *Uses of Maps*.)
> LISA: Well, road maps. You can find out what routes to take.
> T: *Routes* and *directions*. (She writes these words on the board.) What else?
> EMILY: Like, say, when you're in a place you don't know, like when we were lost in Cincinnati, or like last year in Mrs. _____ class, we had to call up. If you're in a place and you're lost, you can look it up and find out where you are.
> ROGER: Like you can know how much gas you use for so many miles. Some maps have little things, 5 or 10 miles they say, tell you how far to go.
> T (adds *mileage* to list of words): What else?
> ANDY: Maps can tell you places to stop, historical interest, to eat, hotels.
>
> There is an interruption as another T enters with an announcement for the children.
>
> T (bringing class back to maps): What else do we use maps for?
> HARRY: Heights, well, levels.
> ANDY: Have colors on maps or on slides sometimes to show heights.
> T: Yes, they are called contour lines which are used to give the same effect as colors.
> TIM: It shows not only differences [in height], but also tells where one state begins and another ends.
> T: Would a map show you if you were going to cross a river?
> CHILDREN: Yes.
> JOY: Also which is north and south.
> DANNY: Tells you where rivers are. . . .

T explains use of color and contour lines, discusses physical features through an analogy with the human face. A girl comments that on large maps you can find places like the Arctic Circle where the climate differs from other areas. The teacher takes up this idea and asks:

T: What about climate? Why don't bananas grow in _____ City?
ANNA: Bananas need a hot place to grow in.
T: If you can show climate and physical features on a map, what else?
DANNY: Vegetation.
ANNA: You can probably determine what kind of clothing people wear if you know the climate.

. . .

BEA: One thing, one real difference between hot places and cold places is in hot places they won't wear outfits like the Eskimos wear.

. . .

ROGER: If you know the vegetation of an area and the animals of an area, you can probably tell what kinds of food the animals eat.

The teacher here wanted the children to learn something about maps—a standard curriculum topic. She wanted them to learn that one can derive specific information from maps and that the kind of information will depend on the nature of the map. She also wanted them to know the specific information. She was using and implicitly teaching an inferential method—that given factual information one can, through reasoning, arrive at valid conclusions.

The teachers from the traditional schools tended to set a problem for the class and then define the steps to solution. When the Dickens and Conrad teachers set problems for the group, they tended to give the children a chance to find the steps to solution themselves. Often they allowed the children to define a problem as well as find the means of solving it. One of the most common teaching modes at Browning and Adams was the simple question-and-answer session in which the teacher often appeared to be putting the children through their paces. In these instances, the children had already had one or more lessons on a particular topic and were, it seemed, being rehearsed in their proficiency with the material. Exercises consisted of multiple examples of short problems; the children were supposed to be brief and concise in their responses, for example, at Adams:

T: Why do so many people come to America?
SEVERAL CHILDREN: For freedom.
T: Why has _____ City grown so?
SEVERAL CHILDREN: Because of the harbor. . . . It is a port and the gateway to the world.

When they told about something, they were given a form to follow. For instance, at Browning, the children were reporting on library books they were reading. Each child was given two or three minutes and two children were appointed as timekeepers. Each child was to cite the name and author of the book; tell how long he had been reading it or how far he had gotten ("Now I'm up to the part where she is going away for a vacation"); convey its general content ("When Florence Nightingale was a little girl she had two nurses. Florence dreamed a lot and this worried her mother. It was suggested that a change of scenery might help Florence. . . ."); give a personal evaluation ("I think it is a very good book"); and recommend it to either boys, girls, or both. When a child departed from the form, the teacher called his attention to it.

The second rating concerned the *leeway the teachers allowed for independent cognitive exploration.* This rating was based on categories that have to do with the teaching-learning climate that the teacher creates. The assumption made here is that certain conditions are conducive to independent thought; the presence of these conditions obviously cannot insure such thinking but does indicate that the teacher is attempting to foster the children's independent attempts. Conversely, the absence of such conditions does not preclude independent thinking but does suggest that little premium is placed upon it and also that when it occurs, it does so outside the mainstream of school life.

In making this assessment the judges evaluated the records in the following terms:[7]

1. Is the subject matter she introduces *close to or distant from* the children's experiences?
2. Is the *scope of content accepted as relevant* wide or narrow?
3. Does she *assist* them when they seem to need or ask for it?
4. Do the teacher's *comments develop* and extend the children's ideas or do they tend to *interfere* with or interrupt the flow of thinking?
5. Is the *pace* the teacher establishes *consonant* with that of the children, or *dissonant?*
6. Is the *atmosphere for learning* that she creates *harmonious* and *task-oriented?* Or is it discordant? Or centered on maintaining order?

The first category concerned the nature of the *subject matter—its closeness to or distance from* the children's realm of experience. The question was not merely whether the curriculum content per se was relevant to the children's experience but rather whether the material was dealt with by the teacher so as to establish—and allow the children to establish—connections with what they already knew. For instance, when the Dickens teacher, in the maps discussion cited earlier, allowed the children to start off by using their own contacts with maps, she was bringing them more effectively to the consideration of all maps, not just road maps. At Conrad, the children practiced arithmetic by doing the accounts of the school store which they ran. (They were interested and also determined to balance the books.) Their social studies program dealt with the history of the west-ward movement; they studied the people of another era in terms of the motivations that had led them to go west; they learned about the small details of everyday life—the kind of food they ate, the kind of clothes they wore, whether the children went to school—that enabled them to make a connection with and give credibility to the idea of a pioneer. On the other hand, although much of the social studies curriculum of the Browning and Adams children concerned the growth and development of the city in which they lived, the content they dealt with seldom touched any aspect of their lives.

What was the *scope of content* that the teacher considered relevant to the classroom? This refers both to the literal factual content that she ac-cepted as pertinent to school work and to her acceptance of children's personal associations and contributions. In discussions at Conrad, the chil-dren were free to bring up topics of personal interest, to pursue a private logic, to respond in emotional terms. Similarly at Dickens, the expression of emotion, as well as the making of symbolic connections, was accepted as relevant to school (compare maps discussion, p. 107).

The teachers of Browning and Adams tended to keep a tighter rein on the content. For example, the Adams teacher had asked the class for infor-mation on Magellan. Allen responded with a long, knowledgeable answer summarizing Magellan's travels, incorporating into his spontaneous reply information on meridians, galaxies, and so on. The teacher made fun of his use of long words and his "more-than-necessary knowledge." (A moment later, however, she softened her ridicule somewhat by remarking: "Allen always tells us a lot, for he does a lot of reading for us.")

Only a small number of these records (16) could be categorized on this dimension; yet it provided a useful way of looking at what the teacher was doing and, when applicable, seemed to offer a touchstone of whether the teacher was in fact giving the children an opportunity to think deeply, creatively, in their own terms (see Biber, 1959).

What kind of *assistance* did the teacher give? Did she give active help or emotional support when the children floundered, asked for help? Did she ignore them, insist they work out problems for themselves, dismiss the inquiry?

The Conrad teacher actively helped the children and kept an eye on those who were not following, as in this arithmetic period:

> T: In the first column write "money received." (She writes *received* on the board.) "Money" you should know how to spell.
> Class busy writing. They look up when finished, then the teacher con-tinues.
> T: In the second column put down "money spent."
> Some children have difficulty spelling "spent." The teacher walks around

pronouncing "spent" very slowly to those having trouble. Then, seeing that others are still stuck on this word, she asks the class:
T: What part of "ten" helps you spell "spent"?
Roy: "En."

Similarly at Dickens, the teacher often gave her attention to those who did not have their hands raised, who needed help.

> Bonny is stuck; she can't do the example. The teacher is encouraging:
> T: You can explain it, think it through.
> Then as Bonny makes no further progress the teacher tells her to use the one's, ten's and hundred's cards that are available in front of the room. Meanwhile, Joe is figuring on his fingers as T asks him how many one's and ten's there are in the number 96. She hands him some wooden splints to count with. Finally he figures out the answer.

The Browning and Adams teachers tended to be oriented more to the class as a group; it was expected that the child would keep up with the pattern set for the class. Of course these teachers were aware of and responsive to differences among the children, and they helped children, answered questions, and gave information. But they were far more likely—often on the basis of a reasoned concept of children's learning—to turn the child away, to tell him to look it up, not to raise his hand if he didn't know the answer, and to heighten the feeling of inadequacy rather than to give support. During an arithmetic lesson at Adams, for example, a number of multiplication problems were on the blackboard. Jay was called on to solve one. He was slow and unsure. The teacher was irritated: "If you don't know your combinations, I can't help you," she said, and called on another child.

A category similar to the one of assistance is whether the teacher's comments developed and extended the children's thinking or tended to interrupt or interfere with it. This aspect of the teacher's comments overlaps also with other categories, such as the scope of content she accepted and the pace she set.

The *pace* of the classroom was set by the teacher; variations were a function of the nature of the material being covered, the type of lessons (for example, review versus new material), and most important for the present analysis, whether or not the teacher took the children's tempo and readiness into account. When the teacher accepted the pace at which the children worked, the tempo from period to period was more variable. And, since there were obviously individual differences in the pace at which children worked and learned, the teacher who paid attention to these differences naturally paid more attention to individual children.

The Conrad and Dickens teachers did not press the children to rush, to complete a lesson within a limited time period. The Conrad teacher gave arithmetic examples to the children, saying, "Do it carefully. Take your time, there's no rush about it." Sometimes the teacher's responsiveness to the children's pace may have resulted in a lack of closure:

> She has posed the problem of why the present century is called the 20th when the year is 19—. It is a difficult question and the children are puzzled. Their initial attempts to solve it are unclear and confused; there are pauses while they sit and think. Some children realize that they don't know how many years there are in a century. The teacher answers this question, but allows them to work on the problem without much guidance. The period ends with the question still unresolved.

In contrast, the Browning and Adams teachers characteristically set a rather rapid pace, hurrying the children along or else keeping them waiting. Frequently, the two patterns occurred as part of the same episode—first the children were hurried, then kept waiting. The following summary description of the transition from one period to another at Adams is characteristic:

> A rapid transition is encouraged by the teacher. She hurries the children along telling them to change books, assigning the lesson, and exhorting them to do all of this "quickly." The children fumble about in their desks, exchanging one set of notebooks for another. In an effort not to get behind, they stuff books into their desks, pulling others out, and as a result most of their desks are constantly in disorder. Invariably, the teacher does not wait for the children, they "scamper" to keep up with her, though after she has told them what page to turn to she may be involved in another activity, keeping them waiting for further instructions, or she may, before all the children are ready, plunge into the lesson asking questions.

Setting a rapid pace is partly a result of pressure to cover a great deal of material, to get a lot done. The traditional school teachers were aware of this and helplessly recognized that such pressures may lead to errors, their own as well as the children's.

It is obviously more difficult for some children to keep up with a rapid tempo than it is for others. But the dimension is not merely one of temperamental incongruence. The sense of hurry—a symbolic clock is ticking in the background—affects the depth with which content can be explored and limits the opportunities to follow an interesting idea. When, for instance, each child's book report must be completed in two or three minutes, there is little chance that any but the most general ideas will be taken up or that another child will be fired with desire to read the book. The following précis of a social studies period at Adams indicates the outer limit of this pressure for speed. Here the children were expected to make rapid decisions, work quickly, learn fast; further and perhaps more important, such a lesson implies that a complex topic can in fact be "covered" in one short exposure.

> In addition to their central social studies content, fourth grade public school children spend briefer periods of time studying two other communities. The lesson today is to choose one of five topics the teacher has selected, join a committee studying that topic, read the section in the social studies book relating to that topic, and together write a report about it. The five topics selected by the teacher are: (1) small farms in China; (2) summer on a farm in China; (3) winter on a farm in China; (4) reading and writing in China; and (5) trade with other countries. The teacher then tells the children: "I'll give you one minute to think about which topic you want to work on."
>
> Committee work involves the children in changing their seats to form small groups. This involves a vast number of decisions and small actions, all time consuming: where to locate the group; dividing up the work; gathering supplies and relocating, etc. The decision as to which topic to select is, for many children, a function of who is going to be in the group, so the decision as to topic is often delayed until the children first decide on whom they want in their group. Further, in order to avoid duplicating topics the children need to confer briefly with other groups.
>
> Twenty minutes later the teacher tells the children to finish their work and report to the class on their topics. For the next fifteen minutes, during which the children again have to change their seats to form a large group circle, they inform the class what work they did and who contributed the most.

The Conrad teacher had the greatest freedom to adapt her pace and could adapt the amount of material covered to meet the capacities of the children. All the public school teachers, however, functioned within the framework of the curriculum directives of the central Board; a prescribed amount of material had to be covered in the fourth grade. It was therefore of particular interest that the Dickens teacher, as much a part of the public educational system as the Browning and Adams teachers, was able to gear the tempo to the children.

This variable, incidentally, could be applied to almost all the records (60 of 67), for usually the relation between the teacher's and children's rhythm was relatively easy to document. Its importance, however, goes beyond indicating the teacher's adaptability to individuals or subject matter by revealing her fundamental attitude to the intellectual experience.

Finally, the records were evaluated in terms of the general *atmosphere for learning* that the teacher created. Was the atmosphere harmonious or discordant? Was it task-oriented? Did the teacher engage the children's interest? Or was she concerned with maintaining order for its own sake? Did she express tension and irritability?

The raters noted that it was more difficult to document a judgment of harmonious atmosphere, easier to record the cues for discord—a problem analogous to the difficulty of describing and defining normal as opposed to deviant functioning. Nevertheless, the working cooperation between teacher and children at Conrad and Dickens was clearly apparent as illustrated in the excerpted reports of the discussion of maps at Dickens (see p. 107), and of the arithmetic lesson at Conrad (see pp. 110–111).

The Browning teacher tended to be concerned with maintaining order in the classroom, sometimes anticipating disorder:

> The class is preparing for committee work. Before they can get started the teacher says, "I know that on a day like this (i.e., a day for committee work) it's hard not to make noise and bother the next group." Then, looking at a child who had turned around in his seat says, with some strong emotion in her voice, "The way one young man is working in here, he'll soon find out he's working all by himself. I'm not going to have anyone who's not working hard."
>
> The head of each committee then reports on what his group will do during the period. A few moments after the children have begun to work the teacher claps her hands and says, "Quiet," and expresses her annoyance at the fact that she had to clap twice. She tells the class that one committee leader is ready to throw up her hands because she can't get anything done (Gloria's group contains 8 children and she has been trying unsuccessfully to boss them). T advises Gloria to let them read and they'll find something interesting. The teacher continues to work alone at her desk and a few moments later she claps her hands again and calls for quiet. She then briefly helps Gloria, who is complaining, "All the children are walking around and looking at other people's things and not getting anything done."
>
> T asks the class for the first rule written on the board relating to work procedures.
>
> GEORGE: Work and move quietly.
>
> A few moments later the teacher disbands the work groups and asks the committee leaders to report on how far their group has progressed.

One of the teachers at Adams openly expressed her tension and annoyance. Her need for order was less notable than that of the Browning teacher, but her sarcasm often created an anxious atmosphere, though it also afforded the children moments of comic relief, usually at the expense of one of the children.

> The T is instructing the children in the use of the abacus. Norman has been sent to the board and starts counting from the bottom instead of the top.
> T (shouting): Oh, on top.
> Children laugh at Norman's error.

Keith, the next child, after completing his turn returns the beads to their original position.

T (raising her voice): I didn't tell you to put them back.

At this point Neil returns to the room after getting milk, squeezes behind the teacher in an effort to reach his seat without disturbing her.

T (annoyed): Isn't there enough room to walk around me so you don't have to crawl under me and almost throw me down?

Children break out into laughter.

Carla is now asked to demonstrate 32 on the abacus (and probably taking her cue from the T's telling Keith not to return the beads to their original position, she attempts to put 32 up with 900 still on the board). The class laughs at her "error."

T (angry at the class): Now, children, don't laugh at each little mistake. Now Carla, how many beads have you up?

Carla, realizing her mistake, moves the 900 down.

T asks Ray to put 106 on the abacus, then asks Chuck if he is right.

Chuck hesitates, says "yes" then "no," then, "I don't know."

T (sarcastically): What are you on, a seesaw?

Children laugh.

T: Now, children, I want you to stop all this silliness.

Aspects of the Children's Cognitive Behavior

There is an inescapable paradox in any attempt to assess thinking through the method of observation, which is that thinking is by nature implicit while observation is restricted to the explicit. We could not therefore make unequivocal statements about the children's thinking from these data; but we could make some judgments about their verbalized thought and their apparent motivation. An additional attempt, to assess the competence of their intellectual performance in the classroom, had to be abandoned because the teachers' requirements and expectations were so different from classroom to classroom that consistent standards could not be applied.

DATA AND METHOD OF ANALYSIS

The same sample of observational records of academic periods that had been used for the analysis of how the teacher organizes children's learning was used for the analysis of the children's cognitive behavior.[8] Since the reliability of the ratings in the earlier analysis was quite high, only two judges were used in this analysis. Considerable time elapsed between the two analyses. Although the raters recognized some records, they did not recall specific categorizations or ratings.

The analytic scheme yielded two ratings: the extent of the *children's involvement in the work of the classroom* and the *quality of the children's verbalized thinking*.[9] The rating of children's involvement was a synthesis of contributory category judgments, made on a five-point scale; the rating of the quality of children's verbalized thinking was made on a three-point scale without contributing categories.

A subsample of 17 records was selected to assess rater reliability. These records give equivalent representation to each classroom and each curriculum area, and were randomly interspersed in the sample. The reliabilities were quite high, ranging from $r = .67$ to $r = .99$, with a median of $r = .97$, indicating good agreement in the application of the system.

CLASSROOM DIFFERENCES

Comparisons of the ratings of the children's *involvement in the work of the classroom* and the *quality of their verbalized thinking* indicated that on these dimensions the classrooms again fall into two pairs: the children at Browning and Adams were rated as considerably less involved and as showing less evidence of verbalized thinking than the children at Dickens and Conrad (see Table 4–5).[10] This is not to say that the children from Browning and Adams were not busy. Their time was certainly filled with activity; in fact, the rapid pace in their classrooms ensured busyness. For

TABLE 4–5

The Children's Cognitive Behavior in the Classroom: Comparative Ratings of Involvement in Work *and* Quality of Verbalized Thinking
(Total $N = 65$ *records)*

Dimension/ Classrooms	N of Records[1]	Mean Rating[2] (Consensus)	Analysis of Variance
Involvement in work of the classroom (1–5)			Between classrooms:
Browning	7	2.86	$F = 22.98**$
Adams	25	2.96	
Dickens	11	4.27	[For B + A versus D + C, $t = 8.15**$]
Conrad	19	4.68	
Total	62		
Quality of verbalized thinking (1–3)			Between classrooms:
Browning	7	1.57	$F = 8.56**$
Adams	25	1.64	
Dickens	10	2.30	[For B + A versus D + C, $t = 4.81**$]
Conrad	12	2.42	
Total	54		

1. *The variation in N's is due to the fact that not all records could be rated on all dimensions.*
2. *Reliability of two judges' ratings was computed by analysis of variance; reliabilities for the two scales are .99 and .97, respectively.*
** $p < .01$

example, when the teacher asked a question there was usually a show of hands, some waving frantically, the children eager to be called on. Often, when called on, a child would have nothing to say or would not know the answer, suggesting more involvement in making contact with the teacher than in the work itself.

Similarly, comparison of the classrooms on some of the contributing categories yielded supporting differences (see Table 4–6). The children's *affective response* was evaluated in terms of whether they seemed to be enjoying the classroom activity or seemed passive or restless. Those at Dickens and Conrad were more often judged to be enjoying the class activity, while children at Browning and Adams were judged as restless and uneasy, or passive ("docile," in Jules Henry's terminology, 1955).

TABLE 4–6

Differences Between the Modern and Traditional School Children's Cognitive Behavior in the Classroom (Total N = 65 records)

Dimension (Interrater Reliability[1])	Classroom Frequencies			Comparisons Between B + A Versus D + C
	Traditional B + A	Modern D + C	N^2	
Involvement in the Work of the Classroom				
Children's Affective Response (.98)				
Enjoyment	6	26		
versus			63	$\chi^2 = 26.81$**
Passivity or restlessness	27	4		
Participation (.67)				
By few, or core group	20	17		
versus			61	NS
By most or all	13	11		
Task-Relatedness (.99)				
Related to task	14	23		
versus			64	$\chi^2 = 6.61$*
Unrelated to task or mixed	19	8		
Quality of Verbalized Thinking				
Opportunity to Express Ideas (.71)				
Ample or limited	18	21		
versus			61	$\chi^2 = 1.93$, NS
None	15	7		

1. *Reliability of three judges' categorizations was computed by means of analysis of variance.*
2. *The variation in N's is due to the fact that not all records could be rated on all dimensions.*
 * $p < .05$
 ** $p < .01$

There were no clear differences in the *breadth of participation* in class activities. There were some activities in which only a few children or a central group of children participated, while the others either listened passively or engaged in other tasks. While the occurrence of multiple simultaneous activities was more characteristic of the modern schools, it was also true that in the discussion, when the total group was presumably working on a problem, there was a central group of contributors and a number of sideline nonparticipators who may or may not have been following the development of the ideas. Although the teachers were observed to make a point of trying to engage these peripheral children, the discussions for the most part were carried on by a central group. The same children did not always play a central role, but there is some evidence that the nonparticipators tended to be the same. This is a problem of the discussion method noted by Friedlander (1965).

The children at Dickens and Conrad were also considered to be engaged in *task-related* activities more often—another aspect of their involvement in the work of the schoolroom.

Perhaps we come closer to clarifying involvement when we see a multiplication lesson at Browning momentarily interrupted by someone who enters the room with a message for the teacher. During the interruption, the children became so restless, inattentive, occupied with what was in their desks, or staring out of the window that the teacher had a difficult time restoring attention. In general it was noted—in these and other observations of the classes—that when the teacher at Browning or Adams was called out of the room, the disruption of work was substantial; some children exchanged answers which they were usually not allowed to do, others wandered. There was horseplay and considerable chatter, the limits set to some extent by the power of the monitor whom the teacher left in charge. The children at Dickens and at Conrad, on the other hand, were much more used to working without continuous teacher supervision. At Conrad especially, the teacher often left for short intervals while the children were working, without making any comment about it. At Dickens, too, the teacher left the room without placing a particular child in charge. The children almost invariably went on with what they were doing, without a discernible rise in noise level or irrelevant behavior. The distinction here is quite simply between extrinsic and intrinsic motivation. In one situation, the children required the uninterrupted presence of the teacher because their dependence was upon her, they related to the work only through her, and it was assumed that only she could give meaning to it. In the other situation, the relationship between the children and the work of the classroom was direct. The teacher was a facilitating agent in that relationship, which was not destroyed when she was temporarily absent.

Comparison of the *quality of verbalized thinking* (the second major dimension) indicated that the children in the more traditional classrooms showed less evidence of relationship thinking than those in the modern classrooms. The quality of the children's thinking was also evaluated on the basis of the relevance and coherence of their statements in class and the amount of opportunity they were given to express ideas.

There were no differences among the classrooms in the relevance or coherence of the children's statements; and there was no statistical difference in the judgment of the amount of opportunity the children were offered to express ideas. The latter finding reflects the fact that children in all classrooms had about the same amount of opportunity to express their ideas, though there was considerable difference in the opportunity for *sustained* discussion and elaboration of ideas.

The fact that almost all the children's statements in all the classrooms were judged as relevant and coherent testifies to the businesslike atmosphere of these schoolrooms. The children's statements were almost invariably pertinent to the task at hand and intelligible to the other children as well as to the teacher and the observers.

In assessing the children's thinking, a broad view was taken of relevant content. The raters took into account instances where the children made pertinent observations, asked thoughtful questions, introduced ideas, attempted to make generalizations, as well as when they were working on problems.

As an example of children actively engaged in thinking through a problem, the record of the Dickens children seeing the relations underlying multiplication comes to mind. Or, consider the following excerpt of a discussion at Conrad. The children had been studying the westward movement in the United States. One of their books concerned a fictitious family named Burd:

T: What were the three reasons the Burd Family moved to Ohio?

SALLY: Because of the Indians?

CHILDREN: What? Indians? What did you say?

T: You mean the danger of Indians is their reason for going West? Do you think a family would move West for the reason that there were Indians?

SALLY: No.

ROGER (raising his hand): The land was cheaper. There were too many taxes in the East.

T: That's right. Anyone know the third reason?

CARL: It was too expensive to live.

T: Yes, that's the third reason.

JESS: There was a lot of land for farming.

T: That's what Roger meant. . . . What are taxes?

MEG: You pay them to live.

T: How? (Children seem puzzled.) What kind of taxes are there in the city, Lillian?

LILLIAN: It's like apartment building taxes—you pay them to live there. You pay to use the telephone.

T: Is that what taxes are? (No one answers.) That's rent, not taxes. What's the difference between rent and taxes?

CARL: You pay to build a house. It's hard to explain.

T: Do you pay a tax to build? Not exactly. You pay money for the property. When do you pay the tax, Carl?

CARL: There are taxes after you live there. You pay money to the government.

TOMMY: When you buy in a store, you pay a city tax. Tax goes through the people in the front of the business.

T: Yes, that's right. The owners collect the taxes.

SANDY: Everyone pays taxes. When you buy candy. . . .

SEVERAL CHILDREN (interrupting): Not always, no, not for everything.

T: What kind of candy don't you pay taxes for?

More discussion of sales taxes. T asks if there are taxes on supplies for the store. . . .

SANDY: If you make over $600 you pay taxes.

T: Yes. That's called an income tax. You pay the government so many dollars for all the money you earn over $600 a year.

MARY: Who is Uncle Sam?

T: Do you know what a cartoon is?

Children all say yes and nod their heads. All begin talking at once about Uncle Sam, his clothes, what he looks like, the colors in his clothes.

ONE BOY (calls out): Where did he come from?

ANOTHER: Why was he called Uncle Sam?

MARY: He's like the mystical (sic) uncle in our story.

T: What is a mythical uncle?

CAROLINE: It's one you've never seen, only heard about—you know, like letters and talking.

This discussion moved from child to child, from children to teacher and back again. The teacher guided the discussion, giving the children the facts necessary to keep the thinking active. The children grappled with the part that taxes may have played in the westward migration in early American history by bringing out their own information (and confusions) about taxes today.

There is no question that this record would serve equally well in the previous section as an illustration of the way this modern school teacher created an environment conducive to the development of ideas. In this environment, the children were coping with ideas and symbols, one child even making the connection between ". . . the symbolism inherent in the

Uncle Sam figure and the intrinsic symbolism of spoken and written language. . . ." (See Biber, 1959, p. 285.)

The children at Browning and Adams did not have the opportunity to engage in sustained discussion though they did discuss what topics to take up in debate time, and they discussed news items and gave reports on current events or books they had read. The required form, however, often gave them little chance for anything but declarative statements of fact. The reports were sufficiently alike to appear to have been based on identical sources. Two written reports from the Adams classroom on the topic of games, at the time when America was a Dutch colony, illustrate this point:

> Bowling was a favorite game of the Dutch. It was played on level grass. They used a number of hard balls which they rolled on the grass and tried to knock down some wooden blocks or pins. Bowling Green in New York City is one of the spots where this game was played.
>
> The most popular game was bowling. It was played on what the English call a green. Where the Dutch played now stands Bowling Green Park.

In general, the children from the traditional schools seemed extremely competent in dealing with the subject matter they were given. But many hours of recorded observation gave little indication of their ability to develop ideas; there was more stress on remembering, recognizing, and identifying.

Aspects of Interpersonal Relations in the Classroom

The classroom, especially the self-contained classroom of the public schools, can be viewed as a closed social system in which the quality of interpersonal relations will depend on the climate the teacher creates and the predisposition and expectations of the children. Many studies of classroom interaction have dealt with the effects of single variables, such as the characteristics of the teacher or the children, or with more complex dimensions, such as the patterns of social interaction and communication, or the social structure of the classroom. Recently, a more dynamic view of classroom processes has been urged; Getzels and Thelen (1960), for instance, describe the classroom as a social "system in motion, or, if you will, in dynamic disequilibrium." Recent reviews of the literature (see Withall and Lewis, 1963; Glidewell, Kantor, Smith, and Stringer, 1966) suggest that adequate characterization of the complexities of the classroom will require more comprehensive theoretical formulation and supporting data than are at present available. The analysis presented here deals with only a limited aspect of interpersonal relations in the classroom—the kind and frequency of contacts between teacher and children and among the children.

No formal hypotheses were made about these data, although the quality of interpersonal relations was expected to vary with the modern or traditional character of the classroom. We have already seen that certain types of teacher behavior are more likely to occur in the modern classroom, others in the traditional classroom. In the preceding analyses, the focus was on the teacher's approach to her central task—the teaching of substantive material to the children—and on characteristics of the children's responses. Here the focus is on details of the transactions between teacher and children and among the children. There is some overlap with the analyses of cognition but the approaches are different.

DATA AND METHOD OF ANALYSIS

A sample of 49 observational records of class group activity, representing all classrooms, observers, and curriculum areas, was selected for this analysis. The sample included 30 observations of academic periods (language arts, social studies and arithmetic), and 19 nonacademic periods (arts and crafts, plays, gym). The distribution of records by classroom, type of activity, and amount of time is seen in Table 4–7.

TABLE 4–7

Distribution of Sample of 49 Records by
Classroom, Type of Class Activity, and Time

Type of Class Activity	Classrooms						
	B	A	(B + A)	D	C	(D + C)	Total
Academic	6	10	(16)	7	7	(14)	30
Nonacademic	2	6	(8)	3	8	(11)	19
Total	8	16	(24)	10	15	(25)	49
Time Covered (hours and minutes)	4′ 35″	9′ 35″	(14′ 10″)	4′ 20″	9′ 05″	(13′ 25″)	27′ 35″

The analysis of interrelations among people required an estimate of the frequency of interchange, identification of the person who initiated contact, and a description of the interchange. An entire record was therefore no longer useful as the unit to be analyzed; instead, an interpersonal incident was chosen as the unit of analysis. An interpersonal incident was defined as any social contact or exchange that took place between teacher and child (or children), child and teacher, or child and child. The exchange might consist of one contact and a single response or it might be a sustained interaction, as for example:

[News reports are being discussed.]

MELISSA: Yesterday President Eisenhower had a heart attack.

T: He had a stroke.

M: The paper said that he had a heart attack.

T: What paper did you read it in?

M: . . . not sure . . . think it was the *Times*.

T: Go down to Miss _____ room [another teacher] and ask her if you can borrow this morning's paper. Then you can show us where it said "heart attack."

Any interpersonal contact which dealt exclusively with academic or management procedure or routine was excluded from the analysis, as for example:

The teacher is working on phonics with a group of children. She asks for words that begin with *ch*, then for words that end with *ch*. The children raise hands and give appropriate words.

The interpersonal incidents were first identified in each record and then coded into the following categories:

1. *Initiation of contact:* teacher or child
2. *Direction of contact:* to teacher, to child, or other (e.g., observer, visitor)
3. *Manifest affect:* friendly, neutral, hostile
4. *Task-orientation:* task-oriented, mixed, personal and/or social

The records were analyzed by one coder, whose judgments were checked by a second. A subsample of 23 records, representing all the classroom and curriculum areas, was selected to check the main coder's judgments. Four records were independently rejected by both coders as containing no interpersonal incidents as defined, thus reducing the sample to 19 records. The two coders differed somewhat in their identification of incidents but 103 incidents were identified by both. In their subsequent categorizing of these 103 agreed-upon incidents, the two coders assigned them to identical categories 81 percent of the time.[11]

A check by inspection showed that there was no systematic tendency to identify more or fewer interpersonal incidents in either the modern or traditional settings. The main coder, therefore, continued to code the records.

CLASSROOM DIFFERENCES

Although the sets of records from the pairs of traditional and modern schoolrooms were balanced for several variables, there could be no assurance that a comparable number of interpersonal incidents would be identified in the two sets. By chance, however, the number of incidents identified in the two pairs of classrooms was almost identical: 117 in Browning and Adams, 120 in Dickens and Conrad.

The comparisons revealed the following clear trends (see Table 4–8):[12]

1. *Initiation of contact:* (a) The ratio of contacts initiated by the teacher and children in the traditional and modern classrooms is quite dissimilar; at Dickens and Conrad, interpersonal contacts were for the most part initiated by the children, while at Browning and Adams they were initiated almost equally by teachers and children; (b) in all classrooms, most contacts initiated by children were directed to another child or other children.

2. *Affect:* (a) The manifest affect of the teacher's communications in the modern classrooms was coded as predominantly friendly or neutral, while in the traditional classrooms the teacher's communications were equally divided between friendly and hostile exchanges; (b) in all classrooms, the child was almost invariably categorized as friendly or neutral, whether he was initiating contact with or responding to the teacher; (c) in all classrooms, when the child initiated contact with or responded to another child, he was usually friendly or neutral (though not quite so consistently as when relating to the teacher).

3. *Task orientation:* (a) Exchanges initiated by the teacher at Dickens and Conrad were predominantly task-oriented, while at Browning and Adams they were equally task- or personally-oriented; (b) exchanges initiated by the children at Dickens and Conrad tended to be task-oriented, while at Browning and Adams they were more likely to be personal and social.

In the traditional schools, teachers and children initiated an almost equal number of interpersonal contacts, while in the modern schools, children initiated many more contacts than did the teachers. This is consonant with the qualitative differences in classroom structure described in the previous sections. Some of the child-initiated exchanges in the Dickens and Conrad classrooms probably originated from the teacher, but a larger number of child-initiated and child-directed responses intervened between the original, teacher-initiated contact and its eventual response. In the traditional school classroom, the more typical pattern was a teacher-child/child-teacher exchange; in the modern school classroom, the teacher's general orientation encouraged a teacher-child/child-child/child-teacher pattern. In general, then, there was more child-initiated communication at Dickens and Conrad than at Browning and Adams, and most of these exchanges occurred within the child group.

The judgments of the teacher's manifest affect indicated that the teachers at Browning and Adams frequently expressed themselves in a hostile way.[13] The teacher comments categorized as hostile often included sarcastic or derogatory remarks. For example:

> A boy goes up to the teacher's desk to tell her something and returns slowly to his desk. The teacher says, "Gary, I wish you'd move as if you were flesh and blood. What's the matter with you?"

The teachers at Adams and Browning also ridiculed a child for inadequate performance more often than the modern school teachers. For example:

> The teacher has asked the children to explain the errors they made in an arithmetic lesson. Jack explains his error, which was merely carelessness. The teacher twists her hands in front of her and says to the group, "What do we do?" The children respond, "Break his neck."

The technique of pitting the children against one another did not appear in the records of interactions in the Dickens and Conrad classrooms.

The children were consistently neutral or friendly in their contacts with the teacher, which may have been simply a reflection of their well-behaved middle-class status as children in schools where respect for social conventions is an established fact. In all the classrooms, communication among the children tended to be friendly or neutral and eruptions were rare.

Another aspect of the quality of relations in the classroom, and one which is central to the character of the classroom as a setting for learning, is the extent to which the interpersonal exchanges were relevant to the task at hand. Comments of both teachers and children in the modern schools tended to be task-oriented.[14] As demonstrated, the children in the modern schools had more opportunity to talk among themselves, and to the teacher, than did those in the more traditional schoolrooms. The bulk of this talk was centered on the work, consisting of comments and exchanges about what they were doing, as the following excerpt from a science period at Conrad illustrates:

> Michael stops by Margery's and Lola's desk. Picks up a pipette and dips it into the beaker of liquid used by the girls for graphite mixture. He is trying to show the two girls how liquid can be drawn into the pipette by first inserting it into the liquid, holding one end closed so that the liquid will stay in the pipette.
>
> MARGERY (watches him with interest): How much can you get into it?
> MICHAEL: No more than the height of the liquid in the beaker; it finds the level of the water.
> JOHN: If you suck you can get more in it.
> MICHAEL: It's air suction.
> MARGERY (continuing to roll the graphite): It's hard to get the clay together.

TABLE 4-8

Analysis of Interpersonal Incidents in the Classrooms

Interpersonal Incidents	Classroom Frequencies						Total[1]	Comparisons Between B + A versus D + C
	Traditional			Modern				
	B	A	(B + A)	D	C	(D + C)		
# Interpersonal Incidents	41	76	117	43	77	120	237	
Initiation of Contacts								
Teacher	20	40	60	17	14	31	91	D + C: Ch > T
Child	21	36	57	26	63	89	146	$\chi^2 = 16.22$**
Direction of Child-Initiated Contacts								
To teacher	3	12	15	7	22	29	44	D + C: Ch-Ch > Ch-T
To child(ren)	10	15	25	19	37	56	81	or Ch-Ad
(To other adults)	8	9	17	0	4	4	21	$\chi^2 = 18.23$**
Manifest Affect								
TEACHER TO CHILD								
Friendly or neutral	8	18	26	10	13	23	49	B + A: Fr = H;
Hostile	11	18	29	2	0	2	31	D + C: Fr > H
								$\chi^2 = 12.66$**
CHILD TO TEACHER								
Friendly or neutral	1	9	10	6	20	26	36	NS
Hostile	1	1	2	0	1	1	3	
CHILD TO CHILD								
Friendly or neutral	3	11	14	14	30	44	58	NS
Hostile	3	3	6	1	4	5	11	
Task Orientation								
TEACHER-INITIATED								
Task-Oriented	4	13	17	8	13	21	38	B + A: T = M = P;
Mixed	6	14	20	5	0	5	25	D + C: T > M, P
Personal/social	9	13	22	3	1	4	26	$\chi^2 = 13.98$**

	Classroom Frequencies							
Interpersonal Incidents	Traditional			Modern			Total[1]	Comparisons Between B + A versus D + C
	B	A	(B + A)	D	C	(D + C)		
CHILD-INITIATED								B + A: P > T, M;
Task-Oriented	5	12	17	16	29	45	62	D + C: T > P, M
Mixed	1	2	3	1	8	9	12	$\chi^2 = 10.6$**
Personal/Social	12	18	30	7	18	25	55	

1. Variation in N's is due to the fact that not all incidents could be coded for each category.

** $p < .01$

MICHAEL (examining the beaker of liquid): Interesting thing about
this beaker . . . silver in the water. It's oxygen.

MARGERY: It's not silver. It's the graphite.

MICHAEL (holding pipette up, examining it): See, it's inside the tube.
Oxygen turned to silver.

The children at Browning and Adams also talked about the task at hand
but more of their exchanges with other children and the teacher were
personal or social.

We should remember that work was defined differently in the modern
and traditional classrooms. As we have seen, the modern schoolrooms encompassed a broader range of topics and a greater variety of activities,
giving the children a wider field of school-related activities in which to
operate. The work life of the children in the traditional schoolrooms was
more circumscribed; perhaps it was partly because their field was so much
narrower that they left it more often.

Summary and Discussion

The teaching performance of these fourth-grade teachers was judged to
be congruent with that of other teachers in the school. This is important
since, although the children were considered to reflect the cumulative impact of their experience in school, if their teacher at the time of the study
had not been representative, the influence of school experience would
have been more difficult to trace.

Informal characterization of the classroom teachers showed that, in
spite of differences in personality, each teacher's way of teaching reflected
her basic alignment with the modern or traditional mode. The modern-
traditional frame of reference was also apparent in the ways the teachers
arranged the furniture and equipment in their classrooms and in the kinds
of educational and decorative material they considered appropriate for
display.

Three analyses of classroom behavior have been described. The first is
an analysis of the way the teacher organized the children's learning situation, the second, of the children's cognitive functioning and observed
thinking processes, and the third, of aspects of the way teacher and children related to each other.

The teachers varied considerably in the way they organized the children's learning experiences. The modern, more than the traditional, school teachers encouraged the children to think relationally, to make connections among facts and ideas, to "go beyond the information given." Similarly, the traditional school teachers offered less leeway than the modern school teachers for the children to explore and work out ideas on their own.

The children, for their part, differed in their involvement in the ongoing work of the classroom. At Browning and Adams, they were very busy and not at a loss for things to do but were judged to be less directly involved in the work and motivated more by extrinsic demands; the children at Dickens and Conrad, on the other hand, were seen as intrinsically more involved in the work itself. Furthermore, in the modern schools, the children gave more evidence of relationship thinking and the ability to generalize, while in the traditional classrooms, the children's verbal expression was more often restricted to memorization and recitation.

Interaction between teachers and children and among the children differed substantially in the modern and the traditional classrooms. At Dickens and Conrad, contacts between teachers and children were, for the most part, initiated by children, while at Browning and Adams, they were initiated more or less equally by teachers and children. The teachers in the traditional schools more often than those in the modern schools made hostile remarks to the children. Children's contacts with the teacher or with other children were primarily friendly or neutral in all classrooms.

As might be expected, there was considerably more interaction among children in the modern than in the traditional schools. In the modern classrooms, these interactions mostly concerned the work at hand, while those at Browning and Adams were more likely to be about personal or social matters.

The consistency of these findings is paralleled in other research. While the generic terms applied to the analysis of teaching may differ from study to study—dominative versus integrative, authoritarian versus democratic, direct versus indirect, traditional versus modern—there is sufficient overlap in these concepts to make comparisons useful. The striking thing about these studies is that the traditional teacher seems to predominate in the study samples and is similarly characterized from study to study. In Anderson's early study (1939) of kindergarten teachers, over 59 percent of the teachers' time was spent in "Dominative" acts. Twenty years later, Marie Hughes and her associates (1959), in a study of 41 elementary school teachers, report that over 40 percent of teaching acts were coded as "Controlling" and "Directive." When Controlling acts were added to those involving Imposition and Negative Affectivity, 80 percent of the teachers were characterized as Dominative in over half the total number of teaching acts in the classroom. Furthermore, many limits were placed on the children's independent pursuit of ideas: most of the teachers spent less than 20 percent of their teaching "functions" on developing content introduced by a child, elaborating a response, or inviting the children to think in complex rather than simple terms.

Perkins (1964), in summarizing his study of 14 fifth-grade teachers, notes:

> . . . the extensive use of seat work (75 per cent of the time) and the infrequent use of discussion (5.5 per cent), individual work, group work, and oral reports . . . the low incidence of praise (1 per cent), asking "thinking" questions (1 per cent), and using pupil's answer or idea (4 per cent). [p. 256]

Perkins put the teachers in his study together with Hughes' elementary school teachers and Flanders' (1960) seventh- and eighth-grade teachers and, on the basis of the categories common to all three studies, he compared the amount of time the teachers spent in different kinds of teaching behavior. Though necessarily crude, his comparison shows many similarities among the three groups of teachers.

Although teaching performance was not subjected to a time analysis in this study, the Browning and Adams teachers conformed to the general picture that these researchers have drawn.[15] It was only in the Browning and Adams classrooms, moreover, that the shaming techniques and training in docility, described by Jules Henry (1955; 1957), were observed. Henry's indictment of the elementary school focuses on the way the teacher gets the children to give the responses she wants, encouraging docility of thought as well as behavior. Henry shows how the development of critical skills becomes a travesty, an exercise in destructive comment on the work of one's peers, with the teacher pitting the children against each other to win her favor. The Dickens and Conrad teachers did not use these techniques; while they may have had their counterparts in some of these studies, they are definitely overshadowed by a majority which is much more traditional in outlook and practice.

The consistency of teaching behavior shown in other studies is corroborated in the present analysis. The ways in which the teachers engaged the children in learning and interacted with them in the classroom were coherent and distinctly different. It was assumed, and confirmed by the findings, that this consistency is due to the fact that the teachers operated on the basis of principles—their conception of the teacher's function—and taught in the way that they believed would best bring the children's learning to a maximum. It is unlikely that the consistency of this behavior was due to chance and that these teachers were selecting approaches blindly. The differences between the modern and traditional classroom teachers were reflected with equal consistency in the responses of the children.

While halo effect may have been operating here, a more plausible explanation is that the climate the teacher created would be the framework of the children's response. Children quickly learn what is and what is not permissible, and Jules Henry's observations of this phenomenon have recently been extended by Leacock (1969) in her study of second- and fifth-grade urban classrooms.

In their intellectual and social behavior, the children in these classrooms were constrained or encouraged by the teacher. Together they created a distinctive style of classroom life which reflected the dominant educational outlook of the school as a whole.

NOTES

1. Only the Conrad teacher participated for the full observation period. The Browning teacher joined with other teachers at Browning in asking that classroom observations be ended after the first year. Dickens was added to the sample only in the second year. At Adams, the principal shifted the first teacher in the study to another grade level and another fourth-grade teacher agreed to participate for the second year.
2. See Gussow (1964) for a discussion of the dynamics of the observational process and the relationship between the observer and the observed.

   The problems and processes he describes could apply equally to narrative and precoded recordings, though in the latter method observer reaction and bias are embedded in what purports to be an objective system.
3. The public address system was used by the principal for sundry announcements and some broadcasts of educational material.
4. The ratings, incidentally, offered an opportunity to check on the similarity between the two Adams teachers. In effect, on only three dimensions were the ratings more than one scale point apart.
5. Ratings of the different classrooms were compared by means of analysis of variance, and category judgments by chi-square technique except for those cases in which the data did not meet the requirements for chi square, when Fisher's test of exact probabilities was used. The latter, it should be noted, is a one-tailed test (McNemar, 1962).
6. See Appendix B for detailed schema.
7. See Appendix B for detailed schema.
8. Two records were eliminated (one from Adams, one from Dickens), reducing the total number of records to 65 (see Table 4–2, for distribution).
9. See Appendix C for detailed schema.
10. As in the previous analysis, ratings were compared by means of analysis of variance, categorizations by chi-square technique.
11. Where there was disagreement between two coders on these 19 records, the coding was adjusted to take both judgments into account.

12. Statistical comparisons were based on the combined frequencies for the two traditional classrooms, Browning and Adams, and for the two modern classrooms, Dickens and Conrad. In general, comparisons were based on chi-square technique, except in one instance when chi square was not appropriate and Fisher's exact test of probabilities was used (McNemar, 1962).

13. Hughes (1959), by contrast, in her study of teaching patterns, found that, while teachers in general make many negative remarks to the children in their classes, positive remarks outweigh negative ones in the long run. In the present analysis, comments relating exclusively to instruction were not coded, thus eliminating many of the teachers' communications of factual or management matters, for example, "Now we'll do spelling," "Open your books to page —," which tend to be neutral in tone. Had they been included, the teacher's remarks would have been predominantly neutral or positive, concurring with Hughes' general conclusions; however, the proportion of hostile comments would still have been greater in the traditional than in the modern classrooms.

14. This finding corroborates the greater task-relatedness of the children from Conrad and Dickens, found in the analysis of cognitive responses (see discussion on children's cognitive behavior, pp. 115–121).

15. The ritual and trivia that Hughes brings out, for example, accompanied much of the learning in Browning and Adams, where great pains were taken with the ritual that surrounds the writing down of things (arithmetic problems, spelling words, and such). Each child had to write his name, school, date, and class in specific places at the top of the page. The paper had to be folded in half, lengthwise, each work item numbered, and care had to be given to penmanship. ("Oh," said Angela toward the end of an arithmetic lesson at Adams, "I've just done a horrible thing. I wrote the numbers in the wrong place.") In contrast, the child's name and the date were considered sufficient at Conrad. The fact that the Dickens teacher also made few such requirements indicates that this ritual is not a necessity in public schools.

CHAPTER

5

THE FAMILIES

In this study, with its central focus on schooling, the analysis of family life is necessarily secondary, although the primary role of parental influence in shaping child behavior cannot be minimized. Here, however, the study of parental variables has been seen as complementary to and as an essential step in the delineation of school influence.

We could not study the families with the same scope and intensity as the schools. A comparable highlighting of the family would have involved home visits and multiple interviews. The methods used here were necessarily more limited, but they made it possible to select children for study whose families were of comparable socio-economic status and to assess aspects of the families' attitudes to the rearing and development of their children and of the relationship between parent and child.

The parents of the children in the study were in their thirties and forties.[1] Born in the first quarter of the century, many had participated in the Second World War, marrying and raising their families in the immediate postwar period. Almost all had attended college and many of the fathers, in particular, had had advanced professional training. They were generally established, successful people, working in high-status, well-paying occupations. They were raising relatively small families, usually of two or three children, and were offering these children privileged, stable life environments.[2] They lived in urban neighborhoods, where they had usually been living through the lifetime of the nine-year-old child under study. With their children now in the middle childhood years, they were providing a multitude of experiences for them, including both informal family excursions and more formally scheduled extracurricular lessons. Most of the children had a busy schedule of lessons in art, music, dance, or religious instruction—a function of the parents' interest in providing opportunities over a broad spectrum and of their ability to organize and support the development of special skills.

An intelligent and educated group, these parents were in a position to make conscious decisions about the nature of family life and the rearing of their children; they were interested in their role as parents and prepared to seek and use advice. In this, they were subject to the shifting emphases that had characterized advice to parents over the preceding decades, from the Watsonian rigidities—by which some of these parents were themselves brought up—through various versions of permissiveness to an approach that was more balanced and psychologically sophisticated (compare Wolfenstein, 1953). By the time of the study, sources and streams of advice to parents were myriad and sometimes confusing; the syndrome of both the knowledgeable and the "guilty" or puzzled parent was more than familiar. Many of the parents felt some uncertainty about their ways of rearing their children—perhaps an inevitable by-product in an era that focused on the child, stressed the importance of the early years and relationships, but left the parent to resolve the many complexities that conflicting ideas, his own life history, and his daily experience as a parent might bring.

It should be noted, however, that the parents of the children in the study differed among themselves in their awareness of these larger social trends and in their reactions to them. The resultant differences in child-rearing philosophy and enactment are of central importance in understanding the study's findings.

This chapter will present the dimensions studied, the methods of collecting and analyzing the data, the characteristics of the parents, and the particular qualities of the four groups of parents whose children attended each of the four schools.

Method

Dimensions of Study

The study of the families was focused primarily on psychological dimensions—on parental ideology with respect to child rearing and education and on the mother-child relationship as it might be expected to affect child personality and behavior. Two considerations guided the organization and analysis of the parent data. First, while we could not hope to encompass the span of meaningful parent behavior without more intensive study, it was essential to assess dimensions of the parent-child relationship that could be assumed to bear on those aspects of the children's functioning to be tested. Second, it seemed important to structure the study of the parents in terms comparable to those used in the study of the schools. Consequently, the concept of modern-traditional orientation was applied to the analysis of the parents as well as the schools. It obviously encompasses some important aspects of parent attitudes and behavior; at the same time, it provides dimensions and a framework parallel to those considered salient for the schools.

Modern and traditional modes of child rearing were organized in terms of four governing value hierarchies and conceptions of parental role, in each of which the modern and traditional orientation are characteristically different: (1) view of the authority role, (2) emphases in the socialization process, (3) ways of understanding the growth process, and (4) evaluation of child achievement and behavior. A full statement of these concepts appears in Appendix D. This statement served as the conceptual framework guiding the construction of the parent instruments (questionnaire and interview).

The traditional parent was seen as one who places greatest value on the child's adaptation to society's demands. He sees the child's behavior and achievement in terms of this goal. He considers it his right and responsibility to train his child directly to meet standards and to behave in socially acceptable ways. The modern parent was seen as one who places greater value on a balance between the child's capacities, impulses, unique rate of development, on the one hand, and the requirements of socialization, on the other. He considers it his responsibility to facilitate the process of individual growth, fulfillment, and adaptation through means that are flexible and functional, allowing the child's own modes of resolution to develop and take over as he increases in maturity.

It is obvious that in the primary and deeply affective relationship of parent and child, aspects beyond the parent's ideology or his enactment of his child-rearing philosophy are important and influence the child's development. Such aspects could not be observed and evaluated in any comprehensive way, but the mother's feelings about her child and an evaluation of the consistency and integration with which she carried her role as a mother were included. They are not identified with either the modern or traditional stance.[3]

In general, the structure and conception brought to the study of the parents depart somewhat from prevailing approaches. Most investigators in recent years have attempted to understand parent behavior along two axes: (1) the parent's affective or emotional reaction to children—warmth, acceptance or rejection, love or hostility; and (2) the parent's techniques of socialization and control—"love-oriented" or "psychological" techniques versus authoritarian, power-oriented, direct, or restrictive techniques (see Becker, 1964; Schaefer, 1959; 1961). This study belongs with those that have probed the second axis. We have dealt primarily with the parent's style of socialization, with little emphasis on affect per se. But although the study can be placed within this framework, the question of socialization style is posed somewhat differently from most investigations.

In most studies of parent attitude and behavior, the goal of socializing the child toward general standards is taken as a given and the stress is on evaluating different procedures for achieving this goal. Parents who use direct, authoritarian, and object-oriented techniques are contrasted with those who use psychological or "love-oriented" techniques. But the basic question posed, usually, is whether removal of love, production of guilt, or the use of rational explanation is more *effective* than power, punishment, or strict rules in teaching the child to adopt behavior that is socially conforming and/or acceptable to the parents.

This study takes a different perspective. Modern parents are seen as differing from the traditional parents not only in the techniques they use but in the very goals of what they hope to accomplish with their children. For those parents attuned to complex dimensions of personality development and the corollary concept of psychological maturity, there is an attempt to foster in the child a growing sense of self-definition, development of inner resources, and a set of standards that have personal meaning. While such parents also monitor child behavior toward socially acceptable forms, their view of child rearing gives central emphasis to the child's needs and abilities as he develops. The traditional parents may be as benign and loving but they have different goals, a different concept of maturity, a different hierarchy of values, and consequently, different ways of handling the incidents of daily life. What has been called "love-oriented" or psychological in other studies might sometimes be labeled traditional by the conception presented here, particularly if it depends on a constant, albeit gentle, coercion toward impersonal behavioral standards. The modern orientation also uses the psychological approach but its techniques for control, discipline, and socialization serve to teach the child more than conformity; they are geared to foster the child's own strength and his capacity to resolve situations by means of principles and resources of his own.

While this conceptual framework for studying parents is relatively different, it is not unique. In recent years, two other studies have highlighted similar aspects of the parent role. Loevinger and Sweet (1961) formulated a composite called "authoritarian family organization," in which they included: (1) hierarchical family organization; (2) inability to conceptualize inner life, both one's own and that of others; and (3) emphasis on external as opposed to internal controls. Hoffman and Saltzstein (1964) appear particularly similar in their ways of differentiating parental style. They were searching for parental child-rearing antecedents of moral development. They focused on different kinds of internalized conscience—humanistic, flexible, and well integrated versus conventional, rigid, presumably based on repression—and they attempted to conceptualize the kind of parental patterns that might foster an integrated, humanistic conscience. They describe their conception of patterns that

> . . . minimize frustration and thus the accumulation of pent up impulses; . . . that introduce limits firmly but gradually, in line with the child's increasing ability to understand them and control his behavior, and accompanied by explanations and substitute outlets where possible; . . . that capitalize on the child's potential for empathy by indicating similarities in the way the child reacts to situations and the way that others react; . . . by fostering development of an ego ideal based on identification, the motive for which is not anxiety over loss of love but something more positive, such as personal love and respect for the parent or the desire to possess the parent's capacity for need gratification. . . . [p. 65]

These formulations, in common with the modern-traditional distinction used in this study, attempt to differentiate among benign parental approaches, separating those which teach general behavioral standards from those which view the child as a complex individual in whom internal processes are developing which become increasingly accessible to him as he grows. It has been our assumption that such distinctions may have profound and subtle influence on the course of child development. We attempted, therefore, to study the parents in these terms, though within the limits set by the secondary role of the parent data in the total economy of the study.

Data Collection

CONTACTS WITH THE PARENTS

The first contact with the parents took place at a meeting called by the principal of each school at the beginning of the school year. The project was described and the parents were acquainted in general terms with the content of sessions to be held with the children. After an open discussion, the parents were asked to consider voluntary participation in the project. During this meeting, the parents answered the Parent Attitude Questionnaire (described below). Of the 199 parents who attended these meetings and filled out questionnaires, 82 percent agreed to participate, but because some families or children did not meet some of the selection criteria, the number of families who actually took part in the project was further reduced.

During the course of the school year, interviews were conducted with the mothers of children included in the study.[4] These interviews were held in the school building during school hours, unless this was inconvenient for the mother, and were usually from one and a half to two hours long.

It is particularly regrettable that there was no contact with the fathers, beyond their attendance at the original meeting, and no direct means of estimating their attitudes and roles as these influenced the personality development of their children. A growing body of literature and research attests to the changing and more interactive role of the father in the life of the child. Whereas, previously, the tendency had been to neglect or ignore the role of the father, current opinion is that the attitudes and relationships of the father deserve systematic study (see Nash, 1965). Beyond this, recent developments in the study of families, a rapidly growing field, suggests that many aspects of family structure and interaction can best be understood through contact with the family as a total unit (Ackerman, 1958; Bell and Vogel, 1960; Minuchin, Montalvo, Guerney, Rosman, and Schumer, 1967; Parsons and Bales, 1955). The practical limits of the research made such study impossible, however. The trends and relationships described are to be understood as maternal rather than parental, therefore, except where the mother could act as a clearly reliable source for factual material concerning both parents or the family as a whole.

TECHNIQUES

The construction of the questionnaire was based on the descriptions of modern and traditional child-rearing ideologies referred to earlier (see Appendix D). The questionnaire consists of two sections (see Appendix

E). The first section covers facts about the family's background and socio-economic level, the pattern of family life, and aspects of the child's developmental history. The second and longer section contains 50 questions about attitudes to child rearing and the purpose of education. Parents were asked, for instance, whether they agreed or disagreed with such statements as the following: "The best reward for parents' efforts is the gratitude of their children"; or "It is better for a child to live up to his own standards of right and wrong, even if immature, than to live completely by his parents' more mature standards." The questions required different response forms—agree/disagree, multiple choice, ranking—all relevant to ascertaining positions on the modern-traditional dimension.

The interview with mothers of the children in the study followed a prepared guide (see Appendix F), but was not tightly structured and was informal in tone. It covered a variety of topics, including the mother's perception of her child, the things about the child that caused tension and pleasure, her views and practices concerning punishment and control, her feelings about being a mother, and so on. The interview was machine-recorded with the mother's knowledge and usually lasted, as noted, from one and a half to two hours.

Data Analysis

The questionnaire and interview were analyzed according to three areas: (A) Modern-Traditional Orientation; (B) Maternal Satisfaction and Role Coherence; and (C) Socio-Economic Level. The component dimensions of each of these areas are defined below.

A. *Modern-Traditional Orientation*
1. *Modern-Traditional Ideology:* The extent to which the mother's view of the socialization process, the authority role, the meaning of behavior, and the nature of pertinent standards reflects a modern or traditional ideology, as defined in this study (questionnaire and interview).
2. *Enactment of Authority Role:* The quality of authority enactment, in terms of the compliance expected from children, the tendency to explain rules and restrictions, the maintenance or relaxation of adult-child distance, and the use of punitive methods of control (interview).
3. *Standards of Behavior and Achievement:* The nature of standards, in terms of the tolerance for impulse fulfillment, the extent to which motivational and situational factors enter into evaluation, and the emphasis placed on meeting standards of behavior and achievement (interview).
4. *Encouragement of Individual Interests:* The mother's attitude and

relationship to the child's individual interests and to the initiation of his leisure time activities (interview).

Composite Rating: Modern-Traditional Orientation (MTO): This score was based on the four dimensions described above and includes both child-rearing attitudes and practices.

B. *Maternal Satisfaction and Role Coherence*

1. *Satisfaction with Child:* The degree and quality of mother's satisfaction with the child, as expressed through her affect and emphasis in discussing the child's positive and negative characteristics (interview).

2. *Integration of Mother Role:* The mother's comfort with and resolution of her role, in terms of her confidence, her enjoyment, her success in her own terms, and the centrality and resolution of this role vis-à-vis conflicting demands (interview).

3. *Consistency of Child Rearing:* The extent to which the mother's viewpoints and practices are consistent with each other, in terms of various components and over periods of time in the child's life (interview).

Composite Rating: Maternal Satisfaction and Role Coherence: This score was based on the three dimensions described above.

C. *Socio-Economic Level*

Socio-Economic-Cultural Index (SEC): A composite index of the family's socio-economic level, based on income, parents' education, and the status of their occupations (questionnaire).

SCORING AND RATING PROCEDURES

The questionnaire was scored for two dimensions: Modern-Traditional Ideology and Socio-Economic Level. The Socio-Economic-Cultural Index (SEC) gives equal weight to parental education, occupational status, and family income on a six-point scale. Separate scores on each of these factors were summed to yield an index of socio-economic-cultural level for each family (see Appendix G for scale-point criteria). Modern-Traditional Ideology was scored on the basis of the precoded meaning of response choices. The theoretical range of questionnaire scores is 0–120, the higher scores representing the more modern ideology.

Interviews were rated for the seven dimensions of attitude, relationship, and role, defined under Modern-Traditional Orientation and Maternal Satisfaction and Role Coherence above. The three interviewers helped to systematize the rating schema, but only two of them rated the interviews. Each rater analyzed the transcripts of her own interviews; the remaining interviews (22) were divided between them.

No effort was made to mask the interview transcripts. Selection of the interviewers as raters was deliberate. Despite the risk of halo effect, it was considered an asset to maximize the use of information and impressions about the mother. It was assumed that parent attitudes would not necessarily vary according to the ideology of the school, but would be distributed across the sample; the procedure involved no risk, therefore, of systematic school-related expectations on the part of the raters. By design, raters had no knowledge of the material concerning schools, classrooms, or children during the period of data collection and analysis (see Chapter 2); their analysis of the mother interviews was also made without knowledge of the mothers' Modern-Traditional Ideology score on the questionnaire.

The interviews were rated for seven dimensions. The Modern-Traditional Ideology rating (A.1 above) was based on an overall judgment, but the rating of the remaining six dimensions (A.2–4 and B.1–3) depended on a series of contributing subscales. All ratings were made on a nine-point scale.[5] Interview material relevant to the subscales was rated prior to the rating of the seven dimensions. Appendix H lists the subscales contributing to each of the seven dimensions.

The Modern-Traditional Orientation (MTO) composite score was derived from a combination of four interview ratings and the Modern-Traditional Ideology score on the questionnaire. These scores were combined according to a quantitative system which was checked by a review of the qualitative material and yielded a rating on a seven-point scale. Appendix J describes these procedures. The composite score of Maternal Satisfaction and Role Coherence is a simple arithmetic average of the ratings of the three contributing dimensions.

Despite the intensive process of training and revision, interrater agreement on a sample of cases was disappointing.[6] It proved particularly difficult to rate the mother's Consistency of Child Rearing with acceptable reliability, and the median correlation of all seven dimensions was $r = .52$ (see Appendix H for reliabilities of individual dimensions). Protocols which presented rating problems were therefore analyzed by both raters, and consensus ratings were assigned.

INTERCORRELATION OF PARENT DIMENSIONS

The intercorrelation of parent dimensions is presented in Appendix K.

The component dimensions of the modern-traditional composite correlate highly with the composite MTO rating (range: $r = .61$ to $.76$), as might be expected, and correlate significantly with each other. Though it seems clear that the different dimensions measure somewhat different aspects of viewpoint and behavior, they constitute a meaningful constellation.

There are substantial correlations among the three components of the Composite of Maternal Satisfaction and Role Coherence.[7] This composite is relatively independent of modern-traditional dimensions and therefore of the MTO composite (correlation of the two composites is $r = .27$), and the components correlate more highly with each other than with aspects of modern-traditional orientation.

For the total sample, there is virtually no connection between the family's socio-economic level and child-rearing or maternal role dimensions, though there is a slight tendency for mothers of higher socio-economic status to be more modern in their attitudes toward girls.

Intercorrelations among particular dimensions, though influenced by reliability coefficients, are also an indication of parental functioning; they suggest which elements are most closely associated in the actual functioning of the parents as they carry their roles and project their orientation. Implications of the correlations are discussed later in this chapter.

Salient characteristics of the parents in the study are described from two points of view: (1) characteristics of the total parent group and (2) characteristics of the parent groups from each of the four schools.

Characteristics of the Parents as a Group

General characteristics of the parent group, as ascertained through their responses to the information section of the questionnaire, have been described. This group of capable adults, articulate and cooperative, seemed generally representative of well-educated, comfortable, middle-class parents living in large urban centers during the middle 1950's. It should be noted, however, that while direct questioning of religious association was not possible for the public school population, indirect information about affiliations and activities suggested that the majority of the families was Jewish. This, of course, is atypical for the country at large, though not so atypical for many metropolitan centers.

Socio-Economic Status

Most parents, both fathers and mothers, had been to college. Sixty-two percent of the fathers and 48 percent of the mothers were college graduates and a sizable group had continued their education beyond the college level.

Occupationally, there was a range in the sample, but there were no fathers with occupations below white-collar status and a considerable number with executive or professional positions, for example, physicians, lawyers, business executives, educators, professionals in the arts. Family income, for most of the families (64 percent), ranged between $10,000 and $25,000.

Eighty-seven percent of the mothers had worked at some time in their adult lives, but at the time of the study, only 37 percent were working. These were engaged mostly in professional positions or in some branch of the arts, though a few held white-collar jobs.

As has been noted, there is little connection between these elements of socio-economic status and the child-rearing dimensions discussed below. In the culture at large, modern child-rearing attitudes tend to appear more among families of higher status (Bronfenbrenner, 1958; Erickson, 1947; Kohn, 1963; Sears, Maccoby, and Levin, 1957). The fact that such an association does not systematically appear in this sample is probably a function of the restricted socio-economic range among families of the study—all of whom qualify as middle class. It should be noted, however, that child-rearing patterns and socio-economic status are not completely independent even in this group: more modern child-rearing ideology appears to some extent among families of higher occupational status, at least for parents of girls (see Appendix K), though the association does not apply to families of boys nor does it hold for all aspects of the modern-traditional orientation. The association is not powerful, but to the extent that it appears it supports the observations reported in other research.

Modern and Traditional Orientation

The group of 102 mothers seemed in general to endorse a viewpoint about child rearing that is more modern than would probably be typical of most American mothers. Although there are no comparative data from other parent groups, indications from other studies support this inference (see, for example, Levinson and Huffman, 1955; Gurin, Veroff, and Feld, 1960). On the other hand, the data of this study indicate that the parents' enactment was more traditional than their expressed attitudes. This is consistent with the findings of attitude research which have in general shown that the statement of attitude or belief does not necessarily imply parallel enactment.

The questionnaire drew from the parents their more conscious and public philosophy. Without the complications of interaction with an interviewer, or talking about personal matters concerning their own children, the mothers responded to the questionnaire in terms of the philosophy they held and/or were willing to present publicly. The prevailing attitudes under these circumstances were considerably more modern than traditional.[8] Most of them (83 percent) agreed with statements like "It is better for a child to resist a parent's orders openly than to obey and hide his angry feelings." In the same proportions, they *disagreed* with such ideas as

"Children owe it to their parents always to do their best to meet their parents' wishes" (75 percent) or "If parents want to keep their children's respect they should not admit their ignorance too readily" (83 percent). Taken at face value, these are viewpoints that tolerate impulse expression, imply some autonomy for the child, and do not stand on parental prerogatives or dignity as the basis of adult-child relations. There was range within the group's responses: Not all items mobilized this much "modern" opinion, and the spread of questionnaire scores (36–113 out of a possible 0–120) is ample evidence that these mothers were neither all "modern" nor completely likeminded in their viewpoints. Judging from the content of what the majority endorsed, however, they were predominantly allied with "modern" principles of child rearing.

Interview responses, which deal with the daily interaction of parents with children, show less concern for individual development, rational authority, and complexly balanced standards.[9] To some extent this difference must reflect the different level of response to questionnaire and interview.

It is probably also true that it is more difficult to live out the complex tenets of a modern role and relationship with children than to maintain a modern viewpoint, no matter how sincerely held or clear the concepts. Mothers described the difficulties of evaluating the child's need and of finding the balance in any given situation.

> There was one night a couple of weeks ago when she kept getting out of bed . . . and I kept going back with her and tucking her in again, and getting very annoyed because I began to feel that it was for real, because she was asking for something, but not for *real* real. You know, it was real because all her behavior is real but she was also using it because it had worked before. . . .

They also described the interference of their own pressures, preoccupations, and anxieties:

> Some of the times I've blown my top when I'm tired or I'm upset. . . . I mean I was irritated with her, you know, but later on I would think about it and know that I have been irritated at the same thing other times and I didn't hit her . . . worked it out some other way.

> I think that being a little more secure and therefore a little less afraid of doing the wrong thing with my child, a little less fearful that practically anything I did would mar her for life—now that's an exaggeration but you know what I mean—that I wouldn't take things, myself, things I said, my own actions, my own effect on a child so very seriously now.

It is perhaps a function of this fact that it was more difficult to find consistent modern mothers than traditional ones. In a separate analysis

(Minuchin and Shapiro, 1964) mothers were identified who were clear
and consistent both in their philosophy and enactment, whether modern
or traditional. Less than half the sample could be so characterized—a total
of 47, of whom 27 were traditional and only 20 modern. Thus, in a total
sample that included many mothers with relatively modern ideas about
child rearing, a sizable proportion presented a picture of daily life and
interaction with their children that was more mixed in quality than their
system of ideas.

The child-rearing model formulated for this study contrasted socialization of the child toward general societal standards with an approach that
stressed individual complexity and growth patterns. Speaking in terms of
their particular children and the events of daily life, the mothers brought
this contrast into concrete form. As illustration, two mothers, who exemplify polar positions in respect to this formulation, described their children:

Eric's mother saw her son's personality in terms of its moral and social
meaning. When asked about his *best characteristic,* she said:

> Well—both my husband and I are very grateful that he's very conscien-
> tious and religious . . . he knows right from wrong and he will even call
> to my attention when I say something wrong.

About his *greatest shortcoming,* she says:

> I think he has a tendency to be somewhat lazy. Well for instance when
> he comes home after school . . . I always have to ask him what he has
> for homework. He doesn't take it upon himself to apply himself in the
> evenings.

Carol's mother saw her in very different terms. Her *best characteristic:*

> Well I can tell you what comes to me. . . . A kind of clear capacity
> to look at life and to enjoy it. She doesn't flit around on the clouds all
> the time. But she—she *really* can be *happy* when she's happy, and
> when she's not, she has, for her age, a pretty doggone good ability to
> try to get hold of what it is, in her own way, in a child's way. I think
> this is going to stand her in good stead.

And her *greatest shortcoming:*

> I've seen recently that she doesn't really know how good she is. Now I
> use "good" about all kinds of things. When I saw [her teacher] at school
> we talked about this a couple of months ago and she had seen it too.
> She'll turn out, you know, a perfectly satisfactory—sometimes more than
> satisfactory piece of work and just be completely aghast at the fact that
> she made some erasures on it—that it isn't perfect penmanship. As
> soon as I say that I wonder. I think of her and how she sounds, and I
> wonder if she *really* doesn't know how good she is, or is she just trying

to get us to tell her. I think part of it, though, is that she really doesn't. She feels some sort of inadequacy these days.

This mother sees strengths and deficits from the child's point of view—her pleasure, her pain, her capacity to develop and to cope with life.

These graphic contrasts appeared in other ways. The goals, methods, and expectations of the socialization process, for instance, were expressed in different forms. More traditional mothers reacted to behavior that's "real loud and boisterous," or "the arguing of a known command," as something that required punishment. Punishment itself was a complicated problem for almost all parents, but more often took an external, pleasure-depriving form with parents who defined transgressions in these ways. A parent might feel clearly effective or not, within this philosophy, but even where she felt that her methods might not be working, her goal was to convince the child that disobedience did not pay.

> A couple of weeks ago, I've forgotten what it was that he did, and he had an argument with his father, and his daddy said he couldn't have his allowance that week. But I don't think it bothered him *at all.* . . . And then in the food line, depriving him of dessert or what have you, doesn't . . . it never works because dessert is not that important to him. It isn't really, in the sense of having particular things that he just adores. As I said, I believe in it in theory but I haven't found the right thing.

Such mothers saw their role with their children as laying down a system of values and behavior that would essentially mirror their own. Some, in fact, defined the success of their parenting role in terms of the eventual identity of values between parent and child. *In what ways would you expect his values and way of life to be the same or different from yours?*

> Well, I don't know how they would differ. I think that children that are brought up as closely as they are to us, I think they usually follow the same pattern.

Another mother expressed a different view of the socialization process. She described herself as having "no specific punishments. I would say I have a fundamental plan of discipline that just is out of what I am but—no plan of punishment." She described her attempt to understand the depth of distress behind a temper tantrum and the fact that this influences whether she actively comforts the child or is more quietly neutral, but noted that it was not a question of punishment. She said she had lost her temper with her child—a fact she considers a reality but not part of her philosophy ("I can't offhand remember a time when it wasn't because I was really mad at something else")—and had deprived her in ways she did consider consistent with her viewpoint.

She lost her subway pass, and we agreed last time this happened that next time it occurred she would pay a nickel toward each subway token she had to buy. And I explained to her why. We added up what the tokens cost, five days a week, for a month, and what the subway pass costs. So I'm depriving her . . . I think I'm also teaching her something.

For the most part, however, she described her socialization philosophy in ways that were little tied to specific transgressions or punishment techniques. She taught her what she needed to know

. . . primarily by what I am. This I know for *sure* and you can't get away from that no matter what you do. Secondarily, by explanation. Third—and I don't plan this—by withholding love—in the sense of disapproving of whatever it is. And somewhere in there comes just letting her experience certain things, if I think it's a consequence she can pretty well take. I never let her cross the street and get hit by a car so she'll learn not to cross the street, but some things . . . hell, she has to *live.*

For this mother, socialization was not fundamentally a matter of direct inculcation or training and her view of what she transmits was geared partly to change and the child's own course of development.

When she grows up? The world's going to be different. When the world changes, values change too. . . . Some things I think should last . . . I hope the things that we think matter . . . because I think my values about that are pretty good. [But] she may well have different ideas . . . because it's going to be what it's going to work out to be. You affect it and you influence it, as you live too, but it sure is changing, and it's going to change some more. So she could well have different values. Thirty years from now mine could be very different, and hers can very well be very different.

Components of the Modern-Traditional Orientation

The modern-traditional concept has three component dimensions besides ideology: Enactment of the Authority Role; Standards of Behavior and Achievement; Encouragement of Individual Interests. It is of some interest to consider whether the parents were consistent in these respects and whether any of the three dimensions distinguished modern and traditional mothers more clearly than the others.

The parents apparently found it easier and more acceptable to encourage the individual interests and initiative of their children than to follow a flexible, functional authority role or to maintain an individually-oriented set of standards (see Table 5-1). Their children were active, energetic, moving into an age level where interests and the wish to develop one's skills are burgeoning, and these parents were generally supportive of this extension. There were still differences between basically modern and basi-

TABLE 5–1

Comparison of Parents of Children Attending the Four Schools
on Aspects of Child Rearing and Socio-Economic Level

MEASURE[1] Source, and Scale Range	Sex §	Browning	Adams	Dickens	Conrad	Total[2]	Analysis of Variance
MODERN-TRADITIONAL ORIENTATION (MTO) (Composite) Scale Range: 1–7	b	3.00	2.94	3.83	5.00	3.75	Schools: 6.88** Sex: 1.29 NS Schools × Sex: 2.88*
	g	4.00	4.19	2.92	5.00	4.04	
	T	3.44	3.53	3.38	5.00	3.89	
MODERN-TRADITIONAL IDEOLOGY Questionnaire Actual Range: 36–113	b	64.00	69.22	80.75	91.65	77.42	Schools: 9.34** Sex: .26 NS Schools × Sex: 2.82*
	g	76.38	75.94	67.00	95.33	78.63	
	T	69.50	72.38	73.88	93.17	77.97	
MODERN-TRADITIONAL IDEOLOGY Interview Scale Range: 1–9	b	3.80	3.39	4.17	5.24	4.18	Schools: 3.74* Sex: .17 NS Schools × Sex: 1.54 NS
	g	4.50	4.31	3.25	5.08	4.27	
	T	4.11	3.82	3.71	5.17	4.22	
ENACTMENT OF AUTHORITY ROLE Scale Range: 1–9	b	3.70	3.17	3.58	4.24	3.67	Schools: 3.00* Sex: 1.45 NS Schools × Sex: .54 NS
	g	4.62	3.50	3.33	4.83	3.98	
	T	4.11	3.32	3.46	4.48	3.81	
STANDARDS OF BEHAVIOR AND ACHIEVEMENT Scale Range: 1–9	b	2.50	2.72	3.67	4.41	3.39	Schools: 2.92* Sex: 3.80 NS Schools × Sex: .85 NS
	g	4.00	3.75	3.67	4.75	4.02	
	T	3.17	3.21	3.67	4.55	3.68	
ENCOURAGEMENT OF INDIVIDUAL INTERESTS Scale Range: 1–9	b	5.50	4.83	6.42	6.82	5.88	Schools: 3.32* Sex: .03 NS Schools × Sex: 2.65 NS
	g	5.63	6.25	4.75	7.17	6.00	
	T	5.56	5.50	5.58	6.97	5.93	
MATERNAL SATISFACTION AND ROLE COHERENCE Scale Range (Composite): 1–9	b	6.37	5.11	5.53	5.35	5.49	Schools: 2.59 NS Sex: .83 NS Schools × Sex: .15 NS
	g	6.21	4.77	4.78	5.25	5.13	
	T	6.30	4.95	5.15	5.31	5.33	
SATISFACTION WITH CHILD Scale Range: 1–9	b	6.20	5.56	6.00	5.76	5.82	Schools: .39 NS Sex: .39 NS Schools × Sex: .24 NS
	g	6.00	5.50	5.17	5.83	5.58	
	T	6.11	5.53	5.58	5.79	5.71	
INTEGRATION OF MOTHER ROLE Scale Range: 1–9	b	6.50	4.67	5.33	5.18	5.28	Schools: 2.50 NS Sex: 1.40 NS Schools × Sex: .10 NS
	g	5.88	4.38	4.42	4.83	4.75	
	T	6.22	4.53	4.88	5.03	5.04	

	Mean Scores for School Groups						
MEASURE[1] Source, and Scale Range	Sex §	Browning	Adams	Dickens	Conrad	Total[2]	Analysis of Variance
CONSISTENCY OF CHILD REARING	b	5.40	4.11	4.25	4.12	4.37	Schools: 3.49*
	g	5.75	3.44	3.75	4.08	4.06	Sex: .26 NS
Scale Range: 1–9	T	5.56	3.79	4.00	4.10	4.23	Schools × Sex: .26 NS
SOCIO-ECONOMIC-CULTURAL INDEX[3]	b	4.20	5.32	4.17	4.76	4.71	Schools: 2.73*
	g	4.19	4.53	4.33	5.08	4.56	Sex: .17 NS
Scale Range: 1–6	T	4.19	4.95	4.25	4.90	4.64	Schools × Sex: .96 NS

1. Low scale points indicate more traditional positions, high scale points more modern positions.

2. N = 105. The three sets of parents who had siblings in the study are represented twice—once for each sibling.

3. N = 103. The two missing cases—parents of a boy and parents of a girl—are from the Adams sample.

* p < .05
** p < .01
§ b = boys
g = girls
T = total

cally traditional parents. The 27 traditional and 20 modern parents selected for special comparative study differed significantly in their ratings on this quality (see Appendix L). Within a general attitude of fostering individual interests, there were subtle but important differences between the piano lessons that reflected a parental conception of what a child should become skillful at and those that reflected something individually meaningful to the child. For the total sample of parents, however, the attunement to such interests and the fostering of their development was relatively high. Perhaps this aspect is most clearly an intra-family affair. Variations in this attitude reflect variations in sensitivity to the child's inner organization and purposes, but the maintenance of a modern viewpoint, as here defined, runs little social or interpersonal risk.

Both the quality of authority and the parental reaction to the child's behavior and performance involve a good deal more that is personally demanding for the parent and important in its implications for other people's reactions to the child. In these aspects, parental reactions appeared more variable and were less consistently modern for the group of parents than either their expressed ideology or their ways of encouraging development in areas that were relatively conflict free.[10]

Traditional and modern parents differed significantly with respect to these two dimensions. The dimensions are core elements in the contrast between modern and traditional orientations toward child rearing and the parents identified as modern were geared to a set of standards and a mode of authority that responded to change, circumstance, and the quality of the individual child. Within this framework, however, attitudes to the child's behavior were relatively variable; they ranged in the expectations they set up, the leeway they gave, the kind of balance point they set. To some extent the range among them can be explained through an important factor: modern mothers appeared somewhat more lenient in the standards they set for their daughters than their sons.

In later chapters, which report child study findings, it will be clear that sex differences were an important factor and that the modern or traditional quality of the children's environments seemed to affect the pattern of differences between boys and girls. In parent interviews, mothers were not directly asked about their attitudes toward boys and girls, and the content of their standards or their own view of how their child rearing might differ for the two sexes is not known. In retrospect, this would certainly have been useful. There are limited data available, however, from comparing mothers of boys with mothers of girls on those attitudes that were measured. By and large, there are no great differences, though on most dimensions there is a slightly more modern orientation toward the rearing of girls. The greatest difference was found for standards of behavior and achievement ($t = 2.73$; $p < .05$). Mothers of boys present an image of interaction that is somewhat tougher, less apt to consider the role of impulse or situational factors. Perhaps it is the mothers' experience or expectation that one can allow the girls more leeway, that boys push the boundaries harder and must be reined in—but the balance for boys is toward a firmer line, with more emphasis on the boundaries of their behavior. Modes of carrying authority are consistent with this, leaning toward more arbitrary authority for boys, but the difference is slight.

Among the small sample of clearly modern mothers, this pattern occurs in the framework of their shared orientation. These mothers were altogether less distant and arbitrary than most, more likely to accept fluctuations, more apt to exaluate behavior from the viewpoint of the child as well as in terms of its impact—but the data suggest that this occurred most easily and consistently with girls.

Traditional mothers did not show this difference. This is somewhat surprising, since sex-linked expectations are generally part of a more traditional orientation. Perhaps this lack of difference is accountable to the fact that the ratings did not cover the *content* of expectations. Possibly the traditional parents differed greatly in the content of their expectations and standards for boys and girls but not in the fact that they were externally derived nor in the pressure exerted on both to live up to these expectations. On this the data are sufficient only to suggest an interesting direction for more pointed inquiry.

Components of Maternal Satisfaction and Role

By and large, these mothers conveyed a sense of pleasure and positive satisfaction concerning their children. While some were concerned with the child's problems, focusing on what was negative, annoying, or required change, the prevailing tenor of their responses was appreciative and positive. Perhaps it was relatively easy to feel gratified and content with these healthy, successful, intelligent children, no matter how high the parental standards.

The questions of role, however, were more complex and marked for many by conflict. It seemed relatively difficult for the mothers to carry the responsibilities and complexities of the parental role with ease, self-satisfaction, and a sense of balance with conflicting demands. As already noted, a fair number were inconsistent in their child rearing, with at least partial awareness of that inconsistency.

These aspects of the maternal role were assumed to be relatively independent of the child-rearing orientation. Theoretically and by common observational knowledge, it is quite possible for either modern or traditional mothers to be satisfied with their children, to feel resolved and integrated as parents, and to carry through their beliefs with general consistency. On the other hand, we expected that it might be harder to integrate the modern role and to maintain it consistently—because it required more constant flexibility of judgment, provided fewer specific guidelines, and had no continuity, for most of these mothers, with the parenting model from their own childhood.

For the total parent group, the relationship between child-rearing orientation and these role aspects is, in fact, not high. The correlation between the MTO and the composite rating of Maternal Satisfaction and Role Coherence was $r = .27$, indicating some positive association between modern orientation and greater role satisfaction and coherence, but obviously with much room for variation.[11] The relationship was due mostly to the feeling of satisfaction the mother conveyed about her child (see Appendix K). Mothers who were centered most strictly around the socialization of their children tended to be more critical and dissatisfied with them. Perhaps the mother's personality organization shaped both the formation of her child-rearing attitudes and her acceptance and open appreciation of her child. Perhaps it is more difficult for children to live up to standards that are unbending and relatively external in ways that satisfy their mothers. There was, at any rate, a connection between a mother's tendency to accept her child in a satisfied way, delineating his strength and positive qualities, and a relatively modern child-rearing orientation. For the group in general, there was no observable connection between the nature of the orientation and the consistency with which the mothers carried it out.

With the subsample of the 47 clearly modern and traditional mothers, the relationships are clearer. By definition, these were mothers whose orientation was most consistently worked out and enacted. The modern group of mothers were reliably more accepting and positive toward their children (see Appendix L). In addition, they were more resolved in their role, deriving more enjoyment from it and evidencing more sense of confidence and success in their own terms. Traditional mothers varied more in this respect and were, on the average, less resolved. It is clear that the modern orientation does not necessarily carry this integration with it. In the sample at large, many mothers told of their doubts and difficulties, much along the lines that we had expected. It may be true, however, that where the modern orientation is stable and integrated it is especially so, carrying with it implications for the mother's perception and enjoyment of the child as he is and of her role as a mother.

Traditional and Modern Mothers

The data yielded no simple composite of the "traditional" or "modern" mother. Not only did the mothers differ as individuals but those with the clearest and most consistent orientation in either direction differed in some respects from those who had leanings, mixed or vague philosophies. Yet some of the tendencies can be summarized.

The more traditional mothers of this sample might best be identified through the central enactment of the socialization process—the way they related their child to society, set and enforced their standards, carried their power and authority vis-à-vis children. In other respects, they overlapped somewhat more with modern mothers. They accepted some tenets of a modern ideology, at least in their more public statements (for example, the questionnaire), and they were geared to fostering the skills and tastes of their children. They were centrally different, however, in their daily reactions to child behavior and the way they shaped and handled it. They set their standards for the most part by a social code, evaluated behavior in terms of this, expected and enforced compliance. They saw themselves as teachers in a rather specific sense, training their children to certain acceptable standards. It is of interest that this central organization and emphasis had elements of consistency, often, with the child's earliest infancy. The clearly traditional mothers described an emphasis on molding behavior in the days of the child's infancy: they followed fixed schedules of feeding, were apt to let their children "cry it out," apparently concerned with impulse control and early training.[12]

Within this framework, mothers might be well satisfied and contented with their children. Perhaps the set qualities of their system had special pitfalls, however, since more of these mothers tended to be critical or dissatisfied with their children.

These mothers felt a specific continuity with the practices of their own parents, just as they projected such a continuity onto the future of their children. Perhaps this fact, together with the relatively clear-cut guidelines of their philosophy, made for more frequent consistency in child-rearing orientation. Yet even the most consistent of these mothers did not necessarily appear resolved in their role nor fully satisfied. Perhaps they pressured themselves and their children in ways that were hard to fulfill, leaving themselves somewhat less than integrated or satisfied as mothers.

Among modern mothers, the questions of balance and flexibility appeared central to their orientation. They saw themselves reacting at the same time to the child's inner organization, the circumstances of his behavior, and the nature of the world toward which they were socializing him; they saw themselves more as guides than specific training agents. For many of these mothers, a modern child-rearing orientation was well worked out at the level of an articulated philosophy. Within the realm of enactment, it was relatively easy for them to foster the development of their children in areas of skill and interest, bringing to this their general orientation which emphasized the initiative, urges, and inner style of the child. More difficult were the areas where parent, child, and the real world formed a complex triad.

These mothers were discernibly different from traditional mothers in the aspects that define their orientation, but they differed most among themselves in the way they set and enforced standards—the degree of firmness and the circumstances for leeway. Perhaps this aspect of interaction with the child presents the most complex forces to balance and depends most clearly on the nature and response of the child or the realities of his world as the parent sees it. There is some suggestion that modern mothers set a firmer line for boys, placing less emphasis on what they expected of girls and allowing them more leeway.

Though some mothers described a subtle shift in their attitudes during the lifetime of the child—usually toward greater confidence as a mother and an easier firmness with the child—there was again an evident continuity between early infant care and child-rearing philosophy in the middle years. Modern mothers, more than traditional mothers, had breast-fed their babies, had followed a demand feeding schedule, and had picked up and comforted their infants when they cried. The underlying orientation toward need, impulses, and comfort appears consistent over time.

In general, however, consistency and integration were difficult for modern mothers to achieve, though for different reasons perhaps than traditional mothers. They felt a gap between their parents and themselves, and they described considerable groping and uncertainty. Among those who had worked out a discernibly consistent approach, however, there was indication of considerable integration and satisfaction. These mothers expressed certainty about their point of view and their feeling that it was best for their child; while they had doubts about some of their methods of enacting their role, they were relatively stable and confident as parents. Modern mothers were generally somewhat more satisfied and positive toward their children. These most consistently modern mothers emerged as the most clearly accepting of their children and themselves, the most resolved and satisfied in their role as mothers. Such a resolution, as noted, is not inherent in the orientation, which was uncertain and unresolved for many. For those, however, who had worked through their complex and individually-oriented child-rearing philosophy, the resolution of role, feeling, and practice seemed particularly successful.

Characteristics of Parents of the Four School Groups

It was particularly important to assess the comparability of the home backgrounds of the children from the different schools. As noted earlier, the schools and the children in the study were originally selected on the basis of general socio-economic comparability. They were compared on other variables, however, and this section reports the differences among the four parent groups and the salient qualities of each.

One point should be emphasized. It is important to keep clear that the characteristics of the parent group of a school are not to be equated with that school's position regarding modern or traditional viewpoints. The parents of Browning, for instance, were not more traditional than those of Dickens simply because the school was. The important exception was the parent group of Conrad. This group had consciously chosen a school with a definite orientation and their prevailing views were not randomly or accidentally related to the position of the school. The range in attitude among parents of the other schools was not causally related to the qualities of the schools their children attended.

Socio-Economic Status

The schools and children in the study were selected to match the inevitably privileged status of parents who could send their children to a private school such as Conrad. Though all families were middle class and the range was limited, there were reliable differences among the four parent groups. As Table 5–1 indicates, the parents of Adams and Conrad were of a higher status than those of Browning and Dickens.

In breaking down the SEC Index into its component parts, it became evident that the difference lay in occupational level. The parent groups did not differ in education or income, but in their occupational status: both the fathers and mothers of Adams and Conrad tended to hold more professional, artistic, or executive positions. In some sense, then, the children of these two groups were living in homes that may have provided subtly different environments, though their parents were not necessarily more affluent or educated.

The research staff members who visited the homes felt there was some validity in pairing Adams and Conrad versus Browning and Dickens with respect to sophistication, complexity, and central urban quality, even though there were many differences between them. For the purposes of the study, it is fortunate that these distinctions do not follow the position of the schools on the modern-traditional continuum; if Adams and Conrad were the two modern schools, comparisons of the children would have been confounded in part by this home-background factor. There are places in the child study data, however, where the children from Adams and Conrad seem different from those of Browning and Dickens, and at such points family background may be relevant.

Attitude, Relationship, and Role: Major Differences Among Parent Groups

There are two primary differences among the parent groups of the four schools: (1) mothers of Conrad children were the most modern in their orientation and (2) mothers of Browning children were the most coherent and integrated in their mothering roles. Table 5–1 presents the means of each parent group on each dimension and the statistical evidence of their comparability.

It was not unexpected to find the Conrad mothers more modern in their child-rearing orientation. As Table 5–1 indicates, their special position is exceedingly clear; they differ from other parent groups on every aspect of ideology or enactment that pertains to the modern-traditional orientation. A number of factors probably made this finding almost inevitable. As already noted, these parents had selected Conrad, with its clear and evident modern philosophy, as the school for their children. Mutually held attitudes were probably further reinforced after the child was attending. In addition, these parents may have felt some pressure to express views syntonic with those held by the school. To some extent the distinctly modern stance of the Conrad parents confounds those study findings that predominantly involve Conrad children and must be held in mind as a contributing influence in such school differences. It is important, however, that the other parent groups do not differ from each other and that there is overlap between the prevailing orientation of Conrad parents and those of parents in the other groups.

The finding concerning the Browning mothers concentrates on role consistency and integration. They were not significantly more satisfied with their children than other groups but they were more consistent and more resolved in their role, particularly in comparison with the Adams mothers. It is possible that their consistency and resolution as mothers was related to their way of life, as cause or effect of their decision and experience in living out of the center of the city, for instance, where they may have had a less complex life. Whatever the reason, it is a fact that the Browning mothers varied in their child-rearing orientation but were, as a group, relatively consistent, resolved, and comfortable in their roles as parents.

The brief sketches below summarize the salient features of home background for each school group.

BROWNING FAMILIES

Browning families were living in small homes in a middle-class neighborhood, somewhat out of the center of the city. Like most of the families in the study, their average income was high and the majority of the parents were college graduates. Approximately half the fathers were professionals —many of them physicians; others worked as executives or owned small businesses.

Almost all the mothers had worked at one time, but primarily in white-collar jobs (receptionist, bookkeeper) or helping their husbands. Very few had careers. At the time of the study one third were working (33 percent). As a group, these mothers lived in a relatively stable, unsophisticated, homogeneous, and family-oriented community.

In modern-traditional orientation, Browning mothers varied over the full range, though more were traditional than modern. They tended to be more modern with girls than boys.

As noted, this was the group that carried their roles with most ease— least conflict and contradiction. Perhaps their environment was most stable and their career versus motherhood struggles least pressing.

ADAMS FAMILIES

Adams families were living in high-rise apartment houses in a relatively privileged area of the city's center. Family income was high and parents were well educated, often at professional levels. Approximately half the fathers, again, were professionals—physicians, attorneys, dentists, and so on—or worked in the commercial arts or as business executives.

Many of the mothers had worked at one time—more of this group in such careers as advertising, interior decorating, or clothes design—but it was the custom in most of these families for the mother to stay at home once she had children. Only 29 percent were working at the time of the study. The general milieu of this parent group was felt to be sophisticated; the parents led busy lives and were very much involved in the activities of the city.

Adams mothers also varied along the modern-traditional range, but were more traditional than modern. They were also more modern in the rearing of their girls than their boys.

This group held the low point in role coherence and integration. A high proportion of these mothers were inconsistent and conflicted in their child-rearing ideology and practices and were uneasy in the way they carried their roles. There is a sense of complexity and flux in this group.

DICKENS FAMILIES

Dickens families lived in the center of the city in a housing development for moderate- or upper-income families.

A high proportion of these parents had college degrees. They tended to be somewhat younger, as families, than other groups, and family income was slightly lower. More among them were in the teaching profession rather than in medicine or law.

Almost all the mothers had worked at one time, either in white-collar jobs or in such professions as teaching, psychology, writing, the arts. As in Adams and Browning, a relatively small proportion (26 percent) were working at the time of the study, principally in career jobs, and many of these worked part-time. Dickens families lived in something of a protected community, albeit in the heart of the city, and to an extent there was more affinity of flavor with Browning mothers than with those of the other groups.

Dickens mothers were more traditional than modern. They were the only group more modern with boys than girls—a finding which can only be noted and for which we have no explanation other than chance. Among mothers of boys, there was variation across much of the modern-traditional range.

In comparison with the other groups, Dickens mothers were unremarkable with respect to role coherence; they were neither so integrated as the mothers of Browning children nor so fluctuating as the mothers of Adams. For whatever reason, the mothers of boys at Dickens tended to be not only more modern in orientation than mothers of girls but more resolved as mothers and more satisfied with their children.

CONRAD FAMILIES

Conrad children were drawn from around the city, but about half the families lived near the school, in small houses or apartment buildings in a varied urban neighborhood.

Family income was high and parents well educated, at levels comparable to the other groups. Fathers were in the professions—medicine, law, teaching—in the arts or theater, or worked as business executives.

It is in relation to the mothers' work history and attitude that this group differed most from the others. Well over half (58 percent) of the mothers were working at the time of the study, usually at careers in the professions or the arts. The children, therefore, were usually living in homes where both father and mother worked and where role images of adult life were thus different from those presented in other parent groups.

The families of Conrad children had consciously chosen this school and, as noted, their child-rearing orientation was *essentially* syntonic with the orientation of the school. There was some range in the group, including a very few quite traditional mothers. Most mothers, however, were modern in their orientation, and this included mothers of both boys and girls.

In role resolution, Conrad mothers varied. Approximately half the women classified as clear and consistent modern mothers came from this group. At the same time, the group as a whole was less resolved and integrated than mothers of Browning children.

Many of the points discussed above in connection with modern mothers apply in essence—though not uniquely—to the Conrad group, since they tend to cluster around this orientation. At the very least, considering their child-rearing orientation and their working status, they were the group who had taken on the greatest complexities; they presented to their children the most complex models of life and behavior.

In understanding the structure of the study, it is important to remember that children from any one of these school groups came from homes that varied. What they shared were the essentials of their school experience. It is for this reason that it is possible to make a comparative study of school effects. In the chapters to follow, the relation between family influence and child behavior is assessed for the various dimensions, and the nature of home-school interaction is probed as far as possible. In the last analysis, however, the central and fullest material concerns the schools and the nature of their effects on children.

NOTES

1. These introductory comments concerning the parent group are based on data obtained from the parent questionnaire (see pp. 138–139).
2. There is a parallel here to the analysis of the schools, which also includes dimensions not considered central to the modern-traditional ideology.
3. Of the 102 mothers in the study, 11 had been divorced and, of these, three

had remarried; in addition, there was one widow. All but one of these mothers were in the Adams and Conrad parent groups (six in Adams, five in Conrad); one mother in the Dickens group was divorced and none in the Browning group. It might be noted that these mothers varied in their child-rearing philosophies.

4. Though the sample of children numbers 105, there are two sets of twins and one pair of siblings. The parent sample, therefore, is 102.

5. Some scales had a tenth point for indicating "laissez faire" attitudes or behavior.

6. For four variables, N = 35; for three others, N = 23.

7. Satisfaction with Child × Integration of Mother Role, $r = .74$; Satisfaction with Child × Consistency of Child Rearing, $r = .44$; Integration of Mother Role × Consistency of Child Rearing, $r = .61$.

8. Even some of the parents considered relatively traditional in this sample would probably not score as extremely traditional on such scales as the Traditional Family Ideology Scale devised by Levinson and Huffman (1955), which is less skewed toward the modern end than the scale developed for this study.

9. The summary score of Modern-Traditional Orientation (MTO) yielded a group average slightly to the traditional side of the midpoint. Comparison of central tendencies on these measures must necessarily be tentative, of course, since the definitions have no absolute status. From inspection of the material, however, the suggested difference between philosophy and enactment seems essentially valid.

10. Enactment of Authority Role and Standards of Behavior and Achievement correlated more highly with each other ($r = .59$) than either correlated with Encouragement of Individual Interests ($r = .39$ and $r = .41$, respectively).

11. Boys, $r = .26$; girls, $r = .31$.

12. Chi-square analysis of clearly traditional and modern mothers on these factors were all significant at $p < .05$.

Effects on Children

C H A P T E R

6

APPROACH AND TECHNIQUES

General Orientation

In this section, the reader comes to the core of the study, the presentation of the reactions of the children who attended the modern and traditional schools. In an age of educational re-evaluation, we have felt the detailed description of schools and classrooms to be important in and of itself, but the comparative assessment of children educated in these different kinds of schools constitutes the *raison d'être* of the study.

The scope of assessment, as already indicated, was broad. We have accepted the proposition that the child's daily, accumulating experience in school—with teaching and learning, with other people, with the fate of his own efforts—has a potential effect on many aspects of his development. In the course of the following chapters, we report measures of child functioning in a number of areas. Chapter 7 reports the children's attitudes toward and identification with their schools. Chapters 8 and 9 present cognitive reactions—both to goal-directed, problem-solving tasks and to more open-ended situations involving imagination and the communicable aspects of fantasy life. Chapter 10 presents the child's perception of family adults. Chapter 11 concerns his attitude toward the authority structure of the school and presents material on the development of social codes and concepts. Chapters 12 to 14 deal with self-image: the child's concept of himself as an individual; as a child moving from infancy to adulthood; and as a boy or girl establishing a sense of sex membership and a conception of the male or female social role. In each of these areas, we had theoretical reason to expect some differential functioning on the part of modern and traditional school children.

A roster of predictions specifies the expected effects of modern and traditional education on the children. The predictions were formulated early in the study through a series of meetings involving both project staff and educational consultants familiar with the range of educational institutions we were dealing with. The prediction roster includes both those effects which modern and traditional schools would articulate as their goals and effects which were considered as possible by-products or concomitants, whether desirable and recognized or not.

It would be misleading to present our work as a tightly organized prediction-testing study. There were many conceptual and practical limitations on such an approach and, beyond this, our multiple purposes led us to explore emergent areas for which we had no clear prior predictions. In general, however, this roster of expectations shaped the data analysis and in the chapters to follow the data are presented—at least in part—in the contexts of our expectations.

The predictions were grouped into three categories: Intellectual Mastery, Interpersonal Perception, and Self-Image. The theoretical position and ideas which governed the predictions in each category follow.

A. INTELLECTUAL MASTERY

All children are involved in trying to achieve an increasingly clear and meaningful picture of the world around them and in trying to master the known facts, forms, and techniques of their culture. While this process reflects family influence, it is expected that children who have experienced different educational atmospheres will differ qualitatively in their organization of concepts and techniques, points of emphasis, areas of strength and strain.

Among *modern school* children, there will be a discernible orientation toward free and open-ended exploration of problems; they will tend to expect complexity in the world, to search for interrelationships among elements and ideas, and to tolerate nonabsolute resolutions of problems; they will more consistently attempt to achieve understanding by relating facts and concepts to their own experience.

Among *traditional school* children, there will be a greater stress on the conclusive mastery of known, culturally established, and accepted modes of solution and codes of conduct; they will have a more pressing orientation toward the achievement of clarity and closure.

B. INTERPERSONAL PERCEPTION

All children are centrally involved in working through personal relationships with other people: they are concerned with the reactions and approval of adults and children; they are exploring appropriate boundaries for the expression of feeling; they are seeking acceptable areas for autonomous activity and for dependent behavior. In working through such relationships, they are strongly and fundamentally influenced by family patterns and experiences. It is expected nonetheless that children who have experienced different educational atmospheres will focus on different aspects of interpersonal relationships and will vary both in their assumptions about how people interact and in the flexibility of their perception of people's roles.

Among *modern school* children, there will be a relatively pervasive assumption of acceptance and understanding in human contacts; they will assume a broader, more flexible range of behavior to be appropriate and possible, both in interpersonal relationships and in independent expression and activity.

Among *traditional school* children, there will be a greater tendency to perceive relatively fixed qualities in the roles carried by adults and children; they will be more persistently concerned with the reception of their reactions and behavior, more alert to the formal and disciplinary aspects of interpersonal contacts, more apt to focus on adaptation and compliance as important qualities.

C. SELF-IMAGE

In the course of maturing, all children are involved in a search for identity: they are trying to form coherent images of themselves as well as of others; from the ideas, values, and available roles in their environment, they are implicitly deriving, selecting, and attempting to assimilate aspects which seem consistent with the developing self. In this area of growth also, all children are basically influenced by the culture of their homes. It is expected, however, that children who have experienced different educational atmospheres will differ in the intensity of their search for individuality, in the content of what they value and strive for and in the style and force with which they attempt to resolve conflicting elements.

Among *modern school* children, there will be a greater tendency for individuality to operate as a central and organizing concept; they will be more concerned with developing a unique and differentiated sense of self, will tend to differentiate other people in terms of individual qualities, and will highly value forms of expression that are unique and original.

Among *traditional school* children, there will be a lesser concern with self-differentiation and self-expression; they will be more concerned with delineating and understanding individuals in terms of congruence with established and valued models and ideals.

The predictions themselves were at a more specific level; for example, a prediction in the Self-Image category reads: "Traditional school children will tend to perceive more clearly defined boundaries between masculine and feminine social sex roles than will modern school children."

We have been able to approach only some aspects of the major developmental areas which concerned us. Limitations were set by the kind of material that could be obtained from the children, the instruments used, the degree to which ideas were amenable to specific statement, and the problems of measurement. We have taken pains to specify the measures used in some detail, in the following chapters, so that the reader can evaluate the relevance of the measures to the ideas we discuss. No researcher who tackles the more complex aspects of human behavior is unfamiliar with the depressing discrepancy between the subtlety of the concepts under consideration and the crudity of the behavioral measures used, in the end, to stand in for them. Dealing with areas where there were few established precedents for measurement ("self-differentiation," "relationship thinking," and so on), we adapted and developed measures, as best we could, using multiple measurement as a rough check on the stability of a trend. Some readers may wish to translate our discussions into more operational terms. We have felt it important, however, to probe varied and subtle areas of development even where measures must still be crude, since our hypotheses suggested that these might be important areas of differential school effects.

The Sessions and the Child Study Material

In order to familiarize the reader with the roster of child study techniques, the following is a summary of the content of each individual session. Annotations indicate the general nature of a technique or task, and the reader with more detailed interest is referred to Appendix AA, in which techniques are reproduced or described in full. The measures derived from the techniques or tasks are reported in the context of the relevant chapters.

Each child had a primary interviewer who saw him for at least three sessions and established an ongoing relationship; other sessions were administered by other primary interviewers or by auxiliary interviewers.[1] All techniques were verbally administered and recorded by the interviewer. The child did not write any of his responses.[2] In addition, all sessions were machine-recorded.

SESSION ONE (PRIMARY INTERVIEWER)
The first session consisted of open-ended interviewing and five specific

techniques. It was approximately an hour and a half in length and was sometimes administered in two parts to avoid fatigue.

The interview covered a range of topics: the child's family life, his interests, out-of-school activities, friendships, opinions about world problems, feelings about school. An interview guide established the coverage and general form of questions. Included in this interview were the following questions:[3]

The future and the past. "Have you ever thought about being grown up? What do you think you'll be or do?" and "How about when you were little—can you remember things about that?"

Best age. "What do you think is the best age to be? Why?"

Best sex. "Suppose you could choose, which do you think it's best to be, a boy or a girl? Why?"

Million dollars. "Suppose that one day someone came up to you and said, 'I'm going to give you a million dollars and you can do anything at all that you want with it—the only thing is, you're supposed to spend it all in one day.' What would you do with all that money? How would you spend it?"

The five techniques were interspersed with sections of the interview. They were usually administered in the sequence listed below.

Similes.[4] * The child was presented with a word and asked to "think of something that's like it." (For example, as *hot* as . . . , as *helpless* as . . . , as *lovely* as . . .) There were 19 items in all.

Stick Figure Scale (SFS).[5] * The child was asked to describe or evaluate himself by placing himself on a series of continua, the two end points of which were described in contrasting or opposite terms and concerned feelings about the self, impulses, styles of life, and so on. There were ten items. In each case, the interviewer sketched two stick figures to mark the end points of the continuum, describing them at the same time. For example:

| "Here's a boy who's pretty sure all the kids like him, that he's popular." | *versus* | "Here's a boy who lots of times isn't so sure the other kids like him so much." |

"Which one is more like you?"

Moral Judgments.[6] The material was gathered in three sections, using different forms of presentation.

    1. *Questions.* The child was asked four questions: ("Who is the *best person* you can think of?" "Can you think of something that you would call *unfair?*" "What's the *worst crime* that you can

think of?" "What's the very *worst thing a child* in your class could do?") The last three questions were followed by discussion of consequences and punishment.

2. *The Child as Judge.** The child was given a puppet in judge's gown to manipulate and told that two children (dolls) would tell him their stories and he was to judge which doll did something "more wrong." There were three stories in all.

In the first story, the child had to judge between amount and intent, between the doll who did a lot of damage accidentally and the doll who did a little damage while breaking a rule. The second story presented a means-ends problem; the child had to judge between the doll who stole a lot of money for an altruistic end and the doll who stole considerably less money for a self-indulgent end. In the third story, both dolls cheated in a test but only one was caught. The three situations involved differential considerations of intentionality, motivation, and retribution in making judgments.

3. *Incomplete Stories.** The interviewer told a story to a point of dilemma and the child was asked to react with an appropriate continuation. The three stories involved social codes (loyalty, fairness, retribution) operative in relationships between adults and children and within the child group. (For example, when a child does not admit a misdemeanor to the teacher, do other children tell? Under what conditions?)

Sentence Completion Test (SCT).* A standard psychological technique, verbally administered, with items constructed for the study. The child was asked to complete 18 sentences "with the first thing you can think of." (For example: "My mother always . . ." "According to Ruthie, most boys . . .") Sentences concerned family, authority, school, boy-girl attitudes, past and future, self-image.

*Picture Titles.** This technique was developed for the study. The child was asked to imagine he was the director of an art museum, with a beautiful new building but no pictures. He was shown a set of pictures and asked to sort them according to his preferences. He was then asked to give each picture a title.

There were three sets of pictures, with 12 pictures to a set. The pictures were museum postcard reproductions of paintings and sculpture, predominantly from the twentieth century. Each of the three sets had a theme (Designs; People; Still Life and Abstracts). The pictures varied in style, use of color, reality-distortion, and level of abstraction.

SESSION TWO (PRIMARY INTERVIEWER)
The second session consisted of the Children's Picture Story Test and Figure Drawings. The session was between 45 minutes and an hour in length.

> *Children's Picture Story Test* (CPST).* This test is an adaptation for the age level of the familiar Thematic Apperception Test. It consists of 12 pictures, selected from other tests[7] and from magazine illustrations. Pictures depict children alone, with other children, in school, and with adults. Four cards had boy-girl alternates. Standard instructions were given, with the child asked to make up a story for each picture.

> *Figure Drawings.*[8] The child was asked to draw a picture of a person. On completion, he was asked to draw a person of the opposite sex. ("Now draw a girl"—if he had drawn a boy first.) Both pencil and crayons were supplied.

> Drawings were done in the middle of the session, after the child had responded to 7 of the 12 cards in the CPST series.

SESSION THREE
The third session consisted of the Rorschach and portions of the WISC. It was approximately an hour in length.

> *Rorschach.* Standard test and administration.[9]

> *WISC Performance Scale.* Three Performance Subtests of the WISC were routinely administered after the Rorschach: Object Assembly, Coding, Block Design. In cases where the Rorschach was short, the remaining subtests of the WISC Performance Scale (Picture Arrangement and Picture Completion) were also administered during this session. In other cases they were administered during Session Five.

SESSION FOUR
The fourth session consisted of Play with Miniature Life Toys. It was approximately an hour in length.

> *Play with Miniature Life Toys.*[10] * This technique presented each child with a wide variety of toys, including people, animals, vehicles, furniture, and so on. A table was provided on which the child played out one or more stories with the objects he had chosen from the collection. If he did not verbalize as he played, he was asked to tell the story after he had finished. The play period (30 to 45 minutes) was followed by a short interview about toys and play, past and present.

> Two adults were present. One served as interviewer and intro-

duced the materials and explained what the child could do; the other acted as an observer and did not participate. The interviewer recorded the action (placement, organization, sequence, objects) of the child's play and the observer recorded verbalizations.

SESSION FIVE (PRIMARY INTERVIEWER; SECOND YEAR ONLY)

A fifth session was added for children in the second year sample. It consisted of the four problem-solving tasks described below.[11] (The Picture Arrangement and Picture Completion subtests of the WISC were also included if these had not been completed in Session Three.)

Cylinder.[12] * The child was asked to solve the problem of removing a wooden cylinder from a tubular container without turning the cylinder over. He was first asked only to suggest possible solutions, then provided with tools and objects that might help him solve the problem and again asked for suggestions only; and finally he was encouraged to use the tools. A pitcher of water on the testing table, which was never specifically indicated by the interviewer, provided the most effective solution.

Meaning Context.[13] * The child was asked to solve the riddle of a nonsense word embedded in a series of five sentences. The context provided by each sentence was the clue to the meaning, and as the series progressed the range of possible answers became increasingly narrow. There were four nonsense words in the test.

Spies.[14] Twelve wooden doll figures were presented to the child. He was told that these represented people standing in a marketplace during the time of the American Revolution and that among them were three spies for the Americans. He was to find the three spies in order to deliver a message to them. All he knew was that all three were alike in some way; he did not know in what way, but he was to look the people over and find three who were alike in some way, had something in common. The child was encouraged to ask the interviewer as many questions as he wanted, but which could only be answered yes or no. The solution principle follows that of the Vigotsky Concept Formation Test in that it is the relation of two elements that constitutes the common factor.

Uncommon Uses.[15] * The interviewer mentioned a common object and asked the child what it was usually used for. The child was then asked to think of other uncommon uses. There were nine objects (for example, tire, newspaper, penny, lipstick).

FINAL SESSION (PRIMARY INTERVIEWER)

The final session consisted of an interview and four techniques. It was approximately one hour in length.

The interview covered the child's reactions to the school year that was finishing and his expectations of the year to come. It also covered his reactions to being a subject of the study. The four techniques were interspersed with sections of the interview. They were usually administered in the sequence listed below.

Dictated Letter. The child was asked to imagine that he had a pen pal in a foreign country to whom he was writing for the first time. He was asked to dictate a letter about himself and his life.

Personal Questions.[16] * The child was asked a series of questions concerning his emotional experiences, for example, involving feelings of pleasure, anger, embarrassment.

Three Wishes. The child was asked what he would wish for if he had three wishes.

Family Drawing.[17] The child was asked to draw a picture of a family. Both pencil and crayons were supplied.

GROUP SESSIONS

In addition to the individual sessions, there were four group sessions with each class, interspersed through the year, during which the following techniques were administered:

Kuhlmann-Anderson Intelligence Test.

Stanford Achievement Test. Five subtests were administered: Word Meaning, Paragraph Meaning, Arithmetic Reasoning, Science, Social Studies.

Sociometric Questions.[18] *

Russell Sage Social Relations Test (RSSR).[19] This is a group problem-solving task in which the group plans and constructs duplicates of block-structure models (house, bridge) presented to them.

Presentation of Findings

In analyzing the child study data we had, as indicated earlier, several purposes. The primary purpose was to compare the school groups. In addition, we wished to describe the recurrent themes and range of reactions in this population of nine-year-old children; assess the differences in reactions of boys and girls; and establish the relationship of child reactions to maternal variables. These other lines of analysis also provided an essential framework against which to understand and evaluate the differences between modern and traditional school groups.

All these levels of analysis have made for a complicated study. They have strained our own power to master the material, even while we value the perspective they have given us, and they present a challenge in the process of communicating with others. We have striven, therefore, for a chapter format that will acquaint the reader with the findings at each of these levels, while drawing together the main points in summaries and discussion.

Most of the chapters to follow are divided into two or three sections; these sections cover aspects of the chapter topic. (Thus, Chapter 8, "Cognitive Functioning," has two sections: Standardized Tests of Intelligence and Achievement, and Problem Solving. Chapter 12, "The Concept of Self," also has two sections: Self-Confidence and Satisfaction, and Self-Knowledge.) Within each of these chapter sections, there are three subsections: Techniques and Measures; Group Characteristics and Sex Differences; School Group Differences. Relationships to Home Background is sometimes added as a fourth subsection and sometimes discussed for the chapter as a whole. Brief summaries usually appear at the end of each chapter section and the main points are drawn together and discussed at the end of each chapter. It has been our hope that the advantages of this organization outweigh the disadvantages; the intention is to keep the reader well oriented to the particular prism through which the data are being examined at any particular time.

The statistical analysis of the material has been handled and is presented as follows.

A section on intercorrelations among measures is routinely included in the chapters because of our reliance upon multiple measures for most of the variables which were studied. Intercorrelations among conceptually equivalent measures are given in tabular form in Appendix BB. The reader will observe all too frequently that measures which appear on the basis of their content to be equivalent or highly interrelated failed to achieve substantial levels of intercorrelation. Since it was impossible to determine in such instances which member of the pair or group of measures contributed the irrelevant variance, both or all measures were routinely subjected to further analysis.

The most salient data of the study, the school group means, are presented in tables within each chapter, together with means for boys and girls. These tables also include the results of the basic statistical analysis of these data—the main effects for the school and sex variables, as well as the sex by school interaction, according to an analysis of variance procedure which utilized an approximate method to adjust for unequal frequencies of subclasses (see Walker and Lev, 1953). When the data are presented in the form of frequencies of nonordinal categories, a chi-square test was used to compare groups. Occasionally, the results of t-tests comparing the means of the modern schools with those of the traditional schools, or within-school sex differences, are cited in the text to supplement the basic analysis of variance results.

The correlations between dependent variables and home background variables are presented in tables in Appendix CC. Because of uncertainty regarding the appropriate weighting of the home background factors, as well as the possibility that some of the home background scores may themselves have been influenced by the child's school experience (for example, a parent's description of her own child-rearing behavior may be influenced by modes and standards implicitly established in her child's school community), it was decided not to employ a multi-variate analysis of covariance procedure. The use of such a procedure would have implied that our data regarding the role of home influence were more precise than they actually were. Instead, only a descriptive analysis of the degree of relationship between each child variable and each home background variable is presented.

NOTES

1. The five primary interviewers, of whom one was a man, saw approximately the same number of boys and girls in each school. Although the influence of the interviewers' sex on the children's responses was not systematically tested, inspection of the data indicates that there was no noticeable overall difference in the response patterns of boys or girls to male or female interviewers.
2. In the description of the sessions, for the sake of simplicity the child is always referred to as "he," though stimuli and instructions were altered appropriately according to whether a girl or boy was being tested.
3. Interviewers were not always able to cover the complete roster of questions. It will be noted in the following chapters that responses are not always available for the total sample, on such questions. This is a regrettable but random function of the fact that the hierarchy of interest for purposes of data analysis had not been established at the time of data collection with respect to interview questions; interviewers sometimes eliminated questions in the interest of time and the primary instruction to cover the five formal techniques.
4. Adapted from Sanford, Adkins, Miller, and Cobb (1943).
* Techniques marked with an asterisk are presented in full in Appendix AA.
5. Based on an idea developed by Mary Engel (see Engel and Raine, 1963).
6. Based on the work of Piaget (1948) but freely adapted; see also Trow (1954).
7. The Thematic Apperception Test (see Murray, 1943) and the Adult-Child Interaction Test (see Alexander, 1952).
8. See Machover (1948).
9. Rorschachs were administered by the child study staff and by psychologically trained assistants. On inspection of the data it was felt that administration and inquiry differed to an unexpected degree and that comparative assessment of the protocols, in this complex and intricately stand-

ardized technique, was thereby jeopardized. Consultation with Rorschach experts confirmed this impression. Rorschach data will not be reported in this book, therefore, though many protocols are useful for individual case analysis.

10. See in particular Murphy (1956) and Meissner (1954).
11. The development of the problem-solving battery was not completed in time for administration to the first year sample.
12. Adapted from the work of Saugstad (1952).
13. Adapted from Werner and Kaplan (1952).
14. Developed by Edna Shapiro.
15. Based on the work of Guilford (see Wilson, Guilford, and Christensen, 1953; Guilford, 1956).
16. Idea adapted from Adorno, Frenkel-Brunswik, Levinson, and Sanford (1950).
17. A commonly used technique, but suggested primarily by Wolff (1946).
18. Not routinely administered to all groups.
19. See Damrin (1959). This test was administered in Year I only.

CHAPTER

7

ATTITUDES TOWARD SCHOOL

The four schools handled the basic educational task of teaching children in quite different ways. The nature of the curriculum, the limits of permissible behavior, the quality of personal relationships, and many other factors varied considerably from school to school. It was the primary concern of the study to determine how these differences in schooling were internalized by the children and affected their behavior. We were also interested, however, in an intermediate question: How did the children themselves perceive the experiences offered in school? To what extent were they resistant, passively conforming, or positively identified with their schools? Such material did not necessarily reflect psychological growth, but it seemed important to know whether children exposed to quite different educational experiences were developing different allegiances and attitudes. This chapter presents material concerning the ideas and feelings of the children in the study toward their schools. It constitutes a prologue, in a sense, to the more internalized material reported in the following chapters.

We expected children of the modern schools to be more actively involved with the experience and more positively identified with their schools; we expected children of the more traditional schools to be less identified and involved—closer to the classic stereotype of the school child who regards his schooling as a necessary burden or who accepts its procedures without becoming truly engaged. Our expectations stemmed from the fact that the modern schools were more centrally focused on the child's own experience. They considered the child's investment and satisfaction in the activities of the school world to be both catalyst for his learning and sign of his growth, and they geared much of their learning atmosphere toward engaging his interest and involvement. The traditional schools were concerned, certainly, with the child's participation and progress, but they were less apt to think of his involvement or feeling as an essential part of his school experience. They did not structure the learning program toward maximizing the child's personal involvement; rather, it was the task of the child to meet the situations presented by the school and to prove himself in the school's terms. In the face of the distinct environments generated by these contrasting philosophies, we expected the children to have different attitudes toward school, and we assessed these attitudes through interview and test material.

Techniques and Measures

The children's attitudes and feelings about school were tapped through four techniques:

Sentence Completion Test. Six of the 18 items had school-related stems:

Item 2:   *One good thing about school . . .*
Item 7:   *When the teacher leaves the room . . .*
Item 8:   *The day (Betty/Ben) was late to school . . .*
Item 10: *Waiting in the principal's office, (Emily/Eddie) . . .*
Item 12: *When visitors come to (Mary's/Jim's) class . . .*
Item 14: *Whenever the teacher asked for quiet . . .*

Interview Questions. Questions about school life were included in the general exploration of the child's experiences and opinions. Such questions as the following yielded particularly relevant data: "Suppose you were the principal of a school like this; then what you thought about school would be taken very seriously. What kinds of things would you like to change? What kinds of things would you be sure to keep the way they are?"

Spontaneous comments about school, made in the course of the individual sessions, also provided relevant material.

Children's Picture Story Test. Picture #7, depicting a boy writing and a female adult standing in the background, was included as a schoolroom scene and provided school-related data.

Dictated Letter. The children's descriptions of themselves and their lives often included school-related material.

A composite rating of the child's *attitude toward school* was based on evaluation of material from the four techniques.[1] Composite ratings were on a four-point scale. The points were defined as follows:

1—negative attitude (child expressed a clear dislike of school)
2—ambivalent attitude (child expressed a mixture of conforming and negative feelings)
3—conforming attitude (child accepted school, but without enthusiasm, challenge, or active involvement)
4—positive identification (child expressed strong positive feeling and active involvement)

Group Characteristics and Sex Differences

There was a wide range and a good deal of variety in what the children told us directly about school. Asked for *One good thing about school* (SCT), some reacted with a general appraisal ("I enjoy it this year"; "You learn things"; "Sometimes they have good teachers . . .") while others were very specific ("arithmetic"; "reading"; "gym"; "I like to do plays"; "My teacher and many others don't yell and that makes it pleasant . . ."). Many children responded in terms of the core learning aspects of school; others were concerned with the qualities of teachers; some highlighted the opportunities for action and play (yard, gym). These obviously were the salient aspects of school, as they came to mind for this group of children. A very few—perhaps surprisingly few—mentioned peers and social opportunities ("the friends I meet . . ."), and a few children avowed that what was good about school was that it did not cover all of life (*One good thing about school* . . . "is that we have vacations!"; ". . . is that you have recess").

In their suggestions for change, the children touched on both the seemingly trivial and the obviously important: less crowding, different desk arrangements, more time for physical activity and play, different teaching methods, different ways of grouping the children, teachers who would be more lenient or fairer in their treatment of children or who "taught you more than you were supposed to learn if you had learned everything that was in the book." Some of their ideas of what to change in the school were sheer criticism, some were thoughtfully constructive.

A relatively small number of children (15) were consistently negative in their attitudes; for these children dislike and criticism of school ran through the direct and projective data as a steady theme. For example, one child, when asked about keeping and changing things in the school, launched a detailed and articulate criticism of the teacher as an inattentive and arbitrary umpire in the children's games and as playing favorites among the group in the classroom (". . . the teacher calls one person and keeps on calling him and calling and calling and nobody else gets a chance . . ."). His story to the CPST card revolved around restriction and interference with the child's real wishes (". . . He's got to stay in after school and the teacher is waiting for him to get through and he's hurrying because he wants to go play . . ."). His response to the one good thing about school was terse and explicit: "I hate it." As noted, however, such an attitude of open negativism toward school was relatively rare in this group of children. They came, after all, from life environments where parents prepared them for school, valued the contribution of the school to the child's growth, and imparted to their children the sense that school was a pivotal life experience. Further, these children were generally successful in school or at least adequately adapted to the school situation. Though their various schools offered them very different experiences, most were able to master these experiences in the terms presented. In contrast to disadvantaged, "inner city," minority group children, they were not apt to see any of these schools as alien to their lives and purposes; they did not play hooky, were not "problems" in school, and were not apt to be the future high school dropouts.[2] It was a legitimate and explainable finding, in such a group, that most children were not consistently negative in their attitudes toward school. The negativism they did feel, of course, may have been partly inhibited, since many of the children in this sample—as indicated in later chapters—did not easily express resistance or criticism to adults.

Many children (37) gave mixed reactions: they liked some aspects of school and disliked others but gave no evidence of thought or concern about changing the aspects they disliked; they expressed acceptance of school but gave indirect evidence, in projective material, of their restlessness or dislike; or they were aware of rebellion in other children and vicariously identified with such feelings and reactions.

About a fourth of the children were consistently conforming. They were uncritical of the school, accepting its ways of doing things, its rules and programs, without any concern for rationale or larger goals. For some of these children school was important; they felt comfortable or successful and tended to like it, but their attitude was passive and compliant.

As an example, one boy said: *One good thing about school* . . . "is that I like it," but he had no suggestions for change in the school and gave no evidence of active involvement. His CPST story seemed to capture the essence of his attitude: "I guess some teacher asking a boy to write something down and the boy is writing it down."

One fourth of the children were actively involved and positively identified with their schools. They seemed to have made an identification with the school and its purposes and they evaluated its procedures with some independence. One child noted *One good thing about school* . . . "is that it teaches me new things." Her CPST story involved a boy who was writing an elaborate adventure story as a composition for school. Her general attitude toward school was certainly positive, but within that context she had several suggestions (". . . larger rooms, and more easels . . . and more space to keep things. And I would allow animals in the class . . . not every day of the week; I'd have a pet show or something"). Another child commented that what was good about school is that "you learn and have fun." He suggested, however, that his school distribute its work and learning assignments differently through the grades so that children would not be piled up with so much work in the upper grades. These children, when they were critical, seemed to be measuring existing conditions against some image of an ideal and to be thinking constructively about implementation and change.

In general, girls were more positive in their attitudes toward school than boys (see Table 7–1). A higher percentage of boys were directly negative and a lower percentage of boys were actively involved. This sex difference describes the three public schools, however, rather than Conrad.[3] There was a significant interaction effect between school and sex (see Table 7–1), due to the distinct reactions of boys and girls in the Conrad group, and this pattern is discussed below as part of the syndrome of school group differences.

TABLE 7–1
Extent of Positive Identification with School

MEASURE Source, and Scale Range	Sex §	Browning	Adams	Dickens	Conrad	Total [1]	Analysis of Variance
Mean Scores for School Groups							
EXTENT OF POSITIVE IDENTIFICATION WITH SCHOOL Sentence Completion Test, Interview, CPST, Dictated Letter Scale Range: 1–4	b	1.90	2.11	2.25	3.24	2.44	Schools: 3.57*
	g	2.38	2.75	3.17	2.67	2.77	Sex: 3.91 NS Schools × Sex:
	T	2.11	2.41	2.71	3.00	2.59	3.09*

1. $N = 102$.
* $p < .05$
§ b = boys
 g = girls
 T = total

School Group Differences

The main finding concerning the school groups is clear: children from modern schools were more positively and actively identified with their schools than children from traditional schools (see Table 7–1). The extent of positive identification, in fact, followed the exact order of modern-traditional philosophy in the schools, with Conrad children most positive and Browning children least so. As already noted, none of these privileged children was bitterly alienated or bewildered in relation to his school, but, on the comparative scale that was used, the percentage of negative and ambivalent children was particularly high in the most traditional school. A relatively high proportion of Conrad children, on the other hand, were positive and enthusiastic.

It might be noted, as impressionistic substantiation of this finding, that the research staff felt the children of Conrad to be more ambivalent about our testing program than many children of other schools, principally because it took them away from ongoing class activities. Children in all schools varied in their attitudes toward the project; some were openly delighted to leave their classrooms, some curious or pleased at the attention, some anxious and uneasy, some polite but guarded, and so on. This variety existed among Conrad children as well, but it was also evident that Conrad children more frequently felt "interrupted" when called to a session than other children, leaving school activities with some reluctance.

The pattern of boy and girl attitudes was different in the several schools (see Table 7–1). Girls of the three public schools were generally more positive in their feelings than boys, and the girls of Dickens were more positive than any other public school group. In Conrad, however, the pattern was reversed. Conrad boys were clearly more positive toward school than other boys and were even more positive than girls of the same school.

It has sometimes been said of schools such as Conrad that the curriculum is geared more to the interests of boys than girls; by the same token, it has sometimes been noted that the structure and demands of traditional public schools are more compatible with the temperament and potential docility of girls. Such generalizations must be taken with considerable caution, but they may offer some partial explanation of our findings. Whatever the explanation, it is particularly interesting that Conrad boys were so identified with their school. In the chapters to come, the material presented will suggest particularly strong effects on Conrad girls and raise some question about the impact of Conrad on the boys. It is thus of special interest that Conrad boys were so notably positive in their attitudes toward their school.

The material that has been presented, as a prologue to the coming chapters, establishes a difference among the children in their attitudes toward school. Is such a difference important in and of itself? Perhaps the answer to such a question depends, in itself, on the educational orientation. Within a traditional framework, indifference or dislike of school might be accepted as regrettable but as an unavoidable by-product, in some children, of the necessary emphasis on the work, effort, and discipline involved in the educational enterprise. Within the more modern framework, however, the fact that a child disliked school would be disturbing, and the knowledge that he was positively identified would be taken as gratifying evidence that an important cornerstone had been laid. It would be considered that a pivotal condition for learning had been established. Perhaps within each framework, however, the full meaning of the child's feeling about school would have to be evaluated in the context of other material about his functioning.

In the material reported in the following chapters it will be evident that the internalized effects of schooling, as we measured them, were sometimes consistent with expectations and sometimes not. To this point, however, we have established certain basic differences in the experiences, reactions and attitudes of children from traditional and modern schools: their experiences in the classroom were different; their reactions in the classroom differed accordingly; and, by the data presented here, their sense of positive identification with their schools differed predictably as a function of the school's philosophy and orientation.

NOTES

1. See Chapter 11 for children's attitude toward other aspects of school life.
2. It is evident, of course, that the articulate alienated youth, the college dropouts, the avant garde "beats" and "hippies," do come from such populations, but they repudiate the value of their schooling at a more advanced stage.
3. A separate statistical analysis of the three public schools indicated that girls from Browning, Adams, and Dickens clearly expressed more positive feelings than the boys of these schools ($F = 10.14$; $p < .01$).

C H A P T E R

8

COGNITIVE FUNCTIONING

The school's effect upon the child's cognitive behavior goes beyond the acquisition of academic skills. It influences his style of thinking and the meaning and value he assigns to intellectual activity. Because this influence takes many forms, and may affect each child differently, it was necessary to use a variety of media for assessing cognitive behavior to be sure that representative aspects of school impact would be identified.

It had been predicted that the children from the modern schools, more than those from the traditional schools, would tend to search for relationships and implications; try many approaches in solving a problem; value the process of thinking as well as its end product; rely on internal standards and evaluation in defining intellectual success and failure. It is evident from these expectations that we did not wish to confine ourselves to cataloguing the academic skills and factual information acquired by the children. We were interested in styles of thinking and problem solving, but also in the values associated with the actual process of intellectual exploration; with the imaginativeness and originality of thought as well as its efficiency.

The decision to go beyond the mere gathering of test results parallels trends in the work of other psychologists interested in expanding existing strategy for the study of cognitive functioning. Klein (1954) and Gardner (1953; 1959) and their collaborators were among the first to conduct a series of studies which focused on qualitative features of cognition. Their explorations of cognitive style, of recurrent formal characteristics of thinking evoked by diverse stimulus situations, represented a significant departure from the traditional emphasis on the way in which specific response tendencies are learned. Recently, the work of Kagan and Sigel (see Kagan, Moss, and Sigel, 1963; Kagan, Rosman, Day, Albert, and Phillips, 1964; Sigel, Jarman, and Hanesian, 1967) has directed attention to stylistic variation in the cognitive behavior of children, introducing new methods for differentiating among their modes of ordering stimuli. Following the pioneer efforts of Guilford (1956), the need to further differentiate among components of the intellectual domain has also been a major emphasis of Getzels and Jackson (1962) and Wallach and Kogan (1965) in their studies of the distinctive characteristics of creative thinking. Bruner (see Bruner, Goodnow, and Austin, 1956; Bruner, Olver, and Greenfield, 1966) has been a dominant figure in recognizing the importance of processing and organizing information in the acquisition process, in calling for the study of thinking as well as of learning, and in actually applying the findings of his studies to the analysis of educational practice. Many of these developments represent overdue recognition of the work of Piaget (1928; 1929; 1950), of his developmental analysis of cognitive functioning and his interest in reflective thinking and logical reasoning rather than associative learning.

At the time of the study, much of this work was in its earliest stages. While it helped to suggest the experimental procedures most likely to evoke the cognitive behavior we wished to assess, this work was not sufficiently developed to offer a comprehensive statement of the significant dimensions of children's thinking or an established and refined methodology for measuring specific variables. Our final choice of measures was based upon the need to have conventional baseline information of the sort provided by standardized tests, as well as data which would reveal characteristics of the thinking process. Therefore, the methods of study included standardized group and individual tests of aptitude and achievement, and individual and group problem-solving situations.

Standardized Tests
of Intelligence and Achievement

Techniques and Measures

Group measures of intelligence and achievement were obtained from all subjects.

(i) **Stanford Achievement Test.** Five subtests were administered to provide an index of academic achievement according to traditional standards and methods of measurement. It was important to establish the school achievement of these children as such accomplishments are customarily assessed, while recognizing that the schools in the study differed sharply on school curriculum and the nature and objectives of child learning. The five subtests were:

Word Meaning
Paragraph Meaning
Arithmetic Reasoning
Science
Social Studies

(ii) **Kuhlmann-Anderson Intelligence Test.** Form E from this test was first included to accompany the appraisal of other more specific phases of cognitive functioning in the Year II sample, to establish the level of intellectual aptitude among the children in the study and thus provide perspective for examining their problem-solving performance. Preliminary informal evaluation of the study samples in each of the four schools, based on school records and teacher assessments, indicated that the four groups were all of above-average intelligence; no remarkable differences among them in intellectual endowment were apparent. The failure to confirm this expectation through intelligence testing during the second year of the study led to the belated administration of the Kuhlmann-Anderson Test to the Year I sample as well (Form F, because the test was administered one year later). As a result, the entire study sample was either administered Form E or F of the Kuhlmann-Anderson Test.

(iii) **Wechsler Intelligence Scale for Children, Performance Scale.** The five subtests of the WISC Performance Scale were administered to the Year II children to provide a less verbal index of intelligence, as it is defined by test performance, and to help clarify the group test findings:

Picture Arrangement, Block Design, Picture Completion, Object Assembly, Coding.

INTERCORRELATIONS AMONG MEASURES

The intercorrelations among the three standardized tests are presented in Appendix BB, Table 1. The largest correlations are almost always between the Kuhlmann-Anderson and the Stanford Achievement Tests despite the fact that they ostensibly measure different attributes—aptitude and achievement. Clearly the similarity of their format and the overlap in test-taking skills requisite for successful performance on each test account for the correlation among the scores.

Group Characteristics and Sex Differences

The group test performance of most of the public school children tended to be in the above-average to superior range (see Table 8–1). Their

TABLE 8–1

Standardized Tests of Intelligence and Achievement

Source	(N)	Sex §	Browning	Adams	Dickens	Conrad	Total	Analysis of Variance
KUHLMANN-ANDERSON IQ SCORES (Form F, Year I Ss only)		b	130.80	134.40		114.17	125.69	Schools: 8.27** Sex: .05 NS Schools × Sex: .26 NS
		g	132.50	129.50		114.80	125.88	
	(33)	T	131.56	131.38		114.45	125.79	
KUHLMANN-ANDERSON IQ SCORES (Form E, Year II Ss only)		b	125.25	119.78	116.25	102.10	114.14	Schools: 4.07* Sex: .01 NS Schools × Sex: 1.95 NS
		g	108.50	126.57	120.00	106.83	117.28	
	(64)	T	116.88	122.75	118.13	103.88	115.56	
STANFORD ACHIEVEMENT TEST (Composite of transformed raw scores of 5 subtests)		b	56.40	55.60	49.40	41.70	50.40	Schools: 11.30** Sex: 1.35 NS Schools × Sex: 2.12 NS
		g	48.30	53.60	50.50	43.50	49.60	
	(102)	T	53.11	54.70	50.00	42.40	50.10	
WISC PERFORMANCE SCALE IQ SCORES (Year II Ss only)		b	114.75	117.55	117.08	114.40	116.17	Schools: 1.92 NS Sex: .33 NS Schools × Sex: 1.05 NS
		g	103.50	124.28	115.75	112.00	115.23	
	(65)	T	109.13	120.50	116.42	113.41	115.74	

* $p < .05$
** $p < .01$
§ b = boys
   g = girls
   T = total

Kuhlmann-Anderson IQ scores were generally more than one standard deviation above the mean of the standardization group. Correspondingly, their grade equivalent scores on each of the Stanford Achievement Subtests ranged from one to three years above their chronological age level (see Appendix M). The results of the WISC Performance IQ, administered only to the second year sample, also revealed a superior level of functioning. For the most part, they performed smoothly and effectively, with a clear understanding of what the test required of them.

The children from Conrad—who had never been given a group test in school—performed quite differently. Their scores on the Kuhlmann-Anderson were only slightly above average, and their achievement test scores ranked them less than a year ahead of their age level. It was only on the WISC Performance Scale that they showed levels of superiority comparable to that achieved by the public school children.

Sex differences were not prominent among the results of the standardized test performance.[1] In general the girls tended to work slightly faster than the boys on the group tests; they attempted more items and also omitted more. On the Object Assembly Subtest of the WISC, boys scored higher than girls, exhibiting a similar but lesser tendency on the Block Design Subtest. Girls tended to score higher on the Coding Subtest (see Table 8–2).

School Group Differences

Table 8–1 presents school group means of the Kuhlmann-Anderson scores. Year I and II data are presented separately because they are based on different, though overlapping, forms of the Kuhlmann-Anderson.[2] The greatest difference among the school group means involved the Conrad school and was statistically reliable at both year levels. The trailing position of the Conrad school group was totally at variance with expectations; taken at face value, this measure would appear to negate the assumption that intellectual ability among the four groups was equivalent. Only the second-year girls from Browning approached the relatively low mean scores of the Conrad school group. Whereas the sex difference found in the Browning school occurred only in the second year and may have reflected a sampling anomaly, the low scores of the Conrad school involved both sexes and both years' samples.

The IQ units merely summarize the outcome; they do not identify the essential features of the marked difference in performance found between the Conrad school groups and the other school groups. The mean raw scores of each of the subtests constituting Form E and F of the Kuhlmann-Anderson are given in Appendix N, accompanied by other data which elaborate the findings. The data indicate that the lagging position of the Conrad school group was pervasive, although somewhat greater for Year

TABLE 8–2

Standard Scores for WISC Performance Scale Subtests

Subtest	Sex §	Mean Scores for School Groups					Analysis of Variance
		Browning	Adams	Dickens	Conrad	Total [1]	
Picture Completion	b	12.00	12.22	12.33	10.90	11.86	Schools: .54 NS
	g	11.00	13.43	10.33	12.29	11.60	Sex: .01 NS
	T	11.50	12.75	11.33	11.47	11.74	Schools × Sex: .80 NS
Picture Arrange-ment	b	12.00	12.78	11.75	12.50	12.26	Schools: 4.12*
	g	9.00	15.29	13.08	11.71	12.73	Sex: .00 NS
	T	10.50	13.88	12.42	12.18	12.48	Schools × Sex: 2.88*
Block Design	b	11.75	12.44	13.00	13.30	12.80	Schools: 1.28 NS
	g	9.75	13.00	12.08	13.14	12.23	Sex: .44 NS
	T	10.75	12.69	12.54	13.24	12.54	Schools × Sex: .33 NS
Object Assembly	b	12.50	12.56	12.58	13.70	12.89	Schools: .98 NS
	g	9.00	11.00	11.42	11.57	11.03	Sex: 6.92*
	T	10.75	11.88	12.00	12.82	12.03	Schools × Sex: .41 NS
Coding	b	12.25	12.56	12.50	9.89	11.79	Schools: 6.18**
	g	13.75	14.71	14.33	9.50	13.34	Sex: 3.68 NS
	T	13.00	13.50	13.42	9.73	12.51	Schools × Sex: .54 NS

1. N = 65 *except for Coding Subtest, where* N = 63.
* $p < .05$
** $p < .01$
§ b = *boys*
  g = *girls*
  T = *total*

II than for Year I, and considerably greater for some subtests than for others. Nearly all the Kuhlmann-Anderson subtests which the Conrad group found most difficult required the child to search short lists of nouns and identify those which he was told were related in some specific way: pairs which constituted opposites, single words which were not members of the general class to which the others belonged, trios which had a common class membership, and so forth. The Conrad children in both years had difficulty with these subtests, but they posed the greatest hardship for the Year II sample, particularly the boys. This group of boys appeared to be least able to cope with the new tasks introduced by the test; their performance on the very first item of each subtest tended to be unusually low. The Year II Browning girls performed relatively poorly on many of the same subtests, but here the difficulty was restricted to the small sample from the second year; it was not evinced by the Year I Browning girls or by any boys from Browning.

It is apparent that much of the discrepancy between the Conrad school and the remaining groups is traceable to the much slower working pace of the Conrad children—which in turn probably reflected both the testing situation per se and the fact that they had had less continuous practice in the skill subjects. They consistently attempted many fewer items (see Appendix N). For the most part, the proportion of their correct responses was indistinguishable from that of the other groups. The proportion of items answered correctly was independent of the number attempted, except for the Year II boys from Conrad and the Year II girls from Browning. There was a greater tendency for the Conrad school children to omit items; as noted, this did not result in greater accuracy for this group.

The Stanford Achievement Test results yielded essentially the same pattern of performance. Some of the difficulties encountered by the Year II Conrad group on this longer, and therefore more demanding, test became accentuated. The Year II children from Conrad had never experienced any form of group testing prior to their participation in the study. The stress created by this more difficult test battery became so great that a contagious banter and protest gradually developed during two of the subtests to the point where the test administration had to be curtailed just short of the allotted time period.[3] Although existing scoring norms could therefore not be applied to the results of these two subtests, the pattern of performance on them was not qualitatively different from that on the remaining subtests.

The mean grade equivalent score for each school group of boys and girls is presented in Appendix M. In close correspondence with the Kuhlmann-Anderson testing, the most salient features of the Stanford Achievement Test results is the trailing position of the Conrad school group. This occurred to approximately the same degree in each of the subtests. In general, it may be observed that the three public school groups were about two years in advance of the national norms, whereas the Conrad school group was performing at its grade level or just slightly above. All the groups were most advanced (relative to the norms) in the verbal subtests of Paragraph Meaning and Word Meaning and least so in the Arithmetic Reasoning and Science.

A more detailed analysis of the Achievement Test data is summarized in Appendix P and indicates a close resemblance to the pattern found in the Kuhlmann-Anderson Test. The children from the two traditional schools (Adams and Browning) consistently worked most rapidly and always attempted the most items. The modern public school children (Dickens) usually trailed them and Conrad was a distant last. The proportion of items of those attempted which were answered correctly is remarkably similar for the three public schools on most of the subtests, with the mean proportion for the Conrad school falling slightly below the public school groups' level. Again, there is no inverse relationship between speed and accuracy as might have been anticipated. Here, too, the most traditional group (Browning) omitted the fewest items while the Conrad school group was most prone to omitting items.

Item analysis of the Stanford Achievement Test data did not reveal dramatic variations in performance on individual items as a function of school group membership, although there were some differences between the children from the Conrad school and the three public schools. The Conrad group seemed to have more detailed information about material they had studied intensively, such as that concerning Colonial and Revolutionary times; they had slightly less general knowledge. They were less facile in arithmetic operations involving subtraction, division, and multiplication and were less clear about word meanings than the other children.

By far the most prominent difference among the school groups was the less efficient test-taking pace of the Conrad children. If only those items are considered to which all four groups responded, differences among the groups are slight and in no way anticipate the striking differences among their total scores. It is apparent, both from direct observation of their behavior while taking the tests and from the pattern of their test scores, that the Conrad children were markedly deficient in test-taking ability. The nature of this deficit is partially clarified by the WISC Performance Scale data.

The results of the WISC Performance Scale, administered to the 65 children comprising the Year II sample, are presented in Table 8–1. They show a startling shift in the relative position of the Conrad school group. The overall group means of the four schools are no longer reliably distinguishable from each other. When compared with the pattern of group test findings, only the markedly trailing position of the small number of Year II Browning girls remains intact.

The change in the Conrad group's performance pattern would have been even greater were it not for the WISC Coding Subtest scores (see Table 8–2). This subtest presented a paper-and-pencil task very similar in content to the Kuhlmann-Anderson Test.[4] The data clearly indicate that the relative position of the Conrad group on the Coding Subtest is very similar to their standing on the group tests. When this link in content with the group tests is excluded, the relative standing of the Conrad school on WISC scores is even more enhanced. They scored highest of all groups on the Block Design and Object Assembly Subtests. Their performance ranked ahead of the other school groups on the trio of WISC scales designated by Witkin (1962) as the "intellectual index" in his study of the analytic field approach in psychological differentiation.[5]

The inferences which may be drawn from the standardized test data are not easily reconcilable. The written group test findings clearly indicate that the Conrad school children were less prepared, both technically and emotionally, to take these tests. The surge of protest and disorganization which led to the disruption of the Achievement Test administration demonstrated that they felt inadequate to the task. In the light of the WISC findings, however, it would appear inappropriate to conclude that the Conrad children as a group possessed less innate ability or that they were pervasively less competent to cope with cognitive tasks.

In accounting for the discrepancy between the WISC and Kuhlmann-Anderson scores, one would ascribe greatest significance to the form of administration (individual or group), the medium (verbal or written), and the speed factor. The public school children, particularly those from the two traditional schools, had learned to mobilize their resources to meet a prescribed speed of functioning; the equation of speed with excellence is a value to which the traditional school child is exposed early. The group tests, moreover, are similar to the written, workbook tasks which they are given as part of their daily classroom activities. Although many of the WISC subtests are also timed, the totality of items to be answered are not visible—as they are in a group test—to serve as an incentive to the speed response.

Practice in working at speed, along with the emotional readiness to respond rapidly, are not the only factors differentiating the groups. The group tests call for a response in which words and ideas are divorced from conventional context. Such a skill was not cultivated in the Conrad children, who were much more accustomed to dealing with words and concepts within meaningful contexts and wholes and who experienced words in isolation infrequently. In their earlier schooling, there had been little emphasis on the learning of individual words, on writing or spelling drills, on exercises involving the listing of synonyms and antonyms. Instead, they had from the beginning been exposed to experiences in which words were introduced to serve specific purposes in a meaningful framework.

On the other hand, the Conrad school group's performance cannot be interpreted as showing a generalized deficiency in abstract thinking. Their high scores on the Block Design Subtest of the WISC, commonly regarded as the best index of abstract reasoning ability in the WISC Performance Scale, demonstrated their skill in this area when the context was more in accord with their previous experience. Their superiority in the Block Design and Object Assembly Subtests illustrates, too, the importance of motor activity as an accompaniment to their thinking patterns. Their school programs placed much greater emphasis upon multiple media of experience: on directly acting out and living through those aspects of reality about which they were learning, on manipulating materials as part of the path toward understanding. Their success in these WISC subtests can at least partly be accounted for in terms of the sheer amount of experience they had had in manipulating objects as part of a problem-solving situation. It suggests, too, that these children had been taught different styles of thinking and that they emphasized different media for interacting with ideas.

Intercorrelations among these three standardized tests within each school group offer another view from which to examine differences among the school groups (see Appendix Q). In the Conrad school, the high degree of intercorrelation between the Kuhlmann-Anderson and Stanford Achievement scores underlines the common problem evoked by both instruments in selected members of the group. Also, according to expectations, their performance on the WISC is virtually unrelated to the outcome of the group testing. If their scores on the group tests were a true indication of general intellectual ability, they should have shown a greater degree of relationship with WISC performance. Dickens, the modern public school, presents a pattern of interrelatedness somewhat similar to Conrad, but shows more intercorrelation between the two tests of intelligence (Kuhlmann-Anderson and WISC).

The contrasting patterns of interrelatedness found within the two traditional schools was unexpected. In the Adams school there is a startling absence of interrelationship among the scores of the three standardized tests, whereas all the intercorrelations in Browning are very high. Differences in variability within the two groups probably account for part of this disparity. In addition, the high degree of interrelatedness found in Browning may be consistent with the global way in which children are characteristically evaluated in the traditional school. The Browning results suggest that children begin to respond to all tests in accordance with expectations set by their relative position in the prevailing system of evaluation. The contrasting set of findings from Adams do not at all adhere to this pattern.

Relationships to Home Background

The correlation between home background variables and standardized test scores tends to be low (see Appendix CC, Table 1). Because of the special relevance of the educational background of parents to the cognitive functioning of their children, the correlation between standardized test scores and educational level of parents is presented as an addition to Table 1 of Appendix CC. Correlations between group test scores and parent educational level are positive but low; they do not account for substantial sources of the test score variance. In the light of these findings it seems evident that school experience—as it mediated acquisition of knowledge, test-wiseness, and other attributes associated with successful test performance—intervened and formed a decisive influence in this particular instance.

Problem Solving

A set of problem-solving situations was introduced in order to evoke samples of the children's thinking behavior. In contrast to the rapid fire, multiple-item approach of standardized testing procedures, with its emphasis on visual attentiveness to printed detail, the problem-solving tasks allowed the child a greater range of unhurried exploration. The children were encouraged to ask questions, offer ideas, and think out loud. In some cases they were required to deal with real objects. All the tasks were sufficiently open-ended to permit the emergence of stylistic expression such as pace, flexibility/rigidity, and associative flow; they provided the opportunity to observe goal-directed thought in microcosm. A group problem-solving situation, in addition to four individually administered tasks, were given. All are presented and discussed separately below.

INDIVIDUAL PROBLEM SOLVING

Four problem-solving tasks (see Appendix AA) were administered to the entire second year sample ($N = 65$) in order to assess process aspects of cognition.

Techniques and Measures

In order to sample a wide assortment of intellectual behaviors, problems were selected which varied in the nature of their cognitive demands. The four problem-solving tests were: Cylinder, Meaning Context, Spies, and Uncommon Uses. The responses to each of these four problem-solving situations were given two ratings: (a) for the degree of relationship thinking they demonstrated, according to a number of criteria established for each technique; and (b) for solution success. The relationship thinking measure attempted to assess the *process* which mediated the outcome, such as the use of reasoning, the flow of ideas and connections, the organization and strategy used to analyze and fulfill the demands of the problem. The relationship thinking rating is an attempt to distinguish formal aspects of the intellectual process from a single index of its efficiency—problem solution.[6] The solution success rating was an assessment of the *outcome* of the cognitive problem—whether or not a correct solution was finally arrived at irrespective of the quality of the performances leading up to the solution. In all but the Spies task it was possible to solve the problem in more than one way; alternative solutions and partial solutions were therefore credited. In addition, there were two composite ratings—the degree of relationship thinking and solution success—of performance on all four problem-solving tasks.

(i) **Cylinder.** Adapted from Saugstad's work with adults (1952), this is a nonverbal problem in which the child is presented with the task of removing a wooden cylinder from a tubular plastic container without overturning the container. The fit of the cylinder inside the container is such that it cannot be grasped and removed with the fingers. The task is divided into three stages: stage 1, in which the child is asked to give his ideas for solving the problem; stage 2, in which he is shown (but may not touch) a screwdriver, thimble, thread, pencil, magnet, and a pair of pliers and asked to suggest ways of getting the cylinder out with these objects; and stage 3, in which he is encouraged to try to get the cylinder out, using any of the objects or any ideas he may have. If he does not arrive at the preferred solution, that of displacing the cylinder with water from a pitcher standing unobtrusively on a different part of the table, he is given a suggestive clue—he is shown a boat floating in a dish of water, into which more water is poured so that the level of the boat rises.

This technique requires the resourcefulness and flexibility to overcome functional fixedness—that is, to perceive the casual pitcher of water as a usable aid. The different stages of the problem provide an opportunity for comparing problem-solving ability under varying degrees of structure and to assess how important it is to be able to manipulate the implements in solving the problem. The technique also tests the ability to produce goal-directed ideas, judge and criticize their usefulness, tolerate restrictions and, possibly, frustration, and follow through and relate ideas in different contexts.

(a) *Relationship Thinking*—A rating on a five-point scale, based on the quality of verbal reasoning, the number and adequacy of suggested solutions during stages 1 and 2, the reasons given for rejection of tools, the fertility of ideas, the degree to which ideas were carried through, the stage when solution was achieved and its nature (that is, whether by using the water or some other, acceptable method).

(b) *Solution Success*—A rating on a five-point scale, based on the number of acceptable ideas offered to solve the problem; the water solution was given double credit in the tabulation of the number of suggestions.

(ii) **Meaning Context.** Adapted from the work of Werner and Kaplan

(1952), this is a verbal technique in which the same nonsense word is embedded in a sequence of five sentences. There are four non-sense words and 20 sentences (as well as a demonstration item with three sentences). The child is asked to supply the real meaning of the nonsense word after each sentence is presented. (The first sentence in the demonstration sequence is "You cannot be a *dinrep* until you grow up.") The context of each sentence in one sequence is the clue to the meaning of the nonsense word.

At the beginning, the child's guess may have a wide range since there are many sensible, though not necessarily correct, responses to the first one or two sentences. As the task progresses, he has to exercise greater flexibility and must be able to change his concepts, integrate various kinds of information, and check the feasibility of his present response against all previous clues.

(a) *Relationship Thinking*—A rating, on a five-point scale, of the number of sequences successfully solved, the number of violations (that is, when the word offered made no sense of the sentence or previous sentences), the quality of verbalized reasoning, and the proc-ess of reaching solution.

(b) *Solution Success*—The sum of correct responses to all 20 sen-tences (that is, appropriate to a sentence and all previous sentences within each sequence). Double credit was given for correct responses to final sentences.

(iii) **Spies.** Patterned after the Vigotsky Concept Formation Test, this task consists of identifying three "spies" from a group of 12 dolls. The child is asked to imagine himself living at the time of the Ameri-can Revolution and to imagine that he has a very important message to deliver to three American spies. He has come to a marketplace to find them. There are 12 people in this marketplace and he does not know which three are the spies. The only thing he knows is that in some im-portant way they are alike and that it is possible to see how they are alike by looking at them. The child is encouraged to ask questions as long as they can be answered yes or no.

The problem demands that he be able to ask questions that will tell him what he wants to know, that he retain and organize what he learns, that he adopt new hypotheses, check their apparent validity, and relin-quish those which don't work. Success in this test depends a good deal on the coherence and effectiveness of his conceptual approach. The test throws into relief the problem-solving *process* and separates the charac-teristics of strategy from the end result.

(a) *Relationship Thinking*—A rating on a five-point scale which assessed the general approach to and handling of the task, including the use of logic and sequence in the questions asked, the level of ab-straction, and the use or misuse of the information obtained in the light of the evidence.

(b) *Solution Success*—Whether or not the problem was solved (that is, the three dolls identified as a group, distinct from others in appearance).

(iv) **Uncommon Uses.** This is a variation of a technique developed by Guilford (see Wilson, Guilford, and Christensen, 1953) in his studies of creativity in adults. As it was administered in the present study, the problem calls for the examiner to mention nine objects, one at a time (for example, newspaper, salt, lipstick), asking the child what it is usually used for. The child is then asked to think of other, uncommon uses for each of the objects.

(a) *Relationship Thinking*—A rating on a five-point scale, based on the tendency to explore physical aspects of the object itself, experiment with ideas which would alter its size, quality, and quantity or differentiate and elaborate the function of the object.

(b) *Solution Success*—A weighted score, based on the number of adequate nonrepetitive responses. A truly new idea, representing a major shift from the previous response, was given full credit; minor changes were assigned half-credit.

INTERCORRELATIONS AMONG MEASURES

The correlation among problem-solving measures for all groups combined was low, although in several instances the coefficients were significantly different from zero (see Appendix BB, Table 1). The common variance shared by any two relationship thinking ratings or any two solution success ratings never exceeded ten percent. This attests both to the specificity of each problem and the limited reliability of problem-solving performance, facts well documented in the research literature.

The correlations between problem-solving ratings and standardized test scores were as high, and even somewhat higher, than those among the problem-solving ratings themselves. This is probably attributable to the greater reliability of the multi-itemed standardized test scores. It is not surprising that the solution success scores of the problem-solving behavior correlate more highly with standardized test scores than do the relationship thinking ratings, since standardized test scores are essentially solution scores. Nor was it unexpected that the Meaning Context solution success ratings correlated most highly with the standardized test scores, since they were based on responses to the most verbal of the problem-solving tasks. In general, the relationship thinking and solution success rating overlapped substantially; the correlation between these two scores for each of the four problems was high.

Group Characteristics and Sex Differences

All four problem-solving tasks contained an element of surprise, introducing some form of irregularity to which the child had to accommodate. The Cylinder problem required that a pitcher and a glass of drinking water, never referred to, be perceived as useful for solving the problem, while the Uncommon Uses task called for the child to think of unfamiliar ways of using familiar objects. The Meaning Context test presented sentences which were entirely meaningful except for a single, unexpected nonsense word. The Spies problem seemed straightforward in asking the child to find the three dolls which were alike in some way. But in order to solve the problem, the child had to abandon his natural expectation that the trio would have a single form or color in common and move to a more abstract basis of commonality—namely, one that combined two specific aspects of the figures into a relationship (shared color). Despite these intricacies, the cognitive reorganization required for solving these tasks was shown to be well within the potential of most of these children. By age nine, they were familiar with the form and demands of an intellectual puzzle and, in most cases, the intellectual challenge was sufficiently compelling to sustain highly motivated and goal-directed problem-solving behavior of substantial duration.

The Cylinder problem was clearly the most concrete problem of the set. It involved real objects, made available real implements, and sought a very concrete outcome. Taken as a whole, the performance of these children on the Cylinder problem was an impressive demonstration of the level of mastery and competence they had achieved by age nine. Their responses were swift, thorough, and complete. They cited a full array of plausible (but not necessarily possible) solutions, quite often commenting upon the contingencies or special difficulties associated with each method. The problem posed by the cylinder was relatively familiar; it offered a task they could fully understand, and required a set of instrumental behaviors well within their repertoires. The force and effectiveness of their performance well illustrated Piaget's characterization of their age level as one concerned with concrete operations.

Some of the children could accurately gauge the potential usefulness of the tools made available before they tried them out. They would preface the trial with an accurate forecast of the ultimate inefficiency of the tools for solving the problem. The response of one child illustrates this pattern:

> A pencil wouldn't stick—not good; screwdriver—you couldn't make a hole; the thimble would make it harder to get your hand in; a magnet only sticks to metal; pliers aren't good because there's not enough room to stick the pliers in; the rope—you couldn't tie, it's too hard to tie, you might as well take it out with your hands if you could get your hand in to tie the string.

Some children combined such an analysis with speculations regarding the kinds of tools that were needed, occasionally devising a new instrument in their minds to meet the specific demands of the problem. Others, however, behaved as though the usefulness of the tools could not be judged without actually using them. They would methodically try each tool without anticipatory judgments of their usefulness.

The Meaning Context test is an unorthodox form of presenting what is actually a riddle, to which the subject is asked to give a tentative answer on the basis of a set of defining clues. As the problem progresses, it becomes increasingly necessary for the child to coordinate and integrate information from previous sources, all within the verbal realm. Some children recognized these demands at once, and were flexible enough to change their response according to each new clue while checking the specifications of previous clues. The (correct) response to one item, by a child whose checking procedure was completely overt, is given below:

1. A *corplum* may be used for support.
ARCH. Or something to hold you up. A CANE or an ARCH.
2. *Corplums* may be used to close off an open place.
A DOOR. Couldn't be used for support—but it could be used for an open place. But it wouldn't make sense.
3. A *corplum* may be long or short, thick or thin, strong or weak.
It *might* be . . . CLOTHES. They could be strong or weak, etc.; if in a closet, on hangers, they could close off an open place. And for support, they could be warm. And could be long or short, thick or thin.
4. A wet *corplum* does not burn.
Ohhhhhh. (Silently checks all the sentences.) Heh, I know what it is, I think. It could be OURSELVES, our SKIN. SKIN could be . . . could close off an entrance. And for support, if you didn't have SKIN, you wouldn't be alive. And you could be long or short, thick or thin, strong or weak. And when you're wet, you can't burn. When people are on fire they go into a lake, a nearby lake, so at least they won't burn.
5. You can make a *corplum* smooth with sandpaper.
Ooh. (Silently checks each sentence and nods after each one.) WOOD! Because you can make lots of things out of wood—a door for closing off an open space—and for support you can make canes out of wood. And wood can be long or short, thick or thin, strong or weak. And wet wood doesn't burn . . . I'm not sure . . . And you can make wood smooth with sandpaper.

However, not all the children could cope so effectively with this problem. Some would not alter their initial response despite the contra-indicating clues from subsequent sentences, while others responded anew to each sentence, unconcerned with the requirements of previous sentences. A few could not free themselves from the notion that the nonsense word was real and kept guessing its meaning on the basis of its spelling and sound. For example, their response to "Some people always *ashder*" would be "answer" or "shudder." Others offered synonyms for the context, ignoring the fact that the nonsense word contributed an extra element to the meaning of the sentence.

In many respects the Spies problem was the most difficult. It called for the most concern with strategy of approach, and offered the greatest opportunity for re-evaluating strategy as experience with the problem increased. It not only required astuteness in eliciting useful information, but the ability to retain and organize data once received and to deduce the solution from the body of accumulated information. Finally, a good deal of flexibility of thought is necessary to conceive of the relational category required for solution.

This problem offered the greatest opportunity to observe the diversity of problem-solving styles within as well as among the children. Some of them worked for as long as thirty minutes without success, whereas a small number solved the problem almost at once. Most indicated that they understood what the problem required, that is, they attempted to identify relevant attributes and/or gave reasons for the solutions they offered; many children, after they had experienced a certain amount of failure, abandoned more systematic procedures for less organized approaches. Others began chaotically and then moved into a more systematic pattern of inquiry. Others simply began to select trios of figures in rapid fire, attempting to identify the spies by way of a direct onslaught on the whole group.[7] Some children limited their questioning to the identification of possible relevant attributes. The more elegant problem solvers did not always find the solution. Some lacked the perseverance to continue their line of questioning, while others failed to move their exploration outside a circumscribed realm of ideas. Some asked very good questions but paid scant attention to the answers, while others gave less thought to their questioning but were good processors of the information they managed to receive. There were a few children who believed the distinctive identifying feature of the spies to be a psychological trait which could be detected by the figure's facial appearance. They chose figures because they looked "smart" or "bold" or "sly." A small number apparently did not understand the problem from the outset, worked maladaptively for a brief period, and then gave up. The Spies problem data demonstrated graphically that nine-year-olds are capable of deep and sustained involvement in the problem-solving process, that there is enormous variation in the style of approach among children by this age, and that within themselves they operate at different levels of efficiency and sophistication during the course of a single brief problem-solving episode.

It was the rare nine-year-old child who could not offer some form of response to most items on the Uncommon Uses task, even though many of the children tended to give routine, rather obvious responses. For those who enjoyed the opportunity to associate unorthodox uses to familiar objects, the test became an opportunity for flights of the imagination. Salt was seen as something to glue on paper to make a snowy scene; a hammer, to get order in the court or for chopping down dead logs; a penny, for settling arguments by way of heads or tails; a brick as a doorstop; tires could be used as hoops for training dogs or could be piled up to form a clubhouse. For a few, the test represented an opportunity to suggest ways of altering objects, of taking them apart and transforming their physical appearance. A newspaper could be used to build a fire, a blanket could be unthreaded to use its wool, a penny could be melted to obtain the copper. A few answered in personal terms, calling upon their own experience with each object. "When you play ball, you put it on your hands (salt) to make your hands sticky to hold the bat better; sometimes we trade pennies—old for new—or we spin it to see who's tails; when we have a Cub Scout pack meeting we use a blanket for a curtain."

Differences between the boys and girls varied with the problem situation (see Table 8-3). The mean ratings of performance on the Cylinder problem were substantially greater for the boys than the girls in the two traditional schools. These sex differences did not appear among the children from the modern schools. Similarly, of the eight children from traditional schools who achieved the water solution without clues, seven were boys, whereas among a like number achieving the solution in the modern schools, there was equal representation of the sexes. Performance on the Meaning Context test yielded a similar pattern, except that boys scored higher than girls in the Conrad school as well as in the two traditional schools.

Sex differences in mean ratings on the Spies problem were small. In every school group, however, the girls asked many more questions than the boys despite the fact that they worked on the problem for slightly less time. Their greater number of questions, accompanied by a greater tendency to repeat questions, led them to identify more attributes. Nevertheless, the boys offered more solutions.

In the Uncommon Uses task, the mean ratings of boys, similar to the Cylinder problem, exceeded those of the girls in the traditional schools; but the girls in this case outperformed the boys in the modern schools. The girls gave more responses on this task and, correspondingly, were more repetitious. In each of the four school groups, they spontaneously offered more verbal elaboration of their response, explaining how or why objects could be used in various ways.

Composite ratings of performance on all four problem-solving situations summarize the trends of sex differences which were obtained on individual tasks: in the traditional schools the boys had a higher mean rating and in the modern school the girls scored higher; in neither case was this difference statistically significant.

TABLE 8–3
Problem-Solving Performance

MEASURE Source, and Scale Range	Sex §	Browning	Adams	Dickens	Conrad	Total [1]	Analysis of Variance
RELATIONSHIP THINKING Cylinder Scale Range: 1–5	b	4.25	3.66	3.50	2.70	3.40	Schools: 2.12 NS Sex: 4.50* Schools × Sex: 1.56 NS
	g	2.75	2.85	3.54	2.57	3.03	
	T	3.50	3.31	3.52	2.65	3.23	
RELATIONSHIP THINKING Meaning Context Scale Range: 1–5	b	3.00	3.11	2.91	3.20	3.06	Schools: 1.05 NS Sex: 1.16 NS Schools × Sex: 1.44 NS
	g	2.00	3.00	3.50	2.42	2.93	
	T	2.50	3.06	3.21	2.88	3.00	
RELATIONSHIP THINKING Spies Scale Range: 1–5	b	3.50	2.44	3.00	2.50	2.77	Schools: .57 NS Sex: .04 NS Schools × Sex: .36 NS
	g	3.00	3.00	2.91	2.71	2.90	
	T	3.25	2.69	2.96	2.59	2.83	
RELATIONSHIP THINKING Uncommon Uses Scale Range: 1–5	b	3.75	3.44	2.75	2.10	2.86	Schools: 2.43 NS Sex: 1.07 NS Schools × Sex: 3.38*
	g	2.25	2.85	3.41	2.42	2.90	
	T	3.00	3.19	3.08	2.24	2.88	
RELATIONSHIP THINKING Composite Rating Scale Range: 1–3	b	2.50	2.00	1.91	1.50	1.89	Schools: 1.05 NS Sex: .49 NS Schools × Sex: 2.23 NS
	g	1.50	1.85	2.25	1.71	1.93	
	T	2.00	1.94	2.08	1.59	1.91	
SOLUTION SUCCESS Cylinder Scale Range: 1–5	b	3.00	2.44	2.08	1.90	2.23	Schools: 1.92 NS Sex: 2.17 NS Schools × Sex: .58 NS
	g	2.25	1.85	2.18	1.71	2.00	
	T	2.62	2.19	2.13	1.82	2.13	
SOLUTION SUCCESS Meaning Context: Total number of correct responses all sentences Actual Range: 7–23	b	17.00	17.77	16.66	16.50	16.94	Schools: 1.74 NS Sex: 2.42 NS Schools × Sex: 1.42 NS
	g	14.00	16.42	18.33	13.29	16.13	
	T	15.50	17.18	17.50	15.17	16.57	
SOLUTION SUCCESS Spies Scale Range: 1–2	b	2.00	1.33	1.42	1.40	1.46	Schools: 1.27 NS Sex: .00 NS Schools × Sex: 1.81 NS
	g	1.50	1.71	1.50	1.42	1.53	
	T	1.75	1.50	1.45	1.41	1.49	
SOLUTION SUCCESS Uncommon Uses: Total number of nonrepetitive responses Actual Range: 13–68	b	28.50	34.88	30.08	25.30	29.77	Schools: .59 NS Sex: 1.54 NS Schools × Sex: .62 NS
	g	30.25	33.85	34.08	35.00	33.73	
	T	29.37	34.47	32.08	29.29	31.60	
SOLUTION SUCCESS Composite‡ Actual Range: 37–60	b	54.50	51.89	49.17	47.60	50.03	Schools: 1.44 NS Sex: .54 NS Schools × Sex: 1.44 NS
	g	48.25	51.00	52.00	47.29	50.17	
	T	51.38	51.50	50.58	47.47	50.09	

Mean Scores for School Groups

1. $N = 65$ except for Cylinder Problem, where $N = 64$.
* $p < .05$ T = total
§ b = boys   ‡ Based on adjusted mean Z scores
  g = girls

School Group Differences

The mean ratings of performance on the Cylinder problem, presented in Table 8–3, are of a pattern whose essential form is repeated in the results of the other problem-solving ratings. None of the differences among school groups was reliable, though the three public school groups were rated above the Conrad school. The ratings of relationship thinking and solution success were in close correspondence, the greatest discrepancy in rank between relative standing in relationship thinking and solution success occurring in the Dickens school. As expected, these children's relationship thinking ratings were relatively higher than that of solution success.

All four school groups were similar in the qualitative features of their performance—in mean number of instances and adequacy of verbalized reasoning; in the number of suggestions which were made during the first phase of the problem when no implements were presented as well as in the total number of workable suggestions offered once implements were available; in the total number of ideas they put into practice once they were free to manipulate the implements and in the rating of their carry through of ideas into action once manipulation was possible. The children from Conrad presented slightly fewer suggestions and less verbalized reasoning during the first stage of the problem. Once the tools were shown to them, their level of performance became indistinguishable from the other groups. They were rated as somewhat less effective, however, in carrying out their expressed ideas once they were given opportunity to work with the implements.

The mean ratings of Meaning Context performance (see Table 8–3) indicate an absence of reliable differences among the school groups along either dimension of evaluation. Once again, as in the Cylinder problem, but by a slightly greater margin, the highest rating of relationship thinking was achieved by the Dickens school.

The basis for the low scores of the Browning school group on both dimensions of this test can better be understood by examining the qualitative features of their performance. Their responses to any given item were most often incorrect, and when they were responding correctly to current items they were more likely to ignore the context requirements of previous items. The Conrad children, particularly the boys, responded most cautiously. They more often refused to respond when they did not know the answer (an adaptive trait in this particular problem, where wrong guesses mislead the problem solver), and when they did respond, their response least often contradicted previous clues.

Table 8–3 presents ratings of relationship thinking and solution success in the Spies problem. Differences among the school groups were very small and unreliable for both ratings. The Browning group ranked first and Conrad group lowest. The modern school groups, Conrad and Dickens, asked fewer questions, repeated themselves slightly less frequently, and identified somewhat fewer attributes. They did not, however, offer fewer solutions.

The results of the Uncommon Uses task are given in Table 8–3. Here the trailing position of the Conrad school reached significant proportions. In addition, a reliable school-by-sex interaction was found among the relationship thinking scores.

The trailing position of the Conrad school group, particularly in the measure of relationship thinking, was not expected. The greater emphasis on resourcefulness and flexibility of thought encountered in the Conrad school would appear to be an asset in dealing with this task, yet the boys, at least, performed less well. If they were at a disadvantage in coping with this task, it was not because their school experience was unrelated to the cognitive processes required by this problem; more likely, it was because the problem implicitly required the child to respond volubly on demand.

Differences among the four school groups were not statistically significant on either of two composite ratings which summarize relationship thinking and solution success on all four problem-solving tasks. Of greatest significance among these relatively small school group differences is the fact that the most modern school of the continuum, Conrad, ranked last on both ratings and that the Dickens school, the most modern of the public schools, ranked slightly ahead of the two more traditional schools in relationship thinking, but trailed them in solution success. The consistently trailing position of the Conrad school was not predicted; the differential rank of the Dickens school was in accordance with expectations that modern school children would show relative strength in relationship thinking.

The intercorrelations among the problem-solving ratings, along with their degree of relationship to the standardized test procedures, are given for each school separately in Appendix Q. It may be observed that in most of the school groups the interrelatedness among the problem-solving ratings was low, the pattern of interrelatedness among problem-solving ratings closely paralleling that found among standardized test scores. There was virtually no communality among scores in either the Adams or Conrad school groups. The Browning group, on the other hand, continued to show marked degrees of interrelatedness among the problem-solving ratings as they did among the test scores. The Dickens group once again occupied the middle ground, showing a mixed pattern of interrelatedness.

Following essentially the same pattern, the relationship between the problem-solving ratings and the standardized tests varied with the school group studied. There was considerable correlation between three of the four problem-solving situations and the standardized tests in the

Browning school, with lesser but substantial coefficients found in Dickens. In both Adams and Conrad, virtually all the correlations were of zero magnitude.

These findings, together with the earlier results of the intercorrelations among standardized test scores, indicate that individual differences among any of the cognitive measures employed tend to possess relatively little generality. The important exception to this pattern is the Browning group, where relative standing on any one of the cognitive measures is a fairly good predictor of rank on any other.

Relationships to Home Background

Correlations between the problem-solving measures and home background variables tend to be low (see Appendix CC, Table 1). They account for only small portions of the variation found in problem-solving performance. The highest relationship between home background and problem-solving behavior was found among the boys, indicating some association between traditional home background and more effective performance on the Cylinder and Uncommon Uses problems.

GROUP PROBLEM SOLVING

In order to study cognitive functioning in a group situation, requiring joint planning and execution, a modified version of the Russell Sage Social Relations Test (see Damrin, 1959) was administered.

Techniques and Measures

The Russell Sage Social Relations Test was administered to all children in the classrooms in the study during the first year. Three groups, thus, were involved: Browning, Adams, and Conrad.

Russell Sage Social Relations Test (Group). This test is designed to assess the skill of a group of children in a classroom with regard to (a) devising a plan which is to govern their behavior in a defined problem-solving situation and (b) carrying out their plan and solving the problem. The test, therefore, has two distinct parts: the *Planning Stage* and the *Operations Stage*.

The classroom group is presented with the problem of building a house (and then a bridge) made of plastic blocks to match a demonstration model. Each child is given one or two blocks. The test involves, first a discussion among the children (the Planning Stage), then the actual building operation (the Operations Stage) which has a time limit.

Three observers recorded the group's behavior along certain dimensions, such as the participation, involvement, and communication among the children and their organizational technique. Time for completion of the construction was recorded and the accuracy of the reproduction was evaluated.

School Group Differences

A qualitative description of each group's performance, based upon the reports of the three observers, is summarized below:

BROWNING

This group was marked by the greatest tension and competition, the greatest rigidity of group structure, and the highest proportion of nonparticipants. Planning was hasty, with little interplay among participants. Once building began, a division of the class into three groups quickly emerged: a small central ring of builders, an outer ring who watched, and a remaining group of children who were completely excluded. At no time during the session were there any girls in the central group and few were in the ring of watchers. The building activity was accompanied by much bickering, tension release in the form of shouting, and a preoccupation among principal performers with claiming major credit for the accomplishment. ("I did most of it, with Harry"; "You did it, but I had to fix it.") The children completed the second construction accurately, but were not able to complete the first within the time limit.

ADAMS

In Adams, the performance had mixed features: evident talent, constructive activity, and effective attempts to mobilize a large group for a united effort, combined with processes destructive to the group's efforts, a general deterioration over time, and a failure to judge and revise their work independently.

There was a constructive exchange of ideas during the planning period, with children developing each other's plans and offering alternative possibilities for dividing and coordinating the work. Both boys and girls participated actively in the building. There were central and peripheral figures but much of the competition was centered in subgroups, with children committed to completing their subsection first. The Adams children had the greatest tendency to turn their work over to the adult for evaluation. They were not systematic or effective in judging their own performance or in revising their product. The group completed both constructions to their own satisfaction within the time limits, but their constructions were inaccurate in both instances.

CONRAD

The performance of the Conrad children had the qualities of an effective group effort, carried through with considerable *esprit de corps*. Planning was vigorous and relevant; building was self-propelled, effective, and technically accurate.

There were central, active figures here, as in the other schools, but less active members were also involved in the general effort. All the children found roles—some to analyze and communicate about patterns, some to spot the current needs, some to build. The general mood was less tense and competitive than in the other schools. The group saw itself as a working unit, dependent on the cooperative efforts of all members. Furthermore, they accepted the responsibility for reviewing their own work and finding their errors; they conducted a systematic check of the correspondence between their construction and the model before declaring it finished. They completed both models accurately within the time limits.

The spontaneous activity which followed completion of the second construction bears mention. The children re-formed the test blocks to fashion the figure of a man, likened it to George Washington, and finished by adding a "wig" which they shaped out of cotton lying on a nearby shelf.[8] The activity was characterized, as was most of the session, by a sense of productive autonomy, a flow of ideas that built on each other, harmonious relations among the children, and general pleasure in what they were doing.

The differences among these groups, while not expressed in quantitative form, are striking enough to indicate that group functioning and group problem solving constitute a completely distinct dimension of school impact. To be sure, the smaller size of the Conrad class placed this group in a very advantageous position with regard to the group problem-solving task. This circumstance does not fully explain the success of the Conrad group, however, nor the contrast between their performance and that of the Browning and Adams groups. The Conrad group was clearly experienced and predisposed to meld their efforts toward a single goal, with workmanlike attitudes and methods for managing the task at hand. Probably a number of features in their school life were relevant to their performance in this situation: the importance of the child group as a functioning and responsible unit; repeated experience in mediating relationships in a work context; the frequent use of nonverbal media as tools of thought; relative freedom from authoritative control; and the conception that child initiative and the extension of ideas are the core of learning. In the two traditional schools, the group task aroused an intense competitiveness which, together with lesser experience in modes of management, militated against successful group effort. In the most traditional school (Browning), the striving for personal dominance resulted in the exclusion of potential contributors. In Adams, the goal and expectation of final adult judgment resulted in abdication of the group's own work process short of evaluation and revision, thus undermining a potentially skillful performance.

Discussion

The exploration conducted with these children points to the impressive level of competence in selected areas of intellectual functioning they had already achieved, the specificity of these accomplishments from an individual difference point of view, and the profound but not completely predictable or consistent effect of school influence. Unfortunately, unresolved issues regarding the general nature of intelligence and the mapping of specific abilities becloud the answers to questions about the consequence of school experience for cognitive functioning. The cognitive domain has not undergone the degree of differentiation, both with regard to concept and method, required for a really comprehensive assessment of school effects. This state of affairs has produced gaps and ambiguities of assessment in the present study. In addition, owing to the skewness of the cognitive psychologist's armamentarium of measuring instruments, some differences among the school groups have been dramatically exposed, while other presumed differences may have gone unnoticed for the same reason.

Some of the most clear-cut quantitative differences among school groups found in the entire study are those involving the standardized test scores. The very gross and sweeping nature of the differences in group achievement and intelligence test scores found between the Conrad school group and the three public school groups appears to suggest the existence of a sharp and unequivocal difference in both general intelligence and school achievement. But contrary data from other sources, most notably those obtained from the WISC Performance Scale testing, must be taken into account. These additional dissonant data suggest the need for a basic reappraisal of the meaning of the standardized group test scores.

It is probably true that public school children were more accustomed to impersonal forms of testing while Conrad children flourished under conditions of more direct and personal confrontation; that the former were more advanced in reading skills while the latter were more experienced with objects and materials; that Conrad children were less test-wise in general than their public school counterparts. Other less concrete facets of school experience were probably also relevant, however. Children of the more traditional schools, for example, were well primed to meet the continuous sequence of challenge and response represented by standardized group tests. In general, the subject matter of the traditional schools was more elementaristic in character, with facts and skills presented in discrete units that could be efficiently learned. The child was expected to meet adult demands; to react with speed and accuracy to exercise, drill, and question.

The child's experience at Conrad was very different. Here the emphasis was more holistic and experiential. The school sought to engage the child in learning *about* something which he would find interesting and meaningful. Units of work were not cut to fit the material which needed to be learned; what needed to be learned was the relation of facts to each other and to more general ideas.

There were, then, important differences in the children's readiness to mobilize energy to meet an extrinsic, unrelated demand. Perhaps more fundamental, there were differences in what they focused their thought on and in the style and pace of thinking. For the traditional school child, the standardized psychological test reflected essentially the same approach to thinking and learning as the traditional school. Such tests are based on a conception of a field of knowledge as a universe of discrete items, a limitlessly large collection, of which the test itself constitutes a representative sample; they offer the child a series of such units for his rapid and efficient reaction. For the Conrad child, such a situation represented a decisive departure from school regimen. A sustained question-and-answer format was quite different from the coherent framework in which he normally encountered content and from the pace and style of inquiry to which he had grown accustomed. In taking a standardized test, the children from the traditional schools were undergoing an experience far more continuous in organization and epistemology with their pretest experience.

It is only comparatively recently that psychologists have begun to reevaluate critically the meaning of a standardized test. Getzels and Jacksons' (1962) study of differences between the high IQ and creative child began with the premise that the two were not necessarily synonymous. More recently, Wallach and Kogan (1965) report consistently low relationships between a battery of intelligence and creativity tests in a heterogeneous group of children. Thus, the need to examine other dimensions of intellectual functioning besides the classical variable of intelligence is gaining acceptance. But so far this trend is proceeding by examining dimensions in addition to intelligence rather than by revising the concept itself; the essential fabric of the concept of the intelligence test has remained intact.

At the same time, it is important to ask whether the greater difficulty with standardized tests encountered by the Conrad children may be indicative of a set style of functioning which adversely affected performance on tasks that were different from those they were accustomed to in school. Does the supportive setting of the modern school jeopardize the intellectual coping skill of the child? Will the disparity between how learning is presented in the modern school and its form outside and beyond school interfere with the child's ability to meet the demands of reality? The fact that Conrad children, tested at a somewhat older age, did not differ so greatly from the other groups suggests that some of their disability was beginning to dissipate.[9] It is reasonable to suggest that the Conrad children, by virtue of their particular mode of school experience, were less developed, at the point of fourth grade, with regard to the skills and emotional readiness associated with effective test behavior. It is also possible that the test-taking deficit was not permanent. The issues of later development and of the role given to test performance skills in the total conception of intellectual competence are important psycho-educational matters. They are considered more fully in the summarizing chapters.

Whatever questions they may raise, the group IQ and Achievement Test findings are interpreted as reflecting important differences between the modern and traditionally schooled children. As in the case of the WISC findings, where the Conrad children excelled on several of the subtests, performance appears to reflect a composite of specific experience, general test-taking skills and attitudes, and more complex aspects of the relationship between the organization and definition of learning implicit in the content and form of the test and that previously experienced by the individual. The WISC Performance data demonstrate that the Conrad children were capable of high-level performance when the task presented followed their previous experience. Their extraordinarily low Coding scores (relative to the rest of their WISC performance) illustrates how unprepared they were to engage in routine clerical tasks. The truly remarkable degree of WISC scatter among the Conrad children (see particularly the Block Design-Coding discrepancy) eloquently testifies to the unique patterning of their cognitive organization.

The position of the Conrad group on most of the problem-solving scores was surprising. Although it may be argued that in some respects the problem-solving situations perpetuated the pattern of imposing a problem from without, it was also true that they were designed with an open-ended quality that left more opportunity for the free play of ideas and the mobilization of thought within a meaningful framework and over a more sustained period. It was also evident that they aroused general interest and curiosity. The four groups of children were not significantly different in the way they performed on these tasks. For the most part, variation within groups exceeded differences between groups. There was some consistency, however, in the more sparse, somewhat less effective response pattern of the Conrad children, particularly the boys. They tended to be least responsive and showed a greater tendency toward blockage. The children from traditional schools responded more aggressively—they tended to work faster, gave more responses, more actively strove to move toward solution. Discrepancies between the more qualitative relationship thinking rating and the solution score were small. Where they occurred, largely in the case of the Dickens school, they were in the expected direction. The relative standing of the modern schools was greater for their relationship thinking rating than it was for the solution score, but their absolute standing on either of these two scores was not remarkable.

There were some consistent differences in performance between the sexes. On the group tests, and on the WISC Coding Subtest, where rapid, accurate clerical dexterity was called for, the girls tended to excel. These differences dwindled, and were occasionally reversed (for example, Block Design) when items requiring abstract reasoning were presented. In general, the girls gave more responses and were much more ready to elaborate their replies. The boys' response was more measured; they were more sensitive about repeating themselves or giving an improper answer. The girls talked about their ideas and strove for solution more freely. Evidently, this sphere of functioning was more conflict-laden for the boys. It was not expected that these differences between the sexes would be most characteristic of the modern school group. Yet it was here that the more constrained, less effective performance by the boys was most in evidence.

There were some indications that the greater restraint and hesitancy among some of the modern school boys represented a higher personal standard of performance—they did not guess when they did not know the answer and were not prone to repeat or contradict themselves. But aside from selected aspects of performance on the WISC, this process of adaptive screening did not manifest itself in the form of effective functioning on measures of individual cognitive behavior.

The most impressive phase of the Conrad children's performance was their cooperative problem solving. Their decisive superiority of functioning on the group task can probably be attributed to a variety of factors. They were experienced in working as a responsible and task-oriented group, with ways and means of managing their relationships and accomplishing their goals. They were accustomed to thinking with movement and translating ideas into action, as the group problem-solving task required, and were accustomed to a certain independence of decision and judgment. They seemed to have acquired a mutuality of feeling and working which greatly enhanced their effectiveness and enthusiasm in joint enterprises. As a skill, this kind of group effectiveness is not to be underestimated. Hilgard (1964), in discussing the assessment of the effectiveness of any educational enterprise, has included as an important criterion the question of whether "the skills of effective participation with others in solving problems . . ." (p. 139) have been developed. Certainly this facet was well established in the Conrad group. At the same time, we would need to raise a different question. Perhaps, for some children, dependency on the group hampered their individual functioning.

The rather pervasive lack of interconnection among the various cognitive measures obtained from these children is an important finding, which indicates that relative standing among these measures is specific to the instrument employed. The reduction in variance produced by the selective quality of the sample undoubtedly contributed to this absence of covariation. But, interestingly, the degree of intercorrelation was not the same for all groups; in the Browning school, it frequently achieved high levels. Thus, these patterns of interrelatedness cannot simply be dismissed as error. If the Browning scores were consistent and their mean value was not distinguishable from the mean scores of other groups, there seems little justification in denying validity to test scores essentially equivalent to the Browning data. It would seem more proper to regard the other schools as characterized by greater specificity of functioning rather than by unreliability of response.

Wherever significant group differences in cognitive functioning were found, they could not be attributed to variation in home background. The rank order of the group mean ratings of the modern-traditional orientation of the mothers did not correspond to the rank order of group means on standardized tests. In a separate correlation analysis within school groups, impressive relationships between home and test performance were occasionally found within each group—particularly in Browning.[10] For the most part these correlations were higher when they involved WISC performance and were therefore based upon the second-year sample. Although no consistent pattern of relationship is in evidence, the two traditional school groups, Adams and Browning, more often indicated a substantial correlation between home background ratings and problem-solving performance. These findings, together with the higher correlations between home and standardized test performance also found in Browning, begin to suggest that the traditional schools, either by design or happenstance, intervened less in the children's psychological development or were more influenced by home factors in their own evaluation of the children. Either of these possibilities would account for the stronger association between home and child functioning in these groups. By contrast, the modern schools, by consciously interacting with, rather than reinforcing home influences, produced a pattern of behavior in the children whose relationship to home factors is more complex.

The most striking aspect of the findings regarding the cognitive effects of school experience is the juxtaposition of dramatic variation among school groups with instances of complete uniformity of functioning. The imbalance between the gross variation found among group test scores and the virtual uniformity of problem-solving ratings among the four groups has led us to conclude that we were the victims of methodological problems which beset the field of psychological measurement. Particularly in the area of cognition, measures are developed pragmatically and somewhat arbitrarily. The potential usefulness of a prospective cognitive measure is judged on the basis of its ability to evoke variation among individuals consistently. Its relevance to the behavioral process in question is of secondary concern. In the course of development, tests become refined instruments, that is, they become capable of making fine discriminations among people. Their widespread use, in turn, has the complementary effect of sharpening the capacity of people to respond to such instruments, thereby increasing individual differences. Thus the cycle is completed. A format is established and people are trained to respond to the format. The increased precision of differentiation thereby established is used as evidence of the validity of the format. The issue of relevance is sidetracked in favor of consistency and differentiability. Our results are congruent with this pattern. When we were instrument-oriented (that is, when we used group tests), we could observe reliable differences; when we focused on process (as in the study of problem solving), it was not possible to obtain significant variation among the school groups.

NOTES

1. An exception to this pattern occurred in the Year II Browning sample, where the boys scored reliably higher than the girls on the Kuhlmann-Anderson Test, most of the Achievement Subtests, and the WISC Performance Scale. However, the small number of cases involved and the failure of a similar pattern of sex differences to appear in the Year I sample would suggest that these differences are attributable to sampling variation.
2. The constant difference found between mean IQ's of the Year I and II data in each of the three schools, by virtue of its very consistency, would appear to be an artifact of the standardization of the test. There are no data in this study, including those obtained from the Stanford Achievement Test (see Appendix M), which substantiate the implication that an actual difference in ability existed between the two years' samples. For this reason, it has been concluded that these differences are attributable to the test standardization, and the data for the two years have been treated separately.
3. These were Arithmetic Reasoning and Science.
4. The correlation between the Coding scores and Kuhlmann-Anderson raw scores was $r = .64$.
5. These were Block Design, Object Assembly, and Picture Completion.
6. A different but related distinction of this type has recently been reported

by Wallach and Kogan (1965), who scored each of their tests of creativity for uniqueness and number (productivity).

7. This difference in strategy closely resembles the distinction Mosher and Hornsby (1966) have made between constraint questioning and hypothesis scanning, in characterizing the response of middle-years children to a similar kind of problem.

8. The activity invites comparison with the essence of what is called for in the Uncommon Uses task, though here it appears in spontaneous form with tangible materials and in a group context; as indicated earlier, all of these may have been important conditions for the Conrad group.

9. See Kuhlmann-Anderson school group differences between Forms E and F.

10. The data generated by this analysis were too extensive to be presented in this report; they are available in the study files.

CHAPTER

9

IMAGINATIVE THINKING

There is an arbitrary though conventionally accepted distinction between the kinds of thinking skills required to deal effectively with the tasks described in the previous chapter and those to be described here. The latter tasks, designed to tap the children's imaginative thinking, are less structured, but they do have form; there are no right answers, but there are more and less appropriate ways of responding; they allow the free play of ideas, but they do require that ideas be expressed; they do not tap the children's knowledge or problem-solving skills, but they do touch on personal and affective material and require effective coping in that domain. In this chapter, therefore, we are still dealing with the children's thinking processes, but the instruments used are chosen to allow the child to think imaginatively, to give greater opportunity for creative response.

Creativity and imaginativeness are elusive concepts which have been studied by psychologists of different persuasions in many contexts. We have studied the imaginative thinking of these nine-year-olds through several different media, both in order to tap different aspects of imaginative functioning and to offer the children several modes in which to express themselves. The techniques vary in their requirements from those which call for immediate associations or brief synthesizing responses—such as titles for unfamiliar paintings—to those which call for the development and elaboration of imaginative ideas—as in stories told to pictures and in play with miniature toys.

A general question can be raised. What can be considered an imaginative product? Holt (1961) has pointed out that fantasy often occurs spontaneously in a state of dreamy reverie and abstraction, in which continuity and transition are implicit; above all, it is private. He argues cogently that projective stories, such as responses to the TAT, should be viewed as cognitive products and that the differences between the stories an individual tells to TAT pictures and his private fantasies, reveries, and daydreams far outweigh the similarities.

Play sequences come closer to Holt's criteria of pure fantasy since they offer more leeway for primary process thinking and affective components and are less dependent on verbal skills and story organization. Perhaps, at best, no projective technique provides more than fragmentary information about an individual's fantasies. None of the techniques used here elicits pure fantasies in the sense defined by Holt, but what the children do and say can be taken as clues to their more private fantasies and offers material for assessing the nature of their imaginative thinking.

Children of this age are notably inclined to an increased wish for privacy. They have sufficient facility with symbolic skills to be able to internalize their fantasies. They are more cautious about trusting adults and wish to protect their privacy. Furthermore, they are less ready or able to express their needs than they were at an earlier age; in general, their needs and inner life are less accessible to them. Thus, both the child's growing sense of his individuality and his relatively dormant awareness of his inner life mitigate against the open expression of his inner feelings. Instead, he is focused on concrete goals and the industrious cultivation of competence. However, the imagination does not atrophy during these latency years and emerge reborn at puberty. It is a period which should be considered in relation both to the emotional turbulence of the preschool years and to adolescence; a period in which the child is clearer than he used to be about the difference between real and unreal, fact and wish, and can move between the two modes of thinking with security.

It seems likely that nearly all children of this age spend some of their time in imaginary activity, whether self-generated, like daydreaming and dramatic play, or more externally structured, like reading and watching television. Some children seem drawn to invention and fantasy and seem, more than others, spontaneously imaginative in their expression. A number of writers have suggested that certain background and environmental factors may be associated with greater imaginativeness or creativity (for example, MacKinnon, 1962; Biber, 1959; Singer, 1961; Weisberg and

Springer, 1961. See also Stein and Heinze, 1960). Although a clear picture of the antecedents of imaginativeness has not emerged from the research, the evidence indicates that factors other than differences in endowment can play a formative role. Certain life conditions, in other words, are more conducive to the development of imaginativeness. In this study we have hypothesized that the modern school, more than the traditional school, constitutes such an environment.

The modern and traditional schools were subcultures with different views about the role of subjective and creative experiences in the child's life. The modern schools encouraged the expression and transformation of experience in ways that had personal meaning to the individual child. The teacher accepted a wide range of responses as appropriate and adequate and, while she helped the child to socialize communication, she placed less stress on formal and conventional rules of expression. The traditional schools had a different goal. The teacher was less interested in personal meanings and idiosyncratic responses. She tended to stress form and order and valued socialized communication. Furthermore, the traditional school's emphasis on the dichotomy between work and play discouraged the kind of intellectual playfulness that is presumably conducive to creative and imaginative thinking. These differences among the modern and traditional schools were expected to lead to differences in the children's imaginative responsiveness.

In this chapter the findings are reported in two sections. The first, Imaginativeness of Response, concerns the quality of the child's responses: his capacity to invest material with his own imaginative ideas, to go beyond the literal, to develop and elaborate in vivid and diverse ways his responses to the stimuli presented to him. The second, Characters, Themes, and Wishes, concerns the basic thematic content that emerged in the imaginative material. We expected school group differences particularly in the first aspect. It was anticipated that children from the modern schools would be more imaginative in their thinking and modes of expression than those from traditional schools and that the traditional school children would tend to use relatively standardized, conventional forms of expression, with less imaginative flow. There was no a priori expectation that thematic content would differ among the groups.

The findings do not confirm these expectations. In general, there were no school group differences in the extent of imaginative response. There were, however, interesting differences in one aspect of imaginativeness—the tendency to transcend the bounds of the real and possible. There were also some group differences in thematic content.

Imaginativeness of Response

Techniques and Measures

Imaginativeness of response was assessed through four tasks: CPST, Play, Picture Titles, and Similes. Picture Titles and Similes invite responses that transcend the concrete stimulus of word or picture, although the responses are necessarily brief. CPST and Play offer the child an open opportunity to develop and extend his imaginative thinking. Responses to the four techniques were rated for imaginativeness, following general principles of evaluating transcendence of a given stimulus, but responses to CPST and Play also permitted the analysis of qualitative differences in the children's imaginative thinking.

The following definitions are presented in abbreviated form:

(i) **CPST: Imaginativeness.** Protocols were rated on a five-point scale, partially based on criteria derived from Weiskopf (1950). End points were defined as follows:

　　1—flat and/or evasive, descriptive stories not elaborated, static, limited to depicted setting and characters

　　5—stories developed and elaborated, showing transcendence of the stimuli and originality in such ways as diversification of setting and characters, extensions in time and space, attribution of feelings, development of characters, metaphoric language, humor

(ii) **Play: Imaginativeness.** Rated on a five-point scale:

　　1—bare scene with few characters and little action; static play

　　5—richly elaborated play; characters and plot developed, complex; scene, characters, action, handled with vividness

(iii) **Picture Titles: Imaginativeness of Titles.** Rated on a four-point scale:

　　1—descriptive, reiterative, for example, "Design," "Fruit Dish," and/or many omissions, low productivity

　　4—interpretive, integrative, combining real and imagined elements to add a new dimension; high productivity, evidence of humor, for example, "Mr. Complicated" (Picasso)

(iv) **Similes: Imaginativeness.** Rated on a five-point scale:

　　1—low productivity; poor coping with task in terms of adequacy of response; repetition of response word in several items; some responses a synonym of stimulus word

　　5—high productivity and all responses adequate; substantial evidence of personal but communicative responses; frequent evidence of humor and style

INTERCORRELATIONS AMONG MEASURES

Correlations among these measures of imaginativeness are of low magnitude, although many are statistically reliable (see Appendix BB, Table 2). Although similar criteria were used in assessing the imaginativeness of the children's responses, and apparently similar skills were required, it appears that the differences among the tasks were great enough to call forth different kinds of responses.[1]

Group Characteristics and Sex Differences

There was of course a wide range of responses to the techniques. Some children were relatively blocked or were bound to the concrete, given features of the pictures, words, and objects. They stayed close to base in reacting to material. They told literal CPST stories that clung to visual elements, described art work in terms of clear content ("Design," "Lady Dancing," "Fruit Bowl"), used repetitive or conventional similes ("as hot as the sun," "as pretty as a picture"), and played out sparse and static stories. At the other extreme, children used the stimuli as a springboard and supplied original, elaborated material. A vivid Kandinsky abstraction, for example, was titled, "East Moon and West Moon," "Topsy-turvy Sidewalk," "Sunrise Glass," and so on; a Miro, "A Fairy-tale Shadow Dance," "Upside-down Sam," "Messed-up Jester." Approximately one third of the children were rated high in imaginative response on each of the two major projective techniques (Play, 36; CPST, 32).[2] Stories and Play verbalizations quoted later in the chapter offer examples of imaginative responses in these projective situations.

Girls were decidedly more capable of responding to the material in adequate, interesting, and spontaneous ways than boys. The greater imaginativeness of girls was most marked in the CPST stories and in the titles they created for the art prints (see Table 9-1).

Making up titles and responding to similes require what Guilford (1956) has termed "ideational fluency," the ability to express a free flow of associations, to play with ideas; these two techniques and the CPST also require verbal skill. While the girls' greater imaginativeness in telling CPST stories undoubtedly reflects their superior ability to transcend the depicted stimulus and develop characters and motives, it also derived from their ability to produce more material, especially verbal material, than the boys. Longer CPST responses were, in fact, more likely to be considered imaginative.[3] While quantity alone is no guarantee of greater imaginativeness, those children who spun their stories out were adding more than merely words. By the same token, those who were blocked and

TABLE 9-1

Imaginativeness of Response

Measure Source, and Scale Range	(N)	Sex §	Browning	Adams	Dickens	Conrad	Total	Analysis of Variance
				Mean Scores for School Groups				
IMAGINATIVENESS CPST Scale Range: 1–5		b	2.70	2.53	2.17	2.00	2.32	Schools: .85 NS Sex: 15.08** Schools × Sex: 1.23 NS
		g	3.63	2.73	3.58	3.42	3.28	
	(103)	T	3.11	2.63	2.88	2.59	2.76	
IMAGINATIVENESS Play Scale Range: 1–5		b	3.20	3.33	2.92	2.81	3.07	Schools: .21 NS Sex: 1.52 NS Schools × Sex: .34 NS
		g	3.50	3.25	3.33	3.42	3.35	
	(104)	T	3.33	3.29	3.12	3.07	3.20	
IMAGINATIVENESS Picture Titles Scale Range: 1–4		b	2.60	2.13	2.36	1.80	2.17	Schools: .27 NS Sex: 3.73 NS Schools × Sex: 2.82*
		g	2.38	2.94	2.18	3.20	2.71	
	(97)	T	2.50	2.53	2.27	2.36	2.42	
IMAGINATIVENESS Similes Scale Range: 1–5		b	2.30	2.44	2.67	2.53	2.49	Schools: 1.02 NS Sex: 1.07 NS Schools × Sex: .00 NS
		g	2.50	2.63	2.92	2.58	2.67	
	(105)	T	2.39	2.53	2.79	2.55	2.57	

* $p < .05$
** $p < .01$
§ b = boys
g = girls
T = total

evasive prevented observation of the quality of thinking and the play of ideas.

It will be noted as a recurrent phenomenon in this study that the boys were less productive than the girls. They were more literal, sparse, and impersonal and seemed reluctant to produce material based on inner subjective processes.

Given the same set of 12 CPST pictures, the same array of miniature toys to deal with, the range of what the children did with these stimuli was impressive. By definition, the children judged most imaginative were those whose responses were most elaborated and developed. Many of these children who moved out from the pictures and objects with a subjective flow of ideas stayed within the realm of the everyday and the possible (a parent-child encounter; a family trip to the circus; a teenage love story, and so on). Others used characters and locales that were not of their immediate and current world (cowboys and Indians; African safari) yet did not project supernatural elements or leap the bounds of the possible.

Some children, however, did make this leap. In each of the projective situations, a small group of children (seven in each instance) developed magical and supernatural ideas.[4] One girl, for example, constructed an animal town with the miniature toys in which animals talked, had individual characteristics, and were involved in a complex social organization; they performed in the best tradition of the fable. Others invoked ghosts, witches, magic forces and supernatural happenings. Some stories were sheer exploration with the idea of the inexplicable—objects that changed form for reasons and by powers never discovered. For example, the following CPST story:[5]

One night there was a very nice lady. She went to bed. She sat down and she decided she would just read. This is a long time ago. And she heard a noise in the livingroom. No—the dining room or dining room-office. She went downstairs quickly and then she got scared because she saw a pot of flowers with a live chick in the middle. She thought this was very strange. She was open-mouthed. But she got a little box and she put in the skinny little chick. In the morning she had her son, who was quite old, about twenty, go out and make a little pen for the chick. And the next night she went to sleep and she heard a noise in the living-room. She went downstairs, saw a lamp. And this was odd because they didn't have many lamps. And in the middle of this lamp was a pussy. (I don't see this, but I'm making it up.) And the pussy said "meow"—it was a kitten.

In the morning her son fixed up a little room in the big house. They had a twenty-room house. And they fixed it up for her with a pillow and a teensy-weensy couch.

Next night the old lady and her son came creeping downstairs quietly. And then they waited and finally they saw something with a white coat and red earmuffs and a blue feather hanging down from her, on her cloak. She came over and she brought a bookcase. And on the case stood a marble statue of an elephant. It was a miniature elephant. And she took out a little hickory stick and she tapped lightly on the back of the elephant. And it became *real*. She said to the elephant, "Go back to the mantle as a model and in the morning, reappear." And she gave him the piece of hickory stick.

So the old woman got mad and decided she didn't want so many animals. She had enough. So in the morning she covered her hickory stick with blankets and tied them firmly (she only had a couple). And in the morning she found that there was just an ordinary plain box. She looked inside and she saw some books with two little statues of two dogs. But if they had the hickory they would have been real dogs. So she decided she would keep the trees covered. The end.

In other cases, children told stories about magic pencils or magic sweaters that gave power, protection, or competence to their owners. A girl told a story about a painter who, fearing his portrait of a man might come alive and hurt someone, tore it into small pieces and was then haunted by voices asking, "Who tore me up?" A boy told a story about a child who talked and played with animal friends in the forest, then helped them to break the spell of a powerful bear who had mysterious powers over them. Stories such as these had interesting underlying themes of power and vulnerability, competence and dependency—recurrent themes in this sample of middle-years children. They are distinctive, however, in the quality of imaginativeness they showed; they are not merely more elaborate, more interesting, or more colorful versions of other children's themes. Rather, in the invocation of magical power, the dramatic transformation of reality and the transcendence of the possible, they bespeak a qualitatively different form of imaginative thought.

Another basic mode of transforming reality was the introduction of animals as symbolic or displacement figures. In general, animals played a large role in the inner lives of these children. Many children (three fourths of the sample) incorporated animals in their Play, talked spontaneously about animals, or responded with animal associations to Similes stems (*as pretty as* "a bird's voice"; *as ugly as* "an ape"). Sometimes animals appeared important as objects or sources of affection and pleasure, but they also served symbolic or displacement functions. They had human characteristics—mischievousness, aggressiveness—or were carriers of impulse and mood (*as mean as* "a panther"; *as helpless as* "a baby kitty"; *as crazy as* "a hurt lion"). Boys and girls did not differ in the extent to which they used animals projectively, but they used them in different ways: girls used the more domesticated and docile animals; boys the wild and fierce ones.[6]

The supernatural and symbolic were not often invoked. Nevertheless, this phenomenon is interesting and important, partly because it signifies the most dramatic transformation of reality through imagination and partly because it was primarily characteristic of one school group.

School Group Differences

Measures of imaginative response showed no consistent differences among school groups (see Table 9–1). It might be noted that, in Play and CPST measures, it was the boys from Conrad and Dickens whose responses were judged less imaginative, while Conrad and Dickens girls were on a par with their traditional school counterparts. But these findings do not support the premise that the extent of imaginative response would reflect the quality of the schooling.

The data do suggest a stylistic difference, at least among children whose productions were judged to be imaginative. Magical transformations and supernatural elements occurred primarily in the Play and CPST stories of Conrad children. Of the seven children who told CPST stories about ghosts and witches, talking animals, and other supernatural forces, five were from Conrad. Similarly, it was primarily children from Conrad whose Play sequences portrayed dramatic and unreal tales concerning an intimate personal relationship between a child and a nonhuman (for example, a story about a boy, Sean, and his horse, Phantom; a girl whose toys talked to her in the night). Among Conrad children, high imagination seemed to coexist with this style of fantasy, more than in any other group.

Animals, too, appeared especially often in the projective material of Conrad children. They used animals in the Similes task to express images and moods more frequently than any other group, and the girls from Conrad were distinguished from those in other schools by more frequent use of animals in their Play.[7] For the Conrad girls, horses seemed to have a particular significance and served as a kind of group totem animal. Horses appeared in their responses in many contexts, obviously serving an important symbolic function.[8]

The findings concerning imaginativeness of response are provocative and do not conform to expectations. We need to account both for the absence of expected patterns and the suggested presence of others. Despite the high evaluation of creative processes and the encouragement of individually expressive forms in the modern schools, the children of these schools were not more freely responsive to these tasks, as we had predicted they would be. As a group, they did not transcend the given nor develop ideas out of their imaginative processes more fully than the traditional school children. Both elaborate and restricted responses were given by children from all schools. To account for this lack of consistent difference in children whose educational experiences were clearly different, in presumably relevant ways, it would probably be necessary to consider the children's capacity for task effectiveness (as discussed in the previous chapter), differential attitudes toward sharing subjective material with unknown adults, and the possible use of fantasy for compensatory purposes.

In spite of their tentativeness, the findings concerning imaginative style invite speculation. In a sense, those children whose imaginative stories transcended the rules of reality had made the fullest and freest use of the possibilities inherent in the imagination, taking the option to create characters, symbols, and events that were not bounded by their knowledge of the real and the possible. From this point of view, the greater incidence of this mode of imaginative thinking among Conrad children is consistent with our expectation, although this was not the form of imaginative expression that had been predicted.

Characters, Themes, and Wishes

There were two different approaches to the substantive content of the children's imaginative thinking: one dealt with their responses to direct questioning about their conscious wishes; the other dealt with the fictions they created, both in response to the thematic picture series and in the Play situation, which provided more complex though less direct information about their concerns, desires, and fears.

In clinical work, such projective techniques are used to elucidate individual patterns and provide clues to intra-psychic organization. Their value lies in their relative lack of structure, which permits a variety of responses. The analysis of group trends from such material cannot take account of individual patterning—of the child, for example, whose stories to 12 different stimulus pictures or whose Play stories are all variations of a single theme—but it can yield a composite image of the children's concerns and imaginative thinking.

Techniques and Measures

The material was examined for general trends and recurrent themes, but was also systematically coded on the following dimensions:

(i) **Three Wishes: Childhood Orientation Versus Adult Orientation.**
The child- versus adult-oriented quality of the children's wishes was rated on a three-point scale:
    1—child-oriented: wishes for toys, food, pets, trips for child pleasure, for example, Disneyland
    2—mixed
    3—adult-oriented: wishes for household goods, gifts, and attributes of adult life
(ii) **Million Dollars: Childhood Orientation Versus Adult Orientation.**
The way the children said they would spend an imaginary million dollars in one day was rated on a three-point scale which paralleled that for the Three Wishes rating (i above).
(iii) **Play: Enactment of Family Life Themes.** The extent to which children's Play sequences centered on family life was rated on a four-point scale:
    1—no stories dealing with family life
    2—family life one of several themes

3—family life the primary theme (although others may be expressed)

4—family life the exclusive concern of the child's play

(iv) CPST: Incidence of Parent Figures. The frequency with which children introduced parent figures into their CPST stories was converted to a three-point scale:

1—0 to 3 stories containing parent figures

2—4 to 6 stories containing parent figures

3—7 or more stories containing parent figures

(v) Play: Aggressive-Destructive Themes. The expression of aggressiveness and destructiveness in the children's Play was rated on a four-point scale:

1—no aggressive-destructive themes

2—some aggressiveness or destructiveness, but its expression is minor, weak

3—aggression and/or destructiveness expressed in muted form; other themes predominate

4—aggression and/or destructiveness is a predominant theme, openly expressed

(vi) CPST: Prevalence of Achievement Themes. The extent of the child's concern with achievement was assessed projectively through the CPST. The rating scheme was based on the definition developed by McClelland, Atkinson, Clark, and Lowell (1953) concerning "competition with a standard of excellence" and was an adaptation of their rating system.[9] Prevalence of achievement themes was rated on a five-point scale:

1—no evidence of concern with achievement

3—

5—considerable evidence of concern with achievement, as indicated by the prevalence of such elements as achievement imagery, achievement need, anticipatory goal states, instrumental activity, goal attainment, and so on.

(vii) CPST: Primacy of External Standards. An assessment was made of the extent to which stories stressed external and tangible criteria for the evaluation of learning adequacy and academic accomplishment (adult judges, tests, formal marking systems, and so on). Rating was on a three-point scale:

1—no evidence of external standards

2—

3—clear evidence of external standards

INTERCORRELATIONS AMONG MEASURES

The measures are, for the most part, correlated at satisfactory levels with those measures with which they form logical groups (see Appendix BB, Table 2). This pertains for the two CPST measures concerning achievement themes and external standards. The two measures, however, concerning family life themes (one from CPST and one from Play) are not related to each other, perhaps because they are drawn from different techniques. Family life themes and aggressive themes in Play are related, in the sense that the prevalence of the former is associated with low incidence of the latter, and vice versa.

Group Characteristics and Sex Differences

The two direct questions put to the children, about how they would spend a million dollars in a day and what they would wish for if they had three wishes, offered comparable yet different opportunities for playful gratification and hypothetical indulgence. Both engaged the children in conscious formulation of those imaginative processes in which wishing, wanting, and hoping are embedded. The million dollars question presented the possibility for vicariously satisfying desires for whatever money could buy; the three wishes question was more open, carrying the connotation of magical power and omnipotence. Where would these flights carry them? What were they consciously wishing for? Were there pleasures to be deepened or problems to be alleviated? Were the children altogether self-involved or would they show signs of budding identification with a more extended social reality?

The children were not equally receptive to the opportunity to engage in these hypothetical forms of gratification. Some obviously enjoyed thinking up how to spend the million dollars, took it as a game from which they derived playful pleasure; others appeared to find little to enjoy in the experience, accepting it as a task, a job to be done. For most of them, it was easier to make up three wishes than to find ways of spending all that money.

There was a mixture of naivete and awareness in their conceptual grasp of the uses of money, more particularly, money in the amount of a million dollars. Although these children had no experience of needing money to meet elementary needs, they were aware of the social power of money in general. This was evident in the "spending" of their three wishes: one fourth of the group wished for lots of money, to be rich, never to be poor. But realistic understanding of the purchasing power of a million dollars was beyond them: one boy would spend a hundred thousand dollars to buy _____ City. Many children thought concretely, enumerating the desired things of childhood for which they had unfulfilled appetite: "I would spend it on model ships, on boat models, airplane models, ship models . . . ," adding, when questioned about what else, "more models." This boy's reply represents a fairly general tendency to flounder in the attempt to spend the whole amount since most of their childlike desires could have been fulfilled with a fraction of the total.

Occasionally, the responses were as revealing of affect as they were of concept. For example, one girl's associations had the quality of an orgy of fulfillment:

> I'd buy a mansion, a country house. I'd get three dogs for four hundred dollars. I'd get twelve mink coats. I'd get ten wardrobes, twenty bathing suits, fifteen hundred dresses. I'd get sixteen hundred more dresses. I'd get—a toy store . . . a club of my own, four swimming pools . . . if I could get ten million dollars I'd have a castle with twelve hundred and sixty-four rooms, etc., etc.

By contrast, quite a few children were inclined to exchange immediate pleasure for images of future benefits. They had concrete ideas for saving the money, putting it in the bank, or investing in sound stocks. For some, the idea aroused feelings of basic distrust—who would give me a million dollars? Is it stolen money?

In the way they chose to use their three wishes there was often a touching, poignant quality, reflecting loss, deprivation, and sadness about aspects of life impossible to remedy. There were wishes "to have longer, lighter hair," "to be older than my sister," "not to have allergy so I could have a dog," "that my mother and father not be divorced." It is not hard to conjecture what this list might be in a population of socially disadvantaged children whose life situations contain so many deeply traumatic elements; at the same time, it is interesting to note that there is no universal exemption for any child.

On the whole, the wishes of these children had a positive if somewhat pedestrian quality. They were consonant with their stage of development —expressing interest in contemporary competence and, at the same time, a look ahead toward adult status; fluctuating between pleasure in acquisition and discontent with adjustments they were required to make. For example, there were wishes for "a stick ball and bat that no one could take away," "that I could go to the same camp every year until I get to be the director," "to have Yankee Stadium for my own, a lake with boats, to play baseball better than anyone I know"; "to be a millionaire, to be Princess Ann, not to share my room with my sister."

Boys and girls differed in their expressed wishes. The girls had a recurrent wish. Almost half of them (20 of 45) wished for a horse or a dog, a farm, a ranch, or country house; only four boys had this kind of wish. There seemed to be also a general dissatisfaction with city living by both boys and girls—many wished for a room of their own, for a bigger apartment, for all the buildings in _____ City to be only four stories high.

Another kind of wish that came from the boys, especially, indicated a desire to have and to hold power. Nine children in the group wished for pervasive "magic powers" or "to be invisible," "to fly," "to be able to be very very big or very very small"; of these, eight were boys. In line with this, there was a kind of wish convention, used by about one third of the children, to wish for an unlimited number of wishes, or for a genie: "I'd wish for ten million dollars and a million more wishes, and on the last one of the million, I'd ask for a million more wishes." Three times as many boys as girls made this kind of magic wish for extended power.[10]

In raising the question of how far these children might have moved toward the state of balancing self-indulgence with generosity in their "spending" or "wishing," it is recognized that strong tendencies toward altruism at this developmental stage can be looked upon either as a sign of increasing identification with a broader segment of humanity or as premature superego control. Actually, most of the children stayed close to their immediate environment and personal concerns; when other people were included they were likely to be members of the immediate family. Only a small number mentioned giving gifts to charity, to hospitals, to the crippled or offered a wish for world improvement, for the alleviation of disease, for the end of war.

It was possible to score the responses to both the three wishes and the million dollars questions on a dimension that cross-referenced these multiple themes, namely, on whether the replies were childhood-oriented or adult-oriented. Many of the children's wishes were adult-oriented (see Table 9–2), pointed toward the future: "to be happily married with four children," "to be pretty when I grow up," "to have lots of good stock and a good income in the bank." Other wishes were grounded in childhood, geared to enriching or improving present situations. Some of these were relatively superficial, for example, "to have a dog," "that my sister didn't snore"; others reflected deeper feelings, for example, "to have a sister instead of a brother," "for my father to get a job on a ranch," "I wish my mother, when I go into her room, wouldn't say, 'Don't come in,' or 'go right out,' or something like that, you know. She doesn't want me in the room sometimes. . . ."

The more elaborated projective material provided a level of imaginative data that was different from the child's conscious wish life. The content of the children's Play and CPST stories served as indices of their salient concerns and ideas. Here we considered who were the main characters in the stories they invented and played out—parents, children, soldiers, explorers, bandits, Indians—and what themes underlay their actions. The Play situation offered a broad array of material, giving the child a wide choice of theme; the CPST pictures left room for choice but tended to elicit more specific material dictated by their content. We wished in these two situations to see if there were findings common to both. The assumption was that if certain themes predominated in both kinds of material, what they would tell about the child at this age would be relatively reliable and

TABLE 9–2
Themes in Children's Imaginative Thinking

MEASURE Source, and Scale Range	(N)	Sex §	Browning	Adams	Dickens	Conrad	Total	Analysis of Variance
CHILDHOOD VERSUS ADULT ORIENTATION Three Wishes Scale Range: 1–3		b	2.14	1.83	1.67	1.31	1.68	Schools: 3.54* Sex: .83 NS Schools × Sex: .21 NS
		g	1.86	1.56	1.64	1.27	1.56	
	(98)	T	2.00	1.71	1.65	1.30	1.61	
CHILDHOOD VERSUS ADULT ORIENTATION Million Dollars Scale Range: 1–3		b	2.60	2.22	2.17	1.94	2.20	Schools: 4.26** Sex: .23 NS Schools × Sex: .23 NS
		g	2.63	2.44	2.33	1.82	2.30	
	(103)	T	2.61	2.32	2.25	1.89	2.24	
ENACTMENT OF FAMILY LIFE THEMES Play Scale Range: 1–4		b	1.80	1.72	1.42	1.63	1.64	Schools: 2.86* Sex: 48.00** Schools × Sex: 2.71*
		g	3.50	2.75	3.33	2.17	2.88	
	(104)	T	2.56	2.21	2.38	1.86	2.21	
INCIDENCE OF PARENT FIGURES CPST Scale Range: 1–3		b	1.90	2.11	1.92	1.88	1.96	Schools: .24 NS Sex: .24 NS Schools × Sex: .73 NS
		g	2.13	1.81	2.17	1.92	1.97	
	(105)	T	2.00	1.97	2.04	1.90	1.97	
AGGRESSIVE- DESTRUCTIVE THEMES Play Scale Range: 1–4		b	3.20	2.89	2.67	2.50	2.79	Schools: .25 NS Sex: 46.50** Schools × Sex: 1.13 NS
		g	1.25	1.56	1.42	1.58	1.48	
	(104)	T	2.33	2.26	2.04	2.11	2.18	
PREVALENCE OF ACHIEVEMENT THEMES CPST Scale Range: 1–5		b	2.30	2.71	2.25	2.00	2.32	Schools: .36 NS Sex: 4.29* Schools × Sex: .43 NS
		g	3.00	2.87	2.67	2.92	2.85	
	(103)	T	2.61	2.78	2.46	2.38	2.56	
PRIMACY OF EXTERNAL STANDARDS CPST Scale Range: 1–3		b	1.50	1.76	1.67	1.29	1.55	Schools: 1.93 NS Sex: 2.28 NS Schools × Sex: .53 NS
		g	2.13	2.00	1.67	1.42	1.79	
	(103)	T	1.78	1.88	1.67	1.34	1.66	

* $p < .05$
** $p < .01$
§ b = boys
  g = girls
  T = total

useful in describing these children as a group and as boys and girls. Responses in both Play and CPST were therefore examined for evidence of common themes.

To a considerable extent, the characters in the stories were related to each other as members of a family. Parent-child relationships were salient for these children. One third of the Play stories concerned family life; and parents, especially mothers, were the figures most frequently introduced into CPST stories. When two figures, adult and child, were depicted together, these nine-year-olds tended to see them as parent and child. On one of the CPST cards, for instance, a woman is shown standing in a doorway looking into a room.[11] The most common interpretation of this picture was of a mother interacting with a child (48 children; 28 boys, 20 girls).

The family Play of these children, however, was clearly distinguishable from that of younger children. Their imaginative productions brought themes to the surface that reflected frontiers of growth and tides of feeling —including conflict—that characterized their stage of development. Their Play stories had a wide range: from simple to elaborate plots; from basic activities, such as eating and bathing, to the drama and romance of journeys and adventures; from portraying merely the presence of family members to accounts of complex personal interaction. A basic trend, developmentally understandable, could be discerned in many of the stories— namely, the extension of the life space outward, beyond the intimately known, toward far-flung environments, and inward toward increasingly complex and less fixed interpersonal roles and relationships. The simpler type of family Play sequences is illustrated in the following:[12]

> There was this house and there were two bedrooms in it. And a mother and a father and a little baby. A big house. This is the livingroom . . . dining room . . . kitchen, playroom for baby's things . . . and the TV. It wouldn't be complete without a TV and a piano. And the husband went to work at this little office in _____ City. And it made furniture, and here's all the furniture. That's all.

One of the more elaborate stories incorporated a dramatic event into daily life routine and involved back-and-forth movement and complex roles:

> One morning three children were at breakfast. The mother gave them their breakfast. These two went to school, and he is too young to go. So two children go to school and the mother just got the other two twins and so she goes to wake them up. Only one child wanted to eat so she puts him in the highchair and she gives him his breakfast, and he is eating and the mother asks her husband if he is going to work. He says, No, because it is Friday and it is his day off. Then the other child eats. One child is in the carriage and one is eating breakfast.
>
> Now the husband tells the boy at the table to practice his lesson and the boy practices and the mother takes the babies for a walk, and the husband goes along. The boy has been waiting for five minutes. He has to stay home and keep on practicing, while the mother and father take the children for a walk. They take the children for a walk for a couple of minutes. The boy says, "I'd better run away so I won't have

to practice." So he takes his clothes—no, he doesn't take his clothes—
and he goes away.

The mother and father come home and see he isn't there. The father
calls the boy's friend and he wasn't there either. He called the police
to look for him. The children came home and ate lunch and everybody
else ate their lunch. Then they tell their mother that they saw their
brother going far away, and they don't know where he went. The children did their homework. One did homework at the desk in the brother's
room and one did homework on the desk in their own room. The children then did their homework and asked their mother if it was right.
Then the children went out to play, and when they came back they
saw their brother. They go out and catch him and bring him home. The
mother then made the brother practice his lessons for an hour. The
mother and father told the children they didn't have to do their lesson.
The children didn't have to practice. The boy went through his lesson
and got bad marks so he had to practice again.

The children used the Play situation as an opportunity to play out simultaneous roles, to rehearse projectively the shifting focus of their actual
position at this age, of being drawn to the pleasures of dependency on the
one hand and to the privileges of adulthood on the other. One of the
CPST stories is a graphic illustration of the child's urge to establish his
own private world and the distancing between parent and child that this
inevitably involves:[13]

Ooh, she's ugly. The mother is ugly. She's sitting there and thinking,
and the mother is trying to read to her, but she's got her thoughts, and
she's got her little doll. They're sitting on the couch and she's thinking
about her boy friend. She's off in a trance and the mother is trying to
read this sad story and doesn't know that the child isn't listening and
she calls her and calls her, and the child is off in a daze and she doesn't
hear her mother and her mother calls her and then she shakes her. And
then the mother asks what she's been thinking about. And she says:
"Oh, I dunno, I forgot." And the mother says: "You couldn't forget
that easily." Then she says: "Oh, I dunno, stop pestering me." And the
mother stops pestering her, and she's off in a big old daze and the
mother keeps asking her questions and the girl doesn't want to tell. She
thinks she should keep her own thoughts to her own self and the mother
doesn't think so. . . .

The pattern of response to another CPST card gave similar evidence of
another facet of the instability of the children's position at this stage in life
in which the push toward identification with being grown up and the uncertainty of being able to sustain the more grown up status are simultaneous processes.[14] This card, which depicts a small boy standing next to a
crib in which a baby is crying, elicited two predominant interpretations:

that the boy wished to help the baby in his distress or that the boy had hurt the baby and the baby was crying as a result. The first approach was more frequent: 45 children (24 boys, 21 girls) saw the boy as wanting to help the baby; 28 children (17 boys, 11 girls) saw him as having caused the baby's distress. While feelings of guilt, as well as identification with the baby's pain, may have contributed to the higher frequency of the more positive response, this picture, with its howling baby and uneasy brother, certainly suggests that the older child has caused the trouble. It is therefore interesting that so many children responded with empathy toward the baby. Taking, as they did, the more responsible and nurturant role in response to this card is perhaps a demonstration of their movement toward maturity. At the same time, the actual ambiguity of these nine-year-old children's position as one between infancy and adulthood is further borne out by the fact that, though they saw the boy in the card as wishing to take care of the baby, only a few saw him succeeding; they were uncertain and uneasy about his chances of success.

As might be expected, stories built around family life were more characteristic of girls than boys. In the Play situation, where the choice of theme was greater, the girls' preference for family life stories was striking: 40 of 48 girls and only 16 of 56 boys enacted such stories; for 13 girls, as opposed to only four boys, family life themes were the exclusive concern in Play (see Table 9–2). This sex difference did not hold in the CPST stories, where both boys and girls tended to introduce parent figures.

While the adults in the children's fictions were most often depicted in their family roles and relationships, they were also depicted in life situations in which children do not ordinarily participate. The stories of adult experience enacted in Play covered a wide range—ladies in a hospital, a man who runs a furniture factory, a man who makes a round-the-world tour, ladies going shopping, a wedding. One such story had the quality of a folktale: A man unexpectedly acquires riches; he is visited in succession by the maid, the milkman, the babysitter, and the grocer, each demanding payment of debts, and soon he is a poor man again. What seems to characterize these stories is the way in which the children attempted to "take the role of the other," that is, to take the roles of adults—not parents—engaged in activities in which children are not ordinarily included. Unlike the war and adventure stories, which were also peopled by adults, these stories took place in a realistic adult world. While this was not one of the most frequent themes (19 children: 6 boys, 13 girls), its interest lies in the fact that it suggests a trying on of adult roles and adult points of view.

Just as the family life theme typified the girls' Play, stories of war and adventure typified the boys'. Of 56 boys, 30 played some form of war story, 19 some kind of adventure. While six girls enacted adventure stories, only one played a war story and one girl used soldier figures in a dream context. The boys' stories, though in complete contrast to the girls' stories in manifest content, were analogous to them in a more basic sense. They also reflected an extension of the life space, both by their inclusion of a variety of characters in all kinds of roles and positions in life, and in the choice of strange and faraway locales.

These battle and adventure scenes were set in diverse and sometimes exotic places—forests, fortresses, islands, the jungles of Africa, the western plains. They were peopled with bandits, counterfeiters, hit-and-run drivers, as well as with many different kinds of heroes: marines, pilots, knights, explorers, cowboys and Indians. Some of the Play extended into the distant past or remote future, dealing with prehistoric times or science fiction: "This is the Stone Age and all the animals are fighting. The sabre-toothed tiger is trying to kill the buffalo so he can eat it." The foreign milieux and romantic heroes were not mere embellishments but were intrinsic to these stories, akin to those referred to by Lili Peller (1959) as stories for "have-nots"—that is, "nature, mystery, adventure, big game and wild west stories for those who are barred from these experiences in reality." Part of their appeal was their exoticism and part that, in a distant and improbable setting, strong urges may be more safely expressed.

The stories were full of action. Figures were moved about on the stage; events were acted out. The plot lines were about war and adventure; the dynamic movement was the symbolized backward and forward surge of force.

Aggressive-destructive themes were present in most war and many adventure stories—fighting and killing, car crashes and fires, rampant lions, or robots. Some of the adventure stories, on the other hand, concerned such peaceful activities as rounding up cattle or training horses. There was a special quality in the way aggression and destruction were expressed in battle scenes which involved the externalization of an internal power struggle as much as an emotional catharsis. Though there was a high death toll in these Play sequences, death was often instantaneous and affectless, without gore. It was usually indicated by laying the figures prone and often none of the men on the losing side, and sometimes none on either side, was standing upright at the end of the story; sometimes the hero was the lone survivor. The children specified the battle lines, the deployment of forces, and the sequence of killings rather than the details of injury and death. There was no suffering, only winning and losing. The wars depicted by these boys between Americans and Germans or between Indians and cowboys were all variations of good guys against bad guys, or good against evil.

The lacing of Play and projective stories with aggression and destruction was decidedly more characteristic of boys than girls; the boys exceeded the girls in this kind of Play to a marked degree, forming a mirror image of the enactment of family life stories (see Table 9–2). In projective stories, likewise, boys were more apt than girls to depict physical violence (11 of 15 such stories came from boys) and more likely to interpret ambiguous cards in tragic or combative terms. The struggle for power and the expression of aggression were clearly central themes for most of the boys, though the nakedness of the struggle and the amount of intellectual overlay varied considerably.

Other aspects of struggle and aggression were also expressed projectively, especially in response to CPST cards. The stories of adventure and danger that were told to the pictures were more specific to the situations suggested by the stimulus cards. They brought to the surface feelings of fright in the face of danger, empathic response to negatively toned mood qualities, perception of aggression taking place among peers and in a realistic arena. One card, for example, depicts two children with serious watchful expressions suggesting that something troublesome or frightening is happening.[15] This elicited a number of stories in which the figures were described as anxious or frightened because they were in danger or apparent danger. The following story illustrates these qualities:

> There were two Indian boys who lived in Africa and there was war going on against the other tribe. And their tribe in their village was set on fire. So then everybody was taken by surprise and it was at night and the two boys were the only ones that were awake and they rushed out and said "Fire, fire." Everybody woke up but they were tired and didn't do much about it because they were sleepy, so they put water on the fire and rescued all the people who were in the tent. (And then what happened?) They put out the fire and everyone else in the other tribe thought that the other tribe was dead because of the fire so they were rejoicing and the good tribe, let's say, took them by surprise and they won the day.

On another card, showing a figure of ambiguous age and sex reclining against a couch, the negative feeling tone and the implicit aggression depicted in the picture figured in the responses of both boys and girls.[16] On yet another card, where a group of children could be seen as either playing or fighting, there was a tendency, especially among the boys, to see it as fighting, thus projecting an image of aggression among peers.[17] These stories came closer to real life than the distant and fanciful stampedes or the cowboy-and-Indian wars of the boys' Play sequences.

In these CPST stories, there appeared something of a countermelody to the aggression and destructiveness projected in the Play stories. The motif of vulnerability and relatively realistic threats of aggression appeared; the inner surfaces of fear and sadness found expression, adding another dimension to the externalization of the struggle between power and weakness, good and evil.

Another aspect of the vulnerability theme concerned threats to the self and appeared in both Play and CPST stories. Sometimes it was symbolized in terms of physical injury, at other times as basic loss of anchorage in the protection of adults. For example, in 17 Play sequences, fire has occurred: the building was burning and people, adults and/or children, had to be rescued. Half a dozen car crashes required an ambulance. Similarly, in the CPST stories, there were numerous instances of bodily injury, harm, or danger, sometimes expressed as a clear threat and sometimes as a vague unspecified dread. There were threats of kidnapping and, in addition, tales of separation from loved ones and abandonment. These threats to dependence on others seemed to be drawn by CPST stimuli, appearing less frequently in the Play sequences. In general, the children's attraction to themes of danger and adventure was expressed differently in Play and CPST stories. The CPST figures, clearly depicting individual people, elicited more personalized responses.

Girls were more apt to express the anxiety and fright associated with adventure and danger. As already noted, boys more readily expressed the bravado, the action and the violent aspects of aggression. Interestingly enough, there were more stories dealing with guilt over aggression among boys and considerably more blocked responses. It would seem that the struggle for ascendency and power had a defensive as well as an assertive function for the boys, more saliently so than for the girls, and that the guilt associated with the force of these feelings could be expressed by some boys but could not be released even indirectly by others.

It is interesting, when one considers the importance of membership in the peer group at this stage, that there was proportionately little projective material which centered on children's relationships with each other. While child figures were major characters in many Play sequences—siblings in family stories and friends playing together—there were practically no stories of group life and none about the acceptance or rejection of peers. This kind of material seemed to come more easily in the CPST series, which is geared to child life and child-adult relations, and in which ten of the 12 pictures show children or a child and an adult. Some themes emerged in response to these cards that were not represented in Play sequences. Children told stories of loneliness, or of a child's need for friends, or stories in which several children functioned or reacted as a group.

Finally, an achievement theme appeared in the CPST stories which seemed to share an underlying dynamic consistency with some of the Play material already described. In the Play sequences, the theme of overcoming obstacles and the dramatization of opposing forces took the shape of war and adventure; in the CPST stories, it took a closer-to-life form, in the shape of achievement. For approximately one quarter of the children, achievement themes had central importance. Such themes were more characteristic of girls than boys (see Table 9–2). Where the stimulus card shows a boy and his violin, many children focused their stories on mastering the instrument, on performing and achieving: a challenge is posed and one must demonstrate one's competence.[18] Where a boy is shown in a setting that suggests schoolroom and teacher, children told stories of working diligently, receiving praise, or expressed feelings of incompetence and the anxiety of being tested.[19] Competence and mastery were dominant over another possible line of response which was much less frequently called out by this picture, namely, compliance or noncompliance with adult authority.

Along the same lines, there was a particular kind of story in which the hero achieved a superlative reward, became great and famous. Eleven children (five boys and six girls) told CPST stories of this kind. Sometimes the hero achieved fame through diligence or sacrifice of pleasure, sometimes fame was thrust upon him. These stories were reminiscent of daydreaming with its fantasies of being acclaimed and of being the center of laudatory attention. For example:

> There was a boy whose mother wanted him to take violin lessons. He loved to play football and didn't like to play the violin and so in this picture he's looking at his violin and he doesn't want to play it and he's unhappy. All the boys are outside calling to him and saying, "Let's play football." And he wants to.

> The day came when he was supposed to play the violin in front of a very large number of people, a very big audience. He got up and all his friends were watching him and he was very frightened. He began to play and the audience thought this was wonderful and started to clap. He was very excited and he kept on playing, so he took lessons and played the violin for something to do in an orchestra. He was in many great orchestras, and he did very well and one day he began to get very weak and everyone was worried and while he did so well he became very famous. He died a few years later and there was a great big statue of him. Everybody remembers that time when he played the first violin —violin piece—in front of an audience.

In general, the responses of this group of children to these two projective techniques when read thematically, appear consonant with their stage of development in the context of their social-class background. They show that the children were involved, as all children of this stage are, in the intra-psychic struggles associated with the intermediate status between childhood and maturity. These children were also in the special position of being able to draw on the relative richness of their life milieu, which provided them with ideational content through which they could explore a variety of adult roles by psychological trying on, and venture imaginatively into far worlds.

School Group Differences

Children from modern and traditional schools differed significantly in the nature of their wishes and the ways in which they thought of spending a million dollars (see Table 9–2). Adult-oriented wishes, focused on a future, more grown-up stage in life, characterized the traditional school children; the wishes of the modern school children were grounded more in childhood and their present lives. This difference follows the modern-traditional continuum, the strongest orientation toward childhood appearing among the Conrad children.

Some of the manifest content of the children's wishes was also suggestively linked to school background. The place of money in the wish-life was one of these: of the 26 children who wished to be a millionaire (or be very rich, never be poor), only one was from Conrad. Percentages here follow the modern-traditional continuum: Browning, 64 percent; Adams, 32 percent; Dickens, 21 percent; Conrad, 4 percent.[20] This finding may be regarded as further evidence that Conrad children were not taking an adult view of the world, if the premise is that valuing great wealth is basically an adult attitude. On the other hand, the absence of a "lot of money" in the content of their wishes could also be seen as a reflection of the particular adult values that were dominant in the subculture of their school.

The pattern of school group differences in thematic content can be summarized as follows. Involvement with family themes was strongest for girls of Browning and Dickens where Play was most family-centered and parent characters most frequently introduced into CPST stories. It follows that there was no systematic difference between modern and traditional schools (see Table 9–2) but Conrad girls were distinct from the others in that fewer of their stories were placed in a familial context, and only one Conrad girl was exclusively concerned with family life as the core of the Play sequence.

No consistent pattern of school differences appeared in the introduction of parent characters in CPST stories (see Table 9–2). The pictures exerted a powerful influence in eliciting parent-child relationship stories for both boys and girls in all schools. Two subsidiary findings are of interest. At Dickens, girls were considerably stronger than boys in this tendency; the girls of Browning and Dickens were consistently high in their enactment of family life themes in Play and in the introduction of parent figures in CPST.

The incidence of aggressive-destructive themes among boys followed the modern-traditional continuum more closely than did the family life themes among girls (see Table 9-2). The traditional school boys tended toward higher scores than the modern school boys though the difference did not reach statistical significance. The girls' means tended in a complementary direction. Within each school the boy-girl difference was marked, though less so at Conrad than the other schools. The subgroup of high-imaginative Conrad boys was distinct from the boys in other schools in the nature of their war and adventure stories. In contrast to the high-imaginative traditional school boys, whose stories were violent and set in an adult world, theirs were personal stories in which the child was central and violence irrelevant. Two factors—the lower incidence of family life themes among the Conrad girls and of aggressive-destructive themes among the Conrad boys—contributed to decreasing the difference between boys and girls at this school in contrast to other schools.

The prevalence of achievement fantasies in different schools reflected the division between modern and traditional schools, though not at statistically significant levels. The Conrad children, especially the boys, were least involved in these themes. The Adams children were notable for their involvement in achievement mastery and acclaim. In the latter school, high imagination co-existed with a high-rating on concern for achievement. In the other three schools, children with imaginative records might or might not show moderately high concern for achievement. At Adams, every child whose CPST stories were developed and elaborated in imaginative terms turned his hero toward accomplishment and surmounting obstacles. More than half the children who told stories in which the hero achieved spectacular reward and became the center of laudatory attention came from Adams.[21] The imaginative children from Adams stood out in their general concern for achievement, particularly the kind of dazzling achievement associated with great fame.

Relationships to Home Background

It will be remembered that school groups did not differ in the extent of imaginative thinking per se. Correlations between aspects of child-rearing ideology and measures of imaginative thinking likewise offer no very firm evidence of systematic relationships. Associations are relatively few and all are of low magnitude (see Appendix CC, Table 2). It is worth noting, however, that they are consistent in direction. They suggest that, to some extent, boys and girls from homes exerting pressure to meet external standards of behavior and achievement tended to produce more elaborated and imaginative material (CPST and Play). Rather than supporting the idea that modern homes foster imaginative expression, these correlations suggest that traditional homes had some influence in this direction. We might see here the effects of a measurement dilemma. Children more used to external rather than self-generated rules may have tried more diligently to fulfill the requirements of the task and may have less frequently given meager responses. Higher productivity in these situations was inevitably related to higher assessments of imaginative response and these children may have been rated somewhat higher because of their more productive response to the situation, seen and accepted as a task to be handled.

It is also possible, however, that the imaginative stories themselves were compensatory responses to the pressures of authority and demand in the environment. These children may have used the projective situations to express their sense of pressure, to explore alternatives to their reality, or to project various ways of coping with it.

Children whose projective stories included magic and imaginary elements tended to come from the Conrad school. Since this was a small group, whose members came from predominantly modern homes, a separate assessment of the influence of home background was not made.

The association between parent variables and the thematic material referred to in this chapter will be reported and discussed again in subsequent chapters. In some respects, the effects of home background appear consistent with those of the school; in other respects, home background seemed the more systematically influential factor (see Appendix CC, Table 2).

As in the case of the school group findings, adult-oriented wishes and spending were more characteristic of children from traditional environments, in this case the home. Although the correlations are relatively weak, the influence of the home appears consistent in direction with that of the school.

The projective material, however, reflects modern-traditional home influence more systematically than that of the school. The children, particularly the girls, from more traditional homes enacted more family life stories in their Play and introduced parent figures into their CPST stories more often than the girls from the more modern homes, suggesting that family life themes play a larger part in their imaginative expression than they do for daughters of more modern parents. There is also a low but reliable association between the enactment of family life themes in Play and the socio-economic-cultural status of the home, suggesting that in this generally upper-middle-class sample, girls who came from homes of somewhat lower socio-economic status seemed more attracted to family life themes. Perhaps conventionality is the common factor.

Only a suggestive relationship obtained between traditional home background and the enactment of aggressive-destructive themes for the sample at large. It should be noted, however, that boys from the most clearly traditional homes enacted significantly more aggressive Play sequences than boys from clearly modern homes and that the combination of traditional home and school background was conducive to such projections.[22]

Inspection revealed that children from Adams who were especially concerned with themes of achievement and success tended also to come from traditional homes; since the group was small, no statistical assessment was made.

Summary and Discussion

In this chapter, the study of cognition was extended to include thinking processes that are essentially imaginative and creative rather than goal-directed or problem-oriented. The imaginative productions and responses of the children were considered to be part of their cognitive life, though they drew more upon personal and subjective experience and required a different intellectual processing than the responses reported in the previous chapter.

The children of this sample were relatively effective in coping with the tasks presented. They varied a good deal, however, in their attitudes toward open intellectual opportunity, as embodied in the invitation to play, to weave their own stories, to put their own verbal stamp on artistic productions, to indulge their wish life. For some, these were difficult chores, while others enjoyed the opportunity to invent. Those who were competent and relaxed in the problem-solving situations were not necessarily those who took on these more open-ended opportunities with greatest ease and pleasure. Children varied not only in their affinity with these situations but in the quality of the material they produced, from literal and sparse responses to highly elaborate and original material.

We expected imaginative thinking to reflect the contrasting modern and traditional environments of the children. Given the factors in a modern school which encourage the expression of imaginative and nonstereotyped thinking and the forces in traditional education which value more formal and prestructured responses, we predicted that children from modern schools would be more imaginative in their thinking and modes of expression, while those from traditional schools would be more conventional and standardized. In assessing the extent of imaginative response, however, these predictions were not borne out; there were no stable group differences.

To an extent, this finding reflects the fact that some modern school children, boys in particular, were not freely responsive to these situations.

There was some general evidence of inhibition in some of these children and caution in sharing their ideas with unfamiliar adults. This bears discussion in a broader context, but it contributed to the fact that modern school children were not more expressive and imaginative, as a group, in the way predicted.

Other relevant factors include those which operate to increase response and productivity in children from the more traditional environments. The full development and expression of imaginative material, for instance, may represent an effective response to a required task—a more highly developed skill in the traditional school children. It may also represent the use of imagination as a compensatory reaction to the exigencies of a pressured environment. The data support the probability that some children used projective situations in this way, since such thinking correlates, to an extent, with the kind of home background that sets strong external standards for behavior and achievement.

In general, it seems likely that elaborate imaginative productions appeared among different children for different reasons; though the quality of the modern milieu may have influenced some children, it was not the sole or overriding influence on imaginative flow, which seemed to have complex and varied determinants.

The data do suggest, however, a stylistic characteristic in the imaginative material of children from the most modern school—a difference in the mode of their imaginative thought and expression. Children from Conrad were more apt than others to invoke the symbolic and the imaginary; some of them created events and phenomena that could have no realistic base. This exploration of the inexplicable was also a way of dealing with the theme of power and its effects through forms that were playful and unrealistic. Other material in the study shows that the issue of power and authority between adults and children was not sharply polarized in the most modern environment and that children of this environment seemed least concerned about adult status and their own position in relation to adults. Perhaps the playful invocation of supernatural forces represented a displacement and symbolic expression of the common and developmentally important theme of power and vulnerability.

Beyond this possibility, it seems likely that the mode of magical and imaginary expression also reflected an educational atmosphere which encouraged the full use of imagination and creative processes without constant commitment to the literal and realistic. The limited incidence of this mode of expression necessitates caution in interpretation, but it is a suggestive phenomenon of some interest.

In this chapter, we have examined the children's responses, not only for their imaginative qualities but for their basic thematic content. In both aspects, there are clear differences between boys and girls. Girls were more reactive, spontaneous, and productive than boys and more imaginative in what they did with the material presented. Manifest content was also different. Girls centered on family themes, boys acted out adventure stories and aggressive-destructive encounters in myriad forms. Even in probing the basic common themes, such as assertion and power, the focus of the boys was different from that of the girls: raw and violent aspects were expressed more openly by boys, for instance, while feelings of fright, anxiety, and vulnerability were expressed more openly by girls.

Despite individual and sex differences, certain major themes appeared often in the projective material, and seem meaningful in terms of the developmental status of the children. (See, in this connection, Pitcher and Prelinger's 1963 analysis of story themes of younger children.)

The dynamic extension of life space was one of the important underlying themes. It involved both an extension outward, beyond known people and immediate places, to distant times and settings, and an extension inward to the exploration of new roles and relationships among people. It seemed a clear expression of the child's exploratory movement at this life stage: from the familiar home setting and young child's role to a more extended and complex environment. It is an exploration made possible by the child's growing intellectual understanding of extended time and space and by his increasing emotional strength for taking on new roles, new contexts, and new relationships. Not unexpectedly, the children in their imaginative expression probed both the pleasures and conflicts of this extension.

Another, and perhaps related, theme concerned the struggle between power and weakness, assertion and retreat. In the oft-repeated play of opposing forces, the children seemed to express their sense of growing power and the wish to be strong and dominant—a wish in constant interaction with the sense of vulnerability and the dangers of assertion. In these dichotomized battles, they seemed also to express the inner struggle that accompanies the process of socialization. The battles of right against wrong externalized the conflict between socialized and acceptable impulses, on the one hand, and the wishes and impulses that oppose the acceptable, on the other.

Mastery and competence constituted a third recurrent dynamic theme. Like the previous theme, it sometimes involved overcoming obstacles. Primarily, however, it expressed the wish and determination to be competent in ways relevant to the broader society. Certainly this is a known and well-documented focus of the middle-years child, who devotes himself in reality to the industrious cultivation of tangible skills and probes in fantasy the frustrations and pleasures that can accompany this desired mastery. For some children, the theme of mastery and competence was embedded in the tangible symbols of reward: recognition by others, dazzling fame, success and power.

In a variety of ways, these separate themes reflected the life stage of these children expressing and exploring the meaning of their middle status. The themes seemed to express the ambiguity of their position, neither young child nor adult, in forms that were more advanced and realistic than the younger child's, less complex and soul searching than the adolescent's. They explored facets of the broader, more adult world, wishing themselves closer to it in some ways, yet wishing to retain at the same time the limits and the pleasure of their childhood status.

To what extent did children from modern and traditional environments differ in these themes? To a large extent, the themes expressed developmental concerns and were shared by the entire group. The data suggest, however, that their different milieux had already pitched the children in somewhat different directions; what emerged as uppermost in orientation or concern within one group was sometimes less prominent in others.

The themes of achievement and fame that characterized children from traditional environments, for example, were in interesting apposition to the themes of magic and fairyland that distinguished the Conrad children. As the themes of achievement and fame are consonant with the orientation to the future, to adulthood, among the traditional school children, the thematic concern with animals and magical happenings seems to go along with the tendency we have noted for the modern school children to fantasy and deal with a more child-oriented world. Both represent distinctive ways of escaping from or not dealing with the everyday world of the present. In fantasying about being grown up, the child is leaping the barrier of time to achieve a position where he is no longer subject to the strains of his present status or the authority of adults. In fantasying a magical world, the child is leaping the barrier of reality and changing and controlling the rules of power; and insofar as the few adults who appear in the world of magic are either powerless or magic-giving, it is a world for and of children.

In another sense, the different hierarchies and modes in the imaginative material may have represented the internalization of somewhat different value systems. The tangible and conventional symbols of power, influence, wealth, and acclaim in the adult world seemed more important to children from more traditional environments and were the vehicles through which they expressed the universal wish for growth and self-fulfillment. It would be misleading to suggest that adults or adult value systems were not important to children from more modern environments. The nature of the modern value system, however, may have bound these children less to tangible and predetermined images.

The major themes discussed in this chapter, in relation to the processes of imaginative thinking, will appear again as the substantive material of Chapters 10, 11, and 13 which deal with perceptions of family adults, attitudes toward school authority, and life-stage imagery and perspective.

NOTES

1. Another task which also taps associative flow and which is often used as a measure of creativity is Uncommon Uses (see Chapter 8). It is therefore of interest to note the correlations between the two scores derived from responses to Uncommon Uses and the ratings of imaginativeness on Similes and Picture Titles. The correlations for the relationship thinking score are .30 and .13 for Similes and Picture Titles, respectively; for the Solver score (which gives more weight to fluency), the correlations are .38 and .26, for Similes and Picture Titles, respectively.

2. There was, however, little overlap; only 14 children received high ratings on both Play and CPST.

3. The correlation between imaginativeness and protocol length is .83, $r = .74$ for boys and .88 for girls, $p < .01$ throughout.

4. Although seven children told CPST stories involving magic and seven children enacted Play sequences involving magic, only one child used magic in both instances.

5. CPST picture #4 (Standard TAT #5).

6. A 3×2 analysis yielded a χ^2 of 10.83, $p < .01$.

7. The number of animal associations given as Similes was converted into a three-point scale and analyzed by means of analysis of variance. School groups differed significantly ($F = 2.75$, $p < .05$), and the children from Conrad gave an average of five responses to the 19 Similes while children from the other school groups gave an average of three or less.

8. Among Conrad girls, horses figured prominently in their casual talk, their art work, the books they read, their wishes, daydreams, and play. For some of these girls, horses were a preoccupation that overflowed into many areas of responses. In the culture of the modern private school with its small groups and intense personal relationships, it seems possible that a few children's personal symbols, especially when attractive and syntonic with the age level, can come to serve as shared fantasy. At any rate, it is evident that the horse cult in this group accounted in part for the prominence of animals in their imaginative responses.

9. Raters coded the elements described in the McClelland system but assigned a rating on the basis of overall judgment.

10. Children of Conrad and Dickens accounted for most of these magical wishes; no Browning children expressed this kind of wish.

11. CPST picture #4 (Standard TAT #5).

12. It should be kept in mind that these excerpts are the child's verbal explanations which accompanied the action of the Play and do not reproduce the manipulative, nonverbal mode of developing the plot.
13. CPST picture #11G (Standard TAT #7GF).
14. CPST picture #6.
15. CPST picture #2B.
16. CPST picture #10 (Standard TAT #8Bm).
17. CPST picture #3.
18. CPST picture #1 (Standard TAT #1).
19. CPST picture #7.
20. It might be noted that this order bears no relation to the actual incomes of the families in the four school groups (see Chapter 5).
21. In this sample, achievement themes are highly correlated with imaginativeness; $r = .65$ for the total sample and is comparably high for boys and girls and for the four schools considered separately. Although rated independently, both measures are based on CPST data and both are highly correlated with productivity. The correlation for Adams is not higher than for the other schools, but inspection of the low scores shows that in the other schools the correlation is carried by low performance which tends to lead to low scores on both measures, while only at Adams is there a consistent association of achievement and imagination at the upper level.
22. This refers to the subsample of 47 children from clearly traditional and clearly modern homes (see Chapter 5).

CHAPTER

10

PERCEPTION OF
FAMILY ADULTS

A major difference between modern and traditional schools was in the relations between adults and children. Adults had distinctly different ways of structuring children's lives and acting toward them, and their expectations of how children should act toward adults and toward each other were also different (see Chapters 3 and 4). Because their school experiences differed so clearly, we expected children from modern and traditional schools to be forming different views of the adult world, and this assumption was to be tested through the data. In the material reported in the previous chapter about the children's perception of the adult world, it was impressive that their imaginative productions were dominated by family figures and themes. Though nine-year-old children are in a period of transition, moving into a broader world of people and experience, parental figures still loomed large in this group. It is possible, of course, that the parents who figured so prominently in the children's projective material were not the literal parents alone but symbolized adults in general. Since we did not know this to be the case, however, we have assumed that the children's reports and perceptions represented simply their impressions and images of family life. We decided, therefore, to separate the children's perceptions of adults and their relationships with them according to content: family and school. In this chapter, children's perceptions of family adults are considered; the chapter following this one considers in part the children's relation to the authority structure of the school, as mediated through adults.

In considering the salience of the family, no specific a priori predictions were made about differences associated with modern or traditional schooling. There were, however, systematic relationships between aspects of family background and the prevalence of family material in the children's projections. It was also found that Conrad children were less involved in family associations than children from the other schools.

In analyzing the perceptions of interaction between adults and children, predictions were made on the assumption that different experiences with adults would affect children's perceptions and expectations. Children from traditional environments were expected to project controlling and disapproving figures, while children from more modern environments were expected to project more benevolent and accepting figures. This expectation was not borne out and was reversed in some particulars; the probable meaning of this reversal is discussed at the end of this chapter.

The material in this chapter is presented in two sections: Salience of the Family, and Perception of Adult-Child Interaction.

Salience of the Family

The assessment of the child's perception of his family included the extent of family content in projective and self-descriptive material, the potency of family members as models or confidantes, and the child's image of his family and of his mother and father, considered separately.

Techniques and Measures

The techniques and measures indicate the primacy of family and family figures.

(i) **Play: Enactment of Family Life Themes.** A rating was made on a four-point scale of the tendency to develop scenes and stories centered on the family drama (see Chapter 9, p. 222).

(ii) **CPST: Incidence of Parent Figures.** The number of stories using parent figures was converted to a three-point scale (see Chapter 9, p. 223).

(iii) **Personal Questions: Family-Related Material.** The child's responses to questions about himself and his personal reactions, for example, "What makes you happy? What puts you in a bad mood? Do you have feelings you try not to show?" were rated on a three-point scale according to his tendency to bring up incidents and figures from family life:

    1—no mention of family

    2—

    3—considerable material about family

(iv) **Sociometrics, Interview, Sentence Completion Test: Salient Figures.**

    (a) *Sociometric Question:* "Who is the *person you tell your troubles to?*" The number of children were counted who mentioned one or both parents, either alone or in combination with a friend or sibling.

    (b) *Interview Question:* "Who is the *best person* you know (or can think of)?" Responses were categorized as family, peer, or well-known figure.

    (c) *Sentence Completion Test,* Item 17: *My hero is* . . . . Responses were categorized as family, peer, or well-known figure.

(v) **Family Drawing: Replication of Own Family.** A rating was made on a three-point scale of the extent to which the child duplicated the actual composition of his own family:

    1—extensive modification, for example, omitting or adding parent or several siblings

    2—

    3—replication

Whether or not the drawing included a figure of the same sex and approximately the same age as the child was noted.

INTERCORRELATIONS AMONG MEASURES

One would expect the correlations among the measures to indicate that these are varied but overlapping ways of approaching the child's perception of family life. However, the differences among them seem to have operated more strongly than the similarities, for many of the intercorrelations among the measures are strikingly low (see Appendix BB, Table 3).

The three most comprehensive scores—the prevalence of family life themes in Play, of parent figures in CPST stories, and the introduction of family-centered material in response to the Personal Questions—have negligible intercorrelations.

Obviously, the techniques offered different opportunities which children utilized in distinctly different ways. Judging from the correlations, they tapped somewhat different facets of the child's perception of and involvement in family life. The lack of relationship among these measures may represent a real lack of integration and resolution of the psychological dimensions being assessed.

Group Characteristics and Sex Differences

The position of these children developmentally as one of moving away from the family, on the one hand, but not wishing entirely to relinquish their erstwhile protected position in it, on the other, is well illustrated in the family drawings.

Most children altered the actual composition of their own families in their family drawings and more than half of these made a radical change: a parent was left out or the number of siblings sharply reduced or, occasionally, increased. Of the 23 children whose family drawings represented actual composition and age relations, 17 were boys. The majority of the children (63) included in their drawings a figure of the same sex and approximately the same age as the child himself, that is, a figure who could be considered a representation of the self. The remaining 35 children (evenly split between boys and girls) did not put themselves into the picture. As a composite picture, these findings seem to symbolize the child's state of transition, of being in the process of realigning his relationship to the world and therefore his family: a few drawings were complete duplications of the child's own family, but most were altered in some way, and in more than a third the child did not represent himself. The children, in other words, departed from a literal rendering of their family while, for the most part, still staying within it.

There is, in fact, a good deal of evidence that family life and figures were still the central influence in the lives, especially the emotional lives, of these children. This is indicated by their enactment of family life stories and their responses to the Personal Questions.

As described in Chapter 9, the single most frequent theme in Play stories was the depiction of some aspect of family life and this was distinctly more attractive to girls than boys (see Table 10–1). Similarly, parents were the adults most often introduced in CPST stories, and with far more frequency than the stimuli suggested.[1] Both boys and girls introduced parent figures, especially the mother, into their stories, although girls did so more often than boys.

The salience of the family was further corroborated by responses to the Personal Questions (see Table 10–1). In their reports of what made them happy or mad, embarrassed or ashamed, 78 percent of the children drew on their family life experiences, a few making it the center of their responses. Most of those who did not introduce any family-related material were boys (17 of 22).

What the children actually said about their parents and siblings in this context, while often quite commonplace—"(I get mad) when my mommy

TABLE 10–1
The Salience of Family Adults

Measure Source, and Scale Range	(N)	Sex §	Browning	Adams	Dickens	Conrad	Total	Analysis of Variance
ENACTMENT OF FAMILY LIFE THEMES Play Scale Range: 1–4		b	1.80	1.72	1.42	1.63	1.64	Schools: 2.86* Sex: 48.00** Schools × Sex: 2.71*
		g	3.50	2.75	3.33	2.17	2.88	
	(104)	T	2.56	2.21	2.38	1.86	2.21	
INCIDENCE OF PARENT FIGURES CPST Scale Range: 1–3		b	1.90	2.11	1.92	1.88	1.96	Schools: .24 NS Sex: .24 NS Schools × Sex: .73 NS
		g	2.13	1.81	2.17	1.92	1.97	
	(105)	T	2.00	1.97	2.04	1.90	1.97	
FAMILY-RELATED MATERIAL Personal Questions Scale Range: 1–3		b	1.78	2.06	1.83	1.44	1.77	Schools: 3.77* Sex: 5.91* Schools × Sex: .45 NS
		g	2.14	2.13	2.00	1.83	2.02	
	(102)	T	1.94	2.09	1.91	1.59	1.88	
REPLICATION OF OWN FAMILY Family Drawing Scale Range: 1–3		b	1.89	2.00	2.00	1.93	1.96	Schools: .12 NS Sex: 3.68 NS Schools × Sex: .18 NS
		g	1.75	1.50	1.70	1.58	1.61	
	(98)	T	1.82	1.76	1.86	1.78	1.80	

* $p < .05$
** $p < .01$
§ b = boys
g = girls
T = total

yells at me"—was sometimes emotionally laden: "Well, when my mother is happy, I'm happy." Occasionally their comments were amusing: "Well, I must say, my mother calling me so much. Like when I'm pasting and then I answer and she says she didn't hear me and she yells and I have to go with paste all over my hands." Sometimes a response was reminiscent of the inevitable tortures of childhood: "Well (I'm embarrassed) when my mother screams at me out in the street and things like that." Many of their responses reflected a quality of mutual nagging, demand and counterdemand, exemplified to the extremes of refinement by the boy who said: "Like this morning, my mother didn't cut my orange right." Much of the children's feeling was concentrated on the rules and regulations of everyday family existence: "My father says, 'Here comes the ice cream man, let's get ice cream.' And then my mother says, 'Oh no, it's right before supper'"; and a few children said that what made them angry was "when I can't have my own way."

There were signs, also, that for these children, their parents still served as the best refuge and source of consolation. In answer to the question, "Who is the person you tell your troubles to?" 83 percent mentioned one or both parents, alone or in combination with a friend or sibling.[2] Boys, more than girls, tended to mention only one parent; this may have been due to their general tendency to respond with only one name, or they may have felt less expansive than the girls, who more often mentioned both parents or a combination of parent and peers.

In a variety of contexts, then, and to a diversity of stimuli, the children talked about family matters and thought in terms of family imagery. Their responses to these four techniques indicated that for most of them, family-related material occupied a very high position in the hierarchy of their concerns, especially when their emotions were involved. Their responses confirmed the power and solidity of family ties for children of this age.

This picture changed, however, when the children were asked to consider an ideal individual or model. Their reach then extended to figures outside the family. In response to the question, "Who is the best person you know?" slightly over half the children (59) said, "My mother" or "My father" or both and 17 chose members of the extended family (for example, grandparent, uncle). The incidence of such responses, however, was noticeably lower than the 83 percent who chose parents to tell their troubles to. Boys and girls were fairly evenly split in their tendency to select a family member as best person—53 percent of the boys and 60 percent of the girls. Of the ten children who could not respond to the question at all, nine were boys. In considering who their ideal person was (Sentence Completion Item 17, "My hero is . . ."), family members entered radically less often. Over half the children indicated a cultural hero or one of their peers. Only 19 children chose a family member, four of which were siblings. There were 15 choices of parent, 14 of which were for the father, not surprising since "hero" suggests a masculine figure. Out of a rather large group of 23 children who did not answer this question, 17 were boys. The predominance of the boys here is one of the most arresting instances of their greater reserve.

In their answers to these last two items, then, these children, while still offering family material, were also groping for personal models beyond the family.

School Group Differences

The most clear-cut difference among schools is that the children from Conrad stand out from other school groups by their relative lack of preoccupation with family themes and associations. With the exception of the drawings, this is indicated by all the measures.[3]

The primacy of family themes in Play, while not following the modern-traditional continuum, yields the greatest difference between Browning, the most traditional, and Conrad, the most modern school (see Table 10–1). Since this theme came mostly from the girls, the difference is carried by them. Girls from Dickens as well as from Browning were drawn to family themes reliably more often than the Conrad girls. For only one girl from Conrad was this the exclusive concern in Play, while in the other school groups combined, one third of the girls enacted only family life stories.

Introducing parents in CPST stories followed a similar pattern: girls from Browning and Dickens were the most prone to add parents, Conrad and Adams girls did so least often.

Similarly, the children from Conrad brought fewer family-related matters into their responses to the Personal Questions (see Table 10–1). The boys from Conrad were particularly low on the Personal Questions measure, and notably lower than the girls from that school. They tended to be exceptionally resistant to personal questions and this, combined with the general tendency for the children from Conrad to offer less family-related material, may have been operating here.

The small number of children who mentioned a family member— mostly the father—in response to the Sentence Completion item "My hero is . . ." were distributed evenly among the four school groups. However, of the 23 children who did not respond to this item, half were from Conrad. The difficulty that this relatively large group of Conrad children had with this item may be due to their unwillingness to confide or to a particular inability to respond to an idealized label, thus making the words "my hero" something they could not apply to someone they knew in the personal and serious sense required.

The children from Conrad also stand out from the other school groups in their responses to the question, "Who is the best person you know?" Here a choice of parent was most characteristic of the children from Conrad: 80 percent chose mother or father, compared to 62 percent from Adams and 50 percent from Browning and Dickens. This is of interest because it reverses the general trend for the children from Conrad to be least concerned and those from Browning and Dickens to be most concerned with family matters. Not only have the Conrad children reversed their own general trend here, but they have also reversed the general group trend, which, it will be remembered, was to mention family figures less often in answer to this question. Whom one considers an ideal figure or model is clearly different, in terms of family associations, from the figures that may come to the fore in Play, CPST, and the Personal Questions. The children from Browning and Dickens seemed to be saying that their parents and the events that transpired in their families were the most salient in their lives. The reactions of the Conrad children were more complicated. Family figures were not particularly salient in most of their material but they seemed to have a very high opinion of their parents considered as individuals.

Family associations, then, recurred consistently in the projections of these children (especially those of the girls), though less so when they were considering an ideal figure or model. The children from Conrad offered notably less family material and seemed less family bound than the children from other school groups.

Perception of Adult-Child Interaction

The prediction that children from traditional environments would project controlling adults and those from modern environments more benevolent figures was based on the different roles assumed by the adults in these two environments. It was expected that the children's direct experience with these adults would be reflected in their projected encounters with them.

Techniques and Measures

The assessment of the children's perceptions of the extent and quality of child-adult interactions was drawn from the Sentence Completion Test, CPST, and Play. Measures (ii) and (iii) concern the children's projection of adult → child relations; the last two measures, (iv) and (v), concern the child's projected role vis-à-vis adults.

(i) **Sentence Completion Test,** Items 3 and 5: *My mother always*
. . . and *Lots of times my father.* . . .
   (a) *Relatedness of parent and child.* The children's responses were categorized according to whether they
      expressed a relationship between parent and child, for example, *My mother always* helps me, cooks for us, makes me practice; *Lots of times my father* plays with me, works on my toys that are broken, drives us different places
      referred to the parent as a separate, independent person, for example, *My mother always* shops, goes to the office, wears a hat; *Lots of times my father* is very busy, reads the newspaper, goes to work
   (b) *Quality of relationship expressed.* Responses in which a parent-child relationship was expressed were categorized as

Giving, nurturing, for example, does nice things for us, takes me swimming, plays with me

Socializing-mild, for example, tells me to set the table, makes me take a bath before bed

Angry, for example, yells at me

ADULT → CHILD RELATIONS

(ii) **CPST: Benevolence of Adult Attitudes and Behavior Toward Children.** Each adult → child interchange was annotated and a rating made on a four-point scale of the extent to which adult behavior was seen as nurturant, affectionate, benevolent.[4]

1—nonbenevolent adult-child relations, annotated for:

1a—stress on authoritative, impulse-controlling, or punitive aspects

1n—stress on nonavailability, nonresponsiveness of adult

2—

3—

4—stress on benevolent, supporting, nurturing, affectionate adult in relation to child

(iii) **Play: Interaction Between Adults and Children.** The children's Play protocols were categorized as follows:

1—no adult-child interaction

2—adult-child interaction depicted. Annotated for

Benign nurturance. Adults and children are present together and the adults explicitly or implicitly care for the children

Giving. The adult gives concrete gifts, trips, or advice and instruction

Mixed. The adults nurture or give but also control or reject

Negative. The adults control or attempt to control, deprive, reject, or fail the child

CHILD → ADULT RELATIONS

(iv) **CPST: Child-Initiated Contact with Adults.** The number of times a child figure instigated contact (of any kind) with an adult figure was converted to a four-point scale:

1—no approach clearly initiated by a child

2—one or two child-initiated approaches

3—three or four child-initiated approaches

4—five or more child-initiated approaches

(v) **CPST: Direct Expression of Opposition to Adults.** A rating of the presence or absence of a child's direct challenge of an adult:[5]

1—absence of directly expressed opposition

2—presence of directly expressed opposition

INTERCORRELATIONS AMONG MEASURES

On the whole, these measures correlate at statistically significant levels and present an acceptable series (see Appendix BB, Table 3). The tendency to project child-initiated interchanges is correlated both with the projection of adults who were more benevolent in their interactions with children and with the expression of child opposition to adults. In the first case, the correlation supports the common-sense notion that those who expect benevolence are more likely to initiate contact; in the second, the correlation underlines the fact that both initiation and opposition are signs of a more active stance in the adult-child relationship.

Group Characteristics and Sex Differences

The children's portrayal of interactions between adults and children fluctuated both in amount and quality. This unevenness is probably related in part to the differences presented by each task and in part it probably also reflects the particular, complex, and fluctuating attitudes and feelings that children of this age have about their families.

In response to the Sentence Completion stems about the mother and father, more children saw the mother (69 percent) than the father (48 percent) in some relationship to themselves (see Table 10–2). The mother was variously described as giving, withholding, guiding, punishing, feeding, or scolding, but she was usually in interaction. A frequent response concerned the mother as provider of food (20 children): "(My mother always) gives me hot cocoa in the morning," "fixes dinner for me." When she was described without reference to the child, the mother was portrayed as busy, taking care of the house, shopping, going to work, or sometimes in terms of a personal characteristic: wears a hat, makes Christmas cards. The father, too, was often seen in a relationship, but what he and the child were described as doing was rather different: "(Lots of times my father) takes me to the movies," "brings me toys," "plays checkers with me." When mentioned without reference to the child, he was often described in terms of his work; as one child put it, he "disappears downtown to his office." While more boys than girls described the father in relation to themselves (54 and 40 percent, respectively), a more or less equal proportion of boys and girls described the mother in such terms (70 and 67 percent, respectively).

The category of mild socialization was uniformly attributed to the mother. "(My mother always) makes me practice," "says no TV till 6:00," "tells me to clean my room." There were no comparable responses concerning the father. Although the father presumably also meted out discipline in these households, the mother set the terms for the simple do's and don'ts of daily family living. On the other hand, while parents were rarely perceived as angry, the father was described as yelling or mad more often than the mother.

This task, then, which specifically called for comments about each par-

TABLE 10–2
Projected Relatedness of Parent and Child

MEASURE Source, and Scale Range	(N)	Sex §	Mean Scores for School Groups					Analysis of Variance
			Browning	Adams	Dickens	Conrad	Total	
RELATEDNESS OF MOTHER AND CHILD Sentence Completion Item 3 Scale Range: 1–2	(103)	b	1.70	1.50	1.75	1.80	1.67	Schools: 1.11 NS Sex: .00 NS Schools × Sex: 1.11 NS
		g	1.88	1.69	1.75	1.58	1.71	
		T	1.78	1.59	1.75	1.70	1.69	
RELATEDNESS OF FATHER AND CHILD Sentence Completion Item 5 Scale Range: 1–2	(104)	b	1.40	1.44	1.75	1.71	1.58	Schools: 1.50 NS Sex: 3.00 NS Schools × Sex: 1.00 NS
		g	1.38	1.40	1.25	1.58	1.40	
		T	1.39	1.42	1.50	1.66	1.50	

§ b = boys
g = girls
T = total

ent, showed a response in which the parents were depicted both as exercising authority and as giving and loving.

These findings concur with other research in which it has been generally reported that mothers are viewed by both boys and girls as friendlier, more loving, and more affectionate than fathers, and fathers as stricter than mothers (Droppleman and Schaefer, 1963; Becker, 1964). Furthermore, these findings make it clear that the content of the child's behavior that each parent characteristically deals with is different and that the sheer amount of interaction is usually much greater for the mother. While this may be a common-sense observation, it is often overlooked in assessments of differences in children's perceptions of each parent and in parents' perceptions of boys and girls.

In their Play dramas a sizable number of the children (39) did not include any kind of interchange between a child and an adult; approximately half the boys (30) invented no stories in which adults and children appeared together (see Table 10–3 for mean differences). Their stories, it will be remembered, were about war and adventure, in which there was much interaction and both comradely and aggressive encounter, but among adult co-equals.

The remaining two thirds of the children did project adult-child interaction in Play. One third (34 children) enacted stories in which adults and children were depicted together in pleasant but emotionally bland situations, with the details of their relationship left unspecified. The adults in

TABLE 10–3
Children's Projections of Adult → Child Relations

MEASURE Source, and Scale Range	(N)	Sex §	Mean Scores for School Groups					Analysis of Variance
			Browning	Adams	Dickens	Conrad	Total	
BENEVOLENCE OF ADULT ATTITUDES AND BEHAVIOR TOWARD CHILDREN CPST Scale Range: 1–4		b	1.30	1.18	1.58	1.38	1.35	Schools: 3.70* Sex: 23.15** Schools × Sex: 1.91 NS
		g	2.38	1.93	2.75	1.55	2.13	
	(100)	T	1.78	1.52	2.17	1.44	1.70	
INTERACTION BETWEEN ADULTS AND CHILDREN Play Scale Range: 1–2		b	1.40	1.39	1.58	1.53	1.47	Schools: .50 NS Sex: 13.00** Schools × Sex: 1.00 NS
		g	2.00	1.69	1.91	1.75	1.81	
	(104)	T	1.67	1.53	1.74	1.62	1.63	

* $p < .05$
** $p < .01$
§ b = boys
  g = girls
  T = total

these stories were usually benign and nurturant, primarily engaged in caretaking functions: the mother may have been preparing food or taking care of the babies. The remaining third depicted adult-child relationships in which the adults' behavior and attitudes toward children were predominantly negative, or mixed negative and positive.

In sum, the sample falls into three more or less equal groups. The first consists of children who did not choose to depict adult-child relationships; the second, of children who left the relationship implicit, though benign; and the third, of children who detailed the relationship and depicted adults with negative or mixed attitudes toward children. More girls than boys detailed the relations between adults and children, but both boys and girls who did so, more often invented adults who scolded and punished, denied, or failed to take care of the children.

In their CPST stories, the children, by and large, projected adults who were controlling, disapproving, or unavailable in their relations with children (see Table 10–3). In general, they used the CPST to project problems and difficulties, exploring situations that required coping rather than ones that gave pleasure. The children invented mothers and fathers who "speak harshly," who administered both unspecified and particular punishments: the child was sent to his room, or spanked and sent to bed without supper, or made to throw away his rock collection; story parents were often too busy to play or not there when the child needed them. These stories might be contrasted with some obtained by Witkin (see Witkin, Dyk, Faterson, Goodenough, and Karp, 1962) from a heterogeneous sample of ten-year-old boys in which parents were described as "physically aggressive, brutalizing and overpowering towards their children" (p. 331). While both these groups presented an exaggeration of their actual experience, the children in the present sample seldom portrayed physical aggression. The negative attributes of their parent figures were less extreme and more subtle.

Boys' stories were most dramatic in their projection of non-benevolent adults: 75 percent of the boys, as opposed to 32 percent of the girls, invented stories in which such figures appear. This is in contrast to Play, where there were no sex differences in the quality of adult-child interactions when these were projected. Boys and girls also differed in the kind of nonbenevolence they portrayed. The boys who projected nonbenevolent adults more often described them as controlling and authoritative rather than absent or remote, while the girls who projected nonbenevolent adults were equally likely to describe them as controlling or absent. In effect, the boys not only portrayed more such figures but seem, in these projections, to show concern about coercion, the threats to *in*dependence. Fewer of the girls projected such figures at all and when they did so, seem equally concerned with fears of abandonment, the threat to *de*pendence.

The interchanges projected by the children were most often initiated by adults. Although about two thirds of the children told a CPST story in which a child initiated an interchange with an adult, most offered only one or two such instances throughout their 12 stories. Children of this age perhaps perceive themselves as responders rather than initiators in relation to adults. Even fewer were the number of incidents in which a child took exception to some adult opinion or rule or directly challenged an adult. Only one third of the children invented such a sequence. While there are no differences between boys and girls in the frequency of child-initiated contacts, more girls than boys told stories involving child opposition (see Table 10–4).

School Group Differences

The characteristics attributed to adults in interactions with children do vary with schooling, though not as a function of the modern-traditional dimension. The children from Dickens and Browning, especially the girls, tended to project benign adults, while the children from Adams and Conrad more often projected adults who were nonbenevolent (see Table 10–3). The boys from all schools more often told CPST stories in which the adults were socializing and nonbenevolent, and in this respect the Conrad girls were most like them. Both in the general pattern of projected

TABLE 10–4
Children's Projections of Child → Adult Relations

MEASURE Source, and Scale Range	(N)	Sex §	Browning	Adams	Dickens	Conrad	Total	Analysis of Variance
CHILD-INITIATED CONTACT WITH ADULTS CPST Scale Range: 1–4		b	1.80	1.88	1.92	1.88	1.87	Schools: .05 NS Sex: .08 NS Schools × Sex: .04 NS
		g	2.00	1.71	2.33	2.27	2.07	
	(100)	T	1.89	1.81	2.13	2.04	1.96	
DIRECT EXPRESSION OF OPPOSITION TO ADULTS CPST Scale Range: 1–2		b	1.10	1.17	1.33	1.31	1.23	Schools: .89 NS Sex: 5.00* Schools × Sex: .56 NS
		g	1.50	1.27	1.42	1.55	1.41	
	(102)	T	1.28	1.21	1.38	1.41	1.31	

Mean Scores for School Groups

* $p < .05$
§ $b = boys$
$g = girls$
$T = total$

adult behavior and in the particular quality of nonbenevolent adult behavior, the distinction between boy and girl patterns was least sharp in the Conrad group.

There are no differences among school groups in the tendency to portray adult-child interaction in Play sequences, although, again, it was the girls from Dickens and Browning who did so most often (see Table 10–3). There are also no differences among school groups in the extent to which the children projected in CPST stories were the initiators in adult-child interactions (see Table 10–4). However, there is a marked difference between what these children projected and what they actually did in their classrooms (see Chapter 4). It will be remembered that at Browning and Adams, both children and teachers initiated contacts, but at Dickens and Conrad, the children were the initiators for the most part. This disparity is further evidence that a simple parallel between projected and overt behavior cannot be assumed (see Zubin, Eron, and Schumer, 1965).

While the children's responses to the Sentence Completion stems about mother and father showed no differences among school groups, the children from Conrad gave eight of the 13 responses expressing anger between parent and child. The disproportion of this response, even though on a small scale, is consistent with the general tendency of this group to portray adults who, in their interactions with children, were not benign and giving. As such, it is a reversal of the study expectations about the Conrad group.

Relationships to Home Background

The children who were most involved with family matters came from families in which the general ideological orientation and modes of relationship were more traditional, presumably more rule-bound and adult-centered; where there was more emphasis on standards of behavior and achievement; and where the mother expressed less satisfaction with the kind of child she had (see Appendix CC, Table 3).

The introduction of parent figures in CPST stories shows a consistent pattern of relationships, especially for girls, which indicates that the less modern the orientation of the home, the greater the likelihood that the child, especially the daughter, will populate her CPST stories with parent figures. The same trend holds, though less dramatically, for stories enacted in Play. In their drawings, too, the girls from more traditional families more often included a self-representation in the families they drew. In their responses to the Personal Questions, it was the boys, from more traditional homes, who were more family oriented. Whether or not adults were portrayed as benevolent was also related to home background: daughters of more traditional mothers more often invented kindly and giving adults.[6] Several correlations suggest that the children from families at the lower end of the socio-economic-cultural scale, in this generally upper-middle-class sample, were those more preoccupied with family matters; this applies especially to the girls. In general, then, the relationship between these measures and home background factors is most consistent for girls.

Schaefer and Bayley (1963), in an extensive study of the correlations between maternal and child behavior variables at different age levels, found that maternal behavior and sons' behavior were highly correlated (in the nine-to-twelve-year-old stage). In general, they found that "maternal behavior has shown significant correlations only with current behavior of daughters, but with prior, current and subsequent behavior of sons" (p. 95). Schaefer and Bayley take this to mean that girls reflect their current interpersonal situation more than boys do. In this study, all the measures are concurrent. Furthermore, the material considered in this chapter seems more centrally important for girls than boys and drew a wider range of response; the measures therefore reflect a finer discrimination within the group of girls. Probably both factors contribute to the greater consistency between these measures and aspects of home background for girls than for boys.

Summary and Discussion

The deep emotional involvement children of this age have in the details and drama of family life is attested to by the prevalence of family themes and imagery in their projective expressions. Family life themes were more compelling, however, for girls than boys. The background antecedents that determined the primacy of material about family life seemed, in general to reside in variations in family more than school experience, though the children from Conrad were distinguished from children of the other schools by their lesser concern with family themes.[7]

The children's projections of parent-child relations presented many facets, including both the benevolent, nurturing aspects of adults and those that were controlling and denying. In associations about their parents (Sentence Completion Test), children described them—mothers especially—as providing routine as well as special pleasures, but they were also seen as disciplinarians. In the projective play situations, many children invented adults who were benevolent, though when the adult-child interaction in play was developed in greater detail the adult was often depicted as denying or failing the child. Boys were not as apt to enact adult-child dramas in play, but in CPST stories boys in particular portrayed adults who were rather severe or not available when needed. In general, a benevolent image of the adult-child world was more characteristic of girls.

The children, especially the girls, who came from the more traditional homes were more involved with family than were the children from the more modern homes. This may reflect a difference in values in the modern and traditional ideologies. While the underlying theories of both modern and traditional modes of child rearing consider family life and the relationships between parents and children singularly important, there is a sense in which the family per se is valued in traditional family ideology that seems qualitatively different from the way it is viewed in the modern ideology (see Levinson and Huffman, 1955). In the latter, the formative importance of family experiences and relationships is of central concern, but the family is not reified in the same way. We might speculate, therefore, that the traditionally reared children had learned to stress and value family life in and for itself. Such an attitude about family life, combined with the traditional conception of a relatively dependent and family-bound role for women, may account for the family-dominated perceptions of the traditionally reared girls. The constellation of role perception and family context among these girls will be discussed further in later chapters.

The psychological processes involved in parent-child relationships are intrinsically complex and the findings reflect that complexity. These nine-year-old children were all deeply involved with their parents, as indeed is natural for children of this age and circumstance. Livson (1966), too, in his study of children's involvement with their parents across a span of years, rated only nine out of 89 as not showing high involvement. Similarly, the projective measures are complex and their relation to the child's life experience, his needs, or his overt behavior are not necessarily clear. On the one hand, the greater expression of concern with family may be seen as a compensatory way of dealing with an area of life in which there is difficulty, dissatisfaction, and conflict. The child who populates his imaginary stories with family figures, for whom family life concerns seem to serve as an organizing concept in his expression, is perhaps showing a perseverative dependence on the family, dwelling too long on the safety of the familiar and comfortable. On the other hand, his preoccupation with family matters may indicate that he is working through the inevitable conflicts of belonging to and separating from the family. The child who expresses a minimum of concern with family matters, for whom the family drama seems to have less force, may be seen as closer to resolving these conflicts. Yet it is also possible that his lack of expressed involvement represents not a greater degree of conflict resolution, but a denial of the conflict and suppression of the problem itself.

Though family influence seemed the major determinant of variation in the children's reactions, there were certain differences among the school groups which threw into relief the position of the Conrad children. They offered far less family material and seemed less family-bound than children from other schools. As noted, there were no specific predictions concerning modern-traditional effects on the salience of family associations. It seems plausible to infer, however, that the modern environments had facilitated the shift from family embeddedness to broader worlds, in these transitional years, through the nature of what the modern school offered and by virtue of the less binding attitudes in modern families.

A priori predictions in this area centered on the children's perceptions of the quality of interaction between adults and children. It was expected that children from the more modern environments would stress the supportive rather than the controlling aspects of adults. This prediction was not borne out by the findings and, considering the general trend among girls to project a benevolent adult-child world, the contrasting pattern of Conrad girls was particularly striking. More like the boys, they included conflict and struggle in their projections of adult-child interaction. It is possible that they did, in fact, experience more conflictual overt relationships. It is more likely, however, that they were less constrained in their reactions and were freer to express conflict and negative feeling.

NOTES

1. Fifty-two children incorporated between five and nine parent figures in their CPST stories, even though only three of the 12 stimulus cards depicted a (single) parent figure. Introducing parent figures in CPST stories is, as might be expected, correlated with the general tendency to introduce an extensive rather than a limited population ($r_{boys} = .59$; $r_{girls} = .64$; $r_{total} = .60$).

2. This item was administered to 70 children.

3. The sociometric measure was not examined for school group differences because of the small and uneven representation from all groups except Adams.

4. The system of notations followed that reported by Witkin, Lewis, Hertzman, Machover, Meissner, and Wapner (1954). However, in the present study, a summary was made for each child's protocol, based on the notations and on qualitative inspection of the projected interactions. The ratings, therefore, are not identical to those used in the Witkin study.

5. It should be noted that this score does not measure feelings of anger or opposition but only separates those children who expressed direct opposition from those who did not.

6. Girls, it will be remembered, were more prone than boys to depict adults as benevolent in their relations with children, so it is pertinent to note that mothers of girls were not, in general, more traditional than mothers of boys.

7. In the course of assessing the psychological meaning of these findings, we considered the possibility that other factors might have contributed. The three major and most general scores—the prevalence of family themes in Play, parent figures in the CPST, and family material in the Personal Questions—were therefore checked against chronological age, family composition, and family break-up. While the age range of the children in this study was narrow, it seemed possible that the younger among the children might have been more family-centered, the older less involved; or that family life might have been more important for only children than for those with several siblings; or that firstborn children might have been more involved in family matters. However, the correlations between chronological age and these measures are negligible; nor is there any relationship with ordinal position or the presence of siblings. Finally, inspection of the responses of those children in whose family there had been divorce, separation, or the death of a parent showed that as a group they were neither more nor less drawn

to family life themes. Thus, none of these variables shows a relationship to the child's apparent involvement in family concerns, as measured by the three most general scores. This does not gainsay the importance of these factors as influences; it means, rather, that they are not operating systematically here.

C H A P T E R

11

SCHOOL AUTHORITY AND MORAL DEVELOPMENT

As reported in an earlier chapter, the children's general attitudes toward their school experience varied as expected. While none of the children was seriously hostile in his expressed attitudes, the greatest negativism and ambivalence appeared among the traditional school children, and the greatest enthusiasm and positive identification among the modern school children. Such feelings and attitudes toward school arise from many diverse elements in school life, but the way in which the child experiences authority—rules, demands, punishments—is one of the salient influences on how identified or, conversely, how alienated a child feels toward his school. It is this question of attitude to authority and the associated internal processes of conscience and value formation which interest us in this chapter.

We studied the children at a stage of development when important shifts in the complex process of socialization take place. To the parental figures and their mode of authority are added the school figures, whose expectations for control and sanctions against violations may be consistent with or differ from the child's experiences at home. We were interested in examining the possible influence of this extended experience with authority on internal processes: the developing codes of right and wrong behavior, the hierarchy of values, and the strength of allegiances which are in active formation during these years.

The modern and traditional schools differed radically in the regulations they considered necessary, in the image of authority the teachers wished to represent and in their views of how moral behavior is learned. The modern schools emphasized flexibility in rules and regulations, veered away from being overrestrictive, were oriented more to correction than punishment, and expected the child's acceptance of authority to come gradually in response to rational treatment by adults and to involve a growing awareness of its functional necessity. The traditional schools established clear rules and regulations, regarded punishment as the necessary, logical sequel to infractions, and extolled compliance and obedience both as desirable behavior and as essential elements of a moral system in childhood.

It was predicted, therefore, that traditional school children more than modern school children would tend to focus on the controlling and disciplinary aspects of adult authority figures, would tend to more overt conformity and have greater fear of censure or punishment from adults. These expectations were borne out in the finding that Conrad children, in particular, had a relatively rational, objective attitude toward school authorities and were developing codes of relationship and behavior that were less embedded in the context of the school and its systematized structure of controls. The traditional school children had a different perception of school authority figures and the rationality of school procedures; while more resentful of school authority, their judgments and evaluations of behavior were more literally tied to the school's system of rules and sanctions.

The material in this chapter will be presented in two parts: Attitude Toward the Authority Structure of the School, and Codes of Right and Wrong. The analysis employed a categorizing rather than a scaling technique.

Attitude Toward the
Authority Structure of the School

The children's ideas and feelings about the part of school life that involves controls imposed from without and from within were concrete and communicable. Their clearest expression was touched off, as might be expected, by those stems of the Sentence Completion Test which presented school situations that were closely bound to established rules of behavior. But the children did not always need a specific stimulus to involve them in the issues of school authority. In the relatively open situation afforded by the interview, where they had a chance to fantasy and make school over more to their liking, their replies turned often to the fairness and unfairness of teacher behavior, to the kind of teacher they wished for, and to strictness and lenience of rules. The content of these comments was useful in understanding how much they were concerned about proscriptions on their behavior and what their criteria were for what was acceptable, bearable, desirable, or just inevitable.

Techniques and Measures

Sentence Completion. Five of the 18 items of the Sentence Completion Test deal specifically with an established regulation or a figure in authority. These items, listed below, were interspersed among the others.

Item 7: *When the teacher leaves the room* . . .

Item 8: *The day (Betty/Ben) was late to school* . . .

Item 10: *Waiting in the principal's office, (Emily/Eddie)* . . .

Item 12: *When visitors come to (Mary's/Jim's) class* . . .

Item 14: *Whenever the teacher asked for quiet* . . .

The child's responses to the five sentence stems were placed into one of four possible categories, according to the dominant tone of all five. The four categories of attitudes toward school authority were as follows:

1. *Rebellious:* The child reported a pattern or expressed a desire for overt outburst against authority figures or suggested direct flouting of the teacher's decisions or requests.

2. *Resentful:* The child described behavior apparently conforming to the authority of teacher and principal while entertaining feelings of disapproval and desire to rebel.

3. *Conforming:* The child appeared to be uncritically obedient and submissive, without much affect about the rules.

4. *Rational:* The child saw the rules as necessary means toward larger ends in school life and assessed rules and controls in terms of their effectiveness in relation to basic goals.

In addition, a notation was made whenever the child's response carried with it the quality of *fearfulness,* when the child seemed to perceive authority figures as threatening or anxiety-producing.

Group Characteristics and Sex Differences

In the children's responses, rebellious feelings were occasionally expressed openly with no disguise, as, for example, in the reply "I start talking" to the Sentence Completion stem *Whenever the teacher asks for quiet . . .* or, in the reply "we break loose," "the class goes wild" to the stem *When the teacher leaves the room . . .*[1] In these replies, the children seemed to be invested in the primary pleasures of fracturing adult restraints in contrast to the kind of resistance by which circumvention of the law yields some otherwise unattainable "good."

Expressions of resentment were more heterogeneous. A wish, quickly denied, was implicit in the response "we throw everything around—not really, I'm glad we don't" to the situation of the *teacher leaving the room.* A sense of burdensome truth was expressed by "we're quiet, we better be" in response to the *teacher's request for quiet.* The "teacher gets very angry" or the "teacher yelled" at the *child who was late to school* suggests resentment about a teacher's overuse of her superior position. Similarly, the child who said, in the interview, that "teachers are unfair on the playground—she makes us play what *she* wants" is resenting the teacher who oversteps her adult right and intrudes where the children should have the right of decision. Resentment that touches the core of teacher-child interaction was expressed by one child's description of the kind of teacher he wanted and the kind he did not want: "A nice teacher who taught you what you were supposed to learn . . . and who could bring out talent . . . not one of those who yells every time, watches with eagle eyes, and she stares at you and then she lets you have it. . . ."

The responses that indicated willingness to conform to the rules and passivity, in general, had a businesslike, unemotional quality. Rules and punishments for infractions were quoted as intrinsic guidelines for behavior, established by adult authority to be accepted by children. When the *teacher is absent,* "the class president takes over," "I either take out a book, or go on with whatever I was doing except once in a while I say something to my friend and then my name goes on the board." *The girl who was late* "got punished or a 'late' on her report card," "it was the third lateness and she had to go home. It's a school rule." *Waiting in the principal's office* was interpreted as part of a punishment-for-wrongdoing sequence and the *presence of visitors in the room* was seen as an occasion when "everybody acts good," when "we have to be very good." But even conformity cannot be systematically categorized. There was the idiosyncratic quality of the child who said "I don't act good and I don't act bad. I act regular." And another one, cryptically, "we were very quiet but he caught us in the act of spelling." When the *teacher asks for quiet*, the conforming replies were as expected: "I try to be quiet," "I shut up," "I'm always quiet. I shouldn't be noisy." One of the descriptions of a desirable teacher indicated a somewhat extreme level of conformity—an allegiance to the teacher that had an antichild quality: ". . . when she sees somebody talking when she's talking, she just looks at them and makes them look foolish . . . and everybody looks at them, too. And so they stop a few minutes later and . . . everybody's looking at them."

The fourth category of responses, those that indicated acceptance of rules as rationally necessary in school life, did not ascribe arbitrary demand or prerogative to punish to adult figures in school. "We could get more work done," one child said in the interview, "if the teacher made the children stay quiet." The life of the classroom keeps its going pace when the *teacher leaves the room*: "She never hardly does that. We sit down and wait for her or we talk about things we just discussed." When *visitors come into the class*, a child "wondered who they were," and another said, "they sit in the back and write down things that we do." To the *day Betty was late to school*, several replies were entirely free of the possible wrongdoing associations, geared more to attenuating circumstances: for example, "the teacher wondered what happened" and "it was raining so she wasn't late." *Waiting in the principal's office*, one child "saw a book about school," another said, it "can be fun." The situation was projected positively or in terms of practical functions, for example, "I stand there and wait for the principal to give the message."

In brief, the children's responses included widely contrasting attitudes toward school authority. At one extreme, rebellious feelings against restraining adults and regulations were strong, indicating that the children would have been willing to take the consequences of active resistance. At the other extreme, rules and controls, not uppermost in the minds of the children, were seen in terms of their effectiveness in relation to school goals, and school adults were not projected as punitive or predominantly restraining. In between were responses that were authority-oriented, divided between those whose yielding was loaded with resentment or negative criticism and those whose acceptance was essentially passive.

In general, the distribution of attitudes within the group seemed to fit the common impression that, while most elementary school children make their peace with the system of demand and retribution in school, there are a considerable number who harbor negative feelings, of different degrees of intensity, toward teachers and principals. As can be seen in Table 11–1, a small number (11) expressed rebelliousness; a larger number (27) were resentful. Thus, approximately one third of the sample expressed negatively toned attitudes toward school authority. About the same proportion of children expressed attitudes that were uncritically obedient and conforming, without much apparent feeling about the restraints involved. Fewer children, one fourth of the group, were identified with the relatively objective view of the function of rules and a less punitive image of school adults.

There was no substantial difference between girls and boys, contrary to a general expectation that girls would be more likely than boys to express conforming and passive attitudes. In fact, a slightly smaller proportion of girls than boys were judged as conforming.

A certain amount of fear or anxiety was expressed by about one third of the children and more often by girls than boys. Most of the fearfulness (84 percent) was expressed, understandably, in conjunction with either resentful or conforming attitudes. There is a felt and frightening danger in resentment, even when contained, and fear can be both basis and reinforcement for conformity. Nor is the low incidence of fearfulness associated with rebellious or rational attitudes surprising: those who fear are less likely to rebel and those who have a rational attitude toward authority have less reason to be afraid.

Boys and girls appeared to differ in the pattern of association of fearfulness with attitudes to authority, although numbers were too small to regard the difference as anything more than indicative. To be afraid in connection with resentment seemed to be the boys' way; to be afraid in connection with conformity more the girls'.

School Group Differences

The school groups differed clearly in their attitudes. The primary contrast was between the Conrad children and those of the other three schools. Rational, objective attitudes toward school authority and control appeared predominantly among Conrad children (see Table 11–1). Conforming attitudes were school-linked, but in this case did not follow the modern-traditional continuum. They characterized children from Adams and Dickens more than those from Browning and Conrad—a finding that may be due primarily, as noted in the following section, to differences in home background. Openly rebellious attitudes were relatively rare in the sample and were not systematically characteristic of any school group.

The expression of fearfulness, like conforming attitudes, appeared mostly among Adams and Dickens children; three fourths of the children who expressed such attitudes were from these schools. This is to be expected. Fearfulness has been noted as appearing in conjunction with resentful and conforming attitudes, which were dominant among the Adams

TABLE 11-1

Attitudes to School Authority (*Categorized Responses to Sentence Completion Test Items 7, 8, 10, 12, and 14*)

Attitude Categories	Frequencies for School Groups				Total	Chi-Square Analysis
	Browning	Adams	Dickens	Conrad		
Rebellious	2 (b:1 g:1)	2 (b:1 g:1)	2 (b:1 g:1)	5 (b:1 g:4)	11 (b:4 g:7)	
Resentful	7 (b:5 g:2)	12 (b:6 g:6)	5 (b:3 g:2)	3 (b:2 g:1)	27 (b:16 g:11)	Resentful versus all other categories AB:CD $\chi^2 = 5.25$*
Conforming	5 (b:4 g:1)	15 (b:9 g:6)	14 (b:7 g:7)	7 (b:4 g:3)	41 (b:24 g:17)	Rational versus all other categories C:ABD $\chi^2 = 11.89$**
Rational	4 (b:0 g:4)	5 (b:2 g:3)	3 (b:1 g:2)	14 (b:10 g:4)	26 (b:13 g:13)	

* $p < .05$
** $p < .01$
b = boys
g = girls

269

children. In the case of Dickens children, fearfulness was associated more with conformity than with resentment.

Relationships to Home Background

For boys, in particular, home background factors were related to one pattern of attitudes toward school authority. Conformity and fearfulness characterized the attitude of boys who came from traditional homes, in which authority was relatively fixed and role-bound, with less stress on individualized development than on the meeting of generalized standards and expectations (Appendix CC, Table 4). We might see this as a propensity brought into a range of school situations—the home experience acting as a conditioning factor on the boys' ways of perceiving and coping with the reality of the authority structure in school. When they brought with them a sense of greater pressure and inflexible demand, they appeared to project this on to the school and to react, for the most part, with an uneasy conformity to the school authority structure. Boys from more modern homes did not appear to carry a sense of such pressure and demand into the school situation.

There is no systematic relationship between the modern or traditional quality of family life and the presence or absence of rational attitudes toward school authority. Though boys from modern homes were not generally fearful or conforming, factors beyond the family seemed to determine whether or not they held rational attitudes toward school authority.

Attitudes toward school authority, then, appeared to vary with the structure of the school. The fact that Conrad children were the most rational in their attitudes and did not focus on the controlling and disciplinary aspects of authority figures is a confirmation of predictions. Reactions of the children from other schools varied, but tended either to highlight resentful attitudes that focused directly on adult control or fearful conformity that implied a similar concern. While the modern-traditional qualities of the schools accounted in part for the pattern of these other attitudes, the family authority paradigm was also influential, particularly for boys from traditional homes. The more individualized structure of family life and authority of the modern homes seemed to reduce the tendency to cope with school in fearful and conforming ways. The development of an image of school authority that was rational and functional, however, seemed to depend on experience with a tangible model of this nature, such as was provided by Conrad.

Codes of Right and Wrong

To move from being disciplined to being self-disciplined is an important part of the traditional ideology. Though other terms are used, and "inner control" or "superego" is substituted for "self-discipline," such growth is equally important to the modern ideology. The two views differ, however, in their concept of the dynamic processes involved and in their image of what constitutes optimal conscience development.

We were interested in exploring whether the children's qualitatively different experience of authority in school would be reflected in their moral development at this relatively early stage. Would they have different ideas about what is good or bad behavior in childhood? Would they differ in their concepts of what is just or unjust? The findings are presented in three subgroups: the code for restraint, the code for allegiance, and the concept of justice. These three dimensions stem from certain developmental phenomena, principally that the child is making a shift from parental to peer-group allegiance at the same time that more universalized principles are beginning to govern his behavior and judgment.

Techniques and Measures

Responses to six tasks selected from the Sentence Completion Test, Interview Questions, and Moral Judgments were analyzed with respect to the children's behavioral codes and their concepts of right and wrong.

CODE FOR RESTRAINT

(i) **Sentence Completion** (school-related). The children's replies to Item 13, *I try not to . . .* were categorized for the presence or absence of school-related control of behavior (talking, making noise, and so on).

(ii) **Interview Question.** The children were asked, "What's the very worst thing a child in your class could do?" The replies were categorized along two dimensions:

(a) *Type of crime*

Major—for example, driving a car and smashing it, murder, or other crimes usually associated with adults

Minor—for example, teasing, answering back to the teacher

(b) *School-related content*—presence or absence

CODE FOR ALLEGIANCE

(iii) **Moral Dilemma: Identifying the Culprit.** The children were asked whether class members should identify the child who accidentally spilled ink over a teacher's book when the teacher asks, "Who spilled the ink?" and the culprit does not reply. They were then asked if the culprit should be identified when, if he is *not* identified, the class would have to pay for the book.[2] The responses were categorized in two ways:

1—judgment that children should tell
2—judgment that children should not tell

(iv) **Moral Dilemma: Exemption from Chores.** The children were asked whether they thought it would be fair or unfair for a child who had accompanied a group on a hike to be exempt from chores because he had just been sick. The responses were categorized in two ways:

1—judgment that exemption would be fair
2—judgment that exemption would not be fair

The children were also asked which would be the fairest way to decide if the children themselves could not agree.

CONCEPT OF JUSTICE

(v) **Interview Question.** Responses to the question "Can you think of something that you would call *unfair?*" were categorized along two dimensions:

    (a) *Level of generalization*

        General—a principle, or a type of situation

        Concrete—a personal experience, or a particular situation

    (b) *Concern for codes*—presence or absence of concern about violation of codes

(vi) **Moral Dilemma: Evaluation of Cheating.** The children were asked to judge which of two children who were taking an important test did more wrong—the one who was seen by the teacher while looking at someone else's paper or the one who did the same thing but was not seen. The judgments were classified as follows:

1—both were equally wrong
2—one was more wrong than the other

Group Characteristics and Sex Differences

CODE FOR RESTRAINT

The low incidence of rebelliousness in the affect of the children's attitudes toward school authority, referred to earlier, had a counterpart in their ideas about how they should behave in general and especially in school. There was no evidence of anarchy—no expression of "I do as I please and no one can stop me." Instead, they were seriously trying to restrain impulses they had admitted as unacceptable and to systematize ideas of right and wrong on a behavioral level. Thus, they were actively participating in their own socialization and were forming codes of behavior which fitted the expectations of significant adult authorities. This was apparent in our data from two perspectives: one, personal and subjective, as expressed in replies to the stem *I try not to . . . ;* the other, more objective and distant, taking the stance of appraising others' behavior, expressed in replies to the question about the *worst thing a child in your class could do.*

The salience of the socialization process was demonstrated by the predominant interpretation of *I try not to . . .* as referring to forbidden or unacceptable behavior. The need for the kind of restraint involved in not breaking rules characterized 85 percent of the replies. The remainder expressed concern for control of a different kind of behavior: they were either self-protective or directed toward not hurting others' feelings.

About one fourth of the children gave an undifferentiated answer, "be bad." But most were more specific. Some would try not to "spend so much money," "be slow walking home," "stay up too late"—reflecting parental admonitions. Others would try not to "giggle in class," "do bad work," "fool around," and indulge in other behavior disapproved of by teachers. Some seemed to touch a deeper level—the conscious effort to control hostile feelings and impulses. These children wanted not to "get my temper all fused up," "get angry at my sisters," and, frequently, not to "get mad." About one fourth of the children in the study said they would try not to talk or make noise, a finding, as will be seen later, which is related to rules of behavior in the schools they attended.

The question about the *worst thing a child in your class could do* elicited widely differing responses including major crimes usually associated with adults, as well as minor forms of misbehavior more appropriate to childhood. Two thirds of the children gave instances of minor crimes which would be considered serious in the context of childhood. They mentioned cheating, lying, hitting, sexual looking, disobeying parents, and making teachers angry. But one third thought children, as well as adults, capable of committing major crimes, including murder, kidnapping, or hitting someone with a lethal weapon.[3] A majority of the children replied with ideas clearly related to school life, perhaps taking the phrase ". . . child in your class" in its restricted meaning; the others allowed themselves more interpretive latitude. Putting the findings from the two perspectives on restraint of behavior together, it becomes clear that most of these children were establishing codes of behavior expected of children by adults: within this perspective, school-related restraints were important though not all-inclusive.

The boys showed a moderately higher incidence of replies indicating need for restraint than did the girls. More boys than girls tended to give the global reply, "try not to be bad," whereas the girls were more likely to be specific and differentiated and more involved in adhering to school injunctions against talking and noise. Boys and girls were equally represented in replies referring to control of anger. While there were no marked differences between boys and girls on the objective judgment of what constitutes seriously bad child behavior, the boys gave a somewhat higher proportion of major crimes, but it was only for the boys in the most modern school that this was a strong trend. Boys and girls were alike in their tendency to mention school-related rather than general "crimes."

CODE FOR ALLEGIANCE

The psychological importance of being accepted by peers and identifying with the peer group at this stage of development is generally accepted as part of the process of individuation, even while allegiance to parents is still strong. Group allegiance takes varied forms and serves diverse functions. The group may represent protection and solidarity with respect to adult authority; it may support extension of kinship feelings by deepening person-to-person communication; it may become institutionalized so that the group assumes an identity and makes demands on individual members.

The schools in our study had widely differing views and practices about the function of the peer group in relation to learning. In the modern schools, the formulation of codes for group functioning was constantly in process, with active participation by the children and much thinking and talking about elements of fairness and justice in their daily school lives. In the traditional schools, the children had few opportunities to construct codes for managing their own activities or interactions but they had more experience of trying out given forms of social interaction, such as class elections, parliamentary procedures, and mock trials.

Although there were no specific predictions based on these differences in functioning together as children in school, we wished to explore for possible differential effects in the response to two moral dilemma situations invoking issues of allegiance to one's peers. In one, where a child spills ink accidentally and does not admit it to the teacher, the dilemma is the time-honored one of "informing," or, in child vocabulary, "tattling," which is a fairly well-established taboo at this stage of development. The struggle here involved keeping the faith among the children when this ran counter to what is due to the adult and to the children's self-protective impulses. In the second dilemma, where the question is whether to take over the work responsibility of a group member who has recently been ill, the conflict is between an individual child's needs and the collective standards and expectations of the group, between elemental feelings of sympathy and reasoned evaluation of individual responsibility to the group.

The decisions about whether to expose the child who spilled the ink to the teacher represented a true dilemma. The group was fairly evenly divided in their replies, though more of them inclined to "not telling." Quite a few indicated conflict about coming to this decision, shifting their answers and giving alternative reasons for the opposite decision. The children who decided on "telling" also showed wavering inclinations. Quite a few of these expressed the wish that the child would tell on himself, thus saving them from breaking the taboo against tattling. For these children, however, the taboo was not as strong as their need to avoid displaced punishment.

Children who said they would "not tell" were asked what they would do if they were faced with paying a share of the cost of the child's misdemeanor. Most decided that they would then tell, but some were still unwilling to expose another child, even at personal cost, giving the impression that a strong child allegiance code was in formation, even while it was vulnerable to other pressures.

While the simple tattle formula appeared quite frequently as a reason for "not telling," other responses reflected wide variation in ethical considerations and empathic sensitivity. Some wanted to wait for the culprit to confess, with the feeling that this would be the best practical path to less punishment. Some wanted to protect the child from the shame of being exposed before the other children as much as from punishment by the teacher. Others seemed to be on a more advanced level, responding not on the basis of allegiance to a child in opposition to adult authority or of protecting themselves against being stamped as "informer," but because they wished to give the guilty child the leeway to come to terms with his own wrongdoing and guilt; for example: "she will feel bad and eventually tell herself," "let him keep it on his own mind, then he would tell."

The hike situation drew more consensus from the children. Two thirds of the group judged it fair to exempt the sick child from his responsibilities, generally advocating a flexible solution to the dilemma and favoring support of one of their peers more than protecting their own rights or the vested rights of the peer group's operational plans.

The comments they volunteered in connection with their replies showed discomfort at being placed in a bald, either/or position by the form of the question. They wanted to qualify their replies by considerations of how recently he had been sick, what the illness was, and how long it had lasted. In one fourth of the replies, it was suggested that the child do a little work, undertake the easier tasks. For example: "If she is strong enough to walk she could set out the table, unless she had a broken arm," from a girl, and "He should do the light work, not the heavy," from a boy. The tendency to qualify the judgments in terms of specific conditional factors and to offer midway solutions to the problems confirmed that the children as a group had moved away from the absolutism of judgment that characterizes younger children.

The reasons for the judgment that it was fair to exempt the sick child sometimes reflected parental attitudes: "If he gets too overheated, he might get sick again," "He might get sick again and get high blood pressure." The reasons for "unfair" had a sterner quality, applying standards of logic and reason and generally leaning toward the view that an individual has responsibility to abide by a contract he has undertaken. For example: "If she is still sick, she shouldn't have come; if she comes, she should do her job," "If her parents let her go, she should do some of the work." For one child, the situations depicted aroused strong egalitarian protests: "One shouldn't be treated like a king while others slave to work."

When asked how a decision might be reached in the event of disagreement, the children projected an image of a self-determined peer society. Only a minority were ready to cede the decision to the adult. The others relied, in the main, on voting.

For the most part, there were no differences between boys and girls in the decisions they made when feelings of allegiance to another child came into conflict with established attitudes toward authority or emerging concepts of individual responsibility. In the situation of the hike, boys were as likely as girls to think it fair to take over the chores of the child. They were equally likely to offer a middle solution and to put the final decision in the hands of the children rather than the adults. The only difference between boys and girls appeared in the somewhat greater reluctance on the part of girls to reveal the culprit in the situation of the spilled ink.

CONCEPT OF JUSTICE

In the previous pages, we have been interested in codes of behavior which are the tools for coping with the authority of salient adult figures and the codes for allegiance by which a child's society is formed and maintains its cohesiveness. There is, of course, another face to the development of the moral code, namely, the concepts of justice, of moral judgment, which are emerging from the self-referenced, specific paradigms of good and bad behavior. At this level, we had two pieces of relevant data. The question about what the children might consider "unfair" was adopted because "unfair" is a term almost universally used by children of this stage to categorize events. The purpose was to gain insight into how much they were moving toward generalized concepts. In the other instance, a behavioral situation was kept constant—both children cheated on the test—and the question put to the children forced a choice between the concept of right and wrong on the basis of the consequences of the act or, on the other hand, on the basis of a general principle.

The instances of "unfairness" given by the children were not all on the same conceptual level; some were concrete, others relatively generalized.[4]

Those who were thinking concretely described a personal experience or a specific situation. For example: "I found a chisel; my father said it was his but it wasn't and he took it," "My brother eats in his robe but the girls must get dressed," "Just because it was his house, he told us what to do and what not to do." A clear majority of the children, though not quite offering abstract principles, generalized from a series of situations. "Cheating" was a frequent reply in this category, sometimes expanded: "Like in a game of monopoly or checkers. . . ." Some replies had achieved a level of primitively stated principles, often about keeping physical prowess equable: "Not fair to hit a smaller boy than you," "Start fight with someone you know you can beat up," "More than one against one." Others concerned benign interpersonal relationships: "People shouldn't blame things on someone else."

On the whole, the children's responses were predominantly drawn from events, issues, and relationships in their immediate daily lives. Most referred to familiar childhood troubles and issues: cheating, bullying, an ungenerous sibling, teasing or abusing animals, pushing, and hitting. Only very few (eight) responded in terms of broad social or moral issues with replies such as ". . . should let colored people go to school, they're people too" and "When poor people have to pay rent and they have no money and they get thrown out."

The content of the replies distinguished unpleasant or uncomfortable personal injustices from those which concerned the breaking of codes. The personal instances included being falsely blamed, being snubbed, siblings or peers having unfair advantage, being bossed, or another child escaping just punishment for a misdemeanor. In these replies, adults frequently appeared as the perpetrators of the wrong.

A larger number of the children, however, cited instances expressive of a strong middle-years code. They protested violation of the rules of the game, often using athletic situations as manifest content but symbolizing the broader struggle of coming to equilibrium between the socializing rules to be accepted as the common code for all and the conflicting personal wishes and search for personal gain. Thus, cheating again appeared frequently, as did gaining advantage through deceitful means. For example: "When a child knows he's cheated and won't admit it," "Like in a baseball game when the umpire says you're out because he's on the other team," "Not doing things the right way according to the rules," "Having a nice game and boys start making up their own rules."

In the cheating dilemma, the group was split. Although these children had reached the level of development where they were generally influenced more by the motivation than the magnitude of a misdeed, they did not consistently judge this dilemma in terms of motivation.[5] Perhaps the fact that this dilemma was very close to the concerns of children explains why, for almost half the group, judgment was less "pure" and was made contingent upon whether or not the cheating was detected.

Almost half the group judged that the child who *was not* seen in the act of cheating did more wrong; (only three children thought that the child who *was* seen was the more culpable). This seems to indicate that the moral choice about the deed per se was complicated for some children by a sense of injustice in the face of wrongdoing that was not apprehended or punished.

On the other hand, more than half the children rejected the two alternatives set by the question. They judged the children were equally wrong and offered reasons which demonstrated that they were thinking in terms of a principle, a general ethic, independent of circumstantial outcome. One would guess these latter children would have mastered well the principle of conservation in dealing with problems of a physical nature.

The children who judged the undetected child as having done the greater wrong revealed varied constellations of feeling about right and wrong, punishment and guilt, in the comments which accompanied their judgments. The punishment-oriented were most concerned that the child "got away with it"; the confession-oriented judged from the perspective that admitting a deed is, per se, partial expiation for its wrongness. A few were influenced by negative feelings about sneakiness, toward the means used by the child in order not to be caught: "She looked to see if anyone was there, didn't take any chances, she's the guilty one." A few others took the common adult view that detection has a deterring influence: "She didn't get caught, she won't know any better when she grows up," "The teacher caught one—she learned; the other snuck it and might do it again."

There was no consistent evidence of a difference between boys and girls in the extent to which they were beginning to make moral judgments on the basis of principles.

School Group Differences

There were differences among the school groups in the extent that wrongdoing, transgression generally, was associated with the authority of the school world, in ways in which the children were establishing codes of behavior for their own child world, and in the extent to which an ethical principle could be made the basis of a moral judgment. Some findings distinguished the modern from the traditional school children: the modern school children more frequently than the traditional school children took the position that they would refuse to reveal the guilty child to the teacher; they were also more concerned about the violation of the codes of fair play (see Table 11–2). Other findings more clearly separated the children of Conrad from the other three groups: the Conrad children were least involved with the sanctions about child behavior which emanate from school authority and, more often than the other three groups, evaluated the dilemma concerning cheating on a test in terms of a moral principle (see Table 11–2).

The differences between modern and traditional children in the area of peer-group allegiance do not present a clear-cut, internally consistent picture. As noted earlier, where the children faced a choice between their allegiance to each other and what they owed the adult, they were in considerable conflict though, in general, there was an inclination to adhere to peer-line loyalty. The tendency for the modern school children, particularly Dickens girls, to refuse to reveal the guilty child was not altogether expected. Examination of their reasons, however, indicated that their reluctance to tell the teacher who was guilty was not so much an in-group protection of one of their peers from an authority presumed to be punishing. Rather, it involved an inclination to leave the resolution of guilt to the guilty child, to think of a conscience that would do its work if given time. There was little expression of the idea that wrongdoing needed to be dealt with promptly, with appropriate censorship or punishment.

In the hike situation, where the authoritative adult was in the background, other issues became crucial: the decision, for some children, involved an opposite pull between their supportive feelings for each other and their emerging ideas about the obligations of an individual to his commitments. There was no systematic difference between modern and traditional school children in the way they came to a decision on this issue. The Dickens children were outstanding in their supportive impulses to the child who had been sick, a response that would be expected from the modern school children in the light of the active fostering of peer-group affiliation in their school experience. At Conrad, however, there was a conflicting picture in which the boys and girls differed from each other. The boys, like the Dickens children, favored the supportive decision while the girls showed a higher incidence of replies taking a negative attitude toward giving support. The reasons given by the Conrad girls showed greater and sterner expectations for decision making on the part of the individual, albeit a child, with a concomitant expectation that members of a group will carry through what they have undertaken. It is interesting to note that this attitude is the reverse of that of the Browning girls, all of whom thought it fair to take over for the sick friend.

Another finding relevant to the question of peer-group affiliation came through in the analysis of the content through which the children documented their ideas of unfairness. The modern school children, this time particularly the Conrad boys, were most concerned about direct or indirect violations—through deceit or manipulation—of what they regarded as the

TABLE 11-2

Codes for Restraint and Allegiance, and Concept of Justice

Measure (Source)	Frequencies for School Groups					Chi-Square Analysis
	Browning	Adams	Dickens	Conrad	Total	
Code for Restraint						
Control of behavior: related to school (Sentence Completion Test Item 13)	5 (b:3 g:2)	10 (b:4 g:6)	8 (b:3 g:5)	2 (b:1 g:1)	25 (b:11 g:14)	CD:AB $\chi^2 = .75$
unrelated to school	12 (b:6 g:6)	22 (b:14 g:8)	15 (b:9 g:6)	23 (b:14 g:9)	72 (b:43 g:29)	C:ABD $\chi^2 = 4.38$*
Major crime	6 (b:4 g:2)	6 (b:4 g:2)	6 (b:4 g:2)	13 (b:9 g:4)	31 (b:21 g:10)	CD:AB $\chi^2 = 2.83$
Minor crime (Interview)	11 (b:5 g:6)	25 (b:12 g:13)	15 (b:7 g:8)	12 (b:7 g:5)	63 (b:31 g:32)	C:ABD $\chi^2 = 5.58$*
Crimes: related to school	9 (b:6 g:3)	22 (b:11 g:11)	13 (b:6 g:7)	10 (b:6 g:4)	54 (b:29 g:25)	CD:AB $\chi^2 = 2.04$
unrelated to school (Interview)	8 (b:3 g:5)	9 (b:5 g:4)	8 (b:5 g:3)	15 (b:10 g:5)	40 (b:23 g:17)	C:ABD $\chi^2 = 3.32$
Code for Allegiance						
Identifying the culprit: tell (Moral Dilemma)	10 (b:6 g:4)	18 (b:9 g:9)	5 (b:4 g:1)	9 (b:5 g:4)	42 (b:24 g:18)	CD:AB $\chi^2 = 5.50$*
not tell (Moral Dilemma)	8 (b:4 g:4)	15 (b:8 g:7)	15 (b:6 g:9)	16 (b:9 g:7)	54 (b:27 g:27)	
Exemption from chores: fair	13 (b:6 g:7)	20 (b:11 g:9)	18 (b:10 g:8)	16 (b:12 g:4)	67 (b:39 g:28)	CD:AB $\chi^2 = .71$
not fair (Moral Dilemma)	4 (b:4 g:0)	13 (b:7 g:6)	3 (b:1 g:2)	9 (b:4 g:5)	29 (b:16 g:13)	

Measure (Source)	Frequencies for School Groups					Chi-Square Analysis
	Browning	Adams	Dickens	Conrad	Total	
Concept of Justice						
Ideas of unfairness: general	7 (b:2 g:5)	13 (b:8 g:5)	16 (b:9 g:7)	15 (b:12 g:3)	51 (b:31 g:20)	CD:AB $\chi^2 = 3.40$
concrete (Interview)	8 (b:5 g:3)	16 (b:8 g:8)	6 (b:2 g:4)	11 (b:3 g:8)	41 (b:18 g:23)	D:ABC $\chi^2 = 2.64$
Content of unfairness: personal injustice	7 (b:4 g:3)	16 (b:8 g:8)	9 (b:5 g:4)	7 (b:2 g:5)	39 (b:19 g:20)	CD:AB $\chi^2 = 4.32$*
violation of code (Interview)	8 (b:3 g:5)	10 (b:6 g:4)	13 (b:6 g:7)	18 (b:12 g:6)	49 (b:27 g:22)	
Evaluation of cheating: both wrong	7 (b:4 g:3)	19 (b:11 g:8)	10 (b:4 g:6)	22 (b:11 g:11)	58 (b:30 g:28)	CD:AB $\chi^2 = 1.14$
one more wrong than other (Moral Dilemma)	11 (b:6 g:5)	15 (b:7 g:8)	14 (b:8 g:6)	7 (b:6 g:1)	47 (b:27 g:20)	C:ABD $\chi^2 = 5.79$*

* $p. < .05$
b = boys
g = girls

code of fair play in the life that children live with each other. The emerging principles seemed to be expressive of a child society in active formation.

The findings that distinguish the Conrad children from the children of all other schools can be seen as indicative of an emerging trend in their moral development. Their concepts of the restraints they should ask of themselves referred less to school mandates for good behavior than was true of the other children; their ideas of a child's misdemeanors were also less school bound. In addition, they tended, more than the others, to think of children as capable of commiting crimes adults might commit, thus seeming to transcend both the school-nonschool and the adult-child barriers. They were outstanding in their tendency to bring a basic principle to bear on the problem of right and wrong involved in the situation of cheating, detected or undetected. The Adams boys were the only other group resembling them in this last tendency (see Table 11–2).

The finding that Conrad children were least involved in issues of breaking school rules reflects the atmosphere of their school life: sanctions against talking and making noise were minimal, presented to them functionally rather than as absolute rules of conduct. Nor did school content dominate their ideas about the worst things a child could do. In all, they seemed to have a basically different perspective on the place of school in relation to their codes for self-restraint: it was less central in their total scheme of good and bad behavior. Perhaps it might be said that they were thinking of transgressions on a broader plane than the childish misdemeanors of a school child. Their tendency not to draw a sharp distinction between children and adults in the nature of crimes committed supports such an interpretation. In the dilemma that directly invoked wrongdoing in school, the Conrad children based their judgments on an ethical principle, independent of circumstantial sequelae, suggesting again their emerging independence from the pressures of external authority.

Relationships to Home Background

Relationships between home background factors and the dimensions treated here are relatively weak and sporadic, but some trends bear noting (see Appendix CC, Table 4). It is of interest, for instance, that the only dimensions completely unrelated to parent variables are those tapping peer allegiance. While broad generalizations are hardly warranted, in such circumstances, the pattern suggests that peer codes and decisions may have been developing within a framework more independent of family influence than the concepts of justice, infraction, and restraint which pertain to the larger interpersonal world and include adults as well as children.

Among the remaining variables, there are isolated correlations between children's concepts and the socio-economic-cultural (SEC) level of the home or the mother's satisfaction and role integration; girls from families at the lower end of the SEC index tended to see self-restraint in school-related terms, and boys with relatively satisfied and integrated mothers tended to conceptualize justice and injustice in relatively concrete terms.

The remaining correlations, though also relatively low, form more of a pattern and are somewhat easier to understand. Children from homes where there was pressure to abide by externalized standards and where authority was clearly established as the prerogative of adults, tended to be circumscribed about the kind of crimes children might commit, thinking of relatively minor infringements, often in the framework of school regulations. The relation to the quality of authority in the home was especially clear for girls. Perhaps these relationships are a function of the general characteristic of the traditional environment, namely, the qualitative gap between child and adult positions in life, both as to what is allowed and what is conceived as possible.

There was also some relationship between the orientation of the homes and the extent to which concepts of justice involved general principles and middle-years codes. Boys and girls from modern homes tended to see "fairness" and "cheating" more in terms of such principles, while those from homes with more traditional orientation and authority patterns tended to fuse deed and consequence in their judgments. Though these relationships are not statistically powerful, they indicate the same direction of effects as those established for modern and traditional school groups, suggesting that consistent home and school orientation may have had a reinforcing effect on the children's concepts of justice and the principles through which they evaluated behavior.

Summary and Discussion

The schools in the study differed from each other in how school life was regulated for the children—who made the rules, what kinds of behavior they governed, how fixed they were, and what happened if they were violated. There were two ways to probe the effects of these differences. One was a direct way—to examine how the children perceived their relation to the authority structure of the school and the quality of affect associated with their perceptions. The other was an attempt to study the kinds of control systems the children were establishing for themselves, the mores they were setting up to govern their child society, and the extent to which they were reaching for moral principles as their behavior guides. The assumption was that their behavioral codes and emerging moral principles would reflect the nature of their experience with authority in school.

The children from all the schools shared a common intention to live up to codes of good behavior. Recognizing in themselves the impulses that would be transgressions of adult expectations, they all showed signs of internalizing these expectations in some form and making conscious effort to abide by them. There were differences among the school groups, however, in the extent to which they evaluated behavior in terms of general moral principles and in the extent to which their own participation in the socialization process stretched beyond the boundaries of the social demands of school. In general, there was a tendency for the modern school children (most frequently the Conrad children) to reflect less pressure from the workings and meanings of school authority and to be taking on the more complex issues and judgments in the realm of moral development.

For the traditional school children, the authority figures of the school, and the demands they made for control, had great salience and generated considerable emotional charge. That they experienced school authority as a strong outside pressure showed in their criticism and resentment, often accompanied by feelings of fearfulness, even while they expected to conform to the demands of the system. For the boys, a traditional home background was an added influence in the direction of uneasy conformity to school authority. Even though many of the Dickens school children also tended to comply, accepting the role of the adults as the rule setters, their conformity was more passive, less negatively toned, more an unquestioning willingness to accept, in the child role, what the adult prescribed, albeit some of them were also fearful in their position of relative powerlessness.

The children of the most modern school, more than any other school group, had a different perspective on school authority. Teacher and principal were not identified with demands for controls or punishment of infringements. There had to be rules and regulations but these could be assessed for their value in the primary function of keeping the school situation viable or they could be modified to fit attenuating circumstances. This rational attitude toward the authority structure seems a clear reflection of the attempts, at Conrad, to keep authority flexible, reasonable in the children's eyes, and not role-invested in the status of the teacher.

The children of this study were involved in conscious efforts to bring their behavior into alignment with the expectations of the important figures in their lives, at home and at school. Parallel to the restraints they expected to exercise on their impulses, in the personal scheme of things, they were also working out a hierarchy of good and bad, or more and less serious misdeeds. There was an important distinction, again, between the Conrad children and the others. The children from Conrad were far less concerned with the fixed rights and wrongs of a code for school behavior; they were less preoccupied with working out acceptability to school authority. Here, too, they appeared to be reacting to the nature of their particular school experience, where the behavioral codes were flexible and adults in authority did not regard obedience as the most highly desired quality in children. In general developmental terms, it would seem that these Conrad children were in the process of constructing a less fragmented and circumscribed moral system, one in which right and wrong, good and bad, had relevance for all realms of behavior and in which the school was continuous with other orbits of social interchange. Their tendency to think of children committing crimes as serious as adults is perhaps another indication of continuity in that there is less dichotomizing of child and adult on the sphere of moral behavior.

At this stage of development, children become more important to each other and the peer group develops a culture of its own. This takes place either under the aegis of the school, when, as in the modern schools, the peer group is regarded as an important instrument for learning and social maturing; or it takes place outside the school, where the mores microscopically reflect the culture of the neighborhood. The nature of the peer-group code can vary widely. It may be a collective defense to counter the feeling of oppressive adult authority. It may be a proving ground for what it takes to create an equable society. The dilemmas we put to the children were tests of the strength of their feelings of support and allegiance for each other. Their responses indicated a general tendency to keep faith with the child rather than to serve the teacher's interest and to support a friend in trouble, but variations in the responses and underlying reasons suggested that there were important and unresolved issues involved. One such issue involved the loyalty to peers vis-à-vis the relation to adult authority; another, the conflict between the needs of the individual and his responsibility to the group.

The traditional school children were in conflict about revealing a child's misdeeds to the teacher. Their concept that wrongdoing should be punished, allying them with the authority of the teacher, ran counter to the taboo against tattling established in their child group; but, in honoring the taboo, they would expose themselves to the possibility of being punished collectively for the undisclosed child's misdeeds. Thus, when they arrived at the decision to tell the teacher about the child, they were acting in response to the fixed paradigm in which punishment is tied in with wrongdoing and to the individual impulse to avoid punishment themselves. The modern school children, less involved in expecting or avoiding punishment, were inclined toward a different decision, arrived at on a different basis. They more frequently invoked the concept of conscience, wanting to give the child time to come to terms with his own guilt, and thereby dealing with the issue of individual responsibility together with the question of allegiance. If projected against Kohlberg's (1964) schema of stages in moral development, the difference in the issues that are dealt with would place the traditional school children at an earlier stage. Furthermore, by his theoretical rationale, their exposure to a punishment-oriented system of authority would partially account for this relatively immature mode of making judgments.

In dealing with the question of whether to exempt a sick friend from his share of work for the group, the children faced a different constellation of forces. The issue was between extending or protecting the self, between the needs of an individual and the rights of a group, without any involvement with a potentially punishing authority. Here, the differences between modern and traditional children tended to disappear. There was a general tendency to exempt the child. Somewhat unexpectedly, this was least clear for the Conrad girls, proportionally more of whom appeared firm, relatively unsympathetic, and more reluctant to grant exemption. Perhaps they were more involved with the issues of individual responsibility to the group, with stronger expectations that an individual, child or adult, should carry through on an obligation once it had been undertaken.

Despite signs of difference between modern and traditional school children in the issues which influenced their judgments, it was clear that they all wished to find and use the strength of their common association as a group of peers. They did not choose the adult to arbitrate disagreement; they preferred to rely on the collective opinion, arrived at democratically through voting, of their own child group. In this sense, they were all moving away from dependence on adult omniscience. In the case of the modern school children, especially those from Conrad, autonomy was expressed both in terms of the independence of the child society from adults and in terms of the individual's responsibility for his actions and transgressions.

In their concepts of justice, several findings point once more to the greater salience of the authority figures in the moral judgments of the traditional school children. The adult-child power structure was a relevant force in the progress made toward formation of a code of relationship within the peer group. Its salience dominated their ideas about "unfairness." In many of their associations they protested the inequities that followed, directly or indirectly, from the actions and dictates of adult figures. They were significantly less involved than the modern school children with the "unfairness" of children's behavior toward each other or, to put it differently, they were still more involved with a central focus on the adult as the primary force rather than with the construction of a fair world by and for themselves in their activities as children.

Along the same lines, the inability to apply a general moral principle to the act of cheating appeared to be a partial function of how much codes and concepts were taking shape as reactive patterns to a controlling authority system. More children of the three public schools fused the detection with the act itself in weighing the relative "wrongness" of the deed. Their reasons reflected the extent to which their judgments were being influenced by certain values already learned and internalized. One of these, as previously mentioned, was the salience of the wrongdoing-punishment paradigm. Thus, they judged less in terms of a universalized principle and more in terms of the violation of that paradigm as a wrong in itself; or, alternatively, they dealt with expiation through confession to the authority. The Conrad children, especially the girls, judged more frequently in terms of the basic violation of a principle, their judgments uncontaminated by considerations of confession to or punishment by an authoritative adult.

The assessment of moral development in this group of nine-year-olds highlights certain stage-appropriate processes. They were stepping into the role of being active self-controlling participants in their own socialization and, at the same time, building up evaluative criteria for assessing the moral attributes of behavior in general. They were finding and using strength in the formation of a peer group culture as they moved away from predominant dependence upon and allegiance to adults. They were in transition, conceptually, between making moral judgments that were contingent upon consequence and those that rested on a general principle. In both these major developmental transitions, the codes they were formulating and the values underlying them reflected, to a degree, the mode of authority they had experienced in school.

For the children in the most modern school in particular, the course of moral development had a freer, more open quality than was true of the traditional school children. They were less restrained by school mandates and criteria for behavior, less focused on the adult as a prime and permanent source of authority, less tied to an alliance in which wrongdoing is followed by punishment or confession. As a result, they seemed to be moving toward a more mature stage of moral development in which, more autonomously, they were beginning to deal with the force of individual conscience and to think in terms of general moral principles.

In this area of development, it could be expected that the child's experience with family authority figures and structure would have salient influence. The relation to family background factors, as already noted, points to a direction of influence that parallels that of the school: the modern home, like the modern school, appeared to be associated with broader conceptions of right and wrong and clear differentiation of the elements that constitute essential morality in that judgment of an action was not fused with its consequences. In these data, where school reinforces the direction of home influence, it can probably be considered an important determinant in the further course of moral development.

NOTES

1. In the description of the range of responses, phrases which are italicized refer to the content of the stimuli.
2. These moral dilemmas are paraphrased here; they appear in full in Appendix AA.
3. The association to major crimes may have been influenced by the fact that the question "What's the worst crime you can think of?" preceded the question "What's the very worst thing a child in your class could do?"
4. "Unfairness" was a trigger word, which easily touched off descriptions of inequities of different kinds and sources. Not all the children showed a clear understanding of a term they had been using freely. Some cited situations or events which were undesirable but not really unfair and used the concept of unfairness to attack adversity with moral indignation.
5. Sequence in the realm of moral judgment has been formulated developmentally by investigators such as Piaget (1948) and Kohlberg (1964). The responses of the children in the study to two of the Piaget dilemmas requiring evaluation of severity of wrongdoing placed them beyond the most primitive level of moral development and at the stage of "intentionalism," regarded as the second level, according to Kohlberg's analysis. These children, preponderantly took motivational and circumstantial factors into account, not allowing their evulations to be mechanically determined by the magnitude of the crime. Damage to property in one instance and stealing money in the other were the content of these two dilemmas (see Appendix AA, Moral Judgments, The Child as Judge). There were no school group differences in the responses.

C H A P T E R

12

THE CONCEPT OF SELF

The child's self-concept is a central variable in this study for several reasons. First, the modern and traditional philosophies differed in the value they placed on the child's individuality and on his relationship to himself and it was therefore important to explore and compare the developing self-concepts of the children. Second, the emphasis on self-concept reflects the growing importance of this variable in psychological theory and its acceptance, after a long and erratic history, as a legitimate subject for study. Though the methodological problems attached to research in this area remain largely unsolved (see Wylie, 1961), its central role in relation to mental health and the achievement of psychological maturity has been generally established.

The children's self-concepts are also central in this study because of their particular relevance to theories of child development. For many theorists, self-knowledge and feeling are crucial aspects to consider in defining this stage of life. Concealment of wishes, feelings, and other self-related material is seen as dynamically important in the middle years or "latency" child. It is thought to involve both concealment from others—especially the powerful adults—and from oneself, rendering self-perception somewhat nebulous, global, and defensive. There are, of course, theoretical disagreements concerning the scope of necessary repression and the origins and functional meaning of the child's relationship to his inner self at this stage of development. But perhaps more relevant to our research and our data is the fact that there are extensive gaps in empirical knowledge. What does the child of this age think, know, and say about himself? Are there areas of greater and lesser openness and concealment? How much variation is there among children of this age? Between boys and girls? To what extent, and in what areas, are such variations linked to socialization attitudes in the child's life environment?

The latter question leads directly to the modern-traditional variable in this study and the predicted link between modern or traditional orientations and distinctive trends in the developing self-concepts of the children. We hypothesized that children from the more modern environments would have a clearer and more differentiated image of themselves and place greater value on individuality. By implication, it was also expected that various features in the modern environment—personalized contact, acceptance of impulse expression—would occasion more open self-contact, deeper self-awareness, and greater impulse acceptance, even in children of this age, than the more formal, less personalized socialization methods of the traditional schools and homes. It was one of the general aims of the study to explore this area and to draw together the findings concerning the child's relationship to, and communication about, himself as these reflect the nature of the socialization values in his environment.

There are serious methodological problems in this exploration of the self-concept. The child's relationship to himself and his communication about himself are not necessarily the same thing. What he knows, thinks, and feels about himself is different from what he tells about himself, to an unknown degree, and it is difficult to know clearly what we are measuring when we investigate this area. Like most other researchers, we have not solved this problem. Given this situation, we have adopted the view that the data are a mixture of inner reality and self-presentation and that the way the child presents himself to the adult is interesting in and of itself.

In the comparison of school groups we have found that predictions of school differences are essentially borne out. In describing themselves and their feelings, children of the modern schools seemed to reflect not only the schools' focus on the individual but the emphasis on probing and differentiated thought as an approach to understanding. Variations in different areas of self-concept are important, however, and the wide range of reactions among the children from Conrad to these self-probing situations constitutes an important finding.

The material in this chapter is presented in two sections: Self-Confidence and Satisfaction, and Self-Knowledge. Predictions of modern-traditional effects center on the latter category. We have selected the variables subsumed under these headings from a wider roster pertinent to self-concept because of their particular relevance to our study. We have used techniques, for the most part, that tap the child's conscious image of himself, regarding this phenomenological level of data as most germane to our interest in how the child thinks about himself and communicates his ideas and qualities to others.

Self-Confidence and Satisfaction

This section is concerned with the confidence, strength, and satisfaction conveyed by the children in presenting themselves to others. In this area, we did not have clear expectations of school group differences, for reasons discussed further along, but we wished to assess the generally positive or negative stance of this group of children, the possibility of sex differences in the confidence of presentation, and the extent of relationship, if any, to school or home qualities.

Techniques and Measures

The material is drawn from two techniques: the Stick Figure Scale and the Drawings. Both techniques tap the child's assertiveness and confidence, but they differ in level and mode. The Stick Figure Scale is semi-projective and verbal, calling on the child's conscious image of the kind of person he is; Drawings are projective and nonverbal, reflecting the child's unconscious self-conception and his basic body image.

(i) **Stick Figure Scale: Self-Satisfaction Syndrome.** Four items (see below) contributed to the overall rating of self-satisfaction. Responses were coded on a four-point scale. The child's score represented the number of items on which he made a positive or satisfied choice. Middle choices were not included in either positive or negative tallies. A score of four implies the most satisfied and confident presentation of the self.

Item 2: Peer Popularity

"Here's a boy (girl) who's pretty sure all the kids like him, that he's popular."   Versus   "Here's a boy (girl) who lots of times isn't so sure the other kids like him so much."

"Which one is more like you?"

Item 4: Work Competence

"Here's a boy (girl) who   "Here's a boy (girl) who
thinks he's pretty good at   Versus   thinks he's not so good at
his work in school."   his work in school."

"Which one is more like you?"

Item 7: Lucky Life

"Here's a boy (girl) who   "Here's a boy (girl) who
thinks he's got a pretty good   Versus   lots of times wishes some of
life; thinks he's pretty   the things in his life would
lucky."   be different; he thinks other
                                                              kids are luckier than he is."

"Which one is more like you?"

Item 8: Sex Role Preference[1]

"Here's a boy (girl) who   "Here's a boy (girl) who
thinks boys (girls) have the   Versus   thinks it's girls (boys) who
most fun, the best life."   have the most fun and the
                                                              best life."

"Which one is more like you?"

(ii) Figure Drawings: Strength of Self-Presentation. Each child was
asked to draw a person and then to draw a person of the opposite sex
to that already drawn. The combined drawings were rated on a five-
point scale for overall strength and confidence of presentation, five
representing the greatest strength. The rating was based on a synthesis
of standard drawing dimensions (figure size, perspective, location,
force of line, use of color, and so on), set against general normative
data for children of this age.[2]

INTERCORRELATIONS AMONG MEASURES

The two measures are not significantly correlated (Appendix BB, Table
4). As noted, they were probably tapping different modes of self-presentation as well as levels of self-confidence differentially available to consciousness.[3]

Group Characteristics and Sex Differences

Three main points emerge from these data: the prevailing stance in this
group of children was assertive and confident; boys and girls had quite
different ways of presenting themselves, however, and the children felt
more confident of their effectiveness in some spheres of functioning than
others.

Verbally, the children of this study presented a predominantly satisfied
and confident evaluation of their lot in life and their own effectiveness.
Only a handful of children were dissatisfied and self-critical on three
or more items of the Stick Figure Scale, and many children (43 percent)
made positive choices on at least three of the four items.[4] They presented
themselves as having a good and lucky life, as convinced that their own

sex has the most fun and the best life, and as pretty successful in their school work. They were least sure of their peer popularity.[5]

Perhaps the latter exception to the general pattern expresses the frontier quality of peer relations at this developmental stage. Moving out from the family to the newly important peer group is often experienced as both exciting and threatening, with problems of acceptance, status, and friendship. Perhaps uncertain of their success, the children described themselves with less satisfaction and confidence in this area than in others.

The Drawings bear out the general impact of positive and confident self-projections. They ranged considerably, of course, from some which were infinitesimally small, wispily drawn, and poorly delineated to some which covered the better part of the paper, were colorful, forceful in line and posture, elaborate in detail, radiating strength and power. Despite the variation, however, it is possible to conjure up a vision of a typical figure, as drawn by these nine-year-olds—albeit with full cognizance of the violation done thereby to this most personalized form of expression. It is a smiling figure, two to five inches high, reasonably well proportioned, and with recognizable facial features. It faces front and stands alone, usually without grounding or other objects. It is rendered at least in part in color and clothed in some form of suit or dress, complete with buttons and pockets, and perhaps with a handkerchief, pocketbook, or pipe.[6] In its general tone, this composite self-projection is not so different from the generally positive and confident picture that comes through on the verbal level from the Stick Figure Scale.

The positive presentation is assuredly a reflection, in part, of inner feelings and self-evaluation. These were privileged children, whose lives were "good and lucky," who were bright and competent, and who were supported and encouraged in many ways for what they were and what they could do. We do not assume a complete connection between privileged lives and self-contentment, and the children themselves differentiated areas of relative uncertainty, but it is still likely that these children presented something of their actual internalization of a realistic situation—a comfortable and rewarding status and endowment. Another group of less privileged middle-years children might well present a different general pattern in their concept of themselves and their lives, internalized from a harsher environment and a less rewarding set of life experiences.

At the same time, this positive picture probably reflects an additional factor—a workable system of defenses that the middle-years child can maintain and present to questioners. To the extent that he is less free and open in his expression than the younger child, less overrun by unrest and self-criticism than the adolescent, the child of this age can present himself consciously to the adult—and less consciously to himself, if necessary—in the context of "I'm all right, everything's all right—don't touch." The combined effect of confidence and defense, working in the same direction, probably makes for the prevailing tone of positive assertion.

It would be misleading, however, to rest with this general impression of the group's qualities. Separate examination of boy and girl protocols show significant sex differences (see Table 12–1). At the verbal level (Stick Figure Scale) it was the boys who presented the most confident and satisfied image. The boys presented themselves more positively in the three spheres of work competence, sex role, and peer popularity, and only three girls were included in the group of 16 children who described themselves and their lives in completely positive terms.[7] In graphic presentation, however, girls projected the more confident and satisfied image. The composite figure drawing described above must be extended for girls in the direction of greater elaboration, detail, and color. Girls' drawings were significantly larger; from the boys, we got smaller drawings—occasionally small, vague, and evasive to an extent nowhere evident among the girls. Girls' drawings were more consistently full face and colorful and had more expression and detail.[8] An interpretation of this reversal in sex differences must take into account the difference between the two measures and what they assess.

TABLE 12–1

Self-Confidence and Satisfaction

MEASURE Source, and Scale Range	(N)	Sex §	Mean Scores for School Groups					Analysis of Variance
			Browning	Adams	Dickens	Conrad	Total	
SELF-SATISFACTION SYNDROME SFS Items 2, 4, 7, 8 Scale Range: 1–4		b	3.11	2.50	3.00	2.56	2.73	Schools: 1.00 NS
		g	2.38	2.50	2.25	2.17	2.33	Sex: 8.80°°
	(103)	T	2.76	2.50	2.63	2.39	2.54	Schools × Sex: 1.20 NS
STRENGTH OF SELF-PRESENTATION Figure Drawings Scale Range: 1–5		b	3.00	2.72	3.08	2.65	2.82	Schools: 1.53 NS
		g	3.38	2.88	3.67	3.18	3.23	Sex: 3.82 NS
	(104)	T	3.17	2.79	3.38	2.86	3.01	Schools × Sex: .22 NS

°° $p < .01$
§ b = boys
   g = girls
   T = total

The Stick Figure Scale asks clear self-referential questions. It calls on the child's conception and feeling about himself, with his responses under conscious control. Drawing is a projective technique. It calls on a less conscious level of feeling and conception and the child does not know that we consider his figure drawing to reflect body image and self-concept. In

Stick Figure Scale responses we may have been getting some denial and bravado from the boys that was thrown into relief by their uncertain and self-concealing drawings. The girls may have been more able to admit doubts and uncertainties without necessarily being more basically uneasy and self-critical.

Further, the boys and girls reacted differently to the medium involved. For the girls, drawing was a favorite medium of expression, affecting the product we saw and rated. This preference, in turn, was almost certainly related to the deeper meanings that bodily display has for boys and girls and to the fact that the two channels of expression often have a different history for boys and girls. In the general culture, girls are admired for the way they look and visually present themselves; display of oneself is acceptable and encouraged. For boys, bodily display has other, mostly taboo, meanings. They are perhaps generally less willing to be known and looked at, and when asked for concrete forms of body representation, concealment may be especially important. Whether they also know themselves less well is a separate question. In the verbal sphere, represented by the Stick Figure Scale, cultural supports and sanctions work the other way. The boys draw on a general experience that leading from strength, or even assertive bragging, is acceptable and sometimes necessary. For girls, bragging is often thought to be immodest, and many have presumably internalized a sanction against an openly bold and favorable evaluation of themselves. Predominant cultural attitudes would predict the nature of the sex differences we actually obtained: boys more verbally assertive, girls more visually so.

A third factor may have contributed to the discrepancy in sex differences. The girls of this sample, as compared to the boys, had a more precisely articulated response style that appeared in many contexts. On the Stick Figure Scale, the girls were more apt to differentiate the conditions of their popularity, sex role preferences, and school competence (in comparison to the boys, whose responses were more unequivocal); because the girls' responses were not unequivocally assertive, their scores came down. This finer articulation in the Drawings took the form of greater use of elaboration, detail, and color and contributed to the total impact of the drawing, thus raising the girls' scores.

The sex differences, then, are probably best understood as a complex function of the level of consciousness tapped by the two techniques, the modes of expression they call for, and contrasting response styles in the boys and girls.

School Group Differences

There are no reliable school group differences in the measures of self-confidence and satisfaction (see Table 12–1). Neither the verbal assertions nor the figure drawings reflect a school-associated difference in self-presentation.

To what extent do these findings negate our expectations? Certainly, it is a basic goal of modern ideology to educate people who can feel satisfied with themselves and confident of their worth and effectiveness. Despite this, our predictions centered on the variables reported in the next section: awareness of feeling, impulse acceptance, and self-differentiation. We did not directly hypothesize that children from modern schools would be more confident and satisfied. This reservation stemmed from several factors: the complexity of integrating self-feeling, the young age of the children, and the expectation that inner feeling and outer presentation would be inextricably mixed in the data.

The modern philosophy actually sees the achievement of a resolved and confident self-image as a complex matter. Under the best of circumstances, the growing child faces failure, feelings that are difficult to manage, and the challenge of evaluating his abilities and limits in relation to the life requirements he faces. The modern environment actively attempts to support his efforts and feelings, but accepts the likelihood that like all children, he will have doubts and uncertainties. We could not assume that the modern environment—supportive, but geared to knowing and facing oneself—would produce children discernibly more satisfied and confident, particularly at this relatively young age.

The fact that the measures confound inner feelings with public presentation further complicates the situation. For the modern schools, presentation of oneself in confident and satisfied terms is not valued for itself. Where there is a feeling of doubt or distress, the value would be on its expression and handling. Both the modern and traditional school children were educated in environments that valued self-confidence and satisfaction; the difference lay perhaps in the stress placed on the inner feeling as opposed to the outer presentation. The measures reflect what the child presents to the adult but give no clear indication of the relation between this offering and the inner perception. For all these reasons, prediction of modern-traditional effects concerning self-confidence had to be guarded.

The school groups, then, did not differ in self-confidence and satisfaction, but there were a number of interesting findings in this area. The children of this sample presented a general picture of satisfaction and confidence concerning their status in life and the effectiveness of their functioning. This picture varied, however, with the sphere of functioning (peer relations representing a frontier of relative uncertainty), with the mode of reaction (verbal and conscious versus graphic and projective) and with the sex of the children. It is difficult to judge whether the boys and girls differed basically in their internal sense of satisfaction and confidence. It does seem that they had different attitudes toward being seen, known, and admitting conflict, with boys more concerned about holding together a fabric of defense against probing, when they were aware of the intention, and girls less concerned. It also seems clear that the boys and girls were using different modalities for putting themselves forward in strength—an accurate reflection, it would appear, of the sex-typed channels characteristically supported by the general culture.

Self-Knowledge

This section is concerned with awareness of feeling, impulse acceptance, and differentiation in the child's communication about himself. The measures fall into two groups: awareness of feeling and impulse acceptance have to do with the child's relation to his emotional experiences; self-differentiation has to do with the child's capacity to deal with his self-image in differentiated rather than global terms. Predictions concerning school group differences were focused on the dimensions in this section.

Techniques and Measures

The material is drawn from the Personal Questions, the Dictated Letter, and the Stick Figure Scale. These techniques are all semi-projective and tap the child's conscious perception of his feelings, qualities, and reactions as he communicates them to the adult.

AWARENESS OF FEELING

   (i) **Personal Questions: Awareness of Own Feelings.** The children were asked a series of questions: "What makes you happy, makes you feel good? What puts you in a bad mood, makes you mad? Do you day-dream? Do you have feelings you try not to show? What kind of things make you feel embarrassed or ashamed?"

   The child was rated on a five-point scale for his ability to deal openly with this task, to communicate an awareness of feelings and fantasies, to give the sense of a feeling, responding individual.

IMPULSE ACCEPTANCE

   (ii) **Stick Figure Scale**

   Item 5: Style of Reactivity

"Here's a boy (girl) who gets very excited and en- Versus thusiastic about things he likes." | "Here's a boy (girl) who is pretty calm and quiet most of the time."

"Which one is more like you?"

(Score 3)   (Score 1)

(iii) Stick Figure Scale
Item 10: Aggression Anxiety

"Here's a boy (girl) who tries not to lose his temper, Versus feels a little worried and uncomfortable when he does blow up or yell." | "Here's a boy (girl) who feels better when he blows up and lets people know he's mad; he doesn't mind doing it."

"Which one is more like you?"

(Score 3)   (Score 1)

(iv) Personal Questions: Aggression Anxiety. Responses to "What makes you mad?" and "Do you have feelings you try not to show?" were rated on a four-point scale of concern with the control of anger.

1—no mention of the expression or control of anger (the issue is denied)

2—some expression of anger indicated but no mention of concern with or problem about control (or child specifies that it's not a problem or that he feels better after expressing anger)

3—control of temper is stated as a problem

4—child regards temper and the control of anger as a severe problem

SELF-DIFFERENTIATION

(v) Stick Figure Scale: Self-Differentiation. The child was rated on a four-point scale according to his tendency to make gradations of judgment along the continuum defined by the two figures. The most differentiated approach was defined as that in which the child used a variety of gradations as he moved from item to item.

1—child puts himself in the same position relative to endpoints or midpoint—for example, always endpoints, always between end and middle (content irrelevant)

2—child has typical way of using the continuum, departs from this twice or less

3—child departs from typical way of using continuum more than twice but does not use all possibilities

4—child uses all possible positions[9]

(vi) Dictated Letter: Range of Self-Differentiation. The rating was based on the number of categories into which material could be coded (basic descriptive facts, activities and functions, preferences and feelings, memories, plans, and so on).

1—child uses less than two categories

2—child uses two categories

3—child uses more than two categories

(vii) **Dictated Letter: Quality of Self-Differentiation.** The rating was based on the presence of material going beyond basic descriptions of facts and activities.

1—material going beyond basic descriptions not included

2—material going beyond basic descriptions included

INTERCORRELATIONS AMONG MEASURES

These measures are not highly intercorrelated, with the notable exception of the two measures of Self-Differentiation derived from the Dictated Letter (see Appendix BB, Table 4). The latter were intended to tap somewhat different aspects and are, in fact, not perfectly correlated. Use of both measures appears warranted, though they are obviously similar.

Of the remaining measures, awareness of feeling relates most consistently to other measures: for girls, to greater self-differentiation; for boys, to more outgoing reaction style; for both, to greater concern about aggressive impulses. The latter correlation may indicate that children in greater self-contact are more aware of their specific struggle with aggression, but it is also likely that the correlation reflects a scoring artifact, particularly since the higher correlations appear between two measures derived from the Personal Questions. Open discussion of concern about aggressive feelings contributed to the rating of awareness of feeling, though there were, of course, other elements considered as well.

Group Characteristics and Sex Differences

In many areas of the study the range of reactions among the 105 children was impressive. Perhaps this was especially so when they came to tell us about themselves, their lives, and their feelings. Open-ended techniques in particular, such as the Personal Questions and the Dictated Letter, were handled by the children in widely disparate ways.

For some children, the probing, direct, emotionally charged questions we asked were difficult and even distasteful. Ten of the children were completely blocked and resistant and approximately one third were sparse or superficial in their responses. Perhaps these were the prototypes of the latency child, as he is usually conceived. But some of the children found these questions intriguing. At least a third offered personal, emotionally important material. Though formed from the unremarkable events of their daily lives, these responses touched on basic experiences of shame and embarrassment, failure, the wish not to be exposed—faced by the child and shared with the adult:

. . . Well, I was at a concert. . . . Just a few people came but there were kids in my class and I goofed . . . didn't know where I was

> . . . started off with the wrong hand. I was frantic . . . and when I was done I went downstairs and one boy stood there saying, "Ooh . . . you goofed!"
>
> . . . I try not to cry when my friends are around. I'm younger than they are, and they tease me that I'm a baby, and I don't like that. . . .
>
> . . . Sometimes, like when guests came, and they didn't serve me . . . and I took a big handful, and I got screamed at in front of the company. . . .
>
> . . . When I got my pin at cub scout meeting, and my father comes over and started doing a big speech and I just said, "Give it to me!" and he said, "Oh, I have to do this." . . . That was embarrassing.
>
> . . . Well . . . if I insist on something and keep on insisting—and usually I'm wrong. . . . That's when I really feel embarrassed . . . and that's when I lose my temper!

Such material is certainly more naive and less introspective than these same children would produce as adolescents, but it is richer and more open than stereotypes of the age might predict.

By the same token, the Dictated Letters ranged widely. Some were impersonal and factual, giving little range or unique material about the self:

> Well, first we salute the flag and then the class has some arithmetic. Then usually after arithmetic we have spelling. On Friday we have some tests, arithmetic and spelling tests, and we usually have reading in the morning also. Then at lunch time some children go home for lunch and some of them stay in the lunch room and some of them eat out. On Tuesday and Thursday in the afternoon we sometimes have penmanship and sometimes social studies, and then at three the class is dismissed from school and that's all.

Other letters are more personal and communicate something of the child's interests, feelings, ambivalence:

> My name is _____ and I live at _____. I am nine years old. I love horses and stuffed animals. I like school very much. I live in _____ _____ for the summer. That's off the coast of _____. I have a smaller brother who's six years old. My opinion of him is he's a little brat! Not *really*. My hobbies are drawing, painting. On Mondays and Thursdays I have piano lessons. It's my second year of taking them. I hope to get a letter from you soon.

The bulk of the letters were relatively impersonal and undifferentiated, but approximately 40 percent covered a range of ideas about the writer and went beyond the sheerly factual and descriptive.

In general, girls responded in more open and differentiated ways than boys (see Table 12–2), and the most blocked and resistant children of all were boys.[10]

TABLE 12–2
Self-Awareness and Differentiation

MEASURE Source, and Scale Range	(N)	Sex §	Browning	Adams	Dickens	Conrad	Total	Analysis of Variance
AWARENESS OF OWN FEELINGS Personal Questions Scale Range: 1–5		b	2.67	3.22	3.08	2.76	2.96	Schools: .86 NS Sex: 1.14 NS Schools × Sex: .19 NS
		g	2.86	3.19	3.55	3.25	3.24	
	(102)	T	2.75	3.21	3.30	2.97	3.09	
STYLE OF REACTIVITY SFS Item 5 Scale Range: 1–3		b	2.22	2.44	2.33	2.19	2.31	Schools: .15 NS Sex: .15 NS Schools × Sex: .30 NS
		g	2.25	2.07	2.42	2.17	2.21	
	(102)	T	2.24	2.27	2.38	2.18	2.26	
AGGRESSION ANXIETY SFS Item 10 Scale Range: 1–3		b	1.50	1.35	1.25	1.12	1.28	Schools: .56 NS Sex: .56 NS Schools × Sex: .38 NS
		g	1.50	1.27	1.58	1.33	1.40	
	(100)	T	1.50	1.31	1.42	1.21	1.34	
AGGRESSION ANXIETY Personal Questions Scale Range: 1–4		b	2.44	2.94	2.33	1.88	2.42	Schools: 3.75* Sex: .50 NS Schools × Sex: 1.90 NS
		g	2.29	2.31	2.55	2.08	2.30	
	(101)	T	2.38	2.65	2.43	1.96	2.37	
SELF-DIFFERENTIATION SFS Items 1–10 Scale Range: 1–4		b	2.11	2.22	2.33	2.88	2.42	Schools: 2.63 NS Sex: 1.92 NS Schools × Sex: .15 NS
		g	2.25	2.44	3.00	3.08	2.71	
	(103)	T	2.18	2.32	2.67	2.96	2.55	
RANGE OF SELF-DIFFERENTIATION Dictated Letter Scale Range: 1–3		b	1.13	1.22	1.50	1.65	1.40	Schools: 4.55** Sex: 5.00* Schools × Sex: .45 NS
		g	1.25	1.50	2.09	2.00	1.72	
	(102)	T	1.19	1.35	1.78	1.79	1.55	
QUALITY OF SELF-DIFFERENTIATION Dictated Letter Scale Range: 1–2		b	1.13	1.22	1.58	1.41	1.35	Schools: 3.68* Sex: 2.63 NS Schools × Sex: .16 NS
		g	1.38	1.31	1.73	1.58	1.49	
	(102)	T	1.25	1.26	1.65	1.48	1.41	

Mean Scores for School Groups

* $p < .05$
** $p < .01$
§ b = boys
g = girls
T = total

In their attitudes toward impulse expression, the children presented an intriguing pattern. When the context was one of pleasure or general temperamental style (Stick Figure Scale, Item 5), they described themselves as predominantly excitable and enthusiastic, rather than calm and quiet. In an area with little or no taboo component, that is, they indicated a style of reactivity that was direct, childlike and free. Whatever they may have internalized of adult admonitions to be quiet or controlled, and whatever changes toward obsessive, less spontaneous modes of reactivity we may associate with this age level, most of these children—both boys and girls— apparently felt themselves to be impulsive and expressive in their reactions to pleasure, and they felt free to say this to the interviewers. The exceptions, of which there were few, probably represent true temperamental differences or instances where taboo on expressive reactions reached even this area.

When the emotional response involved the expression of anger, on the other hand, reactions were different. In this area, where socialization processes are usually strong, the children had more tendency to control the expression of anger and to feel guilt when it broke through, rather than relief (Stick Figure Scale, Item 10). It is of interest that almost all the children could specify what gave them pleasure and made them happy, on the Personal Questions, but over one fourth could not deal openly with what made them angry or ashamed. In the area of anger, control was more of an internalized value; some children avoided its discussion and some children described their angry feelings in combination with a concern about control: "I go to my room and slam the door . . ." "I take a powder—go downstairs and walk around the block until I can face my sister again." They saw themselves as struggling to manage angry feelings and conveyed the sense of an inner self which must be subjugated: "I say to myself 'Down, James!' " That the struggle does not lead to victory by a smooth path was very clear to some of the children: ". . . Sometimes if I get mad I don't show it, I try to—I really try to keep it in me. But most of the time it's like a volcano. Zoom. I get all red, my blood pressure goes up, whrrr . . . but then I settle down."

Of the ten children rated as showing the strongest anxiety about aggression, nine were boys, though group differences between boys and girls did not reach statistical significance.

School Group Differences

It was with respect to the awareness of feeling, acceptance of impulse, and self-differentiation that differences were predicted among modern and traditional school children. The modern school attempts to know and relate itself to each child; it is assumed that this attitude will provide the model and experience for the child to come to know himself—to differentiate his qualities, face and handle his feelings, and be willing to express and educate his potential. The contrast between this orientation toward the individual and the more impersonal, performance-oriented relation of the traditional school to the child, led to certain predictions: that children from modern schools would have clearer and more differentiated images of themselves than children from traditional schools; that they would be more aware of their feelings and more accepting of their impulses, with less anxiety about the control of expression; that they would think in more personalized ways and would apply to themselves a more differentiated style of thought. In a sense, the modern and traditional school children were expected to differ both in *aspects of self-knowledge* per se and in *modes of cognition* as applied to the self.

For the most part, these predictions are borne out. Children from the modern schools were more differentiated in the way they described themselves and children from the most modern school were more accepting and less anxious about the expression of angry feelings (see Table 12–2). More modern than traditional school children offered very personal and meaningful material in a way that suggested open contact with their feelings, though some among them were particularly blocked and evasive. This variability among modern school children—more accurately, among those from Conrad—was not part of the predicted pattern, but is a recurrent and important finding, worthy of detailed consideration.

To review the data in greater detail: On the most general rating (Awareness of Feeling), school groups did not differ significantly in their average scores (see Table 12–2). Inspection of the distribution of scores suggests clearly, however, that children from the modern schools were more apt to offer open material about their moods, their daydreams, their secret or shameful feelings. More of the modern school children were rated above the midpoint, while such ratings were particularly rare among children of the most traditional school (Conrad 38 percent; Dickens 43 percent; Adams 29 percent; Browning 12 percent). At the same time, the group from Conrad was the most variable by far.[11] Its pattern was unique. More than a third of the children responded with depth and awareness, but a disproportionate number were relatively unresponsive. Eight of the ten children rated lowest on the communication of inner feeling came from this group and seven of these were boys. The Conrad group included children from the extremes of communication about feeling, but relatively few who were given "middle" scores; middle scores signify a response that can pass muster without being unduly revealing. Perhaps this pattern is consistent with the philosophy of a school that offers support for self-contact but does not build the personal-social skills for self-protective communication.

When we turn to a special aspect of emotional life that has to do with impulse acceptance, there were school-related differences in the area of anger, though there were no group differences in the self-report of general reactive style (expressive enthusiasm versus calm restraint). In the specific area of anger where the range of socializing attitudes was relatively broad, concern for control among the children was systematically related to the school variable, with the children of Conrad least concerned.

The children from Conrad were least concerned with control of anger on both measures; significant differences among the school groups were found in the responses to the Personal Questions (see Table 12–2). Reactions to the idea of "blowing up" (Stick Figure Scale) supported this trend, though not at statistically significant levels.

Greater impulse acceptance, it should be noted, was characteristic only of children from the most modern school. Children of Dickens were not demonstrably less anxious about expressing anger than traditional school children, for the most part, though it was a subgroup from one traditional school—the boys from Adams—who stood apart from all others as most deeply involved in an active struggle to control aggressive feelings.

How clear can we be about what we have measured here? It is to be remembered that these are not measures of the amount of internal pressure in the child, nor of the objective degree of angry expression, but of the child's perception of his anger, and of his feelings and concern about the moments when he wishes to express these directly. Are we measuring a difference in the admission of anger or in the denial of anger as a feeling to be dealt with? While we already know that some Conrad children were reluctant to elaborate on their feelings in general, there is evidence that the pattern of reactions concerning anger is not predominantly a reflection of denial. On the Personal Questions, most Conrad children (23 of 28) were rated as talking about anger without involving problems of control— not as avoiding the discussion of anger.[12] Discussion of anger without bringing in problems of control was less consistently characteristic of other groups (16 of 34 in Adams; 10 of 16 in Browning; 13 of 23 in Dickens). The finding seems to relate not to a denial of anger but to a more tolerant view of anger as part of the self.

Are we, then, measuring a difference in true self-perception or in ways of telling the adult about oneself? As noted before, we have no way of knowing or of testing this distinction. Even if we are measuring differences in how children talk about themselves, however, it seems important that some children stress the struggle to control temper when talking with the adult, others note that angry discharge can bring relief or tell the adult what they get angry about without simultaneously describing the attempt at control. The sense of what governs the communication with the adult is itself a fact, related to how the child regards his own anger in himself.

By the basic tenets of the modern philosophy, impulse expression is an acceptable part of life and feeling and development of control is a long-term process. The different schools presented a particularly clear contrast in this respect (see Chapter 3). Aggressive behavior and angry discharge were virtually taboo in the traditional school setting, much less so in the modern schools. It would seem important for the traditional school child to think of himself and present himself as a child who values control and struggles to achieve it. It would be less necessary for the modern school child to incorporate and present this image. We do not see the effects of these school differences in comparing the children of Dickens with those from more traditional schools, but the effects appear as hypothesized in the reactions of Conrad children.

The measures of self-differentiation tap another facet of the child's communication about himself. These measures also indicate a significant difference among school groups (see Table 12–2). As in the Personal Questions, children from Conrad varied widely, but as a group the children from both Conrad and Dickens included a greater range of qualities in describing themselves than traditional school children, and were more apt to touch on feelings, plans, and memories that carried them beyond descriptive accounts of their identity and activities. They also responded to the Stick Figure Scale in a more differentiated way, using the possibilities for gradations of judgment with greater variety and flexibility.

The latter finding has implications both for the nature of self-concept and for the cognitive style with which these children thought and communicated about themselves. The *least* differentiated approach was considered to be one in which the child handled all ten items in a particular way, checking himself off against a given model, so to speak. The *most* differentiated approach was considered to be one that used all possibilities, with children judging that on some items they fitted one of the descriptions as given, on some they were in the middle, and on some they tended in a particular direction.[13] As an example, one girl reacted to the item describing a child who gets very "excited and enthusiastic about things she likes" by saying, "That's me!" immediately, and placing herself at that *endpoint;* she placed herself in the *middle* of the line on the item about losing or controlling temper, however, saying, "Sometimes when you're hurt you don't like to show that you're mad, and sometimes when you're *not* hurt, you feel like *giving* it to someone"; on the item about whether or not she was good at her school work, she described herself as good at reading but not so good at arithmetic and then made an overall judgment that she was *between* the midpoint and the "not so good" alternative. In this most differentiated approach, there appeared to be a good deal of thought and process. The children seemed to be trying for a relatively subtle communication about themselves in relation to a series of ideas. They found that the arbitrary models presented to them varied from item to item in their acceptability as accurate descriptions of their own tendencies.

No great subtlety can be attributed to what a nine-year-old can try for or manage, but certainly this differentiating process is in contrast to the process by which a child accepts the alternative models as given and chooses one as being like himself in each case. It is a difference in the cognitive tendency to restructure a stimulus situation into more meaning-ful terms—an active, flexible, intellectual process—and it is a difference in the extent to which facets of the self are focused and differentiated. Per-haps this is merely to make the obvious point that thought and communi-cation about oneself have both content and intellectual form. It is an important point for our study, however. A more differentiated style of thought about oneself among modern school children may have repre-sented the fused effect of two aspects of the modern school: its attempt to teach a probing, differentiated style of thinking in general, and its focus on the individual as the center of his own life and a legitimate object of knowledge. Our task-oriented problem-solving situations did not show the effects of the different intellectual styles in modern and traditional schools. Perhaps the data reported here are an indication that these styles had taken root, but most firmly so in areas of perception and thought that were relatively self-concerned and personal.

As an extension of this idea, it might also be noted that the children of modern and traditional schools approached the letter-writing task not only with different degrees of articulation about themselves but with generally different styles of response. The letters were rated along a continuum from a relatively stereotyped approach (handling facts and ideas in descriptive, precategorized ways) to a more personalized approach (filtered through the perceptions, feelings, or interests of the child).

As an illustration of the former:

> My name is _____ and I am going to tell you what life is like in _____. Today I want to tell you about the _____ skyline. The tallest building is the _____ Building. It has 102 stories and is 150 feet above street level.[14] Next week I will tell you about the _____ Building.

And of the latter:

> . . . I'm living in _____. It is a lot different from India. There is no sand or desert. It looks sort of like a big valley with all the tall buildings. You'd like to look off the platform of the _____. The cars look like toy ones, and the people you can't see.

The children of modern and traditional schools differed significantly on this measure:[15] children from both modern schools created the more per-sonalized letters, whether they focused directly on themselves or described aspects of their lives and surroundings. Though not directly part of "self-concept," these data also suggest that the modern schools may have effected a different kind of fusion in their children between the inner self and the intellectual reaction style. Teaching on the assumption that ideas have most meaning and can best be integrated when they are related to the child's own perceptions and experiences, these schools may have been building a more personalized style of thought and approach to tasks and stimuli than the traditional schools.

Relationships to Home Background

There can be little doubt that the child's self-concept is influenced by the appraisal and attitudes of his parents. We did not find much systematic association, however, between the nature of self-image projected by the children and particular maternal qualities or attitudes measured in the study. The relationships suggested are rather tenuous and do not account, in significant measure, for the variation among children.

Within these bounds, we can note certain suggested connections (Appendix CC, Table 5):

Girls from traditional home backgrounds were more apt to be assertive in the images they presented through drawings. Perhaps they were more consistently cherished and admired for their appearance than girls from modern families and produced, thus, stronger and more elaborated graphic images at this age.

Awareness of feeling and self-differentiation appeared in conjunction with certain features of the maternal role: more consistency and integration in the mother related to less elaborated self-contact in the children. Surprising on the surface, such an association raises the possibility that mothers who had achieved consistent coherence by virtue of a relatively noncomplicated approach to themselves and their roles may have provided relatively nondifferentiated models for their children. The correlations are tenuous, however, and rather preclude an elaborate search for explanations.

Modern-traditional aspects of child rearing related only weakly to the child's style of self-description. Where they reached reliable levels they were in the same direction as school-related findings: more aware, differentiated, and impulse-accepting children tended to come from homes which valued individualized and internally relevant standards. Children from congruent modern home and school environments, it might be noted, were more differentiated in self-description than those from congruent traditional environments and tended to be less concerned about aggressive expression.

The general pattern of home and school findings implies that family forces were not more systematically evident in these effects but that the combined effects of modern home and school may have made for more differentiated self-concepts and more open, impulse-accepting communication about the self; combined traditional home and school background may have made for more impersonal and global reactions.

Summary and Discussion

This study of the children's self-concepts has been bound in part by problems of conception and measurement, as indeed is generally the case in this area of theory and research. We cannot with certainty distinguish conscious from unconscious self-perception, the child's evaluation of himself from his perception of the appraisal of others, or what he knows about himself from what he communicates to other people. Nonetheless, we have been able to establish trends, at least regarding self-concept as communicated to others, and have traced ways in which the self-concept was related to the sex of the child, the social acceptability of what he was describing, and the nature of the socializing background.

The children of this sample varied greatly in their responses to our techniques. The more we put the burden of response on the child, the more variation we saw. Most of the children could respond to a relatively structured technique, which provided boundaries and asked the child to scale himself (Stick Figure Scale), though some dealt with the material in a self-protective way. There was more evident range, however, in response to the open-ended situation calling for self-description (Dictated Letter) and to the direct questions that went to areas of private experience (Personal Questions). Some of the children were blocked, evasive, or resistant and some were relatively sparse or superficial; at least a third or more, however, were able to respond with personal and meaningful material, beyond the point expected, perhaps, of latency children. The children of this sample, of course, were the offspring of educated, articulate, often introspective parents, and a relatively elaborated level of response would be expected from them at any age. Within this group, however, they varied from those whose blocking, defensiveness, or impersonal quality seemed the epitome of the latency image to those who were by no means out of touch with their feelings, their failures, or their experiences of longing, anger, or shame.

By and large, these well-cared-for children presented an image of satisfaction with their lives, their roles, and their effectiveness, though they were less certain in some areas than others (unsure of acceptance by peers though relatively confident concerning academic competence) and more assertive at more conscious levels (a matter of defense and conscious control).

In their reactions to the expression of enthusiasm and anger, the group showed the effects of the long socialization process to which they had been exposed, with frequent central emphasis, in some cases, on the channeling and control of aggression. The children described themselves as reactive and enthusiastic people, generally prone to express feelings of pleasure. When impulsive reaction involved anger, however, many children described their feelings of anxiety, their search for indirect outlets and their attempts to inhibit and control; for some, there was the clear implication that anger was not a legitimate part of themselves. The extent to which children were concerned about anger, however, varied not only according to modern-traditional background but according to the sex of the child. Boys and girls did not differ in their stance toward the relative acceptability of enthusiasm and anger, but there was a clear distinction in degree and tone of their anxiety about aggression. The greatest concern seemed to occur among boys, more of whom may have felt strong internal pressure and a need to struggle against expression. If boys are often allowed more leeway than girls, they may also be heavily censured for extremes of expression.

The contrasting reaction patterns of boys and girls on the self-concept measures were interesting in general. Children of different sexes seemed to express self-confidence through different modes (verbally for boys, graphically for girls) and they may have had a somewhat different pattern of reactions concerning anger and its control, as noted. There was also a general difference in their willingness to be intimately known to others. The girls were more open and responsive. They gave fuller and more personal material about themselves, provided more details, described more incidents, were more able or willing to discuss experiences that were personal and perhaps painful. The boys were more guarded and defensive, more global, less apt to confide what was personal or difficult to admit. They were less willing to be "seen," both in the literal sense of elaborated figure drawings and in the sense of an image that can be built up through personal talk and relationship. In this pattern, we probably see both a well-studied cultural phenomenon (since females of all ages are often found to be more self-revealing and personalized) and a developmental fact: latency may characterize boys more than girls, if it is taken to mean distance from one's feelings and investment of energy in external things as defense against self-concern and self-knowledge. Further, the importance of the probing adult must certainly be considered. Though most nine-year-olds are moving to peer groups and new confidantes, the girls seemed still to preserve more open and trusting contact with adults, the boys to withdraw more of their personal selves—perhaps to protect the still vulnerable sense of personal strength they were building. We cannot know whether their contact with themselves was actually less close and differentiated than that of girls—it seems possible that they were in reality less introspective—but they did appear more distant from adults. Gathering our data through adult-child contacts, we felt the influence of the difference in these attitudes, particularly in relation to fantasy material and material concerning self-concept.

Our primary purpose in assessing self-concept, of course, was to compare children from modern and traditional schools. We had predicted that children from modern schools would be more differentiated in conceptions of themselves, more aware of their feelings, and more accepting of their impulses. The differentiation of self-concept was seen as a function of the modern school's stress on a probing cognitive style as well as on differentiated relationships to children as individuals. We were also interested in comparing constellations of self-satisfaction and confidence, though several factors, including the mixture of inner feeling and public presentation in the data we could gather, precluded predictions that would express the different educational philosophies.

The findings generally support the expectations, though not in all aspects or on all measures. The children of modern schools were more differentiated in describing themselves and more apt to handle tasks in ways that had personal meaning. While all our groups found it natural to express pleasure impulsively, children from the most modern school were more accepting of angry feelings and discharge than traditional school children; the latter made a sharper distinction between the expression of feelings that were socially acceptable and those that were not. The modern and traditional groups showed no difference in self-satisfaction and confidence.

The school groups did not differ on the average, in the extent to which they communicated an awareness of inner feelings and fantasies. In this respect, however, Conrad children presented a unique and highly variable pattern, providing some differentiated insight into the possible effects of this kind of school. Some of the richest, most insightful and freely communicative material came from Conrad children, but some of the most blocked or resistant children, mostly boys, were also from this group. The modern school tends to focus on the child and his individuality, setting a model of self-understanding and providing little direct reinforcement for impersonal handling of personal matters. For some children this may have been a difficult situation. It sets a value on self-knowledge and directness when, for individual reasons, some children may need distance and defense. Their school may have given them little example or encouragement for coping in ways that were impersonal and prestructured; they may have found that complete evasion, in some circumstances, was their most viable alternative.

It might be relevant to note again that the children were asked not only for open communication but for communication to a relatively strange adult. Though some children from Conrad communicated a general feeling of ease in this situation, others were relatively indifferent, and the more resistant children may have been especially sensitive to probing by adults they did not know, particularly if they had no effective ways of responding impersonally. This may have applied especially to boys. It must in any case be noted that, while the pattern of school effects had general features, the school may have affected particular children in different ways. The school capable of fostering the most differentiated awareness of self may also have threatened a minority of children.

The children from Dickens provided support for some of the predictions, but not for all. Their acceptance of anger was not greater than that of traditional school children, but they did show a personalized and differentiated reaction to probing and self-oriented tasks. The similarity between children of Dickens and Conrad in this respect suggests that the modern educational approach, even when expressed in the different forms exemplified by these two schools, tended to foster this style of reaction.

Qualitative differences between the groups from Conrad and Dickens are interesting and may well reflect differences in the impact of the two modern schools. The children from Dickens presented a somewhat more moderate, less erratic pattern than Conrad children. There were fewer children who showed the clear and pervasive effects of what the modern environment strives to foster, but there were also fewer children who were blocked and defensive. This may constitute a contrast between the particular groups of this sample but may also reflect the more consistent modern atmosphere of a school like Conrad—with its greater possibilities for strong and perhaps polarized effects—versus the more moderate atmosphere of a public school like Dickens.

The contrast may also reflect the parent groups, of course. Dickens parents were more heterogeneous in their philosophy; Conrad parents were more consistent with each other and the philosophy of the school. Correlations with parent data are not strong and do not suggest that parent influence prevailed over school influence in this area, but where there are reliable associations they support the direction of school-related findings. The child living in a congruent modern background was more apt to be differentiated in self-concept and accepting of his impulses; the child living in a congruent traditional background was more apt to be impersonal, relatively global, or restricted in what he told about himself and more concerned about the expression of anger as an unacceptable part of his reactions. Boys from traditional homes and schools seemed to find this a particular problem.

Children of the two traditional schools handled these self-probing tasks adequately, even if impersonally, demonstrating perhaps a certain learned effectiveness in task handling where modern school children demonstrated a learned style of differentiated thinking about the self. The children from Adams were somewhat more self-aware than children from Browning and more intensely involved in concern for impulse control. Browning children were more impersonal and guarded, with a fairly strong presentation of self-satisfaction and confidence, but with the least evidence of self-contact, the least differentiated ways of describing themselves as individuals, and the least personalized approach to these self-focused tasks. It is probably relevant that these children attended the school that was most focused on prestructured approaches to ideas and most apt to consider personal reactions or feelings a tangent rather than a central part of school life and learning.

NOTES

1. This measure is treated more fully in Chapter 14.
2. See Machover, 1948; 1951.
3. The four Stick Figure Scale items contributing to the overall measure of self-satisfaction are moderately correlated with each other. Among boys in particular, there is some tendency to present a consistently positive or negative view of oneself: those who feel they have a "good and lucky life" tend also to consider themselves popular with peers ($r = .24$) and good at their work in school ($r = .25$). Both boys and girls who consider themselves competent at school work tend to feel they are popular with peers (total $r = .35$) and members of the sex with "the most fun and the best life" (total $r = .22$). The relatively modest correlations suggest at the same time, however, that self-evaluation in one area has some independence from self-evaluation in others.
4. Three girls, two boys.
5. Chi-square (x^2) analysis showed significant positive group trends ($p < .01$) on all items except Item 2—Peer Popularity.
6. Less elaborated drawings include such features as stick figures, profile drawings, figures without clothing or facial features—though these elements are rare in the sample; more elaborated drawings include detail and decoration in clothing and features, objects or animals as background, figures in movement, and so on.
7. There were no sex differences on the most general item (Item 7—Lucky Life).
8. Size: $F = 4.81$, $p < .05$; Perspective: $F = 11.43$, $p < .01$; Color: $F = 4.94$, $p < .05$.
9. See page 305 for clarifying illustration.
10. Of the ten children rated as most blocked and resistant to the Personal questions, nine were boys.

11. Comparison of variances: $C > B$, $F = 3.24$, $p < .01$; $C > A$, $F = 2.24$, $p < .05$; $C > D$, $F = 2.71$, $p < .01$.
12. A few Conrad children could indicate what made them angry even though they were not self-revealing or elaborated in their responses to the series of questions about inner feelings.
13. The more differentiated approach (rating 4) characterized approximately one fourth of the sample.
14. The factual approach, obviously, is no guarantee against factual error.
15. School differences: $F = 6.08$, $p < .01$; Sex differences: $F = 5.39$, $p < .05$ (girls > boys).

C H A P T E R

13

IMAGES OF LIFE STAGES

The contrast between traditional and modern environments led us to study another facet of self-development in the children: the sense of investment in past, present, and future stages of their own lives. Modern and traditional schools and homes placed such distinctive value on these different life stages that we expected children from the two kinds of environments to differ in their investment and imagery.

To our knowledge, this aspect of the child's psychological orientation had received little attention or systematic study. The most directly relevant material has been reported by LeShan (1952), who studied time orientation in children of different social classes. He noted that lower-class children live in an environment which is often unpredictable and uncertain, where tension release is a prevalent life style and the socialization of children is expressed predominantly by immediate rewards and punishments, while middle-class children live under conditions that are more predictable, where people deal with long-range goals and reward the child for the postponement of gratification. He predicted that these contrasting environments would be reflected in the time orientation of the children, and that the middle-class children would utilize a time span that extended further into the future than that of the lower-class children.[1]

In our study, however, we have focused on differentiation within the middle class and have predicted differences among children who share middle-class status. Our predictions stem from the different values and socializing processes of their schools and homes. The traditional environments, as we defined them in this study, were perhaps more prototypical of the middle-class image described by LeShan—geared to long-range goals and the postponement of gratification. These environments stressed the importance of childhood as a preparation for adulthood—a "moral futurism," in the words of David Hawkins (1966). They saw the future as a separate and highly important stage, toward which the child's training was to be geared. They transmitted images and values characterizing the successful adult and offered models they hoped and expected the children would emulate. The modern schools and homes, however, were different in orientation. Certainly they did not share the erratic inconstancy or the impulsive socializing of the lower-class environments, but they also did not share the "futurism" of the traditional middle-class environments. They focused by conviction on the importance of the child's current life, experiences, and pleasures. They saw past and future as continuous with the present and the child's future development, therefore, as an individual matter and process.[2]

On the basis of these different orientations, we expected children from traditional environments to be more oriented toward the future and to project future images that were relatively standardized and had little continuity with their current lives. We expected children from modern environments to express a stronger investment in the present and to project individualized future images that were relevant to their current interests. The data support these expectations consistently, though it was the children from Conrad who primarily carried the findings.

The material in this chapter is presented in two sections: Preferences for Older, Younger, or Current Life Stages, and Images of Past and Future. Predictions of modern-traditional group differences apply to both sections.

Preferences for Older, Younger, or Current Life Stages

Techniques and Measures

Direct statements of the child's life-stage preferences were obtained from the interview and the Stick Figure Scale.

(i) **Interview Question: Best Age.** The child was asked. "What do you think is the best age to be? Why?" Responses were coded on a five-point scale:

1—younger (infant to age 8)
2—own age
3—immediate future (10–12)
4—teen age
5—adult (20 and above)

(ii) **Stick Figure Scale: Life-Stage Preference (Item 3).**

"Here's a boy (girl) who thinks it will be wonderful to be all grown up." Versus "Here's a boy (girl) who thinks it was really best when he was a little kid."
"Which one is more like you?"

Responses were coded on a three-point scale:

1—younger age
2—middle choice
3—older age

The *adult or childlike quality* of responses to the Million Dollar and Three Wishes questions, reported in Chapter 9 are also relevant here and will be referred to in this section.

INTERCORRELATIONS AMONG MEASURES

Correlations between the interview and Stick Figure Scale measures were approximately zero (see Appendix BB, Table 5). Adult preference on the Stick Figure Scale correlated positively with adultlike responses to Three Wishes, for girls, and the two supplementary measures (Million Dollars and Three Wishes) correlated positively for the total group.

Group Characteristics and Sex Differences

The children of this sample lent some support to the notion that the middle-class culture is future-oriented and that its children are taught to place high value on life stages yet to come. Many of the children expressed a preference for the future, but their reactions varied with the techniques we used to probe their ideas, as if their feelings were conflicted or in flux, and they did not consistently respond with the same hierarchy of preferences.

When we offered the children an open field of choice (interview), many (over 50 percent) turned to the future—teen and adult stages—as holding the promise for the best time in life.[3] They pointed to various forms of independence, privilege, and physical prowess (can hit the ball and my brother), symbolic signs of status and arrival (can vote, buy a pipe), the fun and lure of teen-age dating, the possibility of study and college. A third of the children chose their current age and the period immediately ahead as best, because they "like it," were "satisfied," had "fun every day." Only a fraction (about 10 percent) turned back to the past, usually infancy, as the best age to be because people "take care of you," "treat you so nice," "you get your way a lot."

When we presented a forced choice between past and future (Stick Figure Scale) the pattern of preference was different. Only a fourth thought it would be "wonderful to be all grown up," while the majority thought it was best to be a "little kid." Approximately 20 percent broke the structure of the technique, created an alternative of "right now," and chose the present.

Aside from the fact that the forced choice did not offer the alternative of the contemporary stage, it seems likely that the idea of "all grown up" brought different images for some children than their own spontaneous projections into the future. "All grown up" may have represented something very final, with much responsibility to carry and too much of the fun already behind one. When children spontaneously chose stages of the future as the "best age" (interview) they offered such explanations as "you're not so young and you're not so old"; "you can already take care of yourself—but you're not really grown up and you're not faced with all those problems"; "you can do a lot of things, but you're not permitted to do all the things that grownups have to do"; "I could buy myself a pipe; that's the easiest thing to smoke—you don't have to inhale." Their comments suggested that *full* maturity was not an irresistible idea, even though some features of teen and adult life were pleasant to contemplate. The privileges of the future are compounded by concomitant responsibilities, and our different ways of probing the children's preferences seemed to call out different aspects of their feelings and evaluations.

It is interesting to note that the reaction style of the children varied in similar fashion when they responded to two semi-projective tasks described in an earlier chapter (Million Dollars and Three Wishes, Chapter 9). When they spent hypothetical money, most children were adultlike in their orientation: sensible, provident, and investment-conscious. They were essentially childlike, however, in formulating Three Wishes. In these instances, too, they seemed responsive to the particular implications of the situation we placed them in—a fluctuation that must betoken a potential range of conflicting reactions within individual children.

Despite this flux, there were clear and consistent differences among children from different backgrounds, as will be noted below, and consistently different preferences expressed by boys and girls. Girls looked more to the future than boys, a trend consistent on both measures though statistically reliable only on the Stick Figure Scale (see Table 13–1). The majority of the girls, when interviewed, thought future ages were best (68 percent), while less than half the boys (42 percent) shared their opinion. For girls, the modal preference was the teen-age stage; for boys, the modal preference was their current stage of life.

TABLE 13–1

Preferences for Older, Younger, or Current Life Stages

Measure Source, and Scale Range	(N)	Sex §	Mean Scores for School Groups					Analysis of Variance
			Browning	Adams	Dickens	Conrad	Total	
BEST AGE Interview Scale Range: 1–5 (→ older ages)		b	4.00	3.11	3.45	2.22	3.09	Schools: 3.68* Sex: .19 NS Schools × Sex: .60 NS
		g	3.50	4.00	3.67	2.25	3.57	
	(61)	T	3.75	3.60	3.55	2.23	3.31	
LIFE-STAGE PREFERENCE SFS Item 3 Scale Range: 1–3 (→ older age)		b	1.00	1.56	1.92	1.69	1.59	Schools: .83 NS Sex: 6.17* Schools × Sex: 5.50**
		g	2.63	1.69	2.00	1.58	1.90	
	(102)	T	1.81	1.62	1.96	1.64	1.74	
CHILDHOOD VERSUS ADULT ORIENTATION Million Dollars Scale Range: 1–3		b	2.60	2.22	2.17	1.94	2.20	Schools: 4.26** Sex: .23 NS Schools × Sex: .23 NS
		g	2.63	2.44	2.33	1.82	2.30	
	(103)	T	2.61	2.32	2.25	1.89	2.24	
CHILDHOOD VERSUS ADULT ORIENTATION Three Wishes Scale Range: 1–3		b	2.14	1.83	1.67	1.31	1.68	Schools: 3.54* Sex: .83 NS Schools × Sex: .21 NS
		g	1.86	1.56	1.64	1.27	1.56	
	(98)	T	2.00	1.71	1.65	1.30	1.61	

* $p < .05$
** $p < .01$
§ b = boys
   g = girls
   T = total

School Group Differences

The orientation of the Conrad children toward their contemporary childhood stage emerges as the most striking fact from these data. As predicted, the children of this modern school were most invested in their current stage of life. Children of Dickens did not share this preference for childhood, however, and our understanding of the findings must differentiate—not for the first time—between the two modern school groups.

The findings are clearest from interview data (see Table 13–1). In selecting a "best age," only one child from Conrad chose the teens as best and none chose adult stages. The uniqueness of this group did not reside in numerous choices of infancy or younger years, however. Such preferences were stated by only six children of the total sample and they were from the four different schools. The investment of Conrad children was in the present. The nine-year-old stage was their prevailing choice, followed by the period immediately over the horizon (10 to 12). In the other three schools, the preferred stages were either teen or adult, and certainly the two combined were the powerful preference. They represented the almost universal choice for girls in the three public schools (91 percent, Adams; 75 percent, Browning; 67 percent, Dickens).

Findings from the Stick Figure Scale are not clear-cut (see Table 13–1), perhaps in part because the alternatives offered no description of the current childhood stage, which had been the spontaneous choice among Conrad children and a relatively popular preference among boys in general. Girls of Conrad were again least likely to choose future stages, but the boys in all schools fluctuated considerably. Browning boys were particularly inconsistent, moving from one extreme to the other. They were clearly geared to the future in their spontaneous choices of a best age (interview), but they turned without exception to the advantages of the "little kid" on the Stick Figure Scale. Perhaps boys from this most traditional school were strongly pressed by the demands as well as the privileges of the adult role, as they were being prepared for it, and they reacted at times with interest and determination but at other times with a retreat from projected responsibilities and challenge.

The childhood orientation of Conrad children, so evident on the interview, was only weakly supported, then, by Stick Figure Scale data. The basic consistency of this orientation was suggested, nonetheless, by related data from the semi-projective sources previously noted: the Million Dollar technique and the Three Wishes. As noted in Chapter 9, these two hypothetical situations invited the children to order the universe to their liking in ways that money could buy or wishes make true. We rated their reactions for adult or childlike qualities of response. In each case, the boys and girls of Conrad were most childlike in their responses and least apt to handle the situation in adult terms. Certainly there are several possible explanations for their reactions, but the basic fact to note is the consistency of the phenomenon. In a variety of ways, Conrad children expressed an acceptance of their childhood status, with little preference for adult and future stages, and in this they were different from all other school groups.

It is clear from the reactions of Dickens children that their modern school had little or no influence in shaping a similar investment (see Table 13–1 and Chapter 9, Table 9–2). These children were easily as future-oriented as children from the traditional schools. The unique atmosphere and curriculum of Conrad may have communicated a high evaluation of childhood and current experience in a form that Dickens did not match, though it was more child-oriented and experiential than either of the traditional schools (see Chapter 3). In explaining the discrepant reactions of children from these two modern schools, however, we would also have to remember the difference in range of family orientation, since family background seems also to have been a factor in the reactions of the children.

Relationships to Home Background

Family orientation was related to the children's life-stage preferences in ways that were predictable. Where reliable associations were established (see Appendix CC, Table 6), they suggested, for the most part, that children from traditional homes were more apt to be future-oriented than children from modern homes.

In summary, there were many children in this middle-class sample who were future-oriented. Despite evidence of some ambivalence and flux in their feelings, they looked ahead to stages of life that would be more powerful, pleasurable, and "best." Such a reaction was more typical of girls than boys. There was considerable support, however, for the prediction that *modern* middle-class environments would shape a firmer investment in the present than the future. The children of Conrad, at least, were consistent in their preference for their current childhood status and showed little tendency to react in adultlike ways. Dickens children did not share this pattern, perhaps because their families were less modern and their school less coherent in its support of child life and experience.

Images of Past and Future

We examined the children's images of past and future with an expectation of wide variation in the material and a prediction that this variation would reflect differences in the children's environments. Projections into the future were, of course, sheer fantasy for the children: wishes, images, and plans based on perceptions of the adults in their surroundings, the values inherent in their world, and the amalgamating force of their own personalities. Our predictions centered, as noted, on this future stage. We expected the children from traditional environments to project images that were relatively standardized, as well as discontinuous with their current lives, while children from modern environments would project more individualized images relevant to their current interests and self-perceptions. We had no definite predictions about the past. We considered it possible, however, that children from modern environments would be in closer contact with their younger selves and less rejecting of earlier stages, and we attempted to explore this possibility.

Techniques and Measures

Material concerning *the past* was obtained from the interview and Sentence Completion Test. Material concerning *the future* was obtained from the Children's Picture Story Test, interview, and Sentence Completion test.

THE PAST
(i) **Interview Question:** The children were asked what they remembered about being little and what their earliest memories were.
(ii) **Sentence Completion Test:** Item 6 tapped ideas and feelings about the past: *When I was little . . .*

THE FUTURE
(iii) **CPST: Older Social Sex Role Themes.** The presence of themes concerning older social sex roles was rated on a three-point scale:
  1—theme not present
  2—theme present
  3—theme recurrent
(iv) **CPST: Fame and Success Themes.** Themes of superlative fame and success were coded for presence or absence.

(v) **Interview Question: Continuity of Future Plans with Present.** The child was asked, "Have you ever thought about being grown up? What do you think you'll be or do?" Responses were coded on a three-point scale:

    1—plans continuous with current interests and experience
    2—mixed elements
    3—plans discontinuous with current interests and experience

(vi) **Sentence Completion Test: Childlike or Adult Orientation to Jobs.** Responses to Item 4, *The best job in the world would be . . .* were coded on a two-point scale:

    1—child-oriented, experiential
    2—adultlike, standardized

Comments and reasons given in response to interview and Stick Figure Scale items about the "best age" also yielded relevant data concerning images of past and future.

INTERCORRELATIONS AMONG MEASURES

Correlations between imagery of the future (interview) and opinions about desirable jobs (SCT) were positive and sizable (see Appendix BB, Table 5). Children whose imagery of the future was continuous with current experiences also saw the "best job in the world" in childlike terms. Those whose imagery was discontinuous with their current lives indicated jobs that were standardized and adultlike. Among girls, the presence of older social sex role themes in projective material (CPST) was associated with more adult orientation on other measures concerning the future (see Appendix BB, Table 5). In general, the correlations indicate consistency in imagery for both sexes, though particularly for girls.[4]

THE PAST

Group Characteristics and Sex Differences

The interest and effectiveness with which children recalled their earlier years varied considerably, from children who rejected the task (rare) or mentioned what street they lived on to children who described vivid experiences and recalled feelings with pleasure and intensity. Some children conveyed a sense of live contact with the experiences they described ("I remember I had a blanket I used to play with all the time and chew it"; "I didn't stay in nursery school long because I didn't want my mommy to leave me there alone"). Others reported what parents had told them or shown them in pictures ("My mother says I was a very good baby." "I had very curly hair"). Some went back to infancy and very early stages, remembering cribs and carriages, being fed, trying to walk. Others spoke in terms of their preschool selves, past the stages of primary helplessness and satisfaction and already possessing rudimentary skills, though far inferior in competence to their current selves. This material was difficult to systematize and we were not able, in fact, to analyze statistically for school and sex differences. Prevailing themes were easily abstracted, however, and provide a vivid documentation of the filtering process as the middle-years child looks at his past.

The two most prevalent kinds of recall were those involving play and pleasure and those involving danger and pain. These themes were present in the material of both boys and girls. The remembrance of fun and play often had the feel of active body experience: jump, run, ride, climb, fall, gallop. It involved the sandbox, the seashore, tricycles, play with animals and other children, make-believe fun with parents. Favorite objects were sometimes mentioned: a doll, a panda, a toy accordion.

In the recall of danger, drama ran high. Incidents were sometimes recalled directly ("It went through here," pointing to the shoulder) and sometimes were part of family lore ("My mother always tells me about the time . . ."). They covered an impressive range: an experience with fire; falling in an open manhole; falling from a carriage or crib; a plane trip when one engine stopped; climbing on boxes that collapsed; nearly being run over; knocking a tooth out and throwing it away "because I didn't like that tooth!"; going into a country bathroom barefoot and finding a crab on the loose; an arm pulled out of a socket; doctors, hospitals, and stitches; and, very rarely, the recollection of nightmares or of "being afraid of tunnels."

Other themes were also recurrent. The birth of siblings was recalled by some, in terms of the mother's going away, the somewhat elusive excitement in the house, the feeling of curiosity about the baby. And a number of children noted the learning experiences of those earlier times, seen in the context of their previous immaturity, limited knowledge, and general inadequacy. One child recalled realizing for the first time, while feeding ducks in the country, that such things were real and not just on television; another described "holding on to my grandmother's dog, just learning to walk, putting my hands on its mouth and walking together"; others remembered inadequacies of speech and concept: "calling a victrola 'eyah,'" "saying 'Empire Steak' for 'Empire State,'" "thinking the sky was like a roof."

In this roster of themes, there are a number of interesting points about the nine-year-old child's contact with his early years as he moves away from them: pleasure associated with earlier years was invested not only in protection, nurturance, and contact with people but just as much in the remembered experiences of play; children could recapture and convey the sense of total body movement, action, and vigor that we consider the basic experiential mode of the earlier years; vulnerability, harm, and frightening events were vividly recalled, perhaps partly because they reflected dynamic psychological experiences, such as the fear of bodily harm as punishment from powerful people, and partly because they were the vivid and realistic experiences of being less capable in interaction with the environment; and, lastly, the past appeared meaningful to the children as a contrast to the present. The weaknesses, mistakes, and simpler learnings of the past seemed to provide a perspective for viewing current power, capacity, and knowledge. They gave the children a sense of pleasure in their growth and a way of perceiving life change in the context of changes already experienced.

School Group Differences

The material offered by the children was characterized by great variety and no one theme or approach drew large enough numbers for systematic comparison. We had considered it possible that contrasting environments would affect the child's perception and description of his past, since modern schools were less apt than traditional to stress "age-appropriate" reactions or to shame the child for occurrences of regressive behavior. Preliminary inspection of the data, however, did not suggest that children from modern schools were in better contact with early experiences than children of traditional schools or that they recalled particular themes or feelings with greater frequency. We did not attempt more systematic analysis but on the basis of our survey we have regarded the children's recall of their past as multidetermined and quite individualized—not systematically reflective of modern-traditional features in their backgrounds and of interest primarily in terms of age level characteristics.

THE FUTURE

Group Characteristics and Sex Differences

In talking about what the future would be like (interview, Stick Figure Scale), the children gave some indication of the capacities and privileges they associated with future stages. These have been alluded to earlier in this chapter and will come into discussion again in the next chapter as part of the constellation of sex role concepts. In brief, the future appeared attractive to some children because it implied independence, the disappearance of bothersome prohibitions, and the fruition of one's capacities. The latter were seen most often as physical (run fast, be tall, be good in athletics), but occasionally as intellectual (will be smart, know what to do). For some children, status and recognition were particularly important. In their imaginary stories (CPST), they projected superlative achievement and fame onto the growth and development of hero figures. In such cases, images of the future had a dominant component of status and acclaim.

Concomitants of adolescent and adult social sex roles were also attractive for some children. The expected pleasures of dating, flirting, parties, marriage, and so on were anticipated by some of the girls, who described the future both directly and projectively in these terms (interview, CPST). Not all the girls were involved in these themes, however, as will be noted below, and boys were drastically different in this respect. Boys seemed to have no image of themselves as husbands or fathers. They did not talk of dating or marriage in the future, and they did not project fantasies that were adolescent or adultlike in these terms.

Ideas of work and occupation were of particular interest. The potential pleasures of work per se were not mentioned spontaneously by the children. Those who chose the future as the "best age" were not impatient to work or produce in particular roles; they had other reasons for their choice. But when we asked the children to talk about their future plans— what they thought they would "be or do," or what "the best job in the world would be"—their responses were interesting and meaningful. Here we might consider two aspects: the images they had of future occupations and roles, and the relevance of those images to their current childhood lives and interests.

To describe images of future occupations, we must consider boys and girls separately.

Boys turned with greatest frequency to three occupations: scientist (13), physician (12), and ball player (9). These were followed by lawyer, engineer, musician, artist, and finally by a range of more individual plans (farmer, pilot, businessman, ranger, train engineer, highway policeman, rancher, lifeguard, soda fountain clerk). The roster was characterized by a sizable percentage of professional, high-status occupations but clearly included individualized and more childlike choices as well. Whatever their particular preferences, however—and even if they were not spontaneously future-oriented—the boys talked centrally about work and occupation when we questioned them directly about the future.

Among girls, the pattern was different. There was a clear division between those who spoke about the future in terms of what their work might be, as the boys did, and those who saw the future in terms of their roles as wives and mothers.

There were 20 girls for whom marriage, family, and social life were the central vision of the future. For these girls, the idea of work was either rejected, passed over, or very clearly secondary. ("I've decided if I get married I'd like the man to do the working." "Just be a mother." "I want to get married and I want a lot of children and I want to live in a house and not an apartment . . . (work?) I think I want to be like my mother; I don't want to work." "I'd like to be a married person, but not having a baby

. . . (work?) No, unless something tragic happened and I had to. . . . My husband should be good looking . . . not very fresh . . . like to go out dancing . . . fairly rich.")

The other group of girls (25) responded to questions about the future by considering what they might be or do in occupational terms. Their choices highlighted the artistic and expressive professions (music, painting, acting, dance) and some of the conventional female occupations (nurse, secretary, teacher), with little stress on formal professions or business involvement. They covered a range, however, and included also ventriloquist, model, champion swimmer, doctor, scientist, advertising manager, and various horse-related occupations like trainer or cowgirl.

When girls of this latter group were asked specifically about marrying and having children, many thought that was desirable or possible, while others didn't know or thought they would wait. One girl said she would marry "but right now I don't feel like getting married to a *BOY*." They did not generally exclude this aspect of their future female role, but it was relatively shadowy and secondary and they thought more spontaneously about what their work might be. It was among these girls that the projection of future activities most often built on the experiences and pleasures of the present.

For the most part, the children of this study saw the future in terms that were prestructured by social convention, adultlike in orientation, and essentially irrelevant to their current interests and activities. There was a prevailing tendency, among boys and girls alike, to value jobs like "president of a gold mine," "banker," "President of the United States," "millionaire"; to imagine themselves in positions that would bring status (scientist, doctor); to choose conventional, sex-linked occupations (salesgirl, secretary); or to talk in terms of direct identification with important adult figures, without any clear image of the content or activities that went with their role ("go into my father's business"). These visions seemed based essentially on standardized models and images.

More experiential, childlike, and personalized images were projected by approximately a third of the children. These children thought a "best job" would be one that was adventurous or was close to childlike experiences that they knew and enjoyed: to sail a ship, be a dancer, detective, ice cream taster, ventriloquist, train driver; and they envisioned their own futures revolving around activities they currently enjoyed and were interested in: to be a champion swimmer; a cello player because she plays and likes it; a puppeteer because he makes puppets and gives shows to friends; an astronomer because "I study astronomy a lot; I know all the planets"; or to find an occupation that combines one's interests ("I like horses and I like to act. I don't know how to combine those two. . . . Maybe in a circus—but not really.").

These two distinct orientations toward the future and one's role in it appeared equally among boys and girls. They did not appear equally among children of traditional and modern backgrounds, however. They were systematically related both to school and family factors, generally in directions consistent with our predictions.

School Group Differences

The school groups differed in two respects: the relevance of occupational plans to current interests and self-perceptions, and the centrality of pre-structured social sex roles in the future projections of the girls. The Conrad group was again distinct from all others, with the girls primarily responsible for its unique pattern of reactions.

The children of Conrad were more apt than any other group to see the future in terms that had current experiential meaning. Whether we asked them about their own plans or what the "best job in the world" would be, they stood apart from all other groups (see Table 13–2). Their orientation was relatively childlike. They responded out of their own interests, wishes,

TABLE 13–2

Children's Images of the Future

MEASURE Source, and Scale Range	(N)	Sex §	Mean Scores for School Groups					Analysis of Variance
			Browning	Adams	Dickens	Conrad	Total	
PRESENCE OF OLDER SOCIAL SEX ROLE THEMES CPST Scale Range: 1–3		b	1.10	1.12	1.33	1.12	1.16	Schools: 1.38 NS Sex: 11.03** Schools × Sex: 2.52 NS
		g	2.00	1.60	1.33	1.33	1.53	
	(103)	T	1.50	1.34	1.33	1.21	1.33	
CONTINUITY OF FUTURE PLANS WITH PRESENT Interview Scale Range: 1–3 (→ discontinuity)		b	2.50	2.06	1.92	1.94	2.06	Schools: 7.20** Sex: .20 NS Schools × Sex: 3.40*
		g	2.75	2.07	2.64	1.27	2.13	
	(98)	T	2.63	2.06	2.26	1.67	2.09	
CHILDLIKE OR ADULT ORIENTATION TO JOBS Sentence Completion Item 4 Scale Range: 1–2		b	1.50	1.79	1.50	1.46	1.58	Schools: .56 NS Sex: .00 NS Schools × Sex: .56 NS
		g	2.00	1.53	1.88	1.00	1.53	
	(83)	T	1.69	1.65	1.67	1.26	1.55	

* $p < .05$
** $p < .01$
§ b = boys
  g = girls
  T = total

hobbies, and skills, with relatively little tendency to gravitate toward pre-structured, socially sex-typed, prestigious occupations. To the extent that they reflected the effects of a modern school, with its emphasis on the recognition and development of individual propensities, their responses suggested strong support for the predictions. These children were not only more firmly rooted in the present but when they looked ahead, their images were more individually conceived and more continuous with their present lives. Such a pattern by no means extends to the children of Dickens, however. Again, they were essentially indistinguishable from children of more traditional schools.

It should be noted that the Conrad pattern was most clearly carried by the girls, who were discernibly different on both measures from girls of other schools; they were, in fact, more rooted in their own experiences and interests than any other group in the sample (see Table 13–2). The boys of Conrad were not so distinct from other boys, nor so apt to eschew established models, but their projections were not among the most structured or adult-influenced on either measure. Boys from the two traditional schools were more likely to choose jobs that were socially defined and prestigious. Here, primarily, were the presidents, millionaires, and "owners of oil wells." It is interesting, and perhaps part of the same pattern, that projective themes of superlative success (CPST) came principally from children of Adams—a school with heavy achievement pressure and much recognition for virtuoso performance—though the number of children was small (7 out of 11) and the traditional nature of their particular homes was undoubtedly a factor.

In the orientation of the Conrad girls, two features were important: the quality of the images they did project and the nature of the images they did not. These girls saw their activities in the future as an extension of the things they cared about in the present: for example, a love of horses; a long-term fascination with ventriloquism; a sense of skill and enjoyment in music, painting, or "making up stories." At the same time, they did *not* see the future in terms of social pleasures or the wife and mother role. Such an orientation was more characteristic of girls from other groups. In imaginary stories (CPST), girls from traditional schools were more likely to project themes that were adolescent or adult in quality, revolving around romantic developments, marriage, babies, and social pleasures, though general comparisons between school groups were not statistically significant (see Table 13–2). In this instance, Dickens girls showed some affinity with those of Conrad.

Only the Conrad girls were consistent in their reactions, however. When we asked the children directly about the future, 20 girls, it will be remembered, were primarily oriented toward marriage, children, and the ideas and fantasies surrounding the wife and mother role. These girls were from the three public schools (Browning 4; Adams 7; Dickens 9). None were from Conrad.

Certainly, factors beyond the school influenced the primacy of the wife and mother role or the presence of an occupational orientation in plans for the future. Conrad mothers were relatively modern in their child-rearing philosophies and a higher percentage of Conrad mothers were working than in any other group. As will be noted in the following section, the philosophy of the home was an influential factor in shaping the orientation of the girls, and the mother, as a model, undoubtedly had some effect. But Conrad strongly supported any orientation in its children toward the recognition and development of their own skills, interests, and pleasures. Further, its view of curriculum brought both boys and girls into active contact with the community and with the working roles of adults. It seems likely that this kind of school experience influenced the individualized perception of the future and the orientation of girls as well as boys toward occupational roles.

Relationships to Home Background

We did not test the relation of home background to recall of the past, since the children's material about the past was not systematically analyzed, but we found family factors to be related to the children's ideas about the future. The pattern of association was different for boys and girls. To the extent that boys' occupational choices were related to home background, they seemed to reflect the socio-economic status of the home and the stability of the mother in her maternal role; girls' choices and attitudes, however, reflected principally the modern or traditional orientation of the mother.

In part, children patterned their future plans directly after the occupations of their parents, but this was true of only about one fourth of the children. Fifteen of 54 boys (28 percent) chose their father's occupations and ten of 45 girls (22 percent) chose occupations their mothers were currently or previously engaged in.[5] Identification with specific parent occupations was not universal even among children oriented toward the acceptance of prestructured models; they seemed to choose on the basis of a general model and an occupational level more than by literal imitation of their parents.

By the same token, girls did not pattern their choice of domestic or occupational roles directly on the working status of their own mothers. It cannot be an irrelevant fact, of course, that more Conrad mothers were working than those of any other group (Adams and Dickens less than 30 percent; Browning 33 percent; Conrad 58 percent) and that their daughters were consistently oriented toward occupational choices. Yet the fact of whether the mother worked or stayed at home was not in itself the crucial determinant.[6] Much more decisive was the modern or traditional orientation of the mother.[7] Girls from modern homes (15 of 17) were apt to see themselves in future occupations, with little tendency to highlight a domestic role, while girls from traditional homes were more oriented toward the wife and mother role.

The child-rearing orientation of the homes was, in fact, consistently related to girls' views of the future—not only whether their vision included an occupation, but whether the images of possible and desirable occupations had continuity with their current lives (see Appendix CC, Table 6). To some extent, these two aspects were associated by logic and the coding rationale. We considered the choice of marriage and family, as sole vision of the future or "best job," to be a discontinuous choice; a vision of a role that was established and waiting in the adult future. While it may have been part of current fantasy, it was, by definition, neither childlike in orientation nor related to the development of current interests and experiences. Continuity with current interests was more evident in the ideas of girls who talked about the work they might do, though in some cases such plans were standardized and also remote from child life. It is evident from Appendix CC, Table 6 that a modern maternal orientation toward child rearing, the encouragement of individuality, and so on, was consistently related to an individualized and child-relevant view of the future and of desirable jobs on the part of the girl. A traditional and more standardized orientation on the part of the mother was associated with child attitudes that gave prominence to domestic, socially prescribed female roles and to standardized occupations.

For boys, the modern-traditional orientation of the home was not associated with the nature of their occupational ideas. As indicated earlier in the chapter, the orientation of boys toward childhood or the future was related in part to the modern or traditional attitudes of their homes. However, the *content* of their future plans seemed to reflect other factors. The more standardized and prestigious occupations were chosen by boys from homes where socio-economic status was high and where mothers were most resolved and consistent in their roles. Perhaps this can best be understood if we consider that fathers in such homes were apt to be powerful models of success and prestige for the boy, while mothers resolved in their maternal roles supported the strength of the influential father. The prestigious occupational choices of the boys, in other words, may have been more a function of privileged surroundings and particular parental models than of socialization patterns that stressed prestructured roles, though the two are by no means mutually exclusive.

We cannot unravel the complexities in these data with any certainty. In general it may be said, however, that the children's projections into the future were affected by family patterns and that boys and girls were affected by different aspects of parental attitude and role.

Summary and Discussion

Life-stage orientation appeared important as an aspect of psychological organization. In addition, it was evident that imagery and perspective concerning life stages required assessment in this study, since traditional and modern environments socialized their children differentially in this respect. Traditional environments were training children more actively toward established roles and effectiveness in the future while modern environments were stressing the depth and meaning of ongoing experience. Certainly traditional and modern schools differed not only in their implicit values concerning child and adult status but in the explicit organization of curriculum and learning: in one situation, the child was primarily to accumulate the knowledge he would later need; in the other, he was to experience the processes and the impact that accompany personally meaningful learning.

In the data we obtained, children of the most modern school presented a unique pattern. In almost all the situations tapping life-stage values and images, Conrad children reacted differently from the children of other schools, and they generally typified the pattern predicted for children from modern environments. They were most consistently invested in their current life stage, least apt to carry an adult orientation into wish-fulfilling situations, most apt to project a future image developed from the realities of current interests and experiences. Girls in particular were consistent and distinctive, personifying the reactions expected of children from modern environments.

If we look at the total group of nine-year-olds, this was not the prevailing pattern. Many children saw the future as the time of fulfillment and built their future images around established and successful adult models. Such reactions supported the idea that the middle-class culture socializes toward delayed gratification—toward a sense that the present serves the future and that the future is the time of arrival and serious living. It would be too gross a generalization, however, to describe this sample of children as consistently oriented toward the future. Positive evaluation of the future fluctuated somewhat in many of the children; almost none of these nine-year-olds yearned to be grown up all the time. In addition, imagery and perspective varied with the sex of the child and the nature of the background.

As has been the case with much of our material, boys and girls were somewhat different in orientation. Their view of future roles differed in content and more of the girls were spontaneously drawn to the future than the boys were. Clearly the panorama of future possibilities took different form for boys and girls. Social reality has it that males are most palpably understood in their occupational roles. Though these nine-year-old boys obviously saw adult males as fathers and husbands in their own homes, they understood the question of what they themselves would be or do almost exclusively as an occupational question. Though they differed in the interest and importance they attached to future plans and in the basic determinants for their choices, their reactions were always centered around working roles.

For girls, the question of what one might be or do posed a prior level of decision: whether the future revolved primarily around a general social sex role, with established functions as wife and mother, or primarily around an occupational role. Our data suggest that the girls most drawn to the future were those for whom teen-age and adult fantasies took the former direction. These girls—approximately half of the female study sample—looked to the future as a time of pleasure, fulfillment, and excitement. Teen-age romance, dating, and conventional adult female roles seemed an active and spontaneous part of their inner life, determining their choice of the best life stage, appearing as a theme in their creative stories, providing the central imagery of their ideas about the future. Though some boys were certainly invested in the future and its meanings of power, independence, and success, no single theme among boys had this much appeal—perhaps because the images projected by this group of girls raised no questions of responsibility or competence.

In summarizing the material of boys and girls, however, it should be noted that they did not differ in all respects. Among boys and girls both, there were children who concentrated on the present and those who looked to the future; children who spun wishes and spent money in playful, childlike fashion and others who were more provident and adultlike; children who projected the future as an organic extension of the present and others who saw the future as a very separate stage, with roles and functions to be arrived at. Where there were sex-linked trends and modal patterns, it was generally true that Conrad girls (and/or girls from modern homes) were less apt than some girls to spontaneously invoke the future and more apt to consider the future, when invoked by others, as a time of occupational choice.

The effect of modern and traditional environments seemed quite consistent, in some respects, and applied to both sexes, even if most clearly to girls. A high evaluation of childhood and a tendency to respond in childlike ways were associated, as noted, with the most modern school, and there was some indication that more modern homes were associated with these phenomena as well.

When we focused on the image of the future, the associations appeared more complex, with different patterns for boys and girls. For girls, reaction patterns were consistent with predictions. Out of more traditional backgrounds, girls seemed to feel, "I will arrive at something exciting, waiting for me, that I can look at now and think about"; out of the more modern backgrounds, they seemed to feel, "I am a person with certain interests and I will be extending my *self* into the future."

Among boys, the viewpoint was not so clear and the predicted modern-traditional effects not so consistent. There was some suggestion that more boys from traditional schools projected the future in terms discontinuous with present experience, but the extent to which their orientation was determined by the home and due to factors that were not ideological is hard to determine. The socio-economic status of the home and the mother's role in relation to her son both appeared influential.

It is more difficult to evaluate the responses of the boys in terms of our selected dimensions than those of the girls. Boys who wished to be train engineers and boys who wished to be surgeons may have been expressing many factors beyond their sense of themselves and its implications for their future. The relationship to socio-economic level suggests that the image of a successful professional father reinforced by a mother coherent in her maternal role may have had power in determining discontinuous and prestigious choices, apart from the modern or traditional orientation of the home. This might be especially influential for boys, for whom the eventual reality of an occupational choice is necessary and not optional, as in the case of girls. Whether or not that future is invested with energy and strong meaning at the age of nine, however, does seem to be a matter of life-stage perspective, involving a difference between "moral futurism" and experiential investment, and this aspect was related more clearly to modern and traditional environments.

As an overview of the findings reported in this chapter, it seems possible to conclude that the predictions concerning modern and traditional effects received considerable support. Though we found no consistent trends concerning the past, other aspects were related to the socializing philosophy of the child's background.

The difference between children of Conrad and Dickens raises a problem and can only be understood in the context of both home and school differences. Families of Dickens children, as often noted, were more traditional than those of Conrad. It is also true, however, that Dickens did not offer as much in its curriculum, adult models, or understanding of individual development to counteract the prevailing orientation of the middle-class culture surrounding the children. Conrad children seemed to reflect a different pattern of influence, comprising both the qualitative features of their school and the consonance of their home and school backgrounds.

NOTES

1. LeShan's findings appeared to support this hypothesis; subsequent re-analysis of the data by Greene and Roberts (1961), however, shows that the findings do not necessarily support the hypothesis.
2. Material from parent interviews, reported in Chapter 5, illustrates this contrast in modern and traditional viewpoints.
3. Sixty-seven children were asked this question.
4. Correlations were not calculated for material that was not systematically coded or for measures with limited distribution in response (for example, fame and success themes).
5. Statistical analysis concerning parent occupations or mother's work status are not presented in tables. Relevant figures are included in the text or footnotes.
6. Mothers' work status versus girls' choice of wife-mother or occupational roles: $\chi^2 = 1.50$ NS.
7. MTO versus girls' choice of wife-mother or occupational roles: $\chi^2 = 11.88$; $p < .01$.

C H A P T E R

14

SEX ROLE AND
SEX TYPING

Sex role identification has been historically the most thoroughly studied aspect of self-image and development. Since the early 1900's, psychologists have been intensely concerned with the dynamic bases for sex role formation. They have been interested in understanding conflict and aberration, in tracing the processes of identification for male and female, and in clarifying the course of normal development.[1] Research psychologists in the area of child development have been particularly diligent in documenting the points at which children firmly perceive their own sex identity, orient their behavior and attitudes to sex-linked objects and ideas, begin to experiment heterosexually, and so on.[2]

Against the background of this accumulated knowledge, we were able to approach the children of our study with some orientation toward areas that might show the effects of their different experiences. We did not expect them to vary in basic awareness of their sex identity. By the age of nine, only seriously disturbed children are in doubt about whether they are boys or girls, and no philosophical differences in child rearing or education would be expected to affect the normal child's grasp of this realistic fact. But the conception of roles—and the values, attitudes, and reactions associated with such roles—constitute a different psychological and cognitive level (see Kohlberg, 1966). These are logically more influenced by environmental values and models; they vary among normal children, and we expected group differences in these areas.

The traditional and modern schools and homes of the study taught and raised their children within different frameworks; they conveyed different values and followed some specifically different practices.[3] Traditional homes and schools emphasized clear delineation of roles, acceptable behavior, appropriate attitudes, and probable futures; the images of male and female roles tended to be dichotomous. The modern schools and homes presented a less polarized viewpoint. There was greater similarity in the relations of adults to boys and girls, and there were less dichotomous, sex-typed expectations concerning children's interests, abilities, and personality characteristics. Modern homes and schools expected angry feelings in girls as well as boys and dependent feelings in boys as well as girls; boys as well as girls were exposed to cooking and girls as well as boys to carpentry. The underlying forces that led to these distinct viewpoints and practices have already been delineated and do not need repeating here. It is clear, however, that we were investigating the effects of influence factors that might well be expected to shape aspects of sex role development in different ways.

Our general expectation in this area, as stated in the hypotheses of the study, was that traditional school children would perceive more clearly defined boundaries between masculine and feminine social sex roles than modern school children and would relate differently to these roles. More specifically, we expected that traditionally educated children would express more conventional sex role concepts, would commit themselves unequivocally to the superior value of their own roles, and project more sex-typed life themes than children from more modern backgrounds. By virtue of the complexity and flux concerning women's roles in modern-oriented environments, we also expected that girls from such environments would have more difficulty in developing a coherent feminine social sex role image than girls from traditional backgrounds. No specific prediction was formulated concerning the expressed feelings of boys and girls toward each other; by the nature of the relationships and work-oriented cooperation fostered more actively by modern than traditional schools, however, we explored the possibility that boys and girls from modern schools would be more accepting and positive toward each other than boys and girls of the traditional schools.

In the data to be presented in this chapter, we found evidence to support the basic predictions. Though many children shared sex role allegiances, conceptions, and themes sanctioned by the general culture, the more open and less stereotyped patterns appeared among children from more modern backgrounds. Differences in pattern depended on the level and form of reactions, however, and applied to some subgroups more than others. School differences were found at the level of role concept and preference rather than in basic indicators of sex identity or at the deep personality levels tapped by play and fantasy. It was particularly among the girls of Conrad that nonconventional reactions appeared consistently. Furthermore, particular attention must be paid to home background factors. Though the comparison among school groups constitutes the major focus of the study, emergent findings indicated some systematic connections between home background and certain of the variables investigated in this chapter.

The material in this chapter is presented in two sections: Sex Role Allegiance and Concepts, and Sex Typical Thema.

Sex Role Allegiance and Concepts

This section deals with three interrelated aspects of sex role formation: Sex Membership and Allegiance, Sex Role Concepts, and Attitudes to Children of the Opposite Sex. Predictions of school group differences centered on the first two aspects.

SEX MEMBERSHIP AND ALLEGIANCE

We assumed that most children of this age would have a firm sense of sex membership—a clear, conscious identity as boy or girl. The measures we employed tapped primarily the assertion of allegiance to one's own sex role as preferable and advantageous.

Techniques and Measures

Direct statements of the child's sex role allegiance were obtained from the interview and the Stick Figure Scale. A projective measure of self-sex emphasis was derived from Figure Drawings.

(i) **Interview Question: Best Sex.** The child was asked whether it was "best to be a boy or a girl." Responses were coded according to whether the child indicated his own or the opposite sex.

(ii) Stick Figure Scale: Own-Sex Preference (Item 8).

"Here's a boy (girl) who thinks boys have the most fun and the best life."	Versus	"Here's a boy (girl) who thinks girls have the most fun and the best life."

"Which one is more like you?"

Responses were coded on a three-point scale:

    1—opposite sex choice
    2—middle, open choice
    3—own sex choice

The measures from these two techniques reflect the child's direct handling of an open comparison of roles—the evaluation he publicly wished to stand by.

(iii) Figure Drawings: Emphasis on Self-Sex Figure. The child was asked to draw a person and then a person of the opposite sex. The drawings were rated on a five-point scale (see below) after comparative evaluation of the two figures on such dimensions as relative size; relative centrality on page; front or profile view; relative force of line; amount of detail, movement; presence of sex characteristics; order of drawing.

    1—figure of opposite sex clearly emphasized
    2—
    3—equal treatment of the two figures
    4—
    5—figure of own sex clearly emphasized

The child's own standard in his drawings was used as baseline. Though a boy's figure of a boy might be small, wispy, and without much detail in comparison to other drawings in the group, he received a rating of four or five if the female figure was yet smaller, vaguer, and less delineated. The measure was not geared to general strength of presentation (as it is in the self-concept measures presented in Chapter 12), but to the relative salience given to the figure of the child's own sex.

INTERCORRELATIONS AMONG MEASURES

No correlations were calculated for interview responses because of the limited spread, but correlations between responses to the Stick Figure Scale and Figure Drawings were approximately zero (see Appendix BB, Table 6).

Group Characteristics and Sex Differences

Given a verbal choice of preferable role (interview and Stick Figure Scale), the prevailing trend among the children was clear: most of these children thought their own sex had "the most fun and the best life" and that it was, in all, better to be of their own sex. In this, the allegiance of the boys was stronger and more assertive than the girls.

This kind of response was particularly clear as a reaction to the direct interview question concerning the best sex. Eighty-five percent of the children chose their own sex as "best," though five, all girls, chose the opposite sex, and a few were uncertain or did not respond.[4]

Responses to the Stick Figure Scale showed the same prevailing trend but were more varied. Most children (61 percent) again chose their own sex as having the more rewarding life, and only 12 chose the opposite sex. The sex difference was pronounced (see Table 14-1), with boys more

TABLE 14-1

Sex Membership and Allegiance

MEASURE Source, and Scale Range	(N)	Sex §	Browning	Adams	Dickens	Conrad	Total	Analysis of Variance
			Mean Scores for School Groups					
OWN SEX PREFERENCE		b	2.78	2.50	2.75	2.63	2.64	Schools: .73 NS
SFS Item 8		g	2.50	2.31	2.36	2.17	2.32	Sex: 5.37*
Scale Range: 1–3	(102)	T	2.65	2.41	2.57	2.43	2.49	Schools × Sex: .07 NS
EMPHASIS ON SELF-SEX FIGURE		b	3.11	3.07	3.42	2.93	3.12	Schools: 1.00 NS
Figure Drawings		g	4.00	3.44	3.92	3.20	3.60	Sex: 3.47 NS
Scale Range: 1–5	(95)	T	3.50	3.26	3.67	3.04	3.35	Schools × Sex: .27 NS

* $p < .05$
§ b = boys
　g = girls
　T = total

consistently committed to the advantages of their own sex and girls predominantly responsible for asserting that the opposite sex had greater advantages (9 of 12). It is important to note that approximately one fourth (28) of the children did not state a clear allegiance to either sex. Responses from these children were sometimes the expression of uncertainty, but they appeared more often as the expression of a relatively complex perspective on the question—"each has advantages," "both have fun," "can't choose because I've never been a girl," and so on—and were qualitatively different, both in attitude and thinking style, from a stated choice for one sex or the other. Aside from these responses, however, the general trend of the data at verbal, attitudinal levels substantiates the findings of other research (see Brown, 1956; Hartley, 1964; Lynn, 1959; Rabban, 1950), which has also noted the prevalence of allegiance to one's own role, by this age, and the stronger expressed commitment of boys.

Drawings present a somewhat different pattern. Some elements of the male and female drawings suggested an emphasis on the child's own sex:

almost all children drew the figure of their own sex first, most drew the same-sex figure larger, and only rarely did a child place the overall emphasis on the figure of the opposite sex. The order of drawing in particular probably points to a basic sense of sex membership; the first figure to issue forth was probably a clear statement of the *self*-image, with its attendant acceptance and affirmation of a particular sex identity. At the same time, however, a child's presentation of the male figure was often not different in total impact from that of the female figure. Almost half the children (48 percent) were judged as drawing the two figures with equivalent emphasis, creating a similar impact in terms of force, detail, perspective, and so on.

It seems probable that this projective, nonverbal technique called forth responses related to deep and not fully conscious imagery concerning body image and power. Relative power of parental figures, in each individual case, unresolved elements in the body image, and attraction to the opposite sex were probably intermingled in the projected figures with affirmation of the child's own sex membership. It seems unlikely that the drawings reflected much of the child's allegiance to the social aspects of his sex role. These aspects were more clearly tapped by the conscious, direct, and verbal responses of the children—responses more obviously shaped by social forces and the child's concept of social roles.

School Group Differences

We predicted modern-traditional school group differences in role allegiance. Sharp role distinctions and social pressure on the traditional school child were expected to shape a necessary affirmation of his own sex and its advantages, at least at verbal levels. In contrast, children from modern schools were expected to maintain more open and exploratory attitudes toward sex role advantages, with modern school girls least definite in allegiance to their own sex. The findings support these expectations in essence, though they must be seen against the background of the prevailing tendency to assert the value of one's own sex role.

There was little variation in response when the children were asked where it was "best to be a boy or a girl." Presented thus baldly, the question seemed to mobilize all that was basically established in sex identity and all the potential in-group loyalty that characterizes the developmental stage. Most children said, in effect, "What I am is best," and there were no differences among school groups.

Drawings of male and female figures likewise showed no group differences (see Table 14–1). Many children, it will be remembered, drew the two figures with equal emphasis. While the children of the most modern school ranked lowest in emphasis on the self-sex figure, differences among groups were not statistically significant. It is most safely assumed that the schools did not systematically affect the relatively deep images projected in figure drawings.

Children from modern and traditional schools reacted differently, however, when they responded to the Stick Figure Scale. Here they dealt with role advantages, as in the interview, but were apparently less challenged to automatic role allegiance than on the direct interview question; there was greater variation in response and the variation was associated with school background.

It will be noted from Table 14–1 that the groups were not different on the basic statistical comparison, where allegiance to the opposite sex, open allegiance, and allegiance to one's own sex were treated as a continuous scale. There is no evidence, in other words, that children from modern schools were more committed to opposite sex roles while children from traditional schools were more committed to their own sex role. There is a qualitative difference in meaning, however, between the direct assertion that the *opposite* sex has the best life and an attitude of open, reserved evaluation concerning the advantages of the two roles. Eliminating the 12 children who directly favored the opposite role, differences between modern and traditional school groups become systematic in the predicted direction (see Table 14–2).[5] Children from traditional schools committed

TABLE 14–2

Choice of "Best Sex"
According to Modern and Traditional School Grouping (SFS Item 8)[1]

	Number of Traditional School Children (Browning + Adams)	Number of Modern School Children (Dickens + Conrad)	Total	
Open Choice	8 (b:5 g:3)	20 (b:9 g:11)	28	$x^2 = 4.34$
Own-Sex Choice	34 (b:19 g:15)	28 (b:19 g:9)	62	$p < .05$
Total	42	48	90	

1. The 12 children who favored opposite-sex roles are not included in this table.
b = boys
g = girls

themselves more consistently to the clear advantages of their own sex; most of the more open, relativistic responses were accounted for by modern school children. The girls of Conrad and Dickens, in particular, typified this stance. In this finding, there is probably a reflection both of thinking style as fostered by the schools—assertive and committed versus questioning and exploratory—and of distinct attitudes toward the boundaries and content of social sex roles.

The systematic distinction between school groups, then, did not include a direct allegiance to the opposite sex role or a direct negation of one's own position. It involved, rather, a distinction between an unequivocal allegiance to the advantages of one's own role and a more open evaluation of roles. As noted earlier, the more open stance seemed at times an expression of uncertainty and at times an expression of the capacity to see ideas from different perspectives and in flexible terms; in some instances it may have been both.

In summary, the children of this study seemed well established in their sense of sex membership and, for the most part, allegiance to their own sex role was strong. This allegiance was clearest at the level of verbal attitudes and was more characteristic of boys. An open stance toward sex role advantages was more characteristic of girls, particularly those from modern schools. A stated preference for opposite sex roles was rare and not systematically related to either modern or traditional backgrounds.

SEX ROLE CONCEPTS

Material presented in this section describes the sex role concepts that had accrued to the idea of maleness and femaleness for these children. Such concepts are presumably based on the models and teachings of the child's environment and form part of the substructure for feelings, attitudes, and role allegiance. We expected that the more conventional concepts of male and female roles and qualities would be expressed more consistently by traditional school children.

Relevant data included material obtained spontaneously from a portion of the children and amenable only to inspection, as well as material that had been systematically gathered and analyzed. Presentation of the findings is therefore in summary form.

Techniques

Sources of data are as follows:

    (i) **Interview:**
      (a) Reasons given for whether it was best to be a boy or girl.
      (b) Responses to questions about adult life and future plans.
    (ii) **Stick Figure Scale:** Spontaneous reasons given for choice of sex having "the most fun and best life."
    (iii) **CPST:** Stories involving themes of adolescent or adult social sex roles.

Group Characteristics and Sex Differences

Not all the children provided concrete images to support their statements of role advantages. Some were simply reiterative—"I'm glad to be what I am"—and some were either evasive or wise—"I don't know what it's like to be a boy"; "I don't think either a boy or girl is better. Both couldn't live without the other"; "If my mother were a boy perhaps I'd say boy."

The majority of the children, however, offered a roster of advantages to support the idea that it was best to be of their own sex (interview and Stick Figure Scale). Boys talked primarily about relative strength, prowess, competence, and courage—the sex-typed masculine ideal valued by the culture at large. They noted that boys are stronger, smarter, have more interesting things to play with, are better in sports, can go into the army and become heroes. Girls, as a group, valued different things. They noted that girls can wear prettier and more varied clothing, that they're "nicer" and better behaved, that they have more enjoyable things to play with, and that they can have children.

Projections into the future (interview, Children's Picture Story Test) carried some of these same qualities but extended to more concrete and role-oriented aspects relevant to the perceived lives of adult men and women (see also Chapter 13). Boys, again, stressed independence, power, and competence along lines similar to the image of current advantages but extended to include the feeling of having "arrived." As adult males, they expected to be powerful and effective because they would know a great deal, be physically mature, no longer be controlled by more powerful authorities. It is interesting that they projected little or none of the husband and father role, nor even of adolescent dating. Boys did not ascribe the advantages of their sex to these aspects and offered very few themes of love and marriage. We would assume that the sexual role is vital, at latent levels, through all of development, but for these middle-years boys, sex, courtship, love, marriage, and children were nowhere apparent in their expressed fantasies and did not define the meaning of "maleness" in any prominent way.

The occupational role, however, was a central and accepted part of the adult male definition for boys, though the image of man as worker was only indirectly connected with pleasure and advantage. The chance at certain working roles was not offered as pleasurable in itself—less so in these children perhaps than in three- and four-year-olds, who act out the doctor, policeman, fireman, or bus driver with some pleasure in the details of the role play. For many of these nine-year-olds, it was the heroic and powerful feelings and the status to which one's work might lead that seemed predominant in their fantasies. In this privileged group of boys, plans and fantasies tended often, though not always, toward occupations that carried social status and power and which lay realistically within their reach.

Among the girls, concepts and plans were different. For approximately half the girls, fantasies about the future centered on dating, love, marriage, children. Girls dealt significantly more with such themes in their spontaneous stories and talked more in such terms when they projected into the future.[6] For some girls the advantages of being female lay in the anticipated pleasures of romantic courtship and dating, the deference and protection accorded adult women, and the enjoyment of children. Included in their projections was a concomitant definition of the desirable male—a wish that their husbands be good breadwinners, steady in their jobs, good looking, and so on, as part of the fulfillment of their own future fantasies. Among the boys, there was no concept of female adults in relation to themselves as adult males.

In accord with this role concept and fantasy, the qualities valued and noted by some girls for their adult selves centered on forms of attractiveness. Even those girls for whom the dating and marriage themes were not salient did not project a female image in terms of power and independence, as boys did, but some projected a role that, like the boys, included work and an occupation for themselves.

The girls of this sample divided approximately in half between those who personified the prevailing concept of the wife and mother adult role and those who did not. Since the school background factors relate systematically to these two groups, it is most useful to discuss them in the following section.

School Group Differences

There was evidence that concepts of maleness and femaleness, and what accrues to the social sex role of each, were developing along somewhat different lines for children of modern and traditional schools, though there was certainly overlap among groups in many aspects of role conception. It was particularly in relation to the *female* role that different backgrounds seemed to influence different concepts and values. Assignment of conventional qualities and roles to the female came primarily from traditional school children, whose attitudes were expressed in relation to that traditional image.

Spontaneous comments did not always accompany role choices (interview and Stick Figure Scale), and not all children gave reasons for their choices even when questioned, but it is notable that among the children who gave such material, only girls from traditional schools projected the female image in terms of prettiness, daintiness, beautiful clothing, and so on, and only boys from such backgrounds based their rejection of the female role on a concept that the lives of girls and women are dull and uninteresting.

It is probably part of this same constellation, seen from a different angle, that girls from modern schools presented an unusual pattern of substantiation for their role preferences. For the total sample of children, positive reasons, specifying the advantages and pleasures of their own sex, were offered twice as often as negative reasons, which specified distaste or disapproval of the opposite sex. Girls from Conrad in particular, however, tended to describe the *disadvantages* of the *opposite* sex in support of their same-sex role preferences rather than directly offering positive reasons. While these girls had not incorporated the prevailing cultural stereotypes of the female image and role, they had not developed, at least by age nine, alternative images that were clear and specific.

Projections into the future (interview, Children's Picture Story Test) showed similar trends. Girls who stressed the wife and mother role, when asked what they thought their future would be like (see Chapter 13), all came from the three public schools; none were from the Conrad group. Projective themes (Children's Picture Story Test) stressing adolescent and adult social sex roles—romantic stories, fantasies of sexual or married relationships, babies born, and so on—appeared mostly in the stories of girls from traditional schools (though school differences were only suggestive). And in projecting ahead to future occupations, children from traditional schools tended to focus on relatively conventional roles, discrete from their current experience and interests, while children from the most modern school envisioned roles more related to their current interest patterns, more experiential, and less clearly part of societally prescribed roles and niches.

In general, then, culturally stereotyped role conceptions were more consistently typical of children from traditional schools. This was particularly evident in relation to the perception of female qualities and roles, as advanced by both boys and girls. Girls from Conrad were least apt to conceptualize and value the conventional female role or the qualities of personality and adornment associated with it.

ATTITUDES TO CHILDREN OF THE OPPOSITE SEX

It is an accepted fact that boys and girls of this age tend to establish separate peer groups, marked by some distance and mutual antagonism. This phenomenon is theoretically understood as a flight from sexuality and an attempt to solidify identity by intense in-group contact and unity. In assessing attitudes toward children of the opposite sex, we were interested in further exploration of role concepts and allegiance and in the possibility of school group differences. Though we did not predict such differences, it seemed possible that the relationships and shared work experiences fostered by Conrad, in particular, might modify feeling and acceptance between the sexes.

Techniques and Measures

(i) **Sentence Completion Test.** Two items on the Sentence Completion Test tapped the child's perception of the attitudes of one sex toward the other, as follows:

Item 9: *According to Donald, most girls . . .*
Item 11: *According to Ruthie, most boys . . .*

In one item, the child expressed the attitudes of his own sex to the opposite sex; in the other item, the child expressed his perception of the attitudes of the opposite sex to his own.[7] Two measures were derived from these items:

Affective attitude to opposite sex. Responses were rated on a three-point scale for positive or negative quality of affect to the opposite sex. (Rating of Item 9 for boys, Item 11 for girls.)

1—positive response (nice, smart, good friends)
2—neutral (like to play baseball, stick together, are different)
3—negative (silly, wild, ugly, stupid, selfish)

Projected attitude from opposite sex to own. Responses were rated on a three-point scale for the extent to which the child expected a positive or negative attitude from the opposite sex. (Rating of Item 11 for boys, Item 9 for girls.)

1—expectation of a positive or approving attitude
2—expectation of neutral attitude
3—expectation of a negative or disapproving attitude

The content of the responses was also inspected and is described below.

(ii) **Stick Figure Scale: Preferred Qualities in Opposite Sex.**

(for boys) "Here's a boy who likes the kind of girl who's a good athlete, strong, likes to play games." Versus "Here's a boy who likes the kind of girl who is sort of sweet, shy, and likes to dress up."

(for girls) "Here's a girl who likes the kind of boy who's a good athlete, strong, and likes to play games." Versus "Here's a girl who likes the kind of boy who is smart, likes to make things, and reads a lot."

"Which one is more like you?"

Responses were coded on a three-point scale:

1—less culturally stereotyped (strong athletic girl; smart reading boy)
2—middle choice
3—more culturally stereotyped (sweet shy girl; strong athletic boy)

(iii) **Sociometric Questions.** The children's responses were analyzed along two dimensions: the *number of children* making cross-sex choices and the *number of cross-sex choices* made.[8]

INTERCORRELATIONS AMONG MEASURES
Intercorrelations among measures of affect (Sentence Completion and Sociometric Questions) suggest a consistency in the attitudes and reactions of the girls, but not the boys (see Appendix BB, Table 6). Girls who expressed relatively positive attitudes toward boys also tended to make more cross-sex sociometric choices and to expect relatively positive attitudes from the boys. Given the negative tone of the prevailing attitudes, as described below, it is perhaps more pertinent to state that girls who expressed more negative attitudes toward boys also expected the feeling to be reciprocated and tended not to choose boys as companions in the situations described in the Sociometric Questions. The attitudes and reactions of the boys did not have this internal consistency.

Group Characteristics and Sex Differences

In expressing their opinions of the opposite sex (Sentence Completion Test), the children were generally negative and unflattering. At least half were clearly negative and only a relative handful had positive things to say. Critical opinions about the opposite sex were expressed more often by "Ruthie" than by "Donald" (girls: 66 percent negative; boys: 45 percent negative), though this difference was not statistically reliable.

The children talked about the opposite sex with the simple and expressive directness that marked them as middle-years latency children: fresh, sloppy, silly, jealous, idiots, jerks, horrid, dopes, stink, and so on. While some comments were sheer invective, others contained elements that reflected familiar sex-associated perceptions (girls as "silly" and "jealous"; boys as "fresh" and "sloppy"). Other data, obtained from interview and Stick Figure Scale, bore out these perceptions, with boys describing girls as sissies, scared of mice, silly and talkative, poor in athletics, while girls described boys as bullies or as wild and fresh.

When the children were forced to choose the kind of opposite sex child they liked best (Stick Figure Scale), the boys, in particular, rejected the sweet, shy, clothes-conscious girl and chose the girl described as strong and athletic—a girl competent in ways they valued in themselves rather than one characterized by the qualities they had attributed to girls and spontaneously rejected.

In these data there is the suggestion of a "reverse" image. The pleasure the boys expressed in idealized strength and prowess for themselves had a negative counterpart in the girls' rejection of roughness and bullying in boys; while the girls' pleasure in feminine daintiness and attractiveness had its negative counterpart in the boys' rejection of adornment and reticence. It is probably true that the very things many of these children would come to find attractive in the opposite sex at adolescence—male strength and assertiveness, female gentleness and beauty—were dull or frightening at this younger stage and cause for negative attitudes on both sides.

When the children speculated about the opinions of the opposite sex toward their own, boys and girls had quite different expectations (see Table 14–3). Most of the boys (53 percent) expected "Ruthie" to think

TABLE 14–3

Attitudes to Children of the Opposite Sex

MEASURE Source, and Scale Range	(N)	Sex §	Browning	Adams	Dickens	Conrad	Total	Analysis of Variance
Mean Scores for School Groups								
AFFECTIVE ATTITUDE TO OPPOSITE SEX Sentence Completion Item 9 for boys, 11 for girls Scale Range: 1–3 (positive → negative)		b	1.67	2.17	2.08	2.38	2.13	Schools: 1.59 NS Sex: 2.46 NS Schools × Sex: .04 NS
		g	2.14	2.21	2.58	2.55	2.39	
	(99)	T	1.88	2.19	2.33	2.44	2.24	
PROJECTED ATTITUDE FROM OPPOSITE SEX TO OWN Sentence Completion Item 11 for boys, 9 for girls Scale Range: 1–3 (positive → negative)		b	1.67	1.72	1.58	1.81	1.71	Schools: .45 NS Sex: 14.55** Schools × Sex: .30 NS
		g	2.14	2.36	2.50	2.55	2.41	
	(99)	T	1.88	2.00	2.04	2.11	2.02	
PREFERRED QUALITIES IN OPPOSITE SEX SFS Item 9 Scale Range: 1–3 (→ cultural stereotype)		b	1.89	2.12	1.55	1.19	1.68	Schools: 3.20* Sex: 13.00** Schools × Sex: 1.40 NS
		g	2.50	2.38	1.92	2.25	2.25	
	(101)	T	2.18	2.24	1.74	1.64	1.95	

* $p < .05$
** $p < .01$
§ b = boys
  g = girls
  T = total

well of boys, but the majority of the girls (61 percent) expected "Donald" to be critical and rejecting of girls. Judging from these two sets of responses, the boys seemed to be saying, "We don't like you so much but we think you like us," while the girls were saying, "We don't like you and you don't like us."

Mutually derogatory opinions between boys and girls of this age are a relatively familiar phenomenon. The difference between what boys and girls expected from each other, however, is more noteworthy and is consistent with other data in the study. It is reminiscent of the boys' attitude when asked to evaluate themselves on items of the Stick Figure Scale; in that instance, they were more assertive than girls in general and far more confident of peer acceptance (see Chapter 12). To the extent that they actually felt more sure of acceptance, it seems possible that they were becoming aware of their ascendant position in society and that they felt their growing male prowess to be a value, while the girls could not yet expect their feminine qualities to be valued as such by boys.

The Sociometric Questions, in response to which children could choose companions from either sex, provide supplementary data which generally support these findings. Children overwhelmingly chose members of their own sex. About half the children never chose a child of the opposite sex for any activity, and the frequency of such choices was very low even among those who did. To the extent that sociometric choices can be considered a behavioral validation of attitudes, there was some support for the boys' expectation that they would be approved of and for the girls' expectation that they would not, though the actual discrepancy expressed in the sociometric choices (75:60) was less striking than the difference in the expectation of cross-sex acceptance expressed by boys and girls (Sentence Completion Test). It is interesting that the girls were somewhat more willing to reach out and name boys as companions even though their expressed affect on the Sentence Completion Test was somewhat more negative. Relatively unsure of acceptance, their assertion of negative feelings toward boys may have had some defensive and retaliatory components.

School Group Differences

We considered it possible that the atmosphere of the modern schools, particularly Conrad, might modify the feeling of boys and girls toward each other; that these children might express more positive feelings and more openly accept children of the opposite sex than their counterparts from traditional schools. The data do not support that idea.

There were no clear differences in boy-girl attitudes among the various school groups (see Table 14–3). To the extent that any difference was suggested, negative attitudes were most direct and outspoken in Conrad and least so in Browning. The choice of companions on the Sociometric questions strengthens this impression of the Conrad group, though Sociometric data, unevenly obtained from the several schools, can only be supplementary. Although half the children of the sample never chose companions from the opposite sex, the children of Conrad in particular seemed involved in an implicit boycott. They were the only group in which no child crossed sex lines to choose a companion from the class. The greatest contrast to the Conrad pattern occurred in Adams, where more than half the children crossed sex lines at least once. In this group a relatively sophisticated, semi-adolescent attitude was more evident. Reflecting more than the other schools a current societal tendency to push adolescent patterns downward in age, attractions and "crushes" brought status for Adams children as well as teasing; this group expressed a mixture of middle-years attitudes and precocious adolescent interests.

We know that the atmosphere in the classroom was different in modern and traditional schools. Conrad boys and girls were often seen in joint productive work and amiable interchange. Their performance on the group problem-solving task (see Chapter 8) involved both boys and girls in a cooperative and constructive effort, in contrast to the Browning group, where in the same situation the exclusion of girls from central participation went unchallenged and perhaps unnoticed. We also know that social role concepts concerning male and female were different among modern and traditional school children, as described in the previous section, and these differences were seen again when the children were asked to choose the kind of opposite sex child they liked the best (Stick Figure Scale). Here the traditional school children were more drawn to general cultural stereotypes of personality and role. They valued the athletic young male and the sweet, shy girl more than children from modern schools did (see Table 14–3). Without exception, boys from the Conrad group chose girls who could be "pals" and rejected the decorative girl. It would follow logically to expect that the stage-typical psychological distance between boys and girls might be reduced for modern school children not only at the level of behavioral interaction but also in terms of affective attitudes and friendship choices, but this latter expectation was not fulfilled.

It seems possible that the most modern school may have reinforced this distance in certain ways. In an environment that presents relatively open and complex role definitions, the children may have been driven toward in-group intensity and out-group rejection, at least temporarily, as a way of clarifying the reference group within which to build identification and role imagery. Also, an atmosphere in which adults foster deep relationships and emphasize meaningful cooperative activity among children, regardless of sex, may have induced conflict and guilt over particularized attractions. Interview data suggested that such attractions were present even in these latency children and that these feelings were experienced with some shame. Perhaps the Conrad children felt a special need to deny and ward off such feelings.[9] Whether, in the long run, relationships between sexes would be modified toward greater empathy and acceptance by such an environment remains an open and interesting question.

In summary, negative and rejecting attitudes toward the opposite sex characterized both boys and girls. Boys, however, seemed relatively sure that they would be accepted by girls, while girls were less sure of acceptance and inclined to feel that negative attitudes were reciprocal. There was no evidence that school environments affected this pattern, even though interaction between sexes was qualitatively different in the classrooms and children from modern and traditional schools did differ in the attributes they valued in the opposite sex. It might be noted that the latter difference is similar in import to the role concept findings reported in the previous section, since culturally sex-typed images were valued more by children of the traditional schools.

Relationships to Home Background

The relationships established between the sex role variables presented in this section and home background factors (see Appendix CC, Table 7) do not appreciably alter the import of the findings already discussed. Correlations are neither numerous nor of a high statistical order, and the impact of home influence does not appear more evident, in general, than that of the school.

To the extent that associations are suggested, they are in different realms for girls and boys. For girls, the direction of association has some consistency: girls from families that were more traditional (and of lower socio-economic status) emphasized their own sex (Figure Drawings) and were more assertive about the advantages of their own role (Stick Figure Scale).[10] Those from more modern families with somewhat higher socio-economic status and a stronger tendency to encourage individualized development were less apt to stress the image of their own sex and appeared to hold more open attitudes toward the advantages of their own role. A similar association was established between modern or traditional school philosophy and these different reactions.

For boys, no association was evident between the orientation of their families and their own role allegiance. There was an association, however, between traditional family background and the expression of relatively positive attitudes toward girls. Perhaps the boys from modern families were either more freely expressive of negative feelings or were more insecure about their status and thus more critical of girls; perhaps the boys from traditional families were more benign in their expressions or actually felt less threatened.

Though correlations in this area are weak, the pattern and direction of association suggest that home and school influence may have interacted to reinforce certain attitudes and concepts of the children.

Sex Typical Themes

In searching for aspects of fantasy and personality formation that might further delineate the social sex role constellation, we went to deeper-level material in the data. For our purposes we focused primarily on the tendency toward sex-typed themes, as expressed through projective material, with particular attention to aggression, on the one hand, and family orientation and dependency, on the other. These particular foci stem from the general expectation—born of common lore, cultural values, and research findings—that aggression tends to be more typical of boys, dependency and family orientation more typical of girls (Kagan, 1964). In explaining these associations, theorists have regarded them as a partial function of intrinsic factors and as a more extensive function of cultural expectation and reinforcement. Our particular interest was in the incidence of these trends in children from modern and traditional schools and homes, since their patterns of expectation and reinforcement were distinct. The modern homes and schools were less bound by conventional cultural expectations than the traditional and considered a wider range of expression and exploratory behavior acceptable and normal for both boys and girls. We therefore expected that children from these backgrounds would be less consistently sex-typed in their fantasies and reactions than children from traditional backgrounds, and we turned to projective data to investigate the connection between sex-typed thema and background factors.

Techniques and Measures

Data were drawn from two projective techniques: the play session and the Children's Picture Story Test.

Aside from Sex-Typed Play, the measures reported in this section have been described previously (Chapters 9 and 10). All measures but Sex-Typed Play, therefore, are simply listed.

(i) **Play: Sex-Typed Play.** Play protocols were coded for whether or not the child's play was exclusively concerned with content considered typical for his sex. This included not only the aggressive and family-oriented themes noted above, but any content that could be considered conventionally characteristic of one sex or the other (for example, cowboy stories).

1—not exclusively own sex-typical play

2—exclusively own sex-typical play
(ii) **Play: Aggressive-Destructive Themes.**
(iii) **Play: Enactment of Family Life Themes.**
(iv) **CPST: Incidence of Parent Figures.**
(v) **CPST: Benevolence of Adult Attitudes and Behavior Toward Children.**

INTERCORRELATIONS AMONG MEASURES
Intercorrelations among these measures are relatively stable (see Appendix BB, Table 6). Some significant correlations, it should be noted, are a partial function of the definition of variables, since the tendency of boys to play aggressively, with little concentration on family-oriented play, contributed to a high rating of Sex-Typed Play, while the reverse pattern contributed to a high rating of Sex-Typed Play for girls. These variables are therefore correlated substantially for each sex, though the correlations are not extreme. Other significant correlations, however, reflect consistencies in the children, rather than by-products of the scoring scheme. As indicated in previous chapters, children concerned with family-oriented play did not highlight aggressive themes, and those who did highlight such themes did not place them in a family context. Further, the tendency to project adults benevolent in their attitudes to children was accompanied by a tendency to highlight parent figures, play out family experiences, and eschew a working out of aggressive or violent drama. Though intercorrelations are not of a high order, the emergence of statistical relationships among these measures lends weight to their use as separate but related indicators of sex-typical reactions.

Group Characteristics and Sex Differences[11]

Sex-typical themes were prevalent in the projective material of the children—a parallel at deeper levels to the previous findings, in which many children stated their preference for their own sex and its role, maintained a stance of same-sex cohesiveness in their loyalties and peer choices, and presented images and plans that ran along the lines of the general cultural format for male and female roles. In their play, boys played out stories of combat, of adventure and action, with boys as central characters. Girls played out stories of family life and interaction, in which girls were central characters. Some children developed play that had no sex-typed characteristics (sagas that evolved through stages of the hero's life, farm and animal play, city scenes, circus performances, trips to a variety of places, and so on), and these became important, of course, in our study of modern-traditional effects; the prevailing trend for the total sample, however, involved stories with identifiable, sex-linked characteristics.

Boys and girls differed from each other both in the *extent* to which play was sex typed and in the *content* of the themes that appeared in their play and projective stories. The incidence of Sex-Typed Play was significantly higher among boys than girls (see Table 14–4). Two thirds of the boys played out exclusively sex-typed themes, while the majority of the girls included some themes that were not clearly typical for their sex. There is,

TABLE 14–4

Sex-Typical Fantasies and Reactions

Measure Source, and Scale Range	(N)	Sex §	Mean Scores for School Groups					Analysis of Variance
			Browning	Adams	Dickens	Conrad	Total	
Sex-Typed Play Play Scale Range: 1–2		b	1.70	1.67	1.67	1.82	1.72	Schools: .63 NS Sex: 8.75** Schools × Sex: 1.69 NS
		g	1.63	1.38	1.58	1.25	1.44	
	(105)	T	1.67	1.53	1.63	1.59	1.59	
Aggressive-Destructive Themes Play Scale Range: 1–4		b	3.20	2.89	2.67	2.50	2.79	Schools: .25 NS Sex: 46.50** Schools × Sex: 1.13 NS
		g	1.25	1.56	1.42	1.58	1.48	
	(104)	T	2.33	2.26	2.04	2.11	2.18	
Enactment of Family Life Themes Play Scale Range: 1–4		b	1.80	1.72	1.42	1.63	1.64	Schools: 2.86* Sex: 48.00** Schools × Sex: 2.71*
		g	3.50	2.75	3.33	2.17	2.88	
	(104)	T	2.56	2.21	2.38	1.86	2.21	
Incidence of Parent Figures CPST Scale Range: 1–3		b	1.90	2.11	1.92	1.88	1.96	Schools: .24 NS Sex: .24 NS Schools × Sex: .73 NS
		g	2.13	1.81	2.17	1.92	1.97	
	(105)	T	2.00	1.97	2.04	1.90	1.97	
Benevolence of Adult Attitudes and Behavior Toward Children CPST Scale Range: 1–4		b	1.30	1.18	1.58	1.38	1.35	Schools: 3.70* Sex: 23.15** Schools × Sex: 1.91 NS
		g	2.38	1.93	2.75	1.55	2.13	
	(100)	T	1.78	1.52	2.17	1.44	1.70	

* $p < .05$
** $p < .01$
§ b = boys
  g = girls
  T = total

in this sex difference, a clear consistency with the attitudinal data, in which boys seemed to maintain a tighter, more committed stance toward their sex identity and role, while girls extended the boundaries and were more open, exploratory, equivocal.

In the thematic content of both Play and the Children's Picture Story

Test there were significant sex differences in the areas selected for special study: aggression and family orientation and dependency.

The incidence of aggressive-destructive themes in both play and projective stories was considerably higher among boys than girls (see Table 14–4). Boys selected aggressive figures more frequently as the carriers of their fantasies and acted out stories of battles and fighting as a modal theme. They projected more direct and violent aggression, more scenes of fighting and bodily harm, more defiance of authority, more situations where discipline was called for or invoked. Though girls in their stories allowed children to express divergent opinions to an adult, it was only among boys that the opposition of child figures was intense, forceful, and bent on victory. This distinct patterning of aggressive expression was certainly in keeping with sex-linked expectations. Whether it represented a basic difference in drive or an observable difference in what the children allowed themselves to express is another of our open questions.

Stories and play that revolved around family life and interaction were also more typical of one sex than the other (see Table 14–4). Girls far more than boys played out family drama, made up stories involving parents, and projected adults who were benevolent and protective in their attitudes toward children. Like the higher incidence of aggressive themes among boys, the higher incidence of these family-centered themes among girls follows general cultural expectations.

School Group Differences

We expected modern-traditional school group differences in the prevalence of sex-typed material but found no evidence of consistent group differences in the data (see Table 14–4).

A special pattern characterized the Conrad children, however. Boys and girls of this school contributed least to the general sex differences; that is, they were less sharply distinct from each other on the various measures of sex-typed themes (aggressive-destructive; primacy of family, and so on) than boys and girls from other schools. Furthermore, Conrad girls were again distinctive in their reactions and concerns. They did not play out the themes of family life nor emphasize benevolent adults as frequently as girls in other school groups. Their productions were wider ranging and less benign and they were, in general, the least sex-typical of all the groups.

Relationships to Home Background [12]

It was in relation to home and family factors that consistent and meaningful associations were established between modern or traditional orientation and sex-typical projections (see Appendix CC, Table 7). The children from traditional homes were more prone to play out themes considered relatively typical for their sex. The linkage is particularly clear for girls. Both the total pattern of sex typing in play and the particular syndrome of family-oriented fantasy shows such a relationship, though there is also some connection among the boys between traditional home backgrounds and the acting out of relatively aggressive play. Girls from modern homes were less likely to play in sex-typical ways or to highlight parental figures and family drama, and when they did, they did not characteristically project a world of benevolent and protective adults.

These relationships were substantiated in the study of 47 children from clearly modern and traditional homes (see Chapter 5). Boys from the most consistently traditional homes showed the highest incidence of aggressive play and differed both from the other group of boys and from girls of equally traditional background; boys and girls from modern homes did not differ significantly in aggressive expression.[13] The difference in these patterns probably reflects the more dichotomous attitude in traditional homes to what is acceptable behavior in boys as opposed to girls. Further, the girls from clearly modern homes were less preoccupied with family-oriented themes and were different from all other groups in the minimal quality of sex-typed concerns in their play.[14] The strong influence of modern homes on the development of these patterns in the middle-years girl seems apparent.

Other qualities in the mother, not part of her modern-traditional philosophy, also appeared effective, especially for girls. Relative dissatisfaction with the child and a low level of coherence in the mothering role relate to the child's projection of benevolent adults and parental figures (see Appendix CC, Table 7). As previously suggested (see Chapter 10), the child may here have been wishfully working through troublesome and unsatisfying aspects of her individual experience; in such cases, these reactions cannot be viewed as predominantly an expression of sex-typical modes. From the correlations with modern-traditional parent variables, however, it is apparent that these reactions were also a partial function of the parents' more general child-rearing attitudes and can be taken as part of a syndrome of sustained family orientation and dependence, typically associated with girls and most consistently evident in our sample among girls from traditional homes.

Summary and Discussion

The children of this study shared many perceptions, reaction patterns, and concepts concerning male and female roles. They had all been part of a general culture, after all, that shapes role perceptions with some uniformity, and they were all in a common developmental stage, with its established sense of sex identity, its strong loyalties to children of the same sex, and its antagonisms to those of the opposite sex. They did vary, however, in terms of role perceptions and attitudes, as a function of their sex and of the different subcultures represented by modern and traditional schools and homes.

There were recurrent sex differences, both in role conceptions and in the extent of commitment and sex typing. It was the boys who asserted a stronger allegiance to their sex role and its advantages and were more consistently sex-typed in their projected fantasies. Girls maintained a more open stance and showed more range in the content of their attitudes and fantasies. These differences confirm the findings reported in other studies (Brown, 1956; Rabban, 1950), which have noted the firmer and earlier commitment of boys, the lesser sex typing and commitment in girls. In the literature, these findings have been discussed in terms of the little girl's perception of male advantages, biological and cultural, and the somewhat greater permissiveness in the population at large for "tomboy" behavior in girls than "sissy" behavior in boys—both factors mediating less committed and more exploratory reactions in girls. There are other current theories that would lead to opposite expectations, primarily those that note the greater identification challenge for boys in the necessity to shift away from the earliest model, the mother, but research findings have tended consistently to find less role assertion and allegiance in girls, and our study clearly supports this finding.[15]

Our data also support the hypothesis, however, that variation in sex role concepts and sex typing is a partial function of the child's subculture—what we have here called a "modern" or "traditional" orientation toward the socialization and education of the child. While the association did not appear on all measures and the statistical order of association, where established, was generally fairly low, it is nonetheless impressive that from a variety of techniques, representing various levels and forms of behavior and a variety of measuring devices, the direction of association was almost invariably the same and was in keeping with predictions. The more committed attitudes and allegiance, the more conventional images, the more sex-linked themes, were most consistently characteristic of children from traditional backgrounds. Departures from these attitudes and conceptions, when they appeared, were generally found among children from modern backgrounds.

It is perhaps more correct to say that these departures principally characterized the *girls* from modern backgrounds, since our findings repeatedly single out the modern girls as relatively open in role evaluation, less resolved in their role conceptions, and least centered on sex-typical images and fantasies. The constellation of reactions in these girls is understandable, perhaps, if we consider several factors: in the culture at large, they were challenged by a sex membership and role valued less than that of the opposite sex; in their own life situations, the attitudes of adults tended to decrease sharp role definitions and to increase the possibilities for individualized integrations; in addition, female models in their environment were often themselves involved in complex and exploratory integrations.

In greatest contrast to these girls, it might be noted, were the boys from traditional backgrounds. In this study we may have identified the segment of middle-class boys who most clearly typify the unambiguous, sex-linked pattern of the young male, as discussed in other research. Role assertion, conventional imagery, and sex-typical reactions were most characteristic of boys who lived in traditional environments, where they were most consistently exposed to dichotomous roles and expectations, images of male advantage, and the necessity of committed choice.

In evaluating our data in any area, we have, of course, particular interest in understanding the influence of the school, or at least in better understanding the interaction of school and home as influencing forces. In the data reported in this chapter, school influence can best be delineated by noting that it was systematic at certain *levels* of reaction and that it appeared in certain *combinations* with home factors.

In terms of reaction levels, there is a pattern in the findings that has a psychological face validity. While the families seemed more systematically influential at levels of inner fantasy and personality organization (body image, thematic constellations of aggression and family orientation, and so on), the schools appeared influential at the level of public attitudes (stated role preferences, admired qualities, role images). Perhaps, at the attitudinal level, children are affected not only by the role-relevant influences in their environment, as discussed above, but by attitudes concerning thought and opinion and those concerning the relative value of committed assertive responses vis-à-vis more exploratory and questioning reactions. Perhaps, in this sense, the data in this area are similar to the data concerning self-image and differentiation (see Chapter 12); both sets of data reflect a style of thought and reaction fostered by modern and traditional schools, as well as a complex of attitudinal content, and in these data, school effects are noted.

There is also a suggestion that certain kinds of schools in combination with certain kinds of home affect child reactions. The special position of Conrad children is evident, even at levels of reaction where home factors were more influential for the total group. The girls of Conrad departed consistently from group patterns at every level; the boys and girls of this school contributed least to sex differences and presented more homogeneous patterns, though the boys were not as atypical as the girls. To some extent, the data from this school are confounded, since a large proportion of its children came from modern homes. It seems evident, however, that the congruence of home and school environments reinforces the experience of the child and co-determines much behavior, and in this combination of forces the particular quality of a school so clearly modern as Conrad seems a highly important factor. School and home are likely to be mutually reinforcing at other points in the modern-traditional continuum as well, however: the boy from a clearly traditional home finds reinforcement for his sex-typical patterns in the values and atmosphere of a clearly traditional school. The differentiated effects of congruent and incongruent home and school on this area of development, as on many others, requires further detailed study.

It might be noted in passing that some of the findings we report have been reported elsewhere and attributed to social-class differences. Sex-typical patterns have been found to be more characteristic of lower-class (and lower-middle-class) children, when middle- and lower-class samples were compared (Rabban, 1950), while sex-typical patterns in our relatively class-homogeneous sample were found to be more characteristic of children from traditional backgrounds. We did note an association, for girls only, between less sex-typical attitudes and homes of higher socioeconomic level, constituting a partial support for the trends described in other research, but the incidence of such correlations was very low. In our sample, the influential factors appeared to be principally psychological. These factors varied within environments that were essentially middle class and affected the extent of sex typing in the children.

NOTES

1. Bronfenbrenner, 1960; Brown, 1956; Emmerich, 1959; Gray and Klaus, 1956; Hartley, 1964; Hartup, 1962; Kagan, 1958; Lazowick, 1955; Lynn, 1959, 1962; Lynn and Sawrey, 1959; Mowrer, 1950; Mussen and Distler, 1959; Mussen and Rutherford, 1963; Sears, Maccoby, and Levin, 1957.

2. Brown, 1956; Hartley, 1964; Hartup and Zook, 1960; Kagan, 1964; Milton, 1957; Parsons, 1942; Pintler, Phillips, and Sears, 1946; Rabban, 1950; Rosenberg and Sutton-Smith, 1959; Sweeney, 1953; Terman and Miles, 1936.

3. We did not assess sex role attitudes of the schools and homes directly in this study, primarily because our understanding of the importance of the area grew with time. Since we did not, differences found among the children must be assigned to the *generally* distinct modern and traditional attitudes of schools and homes rather than specifically distinct attitudes toward sex role per se. Obviously, however, attitudes toward the socialization of sex roles are congruent with the general theories and attitudes held by socializing agents.

4. This question was administered to 87 children of the sample.

5. The nine girls making opposite-sex choices were from Adams (5), Conrad (3), and Browning (1) and the three boys were from Adams.

6. Girls versus boys F = 9.86; $p < .01$.

7. Though Sentence Completion items were thinly disguised with the fictitious names of "Donald" and "Ruthie" to facilitate reactions, responses were essentially direct rather than projected.

8. These are supplementary data since some sociometric items were not given routinely to all groups.

9. A much more extreme form of this phenomenon is seen on the Israeli kibbutzim, where boys and girls who live, work and learn together in a tight, cohesive group through adolescence do not choose sexual or marriage partners from their own group.

10. There is also an association, not noted in Table 7 of Appendix CC, between traditional homes (MTO) and a tendency for girls to project conventional fictive roles of wife and mother ($x^2 = 11.88$, $p < .01$; see Chapter 13).

11. Findings from several of these measures have been reported in other chapters (9 and 10). They are reviewed here in the context of their relevance to sex-typical reactions.

12. Aside from the rating of Sex-Typed Play, which is specific to this chapter, most of the measures and relationships presented in Appendix CC, Table 7 have been dealt with in other contexts. They will be only briefly summarized, therefore, in terms of their meaning for the production of sex-typical thema.

13. Aggressive-destructive themes, traditional boys versus modern boys: $t = 2.61$, $p < .05$; traditional boys versus traditional girls: $t = 2.33$, $p < .05$.

14. Sex-typed play, modern girls versus traditional girls: $t = 3.00$, $p < .01$; modern girls versus modern boys: $t = 3.50$, $p < .01$.

15. Lynn (1959) has suggested that deep-level identity disturbance, as opposed to open role commitment, is more characteristic of boys and may be attendant on failure to make this basic shift.

Synthesis

C H A P T E R
15

RECAPITULATION: METHOD
AND SCHOOL SETTINGS

In this chapter, we take a retrospective look at certain basic decisions and choices that were made when this study was initiated. The first part of the chapter assesses the gains and losses implicit in the decisions that were made for the research design and comments on new insights into research issues as these emerged in the course of the research experience. The second part of the chapter recapitulates the differences among the schools as settings for learning. Here, too, the experience of analyzing the data gathered about the schools yielded further insights into methodological problems.

Research Strategy

Viewed from the standpoint of research strategy, this study was essentially a comparison of four groups of children who had been exposed to different antecedent conditions. Focusing on the nature of school environments, we chose to examine the influence of stable and enduring conditions of life rather than to study abstracted elements produced synthetically under laboratory conditions. We suffered few doubts about the relevance and reality of the independent variable: school environments are shaped and sustained over a period of time because of their presumed value in producing certain specifiable behavioral changes. We studied antecedent conditions as they existed in nature, ordering and delineating the major dimensions of variation in the school environments. We then assessed the differences among children living in their midst.

By focusing on the intensive study of a relatively small number of children, we were able to examine numerous facets of their psychological development and to establish a profile of school influence. Although the children were studied variable by variable, it was possible to resolve some of the uncertainties associated with measuring complex psychological phenomena by examining the interrelation among the various measures and viewing each score within a larger framework of knowledge. We were not dealing with isolated, disembodied scores, but with a network of interrelated data bearing upon an intrinsically meaningful question.

Our study bears a certain resemblance to the body of research concerned with the exploration of national character. Instead of studying people who have lived in different countries, we have studied children who have lived in different schools. The parallel is not exact, of course: our work was more circumscribed, both with regard to the antecedent conditions and to their consequences. Despite their differences in school experience, there was a substantial common base to the lives of the children we studied. So, too, the impact of school experience, while clearly extensive, could not be so vast as that associated with one's total cultural milieu. Nonetheless, the essential question is similar: how have the environmental differences of groups of people living under profoundly different conditions affected their psychological functioning?

There were of course debits to our choice of research strategy. The decision to use a molar level of analysis in defining the independent variable precluded the assessment of the influence of component elements of a child's educational experience. Nevertheless, in a number of instances, we have seen fit to explain differences found between modern and traditionally educated children in terms of particular facets of their school experience. Clearly, this was conjecture; the exact psychological influence of specific aspects of school experience can only be determined through a comprehensive series of studies in which the molar variable is temporarily compartmentalized and the impact of its various parts studied separately. For such work to be effective, however, it should be based upon a thorough analysis of the whole, from which the parts are to be abstracted, and on a continuing conception of the whole into which the partial effects can be recombined. It is hoped that the present study advances the possibility for more differentiated and integrated study of educational antecedents.

The decision to sample only four points on the modern-traditional continuum meant that, in a sense, the number of subjects in this study was not 105, but four. Undoubtedly, the small number of schools placed too great a burden on the representativeness of each school. A study based upon four schools surely cannot be definitive. It can, however, identify salient variables, suggest a viable methodology, and yield a body of findings about school effects. The extent of generality of these findings waits upon replication and further extension involving, among other things, additional sampling along the modern-traditional continuum.

One of the peculiar advantages of this study was that the intensity of exposure to various facets of both the antecedent conditions and consequent events, under informal conditions of observation, generated a host of impressions which formed a background against which the study's formal results, gathered objectively, could be viewed. This framework did not, of course, affect the actual outcome of the study, but it did help us to gauge the validity and completeness of the findings. When considered from this perspective, one of the most important omissions stemmed from the fact that we were not able to conduct a thorough social-psychological analysis of the group behavior of the children. The depth of knowledge children had of each other, their degree of intimacy, the nature of their emotional ties, and certain forms of group behavior, such as patterns of leadership and scapegoating or the intensity of in-group feeling, appeared to be very different in the different schools. The Russell-Sage Group Problem Solving data was the only systematic material that touched upon these important issues. In future studies, this might well be an area of greater emphasis.

In view of the fact that we observed antecedent conditions to be dramatically different and saw major differences in children's actual behavior while in school, the degree of similarity found among the four groups on some dimensions was enigmatic. A great many statistically significant differences were found among the four groups, but we were also often compelled to pronounce a verdict of no difference. In this respect, it was particularly surprising not to find larger variation in patterns of problem solving, considering the very different intellectual lives these children led in school. Along similar lines, the markedly different investment in originality and creativity among the four schools aroused expectations of greater differences in imaginative thinking than were actually found. We have attempted to analyze and understand the lack of differences where we had strong reason to expect them, but we are also aware that our expectations may have been false or that the lack of findings may document, not for the first time, the shallowness of psychological measurement.

A final word needs to be said about the problem of measurement as it relates to this study. With dismaying frequency, the tactic of multiple

measurement produced contradictory outcomes. Often, the various measures of a variable, in this multiple-measure design, failed to produce a
uniform pattern of findings—a problem noted and discussed by other
writers (Bronfenbrenner, 1963; Wallach and Kogan, 1965). One reason
why this problem arises so frequently is that most methods of measuring
complex psychological dimensions only provide occasions for bringing out
the relevant behavior; they offer no assurance that the behavior in question will in fact be evoked. When such discordant results are obtained,
they may also indicate that the particular variable needs to be reformu-
lated, usually in the direction of greater complexity. Ironically, the very
conditions which create the problem—the use of multiple, conceptually
related measures—also provide the opportunity for gaining an understanding of the basis of such inconsistent results. The investigator seems
faced with the choice between restricting his work to narrow concepts
with very concrete referents, thereby undercutting his work before it has
begun, or working with multiple measures of more complex concepts with
the expectation that he will encounter the problem of inconsistencies.

A more unusual measurement problem was introduced by the apparent
interaction between the manner in which these children were educated
and the most effective media for studying them. We have noted that the
conventional testing procedures seemed less applicable to the study of the
Conrad children. This would suggest that established modes of measurement are more appropriate for the assessment of behavior governed by
traditional standards than for the study of behavior guided by less conventional criteria. Here, Piaget's concepts of assimilation and accommodation,
though usually applied to developmental changes in behavior, appear relevant to an analysis of psychological measurement. The psychologist's cognitive structure of a behavioral event gradually accommodates to the
nature of the event, but also, the behavioral event gradually is assimilated
by the psychologist's structure. For example, man's attempt to study
human intelligence has resulted in a model of intellectual behavior which
in turn has affected the shaping of his intellectual development. Thus,
existing conceptual and methodological frameworks reflect prevailing behavioral patterns; at the same time, however, they solidify and deepen
the patterns by their own mode of measurement. This consideration is of
special relevance in comparative studies such as this, which contrast old
and new forms of psychological organization and functioning.

The Independent Variable: The Schools

This study was constructed on one critical assumption: the educational
philosophy of the school and the practices by which such a philosophy is
mediated can have specific effects on the psychological functioning of
children even during the first few years of school attendance. Given the

research decision to work with an independent variable that was complex and naturalistic, such as total school environment, great weight fell upon the selection and study of the schools. It proved heuristically advantageous to deal with the differences among schools according to how far they were identified with newer trends, termed "modern" in this study, and how far they were continuing with previously established purposes and practices, termed "traditional." The selection of the four schools in the study was based on the extent of variation (as far as this could be judged in a preliminary investigation) in the modern-traditional orientation as expressed in the creation of a learning environment. Two of the schools were selected because they appeared to occupy clear and polarized positions on the continuum; two others represented modifications.

This tentative alignment was subjected to subsequent test and revision through the collection and analysis of detailed data. Each school's values, teaching methods, strategies for motivating children and teachers, climate of interpersonal relationships, authority structure, view of process and sequence in individual development, and extent of permeability to new ideas were analyzed and rated according to their relevance to either the modern or traditional orientation. These components of school life were selected as derivatives of a basic ideology, judged to be central in potential impact on the children. They lent themselves successfully to the task of comparative analysis of the member schools in the series. As the outcome of this analysis, Conrad and Dickens were placed on the modern end of the continuum, Adams and Browning at the traditional end. Educationally, the two pairs were clearly distinct, though the members of each of the pairs were not identical.

Conrad and Dickens had in common a preference for those instructional methods—exploration, discovery, discussion—that made learning an active, challenging process, demanding of the child search, experimentation, and complex cognitive maneuver between the beginning and end of intellectual tasks. Classrooms were places where active dialogue, questioning, and cross-questioning between children and teachers took place; the library was an actively used teaching device. The program was diversified. Creative arts were given an important place to serve as integrating experiences between the logical-analytic and the intuitive-expressive domains of thought. In these schools, it was assumed that learning would be personally meaningful and the intrinsic rewards so great that external symbols of relative excellence—grades, prizes, and so on—could be relegated to a minor position.

In both these schools, to different degrees, the teachers preferred methods of regulating school life that were flexible, adaptable to changing circumstance, not so restrictive as to appear unreasonable to the children. The strength of their authority was not to be derived from the role of a punitive superior nor the power of an impersonal system. It depended, rather, on the building of a meaningful relation between teacher and child. Informality in the daily encounters between teachers and children, communication to the children of the teacher's awareness of them as distinct personalities, willingness to work through problems inherent in the conflict between impulse and social requirements—these were the components of the kind of teacher-child relationship Conrad and Dickens tried to construct in order to maintain the social order essential in a learning atmosphere.

At Adams and Browning, the measure of intellectual excellence was in the performance. Teaching was directed to a body of knowledge, as organized in textbooks and curriculum syllabi, to be mastered at a level that would make it available to recall and replication in its original form and meanings. Teaching was equally invested in developing proficiency in the basic operations of the word and number symbol systems, regarded as the essential foundation for more complex cognitive engagement with ideas. These learning activities occupied most of the school hours. They constituted the primary sphere in which success or failure were experienced by the children and in which brightness or mediocrity were attributed to the children by the teachers. A certain amount of variety had been introduced into these programs; thus, at Adams, creative arts had a place as extra enrichment in the curriculum. Several forces were expected to keep the children motivated to learn: wish for teacher approval; high grades symbolizing personal success and competitive strength; and secondary privileges granted to high-ranking children.

The teacher was a figure of authority, usually maintaining personal and status distance from the children, functioning within a clear system of right and wrong behavior. The values which had priority in this educational ideology were reflected in the way the children were perceived and characterized. Their individuality took shape in terms of relative brightness, academic prowess, and behavioral adaptability.

While the greatest differences were found between the pairs of schools, there were also differences, as noted previously, within each pair. These differences were of two kinds: first, the extent to which practices matched educational ideology; second, the nature of life style and ethos of the school as a social institution. Between the modern schools, the disparity in the former category was greater than in the latter. Between the traditional schools, the reverse was true.

As compared to Conrad, Dickens was rated consistently as less modern, excepting only in its responsiveness to new ideas and its incorporation of contemporary social-political content into the curriculum. There were limiting conditions on how closely this school could approximate the modern characteristics of Conrad, if this were its goal. Its position as part of a large public system established the boundaries for what could be changed or tried out. Its large size dictated a certain degree of formalization. It was in a process of transition, with diverse viewpoints having rights to exert influence. The group of teachers who were aligned with the modern convictions of the principal were themselves just learning new methods and trying out new teacher roles.

Yet, in this group, despite the uncertainty of transition and new beginnings, there were qualities of style and perspective and a hierarchy of values that were impressively close to those of the Conrad teachers. The panel teachers expressed and enjoyed individual teaching styles. They had come into teaching as a chosen profession in which they expected to invest their energies and from which they expected to derive personal gratification. They were working for purpose and pleasure; committed professionally, they saw themselves as part of a forward movement of change in education. They did not have the self-conscious awareness of being unique that characterized Conrad, but they did have a special bond in their sense of difference from the majority of their public school colleagues—a sense of difference that was based on their wish to vitalize the learning experience and bring the individual child into the foreground of the process.

Between Adams and Browning there was less difference in educational procedures and greater disparity in life style and values. These two schools had the same goal priorities: to keep academic standing high in comparison to other schools and to be in control of behavior at all times in the school day. The methods of teaching and evaluation, the emphasis placed on accuracy and finish in performance, were fundamentally similar and consistent with traditional techniques as previously described. Adams was occasionally rated as somewhat less traditional than Browning on the basis that it had introduced variety through a program of creative activities, extended opportunity for children to take part in school functions outside their classrooms, and tried to bring the children into some direct contact with their surrounding environment.

Apart from their fundamentally common traditionalism in educational matters, however, these two schools presented a striking contrast as life environments. At Browning, the teachers were the kind of people who naturally created an atmosphere of quiet plainness, conscientious application to assigned tasks, controlled feeling, limited striving, and satisfaction with good performance on goals of limited scope. As a school, Browning appeared self-contained, self-satisfied, unburdened by the tensions associated with striving for acclaim or trying to be successful by criteria other than one's own. The staff maintained a stillwater atmosphere by insulating themselves from the stimulating influences of the changing world of education.

At Adams, not decorum but personal magnetism was a desirable teacher

attribute; in manner, the teachers looked and sounded like the sophisticated parents of their children. They were involved in conflicts of role:
they meant to be clear authority figures but allowed themselves to engage
in personal exchanges to win the children; they were attracted by the superior social position of the parents but decried the lack of the parents'
involvement in the rearing of their children. They were unified in their
strong sense of audience, in wanting to keep their school a showplace in
the public school system, and were willing to work for striking display in
production and presentation. Obviously, children attending these two
schools were exposed to very different models and values of adult living.

In the modern schools, there was more room for variation in procedures
by which theory is applied than for variation in basic ethos and values;
conversely, in the traditional schools, there was likely to be greater uniformity at the technique level and more variation in attitudes and ideals.
Perhaps this is as is to be expected when one remembers two salient characteristics of the modern orientation: first, it has an extended view of the
school's role which consciously includes responsibility for attitudes and
value formation, and second, one of its prime values is exploration and
experimentation to be applied to the way the teacher teaches as well as
how the children learn. The finding that variation *within* the modern and
traditional school pairs involves different dimensions may have implications for other studies of school environments. In a larger series of modern
schools, one might look for or expect considerable variation in educational
procedures while fundamental values, nature of commitment, concepts of
authority, and view of individuality would be relatively similar. In a larger
series of traditional schools, by contrast, one might expect little essential
variation in educational procedures while the human relations climate, the
professional stance and outlook, and the basis for in-group coherence
might be substantially different from school to school.

CHAPTER

16

RECAPITULATION: THE FINDINGS

We began the study with a question concerning school philosophy and its effect on the growth of the children. What difference does it make if a child attends a "traditional" or "modern" school? Does he approach learning differently, think in different ways, perceive or relate differently to people, develop a different image of himself? In this chapter, we present a summary of the study findings, considered first in terms of these questions about school impact and the predictions associated with them. The summary of school effects is followed by sections on home influence and sex differences. In the final section of the chapter, school group profiles are presented, summarizing the functioning of the children in each of the four schools.

Summary of Study Findings

School Impact

The study of school effects was organized into three broad areas: intellectual mastery, interpersonal perception, and aspects of self-image. In all three of these areas, we expected differences in functioning among the study children. We predicted differences in the way children from traditional and modern schools would think, perceive other people, emphasize and shape their concepts of themselves. Perhaps our most confident expectations were in the cognitive area. All schools defined intellectual growth as their central province, but modern and traditional schools handled cognitive experiences in very different ways. In addition, functioning in this area appeared most tangible and most amenable to measurement, at least at first glance. The clearest and most consistent school-related findings, however, were not in the area of cognitive functioning but in the area of self-perception and attitude—matters of personal identity, perception of development and investment in roles.

SELF-IMAGE

We found the children of modern schools to be more differentiated in their self-perception, more accepting of negative impulse as part of the self, more invested in their childhood status, and more open in their conceptions of social sex roles. We found their traditionally schooled counterparts to be more consistently impersonal, future-oriented, and conventional in their images of roles and development. It is of special interest that the pattern of reactions in the modern school children was not extreme. They were not geared to infancy and younger ages, but to their *current* lives rather than the future. They were not oriented to opposite-sex roles but to *open* rather than settled and conventional roles. We have seen not regression or disturbance in these findings, for the most part, but a different value system in formation and perhaps a different style of thought. The intellectual attitude of the modern schools, with their stress on differentiated thinking and open-ended search, seemed to have influenced the ways in which modern school children communicated their perceptions of themselves. By the same token, the traditional schools' stress on structured and established intellectual products may have influenced the impersonal approach and the centrality of pre-established models, as these appeared in the self-related material of children from the traditional schools.

It was principally the children of Conrad who typified the predicted modern pattern and among them it was the girls who emerged as most consistent. Their pattern must be seen against the more general profile of sex differences in this area. Like most girls of the study, they were relatively responsive and revealing and more differentiated than boys in their self-description. Here they typified and extended a pattern characteristic of the girls in general. They reversed the female pattern in other ways, however, being less committed to the conventional female social role and less future-oriented. In all these particulars—whether extending or reversing the general pattern of the girls—the girls of Conrad reacted in ways that fulfilled the predictions. They described their qualities and feelings in individualized terms, centered on the pleasures and values of the present, held open their perception of the boundaries and advantages of social roles, and saw their development as a projection from the present rather than an arrival at an externally formed role.

In all, the assessment of self-image suggested consistent school effects, with particular attention to the children of Conrad for their distinctive attitudes, images, and projections. Though operating differently for boys and girls and for children from different kinds of homes, the complex of a school's philosophy and approach appears to have had a formative effect on the children. The findings confirmed the prediction that the more formally socialized, prestructured, and impersonal images of the self would be expressed by traditional school children, while the more open, differentiated, and individually determined images would be expressed by children from the more modern schools.

THE COGNITIVE SPHERE

In the cognitive area, the findings were more variable. Differences in intellectual performance, problem-solving, and imaginative processes were sometimes school-related, but they did not follow predictions in a consistent way.

In certain respects the data followed expectations quite closely; patterns of intellectual functioning within the classroom and the children's attitudes toward school were of this nature. In their classrooms, children of both modern schools were involved in intellectual activities which gave them scope for independent thinking and the pursuit of ideas. Discussions centered on the understanding of connections and relationships among facts and concepts, providing the children with the kind of experience that current programs of discovery, productive thinking, and so on (see Suchman, 1961; Bruner, 1961; Covington, Crutchfield, and Davies, 1966), are bringing into focus. The evidence from our observations is that the children of the modern schools, where such an orientation was central, were more consistently involved in such experiences than children of the traditional schools and that they responded in class with a different level and style of thought. Further, the children of Conrad were predictably invested in their school as a positive and exciting place, in contrast to children of the traditional schools in particular. When we tested the children for the presumably "internalized" evidence of these patterns, however, the findings were mixed, showing expected effects only under certain conditions.

On standardized group tests of intelligence and achievement, children of the four schools were not equally effective. Children of the three public schools were relatively advanced in their performance, and those of the traditional schools in particular handled test situations with notable efficiency. The children of Conrad scored significantly lower on group tests of both intelligence and achievement. At face value, one might take these findings to mean that they were less "intelligent" than children of the other schools and that they had learned less. In the light of their high average and superior scores on individual intelligence testing, however, it seems likely that the Conrad children shared with the rest of the sample a basically high intellectual endowment. Their performance on standardized group tests seemed to reflect a difference in test-taking attitudes, preparation and motivational structure, for the most part, as well as a uniqueness of school curriculum that affected the applicability of conventional achievement tests. The difference in performance on these standardized tests was not totally unexpected nor was it difficult to understand.

More puzzling was the fact that performance on the battery of individual problem-solving techniques was not reliably different among groups. These tasks were designed with some stress on flexible, connective, exploratory thinking, and modern school children were expected to show relative strength. This prediction was not borne out. Children of modern and traditional schools were not consistently different in their approach or effectiveness; if anything, Conrad children tended to lag behind. The pattern of findings did follow predictions when problem solving took place in a group context. Here, traditional school children were competitive, disorganized, and less technically effective. The children of Conrad were both effective and well fused as a group, working toward task solution with interpersonal warmth and considerable skill and competence. Within the array of task-oriented cognitive situations, then, the pattern was varied; it followed predictions in some respects and not in others.

Thinking processes were also tested in contexts that were more personal and projective, less oriented to task solution. In most situations that centered on self-attitudes, as noted above, thinking styles followed predicted lines. Here the more differentiated, exploratory kind of thought and communication, as fostered by the modern schools, appeared to have taken root; traditional school children offered more stereotyped and global material. In situations that called for imaginative thinking, however, the school groups were not discernibly different, at least in the ways we initially expected. We predicted a relatively transcendent flow of fantasy from modern school children and found no evidence of such a trend.[1] Perhaps our expectations needed to take more sophisticated account of the multiple conditions that can foster the weaving of imaginative fantasy and its communication, on request, to other people. We did find, however, that content and thematic characteristics of the fantasy distinguished the modern and traditional groups: playful, unreal, and "fantastic" creations appeared more often among modern school children; achievement, superlative success and recognition, the imaginary living out of sex-typed fantasies, and adult roles appeared more among the traditional school children. We need to question why modern school children were not more productive and imaginative, as predicted, in these projective situations; we have noted, however, that their fantasies had fewer characteristics of a "social mold" and that these thematic aspects of creative fantasy represented an important differential effect in these groups.

Findings in the cognitive area have, of course, a particular importance in a study of school impact. The pattern of findings in this study has raised a series of questions, particularly where predictions were not borne out, concerning the problems of relevant measurement, the factors affecting the functioning of the children, and the possible implications for educational procedures and processes (see Chapter 15). Aspects of these latter questions will be dealt with in the final chapter.

THE INTERPERSONAL SPHERE

In the interpersonal sphere, we predicted group differences in the perception of adults and in the view of authority. On the basis of differences in the interpersonal atmosphere of the schools, we postulated that children from traditional schools would be focused on the controlling and disciplinary roles of adults, while modern school children would perceive adults in more differentiated terms, expecting from them more acceptance and understanding of child behavior.

The findings in this area were variable, but in a different sense than those in the cognitive area. Here they varied in the extent to which school impact seemed to be a major systematic factor; family influence and the concerns of this transitional life stage seemed to dominate much of the material and consistent school group differences appeared mostly in school-relevant contexts.

The middle-years status of these children was evident in their material. We saw ample evidence of the complexity of adult-child relationships at this stage; of the ascendance of new levels of initiative and autonomy as critical and conflictual issues; of the wish to move toward more responsible roles even while there was a continuing need for the guidance of adults and the support of the family. In varying ways, all children expressed this theme in their projective material and perceived adults partly in terms of this struggle, but girls were more obviously involved with family than boys were and were more apt to project benign and perhaps wish-fulfilling images of adults, while boys were more apt to express conflict, pressure, and clash.

In this area, the girls of Conrad were more like the boys: less family-centered than other girls, less apt to portray benign and protective adults, more vigorous in their portrayal of adult-child conflict. Girls of the other modern school, however, along with those of the most traditional school, typified the pattern of family-centered and benign perceptions. The explanation seems to lie less in school experience, per se, than in the distinctive patterns of the homes. Relationships between these interpersonal projections and home background were consistent, though the reinforcing effect of homes and schools with congruent atmosphere, as in the case of Conrad girls, was undoubtedly strong.

It might be noted that the children from the modern environments, who were presumably exposed to the more child-supportive relationships and guidance, did not project the more benign images of adults. Indeed, girls from these environments were more apt to project conflict and struggle between adults and children. Though such a finding may suggest that these children did not experience adults as accepting and supportive and that the prediction of the study has been reversed, it seems more likely that the prediction was neither confirmed nor upset, but simply that the finding was more complex. Taken together with other findings of the study, it seems probable that children from modern and traditional backgrounds used the projective situations differently and that the portrayal of adult-child interaction, by girls in particular, reflected not only realistic experience and expectations of adults but the child's stance toward appropriate and permissible adult-child roles, the attitude toward compliance and protest, and individual styles of defense and coping.

In some respects, the child's school experience was an important and measurable influence on his perceptions of people and his ideas about their behavior and relationships with each other. There were school group differences in the perception of school authorities and in attitudes toward the structure of rules and regulations in the school. Here, too, the child apparently brought with him certain adaptive propensities from his family experience, since fear and conformity appeared more among children from traditional backgrounds. But the school itself seemed to determine much of the child's attitude. The children of Conrad were distinctly different from other children; they conceived of school authority as a functional and rational matter, and were less apt to feel resentful or to react by passive conformity than children in other schools. By the same token, the data suggested that the evolution of codes and principles by which the child develops his allegiances or evaluates right and wrong, just and unjust, was less tied, in the Conrad group, to the school context and to the structure of rules and regulations within the school. Children of this school seemed less bound to issues of acceptable school behavior or to questions of adult approval, in the daily school context, than children of the two traditional schools in particular. Their developing codes were expressed on a somewhat more generalized plane than those of the children in the other schools.

The summary of study findings to this point offers a topical profile of school effects. The next sections summarize the relative influence of home factors and the contrasting reactions of boys and girls.

Home Influence

It is obvious that any child grows in a complex environment, making his own pattern out of his experiences and influenced by the variety of people and happenings that make up his world. In this sense, it is an impossible task to search for the "relative influence" of home and school. Together they supply much of the grist for the young child's mill and he is always affected by both. We have looked for relative influence on a different plane, however—for ways in which the schools affected children systematically despite a range of family experiences, and for ways in which family constellations affected development systematically despite a range of school experiences. We were also alert to ways in which the school and home in interrelation reinforced a direction of impact. We have had to pursue these themes with particular caution, since the parent material was not comparable in scope, detail, or reliability to that of the school material, but we can pinpoint certain areas of systematic home influence with reasonable confidence.

Home influence appeared particularly systematic in two areas of child-reaction: perception of people and social sex roles. We found the nature of interpersonal perception to be associated with characteristics of the child's family, particularly among girls. Their perceptions were apparently influenced both by modern-traditional characteristics of the home and, to an extent, by the quality of acceptance and satisfaction on the mother's part. In these reactions the atmosphere and experience at home appeared to transcend school experience with more consistent effects on the girl's perception of adults in her life space.

For the girl, perceptions of protective adults and a fantasy life centered on the family formed something of a unit—an orientation toward the forms, interests, and satisfactions of a time-honored female role. The girls who typified this orientation came from homes with traditional attitudes about the process of socialization, obedience to authority, and standards of accomplishment and behavior. The girls from modern homes not only perceived (or projected) adult-child relations in more conflictual terms, closer to that of the boys, but conveyed a fantasy life more diverse in its themes, less centered on family and on the pathways and roles traditional to the female. We saw this role-exploratory orientation primarily as a function of the quality of parental (maternal) attitudes toward the child; in these families, the mothers related to the qualities and growth of the child as a particular individual rather than stressing her role as a girl and potential woman. Other less attitudinal factors were also relevant to this orientation, however: the mother as a female model, and the feeling of satisfaction and acceptance that the mother conveyed to her daughter. Socio-economic factors were also relevant, though the more modern attitudes characteristic of families at the higher levels probably constituted the crucial experiential factor for the child. A complex of home factors, then, seemed to shape the quite different orientations toward roles found among the girls of our sample.

In these areas, then, home influence appeared most systematic. Yet the reinforcing effect of the schools was also indicated. Boys from consistent traditional homes and schools gave the most aggressive fantasies by far; and girls from modern schools and homes were the prototypes of the modern young female in formation. We have little data on the effects of homes and schools that presented the child with contrasting environments, but our data suggest that *congruent* values, models, and experiences in home and school constituted a powerful influence on development, consolidating the effects produced by either alone.

It might be noted that we found no systematic evidence of a relationship between family factors and cognitive performance. Such a finding must be seen in the essentially middle-class context of our study sample. There seems to be ample evidence on a national basis that the children of the vast urban ghettos and the impoverished isolated rural areas come to school disadvantaged in many senses and poorly prepared to learn. The relative academic performance of these children, as compared to more advantaged children, is clearly a function of the conditions of life outside the school. In the population of our study, however, all the children came to school in a relatively privileged condition, well prepared by endowment and the life style in their homes for learning. Given this baseline, our data indicated that the kind of school had a far more powerful effect than the home on the pattern and style of cognitive functioning.

Sex Differences

The emergence of distinct reaction patterns among boys and girls was one of the most striking findings of the study. In many of the areas we tapped, we could make meaningful generalizations about these middle-years children only if we described the boys and girls separately—a fact already obvious in this summary, both in connection with school impact and home influence.

As a general response style, we found the girls to be more open and responsive, more productive, more imaginative in their responses, more personalized in their way of handling things. They were more willing to bring personal material into the open and to react with flights of fantasy when that was appropriate. We found the boys more guarded and evasive, more stimulus bound, more realistic and impersonal. They were less willing to be known in any personal sense.

By and large, the boys and girls were not notably different in intellectual ability or in the tests of achievement or problem solving, but we did find differences in style. The girls were more willing to take risks—to offer more hypotheses, ask more questions, take on and try out more. More important, they were generally more differentiated in the way they approached and handled ideas and in their perceptions. They described themselves and other people in more differentiated ways and seemed to think through questions with more elaboration and detail. If the advantages of caution and precision were with the boys, the advantages of complexity and differentiation were with the girls. To some extent, the more differentiated thinking style we found among girls is in contrast to other research findings (Milton, 1957; Sweeney, 1953; Witkin, Dyk, Faterson, Goodenough, and Karp, 1962). But perhaps it is relevant that we included a span of cognitive activities covering not only goal-directed problems but thought and communication about the self, other people, and inner wishes and fantasies.

In many other ways, the boys and girls of this study were different. They had distinct styles of presenting themselves, different attitudes toward their sex roles, and different emphases on present and future. The boys were verbally more self-confident and assertive about themselves; more unequivocally certain that it's great to be a boy; more centered on the "here and now" of their current lives. Girls were less enthusiastic about the advantages of being a girl and, more often than the boys, looked to their adolescent and adult futures with interest and involvement. They appeared more diffident about their accomplishments, their popularity, and their general adequacy, at least at verbal levels, though they found more covert ways to call attention to themselves. We have understood the difference between the verbal assertion of the boys and the visual display of the girls as reflecting culturally reinforced modes for presenting oneself in strength.

Perhaps of special importance is the fact that boys and girls differed radically in what we might call the core of their inner concerns and organization. As noted above, the girls were more oriented toward people than the boys were; human interaction and relationship constituted a more central theme in their lives. The boys were organized more around power, active assertion, and mastery. They were working out themes of aggression, adventure, victory, and defeat, while girls were filling their fantasy world with people, developing them as individuals, and concerning themselves with family figures and adult approval. The girls were more apt to settle their tensions through conformity, while the boys showed more resistance and anger.

But the situation was yet more complex. We found the pattern of sex differences to be somewhat different in the different school groups. Boys and girls of Conrad in particular did not typify the sex-linked patterns. In some important ways, they did differ a great deal from each other: the girls of this school were more responsive and imaginative, the boys generally more inhibited and self-protective. But they did not differ as much as children from other schools in the central organizing themes that generally characterized boys and girls. The girls were not so oriented to the future, so involved in family, so prone to project the benign side of adult-child relations, and the boys were not so centered around aggressive themes. They were closer together in their reactions than boys and girls of other groups. It might also be noted that children of this school reversed the prevailing pattern of attitudes toward school itself. In the three public schools, girls were more positive and comfortable with their schools than the boys. In Conrad, however, the boys were also highly identified with the school and positive in their feelings toward it.

Profiles of the Four School Groups

The study findings have been presented throughout the book in terms of modern-traditional differences in relation to predictions. In the following section, the findings are presented from a different point of view. Organized by school groups, the purpose is to provide an integrated image of the characteristic functioning of children in each of the schools.

The Browning Group

The Browning group was of considerable interest, despite its relatively small size. In many ways it stood as the clearest and most striking contrast to the Conrad group.

The children of this school presented an efficient and capable picture of goal-directed intellectual functioning. They were quick and efficient, omitted little and tried much, and scored some two years beyond their grade level on the formal achievement tests. They had the lowest rate of omission or rejection of test items among all the groups; perhaps they felt particularly adequate to the tasks or perhaps they had the least tendency to break the given structure by selecting or structuring in their own way. The pattern of efficiency, skill, and high performance characterized the boys of this school in particular.

The children of Browning had a relatively fixed performance level in relation to their classmates. Only in this group was it possible to predict a child's relative performance on other tests of IQ, achievement, or problem solving from knowing his performance on any one. To some extent, this pattern must reflect a greater variation in ability, relevant family factors, or coping skill. We have noted, however, that Browning in particular categorized its children in global and public terms. The consistency of performance may have reflected a general image—"I'm capable," or "I'm not smart"—internalized from this kind of evaluation.

The general picture in this school was of high intellectual endowment coupled with performance efficiency in an individual test situation. With the need to work in a group, however, new forces were set up and some of the underlying strain in this class showed clearer. The group problem solving was tense, somewhat hysterical, poorly planned, and not particularly efficient. An elite core of children, all boys, worked competitively and forced through solutions, but there were many children who did not participate and the central children fought for position as much as for task solution. It seemed a group primed to compete on an individual basis, with little experience in either the value or techniques of mutual effort.

The less goal-structured tasks, where "good performance" would have to be defined in qualitatively different terms from achievement and problem solving, pointed up another area where this basically gifted group was not effective. They handled situations that drew on fantasy and self-contact, or offered a relatively open field, in relatively restricted ways. They were productive but not able to modify or improvise readily, and they leaned toward impersonal mechanisms. The restriction of the boys was the more remarkable, both in absolute terms and in view of their capable goal-directed performance. The Browning girls were at least as imaginative, aware and communicative of inner processes as the Browning boys, if not more so. This was generally true of the girls in the study but is of special interest in this group, where it adds a divergent dimension to the otherwise global impression that the girls were simply less able than the boys.

In their perceptions of people, the girls of Browning, along with those of Dickens, stood out as most oriented toward adults and family and the protective benevolent attitudes of adults toward children. For the boys, this was far less true. The boys showed feelings of aggression accompanied by tension over the control of such feelings. Some of this centered on interaction with adults, and certainly the adult-child world projected by Browning boys did not reflect the benign quality portrayed by the girls. In what we could trace of peer attitudes, however, this Browning group expressed the most mutually benevolent attitude between the sexes. Given the general antagonism between the sexes at this age level, this relatively benign expression of acceptance was interesting—perhaps a function of bland public communication but perhaps also a function of relatively resolved roles. It is surely important, however, to juxtapose these spoken attitudes in the context of companionship choices with the breakdown of working relationships in the group problem-solving situation. Whatever the social attitudes between the sexes in this group, they had not found viable ways for boys and girls to work together productively and with mutual acceptance.

In the various aspects of self-concept and presentation, the Browning children, despite their small number, seemed to have a clearly describable pattern. The boys were fairly assertive, the girls less so, except in nonverbal display aspects. Childish enthusiasm was an acceptable part of their self-image, as for all the groups, but there was concern for the control of aggression and anti-social impulse.

Browning children tended to be future-oriented. This was marked in the girls, who consistently turned toward the somewhat romantic and protected aspects of teen-age and adult life. Both boys and girls saw the future in terms discontinuous with the present. They pictured themselves in conventional adult roles with no elements from their current lives. For girls, the vision of themselves as wife and mother often marked the complete content of their projection into the future.

Both the boys and girls of Browning were strongly committed to the advantages of their own sex. Their imagery was concrete and clear. They had sex-linked modes of reaction and often differed from each other more clearly than the boys and girls of any other group.

This distinction between boys and girls extended to their attitudes toward school. The overall tone of their reactions was more negative than any other group, but the Browning girls were more positive and contented with school than the boys were, despite the fact that the school would rate their relative effectiveness as lower.

A number of factors were surely relevant to this pattern of findings among Browning children: Browning families ran the gamut of modern-traditional orientation; they had the widest socio-economic spread of any parent group (this spread in turn relating to the ideological stance). They were, however, the most consistent and resolved of the parent groups. It is also true that the children had been advancing through a school whose conservative character was clear and consistent. The lack of conflict within home and school environments—even when they were not ideologically consistent with each other—may in itself have been a factor in the pattern of the children's responses.

The Adams Group

Adams children gave a more complicated profile. They reacted with more variety among themselves (perhaps a function of the larger group) and were less often the opposite anchorage point from Conrad children. Like the children of Browning, they came from a range of modern or traditional families, but their families were less consistent and integrated in parental roles, more fully urban in their life interests. Their school was judged as basically traditional, but more "sophisticated," more apt to encompass mixed elements, more geared to display. The total pattern of the Adams children seemed less conservative in tone than that of the Browning children, and perhaps this is consistent with the differences in features of their background.

Like the children of Browning, Adams children were effective performers and achievers. They coped skillfully with formal tests. They worked rapidly, covered ground, scored well. They also averaged some two years of formal achievement beyond grade level. Unlike the Browning group, however, the difference between performance of Adams boys and girls was generally negligible or canceled out. Also different was the fact that Adams children did not fall into such clearly predictable slots from one test situation to another. Even from one goal-directed task to another, the relative position of a child in the Adams group was apt to shift. Endowment and coping ability may have been more evenly distributed among Adams children (allowing a shift from situation to situation), but it may also have mattered that this school categorized its children less globally in comparative terms than Browning, even though its achievement standards were high and pressuring.

Adams children were more effective in a group problem-solving situation than the Browning group. They had more ability to plan and work together, competition among them was less corrosive to the general effort, and fewer children were excluded. But they seemed to have little impulse or method to evaluate their own work or to correct and move it along, and failure struck them with particular demoralizing force. Perhaps this pattern gives a valid flavor of the school atmosphere. The children were gifted and effective and they had developed problem-solving skills over a broader range than that offered to Browning children, but they had been geared to the central position of the adult as the judge of adequacy and progress and to the crucial importance of tangible success. The emphasis of these children on achievement and on dramatic success, accompanied by superlative acclaim, was in fact generally marked—more so than in any other group. We felt this to be a very meaningful finding for the children of this school.

Many of the features of the Adams group have been essentially buried in the previous chapters. This is largely because they occupy a "middling" position in a number of instances, though not necessarily a position without content or features of its own. In their attitude toward adults and toward present and future roles, for instance, the girls of Adams were different from both those of Browning and Dickens, on the one hand, and those of Conrad, on the other. They were not so oriented toward family or adult protection as Browning and Dickens girls, yet more so than Conrad girls. Some of them wove fantasies of teen-age life and looked forward to the pleasures of the future, yet some saw that future with elements of continuity from the present. The reactions of Adams girls were not highly sex-typed, though more among them were sex-typed than in the Conrad group. As nearly as we can understand this pattern, the girls of Adams differed from the more consistent extremes on either side of them for somewhat different reasons: they differed from Browning and Dickens girls because the experiences, attitudes, and models in their families shaped less consistent, conventional young-girl attitudes; they differed from Conrad girls because none of them, by definition, experienced the consistency of modern home and school environment that surrounded the Conrad girl, or the elaboration of these attitudes that was part of the Conrad environment.

Among the Adams children, sex differences were not generally so marked as in Browning, but the boys also had certain distinct features. They were, like most of the boys, relatively committed to their role advantages, expressive of conflict with adults, less pleased with school than the girls, and generally assertive. They emerged as a group with high drive—enthusiastic, striving, looking to the future in terms of conventional roles with high status and the potential for recognized success. Their projection of aggressive feelings was accompanied by marked concern for the control of such feelings, and in this concern they were outstanding.

The boys and girls of Adams were rather open in their social contact with each other and in the extent to which they would express friendship feelings between boys and girls. More preadolescent and sophisticated

than "latency" age in this respect, they seemed to reflect a pattern of interaction that may be on the increase in the general culture but was certainly
most evident in this group of the children in our study.

In matters of self-attitude and description, Adams children were not so
extreme as the Browning children, but they also tended to talk about
themselves in relatively global terms. They were also impersonal, compared to children of the modern schools, and they were comparatively
unable to focus on themselves in a differentiated way. This affinity with
the Browning children seems particularly interesting, in view of their
various differences.

The Dickens Group

The children of Dickens were an interesting mixture. The quality of their
reactions has also been partially buried in the chapter discussions, much
like the reactions of Adams children, and for much the same reason. They
often were less consistent or extreme than either the Conrad or Browning
group. But this school and its group of children have considerable importance in the study. It was a public school trying actively to incorporate a
modern philosophy into its way of life, and its children came from families
more mixed in their views than the families of Conrad. In this sense, the
patterns of this school group have more concrete implications for a large
body of existing schools than the patterns of Conrad children.

Reactions of Dickens children were especially interesting in two areas—
cognitive performance and self-description. In some ways, the children of
Dickens performed intellectually much like the children of the other public schools. They were also some two years advanced in achievement and
they coped well with the various tests and tasks we gave them. They were
not as fast and did not cover as much as the children from Adams and
Browning, but the accuracy of what they did was high. Most interesting
was the fact that they rated relatively high in problem-solving processes;
their solution record was on a par with other groups but they rated higher
in the quality of the processes that they were involved in. We expected
such a pattern from children educated in schools that stress the development and implication of ideas. We did not find it among Conrad children,
but the Dickens children, better able to cope with the tests in general, may
have shown some of the fruits of this kind of school approach, combining
a process orientation with an adaptive ability to cope with external demand.

The Dickens children were also interesting in the way they described
themselves, their lives, their feelings. They shared with Conrad a relatively personal and differentiated style of self-report. While they lacked
some of the livelier qualities of certain Conrad children, they were stead-

ier and more consistent as a group, and the general level of communication about themselves was more personalized and elaborated than that of either the Browning or Adams children.

Among the other features that characterized this group, some were certainly determined more by family than school. Dickens girls, none of whom were from modern homes, were much like the girls at Browning. The world of the family was their world of reference. They saw adults as benevolent and protective. They looked to the future as the time of arrival and they envisioned themselves in the basic female roles, with little extension to other sources of satisfaction.

The children of Dickens were reasonably assertive, committed to their own roles and its advantages, apt to perceive themselves as enthusiastic and reactive people. Their pattern of aggressive themes was not remarkable, but, in comparative terms, the girls treated such impulses with more notable concern and the boys were relatively relaxed. Perhaps the contrasting attitudes of home and school for the girls at Dickens presented a special problem—an uncertainty and concern about the permissible boundaries of negative expression.

Children of this group were more positive about school than the children of traditional public schools, and the girls in particular were actively identified. One can wonder whether the school had helped these traditionally reared girls to a kind of development that was freer and more elaborated than they might otherwise have had. Though quite traditional in many of their role attitudes, they reacted in ways that were imaginative as well as competent and they seemed to be developing an awareness and use of themselves that might not have emerged from a more traditional life experience in both home *and* school. Perhaps their active identification with their school was based on an implicit perception of its supportive attitudes and an appreciation of its lesser restrictiveness, in comparison with their more traditional homes.

The Conrad Group

The children of Conrad have been central figures on these pages. Perhaps that was inevitable from the inception of the study. Conrad had had opportunity to work out the meaning of an educational philosophy that had considerable importance and interest, and as a staff we felt the children of this school to be a main anchorage point of the study. We were particularly interested in whatever qualities or problems set them apart from the others. The fact is, however, that they would have forced the attention of any observer who perused the material. They did stand apart—sometimes in the company of Dickens children but often alone, with features that were unique.

We have not solved the special problems raised by antecedent conditions in this group. Many of the Conrad children lived in a consistently modern life space. There were more modern families in the Conrad group than any other; at the same time, these children were educated in the most modern school, whose theoretical structure and uniquely integrated curriculum set it apart qualitatively. When we look at the pattern of the Conrad children, we need to see its features in this context. They are probably a function both of the combined impact of home and school and the very special quality of the school itself.

Conrad children presented a unique pattern of intellectual functioning, a fact evident from the previous summary of the study findings. The pattern of WISC reactions (high block design and object assembly with very low coding) suggests something of the nature and direction of their intellectual skills. The analytic was more developed than the rote or the mechanical; the fusion of thought and manipulation was more effective than discrete recall and verbal association. It was the total pattern of their test responsiveness, however, that was particularly unique. Conrad children were different in their test-taking attitudes. They were less accepting of the test structure per se, more erratic, more selectively responsive to variations in conditions, material, and interest. They functioned extremely well in a group problem-solving situation, where there were mutual supports and considerable fruitful experience to draw on, but mobilized less well in individual goal-directed situations where, as indicated, they were expected to excel. This pattern seemed clearly a function of their school experience, but in a very complex way; it will be discussed further in the following chapter.

Conrad children were unusual in what they conveyed of self-image—their perceptions of themselves, their images of current and future roles. Like the children of Dickens, they gave a relatively differentiated picture of themselves and tended to filter ideas through their own views and perceptions. Unique among the groups, however, they were relatively tolerant of angry feelings, geared to the present rather than the future, apt to react in ways that were not clearly sex-linked. In a number of ways, they seemed more individualized than the children of other groups and less attuned within themselves to the conventional forms and themes that American society places before its children.

At some levels, the Conrad children seemed geared to conflict in human interchange. They had little tendency to paint a world of benign and protective adults and were negative and defensive in what they had to say about children of the opposite sex. At the same time, they worked extremely well together as a group and were highly identified with their school, with very positive feelings about their teachers—an especially unusual phenomenon among boys.

Sex differences in this group were not marked in areas where boys and girls often differ greatly. On all the themes and reactions we labeled as sex-linked, using the broad cultural model, the boys and girls of this school were closer in reactions than those of any other group. This we felt to be an important finding, reflecting the impact of their consistently modern environment.

The boys and girls were different, however, in other important ways. The boys were generally more guarded and unproductive, protecting themselves either from our tests and our probing or from anxieties deeper within themselves. Both boys and girls tended to select and reject parts of the test battery, but the girls coupled this attitude with enthusiastic, imaginative reactions, while the boys were more often inhibited over the broad range of situations in which we placed them. The Conrad group was a variable group. Sometimes its children represented the extremes of reaction, for example, from the most vital and self-aware to the most restricted and blocked. To some extent, this variation followed sex lines, with a few of the boys appearing recurrently among the blocked and unresponsive children.

The girls of Conrad were among the most interesting subgroups of our study. It was their quality in particular that carried the bulk of the findings about Conrad. They were atypical among the four groups of girls, yet in ways that were predictable. They were clearly recognizable as children who were incorporating the values, attitudes, and perhaps conflicts of their subculture. They seemed generally vigorous and reactive, reflecting more the freedom than the uncertainty of their orientation. Actually, more girls than boys fit the preferred image of children held by Conrad teachers —an expressive, individualized child, selective in interests but searching in style, reactive to people in a differentiated way, and aware of feelings and experience.

NOTES

1. It might be noted that the findings thus do not fall under the rubric of discrepant functioning in creativity and intelligence, as distinguished by other authors (Getzels and Jackson, 1962; Wallach and Kogan, 1965); though there are partial similarities in the conceptualization, we expected a basic cognitive stance to affect both problem-solving style and creative or imaginative thinking.

CHAPTER

17

CONCLUSIONS
AND IMPLICATIONS

The findings of the study, as reviewed in the previous chapter, lead to a
series of conclusions to be presented as the first part of this final chapter.
The first of these conclusions concerns the question we set ourselves at the
start: what difference, if any, does modern as compared to traditional
schooling make? There are, however, three other conclusions to be noted.
These have significance for such issues as the potency of the school as an
influencing social institution, the relation of subcultural forces to the developmental stage concept, and the problem of interaction between school
impact and individual personality. The second part of the chapter points
to implications for education and raises questions for educators while facing frankly the fact that not only the answers but the very questions that
are considered important will differ when projected against the contrasting value systems of the modern and traditional viewpoints.

Conclusions

First, it seems clear that the schools affected the lives and functioning of the children in ways that were pervasive and perhaps profound.

In a sense, the primary question we put to the data was the extent of school impact on the psychological development of the children. The findings suggest that the impact is broad. If we put together the various single strands, children of the different schools seemed to be organized, as people, around different axes. Despite all they shared as the bright, nine-year-old children of successful middle-class parents, they were pointed in somewhat different directions, with a different implicit hierarchy of inner concerns, response styles, goals, strengths, and weaknesses. A connecting thread runs through different parts of the data. Children of the more traditional environments seemed to be organized toward the established and dominant goals of the general culture and toward the successful fulfillment of roles that were conceived in conventional terms and pertinent to their sex and family status. This orientation was the common underlying theme in many of our specific predictions, though they dealt with varied facets of self-image, role orientation, dynamic concerns, and life-stage evaluation. The children of traditional schools, by and large, saw fulfillment in terms of the tangible socially identified criteria of success: social acclaim, recognition, money, attainment of a particular role, and status. By definition, their dreams of power and fulfillment centered on the adult future when such achievements would be possible. In the same way, they were prone to accept the given images of male and female roles, as conventionally presented, and to react in ways associated with their sex. By many criteria, they would be considered well-socialized American children.

This was not the prevailing orientation of children from the more modern environments. There was obviously overlap among children of the different schools, but some quite central aspects of development and attitude were different. Children from the more modern environments were as much the products of their environment as any of the other children and as strongly influenced by the important adults in their lives; they were exposed, however, to different styles and values, including values that regarded conventional rewards, standardized goals, and socially typed roles as only partially meaningful for the individual child. These children appeared to live more in the immediacy of childhood and some larger part of their images and projections partook of their experiences as children and their individual characteristics. They were different in their perspectives of life roles, their relative freedom from conventional images, their con-nectedness with self. The psychological impact of the schools, according to these data, extended beyond intellectual functioning and into the realms of personality development.

Within the realm of intellectual functioning itself, the impact of the different schools was also notable, of course. The schools affected both the patterns of cognitive strength and style and the capacity of the children to mobilize for effective performance, to draw systematically on their reser-voir of facts and concepts, on demand, in standardized situations.

Second, it was evident from the data that the potency of the school's orientation in affecting the children was a function of two conditions: the orientation of the home and its interaction with school influence; and the extent to which the school operated as a total integrated environment.

The relative role of school and home, and the nature of their interaction, presented a complex picture. We were not able to unravel the strands of relative influence, in this study, for a variety of conceptual and method-ological reasons. Families as well as schools varied in their orienta-tion and at times this variation confounded the interpretation of results even where school groups differed clearly. From the nature of the data and our findings, however, there are four points to be made: The first two can be briefly stated; the others bear elaboration.

(a) The school appeared as the most likely prevailing force in some areas, such as intellectual functioning, while the home was apparently dominant in others, such as role orientation among girls.

(b) Where school and home experiences were congruent, the impact on the children was reinforced.

(c) By virtue of the new context it provided, the school might extend or modify attitudes established in the family. The child's understand-ing of authority and his concept of the rules and principles that govern human interaction provide an example of this. In the school context, the child's experience was extended beyond the family; he was exposed to another vision of society, how it works and what it expects of him, and in this context he was somewhat free of the intricacies and deep relationships that are part of family life. Our data suggested that the perception of adults was primarily influenced by the child's family experiences but that the new milieu represented by the school society also affected his perception and development of interpersonal codes. Children of the more traditional schools had a more hierarchial vision of school authority and were more involved with the necessity and implications of living by the adult rules. Their evaluations of behavior were constrained, in a sense, by this powerful framework. Children of the most modern school seemed involved in a more mature search for generalized principles; their approach to the universal questions of right and wrong, just and unjust, was less bound to the reference point of what was acceptable or punishable in the arena of the school. Perhaps this was because the school did not make acceptable behavior the leitmotif of school experience, or because it offered to them a tangible model of rational authority. It does not challenge the primacy of family influence to suggest that the school may extend or modify the quality of codes and judgments as they develop in the child; that it may influence the movement toward either externally based codes or more generalized and internalized principles.[1]

(d) Under some conditions, the uniqueness and power of schooling is such that its impact may be strong even in areas that are usually shaped by the home and even if home and school orientation are not congruent. This point is partly speculative but stems specifically from the unique quality of the Conrad curriculum and atmosphere. Consider, for example, aspects of this school that might influence an area of development usually dominated by the home: role orientation in girls. We have presented the relatively unique orientation of girls from this school as a probable function of their congruent homes and schools, partly because this seems a logical explanation and partly because it is the parsimonious explanation when the backgrounds are confounded. But the curriculum of this school involved both girls and boys in active roles of working and learning, with many media of expression; it exposed them early and often to experiences in the community that offered a variety of possibilities for seeing themselves in various roles; and it put them in contact with adults, both men and women, who functioned actively in many areas. Such a curriculum and environment might well affect the role orientation of girls under any circumstances, even if they came from quite traditional homes.

This study could not go beyond the assessment of differences among the groups and an exploration of factors in school and home that might account for such differences. It does allow for a general conclusion that congruent home and school backgrounds consolidate the direction of effects on children and some speculation that certain conditions of schooling might change the equations of relative impact. It is evident that further research on home-school interaction is imperative and that studies of children from contrasting homes and schools would be particularly valuable.

As has been noted above, the potency of the school's orientation in affecting the children was a function not only of the interplay between school and home influence but of the cohesive quality of the school itself. At the level of sheer consistency, Browning and Conrad constituted a contrast to Adams and Dickens. Both Browning and Conrad created an environment where any single aspect might be considered syntonic with its overall views. Perhaps as a function of this consistency, in educational contexts that were very different, children of these two schools often functioned at the opposite ends of whatever dimension we assessed.

Conrad represented the most integrated philosophy and environment of the four schools, however; it was different even from Browning in that its integration was theoretically broad and consciously developed to cover the gamut of school life. It presented the children with consistent values, models, and kinds of experience in every facet of their school day. At the same time, many Conrad families shared the modern viewpoint. Conrad children, then, usually lived in a consistent atmosphere at home and school, where activities and relationships were built around the goal of potentializing the individual, fulfilling the growth needs and developing the capacities specific to the developmental stage. At the outcome level, this added up to a qualitative difference between these children and children from the other three schools, where no such confluence of common forces existed. It will be clear to the readers of this book that the schools and classrooms were approached and analyzed in pairs: two modern and two traditional. In understanding the effects on the children, however, we often had to discuss the data in a 3:1 model, acknowledging the particular quality of Conrad children. Perhaps we have learned from this study that a distinct, highly integrated, and consistent environment constitutes a particularly forceful influence and is likely to produce a unique pattern of effects.

Dickens represents an interesting contrast to Conrad; its philosophy and approach were basically modern but not in the same total and integrated sense. Similarly, some of its parents were also modern, but not in the same proportions; the Dickens girls of this sample, for instance, all came from traditionally oriented families. As noted earlier, these children were less variable among themselves—perhaps less individualized. Their cognitive pattern represented a mixture: some of the process orientation for which modern schools strive, some of the coping and performance ability which traditional schools stress. They shared with Conrad children a quality of differentiation and personalization in relation to themselves. Yet, in other crucial ways, they were much like children of traditional schools—concerned with adaptation to school authority and with the expression of negative impulse (though they liked school better); they were predominantly oriented toward adulthood and the future; they accepted the images and forms of their social sex roles with comparatively little exploration, adaptation, or unique investment.

It is impressive that a large public school, without a totally integrated philosophy and drawing from a population with mixed values, created the impact it did, affecting aspects both of intellectual growth and of personality development. Where its impact was different from that of Conrad, there might even be disagreement as to where the advantages lay. Some might feel that the general direction of personality development in Conrad children was potentially most healthy and that the partial pattern at Dickens involved some loss, yet that the pattern of cognitive functioning at Dickens constituted a more effective mixture of exploratory style and coping ability than that at Conrad. What is important to note here is that Dickens and Conrad—both modern in their educational philosophy— were not equally potent in moving their children toward the patterns of functioning they espoused; this difference in impact appeared to reflect both the distinct conditions of home-school congruence in the two situations and the extent of integration in the philosophy, atmosphere, and curricula of the schools themselves.

As a third general conclusion, this study suggests that different socializing environments can modify the characteristics assumed to be typical of a developmental stage.

The children of this study were latency or middle-years children, a period often characterized in terms of growing interest in competence and mastery; a new reticence, repression, or concealment of feeling and impulse; a movement to peer allegiances with dichotomous boy-girl groupings and a clear sex typing of behavior and interests; a strong dependence on adults for guidance and approval, even in the context of new strivings for autonomy and independence. If we project the findings of this study against these generalizations, we are led to qualify the inevitability of some of these patterns or at least to suggest that there is a wider existing range of reactions.[2]

These data indicate, for instance, that the range in self-contact and in the expression of personal material was considerable in this group. The children were probably less spontaneously expressive than young children and less elaborately introspective than adolescents, but it would be inaccurate to describe them as uniformly impersonal, evasive, or distant from their own feelings and qualities. Some children personified this image of the latency child but certainly others did not. Neither the generalization concerning self-concealment nor the theoretical assumption of its inevitability seem adequate to explain the range. By and large, the more openly expressive children with freer self-contact came from the more modern environments, where the attempt was made to sustain a close and personal contact with the child. It seems possible that this kind of environment modified what has been assumed to be an inevitable phase of repression, moving the pattern in the direction of greater continuity of self-contact.

The pattern of boy and girl behavior also reflected some variations on prevailing expectations for this developmental stage. The classic antagonism between boys and girls of this age was evident, yet took different forms in different settings. It was modified to a rather open level of interest and interchange at Adams, for instance, where the changing and relatively precocious patterns of the teen and preteen culture had begun to take early root.

Even more striking was the modification of sex-typed patterns in the Conrad group. Boys and girls of this school, as often noted, were not as different from each other as those of the other groups. This is not to say that their functioning was identical—certainly it was not—or that the boy and girl groups had lost their separate qualities. Yet they did not typify the polarization of interests and goals or the sex-typical styles of behavior associated with boys and girls of this age. The probable reasons for this have been discussed at length and do not need repeating. What it suggests, however, is that the commonly described patterns are not only a function of developmental forces but are partly a product of particular environmental conditions.

The relationship with adults suggests a third area where the range of reactions challenges a simple age-level generalization. Characterization of child-adult relations at this developmental stage is in any event a complex matter. Deep conflict between dependence and autonomy is a factor; so are the extent of supportive strength in the peer group, the attitude of adults toward the child's independence, and the child's need to learn from the adults so that he can succeed and be competent in the real world.

Certainly the need for adult encouragement and acknowledgment existed in all the children of the sample in some form. There were qualitative differences, however: children from more traditional environments were more preoccupied with school authority and control and perhaps more fearful; the girls among them were especially concerned with family and with the supportive qualities of benign adults. Perhaps the major difference, however, was not in the sheer need for adult approval and acknowledgment but in the extent to which this was generalized to include all adults. Children of the most modern school were relatively selective in their apparent dependence on adult approval. Taking our research staff as the paradigm of unfamiliar adults, we saw them as relatively independent of our procedures and requests. They were less geared than most to whether we would think well of them and, though some were friendly and interested, they were less disposed to exert strong effort as a matter of compliance or to assure success in the tasks. Perhaps this was a function of their close and in-group world. Perhaps it was a modification of the generalized need for adult approval—a selective dependence on those adults with whom there was a meaningful relationship while maintaining some independence from those adults who were not central figures. Whether this represents strength or an overreaction is not the central issue here. What is primarily suggested is that the pattern of dependence and autonomy in relation to adults was not uniform from group to group but was a partial reflection of differences in environment and experience.

As a general conclusion, then, the study appears to indicate range and differentiation within this developmental stage attributable in part at least to variations in the experiences provided by different school and home backgrounds. Not all the variations reflect modern-traditional differences in background. It does seem possible, however, that characterizations of a developmental stage have implicitly assumed a standardized set of influences on the child or have taken children from essentially middle-class and traditional backgrounds as the subjects of observation and description. A more refined understanding of any developmental stage probably requires both a differentiated analysis of influence variables and a clear recognition that social change can have an important impact on the condition of childhood.

Fourth, the study suggests that the schools have a different impact and meaning for different kinds of children.

To some extent, we can illustrate this point in terms of boy and girl groups, which were differentially affected by the different schools; to some extent, and perhaps more basically, we can illustrate it in terms of the kinds of individuals who were apt to succeed or flounder in the different atmospheres of the traditional and modern schools.

Within the public schools, girls seemed more comfortable and identified, boys more restless and negative. The probability of a more natural "fit" between the style and constraints of the conventional school and the conforming, approval-oriented adaptations prevalent among girls has been pointed out by others. Our study offers some support for this analysis, within the structure of traditional schools in particular and in relation to the more traditionally reared children. It might be noted, however, that adaptation and active accomplishment, even within the schools' own terms, were not identical. In a school like Browning, the girls were more content but not necessarily as effective. They were set aside in a group problem-solving situation, for instance, by the more active, competent and competitive boys. Boys were not highly identified with this school; they chafed at the quality of adult authority (usually female) and the behavioral restraints. Yet some of them found that this competitive and accomplishment-oriented setting presented a kind of challenge and satisfaction, a reaction less prevalent among the girls. The possible correlates in tension, self-image, and style of human interaction are not the issue at this point, though they are psychologically and educationally relevant. What is pertinent here is that this kind of school environment called out a different pattern of reactions, in general, from boys and girls.

We have often noted that the development of boys and girls in Conrad was not so sex typical and distinct as in other groups, yet the impact was clearly different for boys and girls along other lines and the pattern was different from that in more traditional schools. Both boys and girls enjoyed this school and identified with it. This was more unusual in the case of the boys, given the prevailing reactions in other schools. The quality of this school, with its stress on active forms of learning, its informal atmosphere, its encouragement of intensity, its flexible adult-child relationships, and its vital curriculum, seems to have provided a relatively viable environment for boys. At the same time, it is not certain that they had the best of it. When we look at their functioning, as expressed in our material, they did not perform with strength. More than the girls, the boys were guarded and restricted. Some among them were pervasively inhibited, with neither an open communicative quality nor the impersonal ways of managing that characterized the traditionally reared and educated boys. We do not know whether they were blocked in relation to themselves or primarily as they communicated with unfamiliar adults. On the one hand, these boys may not have been representative of boys in this school. On the other hand, these findings may be viewed in connection with the question raised by Bronfenbrenner (1961) of whether the modern boy is in potential trouble, losing some of his male assertiveness—even if it is bravado—without clear alternative sources of strength.

For the girls, the impact of the school may have added up to a more unequivocally positive pattern. Though some of these girls showed evidence of groping and uncertainty, they were generally more responsive, expressive, and effective than the boys. Perhaps as important, they seemed to be developing personal alternatives to conventional and constrained roles, in ways not evident in girls from more traditional backgrounds. Perhaps this school constituted a releasing and expanding environment for girls; its impact seemed generally to be in those terms.

It is equally important in the consideration of differential impact to think in terms of the individual. In any of these environments some children were successful and some floundered, but not the same kinds of children in each, nor in the same ways.

Perhaps the tolls and difficulties of the traditional system do not require much elaboration. We have long been familiar with the problems created for some children by an overstructured and competitive environment. The "unsuccessful" child has little leeway for feeling his strength in areas not identified as relevant. The impulsive child may be subject to discipline and shame. The external orientation and impersonal defenses supported by the environment are brittle in some children and subject to sudden decompensation. The fulfillment of personal potential may be limited by a preordained and circumscribed structure, mildly so in some cases and severely in others.

These conditions did not hold for children in modern schools but for some children the complex and open atmosphere at a school like Conrad may have presented another kind of problem and exacted another kind of toll. This school, with its individual support and pacing, provided the children with meaningful experiences of mastery and pleasure, but it also exposed them early to the sense of the conditional in life and learning. Beyond one set of ideas lay others; for these children, "it depends" became an expression both of their appreciation of complexity and their sense of uncertainty that they had reached closure. In a Piagetian sense, they were young to live with this conditional stance, and some managed and built upon it more successfully than others.

An atmosphere which clearly valued uniqueness, creativity, and self-awareness offered pressures even while it offered supports, especially for children who could not easily exemplify these values. The children who floundered in this complex and open atmosphere may have needed more structure, more definite expectations, and more clearly identified moments of accomplishment, for reasons in themselves and their background. With greater tolerance for a mobile atmosphere, and perhaps with more integrative strength, other children at this school developed and flourished in exactly the vigorous, complex, and differentiated ways the school was trying to foster.

Implications

The implications we can draw for education from the findings and experience of this study are constrained by the complexity of the field. The current educational scene is characterized by a series of new developments, involving theoretical controversy and both practical and theoretical alternatives. For the most part, the ideas we can draw will have relevance to some of these alternatives but not to others. Perhaps the implications from a pilot study such as this must in any event come through as a broadening of horizons rather than as specific recommendations for immediate application in the field. The function of such a study in such an era is both to pose new questions and to point up the relevance of factors which cannot be ignored if the planning and evaluation of educational efforts are to be productive.

A broad educational implication emerges from the study of the four schools. If we can generalize from our material, the key to the nature of educational change, as it is actually incorporated into the classroom experience of the child, appears to lie in the viewpoint and educational purposes of his particular school. The schools in this study not only selected many of their teaching procedures in terms of their prevailing philosophies; they also *shaped* their procedures in terms of their general stance toward learning and children. Child work groups in our data are a case in point. The latter were originally conceived as work experiences in which children would have the opportunity for planning, assigning roles, developing viable rules, and arbitrating conflicts as they arose in the course of the work effort. In the hands of the more traditional schools of our study, working peer groups or committees were often surrounded by so much teacher control and specificity of directives that their purposes, not well understood to begin with, were obviated.

Parallels in the current context are obvious. New materials and curricula have a describable form and purpose as they are developed. As they are absorbed into the schools, however, they become part of the total educational context and partake of the schools' and the teachers' approach. The way in which a programmed course in grammar fits into the school day, and the extent to which the teacher considers himself available for questions and discussion during this period, or freed for other matters, is determined by an educational stance beyond the limits of the particular program, and certainly it affects the impact of the program on the child. By the same token, it is not only possible but in some contexts probable that an innovative curriculum unit—exciting and exploratory in its original content and purposes—will be treated as a new and rigid authority, sufficient unto itself and to be mastered as a package in concrete, teacher-dominated terms. In such an eventuality, its basic purposes are hopelessly distorted. Perhaps a more subtle question arises when the unit is well handled, but is adopted, on the one hand, into a school which is basically fact- and performance-oriented or, on the other, into a school whose prevailing orientation is toward exploration and the discovery process. Would the children of Adams draw the same sense of intellectual quest from such a unit as the children of Dickens—or the children of Dickens the same as those of Conrad?

Our research suggests, then, that schools tend to process new developments in their own way and that the educator and evaluator need to view innovations in the context in which they are in use. An analysis of the orientation of a school would be likely to provide meaningful clues as to the innovations that are syntonic with its philosophy, and illuminate the kind of context and modification with which it is likely to surround any given procedure it incorporates. If we are to understand what happens to children in a changing era, and why it happens, we probably need to take into account not only the nature of the innovations that are offered but the framework of values and goals that mediate their selection and that determine the form in which they will be presented to the child in his own classroom.

Another basic implication of the study stems from its conclusion that schools affect the personality development of children. Our data confirm that schools cannot choose to limit the scope of their impact by fiat—by declaring certain areas off limits and out of bounds (see Biber, 1961; Bower, 1962). We saw some of the clearest effects of the contrasting educational systems in areas related to self-development. Whether they noticed it or wanted it, the traditional schools were affecting the attitudes, styles, and values of their pupils in important areas of development, just as modern schools were, but the nature of their impact was different.

Given these findings, it seems self-evident that the vast array of people concerned with the education of children—educators, psychologists, parents—cannot rest with the idea that the school is in charge of intellectual education, that its impact is measurable through tests of intellectual power and mastery, and that the rest is not its province. It is clearly their responsibility to consider the range of experiences inherent in the child's extended participation in school life; to assess the probable correlates in personality development of the educational procedures he is exposed to; and to make conscious decisions about the kind of development they wish to support.[3] Obviously, some schools—the more modern schools in our study —have been more cognizant of the breadth of school impact, even if they have fallen short of some of their goals, while others—the more traditional schools in our study—have been less interested and less aware.

A similar point, in the context of new educational trends, has been made by Wallach (1966). Impressed by our increasing understanding that creative thought, capable of challenging the nonabsolute postulates of knowledge, requires a playful orientation toward ideas, a suspension of right-wrong orientation, and a willingness to take intellectual risks, he finds it distressing and paradoxical that new developments in programmed instruction, by their very nature, allow for little development or exercise of this stance.[4] Essentially, he is pointing up the fact that any given educational approach carries concomitants beyond its surface qualities and needs to be considered and evaluated in these terms. Extended to include not only intellectual attitudes but many aspects of personality development, the mandate to acknowledge and explore the correlates of an educational approach constitutes one of the major implications of our study.

The study findings concerning the functioning of boys and girls also carry implications and questions for the educational field. The findings suggest that the schools may need to deal with a complex reality, involving at least three aspects: (1) the fact of general sex differences in learning style, motivation, and functioning; (2) the fact that the pattern of differences is not immutable, but may vary from era to era and from one subculture to another, and (3) the evidence that the schools themselves have some influence on the nature and extent of these differences.

Perhaps the fact of general sex differences is the most familiar aspect of the three. To an ever increasing extent in recent years, the research world has been paying systematic attention to such differences, attempting to establish the nature and extent of distinct patterns of functioning (see Maccoby, 1966). There has been some tendency among educators to take a rather literal mandate from this documentation of sex differences and to think in terms of separate education for boys and girls. Obviously this is not the only possible response to the fact of difference, unless difference is taken as inherently negative and disruptive in its impact on learning. From another point of view, one might consider differences in interest, learning style, and perspective as potentially valuable, contributing—as variety often does—to a richer and more complex learning experience for all the participants. Furthermore, if school life and learning are not narrowly defined, then daily interaction in the context of work and learning can provide an important base of communication, respect, and empathy that will be relevant to the later and more complex social-sexual relationships.

Even if the gains are potentially great, however, the accommodation of boys and girls whose interests and styles are different is not simple. It involves administrative, curricular, and attitudinal flexibility. Perhaps it is a special case of the acceptance and management of differences between individuals, presenting the school with analogous problems in handling variety.

If the boy and girl patterns are not immutable, however, as the findings suggest, then the guidelines on sex differences established by research are useful only to a point. The educational field would need to be responsive to the changing trends of the culture, as they modify the development and functioning of boys and girls. The generalization that girls are motivated by affiliation needs and boys by achievement needs, for instance (see Crandall, 1963; Crandall, 1964; Sears, 1962), will probably undergo increasing modification as the culture continues to change, and the relative patterns of interest and expressive style may grow farther apart under some influences and closer together under others. Furthermore, the sex-linked patterns that characterize children in any given school may reflect not the prevailing cultural patterns, whether stable or changing, but the particular subcultural patterns of the population from which the school draws. In any educational situation, then, skillful planning and accommodation for the education of boys and girls probably requires a vigilant and nonstereotyped stance, with the capacity to recognize changing conditions and to experiment with a variety of practices.

The suggestion that the school itself is a formative influence brings another aspect of educational decision into focus. If the school is not simply a reactive institution but one that can shape development, then it has complex decisions to make. Does it recognize and foster the predominant patterns, or does it offer alternatives? To be more concrete, does it honor the espoused wish of boys and girls to be in their own sex groups in as many ways as possible, or does it find some instances where it mixes the groups, perhaps meeting a more latent wish and offering a growth experience? Does it send the girls to cooking and the boys to carpentry because their skills, interests, and sex-appropriate roles lie clearly in these separate directions, or does it expose both boys and girls to both? If it does the latter, is it better done in the context of the curriculum—cooking an old colonial meal, constructing the props for a play—or as distinct periods of training in skills? On what basis does the school make decisions and how does it find the balance?

These are difficult procedural questions. Even when schools are aware that they have impact on role and identity development, adaptations of curriculum are difficult; they involve decisions about appropriate balance and draw on basic attitudes toward the kinds of boys and girls or, more broadly, the kinds of personalities that the school wishes to foster through its educational procedures.

There are, in fact, a host of questions not yet solved by either developmental research or educational experiment that bear on procedural decisions in the schools. Many of these, of course, are directly concerned with the style and pacing of intellectual activity. What are the critical stages for establishing and assuring the development of certain intellectual strengths and skills? What sequences are most effective and with what pacing? What attitudes, knowledge, and skills arise as natural by-products of an active learning process; which require more specific attention and in what form; and is this the same for all children?

The individual problem-solving performance of the Conrad children raises a particular issue in these terms. These children had lived their entire school lives in an educational atmosphere of discussion, probing, the pursuit of ideas, and the weighing and relating of facts to concepts. These were the valued procedures and this was the intellectual model. It seemed logical to expect power and skill in the processes of problem solving. We saw this in the group but not in the individual testing. Leaving aside questions of the appropriateness of our techniques and measures or the relevance of general test-taking skills, we might raise another issue: were these children aware of their own skills? Did they know that they possessed a virtual armamentarium of intellectual tools and experience relevant to the problem-solving tasks? Would it have been desirable or helpful for them to know this?

Current developments in the teaching of problem-solving strategies present an interesting contrast to the practices at a school like Conrad and serve to concretize and sharpen the issues. Aspects of the approach advocated by Bruner (1966) or the Productive Thinking Program developed by Covington, Crutchfield, and Davies (1966), for instance, bring the child through certain problem-solving experiences and make him consciously aware that he possesses a useful thinking tool—a way of proceeding logically through problems, gathering and processing information. Though they dealt daily with problem-solving procedures akin to these programs, the experience of the Conrad children was very different. The process was always in the context of ongoing learning, and there was little tendency to point to the experience or the methods, to extrapolate and make articulate the procedures and sequences by which the ideas of the class were discussed and checked and evolved. The knowledge of "my*self*" approaching an idea to pursue it or a problem to solve it was not the kind of self-consciousness that a school like Conrad customarily worked with, though it attempted to support the general feeling of *self* as one who is capable and competent.

Probably few modern schools would choose to rehearse their children in problem-solving skills for their own sake, as an exercise with material that is not meaningful in itself, nor would they articulate and analyze the experience so actively that the investment and the process become secondary or deflected. Yet without moving to extremes, there may be valid questions for consideration.

A school like Conrad assumes, probably with considerable validity, that intellectual processes which are experienced over and over tend to become more and more functional and that at later stages they become somewhat independent of the context and are observed and understood as processes by the more mature individual. But does this happen inevitably? And are there any advantages, even at younger stages, to more focusing and articulation of such processes? Would Conrad children have been less swamped by the test-ness or the alone-ness in the problem-solving situations, for instance, if they had been more consciously aware of their very relevant experiences, tools, and skills? Would that knowledge be especially useful in situations that touch off a struggle between anxiety reactions and coping patterns?

Here, as already noted, the issues concerning the natural by-products of a process are important, as are the questions concerning optimal stages for fostering new integrations and new strengths. It is suggested here only that there are constant procedural questions in connection with the achievement of desirable goals—questions of educational balance and methodology raised by new developments in the educational field, by information gathered through ongoing observation, and by studies such as this concerning the impact of school experience on child functioning and development.

In the long run, the implications of a study such as this, however, must be filtered through a value system. Educators differ in their conceptions of the successfully educated child, in their definitions of effectiveness, in the kinds of human beings they are trying to foster. In this final section, therefore, it might be fruitful to consider the findings and implications of the study from within the framework of the traditional and modern philosophies.

It seems likely that the traditional schools of this study would be basically satisfied with the performance of their children in response to the study material. For the most part, these children were intellectually competent and achieving at high levels. Furthermore, these schools would probably sanction the general orientation of their children toward the future, toward achievement, toward established roles, and toward a prominent concern with school authority and control. Whether or not they were explicitly concerned with development in all these areas, they might find these trends compatible with their image of a successfully educated and socialized child.

If we apply the modern framework to the performance of traditional school children, however, the findings raise some questions. It is not certain that these children were intellectually well educated despite their high achievement levels. In some senses, the thinking and learning ability of very bright children in the traditional schools of this sample was only poorly challenged and activated—a fact obvious from some of the illustrative material in the Schools and Classrooms chapters. If creative, exploratory, and integrative thought is an educational value, even the high-achieving children at Adams and Browning represented a degree of educational failure. One would need to hope that out-of-school or future experiences would enrich and modify the style of thought encouraged by these schools.

Even more broadly, it is important to ask whether the ultimate purposes of these schools were sufficiently complex and well thought out, considering that the school is not only a "socializing agent" but a formative influence on individual development as well. From within the framework of the modern viewpoint, any school has the responsibility to consider the relationship between the values it imparts, through its ideology and procedures, and the ultimate development of the child into a mature, integrated, emotionally responsive individual, whose modes of relationship to life are not only competent but self-invested and unique. There is little evidence that traditional schools were concerned with these aspects of development, and some evidence that their impact was more constricting than otherwise.

To see the dilemma of the traditional schools from within their own framework, we might need to turn to a different and less privileged population, with whom traditional schools have been less successful. The children of the slums do not achieve, they do not read well, and sometimes they cannot be kept in school. To an extent, the traditional school may need to depend for success in its own terms on children like those of our study, who come into school already well motivated, articulate, ready to adapt to school requirements, and skillful in ways that fit the school culture.

The issues these schools must face, it seems to us, are partly those of technique and partly those of ultimate purpose. Obviously, by any criteria, they must find new methods of instruction for disadvantaged children. This search is already active. For the most part, current choices seem to be moving toward specific teaching devices which do not require much training of personnel and which are aimed at the repair of specifically perceived deficits. In times of crisis and urgency, the more swift and tangible procedures have more obvious appeal. Whether or not they will be truly effective, and what context they will need for optimal effect, is still an open question. Perhaps in the long run, schools with traditional goals will need to adopt more modern methods even to achieve their own aims. They may need to broaden their conception of what motivates learning, provide more active contexts for learning activities, make their material more relevant to the life interests of their children, and modify the more rigid aspects of authority structure in the school, even to serve their own primary purpose of bringing children to adequate achievement levels.

When we consider the modern schools in their own terms, the questions are somewhat different. Here the goals were consciously attuned to concepts of psychological health. The issues lie in how they were fulfilling these goals and whether the findings can offer further leads for thought and experimentation in pursuit of these purposes. How would the modern schools themselves regard the findings of this study?

For the proponents of modern education, many of the findings would appear positive and satisfying. It is likely that they would regard the findings on self-image, on life-stage preferences, on social sex role, on the children's perception of school authority, as basically desirable. In general, this syndrome would suggest a core of individualized development, some sense of possible autonomy in relation to the school and its adults, and a set of interests and values that are not prematurely adult nor excessively convergent.

There are, of course, questions to raise even about these findings, though they would be at different levels from within different frameworks. The traditional educator, for instance, might challenge the basic desirability of an orientation which is not geared to the conventional values and goals of society, asking if this is a disturbing socialization failure. Even the modern educator might have some questions in terms of balance points and individuals. He might ask, for instance, at what point and for which children a strong investment in one's child role and its pleasures becomes a subtle defense against growth and greater autonomy. Yet the modern educator, and the authors, would see basic strength in the evidence of a general investment in childhood. It would seem to be the positive product of a point of view which is countercyclical to the prevailing moral futurism of American culture, as described by David Hawkins (1966), which "accepts the child only as the future adult" and channels choice and experience from increasingly earlier stages toward tangible success in later years. Recurrent postponement of fulfillment to a stereotyped future goal is regarded from this countercyclical point of view as relatively empty and unsatisfactory. It is seen as jeopardizing the foundations on which fulfillment in later life can be built, namely, deep involvement and pleasure in current experience at each developmental stage.

In the same way, other findings concerning the modern school children would seem acceptable and healthy from within the modern ideological framework. Perhaps two aspects of the findings concerning Conrad children in particular, however, raise special questions within this framework and bear some discussion: first, the suggestion that some children floundered unproductively and appeared unable or unwilling to mobilize and express themselves even in their own terms; and second, aspects of the pattern of cognitive functioning, including the fact that performance skill seemed erratic and that exploratory problem solving (in individual situations) and imaginative thinking were less systematically evident than might have been expected.

The question of why some children appeared vulnerable and inhibited may need to be seen in the broad context of the school's atmosphere and approach. Its high tolerance for individuality, for instance, may be a pertinent factor. The encouragement and appreciation of variation among individuals form a cornerstone of the modern educational approach. Both the growth of the individual as a unique person and his firm mastery of knowledge and experience are thought to depend on his opportunities to integrate and re-express what he learns in his own way. Such schools expect and encourage differences in individual styles, interests, patterns of strength and response; the consistent pattern of wide variability in the responses of Conrad children are not only explicable in these terms, in all probability, but would be generally acceptable to the school as a desirable finding.[5] On the other hand, the high tolerance for individual variation may sometimes encompass patterns that are not adaptive. As suggested earlier, the close relationship to adults, the sense of evolving activities, and the value placed on self-awareness and creativity may have constituted pressure for some children even while freeing and encouraging most others. For this and other reasons, some children in the group may have developed patterns that were essentially maladaptive—more defensive than productively unique—and the very tolerance for individual adaptations that characterized such a school may have perpetuated these ways of coping. The few children we saw who seemed to flounder or hold back may have been children who could not integrate their own functioning in effective ways without clear lines to guide them.

It would be regrettable if this analysis were to perpetuate the misconception that the classroom culture of schools like Conrad is laissez faire, chaotic, or without boundaries. To the careful reader of the early chapters, it is clear that this is not so. The classroom had an adult in charge, a peer culture that exercised controls on its members, and a series of learning purposes and functional procedures that shaped the functioning of the individual in his classroom group. It is no accident that the Conrad children formed the most effective problem-solving working group by far, almost certainly because they had experience and disciplined skill in working as individuals within a group structure and toward group goals. At the same time, however, it was basic to the school's purposes that it should have a wide tolerance for individuality in functioning.

Perhaps the implication under discussion here is that positive facets of an educational approach—whether an appreciation of creativity, a tolerance for individuality or a closeness in relationships—can have their negative underside in the way they affect particular children. The school faces the subtle problem of adjusting its approach and devising alternative means to serve its basic purposes for certain children.

The pattern of cognitive functioning raises a somewhat different level of question, since it applies less to a small minority than to the group as a whole. We might consider the aspects of performance effectiveness and problem-solving approach in terms of how they might appear to modern educators and what they imply.

Again, we might best approach these issues in the context of the modern educational rationale. Modern educators have developed their procedures on the basis of certain assumptions about the purposes of primary education, and the course of intellectual development. Like the developmental psychologists—whose research increasingly suggests that some patterns, qualities, and attitudes become relatively stable for many children during this period—educators of all persuasions have tended to see the early elementary years as a critical period, when the basic approach to the world of knowledge and intellectual functioning is laid down. Where the traditional educators stress the technical tools and skills and the three R's as foundation, however, the modern educators see this as a period when it is important to help the child develop many schemata for integrating and expressing knowledge. In a school like Conrad, it was a conscious decision to provide a variety of experiences and many media for their expression rather than to channel the child's early school experience predominantly through practice in the verbal symbol skills and through the repeated evaluation of performance in these terms. They have felt that these skills are not vital at young ages, that overemphasis on their development in the first years of school shuts out other and more generic learning, and that these skills can be consolidated more easily and at less cost in later years. Pertinent also is the fact that they have built their educational approach around a more epigenetic concept of development than the traditional. They have not felt that later patterns depend literally on training in identical skills and that "the earlier the better." Rather, they have assumed that later patterns evolve predictably in more highly integrated forms out of early patterns that are essential for such development but are not literally and descriptively parallel. Within this framework, modern educators might regard the lesser performance efficiency of Conrad children at age nine with relative equanimity.

The basic evaluation of this finding—and the decision as to whether any adaptations are required—depends not so much on the nine-year-old pattern but on the course of later development. The educational goals for these children as late adolescents and young adults would include not only an exploratory and self-directed approach to knowledge and a differentiated sense of self but an ability to integrate their efforts and to function effectively. The issues of stability and change in development, of course, affect both modern and traditional forms of education. One might ask whether, in later life, traditional school children would continue to highlight efficiency and factual orientation, yet be able to apply a more differentiated and open-ended style of thought to their identity problems, just as one might ask whether modern school children would be relatively exploratory in their approach to learning and to life roles, yet be able to function at crucial points in ways that would demonstrate their competence and advance them toward their own goals.

In the final analysis, the impact of education does not lie so much in the tangible performance of the individual at any stage. It lies, rather, in its effect on his continuing efforts to integrate experience into the ongoing processes of his own life and development.

NOTES

1. Hoffman and Saltzstein's (1964) distinction between a humanistically oriented, flexible, and well-integrated orientation versus a more externalized, conventional, moral orientation, or a more rigidly punitive one seems pertinent to this difference.
2. See the following for the expression of a similar viewpoint covering the qualification of the developmental stage concept: Kessen (1962), Flavell (1963), Hunt (1961).
3. For a relevant analysis of educational procedures and associated personality processes, see Biber (1967).
4. Among other writers who have also developed this idea are Schachtel (1959), MacKinnon (1962), Murphy (1956), and Barron (1963).
5. The connection between variability of response and environments which tolerate diversity has been noted by Becker (1964). He summarizes projective studies in which warm and permissive family backgrounds led to a greater variety of response patterns: "such findings are consistent with the common sense notion that permissiveness serves as a generalized reinforcer for a wide range of responses just as restrictive attitudes appear to have a generalized inhibitory effect." (p. 199)

SECTION
V

Appendixes

APPENDIX A

GUIDE FOR OBSERVATION OF CLASS GROUP

I. ACADEMIC PERIODS

A. *Context.*

1. Group constellation. Note subgroups.
2. Structure of the situation. Note:
   - (a) Task set by teacher; what is she trying to teach?
   - (b) What is she trying to get the children to learn, to understand?
   - (c) Materials she prepares for children's use.
   - (d) Formal requirements she makes (clearing desks, sitting still, "no talking," seating arrangements) and any other "management," or control techniques at beginning and throughout lesson.

B. *Content and Nature of Children's Activity.* Note the level that is most characteristic of the group; note individuals markedly outside the mainstream.

1. Nature of the children's involvement in the work. Note:
   - (a) Extent and quality of interest, listening (for example, concentrating and absorbed? compliant, passive, dutifully attentive?), participating (for example, asking questions? making comments?).
   - (b) Signs of tension: strain, discomfort, laughter, joking, clowning, withdrawal, day-dreaming, fiddling with self, with objects.
   - (c) Signs of pleasure: comments, conversation, expressions of adequacy, curiosity, wonder, satisfaction, fun in connection with mastery of ideas, of learning skills.
2. Interaction relationships. Note:
   - (a) Interaction among children: related to the work? extraneous to the work?
   - (b) Interaction between children and teacher (other adults): teacher's acceptance, rejection, encouragement, or discouragement of children's behavior.
3. Content and quality of thinking:
   Ideas expressed, questions asked, comments, remarks, answer to questions set by teacher, answers to remarks made by other children.

C. *Observer's Impression.*

   - (a) Of connection between this activity and previous school experience.
   - (b) Of connection between this activity and the children's out-of-school lives.
   - (c) Of how much teacher demands that the children's form of thinking parallel her own.
   - (d) Of extent of teacher direction, how it moves from children to teacher.

413

(e) Of extent to which children interact with each other's ideas and/or with the teacher's ideas.

II. ARTS, SHOP, MUSIC, PLAY PRODUCTION
  A. *Context.* Note:
    (a) Whether activity is connected with an ongoing project, or curriculum.
    (b) Amount of direction and from whom (follow throughout course of period).
    (c) Subject matter or content children are attempting to express or handle.
    (d) Amount of group-initiated versus teacher-directed activity.
    (e) Whether children are working together on a single task or at specialized jobs.
    (f) Any coordination between individual and group purpose.
  B. *Degree of Interest and Enthusiasm.* Note:
    (a) Level of concentration and absorption.
    (b) Comments, ideas, remarks, relevant to their work.
    (c) Interaction among children, between children and teacher, extraneous to the work.
  C. *Skill, Ingenuity, Inventiveness with Materials, Ideas.* Note:
    (a) General level of competence, deftness with material.
    (b) Amount of difference in expressive qualities of product in progress, uniqueness.
    (c) Help asked for, and from whom.
  D. *Observer's Impression.*
    (a) Of expressive scope for action, freedom of action in this activity.
    (b) Of how typical group's functioning was with regard to other school activities.
    (c) Of how much "groupness" is expressed and in what way.
    (d) Of opportunity given, or taken, for cooperation among the children.

ANALYTIC SCHEME FOR ASSESSING THE TEACHER'S STRUCTURING OF THE CHILDREN'S COGNITIVE EXPERIENCE IN THE CLASSROOM

I. LEVEL OF THINKING AS STRUCTURED BY TEACHER

A. *Approach to Mastery of Symbolic Skills*

1. Emphasis on *memorization;* practice in skills; repetitive, routinized drill-type practices and exercises may be employed, for example, flash cards, blackboard, workbook, work sheets prepared by teacher, and so on. Emphasis on accuracy and/or speed.

2. Emphasis on *understanding* via previously learned or simpler concrete processes; use of concrete aids. Connections with other skill area may be noted or emphasized.

3. Emphasis on understanding of symbolic skills on more abstract level: highlighting understanding of relationships, principles, or logical connections.

4. Insufficient evidence.

5. Doesn't apply.

B. *Variety in Approach to Learning of Skills*

1. (a) Single-format exercise for practice.
   (b) Single-format exercise for clarification, understanding, insight.

2. (a) Multiple-format exercises for practice.
   (b) Multiple and varied exercises for clarification, understanding, insight.

3. Insufficient evidence.

4. Doesn't apply.

C. *Approach to Mastery of Conceptual Knowledge*

1. Absence of conceptualization: emphasis on research skills, for example finding source materials; skill in oral and written reporting, skill in evaluating reports of others; skill in "listening hard."

2. Conceptual facts and information introduced and reviewed as important elements of knowledge to learn and remember per se. No or minimal attempt to explore implications, causal connections or relationships. Activity may be conducted as a recitative, question-answer period.

3. Encouraging or structuring for discussion or activity in which facts and information are used, to go beyond facts learned to arrive at connections, to explore ideas, meanings. Ideational connections with other subject matter areas may be emphasized or noted.

4. Insufficient evidence.

5. Doesn't apply.

D. *Problem-Solving Orientation*

1. Technical skill, or the following of step-by-step directions in the solution of a given problem may be emphasized. No problem-solving orientation.

2. Children are given the opportunity to find steps toward the solution of a set problem. Teacher sets a particular problem.
3. Children are given opportunity to discover their own problem(s) through free manipulation and exploration of ideas or materials. No emphasis on technical skill per se.
4. Insufficient evidence.
5. Doesn't apply.

DEGREE OF EMPHASIS ON RELATIONSHIP THINKING

Scale:

1	2	3	4	5
Very Low	Low	Medium	High	Very High

II. COGNITIVE EXPLORATION
   A. *Orientation of Cognitive Experience*
      1. Teacher challenges interest, stimulates enjoyment. Keeps period running smoothly in terms of task-oriented interest per se.
      2. Teacher expresses or generates anxious tension, sarcasm, irritability; may stimulate disorganized emotional expression in the children.
      3. (a) Teacher prods, pushes, demands attention, punishes inattentiveness. In general, her energy seems predominantly directed toward maintaining order.
         (b) Maintenance of order is task-oriented.
      4. Teacher's time spent checking, correcting, evaluating work.
      5. Insufficient evidence.
      6. Doesn't apply.
   B. *Subject Matter*
      1. Intellectual content draws upon or extends children's realm of experience.
      2. Content or task distant from children's realm of experience.
         (a) Utilization of vicarious experience.
         (b) Formal, stereotyped (for example, practice exercise).
      3. Insufficient evidence.
      4. Doesn't apply.
   C. *Teacher's Remarks*
      1. Teacher interjects remarks or ideas feeding into children's thinking.
      2. Teacher's remarks interfere or interrupt flow of children's thinking.
      3. No interruptions or interjections.
      4. Insufficient evidence.
      5. Doesn't apply.
   D. *Pace Allowed or Tempo Established*
      1. Teacher accepts children's pace, allows time for completion.
      2. Teacher hurries children along.
      3. Children wait for teacher.
      4. Inconsistent (specify).
      5. Insufficient evidence.
      6. Doesn't apply.

E. *Assistance with Problems*
   1. Teacher gives active assistance or emotional support when children flounder or ask for help.
   2. Teacher allows or insists that children work out problems for themselves.
   3. Teacher ignores or fails to give assistance.
   4. Assistance not required in the situation.
   5. Teacher disparages or dismisses child as incompetent.
   6. Insufficient evidence.
   7. Doesn't apply.
F. *Breadth of Exploration*
   1. Teacher permits wide scope of content as relevant, either from children's remarks, or by cuing for multiple approaches or answers.
   2. Teacher permits narrow scope of content as relevant; cues for specific approaches or answers.
   3. Insufficient evidence.
   4. Doesn't apply.

DEGREE OF LEEWAY FOR INDEPENDENT COGNITIVE EXPLORATION

Scale:	1	2	3	4	5
	Very Low	Low	Medium	High	Very High

ANALYTIC SCHEME FOR ASSESSING THE CHILDREN'S COGNITIVE BEHAVIOR IN THE CLASSROOM

I. INVOLVEMENT
   A. *Work Orientation*
      The extent to which the children are interested in and absorbed by the work: that is, do they settle down, concentrate, contribute to the task at hand, or are they slow to settle, distractible, daydreaming, or engaged in task-irrelevant activities?

                     WORK ORIENTATION
   Scale: 1   2   3   4   5
             Very Low Low Medium High Very High

   B. *Affect*
      In general the children seem to be
         a. enjoying themselves _____
         b. passive, flat _____
         c. restless, uneasy _____
      (Annotate aggressive/resistive)
   C. *Interaction of Teacher and Children*
      1. *Extent of class participation in ongoing activity*
         Only a few children, or one child _____
         A core group of children _____
         Most of the class _____
         All _____
      2. *Frequency of children's participation in central class activities*
                              DESIRE   OPPORTUNITY
         Frequent   _____   _____
         Infrequent   _____   _____
      3. *Task-relatedness of interaction*
         Predominantly task-related _____
         Predominantly not task-related _____

             DEGREE OF INVOLVEMENT IN WORK, LEARNING, AND
                       ONGOING ACTIVITIES
   Scale: 1   2   3   4   5
             Very Low Low Medium High Very High

II. QUALITY AND STYLE OF THINKING
   In this record, the children have:
      Ample opportunity to express ideas _____
      Limited opportunity to express ideas; some opportunity to answer specific questions _____
      No opportunity to express ideas _____
   A. *Relevance of children's contributions*
      1. Primarily relevant _____

2. Some irrelevance _____
3. Considerable irrelevance _____

B. *Coherence of children's contributions*
1. Primarily coherent _____
2. Some incoherence _____
3. Considerable incoherence _____

C. *Relationship Thinking*
In general the children seem to think through ideas, attempt to make connections, pertinent observations, offer or ask thoughtful comments, questions, and so on _____
Respond to or ask questions, offer information, and so on, but without extending the topic, connecting or generalizing ideas _____
Other _____

_____

_____

NB if record provides good illustration (e.g., of thinking, peer relations, T action, etc.)

Rater's Confidence in rating process (note any variability)   H   M   L

MODERN AND TRADITIONAL CHILD-REARING IDEOLOGIES

The theoretical descriptions below specify aspects of parental ideology that distinguish between the modern and traditional points of view. The resulting characterization, as in all typologies, is of an ideal, not to be found in reality. Furthermore, the assumption is made that these ideologies may be mediated through different personality structures.

I. CONCEPTION OF PARENTAL ROLE

A. *Investment in Authority*

MODERN

The parent views his authority as temporary, gradually to be ceded as the child's maturity, intelligence, and experience make it possible for him to assume responsibility for his own behavior, to become his own authority.

The parent may be benevolent in his exercise of authority, although he will sometimes consider it necessary to be firm or arbitrary; he holds it as a goal, however, to acquaint the child with the reasons behind his authoritative decisions, in order to encourage rational understanding of, rather than unquestioning submission to authority.

The parent encourages the child in certain par relations with adults, within the limits of the child's experience, without feeling that this will interfere with his authority as a parent.

TRADITIONAL

The parent views his authority as a quality inherent in the role and position of being a parent and does not set himself the goal of helping the child gradually assume authority for himself.

The parent may be benevolent in his exercise of authority but he does not consider it necessary that his authoritative decisions should seem reasonable to the child; he is likely to hold that the child's inexperience makes this an inappropriate goal and that there is no implicit harm to the child in learning to accept authority without question.

The parent sees certain clear-cut boundaries between child and adult roles and regards it as important that the child, being in the inferior position of having less knowledge and experience and of physical and social dependence, shall not be granted the privilege of crossing these boundaries on his own initiative lest, in so doing, he transgress to the orbit of parental authority.

B. *Responsibility for Socialization*

The parent is concerned with the conflict (repeated in different forms

The parent is predominantly oriented toward meeting the requirements of

MODERN	TRADITIONAL

at various stages of development) between the requirements of socialization and the child's need to fulfill his impulses; accepting both, he tries to achieve a balance between them in accordance with the child's gradually maturing capacities for inhibition, channeling, and sublimation.

socialization; he is more concerned with the child's success in controlling unacceptable impulses (after early infancy) than in the possible cost of socialization to the child.

Accordingly, he prefers modes of discipline and control that will support the child's increasing capacity for self-control even though these may not immediately effect changes in the child's behavior.

He prefers forms of control that are efficient in altering the child's behavior toward increased socialization.

II. CONCEPTION OF CHILDHOOD

A. *Meaning of Child Behavior*

The parent tries to understand the meaning of the child's behavior by taking motives and situations into consideration; he is more concerned with the determinants of the child's behavior than with the impact of the behavior on the environment.

The parent is likely to take the child's behavior at face value; he is more concerned with the impact of the behavior on the environment than with the sources from which it springs.

He is therefore less likely to develop fixed criteria for evaluating child behavior since his judgments are made in context for the individual child.

He judges the child's behavior by the extent to which it adheres to established criteria whose common denominator is the behavior itself rather than its determinants.

B. *Childhood as Preparation for Adulthood*

The parent views childhood as a symbolic preparation for adulthood. He views the development from childhood to adulthood partly as a natural, evolutionary process, in which satisfaction at every stage, through experiences appropriate to the maturity level, will be most likely to lead to stable, responsible adulthood.

The parent views childhood as a literal preparation for adulthood. He therefore stresses direct and early training in those aspects of behavior considered essential to successful and proper functioning in adult life.

III. STANDARDS, CODES, AND VALUES

A. *Standards of Achievement*

MODERN

TRADITIONAL

The parent is concerned both with the child's individual abilities and interests and with the adequacy of his performance by objective standards.

The parent is primarily concerned that the child's performance be adequate by objective standards, placing considerably less emphasis on fostering the child's individual abilities and interests.

The child's performance is seen in terms of his particular capacities and rate of achievement.

The child's performance is seen against the background of normative group expectations.

The parent places primary emphasis on the child's ability to think independently and sees this as the most important measure of achievement.

The parent places primary emphasis on the child's mastery of subject matter and sees this as the most important measure of achievement.

The parent hopes that the child's satisfaction in achievement will be derived both from fulfillment of his personal goals and interests and from success according to external objective standards.

The parent assumes that the child's satisfaction in achievement will be guaranteed as a by-product of success according to external objective standards.

B. *Codes of Behavior*

The parent presents his own code of behavior to the child with strong conviction but does not expect his code to serve the child without modification as he grows into adulthood. Rather he expects the child to synthesize the environmental forces contemporary to him with the parents' value system and grow into adulthood with his own code of behavior.

The parent presents to the child what he regards as an established code of behavior. He expects the child to accept and abide by this code and assumes that he will grow into adulthood with the code relatively unchanged.

PARENT QUESTIONNAIRE

The first section of this questionnaire deals with factual information about your family. We need this information for statistical purposes. Your answers will, of course, like all our other data, be kept completely confidential. If, however, you prefer not to answer a question, just leave it blank.

GENERAL INFORMATION

Date _____

Name _____ Sex _____ Age _____

Name of husband or wife _____ Age _____

Number of years married _____

	YOURSELF	YOUR HUSBAND OR WIFE
Place of birth	_____	_____

Formal Education (give name of school and city in which located)

Elementary School	_____	_____
High School	_____	_____
College	_____	_____
Other	_____	_____

Number of school years completed, or highest degree or diploma received	_____	_____
Present Occupation (Specify type of work)	_____	_____
Name or type of Firm or Organization with which connected (if any)	_____	_____
Position with Organization	_____	_____
Part-time or Full-time	_____	_____
Mother's occupation before marriage and/or birth of children	_____	_____

Approximate annual family income (Check one—if fluctuates greatly, check approximate *average* over past five years)

Under $5,000	_____
$5,000–$9,000	_____
$10,000–$14,999	_____
$15,000–$24,000	_____
$25,000 or over	_____

Number of children
(Give name, age, sex) _____

                       _____

                       _____

                       _____

                       _____

How long have you been living in this neighborhood? _____
What community activities are you interested in?

Have you had *major moves* during the past ten years? (Indicate what other neighborhoods or towns you have lived in for a year or more and the approximate length of time you lived in each place.)

What do you and your family usually do during the summer?

Have you done any extensive traveling during the past ten years? (If so, indicate approximate duration of trip and whether your children accompanied you, or what arrangements were made for them.)

The following questions apply to your child in the fourth grade:

Did your child attend nursery school? (If so, please specify the school, its location, and the ages during which he attended.)

At what grade-level (including kindergarten) did your child enter this school? _____
(If your child previously attended another elementary school, please specify for which grades, the name of the school, and its location.)

Do you think your child will attend the public high school in your neighborhood? _____
If not, what high school or schools are you considering?

Indicate the approximate amount of time per week that your child spends in special lessons, and what these are (e.g., music lessons, art lessons, dancing lessons, religious instruction, language instruction, etc.).

Approximately how much time does he spend each week watching TV? _____
                                                          reading? _____
How frequently does he go to the movies? _____
What did your child do last summer?

The summer before?

Please comment briefly on your child's development in each of the following areas:

a) Eating   (Indicate whether bottle or breast fed, demand or scheduled feeding, approximate age of weaning, any special features. Do you now consider your child to be a good eater?)

b) Toilet training   (Indicate approximate age that bladder and bowel training were started and completed, any special features.)

c) Walking   (Indicate approximate age when your child started to walk, any special features of motor development.)

d) Talking   (Indicate approximate age of first real words, approximate age of real talking, and any special features of speech development.)

Were there any special difficulties in any of the areas above? (if not already mentioned)

Did your child have any special sleeping difficulties at any time? If so, please describe.

When your child cried, as an infant, and did not seem to need feeding, changing, burping, etc., did you pick him up and hold him?
Usually or always? _____ Sometimes? _____ Rarely or Never? _____

Indicate your child's general level of *health* during childhood; specify operations and serious illnesses, any special health problems.

Has your child's health been good during the past year?

ATTITUDE SECTION

The following are statements about which people hold varying opinions or convictions. Please try to answer them according to your own real thoughts and feelings. Some are concerned with children at home, and some with children at school.

Read each question carefully, but try not to spend too much time on any one question. In general, try to answer in terms of your first reactions, without too much hesitation.

I

For this group of statements, please indicate the extent of your agreement or disagreement with each one by checking the line under the appropriate column. Do not use the "neutral" column unless you really feel completely neutral about the statement; that is, absolutely balanced between agreement and disagreement, or absolutely indifferent.

	AGREE		NEUTRAL	DISAGREE	
	Strongly	Moderately		Moderately	Strongly
1. The best reward for parents' efforts is the gratitude of their children.	—	—	—	—	—
2. Children will put forth their best efforts to learn only when they are stimulated by competition with others. Such competition prepares them for real life in a competitive world.	—	—	—	—	—
3. Whatever one may think about the importance of enjoyable school subjects like art, music, and dramatics, they should be the first to be cut down in the day's schedule if the children's serious academic work is falling below par.	—	—	—	—	—
4. It is better for a child to try to live up to his *own* standards of behavior, even if immature, than to live completely by his parents' more mature standards.	—	—	—	—	—
5. Children owe it to their parents always to do their best to meet their parents' wishes.	—	—	—	—	—
6. Parents should do something about those junior high school girls who go to school with lipstick, mascara, and high-heeled shoes.	—	—	—	—	—

AGREE NEUTRAL DISAGREE

Strongly   Moderately   Moderately   Strongly

7. Only when children grow up and are able to think and reason clearly are they able to make wise decisions. Therefore it is only fair to children that parents make their important decisions for them until they are really grown-up. — — — — —

8. If parents want to keep their children's respect, they should not admit their ignorance too readily. — — — — —

9. Playing is a child's way of building up interest and desire to work, and therefore it is important to think twice before interrupting his play—even when letting him finish would disrupt such family routines as dinner-time. — — — — —

10. The purpose of a report card is to let parents know how their child is doing in relation to the other children in his class. — — — — —

11. It is most helpful in teaching a child standards of behavior to make him feel that if he behaves well, he will deserve his parents' love. — — — — —

12. There are quite a few times with a nine-year-old when a parent can forget he is a parent and just relax and enjoy himself. — — — — —

13. In preparing a child for citizenship, the school should, first and foremost, teach him respect for rules and the ability to conform to the group. — — — — —

14. If a child spends his allowance as soon as he gets it, instead of saving, he will be building up spendthrift habits for the future. — — — — —

II

Below is a series of situations and questions, each with two or more alternative answers. For each question, please place a *check* beside the alternative you prefer. Sometimes it may be hard to choose between them, but please check the one which comes *closest* to being your choice. Sometimes you may have to choose the alternative which is least objectionable.

15. Which of the following reports from school about a child's social relationships should please a parent more? (check one)
    a. Your child is kind, considerate, courteous, and dependable in his relations with both adults and children. He is unusually conscientious about his social responsibilities and seems very concerned with pleasing others. ____
    b. Your child is direct and warm in his approach to other children, and has formed several vital relationships with classmates. He tends quite often to get into quarrels, and is sometimes inconsiderate of other children. ____
16. Most parents enjoy seeing their three- or four-year-old sing or dance or recite for visitors, but when a nine-year-old insists on being the center of attention, they may react in different ways. Which reaction would you be most likely to have? (check one)
    a. It is important to find out why he seems to need to be the center of attention in adult company. ____
    b. It is important to explain to him that people find this kind of show-off behavior inappropriate and annoying in a child of his age. ____
17. In the "clubs" which children so often form at the age of nine or ten, they frequently develop among themselves codes of behavior which differ, in their extreme emphasis on group loyalty, from those stressed by adults. Which statement best describes your attitude toward those clubs? (check one)
    a. Parents should forbid their children to participate in such groups. ____
    b. Parents should let their children belong, but they should try to counteract the influence of such groups. ____
    c. Parents should let their children participate in some activities in which they work out their own rules of behavior, even if these differ somewhat in emphasis from those which are followed at home. ____
18. Janie, who is 11, began to receive a weekly allowance some months ago. Recently she came home one day with a doll on which she had spent her entire savings. Her parents felt that it was both childish and too expensive. (check one)
    a. They decided, nevertheless, to accept her choice, and let her handle her allowance in her own way. ____
    b. They decided, in the future, to review all purchases with her first. ____
19. At dinner, one night, Sammy's parents and their guests were discussing the coming presidential election. Sammy, aged ten, spoke up against the candidate his father was supporting. What should Sammy's parents do? (check one)
    a. Sammy should be told that he'll have to leave the table if he interrupts again. ____
    b. Sammy should be reminded in a nice way that he really doesn't know enough to participate in the discussion. ____
    c. Sammy's opinions should be included in the discussion. ____

20. Larry had been taunted mercilessly by his older cousin. Then, once, on the occasion of a family birthday party, he let go with a barrage of obscene language his parents had never heard him use before. Which of the following ways of handling the situation would be most like yours in a similar situation? (check one)

    a. Larry's father felt that there was some justification for Larry's feeling though not for his behavior; while, under the circumstances, he felt he couldn't let Larry stay at the party, he decided to leave the party with Larry. ____

    b. Larry's mother felt that this would encourage Larry's behavior far too much and that he should be sent to another room to wait alone until the party was over. ____

21. Everyone agrees that adults should be well informed and able to think for themselves. To achieve this end, which is it more important for school to emphasize? (check one)

    a. Making sure that children learn basic subject matter; only then will they be qualified to think for themselves as adults. ____

    b. Making sure that children learn to think for themselves now; this is the best guarantee that they will finally acquire the facts they need to know. ____

22. When a child is young, he is not concerned as much with others' feelings as he is with his own. Which of the following do you think is the better way of helping him become a truly polite adult? (check one)

    a. Teach him the forms of polite behavior only when he is old enough to want to express his consideration for others in these ways. ____

    b. Teach him the forms of polite behavior as soon as he is able to use them. Through constant repetition they will become an integral part of his life. ____

23. Several mothers were discussing the fact that most children are not interested in being clean and neat. They discovered that, although all were faced with the necessity of dealing with this problem every day, they were actually concerned about different aspects of it. Which of the three following statements comes closest to your experience? (check one)

    a. The greatest difficulty lies in the necessity for constant insistence and reminding about personal cleanliness and neatness, which are essential in a well-brought-up child. ____

    b. The greatest difficulty is the mechanical one of keeping them supplied with clean clothes and picking up after them while they are young, since they will eventually outgrow this need for messiness and dirtiness. ____

    c. The greatest difficulty is in working out how to give them the necessary opportunity to be dirty and messy while they are young, while at the same time helping them learn that it is important to be clean and neat. ____

III

Each of the questions below lists four or more items varying in importance or desirability depending on a person's point of view. Please *rank* these items, as directed for each question, in the order of your preference.

24. Here are eight so-called good traits, possessed by different children to varying degrees. Please number them in the order of your own preference, starting with 1 for the one you consider *most* desirable. Do this first with nine-to-ten-year-old *boys* in mind; then do it again with nine-to-ten-year-old *girls* in mind.

Boys		Girls
____	Easy to handle	____
____	Helpful to adults	____
____	Intense in reactions	____
____	Outspoken	____
____	Normal, average	____
____	Creative, experimental	____
____	Clean and tidy	____
____	Individualistic	____

25. Here are eight so-called bad traits. Number these in the *reverse* order of your own preference: that is, start with 1 for the one you consider *worst* or *most* undesirable. As above, do this first with nine-to-ten-year-old *boys* in mind, then with nine-to-ten-year-old *girls* in mind.

Boys		Girls
____	Unwilling to get dirty	____
____	Easily led by others	____
____	Cautious, unexploratory	____
____	Hard to control	____
____	Subdued	____
____	Somewhat rash, impulsive	____
____	Unwilling to wash or tidy up	____
____	Often impolite	____

26. Number the following in order of preference, starting with 1 for the one you consider *most* desirable.

A child should:

____ Feel that his parents know best.

____ Feel free to tell his parents his real feelings.

____ Learn to obey his parents promptly.

____ Feel entitled to criticize his parents for their shortcomings.

27. A state conference of school principals recently met at Syracuse, New York, and discussed a survey which showed that many teachers consider classroom discipline as their most serious problem.

a. Given the following explanations, how would you rank their importance as factors in this growing problem? Start with 1 for the one you consider *most* important.

____ The progressive education movement, with its emphasis on self-discipline, and an easy-going educational philosophy.

_____ The tensions caused by rapid social changes resulting from war, changing neighborhoods, immigration, etc.

_____ The inability of the schools to get a sufficient number of adequately prepared teachers.

_____ A spirit of revolt and discontent among children of school age directed at parents, teachers, and other representatives of the adult world.

b. The following *solution* was proposed by one of the delegates: "Maybe if we had more men teachers who would take a swing at the unruly kids, the problem would be solved." How do you feel about this? (check one)

Agree strongly   _____
Agree moderately   _____
Disagree moderately   _____
Disagree strongly   _____

IV

For this group of statements, please indicate the extent of your agreement or disagreement with each one by checking the line under the appropriate column. Do not use the "Neutral" column unless you really feel completely neutral about the statement; that is, absolutely balanced between agreement and disagreement, or absolutely indifferent.

	AGREE		NEUTRAL	DISAGREE	
	Strongly	Moderately		Moderately	Strongly
28. A child shouldn't be allowed to talk back to his parents, or else he will lose respect for them.	—	—	—	—	—
29. There is a lot of talk about how difficult it is to bring up children in a rapidly changing world. But parents will find it easier if they just remember that the principles of right and wrong don't change.	—	—	—	—	—
30. School should store away in a child's mind as much as possible of the subject matter which every well-educated person must know. No harm is done if much of what the child learns is not fully understandable to him now. In later years, he will appreciate knowing it.	—	—	—	—	—
31. It is *good*, not bad, for a child to learn that his parents will be more lenient in					

	AGREE		NEUTRAL	DISAGREE	
	Strongly	Moderately		Moderately	Strongly

their reactions to bad behavior if he has been feeling particularly unhappy.

32. Twelve-year-old children often have very definite ideas about the work they'd like to do when they're adult, but since they are not old enough to make a final choice, parents need not take these ideas seriously.

33. When family life is planned with a lot of attention to the children's wishes and needs, the children grow up to be people who expect their husbands, wives, and friends to cater to them.

34. When a child knowingly misbehaves, the reasons that he gives for his misbehavior ought not to influence what is done about it.

35. The old-fashioned "hickory stick" method of keeping order in the classroom might still often be quite helpful.

36. Getting a child to learn the proper manners, which make for social ease and acceptance, is one of the most difficult and time-consuming problems which a parent must face.

37. It is better for a child who is angry about his parent's orders to resist openly than to obey and hide his angry feelings.

38. Above everything else, a child goes to school to learn a basic body of facts.

39. When you meet a young person who has good manners, you can be pretty sure that his parents have trained him to be polite from an early age.

V

Below is a series of situations and questions, each with two or more alternative answers. For each question, please place a *check* beside the alternative you prefer. Sometimes it may be hard to choose between them, but please check the one which comes closest to being your choice.

40. Johnnie had a well-earned reputation for his clever sleight-of-hand in picking up an apple or an orange as he passed the vegetable stand on the way home from school. His ability not to get caught was much admired by his ten-year-old friends. The fathers of two of Johnnie's friends talked to their sons about this. Which father's way of handling this matter would be more like yours? (check one)

    a. Robert's father told him that small wrongdoings often lead to man-sized offenses and that he did not want Robert to have anything more to do with Johnnie.   ____

    b. Peter's father said that there were serious and disturbing aspects to Johnnie's "clever" filching but did not give Peter any definite directions as to whether or not he should continue to associate with Johnnie.   ____

41. Mary, ten, was feeling very angry at her adolescent sister and very scornful of her frilly clothes and new lipstick. She refused to wear anything but bluejeans at all times, a costume to which her grandmother objected on their visits to her home. Which of the following would you approve most? (check one)

    a. Mary's mother asked the grandmother to give Mary time to come around, but insisted that Mary wear a blouse and skirt to grandmother's Thanksgiving party.   ____

    b. Mary's mother felt that she would outgrow the fad and took no action.   ____

    c. Mary's mother insisted that she wear a blouse and skirt whenever she visited her grandmother.

42. Which of the following reports about a child's school work would you rather receive? (check one)

    a. Your child does well in original research and in areas which require independent thinking. But he seems unwilling to apply himself to mastering those subjects—for instance, spelling—in which he is weak. His overall performance is therefore considerably below the top of his class.   ____

    b. Your child's overall performance in his regular school subjects is near the top of the class. But he seems uncomfortable when faced with unfamiliar tasks or problems.   ____

43. Which statement is closer to your own view?

    a. If a daughter has been raised successfully, by patient and understanding parents, she will be able to teach her children basically the same standards of behavior that she learned from *her* parents.   ____

    b. A daughter invariably grows up with temperament, experiences, and circumstances different from those of her parents, and so it is to be expected that she will teach her children somewhat different standards of behavior than she learned from *her* parents.   ____

44. The teacher was explaining her program and goals to the parents of her fourth-grade children. Each parent listened attentively, thinking of his own child and hoping that what she said would answer the important question on his mind. Which question would be closer to yours?
    a. Mr. A. wondered why his boy, David, with his unusual musical gifts, should be expected to keep up with the class in arithmetic. ____
    b. Mr. B. was glad to hear the teacher's explanation of how she had improved the children's spelling but he wondered whether Alice, who needed to improve in spelling, ever had the chance to "tell poems" in school as she did so delightfully at home. ____
    c. Mr. C. thought the program sounded pretty good, on the whole, but wondered if the teacher realized that most children of this age need a great deal of attention to the basic skills and to developing better work habits. ____

45. Everyone wants his children to grow up to be generous adults, but people disagree about the best way to achieve this end. Which way do you think would be most effective? (check one)
    a. Children should be taught as early as possible to share their possessions with each other; they need experiences of this sort to help them develop generosity. ____
    b. Young children should not be asked to share their possessions with others if they don't want to; children need some exclusive possessions before they can be expected to be generous. ____

46. Which of the following best expresses your view? (check one)
    a. A ten-year-old child needs to learn that he must sometimes postpone having what he wants, but a parent must expect the occasional outbursts of temper which accompany this. ____
    b. A ten-year-old has to learn that he must sometimes postpone having what he wants, but if parents are fair in their demands, there is little excuse for him to indulge in outbursts of temper. ____
    c. If parents are satisfying their child's needs, there is little reason to expect a ten-year-old to show any serious frustration, and consequent aggression in the form of temper. ____

47. Ted's parents were visiting Jerry's parents one evening and they were discussing a problem both families have been very concerned about. Ted and Jerry and a few of the other ten-year-olds they pal around with have begun to make jokes and cracks about minority groups. Both families feel strongly about this. Which father would you be inclined to agree with?
    a. Ted's father said, "I certainly don't want Ted to grow up with ideas like this but I don't think we know yet what it means to the boys or where it came from. I'm not sure we can handle it sensibly till we do." ____
    b. Jerry's father disagreed. "That kind of talk is plain prejudice and it hurts other people. I think we've got to forbid it right now at the beginning." ____

48. A group of seventh-grade girls decided one afternoon to go to a movie after school. They didn't notify their parents as to where they were and didn't come home until suppertime. Which of the following reactions would be most like yours?

   a. Mrs. A. was not at all concerned, as her daughter Dorothy was a self-reliant child who frequently made her own plans for the afternoon without notifying her mother. ____

   b. Mrs. B. was quite worried, and felt that Rita should have notified her as to where she was, but felt that an occasional adventure of this kind was important to her daughter's feelings of independence. ____

   c. Mrs. C. was also worried, and felt that her daughter Gracie should not make plans of this kind without first calling her and asking her permission. ____

49. Nine-year-old Ellen is passionately attached to her younger brother, takes care of him, plays with him whenever she can, and doesn't seem to get angry with him. Ellen's parents react differently to this. Which parent's reaction would be more like yours?

   a. Ellen's mother is delighted that Ellen is not developing into a jealous child. ____

   b. Ellen's father is a little concerned because he remembers that he loved his little brother but still got angry with him. He feels he would have been better off if he had not always had to hide his anger. ____

50. Two mothers of children in the same class were talking over the trouble their nine-year-old daughters were having with the teacher. With which mother would you be most inclined to agree?

   a. Mrs. A.: "I find I have to agree with some of the things my Mary complains about—like the time the teacher made the whole class sit absolutely still for 30 minutes after school because she couldn't get anyone to confess to who had taken all the coats off the hooks and put them in a heap on the floor of the closet. I told her that I agreed that was not fair, but I also tried to show her what trouble it was for the teacher and how hard it is for a person to be fair when he feels upset." ____

   b. Mrs. B.: "Yes, I remember that incident. I must say that Miss S. sounds very cranky to me but I don't encourage Suzie to go on complaining about her. After all, she *is* the teacher and I don't want Suzie to get the idea that it's her place to decide whether Miss S. is unfair or not." ____

At times children say or do things that make parents wonder whether their way of bringing up children is really the best way. How often does this happen to you?

Often ____   Sometimes ____   Rarely ____   Never ____

Most people hear or read a lot of discussion about what kind of upbringing is best for children. Which comes closest to your own feeling about such discussion?

_____ Many very basic questions are raised to which I feel I do not know the answers.

_____ Some basic questions are raised to which I feel I do not know the answers.

_____ I feel certain of my own position on most of the basic questions raised.

_____ I feel quite certain of my own position on all the basic questions raised.

_____ I don't hear or read much discussion of this kind.

The following are some sources from which parents get guidance in bringing up their children. Please indicate how helpful each of these sources has been for you personally and how frequently you have used each of them.

	HELPFUL			FREQUENCY		
	Very	*Moder- ately*	*Not Helpful*	*Often*	*Some- times*	*Rarely or Never*
Parents or parents-in-law	___	___	___	___	___	___
Other relatives	___	___	___	___	___	___
Friends	___	___	___	___	___	___
Religious counselor	___	___	___	___	___	___
Teachers, principals, etc.	___	___	___	___	___	___
Doctor, pediatrician	___	___	___	___	___	___
Guidance counselor, psychiatrist, social worker, psychologist, etc.	___	___	___	___	___	___
Radio or TV programs	___	___	___	___	___	___
Newspaper columns	___	___	___	___	___	___
Books or articles	___	___	___	___	___	___

If used, indicate which books or magazines you have found most helpful.

Comparing your own childhood background with the environment you now provide for your children, how different would you say they are, in each of the following respects:

	Slightly or Not at All	*Moderately*	*Considerably*
General standard of living, financial situation	___	___	___
Basic tastes and values	___	___	___

Basic attitude of parents toward
children
Residential situation (i.e., country
vs. city, frequent moves vs. few
or none, etc.)
Size of family

MOTHER INTERVIEW GUIDE

Lead Question	Possible Follow-Up Questions
1. First of all, can you tell me how many of you there are in your family?	Do they all live with you? Does anyone else live with you? Does anybody help you take care of the children? About how often? Do you have any other help?
2. a. Can you tell me a little about X? What is he like?	What kind of child would you say he is? (Follow-up question re older siblings, if any, and mother as a child, if girl. If boy—more like mother or father?)
b. Were there any special features in his development—in eating, sleeping, talking, toilet training, etc.?	Any problems? Were you the one who was mainly taking care of him then?
c. Did he ever do much hitting, biting, kicking?	How did you feel about it? What did you do about it?
d. What did he do when other children attacked him?	How did you feel about it? What did you do about it?
e. Did any of your other children have major developmental or health problems that affected X?	
f. In your opinion, what is X's best characteristic?	Can you give an example that shows how he expresses that quality? Do you think he knows that you like that quality in him? How does he know?
g. What would you consider his greatest shortcoming?	Can you give an example of that? What would you say is the reason for his being (acting) that way? Can you tell me a little of how you feel about that quality in him? How did you act (in instance just cited)?
3. a. In general, what kinds of things do you punish him for?	What do you do if he does something you don't want him to?

Lead Question	*Possible Follow-Up Questions*
	(If M says child does what she wants him to, or has developed self-discipline):
What do you do?	What do you think accounts for the fact that X does what you want him to? or . . . has developed self-discipline?
	What methods did you use in the past?
	(If M thinks child is too good):
	Has it always been that way?
	How do you account for the fact that he is like that?
	Do you ever raise your voice?
	Deprive him of things?
	Use threats?
	Spank?
	Confine?
	(Use following at own discretion):
	About how often do you do that?
	Can you give an example of that?
	How does he react to that?
	How well do your methods work?
b. On the whole, would you say you are stricter or more easy-going than the average mother?	Well, then by your own standards, would you call yourself easy-going?
c. In what ways? Can you give me an example?	How are you about things like noise?
	Messing up the house?
	Fighting with brothers or sisters?
	Fighting with other children?
	How strict are you about mealtimes and bedtimes?
	How do you feel about manners?
	Are there any household responsibilities or chores that you expect of him?
	How do you feel about things like answering back, calling you names, hitting you, etc.?
	How strict are you about matters affecting his safety?
d. Do you and your husband feel pretty much the same about these things?	

Lead Question	*Possible Follow-Up Questions*
e. Have your ideas about child rearing changed since X was a baby?	
4. a. What age or stage of development have you enjoyed the most?	
b. Which did you find most trying?	Why?
5. a. Can you tell me about a time recently when you felt especially good about your child?	(Did you show him in any way how you felt about it?)
b. Can you tell me about a time recently when you felt bad about him?	(Did you let him know that you felt this way?)
6. a. In general, would you say that there have been important changes in ways of bringing up children since you were a child?	What changes? How do you feel about these changes? Do you think that parents used to get more respect from children than they do now? Do you think that fathers used to play a different kind of part?
b. What part do you think a father should play in his children's upbringing?	When child is a baby? With respect to discipline?
7. Now, about X in school—	
a. Did he start school when he was five?	If *yes*—Where? Is there anything that stands out about his reaction to his first year at school? If *no*—What school did he go to when he was five? Is there anything that stands out about his reaction to school that year?
b. Do you think that he likes school now?	What does he like especially? Is there anything he dislikes?
c. How well is he doing in school?	How does *he* feel about how he's doing in school? Do you have any idea where he stands in relation to the other children in his class? What part do you think parents should

Lead Question	Possible Follow-Up Questions
	play in a child's school work, in stressing or encouraging it?
d. What are the things you think he should be getting out of school right now?	What do you think he should be *learning* in school now?
e. Thinking of this school and the one you went to at X's age —in what ways are they different or similar?	Does X see more of his teacher outside of school than you used to?
f. What contact do you have with the school?	What part do you think parents *should* play in relation to the school?
g. (For private school parents) Why did you decide to send your child to private school?	Why this school? Did you ever consider sending him to a public school?
(For public school parents) Did you ever consider sending your child to another school— e.g., in another neighborhood, a private school, a boarding school?	If *yes*—Why did you decide to send him to public school?
h. Do you have any idea what high school he will be going to?	
i. Do you expect that he will go to college?	Is there a particular college you would like to see him go to?
8. Now I'd like to ask you about X's present activities and interests *outside* of school—	
a. Can you tell me a little about how he spends his time out of school?	Does he spend any time in or around the school, after school? On weekends? Does he lead a very different kind of life during the summer? How do you feel about the way he spends his time out of school: What kinds of things would you like to see him doing more of, or less of?

Lead Question	*Possible Follow-Up Questions*
b. How does he get along with other children?	If he *doesn't*—How do you feel about it? Does he have any friends you don't like him to play with? Why? Do you do anything about it? Does he have any friends you particularly like? Why?
c. All in all, what would you say have been his main interests so far?	Do you do anything to help him develop these interests? Do you think it should be a function of the school to help develop these interests, such as . . . ? Do you think these are likely to be his permanent interests?
d. If you were to guess, what kind of work would you think X is likely to go into when he grows up? Or, if you can't guess, what would you like him to do?	How would you feel about that? Is there any kind of work which you would be disappointed to see him choose? (If girl) How about marriage? Do you think that she will become primarily a housewife and mother?
e. In what ways would you expect his values and way of life to be the same or different from yours, when he grows up?	How would you feel if he turned out to have values very different from yours? Does *your* present way of life differ very much from that of your parents?

9. Now I'd like to ask you some other things about yourself—

a. Are you working now? Did you work before you were married?

Before you had children?
How has it been, staying at home with the children after having worked?

or

How has it been, being a working mother?

or

Have you ever thought you might enjoy living some other

Lead Question	*Possible Follow-Up Questions*
sort of life, instead of being primarily a housewife and mother?	
b. Apart from your responsibilities, what kinds of things do you really enjoy doing?	
c. What kinds of people appeal to you as friends?	
10. a. On the whole, what qualities would you say a good mother should have?	Think about it in relation to mothers you've known.
b. What would you say are your strengths and weaknesses as a mother?	
c. What's hard about being a mother?	
d. On the whole, what would you say are the good things about being a mother?	
11. Well, that's about all I have to ask you. Is there anything you feel should be added to what we've said?	

APPENDIX G

SOCIO-ECONOMIC-CULTURAL INDEX:
DETERMINING CRITERIA [1]

The index is a composite score of income, education, and social status of occupation. Each of the component scores includes both parents, i.e., family income, number of years of education of both parents, and social status of occupation of both parents (with more weight given to the father's than to the mother's). Each family is given a score of "0" (low) or "1" (medium) or "2" (high) on each of the three components and the position on the index is the sum of the scores. Examples of this process appear below.

Family income over $15,000 (2). Both parents advanced degrees (2). Father physician; mother psychiatric social worker (2). Index 6

Family income $10,000–$15,000 (1). Both parents college graduates (2). Father vice-president of publishing firm; mother commercial artist (2). Index 5

Family income $10,000–$15,000 (1). Father college graduate; mother high school graduate (1). Father free-lance writer; mother never worked (2). Index 4

Family income $10,000–$15,000 (1). Father college graduate; mother high school graduate (1). Father sales engineer; mother never worked (1). Index 3

Family income less than $10,000 (0). Both parents high school graduates (1). Father owns wholesale hardware firm; mother bookkeeper (1). Index 2

Family income less than $10,000 (0). Both parents high school graduates (1). Father owns retail bakery; mother typist (0). Index 1

NOTES

1. The determining criteria are geared to this middle-class sample and are skewed accordingly. A low rating for occupational status on this study, for instance, would correspond to a much higher point on such generally used scales as the Warner (1949) scale of occupational status.

APPENDIX H

SUBSCALES CONTRIBUTING TO THE SEVEN DIMENSIONS OF ANALYSIS OF MOTHER INTERVIEWS AND INTERRATER RELIABILITY

A. *Modern-Traditional Orientation*
1. Modern-Traditional Ideology ($r = .67^*$)[1]
   (global rating)
2. Enactment of Authority ($r = .53^{**}$)
   Punitiveness of control
   Explanation of reasons for restrictions and demands
   Quality of compliance expected
   Encouragement of par relations with adults
3. Standards of Behavior and Achievement ($r = .45^{**}$)
   Rigidity/flexibility of control
   Amount of impulse fulfillment allowed
   Emphasis on behavior standards
   Emphasis on achievement
4. Encouragement of Individual Interests ($r = .72^*$)
   Fostering of individual abilities and interests
   Initiation of child's activities by child and/or mother
B. *Maternal Satisfaction and Role Coherence*
1. Satisfaction with Child ($r = .56^{**}$)
   Depth of satisfaction re characteristics positively valued by mother
   Depth of dissatisfaction re characteristics negatively evaluated by mother
   Amount of approval/disapproval of child expressed by mother
   Inventory of aspects of child's personality, behavior, etc., liked and disliked by mother
2. Integration of Mother Role ($r = .52^{**}$)
   Success in control
   Confidence in self as mother
   Enjoyment of mother role
   Amount of home vs. career conflict
   Organization of mother's life content and self-image around mother role
3. Consistency of Child Rearing ($r = .09^*$)
   Consistency of control
   Consistency of modern-traditional ideology
   Consistency of modern-traditional ideology through time
   Consistency of child-rearing practices relevant to modern-traditional dimension
   Consistency of modern-traditional ideology and relevant practices

In general, both the major dimensions and their component subscales were rated along nine-point scales, though some had a tenth point for indicating laissez-faire attitudes, or behavior, on the part of the mother. In addition, an annotation of inconsistency was made when there was evidence of considerable inconsistency in the mother's attitudes or reported behavior.

Except for the rating of Ideology, which was done on a global basis, the ratings of the major dimensions were based on an evaluation of the ratings of contributing subscales. The ratings were done by two of the three interviewers.

Interrater agreement, indicated above for each dimension, tended to be relatively low, though there was a range among the dimensions. Many of the final ratings, therefore, particularly of problem cases, were arrived at by consensus, after both raters had made their independent judgments.

NOTES

1. Dimensions marked with one asterisk were tested for interrater agreement on 23 cases; those marked with two asterisks were tested for interrater agreement on 35 cases.

APPENDIX J

MODERN-TRADITIONAL ORIENTATION (MTO): PROCEDURE FOR DERIVING COMPOSITE SCORE

The composite score was based on the following five scores:

1. Questionnaire: Modern-Traditional Ideology
2. Interview: Modern-Traditional Ideology
3. Interview: Enactment of Authority
4. Interview: Standards of Behavior and Achievement
5. Interview: Encouragement of Individual Interests

The procedures for arriving at the composite score were as follows: Scale points 1–4 on the four interview dimensions were considered as traditional, 5 as middle, and 6–9 as modern. The distribution of questionnaire scores was divided into thirds and categorized as traditional, middle, and modern.

Mothers were then grouped on a seven-point scale as follows:

Traditional	1—Clearly traditional:	Five traditional scores
	2—Predominantly traditional:	Minimum of three traditional scores; remaining scores, middle
	3—Inconsistent:	Minimum of two traditional scores and one inconsistency score
Middle	4—Middle, no clear trend:	Minimum of two middle scores; remaining scores maintain balance between modern and traditional; no extreme scores; striking inconsistency between questionnaire score and interview rating or among interview ratings.
Modern	5—Inconsistent:	Minimum of two modern scores; minimum of one inconsistency score
	6—Predominantly modern:	Minimum of three modern scores; remaining scores, middle
	7—Clearly modern:	Five modern scores

A review was made of the qualitative material which included annotations to the ratings, interviewer impressions, and assessment of the verbatim transcript. The purpose of this examination was to check for any apparent discrepancies, e.g., differences between mother's and father's attitudes, past and present attitudes, and differences between ideology and described practices. While no cases were moved from the modern to the traditional categories, or vice versa, 13 cases were moved within the modern or traditional categories and seven cases were moved either from the modern or traditional category to the middle category, or vice versa.

447

APPENDIX K [1]

INTERCORRELATIONS OF HOME BACKGROUND MEASURES

Measure N = 105[2]	Sex §	A	B	C	D	E	F	G	H	I	J	K
A Modern-Traditional Orientation (MTO) (Composite)	b	—										
	g	—										
	T	—										
B Modern-Traditional Ideology (Questionnaire)	b	.78*	—									
	g	.71*	—									
	T	.74*	—									
C Modern-Traditional Ideology (Interview)	b	.74*	.53*	—								
	g	.78*	.50*	—								
	T	.76*	.52*	—								
D Enactment of Authority Role (Interview)	b	.63*	.39*	.61*	—							
	g	.73*	.42*	.66*	—							
	T	.68*	.40*	.63*	—							
E Standards of Behavior and Achievement (Interview)	b	.63*	.57*	.51*	.44*	—						
	g	.65*	.22	.57*	.68*	—						
	T	.64*	.38*	.54*	.59*	—						
F Encouragement of Individual Interests (Interview)	b	.63*	.54*	.51*	.31*	.46*	—					
	g	.58*	.31*	.51*	.46*	.37*	—					
	T	.61*	.43*	.51*	.39*	.41*	—					
G Maternal Satisfaction and Role Coherence (Composite)	b	.26		.33*	.24		.47*	—				
	g	.31*		.35*	.38*	.42*	.20	—				
	T	.27*		.34*	.31*	.26*	.33*	—				

448

Measure N = 105	Sex §	A	B	C	D	E	F	G	H	I	J	K
H Satisfaction with Child (Interview)	b	.32*	.22	.33*	.35*	.21	.46*	.84*	—	—	—	—
	g	.43*		.43*	.55*	.47*	.39*	.83*	—	—	—	—
	T	.37*	.16	.38*	.46*	.34*	.42*	.84*	—			
I Integration of Mother Role (Interview)	b	.19		.30*	.22		.44*	.90*	.71*	—	—	—
	g	.33*		.41*	.30*	.37*	.19	.94*	.77*	—	—	—
	T	.25*		.35*	.25*	.19	.32*	.92*	.74*	—		
J Consistency of Child Rearing (Interview)	b	.16		.22			.30*	.80*	.47*	.57*	—	—
	g					.27		.81*	.40*	.65*	—	—
	T					.16		.81*	.44*	.61*	—	
K Socio-Economic-Cultural Index (SEC) (Questionnaire) N = 103²	b			.37*	-.19	-.19						—
	g	.39*	.36*									—
	T			.20*								—

1. Empty cells in this correlation matrix indicate that the coefficient is less than .16.
2. The three sets of parents who had siblings in the study are represented twice—once for each sibling.
3. The two missing cases—parents of a boy and parents of a girl—are from the Adams sample.

* p < .05 (two-tailed test)
§ b = boys
g = girls
T = total

APPENDIX L

CLEARLY MODERN AND TRADITIONAL FAMILIES: COMPARISON OF MEAN SCORES ON CHILD-REARING DIMENSIONS

| Measure[1] (Scale Range) | Mean Scores | | Statistical Comparison |
	Traditional N = 27	Modern N = 20	
Modern Traditional Orientation: Modern-Traditional Ideology: Questionnaire (Actual Range 36–113)	62.67	99.00	t = 12.36**
Modern-Traditional Ideology: Interview (1–9)	2.56	6.30	t = 11.33**
Enactment of Authority Role (1–9)	2.26	5.50	t = 8.76**
Standards of Behavior and Achievement (1–9)	2.11	5.10	t = 6.95**
Encouragement of Individual Interests (1–9)	4.52	7.55	t = 6.31**
Maternal Satisfaction and Role Coherence: Satisfaction with Child (1–9)	5.37	7.15	t = 3.18**
Integration of Mother Role (1–9)	5.30	6.75	t = 2.30*
Consistency of Child Rearing (1–9)	6.22	6.70	t = .87

1. *Low scale points indicate more traditional positions, high scale points more modern positions.*
* $p < .05$
** $p < .01$

450

STANFORD ACHIEVEMENT SUBTEST GRADE EQUIVALENT SCORES YEAR I AND YEAR II [1]

Subtest			Mean Scores for Year I School Groups			
	(N)	Sex §	Browning	Adams	Conrad	Total
Paragraph Meaning		b	6.93	7.11	5.14	6.44
		g	6.50	6.42	5.50	6.32
	(37)	T	6.76	6.77	5.22	6.39
Word Meaning		b	7.00	7.57	4.75	6.52
		g	6.35	7.54	6.05	6.87
	(38)	T	6.74	7.55	5.23	6.67
Arithmetic Reasoning		b	6.13	6.24	4.50	5.66
		g	6.20	5.36	3.95	5.22
	(38)	T	6.16	5.83	4.30	5.47
Social Studies		b	5.32	7.12	4.77	5.88
		g	5.95	6.78	5.00	6.32
	(37)	T	5.57	6.95	4.82	6.06
Science		b	6.92	6.53	4.13	5.87
		g	5.53	5.73	4.10	5.46
	(37)	T	6.36	6.13	4.12	5.71

Subtest			Mean Scores for Year II School Groups				
	(N)	Sex §	Browning	Adams	Dickens	Conrad	Total
Paragraph Meaning		b	8.23	8.42	6.88	5.36	7.04
		g	5.50	7.73	6.77	5.73	6.65
	(62)	T	7.06	8.12	6.83	5.51	6.87
Word Meaning		b	8.28	8.08	6.23	5.51	6.81
		g	6.17	7.95	6.92	5.54	6.71
	(61)	T	7.37	8.03	6.58	5.53	6.77
Arithmetic Reasoning		b	6.70	5.77	4.96	—	5.53
		g	5.20	6.58	5.87	—	5.98
	(46)	T	6.06	6.09	5.41	—	5.73
Social Studies		b	8.00	7.50	6.38	5.12	6.54
		g	5.30	7.06	5.88	5.13	5.95
	(62)	T	6.84	7.31	6.13	5.13	6.27
Science		b	8.00	6.97	6.19	—	6.76
		g	5.93	7.23	5.96	—	6.36
	(47)	T	7.11	7.08	6.08	—	6.57

1. *The samples for Year I and Year II are presented separately (as for the Kuhlmann-Anderson results, see Appendix N) to facilitate comparison with the Kuhlmann-Anderson scores. The Stanford Achievement Subtests were administered at the same point in the children's development.*
§ b = boys
 g = girls
 T = total

APPENDIX N

ASPECTS OF KUHLMANN-ANDERSON TEST PERFORMANCE FOR YEAR I AND YEAR II [1]

Mean Number of Items Answered Correctly (Based on Ten Subtests)

	N	Browning	N	Adams	N	Dickens	N	Conrad
Year I								
Boys	5	10.64	5	11.04	—	—	6	9.72
Girls	4	10.98	8	10.21	—	—	5	8.50
Total	9	10.79	13	10.53	—	—	11	8.86
Year II								
Boys	4	9.55	9	9.01	12	7.38	10	5.43
Girls	4	7.33	7	9.50	12	8.53	6	6.47
Total	8	8.44	16	9.23	24	7.95	16	5.82

Mean Number of Items Attempted (Based on Nine Subtests)

	N	Browning	N	Adams	N	Dickens	N	Conrad
Year I								
Boys	5	11.20	5	11.84	—	—	6	10.00
Girls	4	11.75	8	11.64	—	—	5	9.16
Total	9	11.44	13	11.72	—	—	11	9.62
Year II								
Boys	4	10.64	9	10.33	12	8.82	10	7.04
Girls	4	9.42	7	10.81	12	9.80	6	7.41
Total	8	10.03	16	10.54	24	9.31	16	7.18

Mean Proportion of Attempted Items Answered Correctly

	N	Browning	N	Adams	N	Dickens	N	Conrad
Year I								
Boys	5	.91	5	.90	—	—	6	.88
Girls	4	.90	8	.85	—	—	5	.89
Total	9	.90	13	.87	—	—	11	.89
Year II								
Boys	4	.86	9	.86	12	.83	10	.74
Girls	4	.70	7	.84	12	.84	6	.84
Total	8	.79	16	.85	24	.84	16	.68

Ratio of Number of Items Omitted to Number of Items Attempted

	N	Browning	N	Adams	N	Dickens	N	Conrad
Year I								
Boys	5	.05	5	.05	—	—	6	.06
Girls	4	.06	8	.04	—	—	5	.06
Total	9	.06	13	.05	—	—	11	.06
Year II								
Boys	4	.02	9	.02	12	.04	10	.09
Girls	4	.12	7	.04	12	.06	6	.04
Total	8	.07	16	.03	24	.05	16	.07

1. The samples for Year I and Year II are presented separately because the difference in age at the time of administration of the Kuhlmann-Anderson Test required the use of different forms, with only overlapping subtests, and different scoring norms. It has already been mentioned that the essential similarity in Stanford Achievement Test performance between the two samples within each school group offers strong support for the conclusion that the pervasive year differences within school groups in the Kuhlmann-Anderson Test were attributable to test norm artifacts.

ASPECTS OF STANFORD ACHIEVEMENT
SUBTEST PERFORMANCE

Subtest	Mean Number of Items Answered Correctly				Mean Number of Items Attempted			
	Brown-ing	Adams	Dickens	Conrad	Brown-ing	Adams	Dickens	Conrad
Paragraph Meaning								
Boys	34.00	34.56	32.25	24.56	47.70	47.67	43.85	38.44
Girls	29.14	33.00	31.83	27.12	48.00	47.50	45.75	42.00
Total	32.24	33.82	32.04	25.42	47.82	47.59	44.79	39.63
Word Meaning								
Boys	38.10	39.11	31.75	23.93	46.40	47.50	40.50	34.27
Girls	31.00	39.21	34.67	27.36	41.57	47.71	35.00	35.00
Total	35.18	39.16	33.21	25.38	44.41	47.59	41.58	34.58
Arithmetic Reasoning								
Boys	30.50	28.39	22.17	18.00[1]	43.30	40.22	34.17	28.29[1]
Girls	27.43	28.00	27.83	13.75[1]	44.00	43.00	40.00	37.75[1]
Total	29.24	28.22	25.00	16.45[1]	43.59	41.47	37.08	31.73[1]
Social Studies								
Boys	50.10	50.56	45.92	29.31	68.30	68.78	61.00	43.88
Girls	39.14	50.06	41.00	31.25	69.71	69.75	64.75	44.13
Total	45.59	50.32	43.46	29.96	68.89	69.24	62.88	43.96
Science								
Boys	37.20	34.06	33.08	21.29[1]	47.50	47.39	43.17	33.29[1]
Girls	30.14	33.81	31.83	20.50[1]	45.57	48.19	46.00	35.50[1]
Total	34.29	33.94	32.46	21.11[1]	46.71	47.76	44.58	33.78[1]

Subtest	Proportion of Attempted Items Answered Correctly				Ratio of Number of Items Omitted to Number of Items Attempted			
	Browning	Adams	Dickens	Conrad	Browning	Adams	Dickens	Conrad
Paragraph Meaning								
Boys	.72	.72	.74	.64	.002	.05	.02	.09
Girls	.61	.69	.70	.65	.01	.03	.06	.14
Total	.67	.71	.72	.64	.006	.04	.04	.11
Word Meaning								
Boys	.82	.82	.78	.70	.004	.06	.04	.16
Girls	.75	.82	.81	.78	.03	.05	.07	.14
Total	.79	.82	.80	.73	.01	.06	.06	.15
Arithmetic Reasoning								
Boys	.70	.71	.65	.64	.06	.08	.10	.14
Girls	.62	.65	.70	.53	.10	.11	.12	.30
Total	.67	.68	.67	.59	.08	.09	.11	.22
Social Studies								
Boys	.73	.74	.75	.67	.008	.09	.05	.13
Girls	.56	.72	.63	.71	.10	.10	.19	.13
Total	.66	.73	.69	.68	.05	.10	.12	.13
Science								
Boys	.78	.72	.77	.68	.004	.11	.04	.17
Girls	.66	.70	.69	.65	.04	.11	.13	.20
Total	.73	.71	.73	.67	.02	.11	.09	.18

1. *Based on Year I data only.*

INTERCORRELATIONS AMONG STANDARDIZED TEST SCORES (A–C) AND PROBLEM-SOLVING RATINGS (D–M) WITHIN SCHOOL GROUPS

Measures		N	A	B	C	D	E	F	G	H	I	J	K	L	M
A Kuhlmann-Anderson IQ Scores[2]	B	17	—												
	A	29	—												
	D	24	—												
	C	27	—												
B Stanford Achievement Test, composite of five subtests	B	17	.60*	—											
	A	34	.27	—											
	D	24	.56*	—											
	C	27	.77*	—											
C WISC Performance Scale IQ Scores	B	8	.81*	.84*	—										
	A	16	.29	.23	—										
	D	24	.42*		—										
	C	17		.21	—										
D Relationship Thinking (Cylinder)	B	8	.50	.81*	.50	—									
	A	16	−.34	−.29	−.29	—									
	D	23				—									
	C	17	−.17	.26	−.28	—									
E Relationship Thinking (Meaning Context)	B	8	.39	.63	.34	.56	—								
	A	16	.21	.40	.28		—								
	D	24					—								
	C	17					—								

Measures		N	A	B	C	D	E	F	G	H	I	J	K	L	M
	B A D C §														
F Relationship Thinking (Spies)	B	8	.73*	.38	.51		.58	—							
	A	16	.36	.19	.26		.28	—							
	D	24	.18				.34	—							
	C	17			.29		.18	—							
G Relationship Thinking (Uncommon Uses)	B	8	.44	.45	.27	.78*	.20		—						
	A	16	.19		-.44			.24	—						
	D	24					.52*	.45*	—						
	C	17						-.19	—						
H Relationship Thinking composite rating	B	8	.71*	.87*	.67	.88*	.79*	.55	.63	—					
	A	16		.17		.38	.51*	.61*	.47	—					
	D	24	.33	.17	.27	.35	.57*	.74*	.73*	—					
	C	17	.29			.44	.32	.34	.43	—					
I Solution Success (Cylinder)	B	8	.28	.72*	.63	.63	.24		.48	.51	—				
	A	16				.67*	.33	.16		.60*	—				
	D	23		.20		.81*			.34	.40	—				
	C	17	-.30		-.27	.54*			.18	.42	—				
J Solution Success (Meaning Context)	B	8	.45	.65	.42	.72*	.91*	.57	.53	.90*	.40	—			
	A	16		.24	.30		.68*			.42	.36	—			
	D	24	.41	.58*	.24		.80*	.19	.39	.47*		—			
	C	17		.20	.24		.89*	.22	.22	.53*		—			
K Solution Success (Spies)	B	8	.63	.68	.58	.58	.78*	.75*	.52	.82*	.52	.88*	—		
	A	16					.19	.77*	.18	.63*			—		
	D	24					.28	.84*	.33	.67*		.27	—		
	C	17			.40		.28	.89*	-.27	.21	.19		—		

Measures	N	D A B C§	A	B	C	D	E	F	G	H	I	J	K	L	M
L Solution Success (Uncommon Uses)	8	B	−.29	.34	.21	.43	.24	−.39		.28	.53	.29			—
	16	A			−.24	.38		.29	.80*	.42	.28		.21		—
	24	D	.39	.28	.21		.26		.40			.36			—
	17	C	.18	.21		.16			.68*	.69*		.26	−.23		—
M Solution Success, composite rating	8	B	.38	.79*	.62	.76*	.73*	.34	.51	.83*	.79*	.86*	.83*	.57	—
	16	A				.49	.49	.54*	.55*	.88*	.72*	.44	.50*	.65*	—
	24	D	.40	.44*	.23	.40	.62*	.55*	.69*	.79*	.40	.69*	.54*	.54*	—
	17	C	.22		.18	.33	.56*	.50*	.36	.83*	.50*	.74*	.47	.48*	—

1. Empty cells in this correlation matrix indicate that the coefficient is less than .16.

2. Adjusted for differences between Year I and Year II scores.

* p < .05 (two-tailed test)

§ B = Browning
A = Adams
D = Dickens
C = Conrad

457

TECHNIQUES USED IN THE STUDY OF THE CHILDREN

Similes, Stick Figure Scale, Moral Judgments, Sentence Completion, Picture Titles, Children's Picture Story Test (CPST), Play, Cylinder, Meaning Context, Uncommon Uses, Personal Questions, Sociometric Questions

SIMILES

Instructions. Interviewer says, "I'm going to read you some words and each time I want you to think of something that's like it. Here's the first one—" If the child does not respond, the interviewer may rephrase the item.

Items

1. as hot as . . .
2. as happy as . . .
3. as mad as . . .
4. as crazy as . . .
5. as rich as . . .
6. as bad as . . .
7. as strong as . . .
8. as dangerous as . . .
9. as ugly as . . .
10. as strict as . . .
11. as exciting as . . .
12. as sad as . . .
13. as mean as . . .
14. as helpless as . . .
15. as dumb as . . .
16. as lovely as . . .
17. as scary as . . .
18. as pretty as . . .
19. as easy as . . .

STICK FIGURE SCALE

Instructions. The interviewer draws a stick figure along one side of a piece of paper and describes the quality of the figure as he draws: e.g., "Here is a boy (girl) who's good at games and can skate very well and likes to do these things after school." He then draws a stick figure on the opposite side and describes the contrasting quality of this figure: "Here's a boy (girl) who likes to read and make up stories and who likes to do these things after school." He draws a line connecting the two figures, thus:

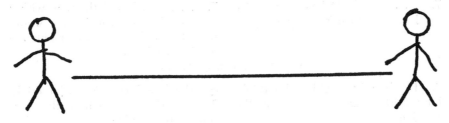

Interviewer asks, "Which one is more like you?" When the child indicates or answers, the interviewer asks him to sketch himself in, so that the child's own figure appears on the sketch.

If the child asks in some form, "Shall I put myself here?" the interviewer answers, "Wherever you like." The child may make middle choices or set himself anywhere along the line, if this occurs to him, but the interviewer never makes such a suggestion.

Items

Here's a child . . .	*Here's a child . . .*
1. . . . who's good at games and can skate very well and likes to do these things after school.	1. . . . who likes to read and make up stories and who likes to do these things after school.

Which one is more like you?

2. . . . who's pretty sure all the kids like him, that he's popular.	2. . . . who lots of times isn't so sure the other kids like him so much.

Which one is more like you?

3. . . . who thinks it will be wonderful to be all grown up—that will be the best time.	3. . . . who thinks it was really best when he was a little kid.

Which one is more like you?

4. . . . who thinks he's pretty good at his work in school.	4. . . . who thinks he's not so good at his work in school.

Which one is more like you?

5. . . . who gets very excited and enthusiastic about things he likes.

5. . . . who is pretty calm and quiet most of the time.

Which one is more like you?

6. . . . who, when he has a report to do or something to learn, likes it best when he works by himself.

6. . . . who, when he has a report to do or something to learn, likes it best when he works with a group of children.

Which one is more like you?

7. . . . who thinks he's got a pretty good life; thinks he's pretty lucky.

7. . . . who lots of the time wishes some of the things in his life would be different; he thinks other kids are luckier than he is.

Which one is more like you?

8. Here's a boy (girl) who thinks boys (girls) have the most fun, the best life.

8. Here's a boy (girl) who thinks it's girls (boys) who have the most fun and the best life.

Which one is more like you?

9. (For boys): Here's a boy who likes the kind of girl who's a good athlete, strong, likes to play games.

(For girls): Here's a girl who likes the kind of boy who's a good athlete, strong, likes to play games.

9. (For boys): Here's a boy who likes the kind of girl who is sort of sweet, shy, and likes to dress up.

(For girls): Here's a girl who likes the kind of boy who is smart, likes to make things, and reads a lot.

Which one is more like you?

10. . . . who tries not to lose his temper, feels a little worried and uncomfortable when he does blow up or yell.

10. . . . who feels better when he blows up and lets people know he's mad; he doesn't mind doing it.

Which one is more like you?

MORAL JUDGMENTS

The Child as Judge. The interviewer says, "Now *you* are going to be *the Judge* (gives child puppet in Judge's gown) and these (dolls) are going to be two children. And these children will tell you their stories and you, Judge, will have to decide which one you think did something more wrong, which one might deserve a bigger punishment."

1. GLASSES: A. What happened was that my mother has a special set of glasses that she always takes very good care of. One day I pushed the kitchen door open without knowing they were on the table and five of them broke.

    B. My mother also has a very special set of glasses, but what happened to me was that I was trying to get at some cookies in a cupboard I'm not supposed to go into, and as I brushed against the glasses, one of them fell down and broke.

Now, Judge, which one did the thing that was more wrong? Why was that more wrong?

2. MONEY: A. Well, one day I was walking down the street and I saw a boy who was very hungry. I felt sorry for him, so I went home and stole $2 from my mother's wallet, and I went back and gave it to him.

    B. I was walking along the street one day too, and I saw a toy in a store window that I wanted very much. I went home and stole 50¢ from my mother's wallet and I went and bought the toy.

Judge, which one do you think did something more wrong, that might deserve the bigger punishment? Why?

3. TEST: A. Here's a child who was taking an important test one day. He (she) couldn't think of an answer so he looked at somebody else's paper. Nobody saw him.

    B. This child was also taking this important test. He (she) couldn't think of one answer so he looked at somebody else's paper too, but the teacher caught him.

Do you think, Judge, that one child did something more wrong than the other? Why?

Incomplete Stories. The interviewer told the following three stories and the child was asked to react with an appropriate continuation.

1. DESSERT: A boy (girl) named Arthur (Grace) who was about nine years old was playing in his room one afternoon when his mother came in and said I'm in a terrible rush and would you mind going to the store and getting some dessert for supper. He said, "Yes," and he meant to go, but somehow he was so busy that when suppertime came, he still hadn't

gone. His parents were pretty annoyed, and they thought he should be punished in some way. They tried to think of a fair way.

What do you think would be a fair way to punish him for that?

His parents didn't happen to think of exactly that, though it seems a fair idea, but they did have two other ideas. Which one do you think would be fairest?

First—they thought they wouldn't let him go to the movies that afternoon when he was supposed to.

The other thing they thought of was that some time when he needed help, they wouldn't help him, like, say he was going to build a kite and he wanted his father to help him (she was going to make a cake and wanted her mother to help her) and they'd say, no, you didn't help the other day and so now I won't help you.

Which do you think would be the fairest? Why?

2. INK: Here's another story about something that happened once in school. You tell me what you think about it.

One day a teacher went out of the room for a few minutes. While she was gone Harry (Jeannie) went up to her desk to get a sheet of paper and as he (she) was reaching for it, he knocked over a bottle of ink and spilled it all over a book of the teacher's. A minute later, she came back and asked, "Who spilled the ink?" Well, the boy must have been scared or ashamed because he didn't say anything.

Do you think somebody should tell the teacher who spilled the ink?

What do you think would happen then?

What do you think the teacher would do then? Well, just suppose the teacher said, "If the person who spilled the ink won't tell me, and nobody else will either, you'll all have to share in paying for the book." Should somebody tell then?

3. HIKE: Now what would you think was fair in this one? A group of children were going on a hike—say five children and a grownup. Just before they started, another child named Jack (Dorothy) decided he (she) wanted to go too, though he'd just been sick. They walked a long time till it was time for lunch. They were pretty hot and hungry, but they had to do something before they could have lunch . . . unpack the food, get water, set things up, etc. One of the boys said, "Let's let Jack rest, since he's been sick. We can all do a little extra work."

Do you think that would be fair? Why? (Why not?)

Suppose they couldn't agree—some thought he should and some thought he shouldn't help, how do you think it should be decided what to do about it? Why would that be the fairest way?

SENTENCE COMPLETION

Instructions. The interviewer says, "I'm going to read you some sentences that aren't finished and I want you to finish them with the first thing you think of. For example, 'On Saturday afternoon I . . .'"

Items

1. On Saturday afternoons, I . . .
2. One good thing about school . . .
3. My mother always . . .
4. The best job in the world would be . . .
5. Lots of times my father . . .
6. When I was little . . .
7. When the teacher leaves the room . . .
8. The day Betty (Ben) was late to school . . .
9. According to Donald, most girls . . .
10. Waiting in the principal's office, Emily (Eddie) . . .
11. According to Ruthie, most boys . . .
12. When visitors come to Mary's (Jim's) class . . .
13. I try not to . . .
14. Whenever the teacher asked for quiet . . .
15. I hate people who . . .
16. When Lucy (Henry) saw the policeman coming . . .
17. My hero is . . .
18. People from different countries . . .

PICTURE TITLES

Instructions. The interviewer says, "Suppose that you are the director of a museum, an art museum, and you've got a beautiful new building, but no pictures. Nothing at all on the walls. Well, I've got a lot of different pictures here and I'm going to show them to you and you pick the ones you'd like best, that you'd like to have for your museum." After the child had sorted the pictures he was asked to give a title to each.[1]

DESIGNS

 Fritz Glarner: Relational Painting
 Wassily Kandinsky: The Black Spot
 Wassily Kandinsky: Improvisation
 Wassily Kandinsky: Composition
 Fernand Leger: The Town
 Jean Bazaine: Landscape
 Ben Nicholson: Aztec
 Paul Klee: Blue Night
 Paul Klee: Autumn Branches
 John Heliker: Of Maine
 Mark Tobey: Transit
 Alberto Magnelli: "Sans crainte"

PEOPLE

 Pablo Picasso: Child with a Dove
 Joan Miro: People and Dog in the Sunlight
 Auguste Renoir: Ritratto di M. Berard
 Fiorella Cesana: I've Got the Blues
 Henri Matisse: Piano Lesson
 E. M. S. Guthrie: Alexandra Danilova in "La Boutique Fantasque" (Year I)
 E. M. S. Guthrie: Pamela May in "Sleeping Beauty" (Year II)
 Edgar Degas: Ballet Rehearsal (Detail)
 Marc Chagall: The Violinist
 Joan Miro: Statue
 Pablo Picasso: Le Fumeur
 C. Carra: La Figlia dell'Ouest
 Albert Giacometti: Chariot

STILL LIFE AND ABSTRACTS

 Attilio Salemme: Inquisition
 Paul Klee: The Red Waistcoat
 Pablo Picasso: Le Torero
 Juan Gris: The Breakfast
 Giorgio De Chirico: Il Trovatore
 Pablo Picasso: Three Musicians
 Pablo Picasso: Still Life with Bull's Head, Book, Palette, and Candlestick
 Pablo Picasso: Still Life by Candlelight

Pablo Picasso: Due Donne Davanti Alla Finestra
Fernand Leger: Yellow Flowers in a Blue Vase
Arturo Tosi: Natura Morta
Jan Van Huysum: Fruchtestilleben

CHILDREN'S PICTURE STORY TEST (CPST)

Administration followed the standard procedure of the Thematic Apperception Test. The child dictated the stories to the interviewer.

Pictures and Sources

PICTURE NUMBER	DESCRIPTION	SOURCE
1	Boy with Violin	TAT #1
2 (girls)	Two Girls	Bank Street College, Research Division collection, #214
2 (boys)	Two Boys	Photography Annual, 1953, p. 68—Barbara Kruck, Roman Urchins
3	Group of Boys in Courtyard	U.S. Camera, 1948, p. 303—Lee Miller
4	Woman in Doorway	TAT #5
5 (girls)	Father and Daughter	David Linton[2]
5 (boys)	Father and Son	U.S. Camera, 1952, p. 365—IPI advertisement
6	Young Boy with Baby in Crib	Bank Street College, Research Division collection, #221
7	Boy, Writing, with Teacher	Parents Magazine, July, 1956
8 (girls)	Girl Alone, on Window Sill	David Linton[2]
8 (boys)	Boy in Doorway	TAT #13B
9	Three Girls, Dressed Up	Photography Annual, 1953, p. 242—S. Szasz, In the Wings, Children's Theatre
10	Figure at Couch	TAT #8Bm
11 (girls)	Mother, Daughter, and Doll	TAT #7Gf
11 (boys)	Mother and Son	U.S. Camera, 1940, p. 229—Valentino Sarra
12	Boy and Girl, Portraits	Adult-Child Interaction Test, #7

PLAY

The Play materials were set up on a shelf with a table nearby at which the child played. They were placed according to category: blocks, furniture, people, animals, vehicles, miscellaneous accessories, and arranged in such a way that the child could see the full array.

The interviewer took the child over to the shelf and said, "Here, you see, we have lots of different kinds of things . . . here are some blocks, furniture, all these people, some bend and some don't (demonstrate) . . . lots of animals . . . things that go, like cars and trains and boats; and here we have a lot of other things you might want to look over for a minute.

"The idea is to use these things—whichever ones you want—to make up a story. You can use this table to make it on.

"Maybe you want to take some time to look these all over . . ."

Unless the child's play was accompanied by a running verbal commentary, the interviewer asked for a verbal description of the story. If a child played a short story, he was encouraged to do another. If his story was very long, he was asked to bring it to a close after 30 minutes.

Miniature Play Materials
1. Thirty-nine assorted *blocks*, including unit blocks, doubles, squares, cylinders, and arches.
2. Seventeen metal, wooden, and plastic *vehicles*, including cars, trucks, boats, a cannon, a train, a helicopter and airplane, a fire engine, and an ambulance.
3. Thirty-seven pieces of *furniture* commonly found in the living room, dining room, bedroom, bathroom, and kitchen of a home. In addition to tables, chairs, chests, and basic bathroom and kitchen equipment, there was a piano, television set, a sewing machine, a lamp, and items denoting the presence of children.
4. Sixty-seven rubber and composition *human figures*, including "ordinary" adult men and women, boys, girls, and babies, in addition to soldiers and role descriptive figures, such as a policeman, cowboy, pirates, and so on.
5. Thirty-six wooden, rubber, composition, china, and woolly *animals*, including farm and wild animals (fierce and nonfierce) as well as pets.
6. The *miscellaneous accessory materials* consisted of household and kitchen equipment, food, books and newspapers, toiletries, tools, weapons, musical instruments and records, baby things, outdoor items, and money.

CYLINDER

Stage 1. The interviewer says, "I'm going to drop this cylinder into the container. Now, how could you get it out without turning the container over? How can you raise the cylinder out of the container without tipping it?" If the child offers only one solution, Interviewer asks, "Can you think of any other ways of raising the cylinder without tipping the container?" When appropriate, "Would you need something to do it with?"

Stage 2. The interviewer says, "Now let's look at the things I have here." Interviewer places the following objects on the table: a screwdriver, thread, a thimble, a magnet, a pencil, a pair of pliers. The interviewer says, "Could you think of some way of doing it—using *anything* on the *table?* Just tell me how, first."

Stage 3. Whether the child has offered no solution or one or more correct or incorrect solutions, the interviewer says, "Now try it. See if you can raise the cylinder out of the container without tipping it."

(A jug of water was on the table during the session.)

MEANING CONTEXT

Instructions. The interviewer says, "Now let's play a game about unusual words. The idea is to try to figure out what the word means. I'll show you a sentence and you're supposed to guess what the word means from how it looks in the sentence. For example . . ." The interviewer shows the child a card with the first sentence of the demonstration item and works through the remaining sentences with him. Each sentence is written on a separate card; the child may check previous cards. The four test words are embedded in series of five sentences each; the demonstration item consists of three sentences.

Demonstration Item. (a) You cannot be a *dinrep* until you grow up.
            (b) There are many *dinreps* in a school.
            (c) The name of your *dinrep* is _____.

Test Items. 1. (a) A *corplum* may be used for support.
        (b) *Corplums* may be used to close off an open place.
        (c) A *corplum* may be long or short, thick or thin, strong or weak.
        (d) A wet *corplum* does not burn.
        (e) You can make a *corplum* smooth with sandpaper.

    2. (a) Some people always *ashder*.
        (b) Jane *ashders* more than she has to.
        (c) People who like to relax don't like to *ashder*.
        (d) Often when you *ashder*, you make mistakes.
        (e) People *ashder* so they won't be late.

    3. (a) You can't fill anything with a *contavish*.
        (b) The more you take out of a *contavish* the larger it gets.
        (c) You can't feel or touch a *contavish*.
        (d) A bottle has only one *contavish*.
        (e) John fell into a *contavish* in the road.

    4. (a) We all admire people who have much *sackoy*.
        (b) *Sackoy* is important in an emergency.
        (c) If you have done something wrong and are not afraid to tell the truth, you have *sackoy*.
        (d) A person who saves a baby from drowning has much *sackoy*.
        (e) You need *sackoy* to fight with someone bigger than you.

UNCOMMON USES

Instructions. The interviewer told the child that he was going to name some things and that for each item the child should tell first what the thing was usually used for and then tell some other ways in which it could be used.

Items

Newspaper
Tire
Blanket
Salt
Hammer
Penny
Lipstick
Brick
Rope

PERSONAL QUESTIONS

The child was asked:

1. What kinds of things make you feel very good, very happy, and pleased?
2. Do you sometimes daydream about things . . . find yourself staring out of the window on a nice day just dreaming about things? What kinds of things?
3. How about the kinds of things that put you into a bad mood . . . that make you feel mad or annoyed and irritable?
4. Most people have some feelings that they try not to show . . . what kinds of feelings do you find it hard to control or hard not to show?
5. Are there some kinds of things you do, or other people do, that make you feel embarrassed or ashamed?

SOCIOMETRIC QUESTIONS

The children were told "We are going to do something with the whole class together, but it is going to be different from the group things we did before. I'm going to ask some questions, and you are going to write down what you think. But this isn't a test—we are asking you for your personal opinion about different people you like to do different kinds of things with. Each person gets a booklet. There are 12 pages and there will be 12 questions. Write your name on the cover where it says Name . . ." etc.

Questions

1. Let's suppose that out of all the children you know, there is one child that you like to be with most of the time. It makes you feel good just to be with him or her. Write down the person you think of first—the person you would like to be your best friend.

2. Now let's suppose you feel in a very special mood—you feel like having a really gay time, laughing, telling jokes, giggling. Write down the child with whom you have most fun doing this.

3. Now, let's suppose that something unpleasant or sad happened. And you feel you need a special kind of friend who will listen to your troubles and be kind and sympathetic. Write down the name of the person who comes to your mind first, the person you like best to tell your troubles to.

4. Suppose somebody gives you two free tickets to a very good movie and your mother says you can take anyone you want. Write down the person you think you'd take to the movie with you.

5. Suppose that your mother and father are going away for the weekend, and they have arranged for somebody, some adult, to stay with you. And they also say that you can have a friend stay over at the house with you for the whole weekend. Write the name of the friend you'd choose to stay over with you.

6. Suppose that in a magazine for children you read about a contest that you want to enter. Only you have to enter the contest in pairs. Write down the child you would pick to be your partner.

7. Who is the person you think knows you best? [3]

8. Who is the person you know best of all? [3]

9. Now let's suppose that one day your whole class gets a letter. It's a letter from a fourth-grade class in another school in another part of the city, inviting your class to come and visit them for a whole day. You are going to spend the whole day there. It sounds like it will be fun and you all decide to go. There will be a lot to do, lots of arrangements to be made. Let's make believe that this really happened and each of you is helping with all the arrangements.

    Well, first of all, you have to arrange about how to get there. Let's say that there will be a lot of cars driving you from (school) to where the other school is. Suppose that there can be *four* children in *each* car. Who will you pick to be the *three other* children in your car?

10. There is going to be a picnic lunch. And each table will have three children

from the class you're visiting and three children from your class. Write down the names of the two other children from this class you would like to sit next to at lunch.

11. Now let's say that in the morning they are going to entertain you, but in the afternoon you are supposed to entertain them. And one of the things you decide to do is give a short play. Which three children would you nominate to be in the committee to work on ideas for the play? [3]

12. And the last thing on the program will be a ball game. Their class is going to pick a team and so is yours. Which three children do you think should certainly be on your class team? [3]

NOTES

1. Only this part of the response was analyzed.
2. Personal collection.
3. These items were given to some groups but not others.

INTERCORRELATIONS AMONG CHILD STUDY MEASURES

TABLE BB-1 [1]

Standardized Tests of Intelligence and Achievement (A–C), Problem Solving (D–M)

Measure	(N)	Sex §	A	B	C	D	E	F	G	H	I	J	K	L	M
A Kuhlmann-Anderson IQ Scores[2]	(97)	b	—												
		g	—												
		T	—												
B Stanford Achievement Test, composite of five subtests	(102)	b	.69*	—											
		g	.76*	—											
		T	.71*	—											
C WISC Performance Scale IQ Scores	(65)	b	.19	.20	—										
		g	.56*	.37*	—										
		T	.38*	.28*	—										
D Relationship Thinking (Cylinder)	(64)	b	.22	.31		—									
		g	.16	.30		—									
		T	.17	.30*		—									
E Relationship Thinking (Meaning Context)	(65)	b	.44*	.41*	.46*		—								
		g	.18	.22	.21		—								
		T			.17		—								
F Relationship Thinking (Spies)	(65)	b	.20		.17		.24	—							
		g		.16			.33	—							
		T	.18				.28*	—							
G Relationship Thinking (Uncommon Uses)	(65)	b	.43*	.27		.45*	.16	.39*	—						
		g	.22	.22	.19	.20	.43*	.23	—						
		T	.33*	.25*		.31*	.28*		—						

Measure	(N)	Sex§	A	B	C	D	E	F	G	H	I	J	K	L	M
H Relationship Thinking, composite rating		b	.32	.31		.60*	.34*	.56*	.54*	—					
		g	.34	.38*	.37*	.40*	.67*	.61*	.72*	—					
	(65)	T	.33*	.33*		.48*	.51*	.58*	.62*	—					
I Solution Success (Cylinder)		b		.17		.63*			.34*	.48*	—				
		g		.32		.74*		.16	.28	.51*	—				
	(64)	T		.23		.69*			.31*	.49*	—				
J Solution Success (Meaning Context)		b		.31			.72*	.18	.32			—			
		g	.53*	.47*	.49*	.24	.85*	.25	.53*	.67*	.28	—			
	(65)	T	.28*	.38*	.30*	.20	.79*	.21	.30*	.50*	.16	—			
K Solution Success (Spies)		b	.20				.17	.82*		.52*			—		
		g		.23	.25	.16	.28	.84*	.37*	.61*	.22	.19	—		
	(65)	T	.16				.22	.83*	.20	.57*		.16	—		
L Solution Success (Uncommon Uses)		b	.35*	.31		.30	.27		.52*	.37*		.17		—	
		g				.18			.60*	.33	.24	.27		—	
	(65)	T	.24	.23		.20	.18		.55*	.35*		.19		—	
M Solution Success, composite rating		b	.32	.40*		.50*	.53*	.50*	.48*	.80*	.49*	.57*	.51*	.56*	—
		g	.35	.46*	.37*	.50*	.58*	.52*	.71*	.84*	.66*	.71*	.58*	.60*	—
	(65)	T	.33*	.42*	.21	.49*	.56*	.50*	.58*	.81*	.57*	.65*	.54*	.57*	—

1. Empty cells in this correlation matrix indicate that the coefficient is less than .16.
2. Adjusted for differences between Year I and Year II scores.
* p < .05 (two-tailed test)
§ b = boys
g = girls
T = total

TABLE BB-2[1]

Imaginativeness (A–D), Themes (E–K)

Measure	(N)	Sex §	A	B	C	D	E	F	G	H	I	J	K
A Imaginativeness (CPST)	(103)	b	—										
		g	}										
		T	}										
B Imaginativeness (Play)	(104)	b	.16	—									
		g	.24	—									
		T	.23*	—									
C Imaginativeness (Picture Titles)	(97)	b	.24		—								
		g	.39*	.30*	—								
		T	.37*		—								
D Imaginativeness (Similes)	(105)	b	.18			—							
		g	.26			—							
		T	.25*			—							
E Childhood Versus Adult Orientation (Three Wishes)	(98)	b					—						
		g					—						
		T					—						
F Childhood Versus Adult Orientation (Million Dollars)	(103)	b					.34*	—					
		g						—					
		T					.27*	—					
G Enactment of Family Life Themes (Play)	(104)	b						.33*	—				
		g							—				
		T						.23*	—				

Measure	(N)	Sex §	A	B	C	D	E	F	G	H	I	J	K
H													
Incidence of Parent		b					.31*			—			
Figures[2]	(105)	g					.16	.29*	.22	—			
(CPST)		T					.24*	.17	.19*	—			
I													
Aggressive-		b						-.26	-.60*		—		
Destructive Themes		g						-.31*	-.24*		—		
(Play)	(104)	T						-.26*	-.62*		—		
J													
Prevalence of		b					.27*			.32*		—	
Achievement Themes		g					-.17			.46*		—	
(CPST)	(103)	T							.17	.39*		—	
K													
Primacy of External		b							-.20		.24	.55*	—
Standards		g						.35*	.37*	.25		.27	—
(CPST)	(103)	T								.18		.43*	—

1. Empty cells in this correlation matrix indicate that the coefficient is less than .16.

2. Correlations for this measure were based on raw frequencies.

* $p < .05$ (two-tailed test)

§ b = boys

g = girls

T = total

477

TABLE BB-3 [1]

Salience of the Family (A–D), Perception of Adult-Child Interaction (E–J)

Measure	(N)	Sex §	A	B	C	D	E	F	G	H	I	J
A Enactment of Family Life Themes (Play)	(104)	b	—									
		g	—									
		T	—									
B Incidence of Parent Figures[2] (CPST)	(103)	b		—								
		g	.22									
		T	.19*	—								
C Family-Related Material (Personal Questions)	(102)	b		.24	—							
		g			—							
		T	.20*		—							
D Replication of Own Family (Family Drawing)	(98)	b				—						
		g			.34*	—						
		T				—						
E Relatedness of Mother and Child (Sentence Completion Item 3)	(103)	b					—					
		g					—					
		T					—					
F Relatedness of Father and Child (Sentence Completion Item 5)	(104)	b					.34*	—				
		g						—				
		T					.16	—				

Measure	(N)	Sex§	A	B	C	D	E	F	G	H	I	J
G												
Benevolence of Adult Attitudes and Behavior Toward Children (CPST)	(100)	b						.26	—			
		g							—			
		T							—			
H												
Interaction between Adults and Children (Play)	(104)	b						.17		—		
		g					.16			—		
		T							.21*	—		
I												
Child-Initiated Contact with Adults (CPST)	(100)	b						.24	.44*		—	
		g						−.26	.29		—	
		T							.35*		—	
J												
Direct Expression of Opposition to Adults (CPST)	(102)	b								.17	.23	—
		g								.30*	.56*	—
		T								.26*	.43*	—

1. Empty cells in this correlation matrix indicate that the coefficient is less than .16.
2. Correlations for this measure were based on raw frequencies.
* p < .05 (two-tailed test)
§ b = boys
g = girls
T = total

Self-Confidence and Satisfaction (A–B), Self-Awareness and Differentiation (C–I)

Measures	(N)	Sex §	A	B	C	D	E	F	G	H	I
A Self-Satisfaction Syndrome (SFS Items 2, 4, 7, 8)	(103)	b	—								
		g	—								
		T	—								
B Strength of Self-Presentation (Figure Drawings)	(104)	b		—							
		g		—							
		T		—							
C Awareness of Own Feelings (Personal Questions)	(102)	b			—						
		g			—						
		T			—						
D Style of Reactivity (SFS Item 5)	(102)	b			.23	—					
		g				—					
		T				—					
E Aggression Anxiety (SFS Item 10)	(100)	b			.26		—				
		g					—				
		T					—				
F Aggression Anxiety (Personal Questions)	(101)	b			.43*		.17	—			
		g			.29	.18		—			
		T			.38*			—			
G Self-Differentiation (SFS Items 1–10)	(103)	b			.21	.16			—		
		g						−.17	—		
		T							—		

480

Measures	(N)	Sex §	A	B	C	D	E	F	G	H	I
H											
Range of Self-Differentiation		b			.24	.30*			.20	—	—
(Dictated Letter)	(102)	g								—	—
		T			.17				.18	—	—
I											
Quality of Self-Differentiation		b				−.18			.18	.79*	—
(Dictated Letter)	(102)	g				.23	.18			.72*	—
		T								.76*	—

1. Empty cells in this correlation matrix indicate that the coefficient
is less than .16.
* p < .05 (two-tailed test)
§ b = boys
g = girls
T = total

481

TABLE BB-5 [1]

Preference for Older, Younger, or Current Life Stages (A–D), Images of the Future (E–G)

Measure	(N)	Sex §	A	B	C	D	E	F	G
A Best Age (Interview)	(61)	b	—						
		g	—						
		T	—						
B Life Stage Preference (SFS Item 3)	(102)	b		—					
		g		—					
		T		—					
C Childhood Versus Adult Orientation (Million Dollars)	(103)	b		−.17	—				
		g			—				
		T			—				
D Childhood Versus Adult Orientation (Three Wishes)	(98)	b			.34*	—			
		g		.33*		—			
		T			.27*	—			
E Presence of Older Social Sex Role Themes (CPST)	(103)	b					—		
		g					—		
		T					—		
F Continuity of Future Plans with Present (Interview)	(98)	b						—	
		g					.27	—	
		T					.18	—	

Measure	(N)	Sex §	A	B	C	D	E	F	G
G									
Childlike or Adult		b						.52*	—
Orientation to Jobs		g					.45*	.78*	—
(Sentence Completion Item 4)	(83)	T					.25*	.65*	—

1. Empty cells in this correlation matrix indicate that the coefficient is less than .16.

* $p < .05$ (two-tailed test)

§ b = boys
g = girls
T = total

TABLE BB-6[1]

Sex Role Allegiance and Concepts (A–E), Sex Typical Themes (F–J)

Measure	(N)	Sex §	A	B	C	D	E	F	G	H	I	J
A Own Sex Preference (SFS Item 8)	(102)	b	—									
		g	—									
		T	—									
B Emphasis on Self-Sex Figure (Figure Drawings)	(95)	b		—								
		g		—								
		T		—								
C Affective Attitude to Opposite Sex (Sentence Completion Item 9 for boys, 11 for girls)	(99)	b			—							
		g			—							
		T			—							
D Projected Attitude from Opposite Sex to Own (Sentence Completion Item 11 for boys, 9 for girls)	(99)	b			.36*	—						
		g				—						
		T			.26*	—						
E Preferred Qualities in Opposite Sex (SFS Item 9)	(101)	b					—					
		g				−.21	—					
		T					—					

484

Measure	(N)	Sex§	A	B	C	D	E	F	G	H	I	J
F Sex-Typed Play (Play)	(105)	b						—				
		g						—				
		T						—				
G Aggressive-Destructive Themes (Play)	(104)	b						.44*	—			
		g						-.52*	—			
		T						.21*	—			
H Enactment of Family Life Themes (Play)	(104)	b						-.69*	-.60*	—		
		g						.56*	-.24	—		
		T						-.22*	-.62*	—		
I Incidence of Parent Figures[2] (CPST)	(103)	b									—	
		g						.22		.22	—	
		T								.19*	—	
J Benevolence of Adult Attitudes and Behavior Toward Children (CPST)	(100)	b									.18	—
		g								.21	.49*	—
		T							.33*	.35*	.34*	—

1. Empty cells in this correlation matrix indicate that the coefficient is less than .16.
2. Correlations for this measure were based on raw frequencies.
* p < .05 (two-tailed test)
§ b = boys
g = girls
T = total

APPENDIX CC

CORRELATIONS BETWEEN HOME BACKGROUND MEASURES AND CHILD STUDY MEASURES

TABLE CC–1 [1]

Standardized Tests of Intelligence and Achievement (A–C), Problem Solving (D–M)

Child Study Measures	(N)	Sex §	Modern-Traditional Orientation (MTO) (Composite)	Modern-Traditional Ideology (Questionnaire)	Modern-Traditional Ideology (Interview)	Enactment of Authority (Interview)	Standards of Behavior and Achievement (Interview)	Encouragement of Individual Interests (Interview)	Maternal Satisfaction and Role Coherence (Composite)	Satisfaction with Child (Interview)	Integration of Mother Role (Interview)	Consistency of Child Rearing (Interview)	Socio-Economic-Cultural Index (SEC) (Questionnaire)
A Kuhlmann-Anderson IQ Scores[2]	(97)	b	-.29*	-.37*	-.37*	-.18	-.26						-.26
		g									.18		#
		T											
B Stanford Achievement Test, composite of five subtests	(102)	b	-.25	-.26	-.33*	-.16	-.16						
		g											
		T		-.18	-.20*								#
C WISC Performance Scale IQ Score	(65)	b	.27	.20			.25				-.17		-.21
		g	.19	.20			.18	.18	.21	.26	.25		.28
		T	.23*	.20			.20			.16			#
D Relationship Thinking (Cylinder)	(64)	b	-.34*	-.43*	-.25	-.27	-.41*				.16		-.18
		g		.20	.16	.17	.19	-.18					
		T											
E Relationship Thinking (Meaning Context)	(65)	b					-.18	.22					
		g		.18	-.18	-.18	-.18	-.25					.31
		T											.17

Home Background Measures

Child Study Measures	(N)	Sex §	Modern-Traditional Orientation (MTO) (Composite)	Modern-Traditional Ideology (Questionnaire)	Modern-Traditional Ideology (Interview)	Enactment of Authority (Interview)	Standards of Behavior and Achievement (Interview)	Encouragement of Individual Interests (Interview)	Maternal Satisfaction and Role Coherence (Composite)	Satisfaction with Child (Interview)	Integration of Mother Role (Interview)	Consistency of Child Rearing (Interview)	Socio-Economic-Cultural Index (SEC) (Questionnaire)
F Relationship Thinking (Spies)	(65)	b	.18	.24				.26	.24	.30	.24		−.17
		g								−.16			
		T											
G Relationship Thinking (Uncommon Uses)	(65)	b	−.33	−.34*	−.26	−.18	−.43*		.23		.31	−.28	
		g	.20		−.20	−.18	−.25*				.17		
		T				−.17							
H Relationship Thinking, composite rating	(65)	b		.22			−.25	.17	.27	.28	.34		.32
		g								.16	.22	−.20	
		T											
I Solution Success (Cylinder)	(64)	b	−.16	−.38*			−.25		.38*	.24	.43*	.29	
		g		.30					−.20		.18	−.27	
		T											
J Solution Success (Meaning Context)	(65)	b	.16						.21	.19			.18
		g											
		T											
K Solution Success (Spies)	(65)	b	.19				.19	.17		.26	.24	.17	
		g											
		T											

TABLE CC-1 (continued)

Child Study Measures	(N)	Sex §	Modern-Traditional Orientation (MTO) (Composite)	Modern-Traditional Ideology (Questionnaire)	Modern-Traditional Ideology (Interview)	Enactment of Authority (Interview)	Standards of Behavior and Achievement (Interview)	Encouragement of Individual Interests (Interview)	Maternal Satisfaction and Role Coherence (Composite)	Satisfaction with Child (Interview)	Integration of Mother Role (Interview)	Consistency of Child Rearing (Interview)	Socio-Economic-Cultural Index (SEC) (Questionnaire)
L Solution Success		b	-.17		-.25	-.16				.21		-.20	
(Uncommon Uses)	(65)	g	.29	.29			-.21	.18				-.18	.23
		T										-.21	
M Solution Success,		b		.29			-.27		.26	.31	.29	-.27	
composite	(65)	g											.20
		T								.17	.18		

1. Empty cells in this correlation matrix indicate that the coefficient is less than .16.

2. Adjusted for differences between Year I and Year II scores.

* p < .05 (two-tailed test)

§ b = boys
  g = girls
  T = total

The correlations between the education component of the SEC Index and the Kuhlmann-Anderson IQ, Stanford Achievement Composite Score, and WISC Performance Scale IQ were .19, .21, and .02, respectively.

TABLE CC-2[1]

Imaginativeness (A–D), Themes (E–K)

Child Study Measures	(N)	Sex §	Modern-Traditional Orientation (MTO) (Composite)	Modern-Traditional Ideology (Questionnaire)	Modern-Traditional Ideology (Interview)	Enactment of Authority (Interview)	Standards of Behavior and Achievement (Interview)	Encouragement of Individual Interests (Interview)	Maternal Satisfaction and Role Coherence (Composite)	Satisfaction with Child (Interview)	Integration of Mother Role (Interview)	Consistency of Child Rearing (Interview)	Socio-Economic-Cultural Index (SEC) (Questionnaire)
A													
Imaginativeness		b				-.26	-.22						
(CPST)	(103)	g					-.27			-.26			
		T					-.17			-.22*			
B													
Imaginativeness		b		-.17			-.21	-.16					
(Play)	(104)	g		.16			-.28*		-.16				
		T					-.22*			-.18			
C													
Imaginativeness		b											
(Picture Titles)	(97)	g	.32*	.42*	.26			.17					.23
		T	.20*	.21*	.18								
D													
Imaginativeness		b			.22								
(Similes)	(105)	g				-.23							
		T						-.18	-.17			-.17	
E													
Childhood Versus Adult		b	-.18	-.25	-.16		-.20	-.19					.16
Orientation	(98)	g											
(Three Wishes)		T		-.18									-.21

TABLE cc-2 [1] (continued)

Home Background Measures

Child Study Measures	(N)	Sex §	Modern-Traditional Orientation (MTO) (Composite)	Modern-Traditional Ideology (Questionnaire)	Modern-Traditional Ideology (Interview)	Enactment of Authority (Interview)	Standards of Behavior and Achievement (Interview)	Encouragement of Individual Interests (Interview)	Maternal Satisfaction and Role Coherence (Composite)	Satisfaction with Child (Interview)	Integration of Mother Role (Interview)	Consistency of Child Rearing (Interview)	Socio-Economic-Cultural Index (SEC) (Questionnaire)
F Childhood Versus Adult Orientation (Million Dollars)		b	-.17				-.30*						
	(103)	g			-.16	-.16		-.17	.19		.21	.25	
		T		-.23*			-.17						
G Enactment of Family Life Themes (Play)		b								-.16			
	(104)	g	.26	-.43*									-.25
		T		-.19*									
H Incidence of Parent Figures[2] (CPST)		b				-.25	-.21	-.16					
	(105)	g	-.33*	-.18	-.33*	-.30*	-.31*	-.16	-.23	-.35*	-.18		-.20
		T	-.21*		-.24*	-.27*	-.24*		-.17	-.25*			
I Aggressive-Destructive Themes (Play)		b	-.22		-.18	-.19							
	(104)	g					-.22						
		T	-.19*			-.17							
J Prevalence of Achievement Themes (CPST)		b				-.23							
	(103)	g					-.29*		-.27	-.35*	-.21		
		T					-.17		-.22*	-.25*	-.18		

490

Home Background Measures

Child Study Measures	(N)	Sex §	Modern-Traditional Orientation (MTO) (Composite)	Modern-Traditional Ideology (Questionnaire)	Modern-Traditional Ideology (Interview)	Enactment of Authority (Interview)	Standards of Behavior and Achievement (Interview)	Encouragement of Individual Interests (Interview)	Maternal Satisfaction and Role Coherence (Composite)	Satisfaction with Child (Interview)	Integration of Mother Role (Interview)	Consistency of Child Rearing (Interview)	Socio-Economic-Cultural Index (SEC) (Questionnaire)
Primacy of External Standards (CPST)	(103)	b	−.23	−.23		−.24			−.24	−.26	−.21		
		g			−.16							.17	−.33*
		T							−.19*	−.19*	−.18		−.16

1. Empty cells in this correlation matrix indicate that the coefficient is less than .16.
2. Correlations for this measure were based on raw frequencies.
* $p < .05$ (two-tailed test)
§ b = boys
g = girls
T = total

TABLE CC-3[1]

Salience of the Family (A–D), Perception of Adult-Child Interaction (E–I)

Home Background Measures

Child Study Measures	(N)	Sex §	Modern-Traditional Orientation (MTO) (Composite)	Modern-Traditional Ideology (Questionnaire)	Modern-Traditional Ideology (Interview)	Enactment of Authority (Interview)	Standards of Behavior and Achievement (Interview)	Encouragement of Individual Interests (Interview)	Maternal Satisfaction and Role Coherence (Composite)	Satisfaction with Child (Interview)	Integration of Mother Role (Interview)	Consistency of Child Rearing (Interview)	Socio-Economic-Cultural Index (SEC) (Questionnaire)
A Enactment of Family Life Themes (Play)	(104)	b	−.26	−.43*						.16			−.25
		g											
		T		−.19*									
B Incidence of Parent Figures[2] (CPST)	(103)	b	−.33*	−.18	−.33*	−.25	−.21	−.16					−.20
		g				−.30*	−.31*		−.23	−.35*	−.18		
		T	−.21*		−.24*	−.27*	−.24*		−.17	−.25*			
C Family-Related Material (Personal Questions)	(102)	b	−.32*	−.25	−.16	−.26	−.35*	−.28*					
		g											
		T	−.18	−.17			−.16						
D Replication of Own Family (Family Drawing)	(98)	b											−.27*
		g					−.19		−.25	−.20			
		T									−.28*		

Home Background Measures

Child Study Measures	(N)	Sex §	Modern-Traditional Orientation (MTO) (Composite)	Modern-Traditional Ideology (Questionnaire)	Modern-Traditional Ideology (Interview)	Enactment of Authority (Interview)	Standards of Behavior and Achievement (Interview)	Encouragement of Individual Interests (Interview)	Maternal Satisfaction and Role Coherence (Composite)	Satisfaction with Child (Interview)	Integration of Mother Role (Interview)	Consistency of Child Rearing (Interview)	Socio-Economic-Cultural Index (SEC) (Questionnaire)
E Relatedness of Mother and Child (Sentence Completion Item 3)	(103)	b	.18										
		g											
		T											
F Relatedness of Father and Child (Sentence Completion Item 5)	(104)	b	.21	.16	.20					−.16			
		g	.16	.16	.16								
		T	.16	.17	.17								
G Benevolence of Adult Attitudes and Behavior toward Children (CPST)	(100)	b	−.29	−.28	−.32*	−.24	−.23	.18					
		g					−.41*	−.24	−.33*	−.41*	−.31*		−.19
		T					−.24*		−.22*	−.26*	−.23*		
H Interaction between Adults and Children (Play)	(104)	b				−.20							
		g										.19	−.16
		T							.18				

493

TABLE CC-3 [1] (continued)

Child Study Measures	(N)	Sex §	Home Background Measures										
			Modern-Traditional Orientation (MTO) (Composite)	Modern-Traditional Ideology (Questionnaire)	Modern-Traditional Ideology (Interview)	Enactment of Authority (Interview)	Standards of Behavior and Achievement (Interview)	Encouragement of Individual Interests (Interview)	Maternal Satisfaction and Role Coherence (Composite)	Satisfaction with Child (Interview)	Integration of Mother Role (Interview)	Consistency of Child Rearing (Interview)	Socio-Economic-Cultural Index (SEC) (Questionnaire)
I													
Child-Initiated Contact with Adults (CPST)	(100)	b								-.19			
		g								-.16			-.27
		T								-.17			
J													
Direct Expression of Opposition to Adults (CPST)	(102)	b		.31*									
		g				-.22				-.16			-.19
		T		.17									

1. Empty cells in this correlation matrix indicate that the coefficient is less than .16.
2. Correlations for this measure were based on raw frequencies.
* p < .05 (two-tailed test)
§ b = boys
g = girls
T = total

TABLE CC-4[1]

Attitude to School Authority (A–D),[2] Code for Restraint (E–G), Code for Allegiance (H–I), Concepts of Justice (J–L)

Child Study Measures	(N)	Sex §	Home Background Measures										
			Modern-Traditional Orientation (MTO) (Composite)	Modern-Traditional Ideology (Questionnaire)	Modern-Traditional Ideology (Interview)	Enactment of Authority (Interview)	Standards of Behavior and Achievement (Interview)	Encouragement of Individual Interests (Interview)	Maternal Satisfaction and Role Coherence (Composite)	Satisfaction with Child (Interview)	Integration of Mother Role (Interview)	Consistency of Child Rearing (Interview)	Socio-Economic-Cultural Index (SEC) (Questionnaire)
A													
Resentful Attitude		b											
(Sentence Completion		g					-.24					-.16	.33*
Items 7, 8, 10, 12, 14)	(105)	T											
B													
Conforming Attitude		b	-.28*	-.28*		-.28*						.21	
(Sentence Completion		g		-.10		-.16	.20						
Items 7, 8, 10, 12, 14)	(105)	T	-.21*	-.19*		-.21*						.17	-.22
C													
Rational Attitude		b	.25	.22	.16	.22	.17						.21
(Sentence Completion		g				.17		.17	.17			.26	-.26
Items 7, 8, 10, 12, 14)	(105)	T											
D													
Fearful Attitude		b			-.21		-.34*	-.36*	-.19			-.18	
(Sentence Completion		g		-.18	-.18				-.23		-.24		
Items 7, 8, 10, 12, 14)	(105)	T	-.19*	-.19*	-.19*	-.17		-.17	-.22*		-.20*	-.19*	-.16

495

TABLE CC-4 [1] (continued)

Child Study Measures	(N)	Sex §	Modern-Traditional Orientation (MTO) (Composite)	Modern-Traditional Ideology (Questionnaire)	Modern-Traditional Ideology (Interview)	Enactment of Authority (Interview)	Standards of Behavior and Achievement (Interview)	Encouragement of Individual Interests (Interview)	Maternal Satisfaction and Role Coherence (Composite)	Satisfaction with Child (Interview)	Integration of Mother Role (Interview)	Consistency of Child Rearing (Interview)	Socio-Economic-Cultural Index (SEC) (Questionnaire)
							Home Background Measures						
E Control of Behavior: School-Related or Unrelated (Sentence Completion Item 13)	(97)	b	-.16										-.16
		g		-.25	-.19	-.19				.17			-.35*
		T											-.26*
F Crimes: Major/Minor (Interview)	(94)	b					.26						
		g		.18			.17			-.16			
		T											
G Crimes: School-related and Unrelated (Interview)	(94)	b	.27*	.25	.27*	.16	.19						
		g	.25		.24	.32*	.26						
		T	.26*	.20*	.26*	.24*	.21*						
H Identifying the Culprit (Moral Dilemma)	(96)	b	.20	.21		.20	.19	-.18					
		g										-.28	
		T		.16		.16	.19		-.19				
I Exemption from Chores: (Moral Dilemma)	(96)	b											.30
		g											
		T											.19

Home Background Measures

Child Study Measures	(N)	Sex §	Modern-Traditional Orientation (MTO) (Composite)	Modern-Traditional Ideology (Questionnaire)	Modern-Traditional Ideology (Interview)	Enactment of Authority (Interview)	Standards of Behavior and Achievement (Interview)	Encouragement of Individual Interests (Interview)	Maternal Satisfaction and Role Coherence (Composite)	Satisfaction with Child (Interview)	Integration of Mother Role (Interview)	Consistency of Child Rearing (Interview)	Socio-Economic-Cultural Index (SEC) (Questionnaire)
J Ideas of Unfairness: Level of Generalization (Interview)	(92)	b	−.22						.37*	.28*	.32*	.35*	
		g							−.26	−.23	−.29		.28
		T											.17
K Content of Unfairness: Concern for Codes (Interview)	(88)	b	.31*	.18	.28	.34*	.31*						.20
		g	.31*	.24	.23	.18	.16						
		T	.30*	.20	.25*								
L Evaluation of Cheating (Moral Dilemma)	(105)	b	.17		−.19	.25				.16			
		g		.53*	.19	.22				.17			.21
		T				.23*				.16			

1. Empty cells in this correlation matrix indicate that the coefficient is less than .16.
2. Because of the low incidence of "rebellious" responses, this category was excluded from the correlation analysis.
* p < .05 (two-tailed test)
§ b = boys
  g = girls
  T = total

TABLE CC-5 [1]

Self-Confidence and Satisfaction (A–B), Self-Awareness and Differentiation (C–I)

Child Study Measures	(N)	Sex §	Modern-Traditional Orientation (MTO) (Composite)	Modern-Traditional Ideology (Questionnaire)	Modern-Traditional Ideology (Interview)	Enactment of Authority (Interview)	Standards of Behavior and Achievement (Interview)	Encouragement of Individual Interests (Interview)	Maternal Satisfaction and Role Coherence (Composite)	Satisfaction with Child (Interview)	Integration of Mother Role (Interview)	Consistency of Child Rearing (Interview)	Socio-Economic-Cultural Index (SEC) (Questionnaire)
A Self-Satisfaction Syndrome (SFS Items 2, 4, 7, 8)		b	-.17										-.25
	(103)	g			-.22	-.28*			-.21		-.18	-.23	
		T											
B Strength of Self-Presentation (Figure Drawings)		b		-.16		-.17	-.20						
	(104)	g											
		T											
C Awareness of Own Feelings (Personal Questions)		b											
	(102)	g				.24		.17	-.23		-.19	-.34*	
		T									-.17	-.17	
D Style of Reactivity (SFS Item 5)		b											-.24
	(102)	g		-.19	-.22	-.17		-.17	-.18				-.26
		T											-.25*
E Aggression Anxiety (SFS Item 10)		b	-.19	-.34*				-.16		.21			
	(100)	g	-.18	-.26				-.29*		.18			
		T	-.18	-.19				-.21*					

Home Background Measures

Child Study Measures	(N)	Sex §	Modern-Traditional Orientation (MTO) (Composite)	Modern-Traditional Ideology (Questionnaire)	Modern-Traditional Ideology (Interview)	Enactment of Authority (Interview)	Standards of Behavior and Achievement (Interview)	Encouragement of Individual Interests (Interview)	Maternal Satisfaction and Role Coherence (Composite)	Satisfaction with Child (Interview)	Integration of Mother Role (Interview)	Consistency of Child Rearing (Interview)	Socio-Economic-Cultural Index (SEC) (Questionnaire)
F													
Aggression Anxiety (Personal Questions)	(101)	b	-.16				-.28*	-.27*					-.17
		g	-.20	-.20	-.22	-.20			-.19		-.17	-.18	-.18
		T	-.18			-.20	-.19	-.20*			-.17	-.18	-.17
G													
Self-Differentiation (SFS Items 1–10)	(103)	b	.17	.18	.20								
		g	.18	.18			.26						
		T	.19*	.18									
H													
Range of Self-Differentiation (Dictated Letter)	(102)	b	.18	.19	.25				-.26	-.21	-.27	-.20	
		g		.16	.16						-.21	-.18	
		T		.18	.18				-.18		-.17	-.18	
I													
Quality of Self-Differentiation (Dictated Letter)	(102)	b		.25	.22				-.16	-.18		-.26	-.21
		g											
		T	.16						-.16			-.18	

1. Empty cells in this correlation matrix indicate that the coefficient is less than .16.
* p < .05 (two-tailed test)
§ b = boys
g = girls
T = total

TABLE cc-6 [1]

Preference for Older, Younger, or Current Life Stages (A–D), Images of the Future (E–G)

Child Study Measures	(N)	Sex §	Modern-Traditional Orientation (MTO) (Composite)	Modern-Traditional Ideology (Questionnaire)	Modern-Traditional Ideology (Interview)	Enactment of Authority (Interview)	Standards of Behavior and Achievement (Interview)	Encouragement of Individual Interests (Interview)	Maternal Satisfaction and Role Coherence (Composite)	Satisfaction with Child (Interview)	Integration of Mother Role (Interview)	Consistency of Child Rearing (Interview)	Socio-Economic-Cultural Index (SEC) (Questionnaire)
A Best Age To Be (Interview)	(61)	b	-.29	-.24		-.30	-.18		-.26	-.16	-.24		-.25
		g		-.31				.20	.19	.27	.22		
		T		-.28*									
B Life Stage Preference (SFS Item 3)	(102)	b	.19				.16						-.21
		g				.23		.30*				-.28*	
		T										-.16	
C Childhood Versus Adult Orientation (Million Dollars)	(103)	b	-.17	-.30*			-.30*						
		g			-.16	-.16		-.17			.21	.25	
		T		-.23*			-.17		.19				
D Childhood Versus Adult Orientation (Three Wishes)	(98)	b	-.18	-.25	-.16		-.20	-.19					.16
		g											
		T		-.18									-.21

500

Home Background Measures

Child Study Measures	(N)	Sex §	Modern-Traditional Orientation (MTO) (Composite)	Modern-Traditional Ideology (Questionnaire)	Modern-Traditional Ideology (Interview)	Enactment of Authority (Interview)	Standards of Behavior and Achievement (Interview)	Encouragement of Individual Interests (Interview)	Maternal Satisfaction and Role Coherence (Composite)	Satisfaction with Child (Interview)	Integration of Mother Role (Interview)	Consistency of Child Rearing (Interview)	Socio-Economic-Cultural Index (SEC) (Questionnaire)
E. Presence of Older Social Sex Role Themes (CPST)	(103)	b											−.27*
		g								−.18			
		T											
F. Continuity of Future Plans with Present (Interview)	(98)	b	−.47*	−.21			−.17		.26	.17	.23	.24	.32*
		g		−.44*	−.22	−.34*	−.18	−.31*				.21	
		T	−.29*	−.32*		−.21*	−.17	−.18	.18			.22*	
G. Childlike or Adult Orientation to Jobs (Sentence Completion Item 4)	(83)	b	−.23	−.22			−.24	−.16					.46*
		g	−.41*	−.38*	−.37*	−.45*	−.20	−.32*	.17		.16	.28	
		T	−.31*	−.29*	−.26*	−.28*	−.22*	−.23*					.20

1. Empty cells in this correlation matrix indicate that the coefficient is less than .16.
* p < .05 (two-tailed test)
§ b = boys
g = girls
T = total

TABLE α-7 [1]

Sex Role Allegiance and Concepts (A–E), Sex-Typical Themes (F–J)

Child Study Measures	(N)	Sex §	Modern-Traditional Orientation (MTO) (Composite)	Modern-Traditional Ideology (Questionnaire)	Modern-Traditional Ideology (Interview)	Enactment of Authority (Interview)	Standards of Behavior and Achievement (Interview)	Encouragement of Individual Interests (Interview)	Maternal Satisfaction and Role Coherence (Composite)	Satisfaction with Child (Interview)	Integration of Mother Role (Interview)	Consistency of Child Rearing (Interview)	Socio-Economic-Cultural Index (SEC) (Questionnaire)
							Home Background Measures						
A													
Own Sex Preference (SFS Item 8)	(102)	b											
		g		−.18				−.18					−.24
		T						−.21*					
B													
Emphasis on Self-Sex Figure (Figure Drawings)	(95)	b											
		g	−.25		−.26		−.22	−.16	−.21	−.23	−.18		
		T			−.18								
C													
Affective Attitude to Opposite Sex (Sentence Completion Item 9 for boys, 11 for girls)	(99)	b	.19	.46*									
		g		.18				.20	−.20	−.19		−.22	
		T	.16	.32*						−.16		−.17	
D													
Projected Attitude from Opposite Sex to Own (Sentence Completion Item 11 for boys, 9 for girls)	(99)	b				.21		.16					−.18
		g				−.28		.16					
		T						.16					

Home Background Measures

Child Study Measures	(N)	Sex §	Modern-Traditional Orientation (MTO) (Composite)	Modern-Traditional Ideology (Questionnaire)	Modern-Traditional Ideology (Interview)	Enactment of Authority (Interview)	Standards of Behavior and Achievement (Interview)	Encouragement of Individual Interests (Interview)	Maternal Satisfaction and Role Coherence (Composite)	Satisfaction with Child (Interview)	Integration of Mother Role (Interview)	Consistency of Child Rearing (Interview)	Socio-Economic-Cultural Index (SEC) (Questionnaire)
E Preferred Qualities in Opposite Sex (SFS Item 9)		b	−.21	−.27*				−.19	−.17			−.26	
	(101)	g	.26				.21	.19					
		T											
F Sex-Typed Play (Play)		b											
	(105)	g	−.32*	−.41*	.21		.20						−.16
		T		−.17									
G Aggressive-Destructive Themes (Play)		b	−.22		−.18	−.19							
	(104)	g					−.22						
		T	−.19*			−.17							
H Enactment of Family Life Themes (Play)		b											
	(104)	g	.26	−.43*									−.25
		T		−.19*						−.16			
I Incidence of Parent Figures[2] (CPST)		b				−.25	−.21	−.16					
	(103)	g	−.33*	−.18	−.33*	−.30*	−.31*		−.23	−.35*	−.18		−.20
		T	−.21*	−.24*	−.24*	−.27*	−.24*		−.17	−.25*			

TABLE CC-7 [1] (continued)

| | | | Home Background Measures | | | | | | | | | | |
Child Study Measures	(N)	Sex §	Modern-Traditional Orientation (MTO) (Composite)	Modern-Traditional Ideology (Questionnaire)	Modern-Traditional Ideology (Interview)	Enactment of Authority (Interview)	Standards of Behavior and Achievement (Interview)	Encouragement of Individual Interests (Interview)	Maternal Satisfaction and Role Coherence (Composite)	Satisfaction with Child (Interview)	Integration of Mother Role (Interview)	Consistency of Child Rearing (Interview)	Socio-Economic-Cultural Index (SEC) (Questionnaire)
J Benevolence of Adult Attitudes and Behavior Toward Children (CPST)		b											
	(100)	g	−.29	−.28	−.32*	−.24	−.23	.18	−.33*	−.41*	−.31*		−.19
		T					−.24*	.24	−.22*	−.26*	−.23*		

1. Empty cells in this correlation matrix indicate that the coefficient is less than .16.
2. Correlations for this measure were based on raw frequencies.
* p < .05 (two-tailed test)
§ b = boys
g = girls
T = total

504

BIBLIOGRAPHY

N. W. ACKERMAN, *The Psychodynamics of Family Life* (New York: Basic Books, 1958).

T. W. ADORNO, E. FRENKEL-BRUNSWIK, D. J. LEVINSON, and R. N. SANFORD, *The Authoritarian Personality* (New York: Harper, 1950).

T. ALEXANDER, "The Adult-Child Interaction Test: A projective test for use in research," *Monographs of the Society for Research in Child Development,* 17 (1952), No. 2.

H. H. ANDERSON, "Domination and Social Integration in the Behavior of Kindergarten Children and Teachers," *Genetic Psychology Monographs,* 21 (1939), 287–385.

H. H. ANDERSON and H. M. BREWER, "Studies of Teachers' Classroom Personalities. I. Dominative and integrative behavior of kindergarten teachers," *Applied Psychology Monographs,* 6 (1945), 109–152.

H. H. ANDERSON and J. E. BREWER, "Studies of Teachers' Classroom Personalities. II. Effects of teachers' dominative and integrative contacts on children's classroom behavior," *Applied Psychology Monographs,* 8 (1946), 33–122.

H. H. ANDERSON, J. E. BREWER, and M. F. REED, "Studies of Teachers' Classroom Personalities. III. Follow-up studies of the effects of dominative and integrative contacts on children's behavior," *Applied Psychology Monographs,* 11 (1946), 101–156.

F. BARRON, *Creativity and Psychological Health* (Princeton, N. J.: Van Nostrand, 1963).

W. C. BECKER, "Consequences of Parental Discipline," in M. L. Hoffman and L. W. Hoffman, eds., *Child Development Research,* 1 (New York: Russell Sage Foundation, 1964), 169–209.

N. BELL and E. VOGEL, eds., *A Modern Introduction to the Family* (Glencoe, Ill.: Free Press, 1960).

A. A. BELLACK, H. M. KLIEBARD, R. T. HYMAN, and F. L. SMITH, JR., *The Language of the Classroom* (New York: Teachers College Press, 1966).

B. BIBER, "Premature Structuring as a Deterrent to Creativity," *American Journal of Orthopsychiatry*, 29 (1959), 280–290.

B. BIBER, "Integration of Mental Health Principles in the School Setting," in G. Caplan, ed., *Prevention of Mental Disorders in Children* (New York: Basic Books, 1961), pp. 323–352.

B. BIBER, "A Learning-Teaching Paradigm Integrating Intellectual and Affective Processes," in E. M. Bower and W. G. Hollister, eds., *Behavioral Science Frontiers in Education* (New York: Wiley, 1967).

P. BOSTWICK, "Inventiveness with Time, Space and Materials," in A. Miel, ed., *Creativity in Teaching* (Belmont, Calif.: Wadsworth Publishing Co., 1961), pp. 140–176.

E. M. BOWER, "Mental Health in Education," *Review of Educational Research*, 23 (1962), 441–453.

U. BRONFENBRENNER, "Socialization and Social Class through Time and Space," in E. Maccoby, T. M. Newcomb, and E. L. Hartley, eds., *Readings in Social Psychology* (New York: Holt, 1958), pp. 400–425.

U. BRONFENBRENNER, "Freudian Theories of Identification and their Derivatives," *Child Development*, 31 (1960), 15–40.

U. BRONFENBRENNER, "The Changing American Child: A speculative analysis," *Journal of Social Issues*, 17 (1961), 6–18.

U. BRONFENBRENNER, "Developmental Theory in Transition," in H. W. Stevenson, ed., *Child Psychology*. The 62nd Yearbook of the National Society for the Study of Education, Part I (Chicago: The National Society for the Study of Education, 1963).

D. G. BROWN, "Sex-Role Preference in Young Children," *Psychological Monographs*, 70 (1956), No. 14.

J. S. BRUNER, J. J. GOODNOW, and G. A. AUSTIN, *A Study of Thinking* (New York: Wiley, 1956).

J. S. BRUNER, "The Act of Discovery," *Harvard Educational Review*, 31 (1961), 21–32.

J. S. BRUNER, "The Course of Cognitive Growth," *American Psychologist*, 19 (1964), 1–15.

J. S. BRUNER, R. R. OLVER, and P. M. GREENFIELD, *Studies in Cognitive Growth* (New York: Wiley, 1966).

J. S. BRUNER, *Toward a Theory of Instruction* (Cambridge, Mass.: Harvard University Press, 1966).

M. V. COVINGTON, R. S. CRUTCHFIELD, and L. B. DAVIES, *The Productive Thinking Program*. Series One: *General Problem-Solving* (Berkeley: Brazelton Printing Co., 1966).

V. J. CRANDALL, "Achievement," in H. W. Stevenson, ed., *Child Psychology*. The 62nd Yearbook of the National Society for the Study of Education, Part I (Chicago: The National Society for the Study of Education, 1963), pp. 416–459.

V. CRANDALL, "Achievement Behavior in Young Children," *Young Children,* 20 (1964), 77–90.

D. E. DAMRIN, "The Russell Sage Social Relations Test: A technique for measuring group problem solving skills in elementary school children," *Journal of Experimental Education,* 28 (1959), 85–99.

L. F. DROPPLEMAN and E. S. SCHAEFER, "Boys' and Girls' Reports of Maternal and Paternal Behavior," *Journal of Abnormal and Social Psychology,* 67 (1963), 648–654.

W. EMMERICH, "Parental Identification in Young Children," *Genetic Psychology Monographs,* 60 (1959), 257–308.

M. ENGEL and W. J. RAINE, "A Method for the Measurement of the Self-Concept of Children in the Third Grade," *Journal of Genetic Psychology,* 102 (1963), 125–137.

M. C. ERICKSON, "Social Status and Child Rearing Practices," in T. Newcomb and E. Hartley, eds., *Readings in Social Psychology* (New York: Holt, 1947).

N. A. FLANDERS, "Teacher Influence, Pupil Attitudes, and Achievement," Office of Education, Cooperative Research Project No. 397 (Minneapolis: University of Minnesota Press, 1960).

J. H. FLAVELL, *The Developmental Psychology of Jean Piaget* (Princeton, N. J.: Van Nostrand, 1963), pp. 442–446.

B. Z. FRIEDLANDER, "A Psychologist's Second Thoughts on Concepts, Curiosity, and Discovery in Teaching and Learning," *Harvard Educational Review,* 35 (1965), 18–38.

N. L. GAGE, ed., *Handbook of Research on Teaching* (Chicago: Rand McNally, 1963).

R. W. GARDNER, "Cognitive Styles in Categorizing Behavior," *Journal of Personality,* 22 (1953), 214–233.

R. W. GARDNER, P. S. HOLZMAN, G. S. KLEIN, H. B. LINTON, and D. P. SPENCE, "Cognitive Control: A study of individual consistencies in cognitive behavior," *Pyschological Issues,* I (1959), No. 4.

J. W. GETZELS and H. A. THELEN, "The Classroom Group as a Unique Social System," in N. B. Henry, ed., *The Dynamics of Instructional Groups; Sociopsychological Aspects of Teaching and Learning,* The 59th Yearbook of the National Society for the Study of Education, Part II (Chicago: The National Society for the Study of Education, 1960), pp. 53–82.

J. W. GETZELS and P. W. JACKSON, *Creativity and Intelligence* (New York: Wiley, 1962).

J. GLIDEWELL, M. B. KANTOR, L. M. SMITH, and L. A. STRINGER, "Socialization and Social Structure in the Classroom," in M. L. Hoffman and L. W. Hoffman, eds., *Review of Child Development Research* (New York: Russell Sage Foundation, 1966), pp. 221–256.

S. GRAY and R. KLAUS, "The Assessment of Parental Identification," *Genetic Psychology Monographs,* 54 (1956), 87–114.

J. E. GREENE and A. H. ROBERTS, "Time Orientation and Social Class: A correction," *Journal of Abnormal and Social Psychology,* 62 (1961), 141.

J. P. GUILFORD, "The Structure of Intellect," *Psychological Bulletin,* 53 (1956), 267–293.

G. GURIN, J. VEROFF and S. FELD, *Americans View their Mental Health* (New York: Basic Books, 1960), pp. 117–142.

Z. GUSSOW, "The Observer-Observed Relationship as Information about Structure in Small Group Research," *Psychiatry*, 27 (1964), 230–247.

A. W. HALPIN and D. B. CROFT, *The Organizational Climate of Schools* (Chicago: Midwest Administration Center, University of Chicago, 1963).

A. W. HALPIN, *Theory and Research in Administration* (New York: Macmillan, 1963).

R. E. HARTLEY, "A Developmental View of Female Sex-Role Definition and Identification," *Merrill-Palmer Quarterly*, 10 (1964), 3–16.

W. W. HARTUP, "Some Correlates of Parental Imitation in Young Children," *Child Development*, 33 (1962), 85–97.

W. W. HARTUP and E. A. ZOOK, "Sex Role Preferences in Three- and Four-Year-Old Children," *Journal of Consulting Psychology*, 24 (1960), 420–426.

D. HAWKINS, "Childhood and the Education of Intellectuals," *Harvard Educational Review*, 36 (1966), 477–483.

J. HENRY, "Docility, or Giving Teacher What She Wants," *Journal of Social Issues*, 11 (1955), 33–41.

J. HENRY, "Attitude Organization in Elementary School Classrooms," *American Journal of Orthopsychiatry*, 27 (1957), 117–133.

E. R. HILGARD, "Issues within Theory and Programmed Learning," *Psychology in the Schools*, 1 (1964), 129–139.

M. L. HOFFMAN and H. D. SALTZSTEIN, "Techniques and Prophecies in Moral Development," National Institute of Mental Health Research Grant m-2333, 1964.

R. R. HOLT, "The Nature of TAT Stories as Cognitive Products: A psychoanalytic approach," in J. Kagan and G. S. Lesser, eds., *Contemporary Issues in Thematic Apperception Methods* (Springfield, Ill.: Charles C Thomas, 1961), pp. 3–43.

M. HUGHES and associates, "Development of the Means for the Assessment of the Quality of Teaching in the Elementary Schools," Office of Education, Cooperative Research Project No. 353 (Salt Lake City: University of Utah, 1959).

J. McV. HUNT, *Intelligence and Experience* (New York: Ronald Press, 1961).

J. KAGAN, "The Concept of Identification," *Psychological Review*, 65 (1958), 296–305.

J. KAGAN, H. A. MOSS, and I. E. SIGEL, "Psychological Significance of Styles of Conceptualization," in J. E. Wright and J. Kagan, eds., *Basic Cognitive Process in Children*, Monographs of the Society for Research in Child Development, 28 (1963), No. 2.

J. KAGAN, "Acquisition and Significance of Sex Typing and Sex Role Identity," in M. L. Hoffman and L. W. Hoffman, eds., *Review of Child Development Research* (New York: Russell Sage Foundation, 1964), pp. 137–167.

J. KAGAN, B. I. ROSMAN, D. DAY, J. ALBERT, and W. PHILLIPS, "Information Processing in the Child: Significance of analytic and reflective attitudes," *Psychological Monographs*, 78 (1964), No. 1.

W. Kessen, "'Stage' and 'Structure' in the Study of Children," in W. Kessen and C. Kuhlman, eds., *Thought in the Young Child,* Monographs of the Society for Research in Child Development, 27 (1962), 65–82.

G. S. Klein, "Need and Regulation," in M. R. Jones, ed., *Nebraska Symposium on Motivation* (Lincoln: University of Nebraska Press, 1954), pp. 224–274.

L. Kohlberg, "Development of Moral Character and Moral Ideology," in M. L. Hoffman and L. W. Hoffman, eds., *Review of Child Development Research* (New York: Russell Sage Foundation, 1964), pp. 383–431.

L. Kohlberg, "A Cognitive-Developmental Analysis of Children's Sex-Role Concepts and Attitudes," in E. E. Maccoby, ed., *The Development of Sex Differences* (Palo Alto, Calif.: Stanford University Press, 1966).

M. L. Kohn, "Social Class and Parent-Child Relationships: An interpretation," *American Journal of Sociology,* 68 (1963), 471–480.

L. M. Lazowick, "On the Nature of Identification," *Journal of Abnormal and Social Psychology,* 51 (1955), 175–183.

E. B. Leacock, *Teaching and Learning in City Schools: A Comparative Study* (New York: Basic Books, 1969).

L. L. LeShan, "Time Orientation and Social Class," *Journal of Abnormal and Social Psychology,* 47 (1952), 589–592. See also J. E. Greene and A. H. Roberts (1961).

D. Levinson and P. E. Huffman, "Traditional Family Ideology and its Relation to Personality," *Journal of Personality,* 23 (1955), 251–273.

N. Livson, "Parental Behavior and Children's Involvement with their Parents," *Journal of Genetic Psychology,* 109 (1966), 173–194.

J. Loevinger and B. Sweet, "Construction of a Test of Mother's Attitudes," in J. C. Glidewell, ed., *Parental Attitudes and Child Behavior* (Springfield, Ill.: Charles C Thomas, 1961).

D. B. Lynn and W. L. Sawrey, "The Effects of Father-Absence on Norwegian Boys and Girls," *Journal of Abnormal and Social Psychology,* 59 (1959), 258–262.

D. B. Lynn, "A Note on Sex Differences in the Development of Masculine and Feminine Identification," *Psychological Review,* 66 (1959), 126–135.

D. B. Lynn, "Sex-Role and Parental Identification," *Child Development,* 33 (1962), 555–564.

D. C. McClelland, J. W. Atkinson, R. A. Clark, and E. L. Lowell, *The Achievement Motive* (New York: Appleton-Century-Crofts, 1953).

E. Maccoby, *The Development of Sex Differences* (Palo Alto, Calif.: Stanford University Press, 1966).

K. Machover, *Personality Projection in the Drawing of the Human Figure* (Springfield, Ill.: Charles C Thomas, 1948).

K. Machover, "Drawing of the Human Figure: A method of personality investigation," in H. H. Anderson and G. L. Anderson, eds., *An Introduction to Projective Techniques* (New York: Prentice-Hall, 1951), pp. 341–369.

D. W. MacKinnon, "The Nature and Nurture of Creative Talent," *American Psychologist,* 17 (1962), 484–495.

Q. McNemar, *Psychological Statistics,* 3rd ed. (New York: Wiley, 1962).

P. B. Meissner, "Miniature Toy Play Situations," in H. A. Witkin, H. B. Lewis, M. Hertzman, K. Machover, P. B. Meissner, and S. Wapner, *Personality through Perception* (New York: Harper, 1954), pp. 376–426.

G. A. Milton, "The Effects of Sex-Role Identification upon Problem-Solving Skill," *Journal of Abnormal and Social Psychology*, 55 (1957), 208–212.

P. Minuchin and E. Shapiro, "Patterns of Mastery and Conflict Resolution at the Elementary School Level," U. S. Office of Education, Cooperative Research Project No. 1401 (New York: Bank Street College of Education, 1964).

S. Minuchin, B. Montalvo, B. G. Guerney, Jr., B. Rosman, and F. Schumer, *Families of the Slums* (New York: Basic Books, 1967).

L. Mitchell, *Young Geographers* (New York: John Day, 1934). Reissued in 1963 by Basic Books, New York.

F. A. Mosher and J. R. Hornsby, "On Asking Questions," in J. S. Bruner, R. R. Olver, and P. M. Greenfield, *Studies in Cognitive Growth* (New York: Wiley, 1966), pp. 86–102.

O. H. Mowrer, "Identification: A Link between Theory and Psychotherapy," *Learning Theory and Personality Dynamics* (New York: Ronald Press, 1950), pp. 573–616.

G. Murphy, "The Process of Creative Thinking," *Educational Leadership*, 14 (1956), 11–15.

L. B. Murphy, *Personality in Young Children, Vol. I: Methods for the Study of Personality in Young Children* (New York: Basic Books, 1956), pp. 9–102.

H. A. Murray, *Thematic Apperception Test* (Cambridge, Mass.: Harvard University Press, 1943).

P. H. Mussen and L. Distler, "Masculinity, Identification, and Father-Son Relationships," *Journal of Abnormal and Social Psychology*, 59 (1959), 350–356.

P. H. Mussen and E. Rutherford, "Parent-Child Relations and Parental Personality in Relation to Young Children's Sex-Role Preferences," *Child Development*, 34 (1963), 589–607.

J. Nash, "The Father in Contemporary Culture and Current Psychological Literature," *Child Development*, 36 (1965), No. 1.

T. Parsons, "Age and Sex in the Social Structure of the United States," *American Sociological Review*, 7 (1942), 604–616.

T. Parsons and R. F. Bales, *Family: Socialization and Interaction Process* (Glencoe, Ill.: Free Press, 1955).

L. Peller, "Daydreams and Children's Favorite Books," *Psychoanalytic Study of the Child*, 14 (New York: International Universities Press, 1959), 414–433.

H. Perkins, "A Procedure for Assessing the Classroom Behavior of Students and Teachers," *American Educational Research Journal*, 1 (1964), 249–260.

J. Piaget, *Judgment and Reasoning in the Child* (New York: Harcourt, Brace, 1928).

J. Piaget, *The Child's Conception of the World* (New York: Harcourt, Brace, 1929).

J. Piaget, *The Moral Judgment of the Child* (Glencoe, Ill.: Free Press, 1948).

J. Piaget, *The Psychology of Intelligence* (London: Routledge & Paul, 1950).

M. H. Pintler, R. Phillips, and R. R. Sears, "Sex Differences in the Projective Doll Play of Preschool Children," *Journal of Psychology*, 21 (1946), 73–80.

E. G. Pitcher and E. Prelinger, *Children Tell Stories: An Analysis of Fantasy* (New York: International Universities Press, 1963).

M. Rabban, "Sex Role Identification in Young Children in Two Diverse Social Groups," *Genetic Psychology Monographs*, 42 (1950), 81–158.

B. G. Rosenberg and B. Sutton-Smith, "The Measurement of Masculinity and Femininity in Children," *Child Development*, 30 (1959), 373–380.

R. N. Sanford, M. M. Adkins, R. B. Miller, and E. A. Cobb, "Physique, Personality and Scholarship," *Monographs of the Society for Research in Child Development*, 8 (1943), No. 1.

P. Saugstad, "Incidental Memory and Problem Solving," *Psychological Review*, 59 (1952), 221–226.

E. G. Schachtel, *Metamorphosis* (New York: Basic Books, 1959).

E. S. Schaefer, "A Circumplex Model for Maternal Behavior," *Journal of Abnormal and Social Psychology*, 59 (1959), 226–235.

E. S. Schaefer, "Converging Conceptual Models for Maternal Behavior and for Child Behavior," in J. C. Glidewell, ed., *Parental Attitudes and Child Behavior* (Springfield, Ill.: Charles C Thomas, 1961).

E. S. Schaefer and N. Bayley, "Maternal Behavior, Child Behavior, and their Intercorrelations from Infancy through Adolescence," *Monographs of the Society for Research in Child Development*, 28 (1963), No. 3.

P. S. Sears, "Correlates of Need Achievement and Need Affiliation and Classroom Management, Self-Concept and Creativity" (Palo Alto, Calif.: Laboratory of Human Development, Stanford University, 1962).

P. S. Sears and E. R. Hilgard, "The Teacher's Role in the Motivation of the Learner," in E. R. Hilgard, ed., *Theories of Learning and Instruction*, The 63rd Yearbook of the National Society for the Study of Education, Part I (Chicago: The National Society for the Study of Education, 1964), pp. 182–209.

R. R. Sears, E. Maccoby, and H. Levin, *Patterns of Child Rearing* (Evanston, Ill.: Row, Peterson, 1957).

J. R. Seeley, R. A. Sim, and E. W. Loosley, *Crestwood Heights* (New York: Basic Books, 1956), pp. 224–276.

I. E. Sigel, P. Jarman, and H. Hanesian, "Styles of Categorization and their Intellectual and Personality Correlates in Young Children," *Human Development*, 10 (1967), 1–17.

J. L. Singer, "Imagination and Waiting Ability in Young Children," *Journal of Personality*, 29 (1961), 396–413.

M. I. Stein and S. J. Heinze, *Creativity and the Individual. Summaries of Selected Literature in Psychology and Psychiatry* (Glencoe, Ill.: Free Press, 1960).

R. Suchman, "Inquiry Training: Building skills for autonomous discovery," *Merrill-Palmer Quarterly* (July, 1961).

E. J. Sweeney, "Sex Differences in Problem Solving," *Technical Reports*

(Palo Alto, Calif.: Department of Psychology, Stanford University, 1953), No. 1.

L. M. TERMAN and C. C. MILES, *Sex and Personality Studies in Masculinity and Femininity* (New York: McGraw-Hill, 1936).

R. R. TROW, "The Relationship of Social Class to the Development of Moral Judgment in Children," M.S. Thesis (New York: Bank Street College of Education, 1954).

H. M. WALKER and J. LEV, *Statistical Inference* (New York: Holt, 1953).

M. A. WALLACH and N. KOGAN, *Modes of Thinking in Young Children* (New York: Holt, Rinehart and Winston, 1965).

M. A. WALLACH, "Creativity and the Expression of Possibilities," An address to the Division of Educational Psychology at the Annual Meeting of the American Psychological Association, New York, September, 1966.

W. J. WARNER, M. MEEKER, and K. EELLS, *Social Class in America* (Chicago: Science Research Associates, 1949).

P. S. WEISBERG and K. J. SPRINGER, "Environmental Factors in Creative Function," *Archives of General Psychiatry,* 5 (1961), 554–564.

E. A. WEISSKOPF, "A Transcendence Index as a Proposed Measure in the TAT," *Journal of Psychology,* 29 (1950), 379–390.

H. WERNER and E. KAPLAN, "The Acquisition of Word Meanings: A developmental study," *Monographs of the Society for Research in Child Development,* 15 (1952), No. 1.

R. C. WILSON, J. P. GUILFORD, and P. R. CHRISTENSEN, "Measuring Individual Differences in Originality," *Psychological Bulletin,* 50 (1953), 362–370.

J. WITHALL and W. W. LEWIS, "Social Interaction in the Classroom," in N. L. Gage, ed., *Handbook of Research on Teaching* (Chicago: Rand McNally, 1963).

H. A. WITKIN, H. B. LEWIS, M. HERTZMAN, K. MACHOVER, P. B. MEISSNER, and S. WAPNER, *Personality through Perception* (New York: Harper, 1954).

H. A. WITKIN, R. B. DYK, H. F. FATERSON, D. R. GOODENOUGH, and S. A. KARP, *Psychological Differentiation* (New York: Wiley, 1962).

M. WOLFENSTEIN, "Trends in Infant Care," *Journal of Orthopsychiatry,* 33 (1953), 120–130.

W. WOLFF, *The Personality of the Pre-School Child* (New York: Grune & Stratton, 1946), pp. 134–142.

R. C. WYLIE, *The Self Concept* (Lincoln: University of Nebraska Press, 1961).

H. ZIMILES, B. BIBER, W. RABINOWITZ, and L. HAY, "Personality Aspects of Teaching: A predictive study," *Genetic Psychology Monographs,* 69 (1964), 101–149.

J. ZUBIN, L. D. ERON, and F. SCHUMER, *An Experimental Approach to Projective Techniques* (New York: Wiley, 1965).

INDEX

academic periods, 35, 101, 115, 122; subjects studied in, 19, 182, 368

accommodation, concepts of, 366

accomplishment, assessment of, 38, 378

achievement, levels of, 7, 9, 13–14, 236, 238, 241, 296, 328, 401; measurement of, 171–172, 183, 190, 208, 211, 374, 381

acting, ability of, 326

activism, educational, 48

activities: classroom, 117–118, 128, 180; out-of-school, 26, 167

Adams School, educational facilities of, 17–18, 21, 27, 29–30, 33, 37–38, 43, 45–46, 91–96, 102, 107–117, 121, 124–125, 128–132, 155–156, 159, 203–204, 210, 235–238, 243, 250, 256–257, 261, 268, 282, 303–304, 319, 329, 349–350, 360, 367–369, 383–386, 393, 395, 404

Adkins, M. M., 173

administrative functions, 25, 30–32, 37–39, 190, 401; see also principal admissions, criteria of, 26

adolescence: phase of, 325, 328, 345, 347, 394, 408; pre-, 350, 384; problem of, 9, 14

Adorno, T. W., 174

adult: benign, 395–396; child interaction, 144, 173, 245, 250, 252–253, 256–257, 261, 375–378, 386, 397; living, 276, 284, 316, 320, 331, 334, 370; non-benevolent, 256–257; role of, 325, 332; 345, 375, 392; status of, 33, 164–165, 225, 239, 241, 244, 331

adulthood, 230, 259, 289, 311, 315, 336, 356, 384, 386, 390, 406–407

adventure, spirit of, 230–231, 240, 380

age-grades, 34

aggressiveness: destructive theme of, 223, 231, 235, 240, 352–355, 360; physical and emotional, 232, 256, 299, 301, 304, 356, 380, 382, 386

Albert, J., 183

Alexander, T., 173

allegiance, unequivocal, 271, 276, 337, 342, 345, 358

analysis, statistical, 9, 15–19; 34, 100–101, 115, 122, 128, 139, 334, 367

anger, expressions of, 302–304, 309, 336

animals, classroom use of, 92–93, 219–221, 277, 323, 353

antecedent conditions, 363–365

anthropology, 18

apperception, tests for, 173

aptitudes, tests for, 183, 185

architecture, school, 27

arithmetic, study of, 94, 101, 103, 105–106, 109, 111, 114, 122, 177, 184, 189, 211, 300, 305

art and artists, 27–29, 31, 33, 37, 47, 101, 122, 157, 242, 325

Asch, Harvey, xii

assembly, school, 32, 91

assertiveness, trait of, 294–295, 386, 397

513

DATE DUE